THE BEST
PLACES
TO KISS

IN THE NORTHWEST
(AND THE CANADIAN SOUTHWEST)

A Romantic Travel Guide

COMPLETELY REVISED
6th
EDITION
AND UPDATED

by

Stephanie Bell, Kristin Folsom,
Elizabeth Janda & Laura Kraemer

BEGINNING

PRESS

OTHER BOOKS IN THE

BEST PLACES TO KISS™

SERIES:

The Best Places To Kiss In Southern California, 4th Edition $13.95

The Best Places To Kiss In Northern California, 4th Edition $13.95

The Best Places To Kiss In Hawaii, 2nd Edition $12.95

ANY OF THESE BOOKS CAN BE ORDERED DIRECTLY FROM THE PUBLISHER.

Please send a check or money order for the total
amount of the books, plus shipping and handling
($3 for the first book, and $1 for each additional book) to:

Beginning Press
5418 South Brandon
Seattle, Washington 98118

All prices are listed in U.S. funds.
For information about ordering from Canada or to place
an order using Visa or MasterCard, call (206) 723-6300.

Art Direction and Production: Studio Pacific, Inc.
Cover Design: Studio Pacific, Inc., Deb McCarroll
Editors: Miriam Bulmer, Laura Kraemer, and Sherri Schultz
Printing: Publishers Press
Contributor: Kristin Folsom

Copyright 1997 by Paula Begoun

First Edition: June 1986
Second Edition: June 1988
Third Edition: June 1990
Fourth Edition: December 1992
Fifth Edition: December 1994
Sixth Edition: January 1997
1 2 3 4 5 6 7 8 9 10

BEST PLACES TO KISS™

is a registered trademark of Beginning Press
ISBN 1-877988-21-9

This book is distributed to the U.S. book trade by:
Publisher's Group West
4065 Hollis Street
Emeryville, CA 94608
(800) 788-3123

This book is distributed to the Canadian book trade by:
Raincoast Books
8680 Cambie Street
Vancouver, B.C.
V6P-6M9
Canada
(800) 663-5714

*"As usual with most lovers in the city,
they were troubled by the lack of that
essential need of love—a meeting place."*

Thomas Wolfe

Publisher's Note

Travel books have many different criteria for the places they include. We would like the reader to know that this book is not an advertising vehicle. As is true in all *The Best Places To Kiss* books, the businesses included were not charged fees, nor did they pay us for their reviews. This book is a sincere, unbiased effort to highlight those special parts of the region that are filled with romance and splendor. Sometimes those places were created by people, such as restaurants, inns, lounges, lodges, hotels, and bed and breakfasts. Sometimes those places are untouched by people and simply created by God for us to enjoy. Wherever you go, be gentle with each other and with the earth.

The publisher made the final decision on the recommendations in this collection, but we would love to hear what you think of our suggestions. We strive to create a reliable guide for your amorous outings, and in this quest for blissful sojourns, your romantic feedback assists greatly in increasing our accuracy and our resources for information. If you have any additional comments, criticisms, or cherished memories of your own from a place we directed you to or a place you discovered on your own, feel free to write us at:

Beginning Press
5418 South Brandon Street
Seattle, WA 98118

We would love to hear from you!

" *What of soul was left, I wonder, when the kissing had to stop?* "

Robert Browning

Table of Contents

The Fine Art of Kissing

Why It's Still Best To Kiss In The Northwest

This is the sixth edition of *The Best Places To Kiss In The Northwest,* and we are proud to still be a regional best-seller and one of the most popular travel books in the area. Our readers are constantly reminding us that our reputation as one of the few travel books that candidly and critically reviews romantic properties is well earned and a breath of amorous fresh air.

We admit a strong bias in our feelings about the Northwest. Without question, this area provides the best kissing territory anywhere in the continental United States and Canada. As is true for every edition, our research is enthusiastic and our criteria increasingly more restrictive. If we're going to recommend a place for romance, we want to be sure your lips and emotions will be satisfied. Disappointment can be a near disaster where the heart is concerned.

Beginning Press also publishes *The Best Places To Kiss In Northern California, The Best Places To Kiss In Southern California,* and *The Best Places To Kiss In Hawaii.* After all this lip-chapping research, we find it even easier to rave about the Northwest.

You will simply relish this glorious part of the world as much as we do. More than any other area in the United States, the Northwest has a splendor and peacefulness that is apparent throughout. And along with the beauty of nature's handiwork, the people here have a style and attitude that are quietly conducive to intimacy and affection. Northwesterners know a secret: the more intimately acquainted you are with the earth, the more intimate you can be with each other. In short, we can't think of a better region for romance.

You Call This Research?

This book was undertaken primarily as a journalistic effort and is the product of ongoing interviews, travel, thorough investigation, and critical observation. Although it would have been nice, even preferable, kissing was not the major research method used to select the locations listed in this book. If smooching had been the determining factor, several inescapable problems would have developed. First, we would still be researching, and this book would be just a good idea, some breathless moments, random notes, and nothing more. Second, depending on the mood of the moment, many kisses might have occurred in places that do not meet the requirements of this travel guide. Therefore, for both practical and physical reasons, more objective criteria had to be established.

You may be wondering how, if we did not kiss at every location during our research, we could be certain that a particular place was good for such an activity? The answer is that we employed our reporters' instincts to evaluate the heartfelt, magnetic pull of each place we visited. If, upon examining a place, we felt a longing inside to share what we had discovered with our special someone, we considered this to be as reliable as a kissing analysis. In the final evaluation, we can guarantee that when you visit any of the places listed, you will be assured of some degree of privacy, a beautiful setting, heart-stirring ambience, and romantic accommodations. What you do when you get there is up to you and your partner.

Rating Romance

The three major factors that determined whether or not we included a place were:

- Privacy
- Location/view/setting
- Ambience

Of these determining factors, "privacy" and "location" are fairly self-explanatory, but "ambience" can probably use some clarification. Wonderful, loving environments are not just four-poster beds covered with down quilts and lace pillows, or tables decorated with white tablecloths and nicely folded linen napkins. Instead, there must be other engaging features that encourage intimacy and allow for uninterrupted affectionate discourse. For the most part, ambience was rated according to degree of comfort and number of gracious appointments, as opposed to image and frills

If a place had all three factors going for it, inclusion was automatic. But if one or two of the criteria were weak or nonexistent, the other feature(s) had to be superior before the location would be included. For example, if a breathtakingly beautiful panoramic vista was in a spot that's inundated with tourists and children on field trips, the place was not included. If a fabulous bed and breakfast was set in a less than desirable location, it would be included if, and only if, its interior was so wonderfully inviting and cozy that the outside world no longer mattered. Extras like complimentary champagne, handmade truffles, or extraordinary service earned brownie points and frequently determined the difference between three-and-a-half and four-lip ratings.

Kiss Ratings

The lip rating following each entry is our way of indicating just how romantic we thought a place was and how contented we were during our visit. The number of lips awarded each location indicates:

No lips	=	Reputed to be a romantic destination, but we strongly disagree
💋	=	Romantic possibilities with potential drawbacks
💋💋	=	Can provide a satisfying experience
💋💋💋	=	Very desirable
💋💋💋💋	=	Simply sublime
Unrated	=	Not open at the time this edition went to print, but looks promising

Romantic Note: If you're planning to celebrate a special occasion, such as an anniversary or birthday, we highly recommend telling the proprietors about it when making your reservation. Many bed and breakfasts and hotels offer "special occasion packages," which can include a complimentary bottle of wine, breakfast in bed, fresh flowers, and special touches during turn-down service, like dimmed lights and your beloved's favorite CD playing in the background to set the right romantic mood. Restaurants are also sometimes willing to accommodate special occasions by offering free desserts or helping you coordinate a surprise proposal.

Cost Ratings

We have included additional ratings to help you determine whether your lips can afford to kiss in a particular restaurant, hotel, or bed and breakfast. (Almost all of the outdoor places are free; some charge a small fee.) The price for overnight accommodations is always based on double occupancy; otherwise there wouldn't be anyone to kiss. Eating establishment prices are based on a full dinner for two, excluding liquor, unless otherwise indicated. Because prices and business hours change, it is always advisable to call each place you plan to visit, so your lips will not end up disappointed.

Romantic Note: The exchange rate for Canadian funds at the time this book went to press was about $1.33 Canadian to $1 U.S. The cost ratings for Canadian establishments included in our book are based on Canadian currency.

Restaurants

Inexpensive	Less than $30
Moderate	$30 to $50
Expensive	$50 to $80
Very Expensive	$80 to $110
Unbelievably Expensive	More than $110

Lodgings

Inexpensive	Less than $95
Moderate	$95 to $115
Expensive	$115 to $155
Very Expensive	$155 to $250
Unbelievably Expensive	More than $250

Wedding Bells

One of the most auspicious times to kiss is the moment after you've exchanged wedding vows. The setting for that magical moment can vary, from your own cozy living room to a lush garden perched at the ocean's edge to a grand ballroom at an elegant downtown hotel. As an added service to those of you in the midst of prenuptial arrangements, we have indicated which properties have impressive wedding facilities. For more specific information about the facilities and services offered, please call the establishments directly. They should be able to provide you with menus, prices, and all the details needed to make your wedding day as spectacular as you have ever imagined.

Romantic Note: If wedding bells aren't in your near future and you are going to an establishment that specializes in weddings and private parties, call ahead to ensure that a function isn't scheduled during your stay. Unless you hope that seeing a wedding will magically inspire your partner to "pop the question," you might feel like uninvited guests.

The Most Romantic Time To Travel

The Northwest is so spectacular, it's hard to imagine any time of the year that would not be romantic. Each season and hour has its own special joy: winter skiing, cuddling by the fireplace on a chilly day (that can be any time of year here), summer sunshine, mesmerizing fall sunsets, the exuberant rebirth of nature in the melting wet spring. Even in overcast conditions (again, any time of the year), if you prepare properly there is no reason to postpone investigating the splendor that hovers around every turn in the Northwest.

So don't be one of those couples who wait until summer to travel and then decide not to go because it might be too crowded. Oh, and about the rain—it does. Enough said.

" *With a kiss, let us set out for
an unknown world.* "

Alfred de Musset

BRITISH COLUMBIA

Vancouver Island

Vancouver Island is ferry-accessible for car and foot traffic from the following ports: Seattle, Anacortes (one and a half hours north of Seattle), and Port Angeles (on the Olympic Peninsula), Tsawwassen (30 minutes south of Vancouver), Horseshoe Bay (in West Vancouver), and Westview (on the Sunshine Coast, north of Vancouver). The Victoria Clipper, a foot-traffic-only ferry, docks in the heart of downtown Victoria after a two-and-a-half-hour passage from Seattle. Another passenger-only ferry travels between downtown Vancouver and Victoria. For information on fares and schedules, contact the British Columbia Ferries, (250) 669-1211; Washington State Ferries, (206) 464-6400; Port Angeles Black Ball Transport, (206) 457-4491; or Victoria Clipper, (206) 448-5000. Be aware that during peak travel times you can spend a long time in line if you take your car. Trial by ferryboat is one of the hazards of summer or weekend travel.

Traveling to Vancouver Island is an unconditional romantic must, simply because it has everything that two people in love could want to share. Covered by deep forests and miles upon miles of wilderness, this enormous island is also known for its rugged beaches, bustling fishing communities, rustic lodges, quaint bed and breakfasts, magnificent hotels, and a mountain range that spans its nearly 300-mile length.

The mostly uninhabited, north-central section is noted for untouched mountain terrain, abundant wildlife, and pristine scenery. The comparatively overdeveloped eastern coastal areas are still marbled with long lazy beaches. Except for the congenial fishing villages of Tofino and Ucluelet, the central west coast is entirely wilderness. Along the southwestern coast, near the towns of Sooke and Metchosin, more unspoiled wilderness is accentuated with rocky beaches and extensive forestland.

Citified Victoria, on the southern tip of the island, presents a stark contrast to the rest of the island. Distinguished by lavish gardens, charming tea rooms, and old-world architecture, the capital of British Columbia also has a multitude of tourist traps and scores of international tourists. (Actually, much of Victoria's English style is self-consciously marketed to attract visitors.)

Romantic Note: Canada charges a 7-percent goods and services tax (GST) in addition to a hotel tax. Most places will warn you about these extra charges, and you'll notice that it can be a hefty addition to your bill. The GST portion of your accommodation bill and some purchases are refundable directly from the government if you are not a resident of Canada. Most places provide the required forms and information explaining how you can submit your receipts for reimbursement. If you have further questions, call the **SUMMERSIDE TEXT CENTRE** at (613) 991-3346 or (800) 668-4748 (in Canada).

The exchange rate for Canadian funds at the time this book went to press was about $1.33 to the U.S. dollar. For the sake of simplicity (and in consideration of the fluctuating exchange rate), the cost ratings for all of British Columbia are listed in Canadian dollars.

Romantic Warning: Signs on this island are not as clearly marked as we would have liked. (In fact, sometimes signs aren't visible at all.) Be sure to bring along plenty of maps and an extra dose of patience. The Island Highway runs north and south along the length of the entire island and can be agony to travel. Being the only main thoroughfare on the island, it gets dreadfully crowded and, unfortunately, not everyone wants to go as fast as you might.

Port Hardy

Outdoor Kissing

CAPE SCOTT PARK AND SAN JOSEF BAY, Port Hardy 💋💋💋💋
(250) 954-4600

Just south of Port Hardy, follow the poorly marked logging road for 28 miles. At the end of the road, you'll pass a government-run meteorology station as you proceed to the parking area at the head of the trail. A very short climb reveals the path.

Cape Scott is on the northwestern tip of Vancouver Island and feels like the end of the world. It is accessible via a dusty gravel-and-stone logging road. Though the park is not very far from Port Hardy, because of the road's condition you'll need longer to get here than you'd think from looking at a map. Once you've arrived, however, you'll be ecstatic that you underwent the ordeal; this park is the epitome of magnificent wilderness.

At the beginning of the hiking trail, you make a dream-like transition from the gravel-pit road to a land filled with the elfin spirits of nature. A flat walkway of wood planks is the only sign of civilization you're likely to see all day; you are guaranteed privacy.

From the trailhead, meander for two miles past trees draped in moss and streamered with sunlight, until the path opens onto an enormous sand-laden horseshoe bay called San Josef, which you can claim exclusively for your-

Cost ratings for British Columbia listings are in Canadian funds. American travelers should check the exchange rate or ask an innkeeper to figure out the cost in U.S. dollars.

selves. Waves breaking on the beach fill the air with a rhythmic pounding. The U-shaped bay is bordered by forested hills where very few people have gone before. At the end of the trail, be sure to mark where you leave the trail or it will be tricky to find that spot again.

Romantic Warning: Because Cape Scott is so remote, acquire a detailed map and complete information from the visitor center in Port Hardy before you head out there. If you plan on backpacking, the need to be prepared for adverse weather conditions cannot be stressed enough. Weather here can be severe and excessively wet, bordering on torrential. Visitors are advised to use caution while camping or hiking here. Cougars and bears are prevalent and the running water is not drinkable.

Campbell River

With a population of more than 16,000, Campbell River is brimming with shopping malls and condominium complexes—definitely not our idea of romantic. Still, it is home to some of the island's best fishing resorts, and very close to the breathtaking pristine wilderness of **STRATHCONA PROVINCIAL PARK** (see Outdoor Kissing).

Hotel/Bed and Breakfast Kissing

DOLPHINS RESORT, Campbell River
4125 Discovery Drive
(250) 287-3066
http://www.vquest.com/dolphins
Moderate to Expensive

If you've got your heart set on fishing but want more seclusion than **PAINTER'S LODGE** has to offer (reviewed below), consider this more intimate, albeit less luxurious, alternative. The 16 rustic cabins here are clustered together on a wooded hillside overlooking Discovery Passage. All of the cabins are comfortable, though nothing spectacular, with outdated colors and fabrics, brick fireplaces, full kitchens, and ample space for relaxation. Most of the cabins have two bedrooms, but some are studios. Special two- and three-night packages include accommodations, 16 hours of guided fishing, tackle, meal service, and flight arrangements.

PAINTER'S LODGE, Campbell River
1625 MacDonald Road
(250) 286-1102, (800) 663-7090
Expensive to Unbelievably Expensive
Closed November through mid-March

It's between 5 A.M. and 9 A.M., and you're sitting in a rocking boat, out in the middle of a serene channel of water, waiting for a slight tug on the end of your fishing pole. Snowcapped summits surround the two of you with silent majesty, amplifying your sense of supreme isolation. Even if fishing isn't your idea of romance (and even if it's raining), the scenery alone is bound to inspire some passionate moments. And keep in mind, there are some who kiss best after they've landed a king or two.

Painter's Lodge is an angler's delight and has been for more than 60 years. Canadians and Californians flock here to test their patience and skill. A fire several years back served almost as a blessing in disguise: the lodge has been entirely rebuilt and the result is an elegant, attractive, modern wood complex nestled right on the water's edge. Wood accents, peaked ceilings, and private decks add charm to the 90 otherwise spartan hotel rooms and four additional cabins. French doors open onto private patios in every room; some face spectacular water vistas while others have views of the outdoor pool and landscaped gardens. Corner suites are particularly enticing, with surrounding windows and slanted wood ceilings. At the end of the day, head down to the glass-enclosed fireside lounge, with its huge stone fireplace and comfortable seating; it's a prime place to gaze at the water and revitalize yourselves for another go-around of fighting off the dogfish and weeds.

Romantic Suggestion: PAINTER'S LODGE RESTAURANT (see Restaurant Kissing) is the nicest place to dine in the vicinity.

STRATHCONA LODGE, Campbell River
Highway 28, 30 miles west of Campbell River
(250) 286-8206
Moderate
Minimum stay requirement seasonally
Recommended Wedding Site

A long, winding mountain road delves into the rugged wilderness of Strathcona Provincial Park and delivers you to Strathcona Lodge, which is like no other lodge on earth. Set at the edge of a crystal-clear mountain lake, the red hewn-log buildings are encircled by an astounding collection of snowcapped peaks. Strathcona is, without question, a visual paradise. There are no other facilities around for miles, and that sort of isolation has an enchantment all its own.

The friendly and professional staff is dedicated to introducing all who venture into this realm to the mysteries and excitement of the outdoor magic of Strathcona Park. They offer guided instruction for any mountain and water activity you could wish for: kayaking, rappeling from cliffs, glissading down glaciers, wildlife viewing, hiking, canoeing, fishing, sailing, and camping. The lodge's brochure lists a rare selection of packaged challenges for all ages and skill levels. (Even if you are not staying at the lodge, the park is a magnificent area to explore on your own, with exquisite vistas and picturesque countryside.)

You may be thinking yes, that all sounds great, but not necessarily romantic unless you're dating Paul Bunyan. But after you have explored the rustically appointed lodge and cabins set around the lake, wandered into the wilderness for a breathtaking hike, and enjoyed three hearty family-style meals served daily, you will be convinced that this is an extraordinary place for nature-loving couples. Your outdoor fantasies will be fulfilled at Strathcona Lodge.

Restaurant Kissing

PAINTER'S LODGE RESTAURANT, Campbell River
1625 MacDonald Road
(250) 286-1102, (800) 663-7090
Moderate to Expensive
Call for seasonal hours.

Floor-to-ceiling windows command brilliant ocean views in this expansive timbered dining room. Tables are well-spaced alongside the windows to ensure that each party has ample privacy and unobstructed views. Fresh flowers, white linens, candles, and fine china give the dining room a formal, upscale appearance. During our visit, the service was gracious and very efficient, but the items on the small gourmet menu sounded much better in print than they tasted in reality. We recommend sticking to the more basic seafood entrées and focusing on the views (and, of course, each other).

Outdoor Kissing

STRATHCONA PROVINCIAL PARK

Campbell River and Courtenay are primary access points to the park. From Campbell River, follow Highway 28 west; from the Island Highway in Courtenay, follow signs to Forbidden Plateau.

Your first sight of Strathcona Provincial Park's 210,000 hectares (over 518,000 acres) of legendary wilderness will take your breath away. Sheltered in the heart of Vancouver Island, far, far from the reaches of civilization, snow-shrouded mountains ascend above sunlit glades and shimmering, crystal-clear lakes. Thick, lush moss clings to bare branches and tree trunks, and rushing waterfalls tumble over rocky summits into lazy, slow-moving creeks that meander through the forest and disappear underground. Roosevelt elk and black-tailed deer forage for food among the forested hillsides, while brightly colored birds twitter in the high boughs of the evergreens. And these are just glimpses. We urge you to come and witness the sights and sounds of the park's spectacular isolation and scenery first-hand. Myriad hiking trails and nature walks allow visitors access to this heavenly region. For maps and detailed information, contact **B.C. PARKS** at (250) 337-5121 or (250) 954-4600.

Courtenay

Just about the time you notice all the logging trucks zooming by, you'll also notice the lack of trees and any sort of natural surroundings. We can't recommend any accommodations in this small industrial logging town, and as far as we can tell there is no reason to stay here overnight. However, a few wonderful dining options make a short visit worthwhile.

Restaurant Kissing

LA CRÉMAILLÈRE, Courtenay
975 Comox Road
(250) 338-8131
Moderate to Expensive
Lunch Wednesday-Friday; Dinner Wednesday-Sunday

This vine-covered Tudor home is one of the most romantic restaurants on the entire island, and its intimate atmosphere is tempered by enough comfort to make it relaxing. Service is efficient and gracious, and the wait staff is attentive to the smallest details. The superior French cuisine here is updated with Northwest flair. Start your meal with the fresh local oysters dabbed with cream, spinach, and bacon, or the flavorful house pâté; both are delicious. For a main course, try the fillet of rainbow trout, pan-fried and topped with roasted almonds and lemon sauce, or the breast of chicken breaded with pistachios, baked, and served with raspberry sauce. Dessert selections change with the mood of the chef and are worth every decadent bite.

THE OLD HOUSE RESTAURANT, Courtenay
1760 Riverside Lane
(250) 338-5406
Inexpensive to Moderate
Breakfast Saturday-Sunday; Lunch and Dinner Daily
Recommended Wedding Site

Don't be too distracted by the neighboring log-processing factory, which operates in full swing during the day; you'll hardly notice it once you've been enveloped by the charming country ambience and lovely garden setting of rustic Old House Restaurant. Willow trees and thick green lawn carpet the backyard, where the Powell River flows by umbrella-shaded tables set on a latticed open-air deck.

Built in 1938, the historic riverfront home has four old-fashioned dining rooms, each one dominated by dark wood beams and wood-burning fireplaces. (Our favorite has an enormous beach-stone fireplace and lots of hanging plants.) Antique furnishings, floral fabrics, and leaded glass windows reflect the building's historic past, although the vinyl tablecloths are less than formal. While the kitchen does a good job with standard items, unusual fresh ingredients turn up in imaginative combinations. Pumpkin pasta, tiger prawn and sole fillet rolls, and a mixed-grain and mushroom timbale are a few of the rare finds on the interesting menu.

Outdoor Kissing

MOUNT WASHINGTON, Courtenay
(250) 338-1386
$40 for an all-day lift ticket

Call for directions.

Be sure to call for directions before you set out for this resort; it took us a lifetime and a half to find it. If you're in an adventurous mood, you'll appreciate the 25-minute drive (it takes much longer if you get lost) along graveled or snow-covered country roads that lead from Courtenay to the ski slopes of Mount Washington. During the off-season (June 5 through September 5), as you dangle above the golden land on the mile-high ski lift, you can study the scenic Comox Valley, the Strait of Georgia, and the Beaufort Mountain Range. During ski season, numerous runs boast great skiing and amazing scenery. It might not be Whistler, but at least the lines are shorter.

Fanny Bay

Hotel/Bed and Breakfast Kissing

SHIPS POINT BEACH HOUSE, Fanny Bay
7584 Ships Point Road
(250) 335-2200, (800) 925-1595
http://www.shipspoint.com
Moderate to Expensive

Minimum stay required seasonally
Recommended Wedding Site

Eagles, blue herons, Canadian geese, seals and sea lions, and other wild-life can be observed from the vantage point of this picturesque beach house perched at the tip of Ships Point Peninsula. If you want to get even closer to Mother Nature, you can launch a rental kayak from the property's sandy beach or ask the gracious innkeepers for a boat tour of the area's wildlife. Nature is the focus of this small but luxurious country inn, encompassed by lush flower gardens and adjacent to a protected forest and bird sanctuary. Panoramic views of the ocean, mountains, and Denman Island are visible from nearly every room in the house.

Hospitality is important to the enthusiastic innkeepers, who welcome you to their home like old friends. Help yourselves to a complimentary drink from the "people fridge," relish the views from the deck, or put on your favorite CD in the airy living room, distinctively appointed with deep red walls and extraordinary modern artwork. Home-baked treats await guests in each of the six small but endearing guest rooms, all with private baths. Native Canadian artwork and gorgeous down comforters lend appeal, even in the rooms with twin beds. For romantic purposes, we recommend Tequila Sunset, with its gorgeous water views, cheery fabrics, and enticing queen-size bed.

Savory appetizers and wine are served at sunset every evening, and for an extra charge the innkeepers are delighted to have you as their guests for a three-course gourmet dinner, served family-style at one large table. Delicious breakfast aromas waft through the halls in the early morning, providing extra incentive to get out of your comfy bed.

Parksville

Sorting through Parksville's overabundance of roadside motels and beachfront accommodations is no easy task, and we wish we had more to show for our extensive research. Parksville's lovely stretch of beach, border-ing Craig Bay and overlooking resplendent views of the mountains, has experienced a condominium/rental explosion. Large signs shout at you from the highway. Some properties have mowed down every tree in sight and now resemble mainland suburbia. The majority of this area's standard economy motels were not included for all the obvious unromantic reasons (outdated decor, traffic noise, and rambunctious children, to name a few). Don't forgo Parksville altogether, however. We did find several eminently lip-worthy locales that should not be overlooked.

Romantic Warning: Summertime in Parksville means family time. Unless you're prepared to deal with sizable crowds, we recommend booking your reservations for the off-season.

Hotel/Bed and Breakfast Kissing

BEACH ACRES RESORT, Parksville
1015 East Island Highway
(250) 248-3424, (800) 663-7309
Moderate to Unbelievably Expensive
Minimum stay requirement seasonally

In the summer, Beach Acres Resort attracts far too many families with children to be considered even vaguely romantic. The 68 Tudor-style cabins are crowded together on a sandy beach and tree-covered hillside, which means your neighbors may be a little too close for comfort. But in the off-season, when the crowds have diminished and children are back in school, a beachfront cabin here can be a cozy and satisfying place for an intimate interlude. Brick fireplaces (you have to purchase the wood), large windows, full kitchens, separate living rooms, patios, and separate (small) bedrooms make these units a comfortable home away from home. Unobstructed vistas of the water and distant mountains are Beach Acres' most redeeming feature, and the beach at low tide is endless.

Romantic Warning: We do not recommend the dreary Forest Cottages, set far back from the water in a woodsy cul-de-sac. None of them offer views of the water, and without water views the tired decor is too overpowering and there really isn't any reason to stay here.

GRAY CREST SEASIDE RESORT, Parksville
(250) 248-6513, (800) 663-2636 (in Canada)
Inexpensive to Very Expensive
Minimum stay requirement seasonally

At first glance, this modern complex of privately owned condominiums doesn't appear to offer much in terms of romance. If it weren't for the resort's spectacular views and reasonable prices, we probably wouldn't have considered it. Fortunately, all of the newly built luxury units have views (some better than others) of Rathtrevor Provincial Park. For kissing purposes, we recommend the suites set on the edge of a wide sandy beach that sweeps down to the water. (Privacy is limited in the units located farther up the hillside, which face the outdoor swimming pool.) Daylight cascades through large windows into one- and two-bedroom units decorated with black-and-gray or pastel color schemes and semi-contemporary furnishings. Though the bedspreads are a little bit drab and some of the appointments look dated, the units themselves are spacious and comfortable. Amenities include full kitchens (complete with dishwashers), ocean-view decks or patios, fireplaces, and a communal outdoor pool, indoor whirlpool and sauna, and a laundry facility. For a slightly higher price, you can request a room with its own private Jacuzzi tub. Breakfast provisions are up to you.

TIGH-NA-MARA, Parksville   😚😚😚
1095 East Island Highway
(250) 248-2072, (800) 663-7373
http://qb.island.net/~tnm
Inexpensive to Very Expensive
Minimum stay requirement on weekends and holidays

With its tranquil setting, myriad walking trails, beach access, stunning water views, and a reliable restaurant, Tigh-Na-Mara is superior to the other accommodations along the eastern coast of Vancouver Island.

Tigh-Na-Mara comprises 142 units; we highly recommend any of the 45 one- or two-bedroom log cabins, clustered together amid tall pine trees. Exposed log walls, peaked ceilings, wood burning beachstone fireplaces, comfortable sitting areas, full kitchens, small private decks with barbecues, spacious bathrooms, and pretty linens contribute to the overall warmth and coziness of these friendly retreats.

Lacking the cabins' rustic ambience, but compensating with luxury and water views, the other options here are individually owned condos that tower over the sparkling shoreline. Each spacious unit features magnificent views, a queen-size bed, stone fireplace, cedar-paneled living room, a full kitchen, and sliding glass doors that open up to a private deck with a ringside view of the water. Because these condos are individually owned, the furnishings in some are standard motel-style, but Tigh-Na-Mara controls almost all of the decor decisions, so most feature attractive contemporary furnishings. Some units are blessed with large Jacuzzi tubs, and a select few have them in the bedroom so you can gaze out at the water as you soak away the evening. If you are traveling on a budget, you can stay in some less expensive units in an adjacent log building, but the interiors are lackluster and the furnishings are outdated, so be cautious when making reservations.

A log mansion with a polished log-and-stone interior houses the lovely **TIGH-NA-MARA RESTAURANT** (Expensive), where the friendly staff serves up consistently good dinner selections seven days a week. Entrées are always first-rate. Try the steamed halibut with sake, pickled ginger, and green onions; chicken in phyllo stuffed with sun-dried tomatoes and feta cheese;

or scallops sautéed in pernod with saffron, mushrooms, and leeks over a bed of fresh pasta. Breakfast and lunch are also served here, but because Tigh-Na-Mara is a hot spot for conferences during the day, the ambience at dinner is much more conducive to romance.

Romantic Warning: Tigh-Na-Mara attracts a lot of families, especially during the summer months, so plan your vacation accordingly.

Restaurant Kissing

HERON'S RESTAURANT, Parksville
240 Dogwood Street, at the Bayside Inn
(250) 248-8333, (800) 663-4232
Moderate
Breakfast, Lunch, and Dinner Daily; Sunday Brunch

Although the Bayside Inn is an average hotel with some great views, its restaurant is a three-tiered showcase with a sweeping view of the water and mountains. Lucky thing: if it weren't for the view, there wouldn't be much incentive to dine here; the food is decent, but could easily be better. English tea is the menu's finest offering; it includes finger sandwiches, pastries, and a steaming pot of your tea of choice. For a real treat, order appetizers and cocktails at sundown, then sit back and watch the sky perform its magic.

MACLURE HOUSE INN RESTAURANT, Parksville
1015 East Island Highway
(250) 248-3470
Moderate
Breakfast, Lunch, and Dinner Daily

Probably one of the last places you would expect to find a romantic restaurant is in the middle of a rustic resort complex, behind the main office and laundry facilities. Nevertheless, here it is, and splendidly inviting too. Originally built in 1921, the Tudor-style Maclure House Inn has been handsomely renovated to retain all of its original charm. The dimly lit interior, bathed in the amber glow of a gas fire, boasts polished dark wood moldings and paneling. Windows draped in lace frame views of colorful gardens and the Strait of Georgia in the distance.

Lunch and dinner are both worthwhile. Our appetizer of hot Camembert rolled in almonds and served with a fresh plum sauce was flavorful, and the classic Caesar salad had exactly the right proportions; unfortunately, the French onion soup was unbearably cheesy. The raspberry torte we ordered for dessert was almost too rich, but we "suffered" through it anyway.

Tofino

A winding 75-mile trip west on Highway 4 cuts across the central mountains of Vancouver Island, taking you to the remote side of the island. For the last few miles of this panoramic drive, the rocky coast ushers you on your descent to sea level. When you finally reach road's end, the highway splits: one road forks north to Tofino, the other south to Ucluelet. Both towns are essentially fishing villages and whale-watching ports of call. They also both pride themselves on being noncommercial places where you can charter boats for fishing and touring. But for heart-stealing pursuits, Tofino is your destination.

Tofino is everything a small town should be: unpretentious and amiable, with streets and neighborhoods set like small constellations along the volatile, rocky oceanfront and the marinas of the calm inner bay. Environmentalists and artists flock here to escape the citified hustle of the island's "other" side. Several waterfront resorts line the shore along the main road into Tofino and have unobstructed views of the beach and ocean. In town you'll find a few basic shops and casual restaurants. Nothing here gets in the way of the scenery. Get close, kick back, and discover a place where time floats by to a melody you can learn to hum together.

Romantic Note: The tourist season in Tofino is brief and intense during July and August. The best accommodations are so difficult to come by during this time, that you should consider timing your visit for a less popular season. In fall or winter, the two of you will practically have the entire area to yourselves.

Hotel/Bed and Breakfast Kissing

BEACH HOUSE BED AND BREAKFAST, Tofino
1297 Lynn Road
(250) 725-3966
Moderate
Call for seasonal closures.

It is not our usual policy to recommend accommodations with shared baths, but we loved the Beach House so much, we decided to break our own rules and include it anyway. Once you've stepped inside the cozy, hand-built wood cabin sequestered among trees, you'll understand why. We weren't surprised to learn that the owner is an artist, given the creative bent of the decor. You'll notice unusual sculptures and colorful crafts tucked in corners or tastefully displayed on walls. A wood-burning stove warms the light-filled common room, where you can enjoy a slice of freshly baked coffee cake and a cup of tea upon arrival, as well as a hot breakfast in the morning.

The three guest rooms share two baths, one of which has a circular two-person soaking tub. The rooms are quite small and borderline plain, but still comfortable, with cushy four-poster beds, plush down comforters, and several pieces of eclectic art. Our favorite room has a small deck and glimpses of the ocean through a stand of trees.

Speaking of the ocean, it's the best thing about staying here. The careening surf and long, long stretches of sandy beach are literally just beyond your doorstep. You can walk forever in either direction and find sand dollars, sea caves, small creatures thriving in tide pools, and all the solitude two people could ever want.

Romantic Note: The innkeeper's private quarters are located in an open loft above the common room, secluded behind shoji screens. Definitely unconventional, though it doesn't appear to pose a problem for guests.

CABLE COVE INN, Tofino
201 Main Street
(250) 725-4236, (800) 663-6449
http://victoriabc.com/accom/cablecov.htm
Inexpensive to Very Expensive

Cable Cove Inn looks like an office building, but don't be fooled. Once you've secluded yourselves in one of the inn's six wonderful guest suites and savored the magnificent ocean views, your doubts will dissipate. Poised high on a cliff, the inn looks out to the surf pounding against the rocks below—quite a magical sight. The guest rooms are just as magical. Gorgeous, richly colored linens drape four-poster beds; sunlight floods through windows and skylights in most of the rooms; and the fireplaces, Jacuzzi tubs, and glass showers are distinctly romantic attractions. Colorful Native Canadian artwork accentuates the stylish flair of every room. In some, sliding wooden doors open to wraparound decks where cedar chairs provide an ideal place to soak in the scenery.

Although this inn has the privacy and professional attitude of most hotels, the innkeepers live right next door and see to personal touches, making it feel more like a bed and breakfast. Hot beverages are served directly to the rooms every morning, and freshly baked goods are available in the common sitting room for all to enjoy.

Cost ratings for British Columbia listings are in Canadian funds. American travelers should check the exchange rate or ask an innkeeper to figure out the cost in U.S. dollars.

FRASER'S VIEW BED AND BREAKFAST, Tofino
1329 Chesterman Beach Road
(250) 725-2489
Moderate to Expensive

Aptly named after the owners' magnificent view of the ocean, this contemporary beige home is situated right on the water, with illustrious views from almost every room. Fortunately, the innkeepers do not rely on location alone, and they have expended an extraordinary amount of time and energy on all three of their guest suites. The units feature private entrances, down comforters, stylish handmade pine furnishings, wood-burning stoves or fireplaces, and private bathrooms. Our favorite is the Storm Suite, with a private entrance from the common deck, wraparound windows with breathtaking views, and a floor-to-ceiling fireplace. The newly added Wolf Suite has an even better view, plus a private balcony, glass-fronted wood-burning stove, a vaulted ceiling, wood wainscoting, and a queen-size bed. A short path in the rear of the house wanders through a stand of trees to the beach, where many treasures await your discovery. If you want to wash off after a beachcombing expedition, a semiprivate outdoor shower adds an adventurous romantic touch, if you can brave it.

Don't worry about dressing for breakfast, because Starbucks coffee, fresh breads with homemade jams, fresh fruit and juice, and smoked salmon omelets are brought directly to your door.

GULL COTTAGE, Tofino
1254 Lynn Road
(250) 725-3177
Inexpensive to Moderate
Minimum stay requirement seasonally

Cottage is a misnomer: this massive green and white country Victorian home with a wraparound porch is far from small. The downstairs common areas and three upstairs guest rooms are filled with contemporary furnishings and local artwork. By far the best choice is the Rainforest Suite, where a beautiful pine sleigh bed is covered with a feather bed and a deep red comforter. Bay windows showcase the serene forested setting, and a spacious bathroom features a large Jacuzzi tub. The other two rooms are more spartan, but still offer four-poster beds, pretty linens, and more views of the forest. A full gourmet breakfast is served downstairs at one large, elegant table each morning.

MIDDLE BEACH LODGE, Tofino
400 MacKenzie Road
(250) 725-2900
Inexpensive to Very Expensive
Minimum stay requirement seasonally
Recommended Wedding Site

Middle Beach Lodge is one of Tofino's more popular romantic destinations, and we can see why. A long, bumpy gravel drive leads you away from the highway and into the forest, where this lovely wood lodge and its newly constructed counterpart are perched above a sandy beach and the roaring Pacific.

Myriad decks and lookouts throughout the original lodge make the ocean seem much closer, and a steep staircase zigzags down to the beach. An immense rock fireplace is the focal point of the main lounge, where guests can relax or cuddle up close on overstuffed sofas. Continental breakfast and dinner are served family-style at two communal picnic tables. If you're not in the mood to socialize, you can take your meal to a cozy private nook. (Dinner is not included in your stay and is also available to nonguests.) Eighteen of the 26 rooms have lovely ocean views, but even those without this advantage are worth mentioning. Simple and almost plain, the attractive European country decor is enhanced with bouquets of dried flowers, wood accents, and puffy down comforters that you can hardly refrain from diving into. Best of all, this section of the lodge does not allow children, so the quiet setting remains tranquil.

Just down the beach, a new lodge and several cabins have been built along a rocky oceanfront bluff. Rustic Northwest charm is provided by the burlap curtains, dried flowers, hand-carved beds, hardwood floors, and wood accents here, and many of the guest rooms have decks that command panoramic ocean views. Private decks wrap around the adjacent cabins, which boast knotty pine walls, antique trunks, and ladder lofts. Several cabins have Jacuzzi tubs and convenient kitchenettes.

A generous continental breakfast is served in the lodge's elegant dining room or can be enjoyed in the living room beside a raging fire.

PACIFIC SANDS, Tofino
1421 Pacific Rim Highway
(250) 725-3322, (800) 565-2322
http://travel.bc.ca/a/pacificsands

Inexpensive to Very Expensive
Minimum stay requirement seasonally

If you're looking for quaint and rustic, this sprawling condominium-style development is not for you. These attractive cedar buildings, bordered by manicured lawns and flower beds on one side and the raging ocean and Pacific Rim National Park on the other, are best described as upscale and refined.

The three-story structures hug a stretch of magnificent coastline, and all 64 units offer fantastic views of the water. In the newer sections, lovely little mini-apartments decorated in soothing pastels feature wood-burning fireplaces, small kitchens, televisions, comfortable living rooms, separate bedrooms, and sliding glass doors that open to private balconies or patios. Two units in the newer section also have hot tubs on their private decks for soaking under the stars. The original section offers units with similar furnishings and decor, and the top-floor rooms sport soaring cathedral ceilings and the best panoramic outlooks. If you can get by without a television or fireplace, the handful of rustic cabins that sit on the water offer the most seclusion.

SPINDRIFT, Tofino   💋💋
1373 Chesterman Beach Road
(250) 725-2103
Moderate to Very Expensive; No Credit Cards
Minimum stay requirement seasonally

Homes that reside directly on the rugged ocean shores of Tofino are envied for their treasured location. Spindrift, a blue-gray wood-frame residence, is sited on just such a corner of forested sand. Inside, the living room, with its hardwood floors, floor-to-ceiling windows, and efficient fireplace, is an ideal spot for guests to watch the daily tidal processions change the shoreline's appearance. For more privacy, seclude yourselves in one of the two attractive guest suites. Though Window-by-the-Sea does not have the luxury of a sweeping view, it does have a peekaboo glimpse. It also has a kitchenette, a private entrance, a cozy dining nook, and plenty of room due to the fact that the bed folds up into the walls. And don't worry about tracking sand in from the beach—this suite has linoleum floors. (Not elegant, maybe, but very practical.)

For the ultimate views, book the eclectic Pacific Suite. Vaulted hemlock ceilings soar above an antique double bed, a fireplace with a raised hearth, and a huge soaking tub set next to windows. Though the decor is mismatched, glorious towering windows display spectacular ocean views from every corner of the room: you simply cannot find better in Tofino. We must warn you that this loft suite does not have a door, so your privacy is limited. Given this fact, the price tag is steep, but it is still almost worth the expense for the views alone.

THE WICKANNINNISH INN, Tofino
Osprey Lane at Chesterman Beach
(205) 725-3100, (800) 333-4604
http://www.island.net/~wick
Moderate to Unbelievably Expensive

At this exquisite, newly built property, set on a rocky cape that juts out from the western tip of Chesterman Beach, guests receive the best of two worlds: frosty white surf crashes against the jagged rocks that front the inn, and the Pacific Rim National Park secludes it in a blanket of tall trees. Visitors will witness this property's outstanding distinction when they open the large wooden doors to the engaging lobby, where elegance in nature is the main focus. Floor-to-ceiling picture windows showcase stunning views of the ocean and wooded surroundings, and attractive contemporary furnishings are accented by copper touches and dark slate floors. Each of the 46 guest rooms is decorated with unique recycled-wood furnishings in rich earth tones, and all offer views of the pounding Pacific through tall windows and private balconies. Other romantic amenities include large soaking tubs, warm gas fireplaces, refrigerators, microwaves, coffeemakers, fluffy robes, and down duvets draped over the king- or queen-size beds. Several room types are available: standard bedroom suites, several-room suites with king queen beds, rooms with two queen beds, and rooms with a queen bed and a double sofa sleeper.

Romantic Note: Don't miss out on the **POINTE RESTAURANT** (Moderate), located on the main floor of the Wickaninnish Inn. It affords panoramic views of the dramatic ocean and untamed natural surroundings. While a circular wood-burning fireplace set in the middle of the room warms the well-spaced tables, you and your sweetheart will enjoy fresh local seafood items prepared to utter excellence.

Restaurant Kissing

ORCA LODGE RESTAURANT, Tofino
1254 Pacific Rim Highway
(250) 725-2323, (800) 725-2320
Moderate to Expensive
Call for seasonal hours.

Tofino is a fishing village, so it isn't at all surprising that the local restaurants have exquisite seafood. Orca Lodge Restaurant's fare is delicious, and its dining room has the most romantic ambience in Tofino. Subtly lit by candlelight, the small, casual room is crowded with small red-clothed tables, and wraparound windows view untamed gardens. A large brick wood-burning fireplace radiates a cozy glow and the friendly service is eager to please. The servings are generous and the fresh seafood is excellent, particularly the king salmon, served with a light pesto sauce, and the steamed prawns. Herbed focaccia is served along with a saucer of balsamic vinegar and extra-virgin olive oil for Italian-style dipping.

Romantic Note: The **ORCA LODGE** also has eight guest rooms, none of which are of any romantic interest.

WEST COAST CRAB BAR, Tofino
601 Campbell Street
(250) 725-3733
Moderate
Call for seasonal hours.

Fresh seafood is abundant in the Pacific Northwest, and we've certainly eaten our share, but we'd never tasted crab quite so succulent or delicious as the crab served here. It doesn't get much fresher than this: you can actually watch the crabs swimming in a tank in the restaurant's front entrance. The casual two-level dining room has peaked wood ceilings and is overflowing with nautical paraphernalia, including tables laminated with maps. Not the most romantic of settings, but the food is so exceptional you won't think twice. Crab-stuffed mushroom caps will warm up your taste buds for the main course: tender, fresh crab served with a cup of drawn butter. Don't hesitate to order a whole crab for each of you, even if you're small eaters. It's a lot of work to crack them and you'll work up quite an appetite. (You'll also make a big mess; ask for lots of napkins.)

Outdoor Kissing

LONG BEACH

Just off Highway 4, on the west side of the road, as you head north toward the town of Tofino.

Located between Tofino and Ucluelet, Long Beach offers everything that restless surf-lovers could want. Several hiking trails run adjacent to the shoreline, which is defined by rocky cliffs, smooth white-sand beaches, old-growth rain forest, and wooded picnic areas. Romantic possibilities here are infinite: you can relax, walk along the extensive beach, hike through the forest bordering the shore, or seek the water for a salty frolic. An amazing number of surfers will be out trying to catch a wave at many spots along the beach; watching them can be quite entertaining.

WHALE WATCHING, Tofino
Jamie's Whaling Station, (250) 725-3919, (800) 667-9913
(in western Canada)
Remote Passages, (250) 725-3330, (800) 666-9833 (in Canada)
Moderate

Everything about whale watching is romantic. Imagine yourself and your loved one staring out from an open Zodiac at the cliff-lined Pacific Ocean and forested islands haloed in shades of deep, lush green. The cool morning air swirls around you as you clasp each other close for protection against the chill. As you scan the calm blue water, your thoughts are overwhelmed with the vastness before you. Then suddenly, in the distance, breaking the stillness of a sun-drenched early spring day, a spout of water explodes from the ocean surface, followed by a giant, arching black profile. After an abrupt tail slap, all is stillness once again. Believe me, even if you're not sitting next to someone you care about, you're likely to grab the person nearest you and yell, "Wow, look at that!"

Maybe it's the excitement of knowing that such an immense, powerful creature can glide so effortlessly through the water with playful agility and speed. Or it could be the chance to "connect" with a civilized mammal that knows the secret depths of an aquatic world we can only briefly visit and barely understand. Whatever the reason, a sighting of these miraculous creatures is best shared with someone special.

Romantic Note: The height of the whale migration season is in March and April, though orcas reside here year-round.

Ucluelet

Hotel/Bed and Breakfast Kissing

A SNUG HARBOUR INN, Ucluelet   Unrated
460 Marine Drive
(604) 726-2686, (888) 936-5222
http://www.virtualcities.com
Expensive to Very Expensive

As this book went to press, the last touches were being put in place on what appears to be a remarkable effort to create a romantic bed and breakfast overlooking one of the most beautiful stretches of land in the Canadian Southwest. The surroundings alone would make this an enviable place to stay, but the scope of the construction and the thoughtfulness of the details demonstrate heartwarming considerations as well. Terraced decks, incredible views, plenty of windows, large rooms, and potentially sexy bathrooms are all waiting to be filled with the owners' decorating skill. What this will all add up to remains to be seen, but we can't wait to find out.

Restaurant Kissing

WICKANINNISH RESTAURANT, Ucluelet
Highway 4
(250) 726-7706
Inexpensive to Moderate
Call for seasonal hours.

Wickaninnish is the name of an outstretched beach with hundreds of weathered logs strewn like toothpicks on the shore. A large wooden building with the same name houses an information center, a museum of Native Canadian culture, and a restaurant, all set on the edge of the sandy shore. The information center and museum, together known as the Interpretive Centre, are educational points of interest but hardly romantic, unless you want to kiss an artifact. On the other hand, the restaurant is exceptionally romantic, particularly during the off-season, when the tourists are home waiting patiently for summer.

The views are the real reason to come here. (Although it is surrounded by windows that showcase the beach and the ever-changing moods of the sea, the wood-crafted waterfront dining room is exceedingly casual.) Threatening winter storms, dramatic high tides, and still summer days make for a scene that at one moment may be languid and silent, and the next violent and thundering. Regardless of what excitement nature is providing, the Wickaninnish Restaurant will serve you tasty fish and chips, salads, and sandwiches while you sit back and watch the show.

Romantic Note: After lunch, weather permitting, hike along the beach or through the woods along nature trails that run behind the building. When you're done, return to the restaurant and drink a toast to the day you've shared together.

Nanoose Bay

Hotel/Bed and Breakfast Kissing

PACIFIC SHORES NATURE RESORT, Nanoose Bay
1655 Strougler Road
(250) 468-7121
Inexpensive to Very Expensive

You don't have to own one of Pacific Shores' ultra-luxurious time-share condominiums to enjoy the resort's spectacular beachfront location for an evening. Everything about Pacific Shores is a dream come true—even the prices. The 52 (soon to be 152) sparkling new units are immaculately and lovingly maintained, and several rental units are available when a time-share space hasn't been taken.

The owners of these units have taken great care to make this place special. Sumptuous twists of fabric beautify bay windows that look out over the ocean. Appointments are contemporary and elegant, including Jacuzzi tubs, fireplaces, and TV/VCRs. Gorgeous linens accentuate four-poster beds in the large master bedrooms. Prices are linked to the size and view of unit you request: the larger the unit and the better the view, the more you pay. And don't forget to request a water view when booking your reservation.

A garden nursery, movie rental shop, and indoor swimming pool are all available to guests. Outside, waves lap at sandstone beaches and strategically placed lighting illuminates the sea-wall nature walk. You'll be so enthralled with this property that you may be almost too distracted to kiss, at least for the first few moments.

Nanaimo

Industrialized and overdeveloped Nanaimo is one of the largest cities on Vancouver Island's east side, and it doesn't offer much for romantic travelers. But once you step outside the city limits, the kissing can begin.

Hotel/Bed and Breakfast Kissing

YESTERYEAR FARM AND GUEST HOUSE, Nanaimo
3005 Quennell Road
(250) 245-4297
Inexpensive

Talk about a change of pace! Once you've settled down on Yesteryear's 33-acre working farm and made friends with the amiable farm animals, the city will feel light-years away. Explore the orchards, admire the flower and vegetable gardens, or relax by a tranquil pond. Learn more about the well-cared-for chickens, rabbits, horses, oxen, and sheep who call this home. Guests are encouraged (but not expected) to participate in seasonal farm activities, ranging from haymaking and fence building to gardening and berry picking.

Two of the three reasonably priced guest rooms here are worth recommending. Both the Gatehouse and the Carriage Room are appointed with attractive antiques, blond hardwood floors, and private baths with glass-enclosed showers. We were especially partial to the Gatehouse, with its queen-size sleigh bed and lush linens. Couples with a sense of humor and adventure are the best candidates for the remaining option: the Hay Loft, situated on the upper floor of the adjacent barn, beside an actual hay loft. The shower for this suite is in the wash rack with the horses. (Hard to believe, but true!) Definitely for horse lovers only!

Complete your experience with a homemade, delicious farm breakfast, served to guests in the cozy main house or on the outside deck when the weather permits.

Restaurant Kissing

OLD MAHLE HOUSE, Nanaimo
Cedar and Hemer Roads
(250) 722-3621
http://www.island.net/~mahle
Expensive
Call for seasonal hours.

If you're ready to escape Nanaimo's overdeveloped core, head out to the rolling countryside for a breath of fresh air at this lovingly restored farmhouse turned restaurant. Hardwood floors, Oriental rugs, and stained glass windows adorn the home's original living areas, which have been converted into charming dining rooms. French doors open to a bright sunroom which functions as a second dining room, surrounded by windows with views of an expansive grassy yard and gardens. At night, wall sconces cast a soft glow on the green wrought-iron chairs, tables draped with floral linens, and colorful modern artwork.

Wonderful smells float in the air, whetting your appetite for the menu's variety of seafood and pasta dishes. Appetizers include tasty choices such as phyllo rolls stuffed with white asparagus, baked pistachio-crusted goat cheese, and prawns served with wasabi mayonnaise. We had difficulty deciding between the fresh ahi coated with black and white sesame seeds and the ultra-fresh vegetarian linguine, so we ordered both and shared. Desserts change daily and are worth saving room for.

Ladysmith

Ladysmith offers few accommodations of any kind, so the serenely beautiful forested surroundings are all but unspoiled. Nevertheless, we did find a couple of romantic possibilities lucky enough to be located in this glorious natural landscape.

Hotel/Bed and Breakfast Kissing

YELLOW POINT LODGE, Ladysmith
3700 Yellow Point Road
(250) 245-7422
Moderate to Expensive (includes three meals and three teas per day)
Minimum stay requirement on weekends and holidays

One of British Columbia's more popular getaways, Yellow Point Lodge is well known for many reasons: its remote location, its extensive beach and secluded coves bordered by 180 acres of forest, the attentive staff, the laid-back ambience, and the huge seaside saltwater swimming pool. There is no need to do anything more strenuous than deciding what to wear to the three hearty family-style meals and three teas (included in the price of your stay) served daily in the handsome main lodge.

Upon arrival the first thing you might detect is the noticeable lack of children anywhere in sight. They aren't allowed here, which is an emphatic romantic advantage. Perhaps the second thing you'll notice, particularly in the warm and inviting main lodge, is the fact that everybody seems to know each other. This is not an illusion—they really *do* know each other. A unique reservation system ensures that guests are guaranteed the same room on the same date one year later (and every consecutive year after that, if they so choose). As a result, many of the people you see have been spending the same week together, year after year, for a long, long time. Most who come here consider it an advantage, but it can feel uncomfortable when you're the only ones who don't know anybody else.

Lodgings here are eclectic. Romantically speaking, we highly recommend the newer white beach cabins that line the ocean shore, tucked among tall pines. Down comforters, sitting areas, private bathrooms with shower, and incredible water views make these the most desirable options. The sprawling property also holds many other accommodations in assorted price ranges, including rooms in the main lodge that offer some water views and unluxurious furnishings, and cottages that feature private bathrooms, beautiful ocean vistas through lofty pine trees, and very rustic decor. The least desirable choices are the barracks and the cabins that share a communal bathroom, unless you're really in the mood to rough it.

Restaurant Kissing

THE CROW AND GATE
NEIGHBORHOOD PUB, Ladysmith
2313 Yellow Point Road
(250) 722-3731
Inexpensive
Lunch and Dinner Daily

If you've never visited the English countryside, this authentic British pub overflowing with rustic appeal and old-world charm is the next best thing. Surrounded by rolling meadows and tall pines, the small Tudor-style house and its captivating rose arbor provide refuge to weary, hungry travelers.

Guests can dine inside at cozy wooden tables arranged near the stone fireplace or outside (where the cigarette smoke is not as thick) at picnic tables shaded by umbrellas. The food, mostly traditional British fare, is better than you might expect.

Chemainus

Many people wonder what exactly the town of Chemainus did to earn its too cute but triumphant nickname, "The Little Town That Did." Once an economically depressed logging community, the small, nondescript suburb was totally transformed by a revitalization project implemented in 1980. World-class artists were solicited from all over British Columbia to paint a series of murals on storefronts throughout town. These impressive illustrations enthralled (and still enthrall) thousands of tourists a year, and, as a direct result, Chemainus is now thriving. Thus, its nickname. Although the murals are interesting, you do have to contend with an overwhelming number of visitors, all flocking here to see the same thing. What most people don't know, however, is that there are other lip-worthy reasons to visit Chemainus.

Hotel/Bed and Breakfast Kissing

BIRD SONG COTTAGE, Chemainus
9909 Maple Street
(250) 246-9910
Inexpensive
Closed January

Fronted by flower gardens and a trickling fountain, this pink stucco home with lavender and white gingerbread trim looks too precious to be real. It is real, though, from the beautiful Victorian furnishings and eclectic collectibles to the larger-than-life oil paintings and the live birds trilling sweet songs. Fancy antique hats and whimsical old-fashioned dresses, part of the innkeepers' ongoing collection, are tucked in every corner.

Bird Song Cottage offers three guest rooms: one on the main floor, just off the common area, and two more upstairs. Nightingale, on the main floor, is outfitted with plush green linens and a crisp white coverlet, pale green walls, a cozy window seat, a private bathroom with a claw-foot tub, and a door that opens to a small patio and colorful gardens. Blue Bird and Hummingbird are smaller, with slanted dormer ceilings, but each has a private bathroom, soothing blue linens, and lots of country Victorian charm.

In the morning, a full gourmet breakfast is accompanied by live piano music in one of the prettiest rooms in the house, an airy garden room awash in flowing white lace and hanging flowers.

LITTLE INN ON WILLOW STREET, Chemainus
9849 Willow Street
(250) 246-4987
http://island.net/~inkeeper
Expensive

Affectionately referred to as "the world's smallest luxury hotel," this entire property is available for rent—in a manner of speaking. Enveloped by lovingly manicured flower gardens, this miniature, red-turreted gingerbread-style castle has only one guest room. A complimentary bottle of chilled champagne is the first of several distinct romantic details you will encounter here. At the touch of a finger, a fire burns in the hearth, illuminating a queen-size canopy bed veiled in richly colored fabric. A Jacuzzi tub, built just for two, is sheltered in the corner of the bedroom, which is furnished with baronial European antiques and a TV/VCR. And for the final romantic touch: a masseuse is available upon request at $40 for an hour and a half of pure bliss.

ONCE UPON A TIME INN, Chemainus
9940 Cedar Street
(250) 246-1059
Inexpensive to Moderate

Once upon a time, a massive mauve Victorian sat peacefully just blocks from the water, until one day it was transformed into an attractive bed and breakfast filled with antiques. Now it provides a setting where the two of you can make up your own romantic adventures. The four guest rooms, located on the first, second, and third floors, are painstakingly decorated with beautiful period antiques and sumptuous floral linens; all boast full or partial views of the water. The Main Suite, embellished with floral wallpaper, hardwood floors, and lace curtains, has a large bathroom with Oriental area rugs and a claw-foot tub. The Angel Room and the Rose Room are smaller and share a detached bathroom with a claw-foot tub and rose-colored wainscoting. On the third floor, the Skylight Suite is filled with contemporary furnishings; it has a spacious bathroom, and the owners plan to add a Jacuzzi tub soon.

On rainy days, you can stay warm by playing a game of pool in the game room, located next door, which also features a TV/VCR, comfy couches, and surrounding windows that showcase the untamed landscape. In the main house, you can relax in the guest parlor, which is filled with Victorian furnishings and knickknacks, or play a duet at the grand piano in the corner. Just off this main parlor is the breakfast room, where guests can enjoy a full breakfast by candlelight every morning.

PACIFIC SHORES INN, Chemainus
9847 Willow Street
(250) 246-4987
http://island.net/~inkeeper
Inexpensive

A sculpted captain with a telescope keeps watch from the rooftop of this light blue gabled inn. Situated on a corner in a residential neighborhood, Pacific Shores Inn is owned by the same company as the **LITTLE INN ON WILLOW STREET** (reviewed above). Although the three suites at Pacific Shores are less luxurious than its sister property, they are still very attractive and the prices are as reasonable as they get. Private entrances ensure your sense of isolation in each room, and tasteful country Victorian furnishings provide an old-fashioned ambience. A lovely Edwardian canopy bed is a particularly enchanting feature in the Duchess Room, which is accented with white lace curtains and beautiful antiques. Amenities include full kitchens and TV/VCRs, and, if you're in the mood to be utterly spoiled, an on-site masseuse is available. Breakfast is not provided with your stay, but the owners offer discount coupons for waffles at a nearby sweet shop.

Restaurant Kissing

WATERFORD RESTAURANT, Chemainus
9875 Maple Street
(250) 246-1046
Inexpensive to Moderate
Lunch and Dinner Tuesday-Sunday

The Waterford's cheerful cafe-style ambience has made it one of the more popular lunch spots in Chemainus. Taking up the main floor of a renovated Victorian home, the restaurant's sunny interior has been sponge-painted blue and white and adorned with watercolors by local artists. Intimate is the last word we'd use to describe the otherwise nondescript decor, and the service can be iffy, but the kitchen's specialty crêpes are among the best we've tasted and well worth stopping for.

Duncan

Hotel/Bed and Breakfast Kissing

FAIRBURN FARM COUNTRY MANOR, Duncan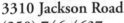
3310 Jackson Road
(250) 746-4637
Moderate to Expensive
Minimum stay requirement on weekends
Call for seasonal closures.

It is essential for those of us who live in cities to reconnect with the earth every now and then, to restore the soul and our capacity to love. Fairburn Farm offers just such an opportunity, and the Archer family with their six children welcome you to share the experience of authentic farm life. A long, meandering drive leading past burnished red barns, grazing cattle, and thriving crops brings you to one of the most beautiful rural settings imaginable: a pretty white farmhouse with a spacious veranda surrounded by rolling green hills, flawless forested grounds, sweeping fields, abundant vegetable gardens, and brilliant flowers.

Built in 1884, the home looks much as it did back then, having under-gone only what you might call necessary changes. All six homey guest rooms have private baths (three are detached), and two of the more romantic rooms have gas fireplaces and bathtubs with whirlpool jets. Fresh flowers brighten the provincial, eclectic decor in each of the rooms.

Breakfast too is a hearty, true-to-life country affair served in the owners' old-fashioned dining room. Almost all of the food served is produced on the farm, including the eggs, vegetables, fresh-churned butter, stone-ground wheat bread, real maple syrup tapped from the trees, and homemade jams. Meals like this soothe and satisfy in a way store-bought fare never can.

Romantic Suggestion: If you really want hands-on farming experience, take the opportunity to milk one of the farm's dairy cows. It's harder than you think!

GROVE HALL ESTATE, Duncan
6159 Lakes Road
(250) 746-6152
Expensive; No Credit Cards

Venerable oak trees usher you to the end of a long driveway, where a magnificent turn-of-the-century Tudor mansion awaits, set on 17 acres of gardens, sweeping lawns, and accessible lakefront. Once you've slipped your feet out of your shoes and into a pair of soft Indonesian silk slippers, you'll feel as if you've been transported to another place and time. Intriguing antiques collected from Asia and the Middle East are tastefully and elegantly showcased throughout the mansion's luxurious interior, where deep red Oriental carpets grace gleaming pine floors. In the evening, gourmet appetizers are served in the formal dining room with views of the lake. Appropriately regal breakfasts are also served here the following morning.

Three exotic guest suites located upstairs are equally impressive. A huge, handcrafted Chinese wedding bed is the star of the spacious Singapore Room (our favorite), accented with stunning antiques and a view of the lake and gardens. An extra sitting room and a private balcony provide even more space in the lovely Indonesia Suite, which showcases art pieces and batiks from that part of the world. Last is the brightly decorated Siamese Room, appointed with—you guessed it—twin beds, which can be pushed together to facilitate a romantic agenda. Indonesian fabrics and prints in all of the rooms are unusual but add authenticity. For the most privacy, rent the self-contained cottage. If you have a penchant for the 1930s, you'll love it; otherwise, the furnishings and linens might feel somewhat dated.

If this picture-perfect escape has a flaw, it can only be the shared bathroom facilities in the main house, although two full baths are available and each is uniquely lovely. In our opinion, this is a small sacrifice to make for the enchantment to be found at Grove Hall Estate.

SAHTLAM LODGE, Duncan
5720 Riverbottom Road West
(250) 748-7738
Moderate to Expensive
Closed January
Recommended Wedding Site

We can't encourage you enough to call for directions to get here. Sahtlam Lodge is situated out in the middle of nowhere, a definite kissing advantage. (Actually, "lodge" is a misnomer; there are only four cabins here.) Located by a surging river and embraced by seven and a half acres of lofty pines, the self-contained cabins are rustic, eclectic, and, most of all, isolated. Best for romantic intentions is the Meadow Cabin, set next to a duck pond; amenities include a fireplace, a kitchenette, and a cedar-and-glass bedroom with a vaulted ceiling. The Log Cabin is a slightly more rustic romantic alternative, with a loft bedroom, glimpses of the river through the trees, and an extra-long 1920s soaking tub. Geared more for families, it has two bedrooms, a full kitchen, and a private small yard. The remaining cabins are too rustic to mention. A breakfast basket is included on the first night of your stay, and after that further baskets can be ordered from the kitchen.

Perhaps Sahtlam Lodge's most attractive accommodations are the "Tent Bedrooms," perched near the banks of the river. Lit by hurricane lamps, these unique, safari-style platform tents have shingled roofs and walls of mosquito netting and canvas. Depending on your romantic inclinations, they may be the best kissing spots on the property. The next best are located across the river, where you are transported by a river cart to 12 secluded miles of riverside walking paths.

During the day, guests can inner-tube or swim in the river; in the evening, a walk in the lighted garden is breathtaking.

Romantic Note: You don't have to get in your car to find a good place to dine. The **SAHTLAM LODGE RESTAURANT** serves excellent food (see Restaurant Kissing).

Restaurant Kissing

INGLENOOK RESTAURANT, Duncan
7621 Trans-Canada Highway
(250) 746-4031
Moderate to Expensive
Dinner Tuesday-Sunday

Set just off the main highway and surrounded by flower gardens, this two-story Tudor home holds one of the nicer restaurants on Vancouver Island.

Reservations are highly recommended; walk-ins are difficult to accommodate, due to nonstop crowds. Rustic yet elegant, the three upstairs dining rooms feature knotty pine walls and an eclectic mixture of watercolors, modern artwork, and vintage antiques. The well-spaced tables are accented by white linens and surrounded by beautifully embroidered chairs. Classical music in the background sets the perfect tempo for a leisurely evening. Service is gracious and efficient, even when they're understaffed.

The kitchen specializes in German cuisine, featuring primarily meat and poultry dishes. During our visit here, the most memorable appetizer was the Brie baked in phyllo, perfectly complemented by a dollop of fruity mango sauce. We were so taken with this dish, we came very close to ordering two.

QUAMICHAN INN, Duncan
1478 Maple Bay Road
(250) 746-7028
Moderate to Expensive
Dinner Tuesday-Sunday
Recommended Wedding Site

What a shame you can't eat charm, because this is one charming location for dinner. Set just off the road on a knoll overlooking the Cowichan Valley, the restaurant's three dining rooms occupy the lower level of a handsome Tudor home, adorned with antiques and glowing fireplaces. Silver candleholders and maroon linens give every table an elegant appearance, although the floral carpeting that runs throughout is a little bit loud. When the weather is clear, the most romantic spot to dine is outside on a rock patio overlooking a verdant lawn, gardens, and a footbridge that crosses a little fish pond. The eclectic menu features meat and seafood; we recommend the latter, particularly the generous seafood taster's platter, overflowing with mussels, clams, scallops, crab, fish, lobster, and every other imaginable delicacy from the sea.

Romantic Note: The inn also has bed-and-breakfast rooms upstairs, but they are not recommended for romantic interludes. Smells and sounds from the restaurant too easily travel upstairs.

SAHTLAM LODGE RESTAURANT, Duncan
5720 Riverbottom Road
(250) 748-7738
Moderate
Dinner Thursday-Sunday

Even if you're not an overnight guest at Sahtlam Lodge, we encourage you to visit the property's restaurant, located in a weathered Tudor home filled with antiques and turn-of-the-century keepsakes. The dining rooms are lined with large windows that command river and forest views, and the handfuls of tables scattered throughout are decorated with floral linens, dried flower arrangements, and other countrified touches. If you arrive early for your reservation, you can start the evening by snuggling up in lounge chairs arranged beside an immense stone fireplace.

Once you are seated, you will not be disappointed: the kitchen serves a four-course gourmet procession of skillfully prepared international cuisine. Menus are seasonal. Your evening repast might include smoked salmon tortellini, creamy carrot soup served with fresh maple bread, and lemon pork with sautéed apples and lentils, or roasted corn and garlic bisque, spring rolls with caramelized chutney, and seafood lasagna. Just remembering our meal makes our mouths water.

Cowichan Bay

Restaurant Kissing

THE MASTHEAD RESTAURANT, Cowichan Bay
1705 Cowichan Bay Road
(250) 748-3714
Moderate
Dinner Daily

With views of bobbing fishing vessels and the forested hills across the water, The Masthead is a picturesque spot to dine (if you can manage to find parking). Colorful flower boxes accent the slightly weathered dockside building that houses the dining room. Inside, white linens and candlelight create a subtle romantic mood. Fresh fish, the kind that jumps from the boat onto your plate, is the specialty here. Succulent oysters; king salmon, and halibut are served with French flair and are remarkably good.

Mill Bay

Hotel/Bed and Breakfast Kissing

PINE LODGE FARM BED AND BREAKFAST, Mill Bay
3191 Mutter Road
(250) 743-4083
Inexpensive
Call for seasonal closures.

Venture 25 miles north of Victoria to experience serene countryside encompassed by welcome quiet. This seven-bedroom manor has an impressive white-pine exterior and an interior that is equally fascinating in its handsome detail and presence (at least in the common areas). Surrounded by a second-floor balcony, the spacious sitting room has an enormous beachstone fireplace and an admirable but cluttered collection of vintage antiques. Unfortunately, the dim, homespun, and small guest rooms upstairs aren't nearly as impressive as the common area or the grounds. Rooms with a peekaboo view of the fields, the Strait of Georgia, and the islands are the only ones worth your consideration. Breakfast is a last-you-all-day enterprise prepared with fresh eggs and homemade preserves.

Malahat

Hotel/Bed and Breakfast Kissing

THE AERIE, Malahat
600 Ebadora Lane
(250) 743-7115
http://www.aerie.com
Very Expensive to Unbelievably Expensive
Minimum stay requirement seasonally
Recommended Wedding Site

In terms of grandeur and extravagance, nothing in the Pacific Northwest or the Canadian Southwest quite compares to The Aerie. This grandiose, sparkling white Mediterranean-style villa with turquoise accents looks as if it belongs in Beverly Hills or Los Angeles. The only reminder that you are still in the great Northwest is the fresh mountain air and serene setting on a remote, forested hillside. The 25-minute drive from Victoria is beautiful, but many guests of The Aerie choose to helicopter in (the resort has two landing pads specifically for this purpose). From the Aerie, views of the distant Olympic Mountains, tree-covered islands, and a peaceful inlet below are absolutely stunning—and sunsets are unforgettable.

From the moment you arrive at the sprawling, multiterraced resort, you are spoiled by luxury. A full-service spa is open for all of your pampering needs, and the glass-enclosed pool, equipped with water jets, is lit by everchanging colored halogen lights. Every inch of the interior is filled with exotic, oversized furnishings. You can get lost in the armchairs, and the ornately carved mirrors, four-poster beds, and handsome buffets are almost too opulent. Many of the 20 rooms have sexy tubs for two, private decks with outrageously glorious views, buttery leather sofas, and other sensuous appointments. And did we mention the ultra-thick down comforters, Christian Dior linens, vaulted ceilings, and peach color schemes found in many rooms?

At the top of the line are the eight lavish, multileveled Aerie Suites, each with a large hydro-massage tub framed by columns in the center of the room, a gas fireplace, a king-size four-poster canopied bed, and an extra-large deck. Unfortunately, some of the decks offer little privacy, and many have views of the tennis courts or parking lot in the foreground. (This may seem minor, but at these prices, you have a right to be picky.) The standard rooms, located one floor below the reception area, are not nearly as grand but still fall in the Very Expensive price category. Some have small balconies with incredible views, but they are right next to the balcony of the neighboring room. Also, these rooms have red exit signs above the patio door (probably for safety reasons but they detracted from the ambience and stated the obvious). Finally, we must mention that the faux marble touches (found in every bathroom and even on some furnishings) look too artificial and compromise the otherwise glamorous fantasy of staying at The Aerie. Despite this, The Aerie still provides a one-of-a-kind experience that will surely inspire many kisses.

A generous full breakfast, included with your stay, is served in the elegant dining room overlooking the inspiring mountain scenery. Dinners here are also a four-lip experience (see Restaurant Kissing).

Restaurant Kissing

THE AERIE, Malahat
600 Ebadora Lane
(250) 743-7115
http://www.aerie.com
Very Expensive to Unbelievably Expensive
Dinner Daily

Who would have thought that a wooded hillside in the middle of nowhere could harbor an extravagant resort? Well, The Aerie is nothing if not extravagant, and you are sure to enjoy a heart-stirring meal at this "castle in the mountains." Located on a Malahat mountainside, The Aerie's dining room possesses a 180-degree view of the Olympic Mountains and the twinkling lights of Port Angeles across the Strait of Juan de Fuca. This awesome vista is enhanced by an elegant interior filled with glittering chandeliers, stately faux marble columns, high-backed upholstered chairs, perfectly pressed white table linens, and massive floral arrangements. Above you is a 14-karat gold-foiled ceiling. If you can't kiss here, it's only because you're too busy getting accustomed to the sumptuous surroundings instead of puckering up.

French-inspired cuisine is the kitchen's forte. Artfully presented dishes such as Caribbean lobster tail in a delectable herb crust and pheasant with juniper-port sauce are exceptional. Try to save room for dessert: the Grand Marnier soufflé and chocolate nougat mousse are satisfying finales.

Romantic Note: There are no dress requirements here, but most guests save up to come to The Aerie for a special occasion. Attire can be relatively formal.

Sidney

Restaurant Kissing

DEEP COVE CHALET, Sidney
11190 Chalet Road
(250) 656-3541
Expensive to Very Expensive
Lunch and Dinner Tuesday-Sunday

This secluded restaurant overlooking Saanich Inlet is quintessentially French and enticingly romantic. A good 30-minute drive north from Victoria, the enchanting wood-frame building is set on manicured lawns dotted with trees and enclosed by low brick walls. Inside, tables draped in white linens stand in stark contrast to dark wood columns, and large picture windows afford stunning views of the inlet. Everything is gracious and elegant, with a congenial, homey feeling.

Prices are high, but every dish is beautifully presented and prepared with the greatest skill. Choice entrées include flavorful lobster bisque, savory crêpes with mushrooms in a smooth beurre blanc sauce, an airy yet rich cheese soufflé, and perhaps the best escargots in puffed pastry to be found anywhere. Meats and fish are always perfectly prepared, and the sauces are light but distinctive.

Romantic Warning: Lunchtime at the Deep Cove Chalet is often plagued by swarms of tourists that arrive by the busload. Dinner may be your best option when planning a romantic interlude.

THE LATCH COUNTRY INN, Sidney
2328 Harbour Road
(604) 656-6622
Moderate to Expensive
Call for seasonal hours.

Tucked away in a residential area, this imposing timber lodge was originally built in the 1920s for one of British Columbia's lieutenant governors. Recent renovations have turned it into a lovely, flower-trimmed country inn where European-style cuisine is served in two handsomely appointed dining rooms. Soft lighting and candles on each table enhance the burgundy accents and light up the polished native woods embellishing the walls. Shelves of antique books in one dining room and a gas fireplace in the other add to the warm ambience. During summer, casual patio seating overlooking the neighboring marina is set up to accommodate guests who prefer the outdoors. The Latch Country Inn is a welcome addition to Sidney's dining scene, and you can expect to find good service and fine meals here.

Romantic Option: Five handsome guest rooms are available on the second floor of **THE LATCH COUNTRY INN** (Inexpensive to Very Expensive). The dark wood paneling continues upstairs, and each room features rich color schemes and Canadian furnishings. Private baths, down comforters, telephones, and televisions are additional amenities. Ask about the inn's "Romantic Gourmet" packages, which include a five-course meal with an overnight stay.

Victoria

As much as possible, this book excludes big tourist draws, and without question Victoria is a sprawling center of tourist activity. But Victoria's charisma is hard to ignore, even in summer when the crowds swell beyond romantic tolerance. The famous Empress Hotel, stately Parliament Building, Butchart Gardens, the parks, museums, cobblestone streets, cozy restaurants, and Edwardian-style shops—combined with a thriving harbor and marina framed in the distance by the Olympic Mountains—make the city an Anglophile's nirvana. And it can be particularly wonderful during the off-season. It may even make you feel lustfully regal.

Romantic Reminder: The cost ratings in this section are listed in Canadian funds and correspond with the chart at the front of the book. For example, an establishment that charges $135 Canadian per night is listed in the Expensive range. American travelers should keep in mind that this price translates into about $100 US per night, so it is actually considered Moderate in U.S. dollars. The rates are listed in Canadian funds due to the fluctuating exchange rate, and for the ease of our Canadian readers. Innkeepers

---

Cost ratings for British Columbia listings are in Canadian funds. American travelers should check the exchange rate or ask an innkeeper to figure out the cost in U.S. dollars.

are used to translating funds for travelers from the States if you need assistance figuring out the U.S. dollar value.

Romantic Suggestion: Victoria is a wonderful walking city and you would do well to leave your car at home. (When you see the summer crowds and read about the hassle and cost involved in bringing your car, you will see what we mean.) If you are staying anywhere within a ten-block radius of Government Street, most of what you'll want to see and do is easily accessible. Victoria's bus system, **B.C. TRANSIT**, can take you anywhere in the city; for questions about bus routes call (250) 382-6161. Rental bicycles and motor scooters are another fun way to explore the city and can be rented from **BUDGET CAR RENTAL** at (250) 388-7874 or **AVIS RENT A CAR** at (800) 879-2847.

The following information and directions may sound complicated, but once you choose your route, it is just a matter of hopping on a ferry and then waiting to cross the water. No matter how you get there, Victoria is definitely worth the trip.

From Seattle: The **VICTORIA CLIPPER**, (206) 448-5000 in Seattle, (250) 382-8100 in Victoria, (800) 888-2535 outside of Victoria and Seattle, operates a passenger-only ferry service year-round. This trip is hardly inexpensive (about $80 US per person round-trip), but the *Clipper's* comfortable, high-speed, water-jet-propelled catamarans will get you there relatively quickly (in about two and a half hours).

VICTORIA LINE, (800) 683-7977 in the United States, (800) 668-1167 in Canada, offers the only car and passenger ferry departing from Seattle. It makes just one round-trip sailing per day, from mid-May through mid-September, so if you are traveling at any other time of the year and need your car with you, skip ahead to another route. It costs to take your car with you (around $135 US round-trip for the car, driver, and one passenger), but the ship is comfortable, with a bar, two restaurants, and a game room. The trip takes about four and a half hours each way. If the length of the trip doesn't bother you and you are not taking your car, you can be a walk-on passenger on the Victoria Line for about half the price charged by the Victoria Clipper.

From Port Angeles: BLACK BALL FERRY TRANSPORT, (360) 457-4491 in Port Angeles, (250) 386-2202 in Victoria, runs a car and passenger ferry between Port Angeles and Victoria. Call for information about fares and sailing schedules. If you do plan to take your car, this route can be a traveler's worst nightmare. During peak season you have to get your car in line at least 12 hours in advance. That's right, *12 hours*! And no matter how slowly you shop, there simply aren't 12 hours' worth of places to browse in downtown Port Angeles. Another time-saving option is to leave your car in a convenient and inexpensive nearby parking lot, and walk onto the ferry fairly cheaply.

The passenger-only **VICTORIA EXPRESS**, (360) 452-8088 in Port Angeles, (250) 361-9144 in Victoria, is an additional option between Port Angeles and Victoria. Call for information about fares and sailing schedules.

From Vancouver via Tsawwassen: The Canadians have it figured out. Perhaps the easiest and most frequent runs are from the Tsawwassen ferry terminal, just 30 minutes south of Vancouver. (This ferry docks in Sidney, about 20 minutes north of Victoria.) The huge, fastidiously maintained ferryboats leave every hour. Summer weekends can be intense, but you only have to wait a sailing or two even at the busiest times. A second nearby option is the Anacortes-Sidney ferry run by the **WASHINGTON STATE FERRIES**, (206) 464-6400, (800) 543-3779 (in Washington). Unfortunately the wait for this ferry is usually long, particularly on weekends and holidays.

Hotel/Bed and Breakfast Kissing

ABIGAIL'S HOTEL, Victoria
906 McClure Street
(250) 388-5363, (800) 561-6565
http://www.getawaymag.com
Expensive to Very Expensive

Abigail's used to be one in a group of three prominent Victoria bed and breakfasts owned by the same company. Although still first-class, this professionally run, country-style inn now stands alone, and the dedicated owners are putting their hearts and souls into keeping it that way. Every nuance of comfort has been attended to (except for an elevator to take you and your luggage up to the third floor).

Surrounded by lovely English gardens, this classic 1930 Tudor mansion is located several blocks from downtown on a tranquil cul-de-sac. It has been renovated into a comfortable, modern inn with all the comforts of a hotel, and finished in pastels and floral prints. Each of the 16 rooms is designed with only two things in mind: romance and pampering. Features include private spa tubs, wood-burning fireplaces, plush carpeting, antique wash stands, and thick goose-down comforters. Even the smaller rooms are sunny and nicely decorated. Of course, the most expensive "Celebration Rooms" are the most luxurious, but they are worth it.

A wood-burning granite fireplace warms the library on the main floor, where champagne and hors d'oeuvres are served each afternoon. In the morning, you and your true love can enjoy a gracious, generous breakfast at one of several tables in the cheery breakfast room. Morning repasts may include fresh fruit, muffins, jalapeño-cheese biscuits, lemon-pecan pancakes, and eggs Victoria. For an additional fee, breakfast can be delivered to your room in a large wicker basket. If you have a special occasion to celebrate, or can invent one, Abigail's is an ideal place to come. Affectionate celebration packages are also available.

Romantic Option: If you're traveling with a family or another couple, ask about **ABIGAIL'S BEACH HOUSE.** This 1928 home, only a ten-minute drive from downtown, is comfortably appointed with two bedrooms, a fully equipped kitchen, a sunroom, and a wood-burning fireplace in the living room. In the morning, you have the option of joining the other guests at Abigail's Hotel for breakfast.

ANDERSEN HOUSE, Victoria
301 Kingston Street
(250) 388-4565
Expensive to Very Expensive

Bed and breakfasts in historic homes typically feature furnishings from the corresponding period, but this turn-of-the-century Queen Anne Victorian is boldly decorated in fresh, artistic style. From the moment you enter the bright and open parlor with its high ceiling, hardwood floor, and original modern artwork, you know that the Andersen House is unique.

Your first impression is confirmed in the four guest rooms, each with a stereo and a selection of compact discs. On the top floor, the sunny Casablanca Room is decorated with Peruvian rugs on the hardwood floors, a four-poster bed, and a casual mix of antique furnishings and modern art; a small private deck shows off distant Olympic Mountain views, and a curved staircase leads down to the garden in the backyard. Also on the top floor is the Captain's Apartment, a self-contained two-bedroom unit with a small kitchenette, extra-long claw-foot tub, eclectic furnishings, and enough space to really get comfortable. Perhaps the most romantic room in the house is the ground-level Garden Studio, which has a marble-surrounded two-person Jacuzzi tub. Colorful flower beds are right outside your window, and you can venture out to the tranquil backyard and enjoy the shade of the 100-year-old weeping willow. (We think this is a great place to kiss.)

Another great kissing site is the Andersen House's completely separate lodging option located at the Victoria Harbour, or, more appropriately, *in* the harbor. The innkeepers rent their 50-foot 1927 classic motor yacht, *Mamita*, to one couple at a time. Polished teak warms the interior, and there is a double bed and views of the setting sun. You can sit on the deck to watch the diverse water traffic passing by or relax in the cozy below-deck salon, with velvet-covered benches and a skylight. *Mamita* truly is a special escape. A five-minute walk from the harbor takes you back to the main house, where you join the other guests for a full gourmet breakfast.

ARUNDEL MANOR, Victoria
980 Arundel Drive
(250) 385-5442
Moderate to Expensive; No Credit Cards

A ten-minute drive north of the town center, this lovely 1912 heritage home sits on a grassy knoll overlooking Portage Inlet. Arundel Manor is a truly classic Victorian-style bed and breakfast, complete with all the appropriate, engaging details: handsome antiques, silver service, English china, and a charming innkeeper who makes gourmet breakfasts. Morning repasts such as salmon-stuffed crêpes with béarnaise sauce are served to guests at individual tables. Ask if the lemon preserves are available; if they are, spread some over her freshly baked goodies or fresh fruit crêpes for a tasty treat.

The four guest rooms upstairs, each done up in a comfortable Victorian manner, are spacious and exceedingly comfortable; all have private baths, although one is detached. The Rose Room and the Plum Room, with private balconies overlooking the water, are the best. Peacefully witnessing a sunset from this vantage point will make you thankful you are several miles from the liveliness of downtown Victoria.

BEACH COTTAGE, Victoria
Reservations through Beaconsfield Inn
(250) 384-4044
http://www.islandnet.com/beaconsfield
Unbelievably Expensive
Minimum stay requirement on weekends seasonally

If waterfront accommodations are what you need to set the proper romantic tone (and if you can handle a lofty price tag), then get out your Gold Card and call for reservations at Beach Cottage. This petite home, set right on Cadboro Bay, could have easily been renovated to house a family or several couples at a time. Instead, it was lovingly remodeled specifically with couples in mind, so you will have the place to yourselves. The single bedroom, which is extremely spacious, holds an antiqued pine king-size sleigh bed and two-person Jacuzzi tub. Pale hardwood floors in the living room set off the country-style decor, and a wood-burning fireplace with a massive river-rock hearth adds ambient warmth. There is another fireplace in the cozy entertainment room, but you will probably prefer gazing through the living room's expansive windows, which cover one wall and provide an outstanding view of the bay and nearby marina. The sunny little Arts and Crafts–style kitchen is equipped with all of the appliances, utensils, and dishes you might need, so you can bring your own groceries and eat in if you so desire; beakfast fixings are left for you in the fridge.

If a moonlight soak strikes your fancy, you can relax in an outdoor Jacuzzi tub beside the house. Another romantic option is to wander along the small stretch of beach that is right outside your door and across a small lawn. Don't get us wrong, we find Victoria thoroughly charming, but we must say that it is nice to feel so removed from the busy atmosphere of downtown. At Beach Cottage you are close enough to go into the city when you please, and then quickly escape when you are ready for peace and quiet.

Romantic Note: Maid service is provided only every third day.

BEACONSFIELD INN, Victoria   💋💋💋💋
998 Humboldt Street
(250) 384-4044
http://www.islandnet.com/beaconsfield
Very Expensive to Unbelievably Expensive
Minimum stay requirement on weekends seasonally

Many inns claim old-world charm, but few can live up to the term. The Beaconsfield Inn not only succeeds, this beautifully restored English manor provides a turn-of-the-century haven to rejuvenate city-tired spirits. Lavish, fragrant flower gardens brighten the inn's classic brown and cream exterior. The garden seems to accompany you indoors as you enter and pass through a plant-filled sunroom. Beyond here, though, rich dark mahogany takes over (at least on the main floor). Black leather love seats, walls of bookcases, and a gas-log fireplace make the library a perfect setting for afternoon tea or evening sherry and a snack.

Seven guest rooms are located on the first and second floors, and two suites occupy the lower garden level. A half split of champagne, cameo chocolates, and fresh flowers from the garden await in each room. The decor varies, but gorgeous antiques, leaded stained-glass windows, fine linens, down comforters, and attractive color schemes appear throughout. On the main floor, the pretty peach-toned Parlor Room has three walls of original leaded stained glass windows, so it is bright and sunny, and the original mahogany floors glow with a high sheen. Upstairs, the especially handsome Emily Carr Suite sports dark houndstooth and paisley Ralph Lauren linens, navy blue print wallpaper, and a massive polished bedframe in the bedroom area. The spacious sitting area features a wood-burning fireplace and two-person Jacuzzi tub, hunter green walls, a high ceiling, and hardwood floors. Even the bathroom is adorned with a sparkling crystal chandelier (how's that for attention to detail?). The Veranda Room, right next door, is considerably smaller. It is the only room without a fireplace, but you'll hardly notice once you discover the jetted tub for two in the corner. On the lower level, the Gatekeeper's Room has a separate sitting area with a gas-log fireplace and corner whirlpool tub for two. Floral linens and a half canopy dress the queen-size bed, and a little patio is connected to the gardens in front. The ground-level location of this room keeps it nice and cool in the summer, but we must note that noise from the room next door can be a problem.

A light gourmet three-course breakfast is served in the inn's original dining room or in the bright sunroom, next to abundant foliage and a small fountain. Tables for two help keep breakfast a semiprivate affair if you so desire. If fancy breakfasts and lounging around this Edwardian oasis make you feel a little too leisured (if there is such a thing), a brisk walk to town may be in order. Since you are only four blocks from the core of downtown, it won't be much of a strain, and you can hurry back to your room in no time.

THE BEDFORD REGENCY HOTEL, Victoria
1140 Government Street
(250) 384-6835, (800) 665-6500
Very Expensive

The Bedford Regency is no ordinary hotel. It has all the trappings of a hotel, such as room service, luggage handlers, a reception desk, and, yes, even elevators, but that is where most of the similarities stop and the heart-stirring differences begin. All 40 rooms are striking and modern, done up in shades of peach and burgundy or yellow and green. Queen-size beds are graced with goose-down comforters, and the bathrooms were clearly built for a couple in love to enjoy together. Some of the rooms have huge tiled shower stalls with two jets, while others have spa tubs; some have wood-burning fireplaces, and a few have everything, including separate sitting rooms and views of the Inner Harbour. The downtown location is convenient for dining, shopping, touring, and just about anything else imaginable.

A complimentary buffet breakfast is served downstairs in the **RED CURRANT CAFE** (Moderate), where tables are draped with peach and ivory linens, and adorned with fresh flowers. The restaurant also features an open bar and a sunny balcony area. Later in the day, the kitchen prepares West Coast cuisine tempered with Asian and European influences.

> *Cost ratings for British Columbia listings are in Canadian funds. American travelers should check the exchange rate or ask an innkeeper to figure out the cost in U.S. dollars.*

Romantic Warning: The courtyard rooms have no views, and because they look directly across to the other units it is necessary to keep your shade pulled if you expect to have any privacy at all. Flower boxes have been added in an attempt to embellish the view, but this is still not the best situation on a hot summer day when you'll want to open a window.

CARBERRY GARDENS, Victoria
1008 Carberry Gardens
(250) 595-8906
http://www.ohwy.com/bc/c/carberry.htm
Expensive

Don't be startled by Max, the huge German sheepdog who will probably greet you—he is wonderfully friendly. Tucked away in a residential area, Carberry Gardens is a comfortably appointed bed and breakfast rich with old-world charm. Three guest rooms are available on the second floor of this 1907 home, two of which are suited for romantic travelers. Each one offers a plush down comforter, hardwood floors, Oriental rugs, and a private bath. The Master's Room has lovely floral linens on the four-poster bed, a wood-burning fireplace, and a claw-foot tub. The Balcony Room, also equipped with a claw-foot tub, is especially nice on summer nights, when you can sit and stargaze from the large balcony.

Rooms are free of modern distractions, but the comfortable guest parlor on the main floor has a stereo and television, and there is a phone available so you can make dinner reservations. Three-course gourmet breakfasts are served family-style in the main-floor dining room. Classical music accompanies your meal of oven-fresh biscuits, seasonal fruit, and a hot dish such as poached eggs or berry-filled crêpes.

THE EMPRESS HOTEL, Victoria
721 Government Street
(250) 384-8111, (800) 441-1414
http://www.cphotels.ca
Expensive to Unbelievably Expensive
Recommended Wedding Site

The words "Empress Hotel" and "Victoria" are usually uttered in the same breath. With its elaborate, palatial elegance and pivotal location, the exalted Empress has always epitomized this European-style city. Long-time patrons who have not visited Victoria lately will remember a somewhat haggard hotel that was begging for some physical attention. Well, several years ago Canadian Pacific Hotels and Resorts spent $45 million to renovate this classic 1908 building. Every detail was attended to, and the result is unequivocally spectacular.

There is the opulent **PALM COURT**, with its $50,000 stained glass ceiling that must be seen to be appreciated; the formal, architecturally grand **EMPRESS DINING ROOM** (see Restauarnt Kissing); the charming **GARDEN CAFE**; and the unique **BENGAL RESTAURANT**, casual only in comparison to the other dining spots here. All are stupendous. You won't be surprised to learn that these public areas feel like a museum, complete with gawking tourists. Still, you would be remiss if you didn't visit The Empress and linger awhile over tea and crumpets or sherry and dessert in the handsome, eminently comfortable **EMPRESS TEA LOBBY** (see High Tea Kissing). Outside, in the perfectly manicured rose garden, potential kissing spots await discovery among the magnolia trees and flower-covered trellises.

As for an overnight stay—is it worth it? Well, if you can afford the steep tariffs, why not? All 474 rooms have private baths, polished furnishings, and down comforters with floral covers. The least expensive rooms are fairly small, though beautifully appointed, but as the price goes up, the rooms increase in size. Eight rooms on the seventh floor, originally the staff quarters, have recently been transformed into "Romantic Attic Suites"; although a bit on the small side, they are accessible via a private staircase and nicely decorated with either canopy beds or round beds set beneath turrets. If you can afford to go all out, request one of the 25 Entrée Gold Suites. These spacious rooms occupy the second and third floors and offer incredible views of the Inner Harbour. King-size beds and large sunny bathrooms are additional enticing amenities. A dedicated concierge goes out of his or her way to attend your every need, while a complimentary breakfast and afternoon hors d'oeuvres and cocktails can be enjoyed in the exclusive Entrée Gold lounge.

THE HATERLEIGH HERITAGE INN, Victoria
243 Kingston Street
(250) 384-9995
http://vvv.com/~paulk
Expensive to Very Expensive
Minimum stay requirement seasonally

This Victorian bed and breakfast has been beautifully restored to preserve its turn-of-the-century charm while providing modern-day comforts few romantics can do without. Located near the south side of the harbor in a rather ordinary neighborhood, this 1901 home still has its original hardwood floors, leaded windows, and intricate stained glass. Handsome light oak wainscoting adorns the parlor. Six unpretentious rooms occupy the first and second floors, each with high arched ceilings, tall windows, separate seating areas, and lace curtains. All of the rooms are exceedingly comfortable, but the best ones are Day Dreams and Secret Garden. Day Dreams is indeed the perfect place to dream the day away, with its whimsical pink and white decor. A cut-lace duvet and a half canopy grace the queen-size bed, and nearby an intricately detailed plaster archway separates the bedroom from the sitting area. In addition, this is the only room with a double Jacuzzi tub (three other rooms have one-person Jacuzzi tubs). Secret Garden, a sunny room on the second floor, features a lacy half canopy over the bed and a small porch affording views of the Olympic Mountains.

A full breakfast is served family-style in the formal dining room each morning. Enjoy a sunny repast of homemade strawberry bread and eggs Benedict among the fresh flowers and friendly conversation.

THE HOLLAND HOUSE INN, Victoria
595 Michigan Street
(250) 384-6644, (800) 335-3466
Moderate to Very Expensive
Minimum stay requirement seasonally

The Holland House has been given a new lease on life, along with a whole new personality. This bed and breakfast has always been a desirable destination: its striking simplicity and modern art pieces were previously showcased throughout the inn. Now, after undergoing a complete refurbishment, the Holland House's ten guest rooms have been warmed up considerably with bold floral prints and stylish color schemes, the modern artwork has been replaced by an eclectic mix of antiques, and the common areas are filled with cozy elegance.

The gray stucco exterior gives little hint of the gorgeous, superior comfort that awaits inside this continental-style inn. All of the guest rooms have elegant baths, hardwood floors with Oriental rugs, and goose-down duvets; some also feature gas-log fireplaces, canopied or four-poster beds, and intimate sitting nooks. Rooms 20 and 30 are particularly spacious and have fireplaces; 30 has deep green wallpaper and a king-size four-poster iron bed, while 20 is done in black and white and has a queen-size iron bed. Room 31 is on a corner, so sun pours in, creating a bright and airy atmosphere. Each tastefully appointed room is decorated differently, so it is hard to specify which ones have the most romantic potential. The staff is extremely service-oriented, and will gladly help you find one that suits your taste.

Morning brings a gourmet breakfast served at one large table in the cheery, wisteria-covered solarium. If you want to burn off calories from your morning meal of stuffed French toast or huevos rancheros, take a short walk along tree-lined residential streets to downtown Victoria.

HUMBOLDT HOUSE, Victoria

867 Humboldt Street
(250) 383-0152
http://www.cbdl.com/humboldt
Very Expensive
Minimum stay requirement on weekends seasonally

Located on a quiet street lined by historic buildings, this beautifully renovated yellow and white Victorian is a short walk from the city center. Inside, everything is perfect for romance. Thick velvet drapes open to a cranberry-colored parlor, where you can help yourselves to sherry as you relax in front of a blazing fireplace. All five guest rooms have inviting down linens, ample space, wood-burning fireplaces, and Jacuzzi tubs tucked away in elevated corners. (The tubs in the three upstairs rooms are spacious enough for two people.) Sunlight streams in through large windows overlooking the neighboring apple orchard.

In the colorful Mikado and Oriental rooms, sexy black Jacuzzi tubs are set apart from the bedrooms by Japanese-style bamboo screens. Edward's Room has a subtle Middle Eastern theme, and the Gazebo Room resembles a garden with its terra-cotta-tiled Jacuzzi area and its hand-painted vines and flowers winding their way up the vaulted ceiling. The Celebration Room is by far the grandest room of all. Lovely white linens grace the immaculate queen-size bed, which is crowned by a sophisticated lace canopy and a lighted archway. Pretty floral prints adorn the elegant drapes and matching sofa. Classical artwork and angelic sculptures abound among the painted ivy and potted plants, and a glittering chandelier hangs overhead. Such pristine splendor will truly take your breath away.

Champagne and truffles welcome you to your room, and champagne is also included with your breakfast. An ingenious feature is the small two-way butler's pantry, where a picnic basket filled with enticing breakfast treats is placed at daybreak for an intimate morning repast. You'll awaken to the wonderful aroma of gourmet dishes like seafood crêpes or eggs Benedict— perfect for breakfast in bed.

JOAN BROWN'S BED AND BREAKFAST, Victoria

729 Pemberton Road
(250) 592-5929
Inexpensive to Moderate; No Credit Cards

The dynamic Joan Brown welcomes guests into her vintage home as only she can. Some may be taken aback by her eccentric personality, but she is right at home in this grandiose Italianate Victorian mansion. Set in a refined neighborhood near Craigdarroch Castle, this stately property has high beamed ceilings, seven fireplaces, gorgeous stained glass windows, formal English gardens, polished wood floors, the original wood staircase, comfortable furnishings, and rooms in a variety of sizes. All of the guest rooms are filled with sunlight and decorated with lovely fabrics; four have private baths and the others share facilities. The larger rooms, particularly the ones with high ceilings on the ground floor, are the grandest. To round out your stay, a generous full breakfast is served in the regal dining room on fine china under a striking crystal chandelier.

LAUREL POINT INN, Victoria
680 Montreal Street
(250) 386-8721, (800) 663-7667
http://www.islandnet.com/~cvcprod/laurel.html
Very Expensive to Unbelievably Expensive

Laurel Point Inn may look just like another massive condominium complex lining Victoria's Inner Harbour; however, this 202-unit hotel contains some extremely stylish suites with phenomenal views. The trick is knowing specifically which rooms to choose. Start by tossing out the brochure; it is entirely misleading, with pictures of only the most exclusive suites. Next, rule out the entire north wing—these boring hotel rooms are more than just rough around the edges. That leaves the south wing to work with. Narrow the choices here by requesting an Outer Harbor view. (The city-view rooms located closer to the water are also acceptable, but if you end up with a room too far back you run the risk of looking directly at the neighboring high-rise.)

What's left are the studio-style south wing junior suites, the south wing one-bedroom suites with separate sitting areas, and the south wing two-story panoramic suites with an amazing amount of space and incredible amenities. Prices start at $235 Canadian in these categories, but again we stress the importance of being choosy here. Peach marble entryways lead into every south wing suite. Creamy color schemes, blond wood furnishings, shoji-style sliding doors, Asian art pieces, and natural burlap-covered walls create an elegantly modern, though somewhat spartan, Pacific Coast feel. Floor-to-ceiling windows open to enormous balconies overlooking glorious views of the Outer Harbor and the majestic Olympic Mountains. Ferries come and go, floatplanes breeze in and out, and all of the harbor's activity can be quietly enjoyed as you sit on your private deck. Guests who rely only on the hotel's brochure will never know what they're missing!

Romantic Suggestion: Laurel Point Inn's Sunday brunch ($18.95 per person) has been voted "Best In Victoria" for at least the past six years. Make a reservation if you would like to join in, and be sure to request a seat in **THE TERRACE ROOM.** The other dining rooms, **COOK'S LOUNGE** and **CAFE LAUREL**, are dated and do not hold a candle to the bright, airy atmosphere of The Terrace Room.

MULBERRY MANOR, Victoria
611 Foul Bay Road
(250) 370-1918
Very Expensive
Closed December through January

Luxury embraces you in this beautifully renovated Tudor mansion set in a landscaped neighborhood. This 1926 heritage home has been given the royal treatment by its dedicated owners, and you will get it too, as guests here. As you enter, the main floor whispers of grandeur with plushly covered chintz sofas and chairs, hardwood floors, and embroidered carpets. A leaded bay window in the parlor allows views of the perfectly maintained grounds. The dining room, where a full gourmet breakfast is served in the morning, is just as ornate, with rich red walls and gold china displayed in an antique cabinet. Anywhere else, all this opulence might come across as gaudy, but here it has been tastefully and beautifully executed.

The three individually decorated rooms are embellished in understated classic English style with thick down comforters and fluffy feather beds. Decorated in yellow and blue, the Jasmine Suite is the largest room, with a huge old-fashioned bathroom, brass bed, wood-burning fireplace, and expansive balcony. The Rosewood Room, with a detached bath, is outfitted in pink floral linens and has a four-poster bed with a half canopy. The romantic Angel Room is done in a black-and-white cherub motif, and features a private balcony. The grounds are as lovely as everything else, with a backyard duck pond that is lit up at night. A tiled solarium/billiard room is set off the meticulous back lawn for couples interested in some friendly competition.

OAK BAY BEACH HOTEL, Victoria   No lips
1175 Beach Drive
(250) 598-4556, (800) 668-7758
Very Expensive to Unbelievably Expensive
Minimum stay requirement on weekends

Long-standing reputations, no matter how undeserved, sometimes never die. The Oak Bay Beach Hotel is known as Victoria's only seaside hotel (that much is true), which explains why it is so popular and often fully booked. The gorgeous setting, overlooking the open waters of the Strait of Juan de Fuca and the often-snowcapped Olympic Mountains, is impressive, and the half-timbered Tudor mansion is striking. Yet inside, the 51 rooms are amazingly second-rate and in serious need of refurbishing. Most have been appointed with down comforters or duvets, but unfortunately they also have dreary colors, unattractive artwork, and a musty odor that seems to permeate the entire building. The third-floor rooms, which flaunt the highest price tags and best views, are the ones that require the most restoration. Even the handful of recently renovated rooms were done poorly and still look tacky.

The parlor is the most attractive part of the hotel (which isn't saying much). Antique sofas, large windows facing the ocean, a blazing fireplace, and a square-beamed ceiling contribute to a distinctive old-world ambience. **BENTLEY'S ON THE BAY** (Expensive) is the hotel's new restaurant. Each table is topped with flowers and green and ivory tablecloths, while a brick hearth glows at one end of the dining room. Despite the wonderful views of Oak Bay, its afternoon tea service is shoddy and the presentation just OK.

OCEAN POINTE RESORT, Victoria
45 Songhees Road
(250) 360-2999, (800) 667-4677
http://travel.bc.ca/o/opr
Very Expensive to Unbelievably Expensive

It used to be that you couldn't miss Ocean Pointe Resort when you arrived in Victoria, but so many condominiums have sprouted up along the Inner Harbour that this sparkling hotel complex is now just one of many buildings along the skyline. Encompassing almost the entire north shore of the Inner Harbour, the massive, contemporary building stands directly opposite The Empress. These two grand dames chaperone the harbor in opposing styles. Whereas The Empress represents European enchantment and tradition, Ocean Pointe represents cosmopolitan luxuries. Amenities include a spa (open to the public as well as to guests) that offers body wraps, massages, aromatherapy, facials, herbal cosmetics, and a glass-enclosed swimming pool. Everything here is ultra-sophisticated and ultra-plush, with a strong concentration on service.

Wondering about the 250 guest rooms? Well, except for the suites, they are just upscale, modern hotel rooms. The even-numbered rooms face the Inner Harbour and the stately historic buildings of Victoria; this view is preferable to the "working harbor" views of condominiums in the odd-numbered rooms. Also, nonsmokers should be sure to request a non-smoking room or they may be unhappy with scents of smokers past. If money is no object (and we are talking about an unlimited expense account here), go for the designer suites. These exquisite, impeccably furnished retreats have outstanding water views, Jacuzzi tubs, private decks, and plush modern furnishings. If sublime privacy and full service are top romantic priorities, Ocean Pointe will be perfect for you.

PRIOR HOUSE, Victoria
620 St. Charles Street
(250) 592-8847
Expensive to Unbelievably Expensive
Minimum stay requirement on weekends

Despite its stately exterior and charming residential setting, the Prior House has seen better days. This 8,500-square-foot Edwardian mansion, once the epitome of grandeur, has become a little frayed around the seams, both literally and figuratively. (Carpeting in the upstairs hallways and guest rooms is in desperate need of replacement.) However, the two plush living rooms on the main floor still have endearing touches like fireplaces, light oak paneling, and stained glass windows. Outside, a carved stone terrace looks out over meticulously groomed lawns and gardens; we found the trampoline in the backyard to be a rather odd touch, but don't let that distract you from such lovely scenery.

Seven guest rooms are spread throughout the three levels and on the ground floor; the most spacious and romantic are the Windsor Suite and the Lieutenant Governor's Suite. The third-floor Windsor Suite has Victorian furnishings, a Jacuzzi tub situated beneath a skylight, and French doors that open to a small private patio facing the Olympic Mountains and the Strait of Juan de Fuca. The Lieutenant Governor's Suite on the second floor has Austrian hand-printed draperies and a wood-burning fireplace. An unusual headboard created from an antique sofa crowns the bed. The most striking feature, however, is the enormous bathroom, which has been lavishly decorated with crystal chandeliers, gold fixtures, mirrored walls, and an air-jet massage Jacuzzi tub in green faux marble. Such modern appointments seem a bit out of place in this historic manor, but who's complaining? Less extravagant (and less expensive) rooms are also available. Each has old-fashioned European flair, with richly colored walls and antique furnishings, and several have fireplaces and views as well.

More contemporary in decor, the two ground-floor Garden Suites were designed with families in mind. Each has a private garden entrance through a stone archway, a private brick patio, full kitchen, two bedrooms, and a living room with a tile fireplace. These suites are thoroughly lovely and engagingly cozy, but can be a tad on the dark side, and you can hear occasional footsteps upstairs. Still, if you are traveling as a group or with children, you can have the entire lower level to yourselves.

A light but proper high tea is served in the afternoon, and sherry and port are always available. In the morning, share a full breakfast presented in the formal chandeliered dining room or arrange to have it delivered to your room.

SWANS, Victoria
506 Pandora Avenue
(250) 361-3310, (800) 668-7926
http://www.islandnet.com/~swans/hotel.html
Moderate to Expensive

If you like being in the heart of the action in every sense of the phrase, you will appreciate the Swans' location. Set in downtown Victoria, on the corner of Wharf Street and Pandora Avenue, this former apartment building has been converted into an appealing hotel. Guest rooms still resemble apartments, with full kitchens, separate dining areas, living rooms, oversized windows, cathedral ceilings, small balconies, televisions, and phones. The 29 units come in three configurations—studios and one- and two-bedroom units—but the studios and one-bedroom lofts are the coziest. Bright original artwork and some exposed brick walls add character, but the televisions at the foots of some beds and the nondescript contemporary decor remind you that this is a hotel. Nevertheless, these are spacious rooms in which to set up temporary housekeeping while touring Victoria, and the location is incredibly convenient.

Romantic Warning: Rooms above the main-floor pub can be noisy. Unless you plan to stay out most of the night yourselves, you won't appreciate the clamor from downstairs.

Restaurant Kissing

CAMILLE'S, Victoria   🔲🔲🔲🔲
45 Bastion Square
(250) 381-3433
Expensive
Dinner Daily; Wine Tasting Sunday Evenings
Closed January

Camille's has been voted "Victoria's Most Seductive Restaurant" in our personally conducted, highly scientific, two-person poll. From the moment you enter this irresistible lower-level restaurant, you'll feel significantly removed from the turmoil of the city. The tables in the front dining room are accompanied by cushioned booths and inviting throw pillows; dimmed wall lanterns and a single candle at each table provide the only light. Hundred-year-old brick walls adorned with contemporary artwork enclose the second dining room. Here you'll find red and ivory linens, hanging stained glass lamps, and a rustic assortment of decorative books and wine bottles. A few individual tables are separated from the rest of the room by wooden partitions that create extremely private booths. As explained on the menu, the affable staff works together to make your experience as warm and wonderful as you can imagine.

A delightful lineup of fresh fish, locally grown produce and meats, and various Mediterranean and ethnic dishes are all prepared in a health-conscious manner. Enjoy the freshly baked sweet buns as you decide between appetizers like the Louisiana vegetable jambalaya or the crab and avocado California rolls. For dinner we recommend the caramel-and-almond-crusted breast of duck, served with a light cranberry-champagne sauce. The broiled fillet of local salmon with dilled yogurt and cucumber on a puff pastry lattice is absolutely celestial. Desserts are just as interesting and just as luscious. Try the bananas flambé for two, with orange, brown sugar, and dark rum, ignited tableside and served over ice cream. Mmmmm ... it's almost as sweet as kisses (almost).

CHEZ DANIEL, Victoria
2524 Estevan Avenue
(250) 592-7424
Expensive
Dinner Tuesday-Saturday

This quaint little restaurant almost blends into the row of shops lining Estevan Avenue; but once you step inside, you'll be in for a romantic treat. Copper pots adorn the walls, and wine bottles abound throughout the tiny dining room. Teal green ceilings, rose-colored trim, crisp linens, and flickering candlelight set the mood for traditional French dining.

Chez Daniel is one of the best French restaurants in Victoria, a claim that will be amply confirmed once you sample the elegantly prepared dishes. Don't miss the choice appetizers, including admirable escargots in garlic butter. Dinners such as filet mignon, veal Madeira, and roasted duck with chestnuts are superior. The table d'hôte menu is reasonably priced and offers an impressive assortment of the kitchen's best efforts. Service is personable but can be slow. Have patience—this meal is worth waiting for.

DA TANDOOR, Victoria
1010 Fort Street
(250) 384-6333, (800) 384-6333
Moderate
Dinner Daily

Savory smells singing of exotic spices will make your mouth water in anticipation when you enter Da Tandoor. There are too many tables to call the dining room intimate, and too many silk plants and fake flowers to call it formal. However, brass hanging lanterns, Persian rugs, Indian silk paintings, and intricately carved wood screens lend authenticity. Tandoori (meaning clay-oven baked) is the house specialty, but the Indian- and Pakistani-style curries are also notable. *Taza sagg,* fresh spinach cooked with green onions, herbs, and spices, is a pleasing side order with the chicken curry in spicy tomato and onion sauce. This is one of the most frequently recommended restaurants in Victoria—dinner will explain why.

EBIZO, Victoria
604 Broughton
(250) 383-3234
Inexpensive
Lunch Tuesday-Saturday; Dinner Tuesday-Sunday

This stylish little restaurant is an intimate, casual place to enjoy first-class sushi. Large windows allow sunlight to filter in, and blond wood trim accentuates the black walls. Wooden tables, each topped with chopsticks and rice bowls, are complemented by chairs with red velvet cushions. Two long tables near the back are elevated for traditional Japanese-style seating. A small sushi bar in the corner offers an extensive selection of sushi, sashimi, and nigiri. You can even request your own special concoctions if you'd like. Don't worry if you're not a sushi lover, because you'll find other Japanese dishes on the menu as well.

Romantic Warning: Sports fans may be distracted by the silent television in the corner above the sushi bar. Those seeking romance should choose their seats accordingly.

THE EMPRESS DINING ROOM, Victoria
721 Government Street
(250) 384-8111
http://www.cphotels.ca
Expensive to Very Expensive
Dinner Daily

Dinner at The Empress is a regal treat. Its formal dining area is separated into two rooms, each appointed with chandeliers, upholstered high-backed chairs, and elegant French fabric-covered walls. Mahogany columns with the original plaster-and-horsehair detailing impart a warm Gothic feel, while candles, fine china, and a single red rose top each linen-draped table. One dining room offers spectacular views of the Inner Harbour; the other room is more quiet and intimate. Enjoy Pacific Northwest cuisine accompanied by live harp music each evening.

HERALD STREET CAFFE, Victoria
546 Herald Street
(250) 381-1441
Expensive
Lunch Wednesday-Sunday; Dinner Daily; Sunday Brunch

People have been raving about the Herald Street Caffe ever since it opened. From day one, the kitchen has been turning out fresh, inventive Euro-Asian cuisine that keeps everyone happy (or at least full). We recommend the roasted chicken breast in a crispy cashew crust with lemon-rosemary sauce sound. Or try the Seafood Splashdown, a concoction of scallops, prawns, mussels, and clams in Hunan barbecue sauce. Seafood is always fresh, and presentations are lovely. Bold artwork, plum wainscoting, taupe walls, and huge floral arrangements lend a stylish edge to the two casual dining rooms, which are always busy. The cafe's popularity means that you should call ahead for reservations, and it also means that the restaurant can be noisy. Ask for a window seat when you make your reservation—the view is just the sidewalk and street, but the active atmosphere seems a little calmer around the edges.

IL TERRAZZO RISTORANTE, Victoria
555 Johnson Street
(250) 361-0028
Moderate to Expensive
Lunch Monday-Saturday; Dinner Daily

Although the tables are a bit too close together and the room bustles with activity, this restaurant's charm will quickly win you over. Exposed brick walls and archways are adorned with colorful artwork, while wrought-iron candelabras hang overhead. Hardwood floors, handkerchief-like floral table-cloths, candlelit tables, and billowy burgundy curtains promote an intimate and casual ambience. Large windows face a quaint brick courtyard filled with hanging flower baskets, marble tables, and wrought-iron chairs. Seven brick hearths are evenly spaced around the patio, and tiny white lights sparkle in the potted trees and surrounding greenery. The courtyard is heated and cozy even on chilly nights, so long as it doesn't rain.

Excellent northern Italian cuisine is served by the knowledgeable wait staff. We recommend the spaghetti with clams, tomatoes, roasted garlic, and black pepper, prepared in a white wine sauce, or the roast duck served on penne pasta with shiitake mushrooms and ginger. You won't be disappointed by anything this kitchen puts together.

THE MARINA RESTAURANT, Victoria   💋💋💋
1327 Beach Drive
(250) 598-8555
Expensive
Lunch and Dinner Daily; Sunday Brunch

In the Northwest, fresh seafood plus a fabulous view almost always equals romance, and that is exactly what you'll find here. The Marina's expansive windows overlook Oak Bay and a colorful marina filled with gently rocking sailboats. From the seahorse-shaped door handles at the entrance to the sculptures of vessels inside, this restaurant is decidedly nautical, but a far cry from the usual fish-and-chips eatery. A striking interior of gleaming African wood is accentuated with brilliant swaths of fabric and local artwork, and near the back stands a circular bar of matching polished wood. Tables set aglow by candlelight are draped in taupe and ivory linens and evenly spaced around the dining room. Although the dining area is a bit too large to feel adequately intimate, the incredible view will distract you from its size.

An extensive menu features cuisine from around the Pacific Northwest: Vancouver Island clams, Dungeness crab, Prince Edward Island mussels, steamed halibut, and other sea-inspired fare. Sound tempting? It is. The daily seafood specials are always fresh and superb. You'll also find a selection of pastas, chicken dishes, and alder-grilled steaks from which to choose. A tastefully decorated sushi bar is tucked away behind the restaurant's entryway; here you can fill up on nigiri sushi, traditional rolls, or a variety of dinner combinations.

Romantic Alternative: Downstairs from the restaurant is the more casual **CAFE DELI**, (250) 598-3890 (Inexpensive), with an espresso bar and glass-enclosed pastry cases sporting the usual assortment of goodies. Whether you grab a light lunch at the deli or decide on a more sophisticated sit-down meal upstairs, waterside dining on the tiered deck is a delightful option on those cloudless summer days.

MICHELINE'S RESTAURANT, Victoria
512 Yates Street
(250) 388-0188
Expensive
Call for seasonal hours.

Micheline's had some rather large shoes to fill when it moved into what was Victoria's oldest French restaurant only a few years ago. Luckily, for Victorians and visitors alike, the results have been excellent. Diners enter Micheline's small, modestly elegant dining room through a charming brick storefront. Soft swing or jazz fills the air on most nights, and the restaurant's pale yellow walls are accented by local artwork and dimmed wall sconces. One wall of exposed brick lends a historic feel, and fresh flowers and votive candles on each linen-covered table provide a personal touch. The overall effect is warm and welcoming, and so is the service.

The menu offers an assortment of fabulous international cuisine. The very freshest ingredients are used in intriguing dishes like smoked local trout poached in Indian-spiced coconut milk, sautéed pork medallions on a purée of spiced pears, and a variety of nightly seafood specials. Presentation is part of the fun, and the kitchen is quite creative. Classic crème brûlée and home-made champagne-lavender sorbet are delicious finales to a totally satisfying meal.

REBECCA'S, Victoria
1127 Wharf Street
(250) 380-6999
Moderate to Expensive
Lunch and Dinner Daily

For a good casual meal in a stylish setting, try Rebecca's. Its handsome interior is composed of exposed brick arches, high-backed chairs, and a white-washed wooden bar (whose patrons can overflow, along with cigarette smoke, into the dining room). Enjoy the kitchen's creative Euro-Asian cuisine, made with fresh Canadian Southwest ingredients. Fusili with fresh charbroiled tuna, capers, and lemon, and the rich banana-curry soup are splendid. A large glass showcase along the edge of the restaurant displays the incredible takeout selections, perfect for a no-fuss meal at home or, weather permitting, an impromptu picnic. Be forewarned: desserts are also on display, and they are hard to resist.

THE VICTORIAN RESTAURANT, Victoria
45 Songhees Road, at Ocean Pointe Resort
(250) 360-2999, (800) 667-4677
http://travel.bc.ca/o/opr
Expensive to Very Expensive
Dinner Daily

Dining is a formal affair at The Victorian Restaurant in Ocean Pointe Resort. This is one of the finest dining spots in the city, at one of the most upscale properties, which is exactly why we cannot understand why the valet parking staff is dressed in such ridiculous uniforms. Obviously, these outfits have no effect on the outstanding quality of the restaurant, but when you are greeted by young men dressed in plaid knickers and riding caps, it makes a rather odd first impression. Inside, however, elegance and sophistication take over.

The restaurant's decor is not Victorian, as the name suggests; rather, it is stylish and modern. A wall of windows looks across the Inner Harbour at the sparkling lights outlining the historic Parliament Building and The Empress Hotel. Special attention is given to the presentation and quality of the European-influenced West Coast cuisine. Dishes such as fresh walnut sourdough bread, a creamy mussel-saffron bisque, and superb grilled beef tenderloin with roasted shallots and green peppercorn sauce are sheer perfection. For dessert, try the smooth-as-silk white chocolate and pear mousse cake or fresh strawberries and shortbread with lemon curd cream.

High Tea Kissing

Sharing high tea is a thoroughly English, utterly civilized way to spend a late afternoon together. And no other town in North America offers this delightful ritual with as much style, dedication, and abundance as Victoria. Presentations differ widely, as do the prices. Some places employ the traditional white gloves and silver service, while others provide a more eclectic display on floral-patterned china. Prices range from $9 to $25 per person, depending on your surroundings, but the customary basics are always the same: fresh fruit, dainty finger sandwiches (held with the little finger up), delectable pastries, fluffy Devonshire cream, and tea properly steeped in a china teapot and kept warm by a cushioned tea cozy.

The ritual of afternoon tea began in China, where tea making was considered an art form. Later, tea was used for meditative purposes by Japanese Buddhist monks. High tea as we know it was initiated in the 19th century, when the Duchess of Bedford noticed a "sinking feeling" each afternoon and decided to ask some of her friends to join her for afternoon refreshments.

Since no trip to Victoria would be complete without a taste of tea, we have reviewed the most well-known places for savoring high tea in the city. Although many of these restaurants serve other meals as well, our romance ratings largely reflect their tea presentations.

BLETHERING PLACE, Victoria
2250 Oak Bay Avenue
(250) 598-1413
Inexpensive to Moderate
Breakfast, Lunch, High Tea, and Dinner Daily

Blethering Place, located in the affluent Oak Bay neighborhood, is a popular place for high tea and chitchat, as the name suggests. Set in a traditional Tudor building, this casual English country–style dining room is appointed with oak chairs, pastel floral tablecloths, and lace curtains. Unfortunately, this very quaint setting is jeopardized by mediocre food, chipped serving-ware, and an inexperienced staff. Most tourists have not heard about the kitchen's shortcomings, though, so the dining room can be very crowded in the summertime.

BUTCHART GARDENS DINING ROOM, Victoria
800 Benvenuto Avenue
(250) 652-8222
Moderate to Expensive
Lunch, Afternoon Tea, and Dinner Daily

Sometimes location is everything. Views of the Butchart Garden's famous flowers from every window make this a refined and regal place for high tea. The dining room, originally the home of Mr. and Mrs. Butchart, is emersed in the colorful beauty of the gardens. Each table is topped with white and burgundy linens and complemented by black lacquer chairs. The solarium is the best room, with its leaded glass windows and abundance of hanging plants. Although tea is a little pricey, the setting is lovely and the presentation is good: finger sandwiches and sweets are delivered to your table on a silver tea tray.

THE CAPTAIN'S PALACE INN AND RESTAURANT, Victoria
309 Belleville Street
(250) 388-9191, (800) 563-9656
Moderate to Expensive
Breakfast, Lunch, and Dinner Daily

If you haven't had your fill of Victoriana, venture into the restaurant at The Captain's Palace for a dessert, or a snack amid turn-of-the-century opulence. (We don't recommend a full meal, as reports have been less than complimentary about the quality of the food and the service.) The four dining rooms are appointed with stained glass windows, frescoed ceilings, stately marble-and-wood fireplaces, crystal chandeliers, antique furnishings, and a sweeping stairway with a carved banister. Each table is topped with fresh flowers and decorated with pale pink and green linens. It's a shame the food isn't up to the standards of its surroundings, let alone those of some of the less ornate, less expensive dining establishments in town. Still, the romantic atmosphere makes this worth a visit.

Romantic Warning: The Captain's Palace is also a bed and breakfast (Expensive to Very Expensive), with rooms located above the restaurant and in an adjacent building. These rooms could be wonderful if care and proper attention were given. Unfortunately, the aroma of cigarettes has permeated the walls, the furniture is worn, and the carpets are rundown, creating an overall tired feel.

THE EMPRESS TEA LOBBY, Victoria
721 Government Street
(250) 384-8111, (800) 441-1414
http://www.cphotels.ca
Expensive
Reservations Recommended
Afternoon Tea Daily

Visitors from far and wide come to The Empress for high tea each afternoon. This is undoubtedly the most formal white-glove tea in Victoria, and the setting is posh beyond words. When we last visited, the talk of the town was the exorbitant price visitors are now expected to pay for high tea. Most agreed that it's not the food itself you're paying for, but the experience of taking tea at Victoria's most beloved landmark.

Once the grand entrance to the hotel, the lobby has been transformed into the main tea room. You can also take tea, along with spectacular views of the Inner Harbour, from the wicker-furnished veranda, and sometimes tea is served under the stained glass dome of the nearby **PALM COURT**; however, the Tea Lobby is the most sought after locale. Two enormous marble fireplaces stand at either end of the room, crowned with portraits of Queen Mary and King George. Intricately carved columns rise upward to an elaborately detailed rose and pink ceiling. From the crystal chandeliers to the hardwood floors, you'll be awed by such stately splendor. As you nestle in one of the overstuffed chairs or floral upholstered couches clustered around the tables, savor finger sandwiches of smoked salmon, deviled egg, cucumber, and watercress; sip The Empress's own blend of tea; and converse contentedly while a pianist or a string quartet plays softly in the background.

Romantic Note: Be sure to make reservations for high tea, especially during the busy summer months. Also, visitors are asked to observe a semi-formal dress code while taking tea at The Empress; shorts just won't cut it.

JAMES BAY TEA ROOM AND RESTAURANT, Victoria
332 Menzies Street
(250) 382-8282
Inexpensive to Moderate
Breakfast, Lunch, Afternoon Tea, and Dinner Daily; High Tea Sunday

Given the state of disrepair at the James Bay Tea Room, you may wonder if we are serious about recommending this little spot. Well, despite the weathered exterior and old interior, this charming Tudor-style home feels entirely authentic. British knickknacks clutter the small dining room, and portraits of the English monarchy, past and present, cover the walls. Perhaps what feels so genuine about tea here is that there is no big production around the event, and the lack of pretension is a welcome change of pace. On the other hand, someone who has never experienced a high tea may want a grand presentation, complete with white gloves. In that case, somewhere like The Empress Hotel would probably be (pardon the pun) your cup of tea.

OAK BAY TEA ROOM AND RESTAURANT, Victoria
2241 Oak Bay Avenue
(250) 370-1005
Inexpensive to Moderate
Breakfast, Lunch, Afternoon Tea, and Dinner Daily

Nestled in a row of small shops on Oak Bay Avenue, this one-room tea house offers a regal setting in which to sip the afternoon away. Pale green walls, needlepoint-embellished chairs, and crystal light fixtures create an old-world air of refined tranquility. Each table has white and floral linens, tiny bouquets of fresh flowers, and enough finger food for any size appetite.

POINT ELLICE HOUSE, Victoria
2616 Pleasant Street
(250) 380-6506
Inexpensive
Afternoon Tea Daily
Closed October through April
Recommended Wedding Site

Some of the best tea in town can be found, well, out of town. A five-minute ferry ride from the Inner Harbour transports you back in time to the peaceful oasis known as Point Ellice. This Italianate villa, built by the prominent O'Reilly family, appears to have remained virtually unchanged since the 1860s, and currently displays a large collection of Victorian antiques and heirlooms. Each room in the house has been re-created to depict the daily life of the O'Reilly family at the turn of the century. You can rent a cassette player at the entrance and take an audio tour of the charming house. Tours last roughly a half hour and can be included in your tea package for an additional $2.

Afternoon tea is served on the croquet lawn, where views of the water and gardens inspire a feeling of serenity. White wicker chairs are clustered together on the lawn, with a few set beneath a shady canopy. High tea consists of fresh fruit, finger sandwiches, and scones with cream and homemade jam, followed by a light dessert of fruit tart, shortbread, and lemon-poppyseed cake. You can choose between coffee, lemonade, or the house tea, a unique blend of Ceylon and China Black. Tea servers wear the traditional dresses of servants in the late Victorian era.

Later, stroll around the grounds, where you'll find a fragrant garden filled with poppies, honeysuckle, jasmine, lavender, hollyhocks, and lilacs. There's also a small gift shop, a heart-shaped rose garden, and a trail called the Woodland Walk leading to the beach through overgrown ivy. Trees and shrubbery enclose the property and serve as a natural insulator from the noisy industrial area nearby. Overall, the excellent food, lovely setting, and reasonable rates make Point Ellice a wonderful afternoon escape.

Romantic Suggestion: The best route to Point Ellice is via the **VICTORIA HARBOUR FERRY COMPANY**, (250) 480-0971 ($3.50 to $12 per person). Your only other alternative is a short but rough-and-tumble drive through Victoria's unattractive industrial district. Simply hop aboard one of the little green-and-white mini-ferries zipping around the harbor. Yes, it is a touristy thing to do, but tourists are everywhere in Victoria, so if you can't beat 'em, why not join 'em?

Outdoor Kissing

THE BUTCHART GARDENS, Victoria
800 Benvenuto Avenue
(250) 652-5256
$14 per adult
Call for seasonal hours.

From north West Saanich Road (Highway 17a), turn west onto Benvenuto Avenue and follow the signs to the gardens.

You really can't kiss here—it's just too crowded. But if you want a preview of what heaven looks like, tour these elysian, astonishing gardens. Each flower seems to have been hand-stroked to full bloom, the hedges could have been trimmed with a scalpel, and the sinuous pathways must have been carved from the earth by artisans who knew how to create a model Eden. All 50 acres are sublime. Especially wonderful are the Rose, Japanese, and Italian gardens. Before descending into the Sunken Garden, once the site of a limestone quarry, stop a moment to take in the incredible panorama of dazzling flowers and sculpted bushes below. Most summer evenings you can enjoy colorful illuminations of the gardens and Ross Fountain. And Christmastime at the gardens will make you believe in Santa Claus again. So ignore the crowds, concentrate on the flowers, breathe in the perfume of fresh blossoms all around, and hold hands tightly.

Romantic Note: If you happen to visit around tea time, **THE DINING ROOM** (see High Tea Kissing) is worth a stop. You can also grab a quick bite at **THE BLUE POPPY RESTAURANT**, (250) 652-4422 (Inexpensive), also located at the gardens. It may not be fancy, but it is the prettiest cafeteria we've ever seen, with cream-colored walls, lush plants, and skylights that allow sunshine to stream in.

ISLAND BREEZE SAILING, Victoria

(250) 361-3773
http://www.islandnet.com/~ibsail
Prices start at $69 per person
Reservations Required

The Strait of Juan de Fuca, with its magnificent views of the Olympic Mountains and Victoria's skyline, provides the perfect backdrop for a day at sea. Leave your cares on shore as you motor out of the Inner Harbour to the deep blue waters of the strait. Once the salty ocean breeze kicks in, you'll be on your way to an unforgettable maritime adventure.

Your 33-foot sailboat, appropriately called the *Island Breeze II*, is comfortably equipped with a galley, heater, barbecue, stereo, sleeping quarters (used during day trips), and much appreciated rest rooms. Cruises last approximately three hours and accommodate small groups of four to seven passengers; however, day trips, overnight excusions, and private cruises for couples can be arranged with your guide ahead of time.

Sail to Albert Head or eastward to Trial Island; friendly winds allow for further exploration near Discovery Island. Herons and other seabirds frequent this outdoor playground, while seals sun themselves on the rocks. And if you're lucky, you might even catch a glimpse of porpoises or orcas in the area. Binoculars for sightseeing, sailing jackets, and fishing gear are all provided, but be sure to bring sunscreen and a jacket to protect you from the elements. Cruises depart from the Inner Harbour at 10 A.M. and 2 P.M. each day.

Romantic Note: Light refreshments, such as drinks and homemade cookies, are provided. Lunch may be included in the future, but for now you may want to bring lunch if you choose the earlier cruise. Then again, those with weak stomachs might want to wait until they're safely on land before eating.

MOUNT DOUGLAS PARK, Victoria

From Highway 17, five miles north of downtown Victoria, exit east onto Cordova Bay Road. Follow this road south to the park.

Although only minutes away from downtown Victoria, Mount Douglas Park is light-years away from tourists and city sounds. This 500-acre rain forest on the ocean's edge is surprisingly quiet and serene. A walk down one of the many beach trails brings you out to a winding stretch of shoreline. From here you can look out across island-dotted Haro Strait. Don't forget to bring a blanket and picnic provisions so you can spend a leisurely afternoon out here without interruption.

ROGERS' CHOCOLATES, Victoria
913 Government Street
(250) 384-7021
Open Daily

If you're trying to woo your beloved while in Victoria, we recommend an age-old tactic: chocolate. Most experts agree that the way to another's heart is through the stomach, or, in this case, the sweet tooth. Simply follow Government Street a few blocks north of the Inner Harbour and there, in the midst of a plethora of shops and cafes, you'll find Rogers' Chocolates. A colorful half-dome of stained glass crowns the entrance, and the large window displays have been known to tempt even the most dedicated window-shoppers. Once you step foot inside, we guarantee you won't leave empty-handed. This old-fashioned chocolate shop is a chocoholic's dream come true, with dark wood paneling, tiled floors, and enough sweets to last a lifetime. Chocolates are handmade fresh every day in the back of the shop,

Cost ratings for British Columbia listings are in Canadian funds. American travelers should check the exchange rate or ask an innkeeper to figure out the cost in U.S. dollars.

according to the original recipes Charles W. "Candy" Rogers perfected in the late 1800s. The creams, almond brittle, caramels, truffles, and other creations are then wrapped in colorful packages and placed seductively in glass display cases. What could be sweeter than a chocolate kiss?

WHALE WATCHING, Victoria
Seacoast Expeditions
45 Songhees Road, on the boardwalk level of Ocean Pointe Resort
(250) 383-2254
$70 for a three-hour trip
Tours Daily May-September

Catching a glimpse of an orca in its natural habitat is truly an unforgettable experience. With Seacoast Expeditions, you can cruise around Victoria's coastal waters in search of marine wildlife and beautiful scenery. Whale-watching trips depart daily from Ocean Pointe Resort on the Inner Harbour and explore 30 to 50 miles of orca territory. Trips last about three hours and accommodate up to 12 passengers, plus a driver and a guide. In addition, each 23-foot Zodiac boat comes equipped with a hydrophone for listening to whale vocalizations. Life suits are provided for your safety (and for warmth), but be prepared to get wet anyway.

June and July are the most likely times to spot orcas, but other wildlife can be seen anytime. Look for porpoises, minke whales, sea lions, harbor seals, bald eagles, and other marine birds. If you have your heart set on seeing an orca, an additional $10 will reserve a pager that will alert you when a whale sighting can be guaranteed.

Metchosin

Metchosin is located roughly midway between the bustling city of Victoria and the rural town of Sooke. Travelers passing through experience the merging of these two distinct worlds, as residential neighborhoods begin to thin out along Metchosin's scenic coastline.

Hotel/Bed and Breakfast Kissing

MARKHAM HOUSE, Metchosin
1853 Connie Road
(250) 642-7542, (888) 256-6888
http://www.victoria.net
Inexpensive to Moderate

If you'd like to retreat to the country after a busy day of sightseeing in Victoria, Markham House is the place for you. This pale yellow Tudor home is located 25 minutes west of Victoria on the way to Sooke. From the moment you enter the circular driveway to the time you depart, you'll be surrounded by abundant gardens and woodlands. Eight gorgeous acres have been landscaped with flowers, greenery, and a small pond; the remaining two acres are filled with rocky outcroppings and winding trails just waiting to be explored.

Afternoon tea is served upon your arrival. Relax by the fireplace in the parlor amidst the innkeepers' eclectic combination of Scottish and Asian antiques, or pass through the French doors to the veranda. Here, among hanging baskets of flowers, city-wearied travelers can peacefully relax. A small boat rests on the shores of a nearby pond, where rainbow trout occasionally ripple the water, and a lovely iris garden is in full view. You can revisit this scene in the morning while enjoying a full breakfast on the veranda or in the nearby breakfast room.

Three guest rooms occupy the second floor of the main house. Although a bit on the small side, they each offer terry-cloth robes, feather beds covered with pretty duvets, and views of the surrounding gardens. The eclectic mix of antique furnishings continues in each of the rooms, and the private bathrooms are rather ordinary (one is detached). However, chocolates and turndown service are much appreciated touches.

From the main house, follow a trail to the Honeysuckle Cottage. Trees excavated from the property now form the bark-covered foundation of this cedar-shingled home. Inside, the secluded cabin is graced with hardwood floors, Oriental throw rugs, a queen-size feather bed, and an ingenious makeshift kitchenette hidden away in a Belgian pine armoire. An old-fashioned woodstove stands in the corner, while the open-beamed ceiling slopes heavenward. The decor is a bit too mismatched for our tastes, but such glorious privacy more than makes up for it. Soak beneath the stars in your own private hot tub, located just steps away on the wooden deck. In the morning, guests at the Honeysuckle Cottage can join the others for breakfast in the main house or they can request that it be delivered to their door in a picnic basket.

SEASIDE BED AND BREAKFAST, Metchosin
3807 Duke Road
(250) 478-1446
http://www.victoria.net
Expensive

A potential deterrent to staying at this contemporary seaside estate is that you might not want to leave: the setting is simply spectacular. A rocky shore with lapping waves frames the front of the peach-colored stucco home; in the distance the snowcapped Olympic Mountains are visible across the sparkling blue waters of the strait.

All three suites feature private entrances, unusual artwork, and terry-cloth robes. Two three-room suites are situated in the main house. One has a living room surrounded by windows, a sliding glass door that opens to a private tiled patio, and skylights that frame the heavens; the other has a bedroom overlooking the beach and ocean. If it's privacy you're seeking, wind your way up the outdoor wooden stairs to the separate one-bedroom penthouse apartment. This suite, which overlooks the entire gorgeous property, has its own deck, a kitchen equipped for light cooking, rattan furniture, and a color TV. Whichever suite you choose, rest assured that all three offer a prime atmosphere for relaxation. The furnishings are comfortable though simple, and some pieces are outdated, but all the proper amenities are seen to with great care.

The crowning glory of this bed and breakfast is a 50-foot-long seaside swimming pool (heated to 85 degrees) edged by natural rock and carved cement, and an oceanside hot tub was recently added. Each morning a full breakfast is served in the dining room of the main house by the amiable innkeeper.

Outdoor Kissing

THE ITALIAN GARDENS AT ROYAL ROADS
UNIVERSITY, Metchosin
2005 Sooke Road (Highway 14)
(604) 391-2513
Open Daily
No entry fee; parking is $1 for two hours

Enter the campus at Royal Roads University through the main gate on Sooke Road. Keep left on the main road and you will see Hatley Castle near the center of campus. The Italian Gardens are located directly beside Hatley Castle.

Who would think that a university campus would be a good place to kiss? Royal Roads University not only has a prime kissing spot, but it has a castle to go along with it. Hatley Castle, otherwise known as the administration building, is the centerpiece of the campus with its ivy-covered stone facade. (Free tours of the castle are conducted daily.) Directly beside the castle are the incredible Italian Gardens, which hearken back to era when gardens were essential elements for romance.

A surrounding stone wall, which keeps the gardens partially hidden, opens near the west end of the castle to allow entry for visitors. Once inside, you'll find a brick pathway that traces the perimeter of the upper level. Columned trellises with flowers and gnarled branches creeping through the latticework create a shady shelter overhead. Continue along the path into the sunshine and into the brilliant colors of springtime. Crumbling statues seem completely at home in this wonderland of lilacs, foxgloves, poppies, and rhododendrons. Descend the steps to the second level, which has larger vegetation and more open lawn space than the previous level. Here, a few benches strategically placed beneath the trees provide excellent sites for private embraces. The gardens are fairly secluded, especially during summer, but don't be surprised if you happen upon one of the friendly peacocks that roam the campus.

Sooke

The undeveloped and reasonably undiscovered town of Sooke lies 35 kilometers (25 miles) west of Victoria. Starting here and continuing for another 65 kilometers (40 miles) north to the town of Port Renfrew, this area has not yet been claimed by civilization for its own purposes, which translates to plenty of wide open spaces for you and yours. Miles of rugged forested terrain, outstanding views of the Olympics across the Strait of Juan de Fuca, rocky isolated beaches, and notable accommodations present many options for enamored travelers seeking solitude and Canadian Southwest beauty. After you've wrapped up all the obligatory tourist requirements in Victoria, be sure to include extra time for this remarkable stretch of coastline and countryside.

Hotel/Bed and Breakfast Kissing

FOSSIL BAY RESORT, Sooke
1603 West Coast Road (Highway 14)
(250) 646-2073
http://www.fossilbay.com
Very Expensive
Minimum stay requirement

Six identical cottages, perched side by side on a rocky cliff bordering the Pacific Ocean, make up Fossil Bay Resort. Each plainly adorned unit has a king-size bed, wood-burning brick fireplace, terra-cotta-tiled floors, full kitchen, a television with videos supplied, an unobstructed view of the glistening ocean, and a partially covered outdoor patio with a hot tub for two. The rooms are too stark to be considered intimate, but the views and the Jacuzzi tubs help compensate for this shortcoming.

Romantic Warning: No food is provided with your stay, not even breakfast fixings or coffee, so be sure to stop at the grocery store before coming— the nearest market is about 25 kilometers (16 miles) away.

FRENCH BEACH RETREATS, Sooke
983 Seaside Drive
(250) 646-2154
Expensive to Unbelievably Expensive

Take your pick: choose the Ocean Treehouse for a cozy liaison in the woods or The Retreat if exclusive use of an 1,800-square-foot oceanfront cedar home sounds more intriguing. Both reside on over three acres of old-growth woods with trails leading to rocky, secluded shores.

The octagonal Treehouse is tiny but inviting, with windows all around, hardwood floors, and Turkish throw rugs. A queen-size bed covered with a sumptuous down comforter is the room's centerpiece, and bookshelves crammed with interesting knickknacks, a stereo, and books line the walls. A fruit bowl, wine, and other goodies greet you upon arrival, and a continental breakfast awaits in the small refrigerator so you can wake at your leisure and encounter only each other.

The Retreat is a steal when shared by several couples (it can accommodate up to eight guests) but still a bargain for just one couple, considering what you get. Like a vacation rental with all the comforts of home, this contemporary coastal property features a full kitchen furnished with all the necessary utensils and initial breakfast fixings, two bedrooms, a sleeping loft, queen-size beds with down comforters, double-sided wood-burning fireplace, two bathrooms (one with a Jacuzzi tub for two), and casual decor. The list goes on, and the longer you stay, the more you'll appreciate the amenities.

Romantic Warning: Children are welcome in The Retreat, which is OK if they're your own but a potential romantic deterrent if you've booked the Treehouse in a quest for peaceful seclusion. The owners assure us that this has never posed a problem, since the areas where kids tend to play are nowhere near the Treehouse. Still, it is something we feel you should be aware of.

HARTMANN HOUSE BED AND BREAKFAST, Sooke
5262 Sooke Road (Highway 14)
(250) 642-3761
Moderate to Expensive

Romance is alive and well and blooming in Sooke, where a lovely affectionate retreat has sprouted up. At first we were skeptical of the location on Highway 14, but once we opened the gate, roamed uphill through a glorious front yard filled with flower gardens, and came upon an English country cottage tucked well away from the road, we knew we had found something special.

Handcrafted cedar furnishings abound throughout the cottage and gardens, and attention has been paid to every detail. A massive Colonial-style fireplace warms the guest living room, where, on cooler days (which aren't unusual around here), you can enjoy complimentary afternoon wine and fruit while cuddling on softly padded wicker furniture. In warmer weather, relax in the tranquil garden on more wicker chairs or on the cedar swing built for two. The foliage is lush enough to create semiprivate sitting areas, a romantic bonus.

Each of the two plush guest rooms has a fluffy feather comforter, lace curtains, hardwood floors, and all the comfort you could ever dream of. The Bay Window Room feels light and airy, with white wicker furniture, white and pale blue linens on the king-size bed, a private bath, and a private entrance. The smaller Garden Room offers a four-poster double bed with a lace canopy and floral linens. Soft lighting in this room may make reading difficult, but kissing shouldn't be a problem. The only drawback is that the bath is across the hall; thankfully, terry-cloth robes are provided.

Sunrise summons a full gourmet breakfast, served at a table for four adjacent to the open kitchen where your gracious hosts work their magic. Spiced rhubarb parfait topped with mint, shrimp omelet with tomatoes and feta cheese, and waffles with strawberry maple syrup and whipped cream are just a few examples of the delectable entrées that may grace your plates. And what could be more romantic than heart-shaped blueberry bran muffins?

Romantic Note: At the time of our visit, a new Honeymoon Suite was being constructed upstairs at the Hartmann House. If all goes according to plans, this spacious suite will outshine the other rooms in amorous amenities. Imagine sharing a soak in an oversized hydro-massage whirlpool tub in the green-tiled bathroom, or snuggling beneath a chintz duvet on a king-size, four-poster canopied Edwardian bed. As you linger over breakfast in your own private sitting area, why not throw open the French doors and take in lovely views of the gardens? Other extras include a butler's pantry complete with microwave, wet bar, and fridge, and a double-sided fireplace that can be enjoyed from both the bedroom and the bath. We can't rate this new suite before it's finished, but it's probably safe to say that the innkeepers have outdone themselves once again.

Cost ratings for British Columbia listings are in Canadian funds. American travelers should check the exchange rate or ask an innkeeper to figure out the cost in U.S. dollars.

OCEAN WILDERNESS, Sooke

109 West Coast Road (Highway 14)
(250) 646-2116, (800) 323-2116
Inexpensive to Very Expensive

An interesting blend of homey comforts and touches of elegance makes Ocean Wilderness an intriguing getaway. Surrounded by old-growth forest and set on an ocean bluff, the log structure has a lovely tree-framed view of the water and mountains. At one edge of the property, a Japanese gazebo holds a Jacuzzi tub that overlooks the ocean through the trees. Private soaking times can be reserved, but before you get wet, be sure to hike down to the wonderful beachfront. A steep but well-kept trail leads down to a rocky, thoroughly secluded beach.

The log cabin's dining room and reception area are romantically rustic. The dark-stained log walls create a cozy, somewhat dark atmosphere, yet settings at the long breakfast table are extremely elegant, with fine china, white linens, silver, and crystal. The nine guest rooms, located in a wood-framed wing that was added to the original log cabin, hold an eclectic mix of antiques, plush furnishings, and handmade canopied beds. Some of the frilly touches and embellished fabrics are a bit much, but you can't go wrong with the second-floor rooms that have two-person soaking tubs, private entrances, and large, private, glass-enclosed sundecks that share in the scenery.

Wake-up coffee is delivered to your room on a silver tray with fresh flowers in the early morning. Full country breakfasts can also be delivered to your door if you request it the night before. Otherwise, breakfast is served next to the crackling fireplace in the log-cabin section of the home.

Romantic Option: From mid-June to mid-September, Ocean Wilderness hosts a Beach Party Seafood Buffet (Expensive) by advance reservation. Depending on what is fresh and available, this casual seafood-on-the-beach gathering may include salmon, crab, prawns, halibut, shrimp, and clams. Driftwood "furniture" is placed around an open beach fire, and gorgeous sunsets accompany your meal.

POINT-NO-POINT RESORT, Sooke

1505 West Coast Road (Highway 14)
(250) 646-2020
Inexpensive to Very Expensive
Minimum stay requirement on weekends and seasonally

Set on one mile of waterfront and 40 acres of untamed wilderness, Point-No-Point has been welcoming travelers since the early 1950s. It all started with just a couple of cabins (still standing and in pretty good condition, considering their age), but today there are 20 units available. Furnishings in some cabins are a little too dowdy for romantic-minded travelers, but each cabin does have a fireplace, full kitchen, and private bathroom. Luckily, none have televisions, phones, or radios, so you should have no distractions except for the ocean view.

The cabins that are specifically suited for a lovers' getaway are the five that were most recently built. Cedar paneling, hardwood floors, and a wood-burning fireplace create rustic ambience, while Adirondack-style furnishings, a pine armoire, and vaulted ceiling lend a modern but still cozy edge. The real draw of these cabins is the private hot tub on each deck that faces the crashing shoreline—now *this* is a place to kiss.

Trails with foliage-covered stone archways lead down to a nearby inlet and a gorgeous sandy beach—another fantastic kissing spot. The pure, rugged beauty of Point-No-Point seems eons away from civilization. It was stormy when we last visited, but regardless of the weather or time of year, the isolation of this place can spell romance.

Romantic Note: Food is not included with your stay, so bring your own breakfast provisions. Lunches, afternoon tea, and dinners are served in the small dining room (Moderate) adjacent to where you check in. The water and mountain views are simply stupendous, and the sunny dining room is charming. Binoculars are placed at every table in case an eagle soars past or a whale happens to swim by in the distant surf. On warm days you can enjoy your meal and the great outdoors on the casual deck.

RICHVIEW HOUSE, Sooke   😙😙😙😙
7031 Richview Drive
(250) 642-5520
http://www.islandnet.com/~rvh
Very Expensive

Poised atop an 80-foot bluff with an expansive view of the Strait of Juan de Fuca and the Olympic Mountains, Richview House is aptly named. It is also one of the most tasteful, sophisticated bed and breakfasts on Vancouver Island. Immaculate lawns border the two-level Tudor home, which has a separate wing dedicated to the three guest suites. Large windows, lofty ceilings, and light wood paneling make the inside as spectacular as the outside.

The three modern suites, decorated with Northwest flair, are incredibly comfortable. Each one has a wet bar, a queen-size bed with down comforter, and polished wood furniture crafted by one of the owners. Both of the upstairs rooms feature beach-stone and slate wood-burning fireplaces, skylights cut out of the slanted ceilings, and radiant-heat floors that give the rooms a rare seductive warmth. These two rooms also have private decks where you can enjoy breathtaking views of the Olympic Mountains while you soak together in your outdoor Jacuzzi tub.

Downstairs, the most spacious suite features attractive Northwest decor and sliding glass doors leading to a small deck. Although this room does not have a Jacuzzi tub, it more than makes up for it with a wonderful steam sauna/shower for two made of green faux marble (essential oils are provided). In traditional European style, this suite is separated from the adjacent dining room by double doors to ensure quiet.

The elegantly served breakfast is equal to the accommodations. Make your way to the glass-enclosed dining room and you may find sweet lemon-yogurt muffins, strawberry-glazed papaya, and fresh fruit crêpes laced with a light maple sauce. (If you prefer, you can stay in bed and have breakfast delivered to your room.) Once your day begins, you'll be pleased to find that the restaurant at **SOOKE HARBOUR HOUSE** (see Restaurant Kissing) is only moments away, while the beach is just a short hike from your front door.

SOOKE HARBOUR HOUSE, Sooke
1528 Whiffen Spit Road
(250) 642-3421, (800) 889-9688
http://www.sookenet.com/sooke/shh
Very Expensive to Unbelievably Expensive
(price includes breakfast and lunch)
Recommended Wedding Site

It is no wonder that Sooke Harbour House has gained nationwide acclaim and earned a stellar reputation for both its inn and restaurant (see Restaurant Kissing). Travelers from all walks of life continue to be surprised and satisfied by the unique experience offered here, at the end of a quiet Sooke road. A fantastic water's-edge setting, subtle elegance, and Northwest charm make Sooke Harbour House an exceptional getaway.

Two buildings (called The Old House and The New House) sit side by side on the property. The Old House, a white clapboard farmhouse, holds the restaurant and three guest rooms, and The New House holds ten more. Fresh cookies, a fruit bowl, and port are set out in all 13 sensational rooms. No detail has been overlooked in the regionally inspired suites, and the views of Sooke Bay, the Strait of Juan de Fuca, and the Olympic Mountains are captivating. The Blue Heron Room has the best view in the house and a large whirlpool tub beside a river-rock fireplace. Totemic designs and Native artwork embellish the expansive Victor Newman Longhouse Room, with its double-sided fireplace, large soaking tub for two and four-poster king-size bed. Regardless of which you choose, you'll find yourselves in the lap of luxury. Our only complaint is that the sofa beds in many rooms show signs of wear and should be replaced or at least recovered. Still, each suite features a wood-burning fireplace, a separate sitting area, views of the water, a vaulted ceiling, beautiful furnishings, and a wet bar. Other amentities include local artwork, king- or queen-size beds, plush linens, balconies or patios, and over-sized tubs or outdoor Jacuzzi tubs.

It will not be easy to leave your sumptuous room. Thankfully, you can lounge around all morning—gourmet breakfasts are delivered to your door. Lunch, also included with your stay, is served in the celebrated dining room or, if you plan to spend the day exploring the region, you can request a picnic basket.

Restaurant Kissing

THE GOOD LIFE RESTAURANT AND BOOKSTORE, Sooke
2113 Otter Point Road
(250) 642-6821
Inexpensive to Moderate
Lunch and Dinner Tuesday-Sunday

What is the good life? Well, that depends. For some it is true love; for others it is fame and fortune. In Sooke, however, The Good Life is an earthy, casual eatery and small bookstore. There is nothing fancy about the un-adorned mix of antique wooden tables in the two dining rooms, which are separated by etched glass windows. The menu emphasizes healthy cuisine with some Mediterranean touches. The Greek chicken baked in phyllo with spinach and feta cheese is tasty, and the lentil burger made with lentils, sun-flower seeds, and veggies—well, it was interesting. Service can be iffy, but you should leave with full stomachs and enough money left in your wallet to buy a book. Maybe that is what The Good Life is all about.

SOOKE HARBOUR HOUSE, Sooke
1528 Whiffen Spit Road
(250) 642-3421, (800) 889-9688
http://www.sookenet.com/sooke/shh
Very Expensive to Unbelievably Expensive
Dinner Daily (Breakfast and Lunch available for guests only)

Prepare yourselves for a memorable experience—Sooke Harbour House has a stellar reputation. The menu reads like an exotic novel, and every dish comes out looking glamorous, sprinkled with colorful, edible blossoms and leaves. It is exciting to see what the chefs will come up with next. Although the presentation is impeccable, reports complain that the dishes themselves can be so overdone (not overcooked, but overly inventive) that flavors get lost in the frenzy of fresh herbs and flowers. Whether this is true or not, the ingredients are undoubtedly the freshest around; an herb garden supplies the seasonings and an outdoor tank houses the shellfish.

The dining room is located on the main floor of a charming two-story country house, where a fire casts a warm glow over the room. Northwest art covers the walls, including everything from totemic carvings to decorated crab shells. Each table is dressed in white linen and adorned with fresh flowers and a single tapered candle. Window seats view the strait and surrounding gardens. The glorious setting and innovative menu almost make up for the service, which can be inattentive on occasion.

Outdoor Kissing

CHINA BEACH AND FRENCH BEACH, Sooke

Follow Highway 14 past Sooke. Ten miles down the road is a sign for French Beach. Reach French Beach via a short tree-lined path that leads down to the shore. Farther along Highway 14, one mile past the Jordan River, look for the China Beach sign. China Beach is accessible via a 15-minute walk through a rain forest.

These two beaches are separated by a few miles, but share similar settings and a rugged character. Ramble through young, replanted forests, visit formidable groves of ancient trees, or explore the white sandy beaches that stretch forever in either direction. Surefootedness is a prerequisite for the hike to China Beach, because you will occasionally have to make your way over projecting headlands of rocky coast and woods. At either location, you can bask on the shore in solitary glory while being lulled by the water's music. Beautiful views are abundant along this relatively undiscovered coastline, about an hour's drive from the bustling town of Victoria.

Romantic Note: French Beach has a well-maintained 69-unit campground set in old-growth forest. It is one of the most picturesque sites on the entire island for setting up a tent for two. Call (800) 689-9025 to make camping reservations.

EAST SOOKE REGIONAL PARK, Sooke

From Victoria, take the Old Island Highway (Highway 1A) to Sooke Road (Highway 14). Turn left onto Happy Valley Road and follow it to Rocky Point Road, which soon becomes East Sooke Road. Follow this road to the park's main entrance.

Whether you're planning a short morning jaunt or a rugged all-day hike, East Sooke Regional Park provides 3,500 acres of wilderness with phenomenal views. Follow one of the many trails that wind through beautiful beaches and pristine forest. Swimming is also recommended at these beaches if you dare take the cool plunge.

WHALE WATCHING, Sooke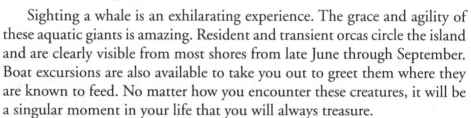
Sooke Coastal Explorations
6971 West Coast Road (Highway 14)
(250) 642-2343
$50 per person for a two-hour trip
Open June through mid-October

Sighting a whale is an exhilarating experience. The grace and agility of these aquatic giants is amazing. Resident and transient orcas circle the island and are clearly visible from most shores from late June through September. Boat excursions are also available to take you out to greet them where they are known to feed. No matter how you encounter these creatures, it will be a singular moment in your life that you will always treasure.

Romantic Suggestion: For an additional charge, you can reserve a beeper that will page you when an orca sighting is reported. When you are notified, simply rush down to the nearby marina, zip up in a flotation suit, hop into the Zodiac, and try to catch a glimpse of the magnificent creatures. It isn't 100-percent guaranteed, but it is the next-closest thing, and the chances of a sighting are pretty good.

Port Renfrew

Outdoor Kissing

BOTANICAL BEACH, Port Renfrew

Thirty miles north of Sooke, just outside Port Renfrew.

Tide pools full of sea urchins, crabs, starfish, chitons, coralline sea algae, and other saltwater animals thrive along this rock-clad beach. At low tide the ocean world opens up for your viewing and entertainment. It is an adventure worth sharing, but please tread lightly and leave the creatures alone; this wonderland is an integral part of nature and should stay that way.

Gulf Islands

Saturna, Mayne, Pender, Galiano, Salt Spring, Gabriola, Hornby, Denman, Quadra, and Cortez islands are accessible via ferryboat from Tsawwassen (just south of Vancouver), from several locations on Vancouver Island, and between the individual islands as well. For ferry information in Vancouver, call (604) 669-1211; in Victoria, (250) 386-3431. Depending on the season and during most weekends, reservations and advance payment may be necessary to assure your place on the ferry. Departure times are limited, so be sure to make your travel plans with this in mind.

Scattered like a heavenly constellation, the Gulf Islands lie nestled between Vancouver Island and mainland British Columbia. There are more than 300 forested isles, whose populations vary from zero to several thousand, and all of them are places of transcendent splendor and solitude. In topography and character, the Gulf Islands resemble the San Juan Islands of Washington State.

A handful of the Gulf Islands are accessible by ferryboat, and all have what's required to give you hassle-free, all-absorbing time away from everything except nature and each other. Whichever island you choose, you will be certain to find bed and breakfasts set on hilltops or hidden in the woods, intimate restaurants where "leisurely" is a way of life, oceanfront parks with sweeping views of the other islands, and miles of meandering paved roads that lead to island privacy. Nothing will be able to distract your attention from the out-of-this-world scenery and the eyes of the person you love.

Quadra Island

Hotel/Bed and Breakfast Kissing

APRIL POINT LODGE
AND FISHING RESORT, Quadra Island
900 April Point Road
(250) 285-2222, (888) 334-3474
http://www.boattravel.com/april
Moderate to Unbelievably Expensive
Call for seasonal closures.

Beginning at 4 A.M., fishing boats of all shapes and sizes race across the narrow channel between Quadra Island and Vancouver Island, leaving a high-pitched buzz in their wake. The early-morning activity is fueled by a passionate, single-minded intent: to hook, at the very least, a respectable-size king salmon or, at the very most, the record catch of the season. With tariffs like these, you'd think people would prefer shopping for fresh fish, but they don't, because fishing like this is utterly civilized.

PAINTER'S LODGE (see Hotel/Bed and Breakfast Kissing in the Vancouver Island chapter), TSA-KWA-LUTEN LODGE (reviewed elsewhere in this section), and April Point Lodge all offer anglers a stylish, extremely elegant getaway where they can chase, and often catch, the elusive Northwest king. If either of you loves fishing, these are the places to do it in style. But if part of your goal is to get some good snuggling in at the same time, your choice should be April Point Lodge.

An eclectic assortment of suites, rustic cabins, and guest houses here provide a wide range of choices. What they all share are scintillating views of the water and mountains, extremely comfortable furnishings with touches of elegance, down comforters, and separate seating areas. Some of the units are remarkably spacious, with large decks, Jacuzzi tubs, TV/VCRs, small kitchens, wood-burning fireplaces, and equally remarkable price tags.

Log pillars, handsome cedar paneling, and wraparound windows that showcase the scenery set a pleasing yet casual mood in the lodge's restaurant. The hearty and delectable meals offer amazing variety: French toast stuffed with Brie and strawberries for breakfast, authentic Texas-style chili for lunch, and sushi for dinner. Extraordinary!

Romantic Note: During summer, the emphasis is on fishing groups, the lodge is packed to overflowing, and the water buzzes loudly with the flurry of boat traffic. From mid-September to May, the crowds are gone, the restaurant is usually closed, the room rates are 50 percent off, the comfort is the same, and your privacy is increased considerably.

TSA-KWA-LUTEN LODGE, Quadra Island
Lighthouse Road, at Quathiaski Cove
(250) 285-2042, (800) 665-7745
Expensive to Very Expensive
Call for seasonal closures.
Recommended Wedding Site

Set on a Native Canadian reservation, this handsome, upscale fishing lodge features a most impressive soaring entryway and an almost cavernous interior supported by massive log beams and pillars. Striking floor-to-ceiling windows look out to a stunning view of the water and the mountains on the mainland. The rooms are hotel-stylish, with high ceilings, tall windows, plain bathrooms (some with a single-person Jacuzzi tub), gas fireplaces, and comfortable, although sparse, furnishings.

Dinner, served in the glass-enclosed waterfront dining room, is a beautiful presentation of gourmet treats. Thin, tender crêpes wrapped around layers of smoked salmon, caviar, and Japanese seaweed are delicious; chanterelles and other exotic mushrooms flavor a hearty soup; and the fresh salmon and halibut combination is perfectly prepared.

Outdoor Kissing

WE-WAI-KAI CAMPGROUND, Quadra Island
Rebecca Spit
(250) 285-3111
Very Inexpensive
Call for seasonal closures.

From the ferry landing, follow the signs to the ferry for Cortez Island or Heriot Bay. When you see the water, start looking for signs to Rebecca Spit. The campground is located on the spit.

Camping is not everyone's idea of a particularly romantic escape. It's not that the outdoors aren't potentially preferable, but campgrounds aren't always the best environment for intimate, tender moments. Kids running about, other campers too nearby, mosquitoes, hard ground, often inaccessible showers, and our personal nemesis—outhouses—tend to keep the mood rustic and neighborly but not private. So when we tell you that We-Wai-Kai campground is one of the most beautiful and well-laid-out campgrounds on the islands, you can be certain this is one spectacular setting.

One group of campsites is located on the beach facing the calm inner bay; another group is just above the shore, surrounded by trees lining the upper bank; and yet another lies in the forested hills overlooking the water. Each one is beautifully maintained and spacious. Even the common facilities are decent. Your privacy isn't guaranteed, but your relationship with each other and nature will be greatly enhanced.

Romantic Note: Just a few feet from the campground is **REBECCA SPIT PROVINCIAL PARK.** This rare parkland has remarkable vistas and short but wonderful trails with the shoreline of tranquil Heriot Bay on one side and the open waters of the Strait of Georgia on the other. The contrast between the two, only a stone's throw apart, is stupendous. There are picnic tables here and a convenient parking area as well.

Denman Island

Denman Island's collection of serene country roads, intriguing rocky beaches, abundant wildlife, and funky art galleries make it a perfect spot for leisurely bike rides with the one you love. **BOYLE POINT PARK** offers a stunning vantage point for viewing the Strait of Georgia and the Chrome Island Lighthouse, and **FILLONGLEY PROVINCIAL PARK** has limited camping facilities and trails that wind through old-growth forests. Directions to these parks can be acquired at the general store in "downtown" Denman or by calling **DENMAN/HORNBY TOURIST SERVICES**, (250) 335-2293. Although you'll find a handful of casual pubs and coffee shops here, we recommend bringing along a picnic lunch and spending the day exploring Denman's wonderful outdoors.

Hornby Island

A visit to Hornby Island is like a visit to Woodstock, New York, circa 1969. The dress, manner, and conversations in the Co-op Center, where most of the island activity takes place, will make you feel as if you've entered a time warp. Two rather good food stands here serve delicious vegetarian fare and decent espresso to boot. But it's the gorgeous sandy beaches, crystal-clear blue water, and gentle coves and bays that make Hornby Island a romantic destination.

Outdoor Kissing

TRIBUNE BAY, Hornby Island

From the Hornby Island ferry dock, follow Central Road to the small Co-op Center and follow the signs a short distance to the bay.

Soft sand under your feet, sparkling surf lapping against the shoreline, a thickly forested backdrop, and cool fresh breezes that blow your cares out to sea: Tribune Bay is the best place in southwestern Canada to spend a summer afternoon.

Gabriola Island

Although it is only a 20-minute ferry ride from the industrialized city of Nanaimo, Gabriola Island is a distinctly rural community of about 4,000 residents. Eagles frequently fly overhead, and deer nibble along roadsides (and in residents' gardens) all over the island. Similar in topography to the other Gulf Islands, Gabriola is lushly forested and has a rugged, rocky coast-line. You'll find ample inspiring opportunities to pucker up on this tranquil island paradise.

Hotel/Bed and Breakfast Kissing

MARINA'S HIDEAWAY, Gabriola Island
943 Canso Drive
(250) 247-8854, (888) 208-9850
http://island.net/~gbrunell
Inexpensive
Minimum stay requirement seasonally

Hidden away on an oceanfront bluff, this contemporary wood-and-glass home, built to serve as a bed and breakfast, commands views of the ocean past a stand of trees. Privacy is the emphasis here. All the necessities are provided to make you feel right at home, but the innkeeper is respectful of your space—a definite romantic advantage. Situated at one end of the home, the two guest suites have sliding glass doors that open onto decks with water views. Fat down comforters and lacy white linens drape king-size beds in the modern rooms, which also feature gas fireplaces, TV/VCRs (accompanied by a small selection of movies), and attractive standard baths. Some of the artwork and accents are a little dated, but you couldn't ask for more privacy or quiet. Due to its location, the top-floor suite has the most privacy, especially since a communal hot tub on the outdoor deck (available to both suites) is just steps away from the bottom-floor suite.

You'll probably have difficulty finishing the more-than-generous gourmet breakfast served in the privacy of your own room, so be sure to ask for a "to go" box and enjoy the leftovers on your trip back to the mainland.

SUNSET BED AND BREAKFAST, Gabriola Island
969 Berry Point Road
(250) 247-2032
http://www.islandnet.com/~sunsetcl
Inexpensive to Expensive

Those looking for an authentic bed-and-breakfast experience will appreciate the warmth and hospitality offered here. Perched on a residential hillside across the street from the water, this architecturally unique wooden home is

Cost ratings for British Columbia listings are in Canadian funds. American travelers should check the exchange rate or ask an innkeeper to figure out the cost in U.S. dollars.

as charming inside as it is outside. A fire crackles in the hearth and classical music sets a tranquil mood in the lovely living room, distinguished by hardwood floors, a sloped ceiling, skylights, and large picture windows with wonderful water views. A generous gourmet breakfast is served at one large table in the adjacent and airy kitchen; the apple cloud is rumored to be a particular favorite. (Some guests return just for this dish!)

Of the three guest rooms, the larger suite offers the most romantic inspiration. Pine paneled and decorated with a mixture of contemporary and antique furnishings, this spacious suite enjoys beautiful water views, a fireplace, and the luxury of a soaking tub set in a beautifully tiled bathroom. The other two rooms are much smaller (and consequently quite a bit cheaper), but don't offer much more than a comfortable night's sleep and quiet views of the home's manicured yard.

Restaurant Kissing

LATITUDES AT SILVA BAY, Gabriola Island
(250) 247-8662
http://www.gulf-islands.com/silvabay
Moderate to Expensive
Call for seasonal hours.

Set at the east end of the island in Silva Bay's bustling marina, Latitudes is the only romantic restaurant to speak of on Gabriola. Floor-to-ceiling windows command pleasant views of the harbor, and when the weather permits, guests can dine outside on the torch-lit deck. Slanted wood ceilings, a fire-place, and Native Canadian wood sculptures lend a rustic, artistic touch to the dining room's otherwise plain, country club–style interior. Though the tables are a little too large for real intimacy, a pianist playing soothing melodies at a baby grand in the corner creates a romantic atmosphere. Service here is exceptionally accommodating and the usually reliable menu features seafood, meat, and pasta. Our favorite item was the appetizer of Camembert baked in puffed pastry and served with herbs and sautéed mushrooms. We were pleased to find clams on the menu, but were very disappointed to discover they were canned, not fresh. The tiramisu for dessert, however, was a smashing success and revitalized our taste buds.

Galiano Island

For many years the Gulf Islands had no elite, ultra-deluxe places for lovers who wanted all the luxuries of a large inn. Now, a handful of prop-erties dotted among the islands offer just such gilt-edged accommodations. Exceedingly small, forested Galiano Island is home to several of our favorites.

Hotel/Bed and Breakfast Kissing

GALIANO LODGE, Galiano Island
134 Madrona Drive
(250) 539-3388
Inexpensive to Very Expensive

Proud Galiano Lodge is visible from the ferry terminal. This means, of course, that all too often the sound of a blaring ferry horn can be a big disturbance to those who are staying here. If you're willing to overlook this fact (and many are), you'll be delighted with the lodge's 17 splendid suites, filled with all the appropriate furnishings and details for a luxurious and relaxing stay. Twenty-four-karat gold-plated fixtures are an opulent feature in the attractive white-and-yellow-tiled bathrooms—just the place for a long, sensuous soak in a spacious Jacuzzi tub. Puffy down comforters cover fashionable wrought-iron beds, and wood-burning fireplaces quickly warm the rooms. Floor-to-ceiling windows overlook the water and views of the ferry's comings and goings, so you'll know just when to expect the horn. (It's really not so startling once you get used to it.)

Romantic Note: The **GALIANO LODGE RESTAURANT** (see Restaurant Kissing) is one of the finest places to eat on the island.

WOODSTONE COUNTRY INN, Galiano Island
743 Georgeson Bay Road
(250) 539-2022
Inexpensive to Expensive
Minimum stay requirement on weekends seasonally

Harry, a South African guinea fowl, is the Woodstone Country Inn's official "meeter and greeter," and he welcomes you with a showy display of tail feathers and a few pecks at your car tires. Set amidst forested farmland, this rural hideaway is nestled in the hills of Galiano Island. Although the inn does not have shimmering water views, the lovely country setting hardly inhibits kissing.

Most of the 12 beautifully appointed rooms have views of the forest and rolling valley, where hawks float effortlessly in the sky and horses graze in distant corrals. Each unit radiates a great deal of warmth, and all are appointed with impressive antiques and attractive floral linens. Ten rooms have fireplaces, and six have large soaking tubs. After only a few hours here, you will achieve maximum relaxation and peace of mind.

A complimentary breakfast is served to guests every morning at two-person tables in the lovely dining room that overlooks the valley. Fine dining options are limited on Galiano Island, so guests staying overnight here will readily appreciate the fact that the restaurant here (see Restaurant Kissing) is one of the best on the island.

Restaurant Kissing

GALIANO LODGE RESTAURANT, Galiano Island
134 Madrona Drive
(250) 539-3388
Moderate to Very Expensive
Afternoon Tea and Dinner Daily; Sunday Brunch
Call for seasonal hours.

GALIANO LODGE (see Hotel/Bed and Breakfast Kissing) is one of the most romantic places to stay in the Gulf Islands, and it has become equally well known for its stylish dining room and impressive menu. Partitioned by a stunning marble fireplace, one side of the waterfront restaurant offers fine dining while the other is a more casual and reasonably priced bistro. You can be assured of exciting combinations of fresh ingredients and expert service at both. Entrées such as penne with chorizo and sun-dried tomatoes, and filet mignon finished with a port wine demi-glace, are as seductive as the surroundings. High tea here is a wonderful midday pick-me-up.

WOODSTONE COUNTRY INN, Galiano Island
743 Georgeson Bay Road
(250) 539-2022
Expensive
Dinner Daily
Call for seasonal hours.

Don't miss this epicurean dining spot on the ground floor of the lovely **WOODSTONE COUNTRY INN** (see Hotel/Bed and Breakfast Kissing). Well-spaced tables draped in lace tablecloths are scattered throughout this gracious, country-style restaurant, where guests partake in serene valley views through floor-to-ceiling windows. Here, excellent four-course dinners are presented by candlelight to the accompaniment of soft classical music. The inn can be understaffed and the service less than efficient, but be patient and you can enjoy such delectable surprises as broccoli-apple soup served with homemade herb bread, oysters gratin, sole stuffed with salmon mousse in a grape cream sauce, and espresso cheesecake.

Salt Spring Island

Salt Spring Island has experienced a bed-and-breakfast explosion. That means a lot of work for a travel writer and a lot of confusion for travelers choosing accommodations. Sometimes having only a few choices is better (or at least easier) than having too many. Still, after exhaustive—and kiss-intensive—research, we discovered the best this wonderful island oasis has to offer.

Romantic Note: Due to Salt Spring Island's size and popularity, we recommend calling the properties you intend to visit ahead of time for reservations and specific directions (it can get confusing).

Hotel/Bed and Breakfast Kissing

ANNE'S OCEANFRONT HIDEAWAY, Salt Spring Island
168 Simson Road
(250) 537-0851
http://www.bbcanada.com/939.html
Expensive to Very Expensive

Perched high above the ocean amid tall trees, this large contemporary home holds four luxurious guest rooms, several cozy common areas, a private exercise room, an outdoor hot tub with views of the water, and two wraparound verandas where you can unwind as you gaze at the peaceful surroundings.

All of the guest rooms are located in a separate wing of the home, with a separate entrance to ensure the utmost in quietness. Each room offers plush linens and affectionate amenities such as massage tubs and soft lighting. In the Oak Room, a queen-size rice bed with Laura Ashley linens majestically occupies the center of the room, and a whirlpool tub sits near the gas fireplace. In the Pacific Yew Room, an octagonal ceiling with windows on all sides allows views of the forest and water, and a whirlpool tub for two sits in the large private bathroom. This is the only guest room without a balcony, but with all its surrounding windows, it really doesn't need one.

Your gourmet morning meal will most likely feature scrumptious fresh muffins, a hot entrée such as sweet French toast or a creative egg dish, and plenty of fresh fruit.

BEACH HOUSE ON SUNSET, Salt Spring Island
930 Sunset Drive
(250) 537-2879
http://www.saltspring.com/beachhouse

Expensive to Very Expensive
Minimum stay requirement seasonally
Call for seasonal closures.

Located on the northwest shore of Salt Spring Island, poised on a rocky bluff above a waterfront cove, this enticing bed and breakfast is miles away from the bustling villages of Ganges and Vesuvius. You can actually watch eagles diving for fish right outside your window.

One of the most romantic options, a self-contained cedar cabin, rests on an incline above its own private cove. Wraparound decks and bay windows allow dramatic views of sensationally gorgeous sunsets over the mountains of Vancouver Island. Although the decor here is slightly dated and rustic, it suits the setting, and the absolute privacy is plenty of compensation. Snuggle in thoughtfully provided bathrobes as you rest on your deck, watching otters and seals frolic in the waves.

Three delightfully plush rooms are located in the main house, and private decks with the same water views make these almost as wonderful as the cabin. All three rooms boast down comforters, feather pillows, lovely floral fabrics, and separate sitting areas. One is furnished in wicker; another has a stunning wrought-iron canopy bed cloaked in white fabric, which contrasts beautifully with the vivid green walls. Sophisticated and subtle, with a taupe color scheme and sumptuous linens, the third and newest suite has a claw-foot tub in the bathroom and a fireplace.

Breakfast is a culinary event at the Beach House; one of the innkeepers was schooled at the Cordon Bleu in Paris. Delicacies such as blueberry coffee cake, salmon quiche, fresh brioche, homemade sausages, and unusual fruit drinks will greet you in the morning.

BEDDIS HOUSE BED AND BREAKFAST, Salt Spring Island 💋💋💋
131 Miles Avenue
(250) 537-1028
Expensive
Minimum stay requirement seasonally
Call for seasonal closures.

We constantly receive recommendations from readers for romantic accommodations to include in upcoming editions of this book. More often than not, these places are wonderfully worthwhile, and Beddis House is no exception. Fruit trees and perennials border the walkway that leads to this turn-of-the-century white farmhouse poised on a rocky bluff; the bed and breakfast is surrounded by more than an acre of manicured lawns outlined by white fences. In the common area, comfy plaid couches sit in front of a wood-burning stove and large windows afford picturesque views of the water through tall trees. The adjacent carriage house holds the three guest rooms, two on the main floor and one perched at the top of the home. Each one has a private bathroom with pedestal sink and claw-foot tub as well as attractive linens, country knickknacks, and private decks with views of the lovely surroundings and the tranquil strait. For the most preferred accommodations, we recommend the top-floor suite, with its king-size four-poster bed, lovingly restored antiques, and spacious bathroom.

In the morning, wander back to the main farmhouse for a full country breakfast of fresh fruit, home-baked breads, and an ever-changing hot entrée, all served at one long table surrounded by views of the gardens. Afternoon tea and baked goodies are served in the guest parlor or out on the expansive front porch when weather permits.

BLENCATHRA HOUSE
BED AND BREAKFAST, Salt Spring Island
125 Mountain View Drive
(250) 537-1606
http://www.cimarron.net/canada/bc/blencathra.html
Moderate

Madrona trees (Canadians refer to them as arbutus) shade this recently built, sprawling cedar home set high on a hillside overlooking the water. A private entrance leads downstairs to two guest suites that share a cozy sitting room and a small kitchenette where cookies and fruit are available at all hours. A private balcony with views of Sansum Narrows is the highlight of the appropriately named Balcony Room, which also features a beautifully appointed king-size bed and an immaculate private bath. Also utterly charming, the Sunset Room is adorned with country floral linens and wallpaper that create an affectionate mood without being too frilly; a private deck bestows glimpses of the water beyond a wooded hillside, and a small private bath with cedar accents ensures privacy.

Breakfast is served family-style in a pretty upstairs dining room that overlooks the water. You won't be disappointed with the homemade, farm-fresh entrées, such as smoked salmon crêpes, apple puffs, and grapefruit with port wine sauce.

Cost ratings for British Columbia listings are in Canadian funds. American travelers should check the exchange rate or ask an innkeeper to figure out the cost in U.S. dollars.

BOLD BLUFF RETREAT, Salt Spring Island
1 Bold Bluff
(250) 653-4377
Inexpensive to Moderate; No Credit Cards
Minimum stay requirement
Call for seasonal closures.

Bold Bluff Retreat is not your typical Northwest getaway, but that's what makes it so wonderful. Nestled on 100 acres of rocky oceanfront land, the only way to reach this property is via the owner's motorboat. While this can seem like a considerable inconvenience, it also guarantees that you won't be bothered by the rest of the world.

Two rental cottages are set at opposite ends of Bold Bluff's sprawling property. Located in a grove of trees behind the owner's private home, the first cottage is best described as rustic, with its creaking hardwood floors, weathered wood walls, and dated (but fully equipped) kitchen. What this cottage lacks in modern conveniences, it more than makes up for in quiet, antique charm. The tiny old-fashioned bath has a claw-foot tub, and the bedroom is furnished with an antique bed covered by a patchwork quilt. A woodstove cranks out heat in the winter.

Farther away, the second, more basic (and cheaper) cottage is poised literally at the water's edge on a rocky outcropping. Floor-to-ceiling windows capture views of the water, herons, eagles, and owls—your only neighbors. Listen to the sound of the waves lapping beneath the cottage's plank floors (yes, the tide actually comes in *beneath* the house). This is the cabin for couples who prefer to rough it, with a composting toilet, a small kitchenette with just the basics, and an outdoor shower. (You'll feel like one with nature after your first day here!) Cozy up next to a woodstove or explore the nearby acres of forest; you might even catch glimpse of an eagle's nest.

Romantic Warning: Meals are not included with your stay, so come prepared with groceries and other personal necessities. Just in case you've forgotten something (inevitable in our experience), the owner will ferry you back and forth to the island's "mainland" for a reasonable charge.

CRANBERRY RIDGE
BED AND BREAKFAST, Salt Spring Island
269 Don Ore Drive
(250) 537-4854, (888) 537-4854
http://www.saltspring.com/CranberryRidge
Moderate to Expensive
Minimum stay requirement

Located on a bluff and surrounded by colorful gardens, the Cranberry Ridge Bed and Breakfast has one of the most magnificent panoramas imaginable, with a mesmerizing view of the islands, inlets, and the imperial snowcapped mountains of the mainland. Charming and immaculate, the three ample guest rooms are located in the bottom section of the house. Cozy sitting areas appointed with wicker and willow furniture look out at the stunning scenery through floor-to-ceiling sliding glass doors found in every room. Two rooms have one-person Jacuzzi tubs, one has a wood-burning fireplace, and all have the added comfort of terry-cloth robes and handmade patchwork quilts. Each room opens onto an expansive deck where a large hot tub sits, perfect for stargazing during late-night soaks.

In spite of all this praise, we should mention that when the shades are opened to let in the beautiful view, you'll feel rather exposed to other guests who are enjoying the deck (especially if you're in the room nearest the hot tub). To remedy this situation, the innkeepers have installed frosted, one-way glass. Although this is meant to ensure your privacy, we were still tempted to draw the shades at times. This is a small price to pay, however, for the endless views and affectionate ambience. And we haven't even mentioned the gourmet five-course breakfast that might include homemade lamb sausage and crab Benedict: utterly delicious and satisfying.

GREEN ROSE FARM 💋💋💋
AND GUEST HOUSE, Salt Spring Island
346 Robinson Road
(250) 537-9927
Moderate
Minimum stay requirement on holiday weekends

Those looking for peaceful tranquility and lovingly decorated accommodations need look no further than Green Rose. Expansive gardens, fruit orchards, and forests surround this crisp white and cream farmhouse. Inside the common area, casual country elegance is provided by white couches, hardwood floors, an antique armoire resting in the corner, and the warm glow of a wood-burning fireplace.

The three snug guest rooms are strikingly reminiscent of an airy seaside inn, with their blue-painted wood floors, soft white walls, and snowy bed linens. The main-floor room features a fluffy down comforter, a brick hearth bordering a wood-burning fireplace, views of the colorful gardens, and a private bathroom with pedestal sink and standard shower. The two upstairs guest rooms have fluffy duvets, dried flowers, and splendid views of the property. Both offer private bathrooms, one with a claw-foot tub, the other with a standard shower.

In the morning, a full gourmet breakfast of a hot entrée, fresh fruit, and homemade breads and muffins is served at a large pine table in the dining room (also with a blue-painted floor); a wall of windows helps to bring the lovely outside in.

HASTINGS HOUSE, Salt Spring Island
160 Upper Ganges Road
(250) 537-2362, (800) 661-9255
Expensive to Unbelievably Expensive
Minimum stay requirement on weekends
Call for seasonal closures.

Hastings House is a sparkling gem of a country inn, poised over Ganges Harbor and set on 30 acres of rolling, wooded hills crisscrossed by inviting bathrooms. Unfortunately, Hastings House will also pull at your purse strings, even if you select one of the smaller, more plainly decorated accommodations. And the strings may break altogether if you want a two-story suite with a classic stone fireplace, two bathrooms, and personalized afternoon tea service. We recommend asking for the latter; the simple decor in some of the smaller units can be a little *too* simple and outdated to warrant the exorbitant price tags, but service and exclusiveness are what you're really paying for.

Every morning, before your four-course breakfast is served in the fireplace-warmed Manor House, a basket of fresh pastries and hot coffee is delivered to your door. As the Hastings House brochure aptly states: "Meticulous attention is given to character, courtesy, comfort, calm, and cuisine," and we can personally vouch for that.

Romantic Note: If your wallet can stand one more splurge, make dinner reservations at the **HASTINGS HOUSE RESTAURANT** (see Restaurant Kissing) or at **SNUG** (Very Expensive), the property's more casual dining room that offers a four-course prix fixe menu. Both are open to the public, although guests do receive reservation priority.

HORSELL HOUSE, Salt Spring Island
1860 Fulford-Ganges Road
(250) 653-9177
Expensive

Views are abundant at this privately owned hilltop home which overlooks a sloping valley, plots of farmland, and Fulford Harbor. Although the common areas are exceedingly homey, the Master Bedroom is lovely and worth recommending. A king-size four-poster bed covered with crisp white linens and a down comforter is the highlight of the small, airy bedroom. A private deck offers spectacular views of the valley, and the spacious private bathroom holds both a steam shower and a large sunken Jacuzzi tub just right for two. Enjoy more valley views over a full breakfast, served on elegant china in the innkeeper's pleasant dining room.

Hersell House offers a second option for couples who prefer absolute privacy and less hands-on service: a small private home set just off the road at the bottom of the driveway. Views of the valley are closer up, but so is the road, which means traffic noise poses more of a distraction. Modestly appointed with mismatched modern furnishings, the home features a full kitchen stocked with breakfast provisions, a comfortable living room with a fireplace and a TV/VCR, and a private bathroom. Down comforters cover wooden beds in the two separate bedrooms.

Both units are available for the same price. While the house offers more space and privacy, we preferred the amenities and the views in the guest suite.

MALLARD'S MILL BED AND BREAKFAST, Salt Spring Island
521 Beddis Road
(250) 537-1011
Inexpensive to Expensive
Call for seasonal closures.

Everything about this bed and breakfast is unique and enticing. Sheltered in a forest grove, the recently constructed wood home is an architectural achievement. Part of the building is supported by cement stilts and propped above a small pond, where water spills from a large rotating waterwheel. An outdoor hot tub and a cabana with a shower overlook this tranquil setting. Guests can even hop on board a miniature railroad that wraps around the house for full-scale views of the property. Like we said, unique.

Profuse daylight floods through skylights in the home's interior, which is appointed with wicker furnishings and hardwood floors. Coffee, tea, and cookies can be enjoyed in this comfortable setting at all hours. Four sparingly appointed guest rooms feature a turn-of-the-century motif; hand-sewn patchwork quilts cover the comfy beds, and several rooms have gas fireplaces and views of the churning waterwheel. All rooms have private baths.

A newly constructed honeymoon cottage called Otter Tail is by far the most appropriate choice for romancing. Secluded in the trees, it offers a king-size bed, fireplace, Jacuzzi tub for two, a dock that stretches out over the duck pond, and the utmost in privacy. A three-course gourmet breakfast is delivered to this unit on the train; the rest of the guests are served in the cheery kitchen or at two-person tables on the outdoor patio, overlooking the pond.

OLD FARMHOUSE
BED AND BREAKFAST, Salt Spring Island
1077 North End Road
(250) 537-4113
Expensive

Nestled among spreading trees, bountiful orchards, and colorful gardens, this revitalized turn-of-the-century farmhouse has everything you'll need for an outstanding getaway. A private entrance leads to four cheerful guest rooms located in a separate building that is attached to the main house by a terra-cotta-tiled hallway. Each room features high dormers, down comforters, a private balcony or patio that overlooks the peaceful landscape, and accents of color that correspond to the room's name, such as blue accents in the Blue Room and peach accents in the Peach Room. Special romantic touches include hot coffee or tea delivered to your door in the morning and a decanter of sherry and two miniature crystal glasses placed on each room's bedside table. Outside, you can relax in the two-person hammock or sip iced tea in the intimate gazebo tucked away in the fruit orchard.

Breakfast here is the talk of the town. Served at one large table in the main dining room, the gourmet country breakfast is meticulously presented, with selections like crème fraîche over kiwis and blueberries, delicious homemade cinnamon buns and croissants, and an orange soufflé with Cointreau crêpes filled with seasonal fruit. Don't worry if you can't finish your bountiful portion; the kind-hearted hosts provide plastic "doggy bags" so guests can snack on unfinished goodies later in the day.

PAUPER'S PERCH
BED AND BREAKFAST, Salt Spring Island
225 Armand Way
(250) 653-2030
http://www.saltspring.com/paupersperch
Expensive to Very Expensive
Minimum stay requirement on summer weekends

Far from being a pauper's perch, this beautifully crafted contemporary home is fit for a king and commands one of the most spectacular views on Salt Spring Island. Ensconced at the top of a steep forested hillside and surrounded by five acres of undeveloped woodland, Pauper's Perch overlooks sloping valleys, lush forests, the Coast Mountains, and the waterways surrounding the island. In this quiet refuge from the island's ever-increasing hustle and bustle, guests can soak up the views from the vantage point of an extra-long claw-foot soaking tub, set outside on the deck. (Due to its public location, however, we recommend wearing bathing suits.)

Private entrances ensure privacy in all three guest rooms, which offer magnificent views from private decks. Though it is slightly more expensive, the Honeymoon Suite is the real reason to come here. A wedding dress adorns the wall above the queen-size four-poster bed in the center of the sun-filled room, which is surrounded by windows. A two-sided fireplace sheds warmth in both the bedroom and bathroom, where you'll find a double-sized Roman soaking tub. A complimentary bottle of champagne accompanies your stay in this suite. Two more suites are available downstairs, but the bright pink color schemes and cutsey touches are a little overdone.

Breakfast is served in the innkeeper's dining room, with views on the side; in the warmer months guests can eat outside on the expansive wooden deck.

SALTY SPRINGS RESORT AND SPA, Salt Spring Island
1460 North Beach Road
(250) 537-4111, (800) 665-0039
Expensive to Very Expensive
Minimum stay requirement

Set on a manicured grassy bank, across the street from the ocean, these peculiar looking "Gothic arch" chalets are unlike anything we've ever seen before. Spiny wooden frames enclose the decks on each of the 12 closely arranged private cabins, creating a strange first impression. However, there is nothing strange about the heartwarming interiors, which all sport knotty pine walls, high arched ceilings, abundant skylights, a full kitchen, and a wood-burning stove. Each unit has an airy living room overlooking the water, and the same views are also visible from the snug bedroom, separated from the living room by shutters. Best of all, guests can soak by candlelight in the large, bright red spa tub set in each unit's red-tiled bathroom.

A new addition to Salty Springs is the spa, which offers shiatsu massage, aromatherapy, hydrotherapy, and herbal wraps. It's the perfect way to unwind after a leisurely bike ride along the quiet country roads.

Romantic Warning: We urge you to only book a cabin that has been recently updated; the older ones feature out-of-date colors and tired linens, and are in great need of new decor.

SOLIMAR, Salt Spring Island
347 Bridgman Road
(250) 653-4418
Expensive; No Credit Cards

A long, winding drive south brings you to one of Salt Spring Island's most secluded waterfront locations. Here, madrona trees reach for the water from rocky outcroppings and small islands dot the horizon. Solimar is Spanish for "sun and sea." Although we can't promise year-round sunshine as its name suggests, you can be assured of total seclusion at this cozy one-bedroom cabin perched just above the water's edge. Overstuffed floral couches, a full kitchen, and a private bath are modern touches in the otherwise very rustic cabin, which features high ceilings, exposed wood beams, and dated artwork and fabrics. Guests can effortlessly appreciate the stunning water views through the cabin's windows or explore the property's waterfront acreage on foot. Breakfast fixings await in the refrigerator (provisions for other meals are up to you), and guests are allowed to pick vegetables and herbs from the owner's organic garden. Laundry facilities are available next door for guests' added convenience.

WESTON LAKE INN, Salt Spring Island
813 Beaver Point Road
(250) 653-4311
http://www.bbcanada.com/172.html
Moderate
Minimum stay requirement seasonally

One of the oldest professionally run bed and breakfasts on the island, Weston Lake Inn is also one of the more reasonably priced. Set on ten idyllic country acres, this contemporary home overlooks the tranquil, forest-lined Weston Lake. Guests can best appreciate this view from the steamy warmth of a hillside hot tub located on a wooden deck just in front of the house.

The three smallish guest rooms are all quite comfortable, with private bathrooms, wonderful down comforters, skylights, and a mixture of contemporary and country touches. Two common areas provide extra space. The upstairs sitting room has a roaring fire in the hearth and is furnished with contemporary overstuffed sofas and local artwork. Downstairs, guests can pop in a video and lazily loll away the hours in the more casual TV room.

After a sumptuous morning meal of a creative juice blend, fresh muffins, and herbed scrambled eggs or lox on a croissant, explore the inn's noteworthy gardens and acres of quiet forest.

Restaurant Kissing

BOUZOUKI, Salt Spring Island
2104 Grace Point Square
(250) 537-4181
Inexpensive to Moderate
Lunch and Dinner Monday-Saturday

Bouzouki is harbored right on the water in the town of Ganges. "Romantic" isn't exactly the best word to describe this casual Greek cafe, but "authentic" is. Good lunch spots are hard to come by on Salt Spring Island, and the Greek food served here is superlative. When the weather cooperates, the outside deck overlooking the water is an ideal spot to enjoy pita bread and hummus, chicken wrapped in phyllo, beef souvlaki, and, for dessert, a gooey slice of baklava.

HASTINGS HOUSE RESTAURANT, Salt Spring Island
160 Upper Ganges Road
(250) 537-2362
Expensive
Dinner Daily

HASTINGS HOUSE (see Hotel/Bed and Breakfast Kissing) is one of the most expensive, exclusive places to stay on the west coast of Canada. If the cost of staying there exceeds your vacation budget but you want a taste of this regal style of living, make dinner reservations at its elegant restaurant. The sumptuous, five-course prix fixe meals feature tantalizing Northwest cuisine made with produce harvested from the inn's meticulously maintained herb and vegetable gardens. Our superb tempura shrimp with nori and exquisite grilled salmon were models of perfection. Regrettably, there is a dress code; men must wear jackets, which is fine if you remembered to pack one. If you didn't, don't fret. Hastings House now has a more casual dining room called **SNUG**, where jackets are not required.

Romantic Note: The inn is devoted to its patrons and allows the public to partake of its sublime dinners only if the guests of the inn don't take the limited reservations first.

HOUSE PICCOLO, Salt Spring Island
108 Hereford Avenue
(250) 537-1844
Moderate to Expensive
Call for seasonal hours.

Once you've sampled House Piccolo's delicious fresh seafood and charming ambience, you'll understand why this dinner spot is touted as one of Salt Spring Island's best. Set in the heart of Ganges, the small blue-and-white farmhouse is wonderfully intimate. Two-person tables covered in ivory tablecloths are scattered throughout two connecting dining rooms appointed with copper kettles and antique dishes. Everything on the menu is enticing, particularly the tender fillet of salmon, and the prawns Provençal flambéed with brandy and finished with herbs and a creamy garlic sauce. Desserts change daily, and are always worth your while.

Outdoor Kissing

ARTISAN SUNDAYS, Salt Spring Island

Visit the travel information center in Ganges or Vesuvius for a map with addresses and other information.

Sundays on the island are loosely organized but exceptionally interesting. Every Sunday the local craftspeople open their studios to the public for browsing and shopping. Every imaginable artistic mastery and innovation can be found in all kinds of hideaways dotted along forested hillsides and settled at the end of long, winding roads. Handmade candles, art glass, knitted items, paper art, ironwork, paintings, pottery, weavings, sculpture, baskets, quilts, and dried flowers are just some of the specialties you can discover during your journey. It might not sound romantic, but once you discover out a place that can create something you will share forever, it will be an affectionate memory for a long time to come.

MOUNT MAXWELL PARK, Salt Spring Island

From the town of Ganges, take Lower Ganges Road south out of town and follow the signs to the park.

Endless views are just the beginning of what you will experience at the end of the dusty gravel road that takes you to the top of Mount Maxwell. If you do nothing else on this island, you must witness the breathtaking panorama from up here and kiss passionately for at least a moment or two. It is hard to describe how magnificent and inspiring the scenery is from this vantage point. To the north are the snow-crowned mountains of the Canadian Rockies; to the south stands the glacial peak of Mount Baker; all around, for 360 degrees, are the forested islands and the sparkling, crystalline waters of the Strait of Georgia. Ahh, the sheer beauty of it all. Kissing isn't really mandatory, but you'll find it very hard not to indulge, the sensory stimulation is that potent.

WELCOME ABOARD SAILING
CHARTERS, Salt Spring Island
Contact Ted Harrison or Susan Evans at (250) 653-4311
$150 per party for a three-hour minimum

Call for reservations and directions.

If you're in the mood for a seaworthy adventure and would like a waterborne look at the Gulf Islands, consider sailing on the sleek and elegant 36-foot *Malaika*. You can help crew the boat as much or as little as you'd like; of course, we suggest snuggling up at the bow and nibbling on the provided cookies and hot chocolate, but it's up to you. Lessons and a prepacked picnic lunch are available upon request for an additional $25 per couple.

Mayne Island

Mayne Island may be more populated than some of the other Gulf Islands, but its peaceful aura and natural beauty are intact, making it the perfect choice for a secluded vacation or extended day trip.

Hotel/Bed and Breakfast Kissing

OCEANWOOD COUNTRY INN, Mayne Island
630 Dinner Bay Road
(250) 539-5074
http://www.gulfislands.com/mayne/oceanwood
Expensive to Very Expensive
Minimum stay requirement on weekends
Closed January through February

Enveloped by plentiful gardens, towering trees, and a sweeping view of Navy Channel, this recently renovated Tudor home holds 12 magnificent guest rooms, four ultra-cozy common areas, and an elegant 30-seat country-gourmet restaurant. Each unit is spacious and exquisitely designed for cherished time together. We don't have space to list all our favorites, but the Lavender Room is certainly one of them; it has two levels of plush carpeting, a queen-size canopy bed with pretty blue linens, a small soaking tub facing a wood-burning fireplace, and a private deck overlooking the water through tall trees. The Fern Room is equally engaging, with a pretty yellow and green color scheme, vaulted ceiling, queen-size canopy bed, large soaking tub, wood-burning fireplace, and private deck that faces the water. If you can tear yourselves away from your room, you'll find the four common areas are just as wonderful. Two of the loveliest are the garden parlor, with a terra-cotta-tiled floor and floral-tapestried chairs, and the library, with soft couches and myriad books; a double-sided fireplace warms both rooms.

Cost ratings for British Columbia listings are in Canadian funds. American travelers should check the exchange rate or ask an innkeeper to figure out the cost in U.S. dollars.

Breakfast (guests only) and dinner are served in the idyllic downstairs dining room (see Restaurant Kissing), where you'll have front-row views of the water and the heavenly gardens. Your morning could very well begin with fresh muffins and breads, pancakes with fresh berries, and freshly squeezed juices. Our earnest recommendation is that you pack your bags right this minute and take advantage of what this first-class inn has to offer.

Restaurant Kissing

FERNHILL LODGE, Mayne Island
610 Fernhill Road
(250) 539-2544
Moderate
Dinner Daily; Sunday Brunch
Call for seasonal hours.

This restaurant is a must for food connoisseurs. You'd never guess that feasts like this could possibly exist on a remote island. Every night between May and October, the menu lists four-course theme dinners based on a particular time in history. The Renaissance is evoked with slivers of smoked eel in fruit sauces, a garden-picked salad with quail eggs, barbecued lamb in sweet-and-sour citrus sauce, and sweet and spicy pear pie. A Roman motif is carried out with dates fried in honey and olive oil and sprinkled with pepper, barbecued pigeon with mustard and nut sauce, lentil-chestnut potage, and cheese and honey balls. The small country-rustic dining rooms are somewhat austere, but they hold a handful of tables set near a warm wood-burning stove and windows that look out to the beautiful flower beds and forested surroundings.

Romantic Note: FERNHILL LODGE (Inexpensive to Expensive) is also a bed and breakfast with eight ethnic-themed rooms. Some are quite comfortable, with pretty linens and views of the pastoral surroundings, but all are too small and dark for us to recommend wholeheartedly.

OCEANWOOD COUNTRY INN, Mayne Island
630 Dinner Bay Road
(250) 539-5074
Expensive
Dinner Daily
Call for seasonal hours.

Housed on the ground level of the impeccable Oceanwood Country Inn, this warm and intimate restaurant is bordered by a brick hearth on one side and a wall of windows overlooking lush gardens and sparkling Navy Channel on the other. Service is exemplary, and the continental prix fixe menu might include such delicacies as purée of celeriac soup with wild mushrooms; braised young carrot terrine with watercress; roast Muskovy duck breast on pepper greens with whipped potatoes; or sesame salmon on a bok choy, ginger, and noodle salad. Top off your repast with the espresso-chocolate torte with lemon crème fraîche and you'll have yourselves an evening to remember.

Saturna Island

Saturna Island is one of the more remote destinations in the Gulf Islands. Ferry schedules are tricky, but it's worth the effort to find yourselves this close to the middle of nowhere. Although the entire island is lush and forested, and wildlife abounds, **EAST POINT** offers particularly impressive views of neighboring Tumbo Island. From this vantage point you're almost guaranteed to see eagles fishing and sea otters frolicking, and sometimes (if you're very lucky) a pod of orcas blowing and breaching on the horizon.

Romantic Warning: Saturna has no romantic restaurants to speak of. Local pubs offer standard salads, sandwiches, and burgers (which can be satisfactory if you're in the mood for fast food), but we recommend purchasing picnic provisions beforehand to tide you over during your stay here. This will also give you a chance to explore the island and find a remote picnic spot where you can dine and warm up your lips.

Hotel/Bed and Breakfast Kissing

STONE HOUSE FARM RESORT, Saturna Island
207 Narvaez Bay Road
(250) 539-2683
Moderate
Minimum stay requirement

For the sake of romance, solitude, and relaxation, you would be wise to sojourn at this 17th-century-style English country home surrounded by 25 acres of farmland and forest. Stone House Farm sits on the banks of Narvaez Bay, fronting a half mile of picturesque waterfront and sandy beach. As the name implies, the formidable tile-roofed structure is built from stone. Inside, the massive Tudor-style wood beams and handsome paneling are equally impressive.

Guests are encouraged to make themselves at home. Cuddle in the comfy sofa as you share a good movie in the upstairs TV room or challenge each other to a game of pool, darts, or shuffleboard in the adjacent game room. You can also accompany the innkeeper (and his faithful canine companion, Flossy) as he tends to his chores, which include feeding two very funny Highland cows and a well-tended flock of woolly sheep. The three guest rooms here are modest but comfortable; private balconies offer stunning water views, and private baths and plush down comforters are satisfying amenities. In the morning, an exceptionally hearty English breakfast is served in the dining room at your own private table.

Vancouver and Environs

Vancouver is a phenomenal example of a big city done right. Towering skyscrapers, flashing lights, steel-girded bridges, and heavily trafficked one-way streets sprawl for miles, but this vintage urban landscape is softened by surrounding snowcapped mountains, forested parks, and the island-flecked Strait of Georgia. International cruise ships ferry passengers from around the globe to this popular Canadian port of call, renowned for its impressive scenery and world-class cultural activities.

There is something for everybody in the Vancouver area. Visitors can take in views of downtown's sophisticated architecture from the forested acreage of Stanley Park or from the peaks of Grouse Mountain (accessible via an aerial tram). Outdoor enthusiasts will be impressed with the area's provincial parks and woodland, nearby ski slopes, and abundant wildlife. If you prefer tamer encounters with nature, seek out the flawlessly manicured gardens scattered in fragrant pockets throughout the city. Those who arrive in Vancouver with shopping in mind (and many do) can wander for hours in the multitude of stores, boutiques, and art galleries crowded around colorful Robson Street, artist-oriented Granville Island, and historic Gastown, where a steam clock regularly pipes out the time. The **VANCOUVER ART GALLERY**, 750 Hornby Street, (604) 662-4719, has a stellar permanent art collection and more than a dozen additional temporary exhibitions every year. The **VANCOUVER SYMPHONY ORCHESTRA**, 601 Smithe Street, (604) 684-9100, and the **VANCOUVER OPERA**, 845 Cambie Street, (604) 683-0222, along with local theater groups, offer outstanding productions year-round. Your options in this lively city are endless. Once you've sampled what Vancouver has to offer, your notions of urban life will never be the same. You're likely to find yourselves making plans to return before you know it.

Like most cities, Vancouver's traffic can pose a serious problem, particularly on the bridges at rush hour. Foot travel and public buses are recommended whenever possible. Another option is the **AQUABUS**, (604) 689-5858, which offers commuter ferry service in False Creek from five terminals. Though it is arguably touristy, the Aquabus is a convenient and interesting way to see the city's sights without having to contend with traffic (a definite romantic plus).

While exploring this vast area, we also highly recommend that you purchase a detailed map. For more personal, detailed travel guidance while in

British Columbia, consult the Visitor Information Centres scattered generously along most major roads and in most towns. The people here are lovely; you should stop in just to say hello and get your first taste of Canadian hospitality. For Vancouver information, contact the **VANCOUVER TRAVEL INFORMATION CENTRE**, 1055 Dunsmuir, Vancouver, BC V7X 1L3, (604) 683-2000.

Romantic Warning: Be aware that timing border crossings to and from Canada at Blaine, Washington, can be exceptionally tricky due to the long lines of cars encountered at varying times of the day and year. Peak travel times during the summer and weekends are the worst, but traffic can be very fickle and there is no telling when you may have to endure a serious wait.

Vancouver

Hotel/Bed and Breakfast Kissing

ARBUTUS HOUSE, Vancouver
4470 Maple Crescent
(604) 738-6432
http://www.bbcanada.com/257.html
Inexpensive to Moderate
Minimum stay requirement
Closed December through mid-January

Arbutus House is harbored at the edge of Vancouver's prestigious Shaughnessy district, but you don't have to worry about the railroad tracks that run adjacent to this property—it's been years since trains have regularly used this route. (Today the tracks are primarily used as a walking and jogging path.) Recent renovations have turned this 1920s home into an ideally romantic hideaway. A fire burns in the hearth (during colder months) in the elegant living room, surrounded by contemporary furnishings and artwork. Guests can also lounge in the comfortable den, where bookshelves brim with novels and a TV with VCR is available.

A magnolia tree shades a private deck that belongs to the appropriately named Magnolia Room, and a large leaded glass window in the Dahlia Room looks out to the backyard gardens. Although both of these rooms share a bathroom, the robes and slippers provided help to ease the inconvenience. Fluffy down comforters and luxurious linens add to your comfort. The Maple Room has its own charming rust-colored bathroom with a pretty glass-enclosed tiled shower. For the most privacy, however, we recommend the Sunset Suite, perched at the top of the house. Sloped ceilings give the room quaint charm, and beautiful floral down linens cover an inviting pine and wrought-iron sleigh bed. Airy and bright, the private blue-and-white-tiled bathroom in this suite overlooks the gardens in the backyard. A gas fireplace warms a separate sitting area, where you'll also find a TV and VCR.

All guests are presented with a gourmet four-course breakfast served at one table in the owner's contemporary dining room or, when the weather permits, outside on the large deck in the garden-laden backyard.

BRIGHTON HOUSE, Vancouver
2826 Trinity Street
(604) 253-7175
Inexpensive to Moderate
Minimum stay requirement seasonally

Location often plays a part in the romantic potential of any accommodation. Scenic water views or access to nearby parks and city life can enhance the appeal (and therefore the lip rating) of almost any country inn or bed and breakfast. That's why we wish Brighton House was a little closer to the city with a more appealing view of the harbor (this water panorama has smokestacks and freight traffic in the way). Even so, the owners have taken great care with their property, and it's well worth a closer look.

The two guest rooms in this neighborhood home, decorated in French country style, are as pretty as pictures, and tucked into alcoves on the second floor. Both rooms are outfitted with oversized willow chairs, down comforters, and handsome fabrics. They also feature large, sun-filled, brightly tiled bathrooms, sitting/breakfast areas near large windows, and nearly spectacular views of the water and mountains. The overall effect is wonderfully relaxing. Breakfast is a bountiful affair of muffins, fruit, egg dishes, and pancakes, proudly presented by the extremely helpful innkeeper.

COLUMBIA COTTAGE GUEST HOUSE, Vancouver
205 West 14th Avenue
(604) 874-5327
http://www.novamart.com/columbia
Moderate to Very Expensive

Despite the overwhelming number of properties in Vancouver, there are very few professionally run, high-quality bed and breakfasts that meet our kissing criteria. That is why Columbia Cottage Guest House is such a find. Located on a corner in a quiet residential neighborhood, this modestly adorned Tudor-style home surrounded by slightly neglected grounds has much more to offer than it appears at first glance.

Chock-full of antiques, the home's interior looks like an English country cottage. Lace curtains, Oriental carpets, and beautiful blond wood floors adorn the lovely common areas, where guests can enjoy a glass of sherry in front of the fireplace. The five guest rooms, four of which are located on the first and second floors of the main house, offer cushy feather beds covered with luxurious linens and down comforters. Bright, contemporary fabrics and color schemes add modern flair to the antique-furnished rooms with hardwood floors. The fifth room, situated in the lower-level converted basement, is called the Garden Suite. It offers the most space and privacy, with a private entrance, kitchen area, and separate living room and bedroom. The wrought-iron sleigh bed is a decisive romantic touch, but we still preferred the authentic charm of the upstairs rooms.

In the morning, the professional chef/host prepares a full gourmet breakfast that might include freshly baked bread, muffins, and croissants, a shrimp-and-vegetable frittata, fresh fruit and juice, and, of course, coffee and a selection of teas.

Romantic Suggestion: QUEEN ELIZABETH PARK (see Outdoor Kissing) is nearby if you are up for a healthy walk after breakfast.

ENGLISH BAY INN, Vancouver
1968 Comox Street
(604) 683-8002
Moderate to Very Expensive
Minimum stay requirement on weekends

Enchanting best describes this eye-catching Tudor-style home tucked between high-rise apartments in the heart of Vancouver's West End, a mere half block from the sea wall. The elegant common rooms are filled with museum-quality antiques, which lend authenticity to the historic home. Although four of the five guest rooms are a bit on the snug side, all are handsomely outfitted and extremely comfortable. Richly colored Ralph Lauren linens grace the seductive Louis Philippe four-poster beds, lavish bouquets of fresh flowers rest at your bedside, and private bathrooms accompany each room. Of particular romantic interest is the spacious suite on the top floor, with an inviting wooden sleigh bed adorned with crisp white linens. Other romantic delights up here include skylights, a separate sitting area with a glowing fireplace, and a large bathroom with a soaking tub. A stunning stained-glass window lets in nothing but the glow of the sun and the moon. In the morning you'll feel quite baronial when you sit down to a delicious breakfast served at a massive Gothic-style table in the dignified dining room. Vacations are the perfect time to be extravagant, and at the English Bay Inn, extravagance rules.

THE FOUR SEASONS, Vancouver
791 West Georgia Street
(604) 689-9333, (800) 223-8772
Expensive to Unbelievably Expensive
Recommended Wedding Site

Run with typical Four Seasons finesse, this 28-floor grand dame exceeds all of the traditional hotel standards in both service and style, although it is still just a hotel. The 385 spacious rooms are all conservatively adorned with refined furnishings and tasteful color schemes, and all of the amenities you could possibly need are either provided in your room or simply a phone call away. Rooms above the 18th floor have unobstructed views of Vancouver and its surroundings; rooms with numbers ending in 01 through 10, on the west side of the building, have the best water views.

Romantic Suggestion: For an extremely fine dining experience, we highly recommend **CHARTWELL** (see Restaurant Kissing), on the hotel's first floor. If you're in the mood for a lighter, less formal repast, try the **GARDEN TERRACE**, where cozy groupings of wood tables are set just off the lobby in an open, airy garden setting.

THE FRENCH QUARTER
BED AND BREAKFAST, Vancouver
2051 West 19th Avenue
(604) 737-0973

Expensive to Very Expensive for this luxurious property. Tucked behind the owner's home, the French Quarter's self-contained private cottage was designed with couples in mind. French doors open onto a small private patio adjacent to a pristine blue pool, which is available to guests and impossible to resist on a hot summer's day. Tile floors and handsome antiques lend a European flavor to the cottage's lovely interior, which also features a full-size wet bar, a welcome basket of goodies, a TV and VCR tucked in an armoire, and a gas fireplace. Beautiful artwork adorns the pale yellow walls, and a green-painted canopy bed is draped with white and green fabric and covered with a thick down duvet. An extra large Jacuzzi tub is the romantic highlight of the bathroom, which also has a roomy, glass-enclosed shower.

A second guest room is available in the owner's upscale European-style home. The room, done in French country style, has a brass bed covered with a fluffy down duvet, green walls, and country antiques. Though the bathroom does not have a Jacuzzi tub, it is very pretty and quite spacious. Breakfast is an affair to remember, served in the privacy of your own room, by the pool, or in the owner's contemporary kitchen (depending on your preference). Morning meals might include banana and mango smoothies, poppyseed and lemon muffins served with strawberry jam, a melon bowl with sliced strawberries marinated in Grand Marnier and sherry and topped with whipped cream, Tuscan-style poached eggs served over polenta cakes, and grilled turkey sausages. You'll probably want to skip lunch after a feast of this caliber!

GEORGIAN COURT HOTEL, Vancouver
773 Beatty Street
(604) 682-5555, (800) 663-1155
Inexpensive to Very Expensive

Renovations are currently underway at this well-known landmark in downtown Vancouver, but the Georgian Court was impressive even before they began. None of the 180 spacious guest rooms has a view to speak of (aside from views of office buildings), but rooms on the third floor offer private balconies. Lacquered wood furnishings, queen-size beds, and up-scale, modern fabrics and color schemes create a pleasant, comfortable climate in all of the rooms. Prices are surprisingly reasonable, and even the two luxurious Penthouse Suites with jetted tubs are less expensive than some of the standard hotel rooms found elsewhere in the city. Guests can make use of the hotel's small workout room and whirlpool, then dine at the famous **WILLIAM TELL RESTAURANT** (see Restaurant Kissing), which defines intimate.

HOTEL VANCOUVER, Vancouver
900 West Georgia Street
(604) 684-3131, (800) 441-1414
Expensive to Unbelievably Expensive

Recognizable from miles around, Hotel Vancouver is one of downtown Vancouver's most venerable properties and nothing like the average high-rise hotel. Built in 1939, the formidable stone building, replete with gargoyles and Old English style, contrasts with the bright, crystal-chandeliered, red-carpeted, lush interior. Recent renovations have turned the hotel's 550 guest rooms into impressive showcases with all the amenities you could ask for. Like most hotels in Vancouver, this hotel caters primarily to business executives, but down duvets, dark wood antiques, and pretty (albeit tiny) marble baths add romantic allure for those with more than business in mind. Though there is an extra charge, guests are welcome to use the large, indoor glass-enclosed pool and full health club.

Optimum service is part of the glamour of staying here. For the utmost in service, we recommend staying on the Entrée Gold ninth floor. Although rooms here are significantly more expensive, they include a complimentary deluxe breakfast, free newspaper delivery, afternoon hors d'oeuvres, free local calls, and complimentary use of the hotel's health club. For an exclusive celebration in an august setting, you couldn't pick a better place.

Romantic Suggestion: You won't have to leave the property in search of an impressive meal, because the Hotel Vancouver is brimming with options. Cozy up in a love seat in the luxurious lobby lounge and enjoy a light snack, afternoon tea, or late-night cocktails. **GRIFFINS RESTAURANT** (Moderate to Expensive), adjacent to the lobby, is another option. Though it isn't exactly romantic, the dining room's tall ceilings, cheery yellow walls, hardwood floors, and remarkable, reasonably priced meals distinguish it from most hotel restaurants. Griffins is especially popular for lunch, due to an outstanding buffet ($12.95 per person) serving gourmet delights. For a truly romantic repast, we recommend the hotel's newly opened restaurant, **900 WEST** (Moderate to Expensive), which was still under construction when we visited. 900 West's floor plans show all the telltale signs of elegance, intimacy, and abundant romantic potential.

JOHNSON HOUSE BED AND BREAKFAST, Vancouver
2278 West 34th Avenue
(604) 266-4175
http://www.bbcanada.com/821.html
Inexpensive to Moderate; No Credit Cards
Minimum stay requirement
Closed December through January

Leafy trees line the shady streets in this exceedingly quiet, upscale residential neighborhood, where the Johnson House is tucked amid flowering gardens. Exhaustive renovations have turned this gray and white Craftsman-style home into a sensational escape from the nearby city. Guests can savor a clear view of the mountains outside on the breezy veranda or relax in the winsome common areas decorated with carousel horses and other eclectic antiques. Sizable brick fireplaces warm both the living and dining rooms, where Oriental rugs grace hardwood floors.

All four guest rooms have private baths, though some rooms are more desirable than others. The Garden Suite feels too much like a converted basement, but the Sunshine Room upstairs is quite charming, with a wrought-iron canopy bed covered with a blue patchwork quilt. Also upstairs, the Mountain Room has glimpses of the North Shore Mountains beyond Vancouver's cityscape. For kissing purposes, the irresistible Carousel Suite is the property's romantic claim to fame. Here, Persian carpets cover hardwood floors and a cathedral pine wood ceiling soars above a brass canopy bed covered with white lace and a patchwork quilt. Views of the mountains are framed by large windows. Nearly equal in size to the bedroom, the sexy bathroom features an abundance of mermaid sculptures, luminous skylights, a large wood-framed tile shower, soaking tub, bidet, and all the room you need for some good clean fun.

All guests are treated to a full traditional breakfast in the dining room at a large, beautifully arranged table. Although there is only one table, guests are served at staggered times, which allows for a little more privacy.

A LITTLE GREEN HOUSE ON THE PARK, Vancouver
1850 Grant Street
(604) 255-3655
Inexpensive; No Credit Cards

Although the neighborhood that surrounds this charming property is somewhat iffy (we wouldn't recommend walking alone in this area after dark), everything else about the Little Green House is praiseworthy. Aptly named, the bright turquoise-green townhouse is situated across the street from a local park. In the backyard, a roomy hot tub is ensconced beneath a trellis and surrounded by beautiful gardens. Inside, the owners have taken pride in decorating their newly built home, which features blond hardwood floors, modern black couches, and a cozy window seat covered with comfy pillows.

Upstairs, the two guest rooms have private baths and a contemporary look. Flower boxes line the small private balcony in Parkview, which faces (not surprisingly) the park across the street. A striped comforter drapes a pretty wrought-iron bed, and French country antiques accent the small but engaging room. A TV and VCR are discreetly tucked away, and the bathroom has a single jetted tub. Aptly named Gardenview, a second room across the hall faces the gardens in the backyard. A little plain but still very comfortable, this room is furnished with eclectic antiques, contemporary linens, and a double steam shower accompanied by complimentary aromatherapy. An elaborate homemade breakfast served in the modern kitchen or the countrified backyard is the ideal prelude for a day spent exploring the city.

THE METROPOLITAN HOTEL, Vancouver
645 Howe Street
(604) 687-1122, (800) 667-2300
http://www.metropolitan.com

Cost ratings for British Columbia listings are in Canadian funds. American travelers should check the exchange rate or ask an innkeeper to figure out the cost in U.S. dollars.

Moderate to Expensive
Recommended Wedding Site

Originally built as a Mandarin Hotel in 1984, the distinguished Metropolitan retains its decidedly Oriental style and design. The elegant marble lobby is adorned with antique artifacts, including an impressively ornate hand-carved wall screen depicting 200 different storyboards. Significantly smaller than many of the other hotels in the heart of downtown Vancouver, the Metropolitan has only 197 guest rooms, which makes it feel more intimate and personable. Although the beige-and-cream color schemes are somewhat conservative and plain, the sparsely appointed guest rooms have attractive oak furnishings and cozy down duvets. In the larger suites, Asian artpieces are beautifully showcased. Spacious and immaculate, the white marble bathrooms contain all the amenities (and a few extras), including a soaking tub and separate glass-enclosed shower. Guests have free access to the small but complete health club, which includes an indoor lap pool under a closed atrium, a weight room, whirlpool, sauna, squash and racquetball courts, and an on-call masseuse. Like most of the hotels downtown, the Metropolitan caters to business travelers, but this shouldn't prevent you from kissing to your hearts' content while you are here.

Speaking of romance, the Metropolitan's "Romance Packages" are worth checking into. For a slight extra charge, your stay can include a bottle of sparkling wine, chocolate-dipped strawberries, and assorted fruit upon arrival. Breakfast in bed or at **DIVA** (see Restaurant Kissing), parking, taxes, and service charges are also included for your convenience.

"Main Event Getaway Packages" are geared for guests planning to attend the theater. Ticket buying is up to the guests, but room rates include a pre-theater three-course dinner for two at Diva, in addition to parking, gratuities, and taxes.

"O CANADA" HOUSE, Vancouver
1114 Barclay Street
(604) 688-0555
http://www.bbcanada.com/919.html
Expensive
Minimum stay requirement on weekends

Set in a calm downtown neighborhood, this beautifully restored 1897 Victorian home has an extremely appropriate name: Canada's national anthem was written in this very home in 1909. Classical music plays in the background throughout the distinguished house, which is brimming with antiques and historic architectural wonders (they don't build homes like they used to). A cheery hearth glows in the living room, where sherry is served to guests in the evening. Mornings begin with a formal gourmet breakfast served in the refined parlor at one large table set with crystal, gold, and fresh flowers.

Characterized by genuine old-world charm, the five guest rooms have original light fixtures, sumptuous designer linens, private baths, and TVs with VCRs. In the East Suite, daylight streams in through huge bay windows. Boutique pillows and embroidered linens cover an enormous king-size bed in the North Suite, where a claw-foot tub is the highlight of the spacious black-and-white-tiled bathroom. Smaller but equally lovely, the West Suite has a brass bed covered with lush beige linens. Sloped ceilings make the top-floor Penthouse feel slightly cramped, but there is room enough for two beautiful sleigh beds covered with choice linens. All guests have use of a small kitchenette, which is always stocked with an abundance of home-baked desserts, cold and hot beverages, and local maps to help you orient yourselves.

PACIFIC PALISADES HOTEL, Vancouver
1277 Robson Street
(604) 688-0461, (800) 663-1815
Expensive to Unbelievably Expensive

Although the lobby here screams large chain hotel, the centrally located Pacific Palisades has a genuinely romantic disposition. For starters, each floor holds only a handful of rooms, which makes the hotel feel small and personal. (You'd never guess there are 233 units.) Better yet, most of the rooms are exceedingly roomy—even the studios. Televisions are discreetly hidden in wood cabinets, and plump down duvets give the beds an inviting appearance. Though the decor is fairly hotel-standard, contemporary artwork and water or mountain views make most of the rooms feel stylish and upscale. Orchids spice up the standard but attractive bathrooms.

Guests have complimentary use of the hotel's health club, which features a 55-foot indoor pool, whirlpool, sauna, weight room, suntan and massage service, and even bicycle rentals (which will save you a lot of frustration when battling Vancouver's ever-increasing traffic).

PAN PACIFIC VANCOUVER, Vancouver
300-999 Canada Place
(604) 662-8111, (800) 663-1515 (in Canada)
(800) 937-1515 (in the U.S.)
http://www.panpac.com
Expensive to Unbelievably Expensive
Recommended Wedding Site

Achieving romance at the enormous Pan Pacific Hotel in downtown Vancouver may seem impossible at first. A regular stream of cruise ships unload thousands of passengers at this expansive waterfront complex that resembles a small city, complete with a shopping mall, multitudes of restaurants, and even a convention center. Needless to say, this gargantuan property has an air of sterile impersonality. Even so, it is an exceptionally stunning, professionally run, and exciting place to stay, offering superbly designed guest rooms that other hotels could learn from. Many of the 506 units have stupendous views, soft color schemes, firm king-size beds with down duvets, and chic marble bathrooms. Four of the deluxe rooms have luxurious sunken jetted tubs, but these are almost always booked. As you would expect, rooms in the Unbelievably Expensive price range are the most luxurious and spacious and offer the most impressive views. All guests have access to the ultra-modern health club, which includes an outdoor pool and sundeck, sauna, Jacuzzi tub, up-to-date weight-training equipment, and even a paddle tennis court.

Romantic Suggestion: The Pan Pacific Hotel is blessed with several excellent restaurants. We recommend **THE PROW** (see Restaurant Kissing) for the most spectacular views and supreme romantic ambience. **FIVE SAILS** (Moderate to Expensive) is much smaller but equally elegant, with floor-to-ceiling windows that showcase views of the waterfront and lights twinkling in the mountain foothills. The seafood here is worthy of praise, particularly the sesame-crusted seared British Columbia salmon served with hot-and-sour carrot-butter sauce. If you want to enjoy the views of the water but don't have much of an appetite, the lobby lounge is your best option. Expansive windows reach from floor to ceiling throughout the lobby, ensuring that every cluster of chairs has a mesmerizing view. A live pianist performs on a shiny black baby grand, enhancing the already romantic mood.

Romantic Note: Pan Pacific's "Romance Packages" might seem Outrageously Expensive at first, but take a second look. The price tag is understandable when you consider what is included: a waterfront room or suite, fresh flowers, sparkling wine, complimentary breakfast or Sunday brunch, and free valet parking.

PENNY FARTHING INN, Vancouver
2855 West Sixth Avenue
(604) 739-9002
Inexpensive to Moderate; No Credit Cards
Minimum stay requirement on weekends seasonally

Ensconced in a charming residential neighborhood, the Penny Farthing Inn is hard to miss with its bright turquoise exterior and pink trim. Gardens and greenery enfold the picturesque Craftsman-style home, where you'll often find a cat or two napping in the sunshine on the front porch. Inside, timeworn turn-of-the-century antiques lend authenticity to the homey common areas, crowded with family photos and family heirlooms. A weathered staircase leads upstairs to four guest rooms done up in daring color schemes that are startlingly pleasant and fresh.

Sophie's Room and Lucinda's Room share a bathroom but are still enticing, with hardwood floors, French country accents, and brightly colored walls. Bettina's Suite is particularly striking, with glowing wood floors, aqua-colored walls, and a veranda that faces the mountains and water. Other amenities include a sumptuous four-poster pine bed, private sitting room with TV and VCR, and a private bath. An operable skylight in the sloped ceiling draws daylight into the top-floor Abigail's Attic Suite. Here, yellow floral linens cover a brass queen-size bed, and a separate sitting room offers views of the gardens in the backyard and the mountains in the distance. This private retreat also has a TV and VCR, and an appealing black-and-white-tiled bathroom.

Breakfast can be delivered to Abigail's Attic Suite upon request. For everyone else, a full breakfast is served on the backyard garden patio in the summer or, on cooler mornings, in the formal dining room, amid stained glass windows, English antiques, and a crackling fireplace.

SUTTON PLACE HOTEL, Vancouver 🙢🙢🙢🙢
845 Burrard Street
(604) 682-5511, (800) 961-7555 (in Canada)
Expensive to Unbelievably Expensive
Recommended Wedding Site

In some regards this is just one more elite high-rise hotel in the heart of downtown Vancouver that specialize in flawless, attentive service, posh restaurants, and attractive rooms. But Sutton Place begins where other hotels stop. European artwork and antiques accent the small but lavish marble lobby, where a gilded chandelier hangs from an ornate cathedral ceiling. Rooms and suites are attractive and bright, appointed with luxurious maroon-and-gold-upholstered furniture, marble-tiled bathrooms, and all the expected amenities. Service is the hotel's specialty, and it is evident from the moment you step inside. Everyone here is concerned with your comfort and offers to help. Nowhere is this more obvious than **LE SPA**, the hotel's health, fitness, and beauty center, which features a year-round pool set beneath a glass roof and a spacious sundeck. Like most hotels in Vancouver, Sutton Place tends to gear itself toward a business clientele, but it is still one of the sexiest properties in the area.

Sutton Place features a truly lavish Sunday brunch—one of the finest in town—at the countrified **CAFE FLEURI**. Breakfast, lunch, and dinner are served daily in this pleasant dining room, highlighted by light pink walls and floral linens. It is also worth a visit for the lavish, 20-item Chocoholic Buffet, served Thursday through Saturday evenings from 6 P.M. to 10 P.M. This sweet indulgence is decadent and wantonly sinful, but worth every mouthwatering, caloric bite and the weeks of repentance that follow. (You can actually begin your penance at the hotel's previously mentioned first-class health club.)

Romantic Note: Cafe Fleuri is not the only dining option here. **LE CLUB** (see Restaurant Kissing) is a superbly romantic venue, which, believe it or not, is considerably less expensive than many other first-class restaurants in the area.

TREEHOUSE BED AND BREAKFAST, Vancouver
2490 West 49th Avenue
(604) 266-2962
http://www.vancouver_bc.com/treehouse
Inexpensive to Moderate; No Credit Cards

Though it is nothing like an actual treehouse, this contemporary bed and breakfast lives up to its reputation as "a rather unique experience" in the best sense of the phrase. A welcome refuge from adjacent (and busy) West 49th Avenue, this ultra-modern home is designed to soothe with its ivory-and-cream color schemes, ethnic baskets, and contemporary artwork and sculptures. Lengths of honey-colored fabric drape white couches in the austere but stylish common living room. All three guest suites have private baths, TVs with VCRs, and views of the slightly overgrown but wonderful backyard, which holds an abundance of trees and a serene Japanese garden.

The spartan Pacific West Room is decorated with plaid linens, Oriental accents, and earthy baskets; it also features a small private bathroom with a one-person Jacuzzi tub. Similarly minimalist, the School Room is a little too snug for an extended romantic encounter, especially since the private bathroom is located down the hall. The Treehouse's most romantic accommodation is the Treetop Suite, which occupies the entire third floor and features a jetted Jacuzzi tub for two (with 100 jets!) in the skylit bathroom.

In the bedroom, white fabric drapes a beautiful wrought-iron four-poster queen-size bed, and a private, spacious outdoor deck overlooks the pretty backyard.

A lavish gourmet breakfast can be delivered to your room (a definite romantic plus) or enjoyed with the other guests at one large table. Breakfast is served on shiny black dishes and sparkling crystal.

WATERFRONT CENTRE HOTEL, Vancouver   ❤❤❤
900 Canada Place Way
(604) 691-1820, (800) 441-1414
http://www.cphotels.ca
Expensive to Unbelievably Expensive
Recommended Wedding Site

Just across the street from the better-known Pan Pacific Hotel, the polished Waterfront Centre Hotel surveys views of Burrard Inlet, where seaplanes and cruise ships come and go against a backdrop of tree-covered mountains. Centrally located but away from Vancouver's intense city center, the Waterfront Center offers the best in big-city accommodations. Gold-tinted marble floors and columns and floor-to-ceiling windows impart an air of luxury to the ornate lobby. The 489 spacious guest rooms are sooth-ingly decorated in tones of salmon, beige, and cream, and all have pretty marble bathrooms. Artistic lamps, lovely watercolors, and original Native Canadian artwork add dashes of color to the subdued color schemes. Although the linens and hotel-style furnishings are rather ordinary, picture windows frame extraordinary water views in most of the rooms. Corner rooms are especially inviting, with an abundance of windows and slightly roomier bathrooms. None of the units feature Jacuzzi tubs, but guests can pamper themselves in the health club's heated outdoor pool, large hot tub, and sauna. An on-call masseuse is also available to knead away the stress you're attempting to leave behind.

For an extra charge, you can reserve one of the 48 rooms on the Entrée Gold floor. These rooms feature down duvets instead of bedspreads, 24-hour concierge service, a complimentary breakfast, and afternoon hors d'oeuvres, among other personal touches. "Romance Packages" are also avail-able for an extra charge and include complimentary breakfast, champagne, roses, and free valet parking. (Isn't your beloved worth it?)

WEDGEWOOD HOTEL, Vancouver
845 Hornby Street
(604) 689-7777, (800) 663-0666

Expensive to Unbelievably Expensive
Recommended Wedding Site

Many hotels want you to believe they specialize in European-style elegance and service; unfortunately, most don't deliver. Blending both romance and five-star hotel efficiency, the relatively intimate Wedgewood Hotel follows through with exceptional grace and finesse. Its white French doors open onto an elegant lobby and an attractive, exceedingly comfortable lounge that has not been taken over by the serious business-suit crowd. Many of the guest rooms have separate sitting areas that make you feel like you're staying in an uptown apartment instead of a downtown hotel. Some suites have fireplaces (which are hard to come by in Vancouver), and all of the beautiful rooms have foliage-draped decks with sliding glass doors to alleviate the claustrophobia that other high-rise hotels tend to induce.

Romantic Suggestion: You probably will want to dine at one of the many notable restaurants in the surrounding area, but don't neglect the Wedgewood's **BACCHUS RISTORANTE** (see Restaurant Kissing).

WEST END GUEST HOUSE, Vancouver
1362 Haro Street
(604) 681-2889
Moderate to Very Expensive
Minimum stay requirement on weekends

Everything about the West End Guest House is wonderful, including its six-block proximity to Stanley Park. This electric pink turn-of-the-century house, dwarfed by two large, modern apartment buildings on either side, resides in a neighborhood that is almost exclusively high-rises. Although the bright exterior is a bit startling when you first see it, it sort of grows on you (especially after you stay a while and get attached). The more subdued interior has been beautifully restored and is decorated with an imaginative blend of Edwardian and Victorian touches. Framed black-and-white photographs decorate the hallway walls, and a gas fireplace warms the downstairs. You'll love the high ceilings, crystal chandeliers, fine antiques, floral wallpapers, and bay windows framed by lace curtains. All eight guest rooms boast soft down quilts under handmade bedspreads, and quaint private bathrooms; most (but not all) also have beautiful brass beds and either a skylight or a ceiling fan. The attic rooms, tucked up and away from the others, are especially cozy.

Breakfasts are quite gourmet and can be enjoyed either downstairs in the dining room or delivered to your room if arranged in advance. An outside sundeck proves to be a splendid area for enjoying summer teatime or sherry, and a brick path wraps around the house to the backyard, where a small tree-shrouded patio seems designed for intimate evening relaxation. Although some of the rooms are a bit on the snug side, this is a warm, tastefully decorated place with all the comforts of home (and then some), but without the cookie-cutter sterility of a ritzy, skyscraper hotel.

Restaurant Kissing

BACCHUS RISTORANTE, Vancouver
845 Hornby Street, at the Wedgewood Hotel
(604) 689-7777, (800) 663-0666
Moderate
Breakfast, Lunch, and Dinner Daily

Although this restaurant is named after the Greek god of wine, the owners are Greek-Canadian, and the chef is English, this is one of the best places in town to indulge in inspired northern Italian cuisine. The food is delectable, the surroundings are exquisite, and everything is carefully orchestrated to make your experience here an enamored one. The lighting is perfect—low and warm—and the decor reminds us of an old Italian villa, with ornate wall tapestries and textured beige walls. Wrought-iron gate partitions separate the four dining areas so each feels appropriately intimate, and live soft guitar or piano melodies flow in from the adjacent lounge.

Let your taste buds begin a love affair with the prosciutto, strawberry, and arugula salad in balsamic vinaigrette topped with shaved Parmesan. Continue with fresh grilled halibut in rich shiitake mushroom essence and ricotta gnocchi or Washington state rack of lamb encrusted in black olives and accompanied by a mint–balsamic vinegar sauce.

Romantic Suggestion: Bacchus is open for breakfast, lunch and dinner, but dinner is definitely the most amorous time to dine. If you're not in the mood for a full meal, the adjacent lounge is a lovely spot for a quiet cocktail or espresso and dessert while listening to soothing live music.

BISHOP'S, Vancouver
2183 West Fourth Avenue
(604) 738-2025
http://www.settingsun.com/bishops
Expensive to Very Expensive
Dinner Daily

Bishop's pastel art deco exterior looks more like it belongs on a California beach strip than on Vancouver's heavily trafficked West Fourth Avenue. It doesn't immediately suggest romance, but don't let first impressions fool you. As you might guess from its standing as one of Vancouver's best-loved restaurants, Bishop's has a lot to offer. Modern artwork and extravagant flower arrangements add a dash of color to the minimalist interior of this highly regarded, two-level bistro filled with a cozy scattering of tables cloaked in white. On the lower level, large picture windows allow in ample daylight, but also look out to the busy street. We recommend the upper level, where the lack of windows enables you to focus your full attention on each other.

The menu features nouvelle cuisine with an emphasis on fresh regional ingredients, and the wine list is extensive (an understatement). Our salad of assorted summer greens topped with crisp goat cheese wontons and tossed with a roasted-garlic-and-tarragon vinaigrette was smashing, and the ravioli filled with Dungeness crab, eggplant, and mascarpone and served with a roasted coriander-and-tomato coulis was simply stupendous. Our compliments to the chef and to the outstanding wait staff, which was gracious from the beginning to the end of our exquisite meal.

BREAD GARDEN, Vancouver
1880 West First Avenue
(604) 738-6684
Inexpensive to Moderate
Breakfast, Lunch, and Dinner Daily

If your sweet tooth is begging to be indulged, you've come to the right city: Vancouver is awash in a multitude of bakeries and pastry shops. Set in a cozy storefront among clusters of other charming shops, the Bread Garden is one of our favorites. A glass pastry case takes up nearly one wall, showcasing a variety of decadent desserts and other temptingly fresh baked items. You can enjoy your treats at one of the handful of tables in the bakery's casual interior or get a "to go" bag and dine at one of Vancouver's scenic outdoor spots. (We recommend the latter; see Outdoor Kissing.)

Romantic Suggestion: Although The Bread Garden is one of our favorites, it is by no means the only good bakery in town. We also recommend **TERRA BREADS**, 2380 West Fourth, (604) 736-1838; **ECCO IL PANE**, 238 West Fifth, (604) 873-6888; **CARMELO'S PASTRY SHOP**, 1399 Commercial Drive, (604) 254-7024; **VITO'S PASTRY SHOP**, 1748 Commercial Drive, (604) 251-6650; and **RENATO'S PASTRY SHOP**, 1795 Commercial Drive, (604) 255-8921. The latter three shops are located in a part of town called **LITTLE ITALY**, located in the east part of town near Commercial and 12th Streets, which is worth exploring for a diverting hour or two.

CAFÉ IL NIDO, Vancouver
780 Thurlow Street
(604) 685-6436

Moderate to Expensive
Lunch Monday-Friday; Dinner Monday-Saturday

Tucked in an alley and set back from the bustle of Robson Street, Café Il Nido provides delectable Mediterranean cuisine in an intimate atmosphere. Rich saffron-colored walls, black accents, green carpet, and a handful of polished mahogany tables covered with white tablecloths and topped with fresh flowers distinguish this small Italian hideaway. Dried flowers displayed in clay pots and contemporary artwork decorate the walls, while the green ceiling with exposed pipes and one green sponge-painted wall are interesting touches. Wall sconces provide soft lighting in the evening, when you can feast on intimate conversation and oven-roasted chicken stuffed with Camembert, scallops, and dried apricots in a romaine sauce, or a pan-seared fillet of salmon accompanied by a trio of melon sauces and garnished with pink-shelled scallops and tiger prawns. Outdoor seating is available on warm summer afternoons. Due to this restaurant's lunchtime popularity with the business crowd, however, you may want to skip lunch and come back for dinner instead, when you can enjoy your privacy to the fullest.

CAFFE DE MEDICI, Vancouver   💋💋💋
1025 Robson Street
(604) 669-9322
http://www.settingsun.com/medici
Moderate to Expensive
Lunch Monday-Friday; Dinner Daily

Robson Street is like a river of specialty shops, bakeries, cafes, bistros, superb restaurants, and designer boutiques, cutting a half-mile course through downtown. Caffe de Medici holds court in one of the swankier clusters of shops, tucked away from the bustle of the street. This elegant northern Italian restaurant is artistically decorated with high arched ceilings, chandeliers, and terra-cotta-tiled floors with Oriental rugs. Plush drapery frame its many large windows, ornately framed oil paintings grace the walls, and each table is topped with crisp white linens, fresh flowers, and a candle to add a soft glow to your evening. The restaurant has grown over the years, but the polished, unmistakably romantic interior remains lovely. Although the traditional Italian entrées are delicious and nicely presented, the appetizers are a bit lackluster. Desserts are exquisite.

CHARTWELL, Vancouver
791 West Georgia Street, at the Four Seasons Hotel
(604) 689-9333

Expensive
Breakfast, Lunch, and Dinner Daily

We believe Chartwell's warmth and refinement can best be appreciated on a chilly winter evening. Stepping in from the cold, snowflakes still in your hair, would make the handsome dining room, with its dark wood paneling, detailed murals, and massive glowing fireplace, seem even more inviting than it already is. Meals are just as warm and tempting. The skilled kitchen offers a varied menu of specialties from such locales as Europe, the Far East, and our beloved Pacific Northwest.

CIN CIN, Vancouver
1154 Robson Street
(604) 688-7338
Moderate to Very Expensive
Lunch Monday-Friday; Dinner Daily

Tiled stairs covered with Oriental carpets ascend to this popular Mediterranean-inspired restaurant, harbored one floor above ever-busy Robson Street. Abstract, colorful murals adorn orange and yellow sponge-painted walls in the upbeat dining room, which features high ceilings, arched windows, and tiled floors. The immense wood-fired oven and grill are the highlights of the open kitchen, whose sights and sounds will whet your appetite for the feast to come. The restaurant is crowded and lively almost every night of the week, so your best bet for romance is the outdoor balcony enclosed with greenery.

Due to crowds, service can be slow and sometimes even discourteous— the couple next to us left in a huff on the evening we dined here. However, you won't be disappointed with the Mediterranean menu, including wood-oven-toasted focaccia topped with baby mozzarella and basil, scallops seared with rotini in a pesto-cream sauce, and fresh fish and shellfish in a saffron-tomato broth. When your meal arrives, lift and clink your glasses as a tribute to good health and old friends, and share a traditional Mediterranean toast: "Cin Cin."

DELILAH'S, Vancouver
1739 Comox Street
(604) 687-3424
Moderate
Dinner Daily

Situated on the lower floor of the Coast Plaza Hotel (no affiliation), Delilah's offers an exuberant blend of fantasy, elegance, and eccentricity. Scalloped banquettes covered with plush red velvet flank dark wood tables in the snug, dimly lit dining room appointed with colorful, fanciful art-work. The place actually looks more like a lounge than a restaurant.

At the beginning of your meal, you are handed a fill-in-the-blank prix fixe menu which you return to the server when you have made your selections. The options are vast, ranging from an orange and blueberry salad with pecans and arugula to steamed mussels with lime leaves as beginning courses. Main courses include options like grilled swordfish with a blueberry-lemon compote, and tiger prawns laced with pepper vodka and served with spinach fettuccine. You won't find fault with anything on the eclectic but superb menu, and the service is both faultless and friendly. With its ornate setting and original cuisine, dinner at Delilah's is a flamboyant must.

DIVA, Vancouver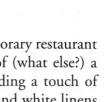
645 Howe Street, at the Metropolitan Hotel
(604) 602-7788
http://www.metropolitan.com/diva
Moderate to Very Expensive
Breakfast, Lunch, and Dinner Daily

A wall of beautifully etched glass separates this contemporary restaurant from the Metropolitan Hotel's lobby. A colorful picture of (what else?) a diva hangs above the open bar in the front entrance, lending a touch of whimsy to the ultra-modern terraced dining room. Beige and white linens drape the well-spaced tables, which are topped with candles and copper salt and pepper shakers. Depending on your mood, you can reserve a table in front of the open kitchen and watch the adept chef prepare your meal, or cozy up in a secluded banquette in the upper dining room (an appropriate spot for a few discreet kisses).

Evening is undoubtedly the most romantic time to dine here, and the food is consistently superb. The baby spinach salad with crisp fried shiitake mushrooms was done to perfection, as was the spicy blue-corn masa tamale with a ragout of three kinds of beans, spinach, and mushrooms. No matter how full you feel, do not pass up the decadent desserts here. Instead, request the dessert sampler, which offers small tastes of everything.

Romantic Note: Diva offers a table d'hote pre-theater three-course menu that is very reasonably priced and includes complimentary parking (a definite plus in this busy city). Guests are guaranteed to make their curtain call, or dinner is on Diva. Guests who arrive late to dinner or simply don't

Cost ratings for British Columbia listings are in Canadian funds. American travelers should check the exchange rate or ask an innkeeper to figure out the cost in U.S. dollars.

have time to enjoy a leisurely dessert can take a rain check and return later to enjoy it after the show. *Bravo!*

GIANNI RESTAURANT, Vancouver
2881 Granville Street
(604) 738-7922
Moderate to Expensive
Lunch Monday-Friday; Dinner Monday-Saturday

Traffic speeds by at a frantic rate on Granville Street, so it isn't at all surprising that the pace at Gianni is equally brisk. Though it can be difficult to get a table and sometimes even more difficult to hear yourselves over the clanking of dishes in the open kitchen, there are several good reasons why this restaurant continues to draw crowds. The lovely narrow dining room boasts cathedral ceilings, and the terra-cotta-colored walls are appointed with handwoven tapestries and Italianesque sculptures. White linens and fresh flowers adorn the well-spaced tables, where you are catered to by the friendly, helpful wait staff. From the antipasto to the interesting gourmet pastas to the consistently fresh seafood, the Italian fare here is some of Vancouver's best. So don't expect the crowds to diminish anytime soon—we have a feeling they're here to stay.

HERMITAGE, Vancouver
115-1025 Robson Street
(604) 689-3237
Moderate to Expensive
Lunch Monday-Friday; Dinner Daily

Situated on fashionably vibrant Robson Street, the Hermitage is a surprisingly quiet refuge and a definite romantic find. Brick walls warm the dining room's French country–style interior, appointed with antiques and country knickknacks. A fire roars in the corner hearth, accented with copper kettles and other vintage cookware. Candle lanterns flicker at fairly well-spaced tables covered with elegant white fabric. The aroma of French cuisine wafting through the dining room will stop you in your tracks. Whether you opt for the medley of poached seafood and shellfish or the sautéed scallops wrapped in a cabbage leaf and served with chive butter, you're in for a seafood lover's fantasy. And then there are the fresh home-baked desserts; forgoing them would be a sin.

IL GIARDINO DI UMBERTO, Vancouver
1382 Hornby Street
(604) 669-2422
Expensive

Umberto has five restaurants in the Vancouver area and two in Whistler. With all these Umberto's competing for attention, one would imagine that the quality might suffer, as it can with most other chain restaurants. Umberto's doesn't have that problem. In fact, most people argue about which Umberto's is the best. Assuredly, this one is the most romantic. A beautifully restored Victorian home with a lavish decor of terra-cotta-tiled floors, plush fabrics, and high slanted ceilings with exposed wooden beams is the backdrop for excellent Italian cuisine. The emphasis is on fresh veal and pheasant with rich, delectable sauces. A tiled garden terrace complete with a fireplace is open for summer dining. One warning: This popular restaurant is packed during lunchtime on weekdays and also on Friday and Saturday nights. When most of the tables are filled, the romantic ambience suffers.

KETTLE OF FISH, Vancouver
900 Pacific Street
(604)682-6661
Moderate
Lunch Monday-Friday; Dinner Daily

It's a jungle in here. Well, almost. Lush flora surrounds you, overflowing from white wicker plant stands, in this plant lover's dream (there's even a tree in the center of the restaurant). An indoor veranda sits at one end of the main dining area, and the open kitchen off to one side is partially obscured by greenery. Lace and floral tablecloths and fresh flowers on each two- and four-person table create an intimate atmosphere amid the foliage.

The restaurant's name is the key to its menu. A daily fresh sheet features tantalizing seafood selections that should satisfy even the most demanding eaters. Mahimahi, Chilean sea bass, Atlantic lobster, local snapper, and sockeye salmon are all served in a variety of ways. Although the menu is impressive, we found the service a bit on the slow side and the food unpredictable: the seafood vol-au-vent was chewy and bland, but the shrimp and avocado sandwich was delicious. Perhaps the best reason to come here is the decor; although the restaurant is located on the corner of a busy downtown street, with so many leafy greens surrounding you, and your beloved so near, you probably won't notice.

LE CLUB, Vancouver
845 Burrard Street, at the Sutton Place Hotel
(604) 682-5511
Expensive to Very Expensive
Dinner Daily

Located in the very opulent **SUTTON PLACE HOTEL** (see Hotel/ Bed and Breakfast Kissing), Le Club is exceedingly posh and dignified. Dinner here is in no way a laid-back dining event. Quite the contrary: it is one of those stately, glamorous affairs where dressing to the nines is a must. (We have been informed by management that dress requirements have been relaxed. It seems they have come to terms with their Northwest location; men no longer have to wear jackets. Still, we wouldn't call this place casual.) Crystal chandeliers cast a soft glow on the silk wallpapered walls, and candles trim the linen-cloaked tables. Dishes like broiled brochettes of scallops and prawns with vegetables, or Nova Scotia lobster on vanilla-flavored corn cream with gingered carrots can be ordered à la carte or as part of a prix fixe meal. If deluxe continental dining is your way of celebrating together, Le Club is de rigueur.

Romantic Suggestions: Also on the premises, the **GERARD LOUNGE** is a handsome mahogany-paneled room with a glowing fireplace and intimate corners where privacy is almost always guaranteed. Those who believe that chocolate can be an aphrodisiac ought to visit **CAFE FLEURI** (see the review of the Sutton Place Hotel in Hotel/Bed and Breakfast Kissing). Also located in the hotel, Cafe Fleuri offers the Chocoholic Buffet, an extravagant 20-item chocolate buffet, on Thursday, Friday, and Saturday evenings.

LE CROCODILE, Vancouver   😙😙😙😙
100-909 Burrard Street
(604) 669-4298
Moderate to Expensive
Lunch Monday-Friday; Dinner Monday-Saturday

Forget every negative French restaurant stereotype you've ever heard: Le Crocodile proves them all invalid. From the gracious staff to the beautifully presented meals, and everything in between, your hearts will be won. Casual refinement describes the warm dining room, with its goldenrod-colored walls, polished mahogany chairs, starched white linens and sprigs of fresh flowers on each table, dimly glowing candle lamps and wall sconces, and saffron half-curtains shielding all this intimacy from the busy street outside. The restaurant is always busy (reservations are a must), but even with a full house, the noise level remains low, service is attentive, and you and yours will be well taken care of.

Authentic French dishes fill the menu, and there is usually an extensive list of daily specials. Roasted duck breast served with a tangy citrus sauce and grilled Atlantic scallops in basil butter presented on black linguine are just two of the remarkably delicious creations offered. Whatever you choose, try to save room for dessert.

LE GAVROCHE, Vancouver
1616 Alberni Street
(604) 685-3924
Expensive to Very Expensive
Lunch Monday-Friday; Dinner Daily

Le Gavroche stands alone when it comes to traditional romantic dining in the Vancouver area. Situated downtown in a renovated Victorian home, this restaurant offers views of the distant bay from tables scattered throughout the home's original dining and living rooms. Hardwood floors, floral wallpaper, impressive antiques, and a glowing fireplace make the restaurant feel intimate yet polished. Fresh flowers and candle lanterns sparkle atop white linens at every table, and when weather permits, guests can dine in the sunshine on the outdoor deck.

Though ultra-formal dining doesn't always translate into romance, Le Gavroche's friendly staff strives to make you feel comfortable and welcome in this formal setting. Not surprisingly, the food is a gastronomic triumph. Every dish is a masterpiece, from the fresh sea bass appetizer served with white beans and spinach to the fresh scallops and prawns with curry risotto and mild chile-citrus sauce. *Bon appetit—et bon amour.*

PICCOLO MONDO RESTAURANT, Vancouver
850 Thurlow Street
(604) 688-1633
Moderate to Expensive
Lunch Monday-Friday; Dinner Monday-Saturday

One block south of lively Robson Street, Piccolo Mondo is an ideally located refuge from the city. White columns and cherry-stained wood floors graced with Oriental carpets lend stylish elegance to the small, two-level dining room. Layers of beige fabric give the windows a fashionable look, lovely artwork depicting Italian scenes hangs on a turquoise wall, and the well-spaced tables are topped with white linens, candles, silver, and fine china.

Although the setting is formal, the gracious staff puts you instantly at ease and makes you feel at home. You'll want to linger for hours, savoring the ambience. Northern Italian cuisine is the specialty here, and the pasta dishes combine the freshest herbs and cheeses with rich, silky sauces. The vegetable terrine and the mushroom risotto are out of this world. Ask the owners to select the right wine to accompany your meal from their award-winning list of Italian wines.

THE PROW, Vancouver
999 Canada Place, Suite 100
(604) 684-1339
Moderate to Expensive
Lunch and Dinner Weekdays; Sunday Brunch

Dinner at this establishment is an indelible romantic event. How can it fail? The three distinct dining rooms overlook Burrard Inlet, set off by mountains, glittering city lights, and imperious ships forging their way through the water. Dressed in pastel peaches and greens, each dining area is pretty and the tables have room to spare. Perhaps the most attractive room is the one that resembles a greenhouse, with tiled floors, expansive windows, and abundant foliage. Outdoor seating in a geranium-trimmed patio is also available. Add to all this a menu featuring seafood as outstanding as the view, and you have a restaurant that almost transcends its touristy location. We say "almost" because the dining room is consistently packed, which interferes with intimacy. Still, the desserts are bountiful—and, well, there's that view again.

Romantic Note: If The Prow is crowded, you can relax awhile next door in the **CASCADES LOUNGE** in the **PAN PACIFIC HOTEL** (see Hotel/Bed and Breakfast Kissing). This immense, airy, echoing bar shares the same astonishing view as the restaurant, through arresting floor-to-ceiling windows. When the weather is warm, we also recommend walking hand in hand along the outdoor walkway that leads to The Prow. You'll find lots of cozy lookout perches seemingly made just for kissing.

SEASONS IN THE PARK RESTAURANT, Vancouver
Cambie and 33rd Avenue, in Queen Elizabeth Park
(604) 874-8008, (800) 632-9422
Moderate to Expensive
Lunch Monday-Friday; Dinner Daily; Sunday Brunch

Sister to Stanley Park's **TEAHOUSE RESTAURANT** (reviewed below), this stunning establishment is a slightly less crowded (but still touristed) alternative, which gives it is a distinct kissing advantage. Roosting high on a hilltop in emerald green Queen Elizabeth Park, Seasons enjoys a sensational view of the park, Vancouver's skyline, clouds hovering above the North Shore Mountains ... and the sunset, if you time things right. Both dining rooms have an enormous live tree as their centerpiece, atrium-style glass ceilings, and walls of windows that showcase the breathtaking scenery. Though the restaurant is open and airy, the atmosphere is intimate and casually elegant, with white linens, low lighting, and tapered candle lanterns at each of the well-spaced tables.

Fresh seafood specials supplement the continental menu. We were especially taken with the vegetarian special of the day: curried lentils wrapped in savory layers of phyllo. Your meal will be good, but a sunset from this vantage point is something to cherish forever.

THE TEAHOUSE RESTAURANT, Vancouver
Stanley Park at Ferguson Point
(604) 669-3281, (800) 280-9893
Moderate to Expensive
Lunch and Dinner Daily; Saturday and Sunday Brunch

It's hard to believe that a major tourist attraction can also be one of the more beautiful places to dine in British Columbia. In spite of the crowds it draws, the Teahouse Restaurant remains a truly extraordinary kissing place. Much of this property's charisma comes from the location: the teahouse rests in the middle of a verdant lawn overlooking English Bay and Vancouver Island. The building itself is dazzling—half of it is an evergreen-colored country home, the other half a glass-enclosed atrium. Here you can watch the sun gently tuck itself into the ocean for a peaceful night's rest—as long as you have reservations, that is. Everyone knows about the Teahouse Restaurant, including busloads of tourists, so reservations are a definite must.

Although the kitchen serves fairly standard Canadian and French cuisine that is a tad too standard and generally oversauced, if you order carefully you'll find that the seafood and pasta dishes can be tasty when prepared *au naturel*. With a view like this to accompany your meal, you'll hardly feel disappointed.

VILLA DEL LUPO, Vancouver
869 Hamilton Street
(604) 688-7436
Moderate to Expensive
Dinner Daily

Benissimo! This charming restaurant immediately won our hearts. In a neighborhood that's almost exclusively high-rises, this little Victorian home turned restaurant looks tiny but promising. Inside you will find three cozy dining rooms, each slightly different but all warm, welcoming, and freshly decorated. There are only about six tables in each area, so they exude intimacy. A wood-burning fireplace makes one of the rooms especially cozy; another has tiled floors and salmon-colored walls with branches climbing up to big red oak leaves on the ceiling. If this doesn't pique your interest, wait until you read about the menu.

Free-range chicken stuffed with brioche, sage, and roasted garlic, then pan-roasted with sweet butter, glazed apples, and pumpkin, is one of the many inventive Italian-inspired specialties offered here. You really should go see for yourselves—you won't be disappointed. *Bene ... molto bene!*

Romantic Note: A wine cellar can be reserved for special occasions. The privacy factor is nice, but the room feels rather claustrophobic and is adorned only by walls full of wine.

VISTAS ON THE BAY, Vancouver
1133 West Hastings Street, at the Renaissance Vancouver Hotel
(604) 691-2787, (800) 468-3571
Moderate to Very Expensive
Breakfast, Lunch, and Dinner Daily

Scenic views don't get much better than this. Located on the top floor of the Renaissance Vancouver Hotel, this circular revolving restaurant surveys panoramic views of the entire Vancouver area. White linens and candles create an elegant mood in the slightly dated dining room, but the service and food (not to mention the views) are usually flawless. The crispy artichoke flower sprinkled with a shallot-herb vinaigrette is a perfect prelude to an excellent meal. We highly recommend the black tiger prawns sautéed with shiitake mushrooms and asparagus, and the seafood roast, which includes salmon, king crab, clams, and prawns baked in white wine and rosemary-garlic butter. Freshly baked desserts almost (but not quite) surpass the view.

Romantic Warning: Though many of the guest rooms at the **RENAIS-SANCE HOTEL**, 1133 West Hastings Street, (604) 689-9211 (Moderate to Expensive) share Vistas' spectacular view, the amenities and decor are far too dated and hotel standard to be even remotely romantic.

WILLIAM TELL RESTAURANT, Vancouver
773 Beatty Street, at the Georgian Court Hotel
(604) 688-3504
Expensive to Very Expensive
Breakfast, Lunch, and Dinner Daily

Renowned for its intimate setting, the William Tell caters almost exclusively to romance-minded couples. Part of the restaurant has been recently converted into an airy, contemporary bistro with an outdoor terrace where tables are arranged under umbrellas. But when the sun goes down, French doors open into the William Tell's heart of hearts, where a crystal chandelier softly illuminates rich green walls and a handful of tables covered with crisp white linens. European artwork is spotlighted by glowing wall sconces in this exceedingly formal and radiant setting. Fortunately, the food is as impressive as the ambience. The menu features an eclectic selection of meat and seafood entrées, such as the grilled salmon with raspberry butter sauce or sautéed prawns and scallops. We particularly enjoyed the vegetarian strudel served with goat cheese, and the homemade ravioli stuffed with ginger and tossed in a soya-orange glaze. Desserts are to die for, but don't expire until after you've tried, say, the white and dark Belgian chocolate terrine set on berry coulis and praline sauce.

Outdoor Kissing

BOTANICAL GARDENS, Vancouver
Recommended Wedding Site

The Vancouver area boasts many acclaimed, exquisite, and lush gardens, but the most beautiful are the **VANDUSEN BOTANICAL GARDENS**, 37th Avenue and Oak Street, (604) 878-9274; the **UNIVERSITY OF BRITISH COLUMBIA BOTANICAL GARDEN**, 6804 Southwest Marine Drive, (604) 822-4208; the **BLOEDEL FLORAL CONSERVATORY**, 33rd Avenue and Cambie Street, (604) 872-5513; and the **DR. SUN YAT-SEN CLASSICAL CHINESE GARDEN**, 578 Carrall (in Chinatown), (604) 689-7133. Each one has its own captivating beauty. Coaxed from the earth by skilled artisans, the verdant presentations are creative and dramatic. Sculpted shrubbery, specially pruned trees, tranquil ponds, and exotic arrangements are all here for your pleasure. Of course, there are the occasional tour buses to look past, but depending on the season you could be the only ones walking through these elysian paradises.

HYAK WILDERNESS ADVENTURES, INC., Vancouver
(604) 734-8622, (206) 382-1311 (in Seattle), (800) 663-RAFT
$95 to $235 per person
Call for information and reservations.
Closed October through April

Trips are available on the Chilliwack and Thompson Rivers.

Located one hour from Vancouver, the Chilliwack River is churning with white water and (if you'll pardon the phrase) a thrill a minute. River rafting through rugged canyons, unanticipated gorges, and momentary still water along riverbanks crowned with cedars and pinery makes for a trip that is nothing short of sensational. Depending on the season, the impact of your excursion can vary from awesome to electrifying. Packages are available for one-, two-, or six-day adventures. It is all an immense amount of fun, even if you've never been in a wet suit before or are afraid of how you'll look in one. Let go and jump in; the surging water is terrific.

QUEEN ELIZABETH PARK
Recommended Wedding Site

At 33rd Avenue and Cambie Street.

Queen Elizabeth Park, home of the **BLOEDEL FLORAL CONSERVATORY** (see the Botanical Gardens entry, above), is located at Vancouver's geographic center. A short, winding, tree-lined drive ascends to a lookout peak where you can enjoy panoramic views of the city and its surroundings. Although this park is popular, it isn't nearly as touristed as Stanley Park, so affectionate hand-holding or an intimate picnic is possible while you enjoy the natural beauty Vancouver has to offer.

Romantic Suggestion: You will see plenty of signs for **SEASONS IN THE PARK RESTAURANT** (see Restaurant Kissing), where you can eat up the view while you dine.

ROCKWOOD ADVENTURES, Vancouver
1330 Fulton Avenue
(604) 926-7705
$45 per person

If you're eager to spend a "green day" in Vancouver, call Rockwood Adventures. Although guided tours preclude truly romantic moments, Rockwood Adventures' friendly guides can only be considered a romantic asset, as they lead you to some of Vancouver's most awe-inspiring (and kiss-inspiring) destinations. You can learn more about the life cycle of the Pacific salmon at the Capilano Fish Hatchery along the spectacularly lush Rain Forest Walk in the Capilano River Canyon. Drink in spellbinding views of a virgin coastal rain forest in Lighthouse Park in Burrard Inlet, seek out spectacular hidden corners of Stanley Park, or take a scenic journey to nearby Bowen Island. Couples who are looking for a physical challenge will enjoy the steep climb up Grouse Mountain (better known as the Grouse Grind). Rockwood Adventures guarantees a scenic perspective of Vancouver you won't find anywhere else.

STANLEY PARK
Recommended Wedding Site

In the West End, just off Georgia Street.

Stanley Park is a spectacular oasis of thick forest, green hilly lawns, and jewel-like lakes, with paved trails weaving through its 1,000 acres of cloistered parkland. Almost an island, the park projects into the water, with English Bay on one side and Burrard Inlet on the other. From the **SEA WALL PROMENADE**, which wraps around the park, to the engaging aquarium, abundant picnic areas, lengthy shoreline at Sunset Beach, picturesque restaurants, and vista after scenic vista, Stanley Park provides a much-needed respite from the cityscape. And it's just moments away! Of course, this means it draws thousands of locals and visitors at all times of the year, which doesn't leave much room for privacy. But the surroundings are so welcoming that you can forgive the busloads of camera-clicking tourists and find yourselves a corner to call your own—at least for a while.

Romantic Suggestion: If you work up an appetite while exploring the park (and if you remembered your wallet), **THE TEAHOUSE RESTAURANT** (see Restaurant Kissing) is an ideal spot for lunch in the park.

West Vancouver and North Vancouver

If you time it right and manage to avoid rush-hour traffic on Lion's Gate Bridge or Highway 1 West, you can trade Vancouver's urban sprawl for more residential and forested North Vancouver or West Vancouver in a matter of minutes. (If you do happen to get stuck in traffic, as we did, rest assured the wait is worth your while.) Nestled in the foothills of the North Shore Mountains, adjacent to several provincial parks, this region features tranquil settings and scenery that are undeniably conducive to our favorite activity: kissing, of course! Better yet, we found a handful of properties designed for couples with just that in mind.

Hotel/Bed and Breakfast Kissing

ARBOR HOUSE BED AND BREAKFAST, North Vancouver
5186 Cliffridge Avenue
(604) 990-5174
http://www.vancouver-bc.com
Moderate; No Credit Cards

Nestled at the foot of Grouse Mountain in a peaceful residential neighborhood, this semi-contemporary private home overlooks beautifully tended gardens and a burbling creek that runs through the adjacent woods. Private entrances enhance the sense of seclusion in the two spacious guest suites here, both of which have views of the quiet, forested backyard. The bright yellow walls in one suite are almost overwhelming, but the king-size bed covered with a fluffy down comforter and floral linens is sumptuously inviting. A fire raging in the hearth offers welcome warmth in the winter months. The second suite is similarly decorated, but has access to a private covered patio. Both suites have small but cheery private baths. A full, delicious breakfast is served in the outdoor garden when weather permits or in the owner's modern, attractive kitchen upstairs.

BEACHSIDE BED AND BREAKFAST, West Vancouver
4208 Evergreen Avenue
(604) 922-7773, (800) 563-3311
Inexpensive to Expensive
Minimum stay requirement seasonally

Nestled in an upscale residential community, this semi-contemporary home is perched literally at the water's edge. Waves lap at the driftwood logs that have settled on the beach fronting this property. Views of Vancouver span the horizon in the distance and can be enjoyed from the vantage point of a large deck or a steamy hot tub set right on the beach. While the Beachside's setting is, without exaggeration, picture-perfect, the five guest rooms could use some major updating. Brown carpeting and mismatched furnishings and linens lend a dated feeling to many of the rooms, several of which lack water views due to their location at the back of the house. Having said that, the oceanfront Honeymoon Suite is still worth your romantic consideration and is the only real reason to book a reservation here. Set overlooking panoramic views of the water, this otherwise homespun suite offers ample privacy, a private entrance to the beach, and exclusive use of a Jacuzzi tub the size of a small swimming pool (you have to see this one to believe it).

All guests are encouraged to make themselves at home in the comfortable fireside living room or dining room enclosed by floor-to-ceiling windows that face the water. In addition to the already mentioned beachside hot tub, guests can also use an outdoor barbecue area that is perfect for nighttime bonfires. In the morning, a full breakfast is enriched by the sound of waves lapping against the shore.

ENGLISH ROSE BED AND BREAKFAST, West Vancouver
2367 Lawson Avenue
(604) 926-1902
Moderate; No Credit Cards
Minimum stay requirement on weekends
Closed mid-October through April

Laurels, cedars, and lavish gardens with more than 50 English rosebushes encompass this unassuming, pocket-size, white frame country home nestled in a quiet residential neighborhood. Guests have exclusive use of the front yard, where they can stop to smell the roses and enjoy the sights and sounds of a tranquil water garden teeming with fish and floating lilies. If you manage to get past the front yard (you'll want to stay here all day), you will be equally pleased with the home's picturesque interior, most of which belongs solely to you during your stay here. (Doors separate the guest quarters from the rest of the owner's home.) A glowing red-tiled fireplace warms your own private sun-filled living room filled with country antiques and a noteworthy art collection. Floral linens and more countrified touches make your bedroom feel especially inviting. Breakfast can be served in the privacy of your own dining room, where bay windows are lined by a pillow-filled banquette. In summer months, breakfast can also be served in the garden by your lovely hostess, who makes you feel right at home.

LABURNUM COTTAGE, North Vancouver
1388 Terrace Avenue
(604) 988-4877
Moderate to Very Expensive
Minimum stay requirement in cottages
Recommended Wedding Site

Haloed by towering evergreens, this picturesque Victorian country home and its separate cottage are as pretty as can be. Miniature bridges traverse a trickling mountain stream and winding footpaths meander through the colorful, manicured English gardens that embrace this one-and-a-half-acre retreat.

Five of the six options for guest accommodations here face the tranquil garden setting, ensuring calm privacy. Unfortunately, years of popularity have taken their toll on all of the interiors, which sport occasional carpet stains and some noticeably dated touches. Despite these drawbacks, we still found this property to be a lip-worthy destination.

The guest rooms in the main house, three upstairs and one down, are quite snug, but still cheery and bright; all overlook the garden in the backyard. The self-contained Summer House, right in the middle of the garden, offers the most seclusion. Appointed with a double-size brass bed and eclectic country accents, this snug cottage is serenely quiet. Although it lacks a garden view, a second private cottage attached to the main house offers a fireplace, kitchenette, and comfortable sitting area. Thick down comforters, floral linens and fabrics, turn-of-the-century antiques, and country knickknacks give each of these rooms quiet charm.

High tea and sherry are served in the formal English-style living room, where windows allow views of the colorful flowers outside. A full breakfast is presented in the nearby terra-cotta-tiled kitchen, which brims with sunlight.

Romantic Note: A mother-and-daughter team ran Laburnum Cottage for years, but several years ago love sparked at the breakfast table. Now it is a mother-daughter-and-son-in-law-run operation. A fitting tribute to the affectionate ambience here.

THE PALMS GUEST HOUSE, West Vancouver
302 Marine Drive
(604) 926-1159, (800) 691-4455
http://www.bbcanada.com/932.html
Moderate to Very Expensive
Minimum stay requirement seasonally

Located in an impressively upscale residential neighborhood, this architecturally unique contemporary home is perched atop a hill and has magnificent water views. Guests are encouraged to make themselves at home in the owner's elegant upstairs living quarters, fashioned with high ceilings and skylights, Corinthian columns, and beautifully finished hardwood floors. Watch the traffic on English Bay from the expansive outdoor deck or lounge on the lawn in the large backyard, surrounded by tall trees. You won't even have the chance to get hungry here; beverages and baked goodies are available at all hours in the small kitchenette adjacent to the common rooms.

The four guest rooms here all have beautiful views of the water and surrounding stands of evergreens. Although some of the color schemes are a little too jarring and dated for our tastes, private bathrooms and access to water-view balconies help to compensate. If you've got serious romancing in mind, the spacious Ambassador Suite is the only real reason to stay here (but it's reason enough). A two-sided fireplace warms the bathroom and bedroom at the same time. Handsome green linens drape an immense four-poster bed and contrast with the spotless, scintillating white carpet. Nearly the size of a bedroom itself, the beautiful white-and-green-tiled private bathroom has a double Jacuzzi tub and a glass-enclosed shower, not to mention an exceptional water view. You can even watch the sun set over the water from the privacy of your own big balcony. Other amenities in this sumptuous suite include a TV, telephone, and stereo.

Tea is offered to all guests in the afternoon, and a generous gourmet breakfast is served in the elegant dining room, which shares the same lovely water views.

Restaurant Kissing

BEACH SIDE CAFE, West Vancouver
1362 Marine Drive
(604) 925-1945
Expensive
Lunch and Dinner Daily; Saturday and Sunday Brunch

Set just off busy Marine Drive in a cheery storefront, the Beach Side Cafe is one of the more "happening" places to dine in West Vancouver. The pace can feel a little frantic at the peak of the evening, but the lovely setting and fabulous fresh food ensure a pleasant interlude. Tiles in the entrance give the restaurant a Mediterranean flair, accented with blond wood, round columns, and jazzy fabrics. White linens drape the well-spaced tables, several of which are cozied into window alcoves that overlook the street beyond. When the weather cooperates (and sometimes even when it doesn't), you can dine on the heated terrace at an umbrella-shaded table with a view of the water just past the parking lot. Sunsets here are remarkable and worth celebrating. The kitchen strives to be creative and rarely disappoints. Exotic fresh fish (one night escolar from Egypt was headlined) and hearty appetizers such as Brie wrapped in phyllo are part of the restaurant's repertoire.

CAPERS CAFE, West Vancouver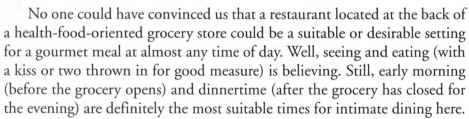
2496 Marine Drive
(604) 925-3374
Inexpensive to Moderate
Breakfast and Lunch Daily; Dinner Monday-Saturday

No one could have convinced us that a restaurant located at the back of a health-food-oriented grocery store could be a suitable or desirable setting for a gourmet meal at almost any time of day. Well, seeing and eating (with a kiss or two thrown in for good measure) is believing. Still, early morning (before the grocery opens) and dinnertime (after the grocery has closed for the evening) are definitely the most suitable times for intimate dining here.

The casual wood-paneled interior is appointed with white tablecloths, forest green accents, and a large glass-enclosed deck with a view of English Bay. Soft classical music adds to the ambience. Not surprisingly, the menu is almost entirely vegetarian (except for several seafood items), and the whole-wheat, organic, al dente pasta is a dream come true. Everything we sampled was excellent, and the service was professional and friendly. We recognize this is an unusual setting for a romantic encounter, but we still think it is worth considering if you admire wholesome cooking served with elegant flair.

Romantic Note: A recently opened second location lacks a water view, but you can enjoy the same friendly service and delicious health-oriented cuisine at **CAPERS KITSILANO**, 2285 West Fourth Avenue, Vancouver, (604) 739-6685.

CHESA RESTAURANT, West Vancouver
1734 Marine Drive
(604) 922-2411
Moderate to Expensive
Lunch and Dinner Monday-Saturday; Sunday Brunch

Snugly tucked into a small storefront on well-traveled Marine Drive, Chesa's garden-like interior is a welcome haven. Oriental carpets cover hardwood floors in the sunny dining room, which is filled with bouquets of exotic flowers. White latticework separates clusters of tables covered with white and red linens and topped with fresh flowers. Primarily meat-based, the menu features Swiss cuisine with a distinctly French touch. Entrées like duck parfait with port wine and Amaretto, linguine napped with a rich basil cream, and the fresh seafood are usually good, but sometimes miss the mark. (One of the dishes we ordered contained an ingredient we were trying to avoid and were specifically told it did not contain.) Desserts, however, are always tantalizing and entirely too good to exclude; if you didn't save room, we recommend kissing until you find room.

LA TOQUE BLANCHE, West Vancouver
4368 Marine Drive
(604) 926-1006
Moderate to Expensive
Dinner Tuesday-Sunday

Don't let your first glimpse of this French restaurant dissuade you from dining here. Located behind a gas station and convenience store, La Toque Blanche has much more to offer than is first apparent. Step inside the softly lit dining room and you'll see exactly what we mean. Tall windows in the dining room face in the opposite direction of the gas station (thank goodness) and offer views of two towering evergreens in the parking lot instead. Almost Oriental in design, the dining room has a low ceiling, dark woodlatticed walls, and well-spaced tables draped with white linens and flanked by shiny black-lacquered chairs. Extravagant flower arrangements lend a colorful flair, and a free-standing black iron fireplace in the center of the room radiates warmth. The traditional French menu offers a selection of exquisite entrées, including breast of Fraser Valley duckling, grilled fillet mignon with scalloped potato tart, and ravioli of lobster and seared scallops with cucumber and ginger. The name of this restaurant, La Toque Blanche, refers to the white "hat" awarded to chefs depending on their talent. We can't give hats of approval, but we can award lips of approval. Both are deserved.

SALMON HOUSE ON THE HILL, West Vancouver
2229 Folkestone Way
(604) 926-3212
Moderate to Expensive
Lunch and Dinner Daily; Sunday Brunch

Sometimes a spectacular view is enough to establish a place's romantic dining credentials, and the Salmon House is a case in point. Poised high on a hillside, the restaurant surveys superlative views of Vancouver and its busy waterways. Much to our delight, the Salmon House also offers an innovative seafood-oriented menu that equals (and sometimes almost surpasses) its impressive setting. Designed to look like an authentic Northwest lodge, the expansive terraced dining room is decorated with Native Canadian artwork, hand-carved canoes that hang from a sloped knotty pine ceiling, and a glowing brick fireplace. Wooden tables and green booths fill the interior, and all have glimpses of the water through the wall of windows fronting the restaurant. Reserve a table near the window, order the savory alderwood-broiled salmon or the Cajun-dusted fried green tomatoes, then sit back and let the evening drift by your ringside view of the world.

SALUTE!, West Vancouver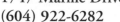
1747 Marine Drive
(604) 922-6282
Moderate to Expensive
Lunch Monday-Friday; Dinner Monday-Saturday

You won't even notice the heavy traffic on Marine Drive as you enjoy the consistently delicious fare served up by this vintage Italian eatery. Reproductions of Michelangelo's Sistine Chapel paintings embellish the walls, and terra-cotta tiles accent the floor of the small but charming dining room. White linens lend elegance to tables aglow with candlelight and surrounded by shiny black-lacquered chairs. Everything on the menu is fresh and worth trying, from the grilled oysters and antipasto appetizers to the penne pasta sautéed with fresh tomatoes and vodka (unusual but wonderful!). Desserts are equally tempting and impossible to resist.

SAVOURY RESTAURANT, North Vancouver
107C-4390 Gallant Avenue, at Deep Cove
(604) 929-2373

Moderate to Expensive
Dinner Daily

Harbored in scenic Deep Cove, in the quiet reaches of North Vancouver, this casually authentic French restaurant is situated at the end of a modern row of storefronts overlooking a peaceful waterfront park. A wall of windows in the airy dining room showcases views of boats bobbing in the marina and majestic mountains ascending above the cove. The relaxed but pretty dining room is colorfully decorated with deep maroon walls, green columns, and a sparkling black-tiled floor. White linens give each table elegant flair, and nearly every seat in the house has a glimpse of the water. In the spring and summer, you can dine on the outdoor terrace, which shares the same views. Savoury's cuisine displays southern French and Basque influences used to enhance the fresh, local ingredients. You won't find fresher seafood anywhere, and the mussels were some of the best we've ever sampled.

Romantic Suggestion: After you've lingered over the views and eaten your fill, take a walk through the adjacent waterfront park or nearby **CATES PARK** (several minutes via car from the restaurant on Dallarton Highway), both of which offer numerous spots to stop and smooch at the water's edge.

Outdoor Kissing

CYPRESS PROVINCIAL PARK, West Vancouver ❤️❤️❤️❤️
GROUSE MOUNTAIN, West Vancouver
MOUNT SEYMOUR PROVINCIAL PARK, North Vancouver

These three mountain areas are accessible from Highway 1 and Highway 1A/99. To get to Mount Seymour Provincial Park, follow the signs from Highway 1 heading east from the Lion's Gate Bridge. Cypress Bowl Road in West Vancouver takes you to Cypress Provincial Park. Capilano Road in West Vancouver leads to Grouse Mountain.

One extraordinary aspect of Vancouver is that in its very own backyard are three separate mountains high enough above sea level to be active ski areas, and they are only about 30 minutes from the city (45 minutes if you take your time or get lost). It is quite feasible to spend an invigorating day on any of these mountains hiking, swimming in lakes (depending on the season), gazing out over the stupendous views, or skiing, and still have more than enough time to get back to the city and dress up for an elegant dinner downtown.

On a moonlit winter's eve, more adventurous couples may consider doing the above scenario in reverse. After an early dinner in the city, gather your cross-country ski equipment, toss it in the car, and drive up to Cypress

Provincial Park. There you can make tracks over the sparkling white snow until the park lights shut off at 11:00 P.M.

Romantic Warning: These park areas are well known. Grouse Mountain tends to be the most touristy of the group, but it also has dining on top of the world overlooking the city lights. For general information about Grouse Mountain or for dinner reservations, call (604) 984-0661. Needless to say, the crowds are worst during the summer and on sunny weekends.

LIGHTHOUSE PARK, West Vancouver

From Highway 1/99 in West Vancouver, take the 21st Street exit to Marine Drive. Follow the signs on Marine Drive to Lighthouse Park.

At the southwestern tip of West Vancouver is a peninsula called Lighthouse Park, a small fragment of granite hanging on to the mainland. From the parking area, the shores of the Strait of Georgia and the cliff tops of the parkland are both only a brisk 15-minute walk over trails through rocky forest. As you stroll along the trails, you can inhale the freshness of sea air mingled with the scent of sturdy fir and spruce trees. At trail's end, you'll get a far-reaching view on a clear day. On a cloudy day, Lighthouse Park obligingly resembles the kind of dense forest that exists deep in the distant Canadian Rockies, enabling you to feel far away from city life. The two of you will scarcely remember how close civilization really is.

LYNN CANYON SUSPENSION BRIDGE, North Vancouver

Take Highway 1 east from the Lion's Gate Bridge and follow the signs to Lynn Canyon Park.

While everyone and their aunt is lining up at the well-touristed **CAPILANO SUSPENSION BRIDGE**, you can discover the bridge less traveled. There are no entrance fees and no tourist shops, and when school is in session you may even have a certain amount of privacy. The suspension bridge across Lynn Canyon hovers and sways (as suspension bridges are inclined to do) over a rocky, forested gorge where a waterfall and river etch their way through the canyon floor below. On the other side of the bridge are trails that lead to a boulder-strewn brook with freshwater soaking pools. You can cross over the rocks and find a refreshing niche all to yourselves.

Romantic Warning: Trails here are periodically washed out, and the crystal-clear pools, which look inviting, can be dangerous due to unexpectedly swift water. Be cautious, stay on the trails, wade in the shallows, and the solitude will be invigorating.

MARINE DRIVE, West Vancouver

Heading north over the Lion's Gate Bridge, turn west onto Marine Drive, which follows the southern shoreline of West Vancouver.

Marine Drive borders, at water's edge, a stellar residential and commercial neighborhood in the Vancouver area. Summertime graces this road with perfect views of the city and Vancouver Island. During the fall, overcast rainy days make this sinuous road more reclusive, emphasizing its dark, rocky cliffs and the thick, moist foliage that veils the houses along the way. Stores and restaurants here have a quaint, congenial style. Major banks and gas stations are scattered throughout, but for the most part this area is a quieter alternative for a stroll or drive than Vancouver.

Besides being scenic and conducive to sitting close (if you don't have bucket seats), Marine Drive has an added attraction: several satellite roads leading northward and connecting with two alternate routes to Whistler— Cypress Access Road through **CYPRESS PROVINCIAL PARK**, and Capilano Road over **GROUSE MOUNTAIN** (see Outdoor Kissing). Let the beauty of the drive lead you wherever your hearts desire.

Romantic Alternative: Adjacent to Marine Drive, just west of the Lion's Gate Bridge, look for a waterfront park called **AMBLESIDE**. The long, winding sidewalk that outlines the park is bordered on one side by a stone sea wall with marvelous views of the water and city, and on the other by grass and playgrounds. This is a much smaller, less crowded version of the sea wall in Stanley Park, and the better romantic option if crowds are something you like to avoid.

Ladner

Set on the Fraser River Delta, Ladner is a quiet farming and fishing community. Located only about 30 minutes south of downtown Vancouver, this is a pleasant alternative to staying in the city, but it's not so far away that you can't take advantage of all the fine dining and entertaining options Vancouver has to offer.

Hotel/Bed and Breakfast Kissing

RIVER RUN COTTAGES, Ladner
4551 River Road West
(604) 946-7778
http://www.achilles.net/~bb/366.html
Moderate

Don't let the cute gingerbread exterior of the little houseboat here fool you: there is much more to this property than meets the eye. A queen-size loft bed, small kitchenette, woodstove, pillowed sitting area, and highly polished wood make up the interior of the *Waterlily*, which rises and falls with the tides and gently rocks on the waves. Three equally alluring onshore cottages, built on pilings, are also available. The Net Loft is a snug, two-level retreat featuring a Mexican tile floor, a woodstove, skylights, hardwood floors, and a built-in queen-size captain's bed on the upper level that showcases views of the river.

Two newly renovated cottages are equally cozy and charming, with French doors that open onto flower-laden private decks that jut out over the river. Like the other accommodations, these two adjoining cottages have fireplaces, CD players, and small refrigerators for your convenience. The Keeper's Cottage is slightly more spacious, featuring a two-person Jacuzzi tub in the lovely bathroom and a massive log bed draped with a down comforter in the separate bedroom. Recently dubbed the Northwest Room, the second cottage features local and Native artwork, an enticing queen-size bed fashioned out of driftwood, and, most intriguing of all, a river-rock and slate bathroom with a sexy walk-in shower that has two shower heads.

To make you feel thoroughly pampered (as if your surroundings haven't already done that), a full gourmet breakfast can be delivered *literally* to your bed in the morning. Later, borrow a rowboat for a quiet tour of your surroundings or, better yet, just relax and cherish the tranquility of life on the river.

Tsawwassen

Best known as a terminal for ferries headed to and from Vancouver Island, the otherwise nondescript town of Tsawwassen has several glorious sand-swept beaches. Because its beaches are not well known, you're almost guaranteed to find a private spot on the sand to sit and watch eagles soaring and blue herons fishing until the sun goes down.

Hotel/Bed and Breakfast Kissing

OCEAN VIEW LODGING, Tsawwassen
246 Centennial Park Way
(604) 948-1750
http://www.max-net.com/business/Ocean.html
Inexpensive to Expensive

Balanced literally on the edge of Boundary Bay, this rambling contemporary home overlooks waves lapping at a vast expanse of sandy beach. In the front yard, a hot tub surrounded by gardens takes full advantage of this view, and after a long, hot soak, guests can cool themselves in the gentle rolling surf just beyond.

An eclectic assortment of antiques, bookshelves, floral linens, four-poster beds, and homey accents fill the eight guest rooms in this sprawling home. For the purposes of our book, we recommend only the three rooms with private baths: the Mount Baker, the Victorian, and the Anniversary Suite. Mount Baker features mesmerizing views of the water and the Victorian offers pretty garden views, but the Anniversary Suite is really the most romantic spot in the house. (Unfortunately, it is also exorbitantly expensive.) It is, however, mostly worth the splurge, with its round 27-foot fireplace, three decks, two lofts, and 16-foot tall bay windows that showcase marine views. A generous home-cooked breakfast is served in the vista-blessed dining room at one table to all guests. It's a perfect prelude to a day spent exploring Boundary Bay's endless beaches.

Point Roberts, Washington

Due to a geographic quirk, the tiny rural town of Point Roberts is actually located in the state of Washington, but because it is so close to the Canadian towns of Ladner, Tsawwassen and Vancouver, we felt this was the most appropriate placement in our book. Even if you don't book a reservation at the lip-worthy bed and breakfast we recommend, this quiet farming community set at the edge of Boundary Bay is well worth an afternoon visit.

Hotel/Bed and Breakfast Kissing

MAPLE MEADOW, Point Roberts
101 Goodman Road
(360) 945-5536
Inexpensive

Get back to nature at this picturesque farmhouse, enclosed by a white picket fence and surveying pastures full of farm animals. An exuberant Doberman welcomes guests at the front gate (don't worry, he's very friendly!) and ushers them into the authentic country home. Inside, Oriental rugs grace the hardwood floors and handsome antiques fill the pleasant common areas. Guests are welcome to make themselves at home here or take a soak in

> *Cost ratings for British Columbia listings are in Canadian funds. American travelers should check the exchange rate or ask an innkeeper to figure out the cost in U.S. dollars.*

the outdoor Jacuzzi tub that overlooks horses grazing under an immense 200-year-old oak tree. Appointed with comfortable patio furniture, the outdoor deck and veranda are wonderful places to sit and fill your lungs with fresh country air. And if you're in the mood for a walk, the beaches of Boundary Bay are just minutes away.

Although two of the three guest rooms here (Knotty and Cedar) share baths, the self-contained Old Pumphouse cottage offers more than enough privacy for romance-minded couples. Homey and snug, the cottage's countrified interior is outfitted with a claw-foot tub, four-poster king-size bed, and embroidered white linens. Naturally, a fresh country breakfast is served in the main house to all guests, featuring produce right off the farm. Guests who are interested can rise early with the innkeepers and accompany them on their farm chores. Your vision of the country will never be the same!

White Rock

Located 30 minutes south of Vancouver, the town of White Rock sits just north of the U.S. border. Though White Rock isn't touted as a romantic destination, its miles of sandy beaches and a beach promenade lined with specialty shops are wonderfully pleasant. We also discovered a bed and breakfast that is worth a stop if you've got romance in mind.

Hotel/Bed and Breakfast Kissing

DORRINGTON BED AND BREAKFAST, White Rock
13851 19A Avenue
(604) 535-4408
Inexpensive to Very Expensive
Minimum stay requirement for the suite

In spite of its location in a not-so-romantic upscale suburban housing development, everything about the Dorrington is impressive. Immaculately manicured grounds envelop the contemporary wood-and-brick mansion, which in turn holds cathedral ceilings and impressive artwork. All three guest rooms are located upstairs and have private bathrooms.

The St. Andrews Room is decidedly masculine, with a mixture of plaid and golf-print wallpaper. A hand-hewn maple-branch four-poster bed is draped with maroon and green linens and fluffy pillows. Though the bathroom for this room is across the hall, it's a showpiece, decorated with a tiled floor, Southwestern color schemes, and several cactus plants. The traditionally elegant Victorian Room contains an antique four-poster bed covered with beautiful pink-and-white-striped linens. Well worth the extra price you're asked to pay, the Windsor is the most romantic room in the house (and the reason this property was awarded three lips). A canopied queen-size brass bed takes up a large part of the spacious suite, which is additionally appointed with Oriental carpets, lovely antiques, and European sculptures. A fireplace warms a cozy sitting area in the bedroom, and the oversized marble bathroom features a large Jacuzzi tub, separate glass-enclosed shower, twin basins, a bidet, and even in-floor heating. A bottle of chilled champagne is a complimentary bonus.

Breakfast is served in the beautifully appointed lounge, adorned with a floor-to-ceiling river-rock fireplace, hunter green walls, and surrounding windows. On sunny mornings, it can also be served outside on the shady deck. This vantage point overlooks the lush backyard, tennis courts, and a small bridge that crosses over a fish pond to a roomy hot tub set beneath the open sky. Is there anything about this property that *isn't* romantic?

Harrison Hot Springs

For more decades then anyone can remember, Harrison Hot Springs has attracted throngs of tourists and locals who want a quick but easy escape from the city. Located one and a half hours northeast of Vancouver, it is a mixed bag of treats. From any viewpoint, the town is located in an idyllic setting. Low-rise buildings (mostly newly constructed condos) hug the shore of Harrison Lake, backdropped by evergreen-clad mountains and foothills. If you can see around the RVs and campers, it is truly a site (and sight) to behold, especially in the off-season (which means anytime but summer).

Where are the hot springs the town is named for? The actual springs burble out of the ground into a holding reservoir, five minutes from the front lobby of the **HARRISON HOT SPRINGS HOTEL** (see Hotel/Bed and Breakfast Kissing). Unfortunately, the water temperature of these springs is far too hot for swimming. But don't let your sore muscles be dismayed; a large public pool in town recycles the hot sulfur-laden spring water into fresh water and cools it down to an agreeable 102 degrees Fahrenheit. You can also stay at the Harrison Hot Springs Hotel, which offers three hot pools for hotel guests only.

Hotel/Bed and Breakfast Kissing

HARRISON HOT SPRINGS HOTEL, Harrison Hot Springs
100 Esplanade
(604) 796-2244, (800) 663-2266
http://www.tourbc.com/travel/harrison

Inexpensive to Expensive
Breakfast, Lunch, and Dinner Daily

Harrison Hot Springs Hotel has long been a local landmark, and for decades it was the lone getaway in this region. Originally built in 1885, then destroyed by fire and rebuilt in 1926, it has undergone several face-lifts and additions throughout the years. Unfortunately, perhaps due to the lack of competition, this sprawling hotel is in desperate need of serious attention. It lacks warmth and style, being little more than a random cluster of nondescript buildings filled with motel-standard rooms and a jumble of restaurants and meeting rooms. Its popularity has not waned over the years, but that speaks more for the surrounding beauty of Harrison Lake and the rolling hills than for the accommodations themselves. Without question, the best reason to stay at Harrison Hot Springs Hotel is the hot spring water, filtered and cooled to a variety of temperatures to accommodate a range of tolerance levels, then piped into one indoor and two outdoor pools reserved exclusively for guests. Tennis courts, massage facilities, an exercise room, a nine-hole golf course, and lakeshore hiking trails provide additional ways to keep busy. During high season you can dance nightly to the rhythms of a local four-piece band that plays rock and roll and country ballads. (The ballroom has a flavor all its own, hovering somewhere between nostalgia and kitsch.)

When it comes to food, we encourage you to eat elsewhere in town. The hotel's two restaurants can be described as mediocre at best, with very steep prices, and the ambience is reminiscent of a 1950s catering hall.

LITTLE HOUSE ON THE LAKE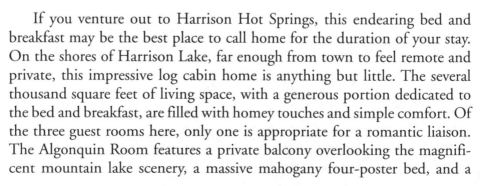
BED & BREAKFAST, Harrison Hot Springs
6305 Rockwell Drive
(604) 796-2186, (800) 939-1116
Moderate to Expensive
Call for seasonal hours.

If you venture out to Harrison Hot Springs, this endearing bed and breakfast may be the best place to call home for the duration of your stay. On the shores of Harrison Lake, far enough from town to feel remote and private, this impressive log cabin home is anything but little. The several thousand square feet of living space, with a generous portion dedicated to the bed and breakfast, are filled with homey touches and simple comfort. Of the three guest rooms here, only one is appropriate for a romantic liaison. The Algonquin Room features a private balcony overlooking the magnificent mountain lake scenery, a massive mahogany four-poster bed, and a fireplace. The other two rooms, though pleasant enough, hold several guests and feel more appropriate for a family than a couple.

Guest are encouraged to relax in a large common room outfitted with a games table, billiards table, VCR, piano, and a number of chairs and couches. Depending on the weather, continental breakfast and afternoon tea are served either in the library or on an outdoor deck with a commanding view of the area.

Restaurant Kissing

AUBERGE LA COTE D'AZUR, Harrison Hot Springs
310 Hot Springs Road
(604) 796-8422
Moderate
Call for seasonal closures.

Although this restaurant was transplanted from France to Vancouver's Robson Street and now resides in Harrison Hot Springs, the owners continue to produce magical French cooking. For the most part, when the chef gets it right, you are in for a treat, with classic presentations, flavorful seasonings, and incredibly fresh fish. The salads and some of the side dishes are lackluster, but that is forgiven once you taste the rich but delicate sauces complementing perfectly prepared filet mignon or fresh reindeer. The restaurant's interior has a delightful rustic charm and warmth lacking in the other restaurants in town. This splendid culinary outpost should be at the top of your dining list when visiting the area.

Harrison Mills

Hotel/Bed and Breakfast Kissing

ROWENA'S INN ON THE RIVER, Harrison Mills
14282 Morris Valley Road
(604) 796-0234, (800) 661-5108
Expensive

Every inch of this stunningly renovated bed and breakfast is almost too picturesque for words. Situated on the banks of the rushing Fraser River, Rowena's Inn will generate romantic aspirations in even the most jaded of city-tired spirits. Quite a saga lies behind this property, which comprises 160 immaculate acres of smooth lawn, towering evergreens, and undulating hillside poised along the rushing Fraser River; the owner will explain at length his family's long-standing history as local land barons. For our purposes what counts most are the five exceedingly affectionate rooms located on the second floor of the main house, and the four nearby, magnificent cedar cabins.

Rowena's is modeled after a quaint English manor. The attention to detail and fastidious elegance is evident throughout, from the glass-walled solarium (where breakfast is served) to the sunken living room adorned with crystal chandeliers, baby grand piano, silk-covered sofas, massive Oriental carpet, expansive marble fireplace, and an enchanting sweep of bay windows. Upstairs, the handsomely decorated rooms, with their thick down comforters, attractive seating arrangements, views, soaking tubs, and generous space, are perfect in every way. Still, as wonderful as these rooms are, they pale in comparison to the cabins, which border a pond just a stone's throw from the riverbank. Towering fireplaces, heated slate floors, striking furnishings, exquisitely cozy beds, and impressive bathrooms distinguish these ultra-romantic retreats. If you can bear to tear yourselves away from all this ease, you can try out the inn's 18-hole golf course, swim laps in the 70-foot blue-tiled pool, or hold hands in the soothingly steamy outdoor hot tub.

Dinner is served nightly in the heritage dining room. Guests are seated first, but reservations are also available to the public. The decor and scenery are sumptuous, and the food is equal to its surroundings. The kitchen's creativity transforms remarkably fresh ingredients into divine meals. Every bite is ambrosial.

Romantic Note: The 18-hole golf at Rowena's was just being completed as this book went to press. This vast undertaking is being handled with the same thoroughness and distinction as the inn, but its effect on the solitude here remains to be seen. It is hard to imagine that golf carts winding their way around the property won't be an annoying distraction—unless, of course, romance and golf are your cup of tea.

Whistler and Environs

For awesome scenery and year-round outdoor sport action, there is no spot in the Pacific Northwest/Canadian Southwest quite like Whistler. When the first serious snowfall of the year blankets the slopes of Whistler and Blackcomb Mountains (elevations 7,160 and 7,494 feet respectively), skiers the world over gather to revel in miles of spectacular downhill skiing. The two mountains offer a total of 7,000 acres of downhill skiing accessed by 28 chairlifts (nine of which are high-speed), and over 200 marked cross-country skiing trails. And when we say that snow "blankets the slopes," we are not exaggerating: the average snowfall at the top of both mountains is approximately 360 feet per year. Even during the summer, glacier skiing is available at the very top of Blackcomb Mountain. You won't find the mile-long runs of the winter season, but then again, in winter you can't wear your bathing suit on the slopes.

Whistler's year-round *raison d' être* is the enjoyment of every outdoor recreational activity you can imagine: alpine skiing, cross-country skiing, heli-skiing, kayaking, canoeing, windsurfing, white-water rafting, hiking, mountain biking, and golfing. The world-class resort facilities of Whistler Village and the surrounding area are unrivaled almost anywhere else in the world. If you like fast-paced fun and an easygoing party atmosphere amid high-altitude grandeur, Whistler delivers in the slickest, most impressive way possible.

The only drawback to this mountain holiday mecca is that the town of Whistler is growing so fast the area has a few disturbing elements of urban sprawl—functional for skiers and highly social, but not necessarily intriguing or charming. Designer homes, mountainside condominium complexes, chateau-style hotels, and an assortment of inns, bed and breakfasts, and lodges accommodate more than 1.5 million visitors to these slopes each year. Starting in April and ending when the first snows arrive sometime in October, you are more likely to hear the roar of development than the call of the wild. We counted more than 50 new construction projects underway the last time we visited. However, if charming and remote are not at the top of your list of mountaintop necessities, you needn't be too concerned with the real estate

Cost ratings for British Columbia listings are in Canadian funds. American travelers should check the exchange rate or ask an innkeeper to figure out the cost in U.S. dollars.

explosion up here. Any time of year, you can find the romantic sparkle and secret solitude that still abound in this part of Canada.

Romantic Note: Bed and breakfasts in Whistler don't have to charge many of the taxes hotels and other rental companies are required to add to your bill. You stand to save over 18 percent, which is no loose change during high season.

Wherever you stay, be sure to ask about discount packages and special seasonal rates. Most places have several different price categories depending on the time of year you venture up here. While the the rest of the world has four seasons, Whistler can have up to eight, at least when it comes to rate changes. It can get very complicated sorting out when all those periods stop and start for the different properties, but you can be assured of one thing: high season is definitely the last week in December and the first weeks in January.

Ski lifts and properties on the mountain are open sporadically during shoulder seasons. For general information, call the **WHISTLER CHAMBER OF COMMERCE**, (604) 932-5528, or **WHISTLER RESORT ASSOCIA-TION**, (800) 944-7853.

Romantic Warning: At some point during your visit to Whistler, or in the mail afterwards, you are very likely to receive a sales pitch from a time-share development company. In exchange for sitting through one of their presentations you will be offered a free or discounted stay during your next visit or a discounted meal at an associated restaurant. There is a great deal of consumer information about time-shares you should know before you deal with a provocative sales performance (and we mean provocative). Do your homework before you inadvertently sign on the dotted line.

Whistler

Hotel/Bed and Breakfast Kissing

CENTRAL RESERVATIONS, Whistler   N/A
(604) 932-4222, (800) 944-7853

CROWN RESORT ACCOMMODATIONS, Whistler   N/A
(604) 932-2215, (800) 565-1444

WHISTLER CHALETS, Whistler   N/A
(604) 932-6699, (800) 663-7711

There are literally thousands of condominium units and dozens of homes available in Whistler. From the most basic one-bedroom condominium units to elaborate log cabin homes and everything in between, the scope and variety to choose from are nothing less than staggering. This deluge of accommodations is due to the large number of nonresidents who buy property here for their seasonal getaways. Rather than leaving them empty, and to help pay off the mortgage, many of these owners list their places in a rental pool. Several management companies in the area handle the marketing, renting, and maintenance of these residences, and most represent the same complexes, only different units. Listed above are three of the largest management companies in the area, which are responsible for many of the properties reviewed in this section.

Romantic Note: Whistler Chalets specializes in house rentals. Although this is not the only company to represent the larger free-standing homes, several of its outstanding selections deserve at least a four-lip rating. Our favorites are identified in Whistler Chalets' brochure as: **NEW DELUXE LOG HOME WITH DEN** (Code #V3257), **DREAM LOG HOME WITH PRIVATE HOT TUB** (Code #H6215), **WHISTLER CAY HEIGHTS LOG HOME** (Code #P6215); **LAKE FRONT HOME** (Code #V3315), and **HORSTMAN ESTATES HOME** (Code #K4965 or #K4914). All of these are large, handsomely constructed, and beautifully furnished homes offer more than enough room for three couples. Everything that could possibly enhance your comfort awaits at these locations, including stone fireplaces, Jacuzzi tubs, stereos, TV/VCRs, designer kitchens, and views. Any of them will meet your affectionate needs, and then some.

Romantic Warning: Checkout times for this rental pool of condominiums and homes can be as early as 10 A.M., and maid service may be limited to every three days or even just once a week. You will want to be crystal-clear on these very important details when making final plans and arrangements.

ALPINE GREENS, Whistler   💋💋

BLACKCOMB GREENS, Whistler   💋💋💋

GLEN EAGLES, Whistler   💋💋

THE WOODS, Whistler   💋💋
Call one of the reservation companies listed on page 154
Inexpensive to Expensive

Undeniably, golfers have their own sense of passion. Many are able to concentrate on kissing only after they've shot below par and successfully negotiated their way past (or out of) all sand traps. Any other outcome and smooching may be out of the question. Depending on your point of view and temperament, golfing may not be the best way to spend romantic moments. Why then would we include three condominium complexes that frame the popular Chateau Whistler golf course? Because during the winter, when snow veils the area in white, some of the most immaculate cross-country ski trails you've ever seen are right out your front door.

Of the three complexes, Blackcomb Greens is by far our favorite. The handsomely furnished two-level condominiums all have smart detailing, gas fireplaces, great floor-to-ceiling windows, single Jacuzzi tubs, and very livable floor plans. Calling one of them home for a mountain getaway is something you could easily get used to.

Alpine Greens and Glen Eagles are both nice Whistler-style condominiums, but their view of the golf-course-turned-snow-covered-meadow makes them first among equals. Comfortable and cozy, they are decked out with all the usual conveniences and amenities, including fireplaces, stereos, TV/VCRs, and designer kitchens; a few also have large Jacuzzi tubs.

CEDAR CREEK, Whistler
Call one of the reservation companies listed on page 154
Unbelievably Expensive

When a brochure boasts that a place offers "the ultimate in luxury," our first reaction is to assume that the management is stretching things a bit—after all, it's hard to be the ultimate in anything. However, when it comes to accommodations in Whistler, Cedar Creek is absolutely as lavish as it gets. The entire complex consists of only six units, and it is designer heaven from top to bottom. Astounding floor-to-ceiling windows fill the rooms with outdoor splendor, massive stone fireplaces cast a glow on the terra-cotta floors, and the artistic furnishings invite you to put up your feet and forget the rest of the world. These units are fully equipped in every sense: you can soak for hours in an oversized whirlpool tub or a private outdoor hot tub while listening to a state-of-the-art CD stereo. Then relax even more while watching a romantic movie on the TV/VCR. If your culinary talents need exercise, you can create a masterpiece meal for the two of you in a kitchen Julia Child would envy.

CHALET LUISE PENSION, Whistler
7461 Ambassador Crescent
(604) 932-4187, (800) 665-1998
Inexpensive to Moderate
Minimum stay requirement seasonally

Whistler has several Swiss- or German-style pensions that cater to visitors who want a more reclusive, less hectic residence than a condominium complex in the heart of Whistler Village. Almost all of these professionally run bed and breakfasts provide a homey environment with a hearty meal served first thing in the morning, just before the lifts open.

Chalet Luise is just such a place, with a little bit of everything for couples who want to be close to the mile-long mountain runs: pine details and furnishings; a huge outdoor whirlpool protected from the elements by a gazebo; and all the extra comforts and crisp, clean detailing you would expect from a European-style bed and breakfast. Some of the quaint, exceptionally neat rooms are a bit on the snug side, one has a fireplace, and a few have views and balconies. A generous breakfast is served in a fireside lounge; individual tables are placed around the room, allowing for a private morning repast of creative juice combinations, waffles, cereals, breads, and jams. Chalet Luise is only moments away from the slopes and cross-country ski runs (ski in, ski out), so once you arrive you may not need to use your car again during your winter stay.

CHATEAU WHISTLER RESORT, Whistler
4599 Chateau Boulevard
(604) 938-8000, (800) 606-8244
Expensive to Unbelievably Expensive
Recommended Wedding Site

In a sea of condos, time-shares, and ordinary ski lodges, it is almost a relief to find a hotel of this quality and sophistication. Chateau Whistler's deserved reputation precedes it via the many accolades and laurels awarded by travelers the world over. For ski buffs the big attraction is location, and this one is ideal: right at the foot of the ski lifts. But to put it in perspective for romantic endeavors, in some ways the Chateau is nothing more than an upscale lodge with very nice but standard rooms (342 to be exact), some of which have exceptional views of the mountains. We think the lobby area, with its soaring glass windows, and the capacious lounge, with comfortable seating and a handsome stone fireplace, are the most exquisite in the area; unfortunately, you can't sleep there.

A notable Chateau Whistler attribute is the day spa, which has fairly good to excellent services and facilities. Take time off from the slopes to enjoy the indoor/outdoor pool heated year-round to a very swimmable but warm 86 degrees. Or soak in the two large Jacuzzi tubs, one indoor and the other outside, both with powerful jets for muscle-sore skiers. You'll also find a fern-clad juice bar, as well as relaxing and therapeutic massages performed by skilled professionals. The only possible negative is the workout room, which is a bit snug and has a limited number of aerobic machines. However, the weight circuit is outstanding in comparison to those in other hotels, and the attendants are knowledgeable and helpful.

Chateau Whistler offers a four-star hotel experience with an exceptionally attentive staff and all the necessary services. But in terms of the heart, it isn't the most affectionate choice in town.

Romantic Note: A meal at **WILDFLOWER** (see Restaurant Kissing), the hotel's country-elegant restaurant, is an exceptional culinary experience, particularly for dinner. It isn't wildly romantic, but the chef makes passionate culinary use of a wide variety of local herbs and vegetables.

DURLACHER HOF, Whistler
7055 Nesters Road
(604) 932-1924
Moderate to Expensive
Call for seasonal closures.

Top to bottom, the Austrian influence is strong at the Durlacher Hof. Elaborate breakfasts and cozy rooms are standard amenities, but where some bed and breakfasts stop, Durlacher Hof is just beginning. The innkeeper here serves a most bountiful morning meal of freshly baked breads and Danishes, homemade jams, cheese soufflé, blueberry and apple pancakes, and fresh fruit—and that is just one morning. Afternoon tea with fresh-from-the-oven cakes is also a delicacy. The rooms are pretty, immaculate, and cheerful; some have spa tubs, one has a gas fireplace, and all are quite spacious. Unfortunately, the inn is a bit too close to the highway for comfort, but once the quiet of night embraces the area, it really doesn't matter.

During the winter, the Durlacher Hof offers five-course gourmet dinners. Chefs from all over the world come to take part in these culinary productions. It makes for an incredible, exclusive evening without crowds or pretense.

EDGEWATER LODGE, Whistler
8841 Highway 99
(604) 932-0688
http://www.whistler.net/accommodate/edgewater
Moderate

If only the rooms here were equal to the views, the two-lip rating for Edgewater Lodge would soar to a ten-lip rating in a heartbeat. The expansive bay windows in each unit offer scintillating, unobstructed views of Whistler's resplendent scenery. Every room is a front-row seat where you can be dazzled by towering snow-clad mountains that entertwine and overlap endlessly in flawless panoramic glory. An occasional floatplane or canoe momentarily breaks the calm surface of the serene crystal blue lake that fronts the vista.

The same incredible scenery fills the floor-to-ceiling windows of the lodge's dining room, where you can enjoy a simple, complimentary continental breakfast. Alas, the view is the main reason to stay at this newly built, 12-room inn, located an appreciated two miles from the hectic center of Whistler Village. The suites and rooms are strictly motel-quality, with impossibly tiny bathrooms and stark, plain furnishings.

Romantic Note: The petite **EDGEWATER LODGE RESTAURANT** (see Restaurant Kissing) serves delectable four-course dinners.

THE GABLES, Whistler
Call one of the reservation companies listed on page 154
Inexpensive to Expensive

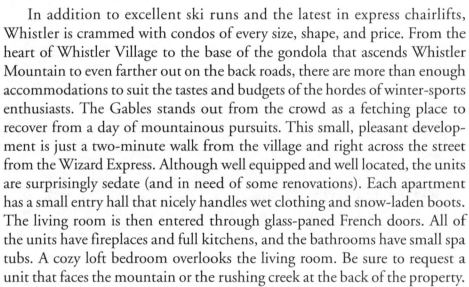

In addition to excellent ski runs and the latest in express chairlifts, Whistler is crammed with condos of every size, shape, and price. From the heart of Whistler Village to the base of the gondola that ascends Whistler Mountain to even farther out on the back roads, there are more than enough accommodations to suit the tastes and budgets of the hordes of winter-sports enthusiasts. The Gables stands out from the crowd as a fetching place to recover from a day of mountainous pursuits. This small, pleasant development is just a two-minute walk from the village and right across the street from the Wizard Express. Although well equipped and well located, the units are surprisingly sedate (and in need of some renovations). Each apartment has a small entry hall that nicely handles wet clothing and snow-laden boots. The living room is then entered through glass-paned French doors. All of the units have fireplaces and full kitchens, and the bathrooms have small spa tubs. A cozy loft bedroom overlooks the living room. Be sure to request a unit that faces the mountain or the rushing creek at the back of the property.

LE CHAMOIS, Whistler
4557 Blackcomb Way
(604) 932-8700, (800) 777-0185
http://www.whistler.net/resort/accommodation/powder
Expensive

Claustrophobia is a new problem in Whistler, and it's getting worse. Everyone wants to be a stride or two away from the slopes, which means the developers do too. New high-rise accommodations are going up everywhere, right on top of each other. In the middle of all these exploding steel girders is Le Chamois, a comparatively small 52-units hotel with sparse furnishings, views in some rooms, nice amenities, an impressive restaurant, and, most important, a location directly at the foot of the Blackcomb ski run. Surprisingly, Le Chamois offers six attractive studios, each with ample space, cozy alcoves, high ceilings, a kitchenette, and a two-person marble Jacuzzi tub in the living area. And these are the least expensive rooms in the hotel! During the summer they are an incredible kissing bargain.

Romantic Note: Le Chamois' restaurant, **LA RUA** (see Restaurant Kissing), is one of Whistler's more provocative settings for dinner. Sometimes its romantic ambience is overrun by tour groups or golf enthusiasts, but it is still an exceptional find and the menu is a work of art.

LORIMER RIDGE PENSION, Whistler
6231 Piccolo Drive
(604) 938-9722, (888) 988-9002
Inexpensive
Minimum stay requirement seasonally

Dignified detailing, majestic mountain views, and welcoming hosts make this bed and breakfast a preferred choice for every taste and budget. Set in a residential neighborhood away from Whistler Village, the eight modest yet cozy guest rooms feature a variety of amenities, but all are equipped with soft comforters and handsome wood furnishings. The large common rooms with wood-burning river-rock fireplaces, the sauna, the outdoor hot tub, and the generous breakfasts will melt cold hearts regardless of the weather conditions.

NORTHERN LIGHTS, Whistler
Call one of the reservation companies listed on page 154
Moderate to Expensive

After a while, all the condominiums in Whistler start blurring together, with little to distinguish one from the other. Even the appealing features seem to be repeated time and time again. Units 2 and 19 at Northern Lights are among the exceptions to that rule (along with the other properties listed in this section). Do keep in mind, however, that these are the only two units in Northern Lights we really recommend. What makes these two particular units so outstanding, aside from the designer kitchens, comfortable bedrooms, sunken living rooms, glowing fireplaces, attractive furnishings, and oodles of space, are the soaring floor-to-ceiling windows with spectacular views of the mountains and ski runs. What's more, Northern Lights is just a short walk from Whistler Village, but rests high enough on the slopes to give a sense of being above it all.

Cost ratings for British Columbia listings are in Canadian funds. American travelers should check the exchange rate or ask an innkeeper to figure out the cost in U.S. dollars.

PAINTED CLIFFS, Whistler
Call one of the reservation companies listed on page 154
Inexpensive to Expensive

As development in the Whistler Village Benchlands continues to move up the mountain, you get the feeling it will never end. For now, it has culminated in this large condominium complex. There are no other buildings around. Painted Cliffs isn't in the wilderness, but it does have a less crowded feeling. It also has some of the more attractive, though small, condos in the entire area. The detailing is attractive throughout, with fireplaces and single-person Jacuzzi tubs, but the units on top with the panoramic views are superior, and the best reason to stay here.

POWDERHORN, Whistler
Call one of the reservation companies listed on page 154
Moderate to Unbelievably Expensive

Given the highly stylized developments we passed on the way through town and the village to get here, we found Powderhorn's facade a bit disappointing. Its exterior is an uninviting mix of black steel and rose-colored cement that makes it look like a rather average apartment high-rise. The single elevator and sterile hallways seemed to confirm our impression. But once we turned the key on our unit, we were shocked: Could this be the same building? Everything was picture perfect. The interior was bright and sunny, with expansive windows, comfortable furnishings, a large kitchen, and a huge amount of space. Actually, our unit was designed for a group of six or more, but we didn't miss those other bodies. If we had come with a group, though, we could still have accommodated our need for privacy. The master bedroom is in a separate wing just off the living room. Its huge bathroom features a large spa tub and lofty windows. Outside on the roof, another spa tub is available for everyone. The moral: Don't judge a book by its cover.

STONERIDGE, Whistler
Call one of the reservation companies listed on page 154
Inexpensive to Expensive

Stoneridge is located in the Benchlands of Whistler Village. Many of the amenities found in this small cluster of townhomes sound enticing; floor-to-ceiling windows, vaulted ceilings, sharp detailing, wonderful kitchens, single Jacuzzi tubs, gas fireplaces, and private decks are all perfect for a mountain retreat. Unfortunately, the units are situated so that most of them face the parking lot or street, which is not desirable when the mountains are the main reason you are here. Try to reserve one of the units with a close-up view of the woods. The view adds to the privacy and makes the interior feel much more intimate.

SUNDANCE, Whistler
Call one of the reservation companies listed on page 154
Inexpensive to Moderate

As you venture into Whistler on Highway 99, you pass the original ski-resort site of Whistler Mountain. Unfortunately, age and fashion have left the area a bit behind in terms of conveniences and polished accommodations, which is why Whistler Village, at the foot of Blackcomb Mountain, is the preferred destination. (Don't repeat that to any of the Whistler Mountain enthusiasts, who swear the slopes here are superior to those of Blackcomb's.) Regardless of your skiing preferences, there is romance to be found up in these hills.

The view units of SunDance (the ones that face the mountain or woods only) are located along one of the ridges just to the south of the ski runs. These impressive condominiums have enormous vaulted ceilings, floor-to-sky windows, wood-burning fireplaces, and hot tubs on spacious outdoor decks. Like all of the condominium accommodations in Whistler, each is individually decorated, but the individual owners of these units have made them quite attractive and comfortable. Don't expect a lot of space; despite the three bedrooms, these are more cozy than spacious. But the windows and decks add immeasurably to the sense of roominess.

WOODRUN, Whistler
Call one of the reservation companies listed on page 154
Expensive to Unbelievably Expensive

Certain celebrations require a splurge. Mountain buffs and ski lovers who also love each other will find luxurious space in a select number of Woodrun's foremost romantic apartments. Each of the most extravagant rooms has cathedral ceilings, floor-to-ceiling windows, wonderful views of the mountains and ski area, a full designer kitchen, marble and hardwood floors, a gas fireplace, and a huge Jacuzzi tub in the master bedroom. The furnishings are casual but plush, and the space is considerable. The outdoor swimming pool and hot tub have a view (to console those in the rooms without the sexy private baths). Woodrun is not a hotel, but it is a sizable lodge set up in the impressive Benchlands (above the base of Blackcomb) with ski-in, ski-out accessibility and a front desk for check-in during limited hours. You can't splurge all the time, but when you do, this should be a strong consideration.

Restaurant Kissing

CHRISTINE'S, Whistler
On Blackcomb Mountain
(604) 938-7437, (604) 932-3141 (in Vancouver)
Moderate to Expensive
Lunch Daily
Closed May through December

Located at the top of Blackcomb Mountain, Christine's awaits you with an impressive four-course, prix fixe dinner. (This is available on selected summer weekend evenings only, so you'll have to call to get the schedule.) As good as the food is, it is only a minor part of your transcendent evening up here. It will take a while for your eyes to adjust to the magnitude of the view from this location. This must be what dining in heaven is like. Summer months up here are filled with visual ecstasy. When the snow has melted (except for the perennial glacier patch at Blackcomb's summit), blazing sunsets seem to linger forever across the face of the endless rugged mountain peaks.

Two seatings are available for dinner; we recommend the 8:30 P.M. seating so you can watch the sunset linger over the peaks. The restaurant is open for lunch during both the winter and summer (the patio also provides visual thrills), and for Sunday brunch between 11 A.M. and 2:30 P.M. in the summer. After brunch you can take the bus from the top of the Solar Coaster lift to the Seventh Heaven high-speed chairlift. From here you can ride up to Horseman Hut, where you can view the perennial glacier atop Blackcomb, Black Tusk, and the towering alpine peaks of this magnificent range of mountains.

Regardless of which time of the day and year you choose to voyage up here, you are guaranteed a heart-stirring experience. There is something about the combination of dinner and sunset that is wildly romantic.

EDGEWATER LODGE RESTAURANT, Whistler
8841 Highway 99
(604) 932-0688
hhttp://www.whistler.net/accomodate/edgewater
Moderate to Expensive
Dinner Daily

Romantic dining is not exactly common in Whistler. The atmosphere of most dining establishments tends to be gregarious and sociable rather than intimate and cozy. That's not the case in the Edgewater Lodge's small dining room, which commands one of the most stunning views imaginable. Although the interior is extremely plain, even austere, the handful of tables, soft lighting, the wondrous terrain surveyed through sweeping floor-to-ceiling windows, and the exceptional cuisine more than make up for it. Prepare your appetites for some of the most creatively and skillfully prepared dishes Whistler has to offer. The fresh spring salmon in a silky smooth béarnaise sauce and the fresh venison drizzled with peppercorn and cognac sauce are sheer perfection. There is little the kitchen can do wrong, so whatever the weekly offerings, jump in and enjoy.

LA RUA, Whistler   💋💋💋
4557 Blackcomb Way, at Le Chamois Hotel
(604) 932-5011
http://www.whistler.net/resort/restaurants/larua
Expensive
Call for seasonal hours.

La Rua's two handsome dining rooms are framed with deep maroon walls and mahogany wood paneling. Terra-cotta floors, soft lighting, black lacquered chairs, and white tablecloths in both rooms complete the striking, intriguing setting. We prefer the room with a mural behind the banquettes; the ambience there is warmer and cozier.

La Rua is actually one of the few restaurants in Whistler where the food can compete with the natural beauty outside the window and sometimes even win. The interesting international menu has a noticeably Californian flair, as does the service. Our roasted garlic and onion soup was remarkable rich and smooth, and the butternut squash in a cream curry sauce with smoked duck was tantalizing. Unfortunately, sometimes the intricate menu gets a bit tricky for the kitchen; the tiramisu was a bit dry and the filet mignon was on the tough side. Still, in spite of the occasional faux pas (and the kitchen owns up to its mistakes), you are likely to be pleased with your repast, and the view is one of the best shows in town.

LES DEUX GROS, Whistler   💋
1200 Alta Lake Road
(604) 932-4611
Moderate to Expensive
Dinner Daily

Les Deux Gros was once our favorite restaurant in Whistler for both romantic and dining excellence. Unfortunately, time has taken this establishment into the Twilight Zone and it would take some amount of passion or at least interest on the part of the owner to bring this place back to life. Our last two dinners here were disappointing almost to the point of embarrassment, the flowers on the tables were either fake or wilting, and the tablecloths needed laundering. What a shame. There's certainly nothing wrong with the site or the room. Located two miles south of Whistler Village, this elegant country restaurant sits on a forested bluff overlooking the woods and the mountain. The timbered exterior is a fitting reflection of the area. Inside, wood-beamed cathedral ceilings, floor-to-ceiling windows, and cascading floral draperies create an atmosphere of casual elegance. There is also an outdoor patio for summer dining.

RESTAURANT ARAXI, Whistler
Whistler Village
(604) 932-4540
Moderate to Expensive
Dinner Daily
Closed October

Restaurant Araxi is perhaps a bit too large to be truly appealing for a cozy discourse over dinner, but the inviting interior and the superior northern Italian cuisine will warm your heart and please your palate. Terra-cotta floors, oversized urns and casks, wooden tables and chairs, and sultry lighting give the room a contemporary but rustic flavor that enhances the ensuing meal. And what a meal it is. Exquisite appetizers such as baked stuffed eggplant with goat cheese, ricotta, spinach, and fresh tomato sauce, and roasted fresh mussels with an incredible vermouth, lime, and honey sauce are nothing less than triumphant. And the entrées are just as wonderful. The penne with freshly smoked turkey in sage butter with roasted vegetables, and the West Coast fisherman's stew, an array of fresh fish and seafood in a rich saffron-tomato broth, are beyond reproach. You won't have room for dessert, no matter what you select, but force yourselves: this kind of indulgence is too good to pass up.

RIM ROCK CAFE AND OYSTER BAR, Whistler
2101 Whistler Road, at the Highland Lodge
(604) 932-5565
Moderate to Expensive
Reservations Recommended
Dinner Daily

Ask any innkeeper to name the best seafood restaurant in Whistler and you are likely to be directed to the Rim Rock Cafe. Two stone fireplaces fill the wood-paneled room with a blushing glow in the winter, and there is outdoor seating on the umbrella-covered patio during warm summer days. The open-beam ceiling and antique tables help establish a provincial setting. The food is unquestionably top-notch: the freshest of fish, napped nicely with light sauces and served with tender vegetables, all flawlessly prepared and served. After a tiring day of skiing or hiking, or a lazy afternoon communing with nature, this is a handsome place to have dinner. Unfortunately, it is very popular and usually full (reservations are a must, sometimes a week in advance). The nearby lounge features a live band playing first-rate rock and roll. The music can be a bit loud and the volume of conversation increases to compete with the tunes, but between the food, the setting, and the music, you will have a delightful evening.

VAL D' ISERE, Whistler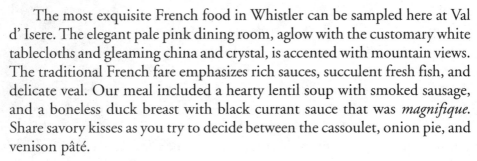
433 St. Andrews Place, at St. Andrews House
(604) 932-4666
Expensive
Dinner Daily

The most exquisite French food in Whistler can be sampled here at Val d' Isere. The elegant pale pink dining room, aglow with the customary white tablecloths and gleaming china and crystal, is accented with mountain views. The traditional French fare emphasizes rich sauces, succulent fresh fish, and delicate veal. Our meal included a hearty lentil soup with smoked sausage, and a boneless duck breast with black currant sauce that was *magnifique*. Share savory kisses as you try to decide between the cassoulet, onion pie, and venison pâté.

WILDFLOWER, Whistler
4599 Chateau Boulevard, at the Chateau Whistler Resort
(604) 938-8000, (800) 441-1414
Inexpensive to Expensive
Breakfast, Lunch, and Dinner Daily; Sunday Brunch

Almost everything inside Chateau Whistler is striking and eye-catching, including Wildflower. Its radiant, bright feeling is enhanced by soft neutral tones, wooden tables, wicker chairs, and floor-to-ceiling windows that look out to the foot of the ski slopes. Service is attentive and considerate, without the slightest hint of haughtiness. In many ways this is one of the most soothing environments for dining in all of Whistler.

As your senses are being calmed by the surroundings, your appetite will be stimulated by the delectably varied menu. The versatile kitchen produces casual fare such as sandwiches and pizzas (the pie with grilled venison sausage and basil pesto is delicious), as well as formal entrées. The chef here is known for his skillful use of herbs and local fresh meats and fish, but he's also brilliant at meeting vegetarian needs. Our meal included a mixed-leaf salad laced with edible flowers and drizzled with an incredible watermelon and fieldberry vinaigrette, a rich and flavorful baked tofu lasagne with three cheeses and grilled vegetables, and an ambrosial crispy duck breast with wild rice crêpes.

Romantic Note: Breakfast here can be relaxing, but the food is disappointingly lackluster and bland. Thankfully, the Sunday buffet brunch is a cornucopia of nicely presented dishes and the kitchen once again lives up to its reputation.

Outdoor Kissing

BRANDYWINE FALLS

Take Highway 99 north to Whistler. A few miles before Whistler, you will see signs directing you to the falls.

A brisk ten-minute walk through lush forest will bring you to a feat of natural construction that deserves a standing ovation. At the end of your jaunt, pine trees open out onto a cliff from which you look across to the top of Brandywine Falls. The water drops down a tube-like canyon into the river, which cuts through a valley of interlacing mountains and meadows. During the summer you can climb down to the rocky ledges under the falls and sit side by side beneath the surging waters as the spray cools your faces.

HIGHWAY 99

From Vancouver, cross into West Vancouver via Highway 1 north over the Second Narrows Bridge, or via Highway 1/99 over the Lion's Gate Bridge. Follow the signs to Squamish and Whistler. Depending on the road conditions, this is about an hour-and-a-half drive. Winter driving conditions can be hazardous.

The combination of perilously dropping cliffs, cerulean glacial flow, dramatic waterfalls, and uninterrupted, fragrant pinery forms the best of all outdoor worlds. The drive along Highway 99, nicknamed the Sea-to-Sky Highway, is so gorgeous that you'll actually be relieved when a curve takes you away from the view and lets you get your mind back on driving. That doesn't happen very often during the first half of your trip, so be sure to agree beforehand about who's going to drive, or else take turns. Both of you should get a chance to gawk at the wonders that line the 90 miles of curvaceous highway from Vancouver to Whistler.

MOUNTAIN HELI-SPORTS, Whistler
(604) 932-2070
Expensive

Free shuttle service to the departure pad from anywhere in Whistler.

We cannot begin to describe to you the literally awesome landscapes you will witness during a helicopter flight over this magnificent realm. The experience will engulf your souls with images that will last a lifetime. Heli-Sports offers various ways to partake in the spectacle of true mountain alpine wilderness. You can sightsee for 20-, 30-, or 45-minute flights. Adventurous souls can opt for guided heli-hiking excursions deep into the heart of this rugged, glacier-crowned terrain. Less strenuous but equally scenic is a heli-picnic that sets you down beside pristine, untouched mountain streams or ridges where you can enjoy a tasty gourmet lunch. But it's really the scenery that will awaken taste buds you never knew you had.

SHANNON FALLS

North of Vancouver on Highway 99, about halfway to Whistler on the east side of the road. Look for signs that identify Shannon Falls.

Highway turnoff sites are practical places to stop for a momentary respite from the road and to review where you've just been or where you're heading. You don't have to hike anywhere, and the big-screen viewing begins the instant you stop. The turnoff to Shannon Falls is a turnoff-lover's view extravaganza.

Immediately after you pull off the main road into the parking area and silence the engine, you'll hear the thunder of a huge waterfall plummeting straight down the face of the mountain. One would expect to find such a spectacle at the end of a long, arduous trail and not in the middle of a rest area, but here it is nevertheless.

Before you leave Vancouver to start your trek up the mountain, be sure to pack a picnic to enjoy at the base of this lofty cataract. Then you can take full advantage of this very accessible scenic paradise.

WHISTLER RIVER ADVENTURES, Whistler
(604) 932-3532
Moderate
Open mid-May through early September

Call for directions and river conditions.

There's river rafting, and then there's river rafting through the stately snowcapped peaks of Whistler's rugged, supernatural terrain. Your memory of the thrilling, scenery-packed journey will linger for months and perhaps even years. It is truly that majestic—well, at least on a clear day. Several different water excursions are available depending on your temperament and budget. Don't miss the excitement.

Romantic Alternative: Not all river expeditions have to be the same intensity. Rather than touring a river roller-coaster style, you can navigate by canoe or two-person kayak down the River of Golden Dreams. This relatively peaceful, meandering river maneuvers calmly around and through some incredible scenery. Several companies provide canoes or kayaks; call (800) 944-7853 for more information.

Pemberton and Mount Currie

Twenty minutes past Whistler on Highway 99 you'll find the teeny, newly alive towns of Pemberton and Mount Currie (population 800). In many respects these villages are not much more than a truck stop along the highway, yet they are slowly becoming a destination for those who feel Whistler has become a burgeoning suburb of Vancouver with ski runs. A lot of the locals up here feel Pemberton and Mount Currie are what Whistler was 30 years ago. Visually stunning and bucolic, the towns are nestled in a mountain valley dotted with farms framed by the snowy peaks of Mount Currie, which rises some 9,000 feet into the air.

For those in pursuit of real country living, it is worth the extra few minutes' drive due north. We urge that you consider making this trip sooner rather than later; civilization is on its way. Pemberton even has an 18-hole golf course, the **PEMBERTON VALLEY GOLF AND COUNTRY CLUB**, Airport Road, Pemberton, (604) 894-6197, and where there's a golf course, the accompanying tourist needs will follow.

Hotel/Bed and Breakfast Kissing

THE LOG HOUSE BED AND BREAKFAST INN, Pemberton
1357 Elmwood Drive
(604) 894-6000, (800) 894-2002
Inexpensive

Some places are just too hard to describe because they are such a mixed bag, and this is one such place. In some ways the Log House is just a nondescript bed and breakfast set in a rather ordinary neighborhood cul-de-sac. In other ways it is a one-of-a-kind mountain getaway in the middle of a lovely country setting. As you drive up the otherwise drab street, an amazing, recently constructed log home seems to appear out of nowhere. Upstairs, two standard bed-and-breakfast rooms feel like part of the owners' home rather than private and unshared spaces. (Both have Jacuzzi tubs, although one has

---

Cost ratings for British Columbia listings are in Canadian funds. American travelers should check the exchange rate or ask an innkeeper to figure out the cost in U.S. dollars.

an en suite bathroom while the other's bath is detached.) However, downstairs is a lovely, extremely secluded apartment/suite. In spite of the basement location, everything is delightfully inviting, with comfortable furnishings, attractive country floral fabrics, a down comforter, and a complete kitchen with elegant china and glassware. Breakfast is an enticing promenade of fresh fruits, pastries, Canadian back bacon, eggs or French toast stuffed with fresh berries, and anything else the outgoing innkeeper can think of.

Restaurant Kissing

SPIRIT CIRCLE TEA HOUSE, Mount Currie
214 Main Street (Highway 99)
(604) 894-6336
Inexpensive
Call for seasonal hours.

This unexpected, beautifully constructed contemporary wood restaurant sits across the street from the Roadside Cafe. It is anything but a traditional British tea house; instead you will find an intriguing menu accompanied by an equally intriguing story. Designed after a Salish longhouse, the building resides on what the locals believe is sacred ground. "Spirit Circle" refers to the influence of Native Canadian (First Nations People) culture in the artifacts, books, and cuisine the restaurant dedicates itself to.

At first glance the menu comprises a simple assortment of lighter fare such as soups and salads. On closer examination, especially when the daily specials are recited, an entire ethnic culinary event begins to unfold. Native foods such as *bannock* (Indian fried bread), *tswan* (wind-dried salmon), various salmon soups (a few have names with no written counterpart), and swamp tea (made from wild herbs that grow alongside alpine lakes) are a few of the house specials, and they are remarkable.

Large communal wooden tables with oversized cushioned willow chairs fill the bright dining area, which features floor-to-ceiling windows and French doors that open onto a deck for summer seating. A balcony is lined with First Nations People books and art that are there for your enlightenment. You may not get in many kisses here, but you will be all the more in love with the area you've discovered.

Outdoor Kissing

PEMBERTON ADVENTURE RANCH, Pemberton
1642 Highway 99
(604) 894-6601, (800) 303-2628 (in Canada)
Moderate to Expensive

This group of outdoor specialists offers a summer agenda that will suit your abilities and preferences in any of a dozen adventures. Horseback riding (including full-day rides), river jet-boat rides, white-water rafting, float-raft trips, kayaking, camping expeditions, and hiking excursions are all available. The best part is that in this neck of the woods, there won't be anyone else on the trails but the two of you and your guide.

Gold Bridge

Hotel/Bed and Breakfast Kissing

TYAX MOUNTAIN LAKE RESORT, Gold Bridge
Tyaughton Lake Road
(604) 238-2221
Moderate to Expensive

An alpine meadow in the heart of the Canadian Rockies, a crystal-clear lake, mountain goats roaming the hillside, and eagles soaring overhead: this is the stuff of a high-country escape. Add to that picture an imposing log building enclosing 28 attractive rooms, rustic private cabins, an outdoor hot tub, and all the outdoor and indoor adventures you can imagine, and you have Tyax Resort. It's all there, along with three meals a day graciously served in the main lodge.

Depending on the package you choose and the time of year you visit, the following activities (and the appropriate gear) are available to assure your outdoor entertainment: snowshoeing, skating, tobogganing, mountain biking, ice fishing, snowmobiling, horseback riding, windsurfing, river rafting, heli-hiking, fishing tours, floatplane fishing, sleigh rides, canoeing, cross-country skiing, tennis, and hay rides. You can even pan for gold, and if you don't find any the excursion is free. This unique lodge 110 miles north of Vancouver is a popular destination for conferences and, during the summer, family vacations.

Romantic Warning: This isn't an easy place to reach by car, so be forwarned it takes a true Northwest trek to reach this destination. Also, the food at the resort is both unavoidable and almost inedible. That is an incredible shortcoming when you're the only game in town. Stay simple when you order and you are less likely to be disappointed.

"*A soft lip would tempt you to
an eternity of kissing.*"

Ben Jonson

Sunshine Coast

The Sunshine Coast is accessible only by ferry from Horseshoe Bay, just past West Vancouver where Highway 1 meets Highway 99. A 40-minute ferry ride takes you through the mountain-ringed waters and islands of Howe Sound to Langdale. Ferries make eight sailings per day, approximately every two hours. For schedules and general information, call the British Columbia Ferry Corporation, (604) 669-1211. For the latest ferry information, including reports of delays, busy sailings, and any other conditions that may affect ferry traffic, call the Sunshine Coast SuperLine, (604) 885-0852.

Whoever named this region was certainly an optimist (or perhaps just a good marketing person). It may not always be clear and sunny, as the name suggests, but this region does provide all the wonderful rugged sights and sounds you could want, and some other getaway opportunities you probably didn't know existed. Regardless of weather conditions—even on a cool misty morning—the Sunshine Coast is breathtaking.

You'll feel as though you've accidentally stumbled onto a remote, lengthy peninsula or a long skinny island, yet this geographically unique area is neither. This section of British Columbia, beginning at Langdale's ferry dock and ending at Powell River, is indeed part of the mainland, but because it is bordered on the north, south, and west by water and on the east by mountains, it is accessible only by ferry. Even when the ferry from Horseshoe Bay is packed and you have to wait awhile to board, the other cars will seem to disappear as you head north along the coast. It is unlikely you will encounter crowds again until you return to the Vancouver area. This ferryboat ride is also one of the most visually glorious excursions you can experience. Get out of your car, walk outside, and breathe in the salt air; the ride is a perfect prelude to the magnificent sights ahead.

Romantic Note: For all its spectacular scenery, the Sunshine Coast is still a fairly remote destination. In other words, come here for the isolation and the incredible seascape, not for lively nightlife or super-fancy restaurants and accommodations. Room rates are in keeping with the low-key atmosphere, making the Sunshine Coast one of the most affordable getaways in British Columbia (and in this book, for that matter).

Romantic Suggestion: If hiking and outdoor activities are part of your romantic itinerary, then the Sunshine Coast is your kind of place. We highlight several of our favorite Outdoor Kissing spots throughout this chapter, but for more detailed information we wholeheartedly recommend purchasing *Sunshine and Salt Air: A Recreational Guide to the Sunshine Coast*, by Bryan Carson and Karen Southern (Harbor Publishing). This handy guide details the type of terrain you will encounter, suggests hikes (and tells you how long each one is), and offers brief but vivid descriptions that will make you even more eager to reach your destination.

Bowen Island

Although it is just a 20-minute ferry ride from Horseshoe Bay, Bowen Island feels worlds apart. There is enough rural charm and serenity here to soothe even the most tense, city-weary traveler. Bowen Island is one of the less touristed of British Columbia's Gulf Islands. This fact alone makes the trip here worthwhile. Although the island is relatively undiscovered, a variety of low-key services and activities are available. A small brewery offers tours and tasting: **BOWEN ISLAND BREWING COMPANY**, 595 Artisan Lane, (604) 947-0822; there are hiking trails for outdoor lovers; and the overall relaxed feel of the island provides unbeatable tranquility. The 23 miles of coastline may be calling you—if so, consider a kayak excursion. One reliable company that offers affordable rentals and guided trips is **WATERWAYS EXPLORERS**, (604) 947-9266, (800) 606-2925.

Hotel/Bed and Breakfast Kissing

THE VINEYARD AT BOWEN ISLAND, Bowen Island
687 Cates Lane
(604) 947-0028, (800) 718-9463
http://ourworld.compuserve.com/homepages/Lary_Waldman
Inexpensive to Very Expensive

If you fantasize about getting away from it all but have only a weekend to spare, then dream no longer. Just a 20-minute ferry ride from Horseshoe Bay is Bowen Island and, more specifically, The Vineyard at Bowen Island, a newly built bed and breakfast where your dreams of seclusion and tranquility can come true.

As you might guess from the name, this bed and breakfast is also a working vineyard. Set on four acres, one of which is devoted to grapes, the guest house overlooks a rolling acre of young vines. Although the grapevines may not look like much at certain times of the year, this plot of land and the additional six acres mid-island will eventually become thick, lush rows of precious fruit. Regardless of how the winery matures, though, the guest facilities are ready year-round, and they are completely worth your affectionate consideration.

In the main house, plush couches sit beside a stone fireplace in the French country–inspired living room. Beyond, a sunny breakfast room has tables for two by windows that face the vineyard. Also overlooking the vineyard and neighboring forest is an expansive brick patio with a large pool and hot tub, located behind the house. Guest rooms are in a separate building next door, and each of the six custom-built units has its own private entrance. On the ground level there are four guest rooms, and the second floor holds two beautifully spacious suites. Every room and suite is equipped with a gas-log fireplace, down comforter, small kitchenette, rich Native Canadian print linens, wrought-iron touches, and exquisite local artwork. Contemporary furnishings blend with warm color schemes, stylish accents, and natural wood to create modern, comfortable rooms. The four main-floor rooms have queen-size beds, while both suites are equipped with king-size beds. Additional extras in the suites include large bathrooms with hardwood floors and a soaking tub for two, separate living and dining areas, and a little garden courtyard. Balconies off every unit survey the property.

Nightlife is pretty mellow on Bowen Island, but there is a television with VCR in every room, and you can borrow a video from the main house. In the morning, generous full breakfasts are served to individual tables in the breakfast room, or you may arrange to have breakfast delivered to your room. As much as we appreciate that couple-oriented option, we found the cheerful breakfast room sufficiently intimate, and we found the smoked salmon and Brie omelet to be outstanding.

Romantic Suggestion: Since there are only a few restaurants on the island, the owners offer dinners by previous arrangement, and we highly recommend that you make a reservation. The prices for this four-course gourmet delight start at $50 per couple (not including wine).

Gibsons

Gibsons is the most densely populated town on the Sunshine Coast. If shopping and browsing are part of your vacation plan, you'll love this little village's array of shops and boutiques.

Hotel/Bed and Breakfast Kissing

ROSEWOOD, Gibsons
575 Pine Road
(604) 886-4714
Inexpensive to Moderate; No Credit Cards
Reservations Required
Recommended Wedding Site

It is hard to believe that this stately home is a reproduction of a 1910 Craftsman-style home, built only several years ago. From the gabled detailing to the antique leaded glass windows, every aspect of this slate blue house is immaculate and authentic-feeling. Profuse flower gardens trim the home in brilliant color, and a charming gazebo is set bear a pond in the front yard. Tender loving care and attention to detail has made Rosewood what it is today.

Polished hardwood floors, Oriental carpets, and gorgeous antiques adorn the interior, and an elegantly appointed sitting room provides a place to relax and savor the view of the ocean and mountains. The main floor holds three guest rooms, but usually only two at a time are rented (the smallest room is designed for the extra person in a party of three). The Orchid Room is attractive, with a queen-size bed in a contemporary bedframe, pale lavender walls, down comforter, floral linens, and shared detached bath. The Sunset Room is the absolute best amorous option, with its soft window seat where you can watch the sun make its dramatic daily exit. A tub is cleverly tucked beneath the window seat so sunset baths are another option; there is also a sink in the room, but other facilities are located down the hall and shared with other guests. This opulent room also has a private entrance, a gas fireplace in a brick hearth, a queen-size brass bed, lace appointments, and exquisite decor. The owners eventually hope to install a private bath en suite, but until then the restroom is across the hall.

At breakfast time, champagne, orange juice, warm croissants, and home-baked muffins accompany the health-conscious, filling meal served in the sunny breakfast room. All of the jams and jellies are homemade. In fact, ask your attentive hostess about the various gourmet delights she creates; her pantry is full of goodies that would put Martha Stewart to shame.

Romantic Suggestion: Your multitalented hostess can also prepare a personalized romantic dinner for two on the picturesque balcony overlooking the gardens, pond, and gazebo. Arrangements must be made prior to your arrival; the price is approximately $95 for two. (Although this price does not include wine, you are welcome to bring your own bottle of wine or champagne if you would like to toast a special occasion.)

Restaurant Kissing

CHEZ PHILIPPE RESTAURANT, Gibsons
Gower Point Road, at Bonniebrook Lodge
(604) 886-2188
Moderate to Expensive
Call for seasonal hours.

What do you get when you combine a French restaurant, a Victorian inn, RV sites, and a tent campground? There is no punch line—the straight answer is Chez Philippe Restaurant at Bonniebrook Lodge. As strange as the combination may sound, all of these varying businesses operate on one property, offering something for every type of traveler. For those with romantic inclinations, however, we specifically recommend an evening at the restaurant.

Abundant flower gardens border the front patio of Chez Philippe, housed on the first floor of a large 1920s home. Quiet country elegance best describes the two dining rooms, each with delicate stencilwork lining the walls, rich mustard-colored linens, and little oil lanterns at every table. Picture windows face the ocean across the street, and a crackling fireplace enhances the already intimate ambience.

Call ahead and reserve a sunset window seat. Even if you arrive a little too early for sunset, you can always linger over your West Coast–influenced French meal. Pan-fried butterflied trout with baby shrimp and sautéed mushrooms, grilled scallops and prawns in saffron cream, and wild mushroom–stuffed chicken breast with port wine sauce are just a few of the items to choose from. If the sun hasn't set by the time you finish dinner, why not linger a bit over dessert? The profiteroles in warm chocolate sauce are a heavenly accompaniment to nature's heavenly show.

Romantic Note: Four country Victorian guest rooms above Chez Philippe comprise **BONNIEBROOK LODGE**, (604) 886-2887 (Inexpensive). Each room has a floral bedspread and striped wallpaper in varying color schemes. Only the Rose Room has a private bath; the other three share two detached baths (not exactly our idea of romantic, but we must say that the prices are quite reasonable). Unfortunately, it is two of the rooms with shared baths that have the best ocean views from the front of the house, although the Rose Room has partial water views beyond the small parking lot. A hearty breakfast, served in the lovely dining room, is included with the price of your stay. Be forewarned that, as with most establishments that rent guest rooms above a restaurant, noise from the dining room can be a problem (especially in the summer months, when Chez Philippe is extremely popular).

Roberts Creek

Hotel/Bed and Breakfast Kissing

THE COTTAGE ON DRIFTWOOD BEACH, Roberts Creek 💋💋❤
3807 Beach Avenue
(604) 885-3489
Inexpensive; No Credit Cards

Do you ever dream of having your own quiet little beach house? Well, even if it is yours for only a few nights, The Cottage on Driftwood Beach will make that dream come true. This modest cottage is set right at sea level; high tide is only 20 yards away. If you arrive on a cool, drizzly day, your congenial hostess will have piping hot soup and homemade bread ready for you—a greeting that is a good indication of the welcoming atmosphere you will encounter here.

The owners' home is right next door and a covered walkway connects the two contemporary buildings, but once you have settled in, you will find the cottage wonderfully private. A large stone fireplace, cedar interior, shelves full of books, and an eclectic mix of artwork and furnishings create a warm, homey interior. There is a full kitchen, two bedrooms, and one bathroom. Two couples could easily share facilities here, but for obvious reasons we think it is perfect for just one couple. One of the bedrooms has a window facing the ocean through tall trees, and the sound of waves lapping against the shore will lull you to sleep. Go ahead and leave the window open to let in the sound of the sea—flannel sheets will help keep you warm and cozy.

In the morning a full, hearty breakfast is delivered to the cottage. After a filling meal of hotcakes and bacon, stroll along the pebbly little stretch of beach just steps away. If you sit very still and wait long enough, you might even catch a glimpse of the eagle that regularly hunts from the ancient Douglas fir right in front of the cottage. Consider yourselves lucky; it isn't every day you find a quiet spot like this.

COUNTRY COTTAGE ❤❤❤
BED AND BREAKFAST, Roberts Creek
1183 Roberts Creek Road
(604) 885-7448
Inexpensive to Expensive; No Credit Cards
Minimum stay requirement on holidays

Country Cottage Bed and Breakfast is a perfectly cozy retreat. Hot tea, freshly baked scones, and a congenial innkeeper invite you to relax and enjoy genuine Canadian country hospitality. You'll realize that you have truly escaped the city after strolling through the gardens, stopping to visit the sheep, and watching the chickens busily move around the henhouse. This charming property is set on two acres; although much of the property is wooded, the innkeepers have created a sort of small farm around their centrally located farmhouse.

Only two units are available here, which helps create a personal experience. The Cottage, adjacent to the main farmhouse, virtually defines country charm. Colorful gardens and window boxes trim the exterior of this little cedar cabin, and touches like hand-loomed throw rugs on the hardwood floors, mixed antiques, a patchwork quilt covering the queen-size bed, and a little woodstove make you feel as if you're at Grandma's house.

Even more privately located at the back of the property is the beautifully rustic Cedar Lodge. Although it can comfortably accommodate up to three couples (which makes it a real bargain), the kissing potential is best when you have all of the wondrous space to yourselves. You'll feel like lighting a fire in the tremendous river-rock fireplace even on a warm day, just to give the knotty pine walls the proper luster. Hunter green and cranberry-colored Adirondack-style furnishings, fishing paraphernalia, and sleeping lofts with fine wool blankets and snuggly flannel sheets create an exceedingly cozy atmosphere that would fit right into an Eddie Bauer or L. L. Bean catalog. If you do happen to be traveling with another couple, you can all have privacy; a tiny cabin, complete with a skylight, private bath, and sauna, is separated from the lodge by a deck and provides additional sleeping quarters.

Both the Cedar Lodge and the Cottage have full kitchens, so you'll need to venture out only if you desire an outdoor excursion. A hearty farm-fresh breakfast, served at one table in the kitchen of the main house amid vintage country collectibles, is also included in your stay. A wood-burning cooking stove crackles in the background as your gracious hostess serves up such delectables as whole-grain Belgian waffles with whipped cream and fresh fruit or savory asparagus crêpes. Whatever the main course, you'll be more than adequately prepared for a full day of outdoor activity.

MARY'S GARDEN BED AND BREAKFAST, Roberts Creek 💋💋💋
1878 Lockyer Road
(604) 885-9270
Moderate

Tucked into the forest, this unique little cottage is a great place to spend quality time together (and, if your vacation time allows, a sizable quantity of time too). Handcrafted woodwork and charming details lend warm, rustic ambience to the interior. From the stained glass touches to the hand-peeled log bedframe to the alder twigs lining the vaulted ceiling, every aspect of this studio-style cottage has character.

> *Cost ratings for British Columbia listings are in Canadian funds. American travelers should check the exchange rate or ask an innkeeper to figure out the cost in U.S. dollars.*

A little woodstove in one corner of the room provides warmth on a cool evening, throw rugs cover the hardwood floors, a queen-size bed is adorned with a down comforter, and the bathroom features an antique claw-foot tub. Settle in, click on the stereo, and get cozy—it won't be difficult here. In case you want to stay in and continue the coziness through dinnertime, a small but functional kitchenette is ready for your use. In the morning, breakfast is delivered to your room. Pancakes with maple syrup and fresh fruit, turkey sausage, and homemade baked goods will give you a hearty start to an adventurous day spent exploring the Sunshine Coast.

WILLOWS INN, Roberts Creek
3440 Beach Avenue
(604) 885-2452
Inexpensive; No Credit Cards

Willows Inn consists of just one little log cabin and you are the only guests, so enjoy—it isn't often that you find seclusion like this. Colorful hanging plants and a well-tended yard separate the picturesque cabin from the owner's log home, enhancing the cabin's intimate potential.

Sparkling hardwood floors, scattered throw rugs, green floral fabrics, comfy rocking chairs, and a woodstove set against a brick hearth furnish a fresh and simple country interior. A fruit basket and chocolate-covered strawberries await you in the small kitchenette area, and fresh flowers are placed around the room. Wake to sunlight streaming through the skylights overhead, and savor the abundant country breakfast served directly to your cottage at whatever time you choose. One morning you may find gourmet omelets with freshly baked scones made for you; next morning's feast could include blueberry pancakes with fresh fruit and a selection of syrups. Once you've tasted the solitude and quiet splendor of this cozy retreat, located only a five-minute walk from the beach, you may not want to leave.

Romantic Alternative: A forested driveway leads to another cottage that you may want to consider: **PEBBLE COVE**, 3431 Beach Avenue, (604) 885-7930 (Inexpensive). Easy beach access and a view of Georgia Strait and the lights of Nanaimo beyond the rooftop of the owners' home make this a serene escape. A Mission-style bedframe and plush down comforter on the double bed is inviting, there is a small private bath with shower, and a full breakfast is delivered to your room (or it can be served on the owner's front deck, where the view is fabulous). The only thing that kept us from awarding lips to this petite country cottage was the slightly musty odor from years of salt air. Still, the price is right and the privacy is wonderful.

Restaurant Kissing

CREEKHOUSE RESTAURANT, Roberts Creek
1041 Roberts Creek Road
(604) 885-9321
Moderate to Expensive
Call for seasonal hours.

What a wonderful surprise to discover that fine dining exists in this unassuming country neighborhood. Windows along two walls of the modest dining room face lush greenery, while dark hardwood floors, potted plants, and high ceilings give the room a casual ambience. French cuisine with an emphasis on fresh local ingredients graces the menu, and the catch of the day is always excellent. Cannelloni stuffed with crab and spinach, then covered with creamy tomato sauce and Parmesan, is one option; or you may want to try the pan-fried salmon with lemon sauce—both dishes are exquisite. Such rich entrées may not leave you with room for dessert, but if you can force yourselves to be decadent, the chocolate mousse and fruit tarts are marvelous. Service is knowledgeable and friendly.

Outdoor Kissing

ROBERTS CREEK BEACH PARK, Roberts Creek

Driftwood benches line each side of this long, thin stretch of beach that juts into Georgia Strait. This is one of the best lookout points for viewing all of the marine wildlife of the Sunshine Coast. Diverse sea birds, bald eagles, seals, otters, and orcas are just a few of the creatures that enjoy the remote splendor of this coastline. You will surely join them in appreciation of this area's natural beauty and tranquility.

Sechelt

Restaurant Kissing

BLUE HERON INN, Sechelt
Porpoise Bay Road
(604) 885-3847, (800) 818-8977
Moderate to Expensive
Reservations Required
Call for seasonal hours.

Pull into the driveway and head down to the water's edge, where the Blue Heron Inn fills the lower level of a family home. This contemporary dining room is adorned with bright floral tablecloths, fresh flower arrangements, heron-inspired artwork, and luminous little lamps at every table. A wall of windows faces the glassy waters of Porpoise Bay, and almost every table shares the magnificent vista. The house specialty is seafood, and it is kept fresh in the cool waters of the bay, off the front dock, until it is prepared.

Try a wonderfully creative appetizer such as artichoke hearts filled and baked with shrimp, crab, and Parmesan cheese, or deep-fried Camembert cheese served with lingonberry sauce. As a main course, we recommend the gently smoked fillet of rich black Alaskan cod accompanied by warm hollandaise sauce, or the grilled salmon steak presented on a bed of sautéed fennel with a fresh thyme-and-garlic wine sauce. Unless you catch it yourself, seafood doesn't get much fresher than this.

Halfmoon Bay

Outdoor Kissing

SMUGGLER COVE

Signs clearly mark the trailhead to Smuggler Cove, in the town of Half-moon Bay.

Dozens of spectacular and isolated watery enclaves adorn the Sunshine Coast, and Smuggler Cove is one of the most easily accessible ones. After meandering a short distance through rain forest, you will be exposed to a wondrous view that is provocative in any weather. A sunny day reveals an entirely private inlet, etched from assorted rocks and jagged coastal formations. Sailboats add to the picturesque beauty as they quietly pass along the outer edge of the bay. In the overcast opaqueness of a fall or winter day, you may imagine an English seaside underneath the clouds. Why not bring along some scones and a thermos filled with tea to snack on while you enjoy this haven? If by chance you hear some sounds emanating from the water or islands, don't be surprised. You've probably just happened upon a group of sea lions or otters lounging in the afternoon sun or playing in the evening tides. (Anyone for amending the name to *Snuggler* Cove?)

Romantic Note: The walk to Smuggler Cove takes about 20 minutes each way. The trail is extremely well maintained by the B.C. parks department, but due to the marshes around parts of the trail, portions of the path are sometimes covered with water. This usually happens only in winter and early spring, but you should be prepared for at least some muddy spots if there have been heavy rains—a not so unlikely circumstance, even on the Sunshine Coast.

Earl's Cove

Outdoor Kissing

FERRY RIDE FROM EARL'S COVE TO SALTERY BAY

The ferry landing is at the northern tip of the Sunshine Coast.

If you don't have a chance to become acquainted with the Sunshine Coast via your own boat or a chartered excursion, then the ferry crossing from Earl's Cove to Saltery Bay is a must. An array of snowcapped mountains frames your tour through Jervis Inlet, where magnificent forested, rocky promontories jut into the water. The soaring peaks all around make you realize the sheer vastness of the area, and a view from the water affords an opportunity to truly understand what makes the Sunshine Coast so unique and special. Have your camera ready—fabulous photo opportunities lie around every corner, and you never know when (or what) marine life might join you in your trip across the bay.

Romantic Note: We suggest that you check the ferry schedule for departure information before making this winding trek up the coast. Sailings are fairly infrequent, particularly in the off-season, and once you're at the ferry terminal there isn't much to do (except wait). Be sure to call **SUNSHINE COAST SUPERLINE**, (604) 885-0852, in advance for the current sailing schedule.

Egmont

Outdoor Kissing

SKOOKUMCHUCK NARROWS, Egmont

The trailhead is located just off Highway 101, on the road to Egmont. Signs clearly indicate where to go.

The Canadian Southwest and the Pacific Northwest are filled with more than enough natural wonders to impress even the most experienced world traveler. Skookumchuck Narrows is one of the more intriguing phenomena.

Cost ratings for British Columbia listings are in Canadian funds. American travelers should check the exchange rate or ask an innkeeper to figure out the cost in U.S. dollars.

Enormous energy passes through this thin portal and is so moving (figuratively and literally) that the experience is nearly indescribable. The trail to the narrows has abundant foliage, the ground is often carpeted in autumn-colored leaves, and trees are wrapped in moss. (The ground can also be extremely wet and mucky when it has been raining, so you will need suitable footwear.) As you make your way out to the tip of the peninsula, you will approach Sechelt Inlet. You can stand almost at the edge of the rock-bordered gateway to this body of water. Through this tiny opening, at high and low tide, the rush of water is so intense that the land actually shakes beneath your feet. This is one time and place when, without even kissing or touching, you can really feel the earth move.

Romantic Note: Optimum viewing times are posted at the trailhead and in the local paper so you can be sure to witness Mother Nature's colossal show. You will need to allow about an hour to reach the narrows from the parking lot, and you may want to plan on arriving an hour before a high or low tide and staying for another hour after the tide changes. After the water violently rushes one way, the narrows flatten, but water rushes the opposite way soon thereafter. Moments like these are worth waiting for.

WASHINGTON

Olympic Peninsula

Taking the ferry from Seattle to Bainbridge Island is one of the more popular ways to begin a trip to the Olympic Peninsula. From Bainbridge Island, cross the Agate Pass Bridge, drive north up the Kitsap Peninsula, and then head over the Hood Canal Bridge. All these efforts bring you to the Olympic Peninsula, where the Northwest's largest national park and some of the state's most spectacular scenery await you.

Seabeck

Hotel/Bed and Breakfast Kissing

WALTON HOUSE, Seabeck
12340 Seabeck Highway Northwest
(360) 830-4498
Very Inexpensive
Closed weekdays

If staying on budget is a consideration, then the price is right at the Walton House. In fact, it's so right, you might find yourselves wondering why a night at this simple country retreat is *so* inexpensive. The answer: it just is.

Set just off the highway (which is not heavily trafficked), the turn-of-the-century farmhouse glories in uninterrupted views of Hood Canal. The bona fide country decor incorporates antiques and family heirlooms, but has been refreshingly executed so that none of the rooms seems the least bit cluttered. White wicker furniture, floral linens, and lovely water views lighten up the bright green (too green) color schemes in the house's two old-fashioned guest rooms. Guests have exclusive use of the comfortable downstairs parlor and an outside porch that overlooks a manicured lawn sloping down to the water's edge. Your stay includes a tasty full breakfast, served family-style in the charming and cheerful country kitchen.

WILLCOX HOUSE COUNTRY INN, Seabeck
2390 Tekiu Road
(360) 830-4492, (800) 725-9477
Moderate
Minimum stay requirement weekends and summers

We're in full agreement with those who think that the Willcox House is one of the premier places to kiss on the Kitsap Peninsula. What we found here exceeded our wildest imaginings. A drive through 14 miles of towering evergreens and rolling countryside brings you to the turnoff for the house, where the road takes a steep turn down to the water and passes under a dramatic log and stone archway. The enormous copper-roofed mansion with terra-cotta tiles is a magnificent sight, resting on a forested bluff with superb views of Hood Canal and the Olympic Mountains. Wisteria climbs the trellis in the backyard, where walking paths wind through palatial gardens, past a swinging hammock, a swimming pool, and a goldfish pond.

Restored at a cost of more than $300,000, the 10,000-square-foot interior is a masterpiece of Northwest architecture (although a bit on the eclectic side). This place has to be seen to be believed! There are almost as many common areas for guests as there are bedrooms. You can tinker with the grand piano in the wood-paneled guest parlor, amuse yourselves with darts in the large game room, or socialize with other guests over wine and cheese in the upstairs library that overlooks the water. All five guest rooms have been diligently renovated and feature gorgeous linens, copper-framed fireplaces, walnut paneling, and wood parquet floors. Some have views of the sweeping lawn and gardens, mountain peaks, and water; two have Jacuzzi tubs; and one has a private balcony.

Breakfast is a remarkable presentation of fresh fruits and waffles with homemade apple and blueberry syrups and butters, served in a glass-enclosed dining room with impressive views.

Romantic Suggestion: On weekends the innkeepers at Willcox House serve a formal four-course dinner that is available to guests as well as to the public. This is a meal you will thoroughly appreciate. Baked Brie with pineapple-mango chutney, a salad with 20 different greens and edible flowers, alder-smoked fresh salmon, and asparagus with kumquat butter are a few of the menu's savory delights.

Poulsbo

Poulsbo has much more to offer than is first apparent, and its distinctly romantic destinations, concealed in the countryside, are not to be missed. This tiny waterfront town is best known for the charming (admittedly touristy) Scandinavian motif of the coffee shops, restaurants, and storefronts. You'll almost certainly be drawn in by the tantalizing aroma of fresh pastries wafting out the door of the popular **SLUYS BAKERY**, 18924 Front Street, (360) 779-2798 (Inexpensive). Once you've selected your dessert (this is easier said than done), head for the boardwalk at **LIBERTY MARINA PARK**. The scenery here is sure to inspire a kiss or two.

Hotel/Bed and Breakfast Kissing

EDGEWATER BEACH BED AND BREAKFAST, Poulsbo
26818 Edgewater Boulevard
(360) 779-2525, (800) 641-0955
http://members.aol.com/edjh20be
Moderate to Expensive

Bald eagles, blue herons, otters, sea lions, pheasants, and songbirds frequent this location, which might be incentive enough to pack your bags and leave the city life behind. If it isn't, this should help: 3,000 square feet of this 4,800-square-foot renovated 1920s beach house are dedicated exclusively to guests, including comfortable sunlit common areas with views of Hood Canal and the ascending Olympic Mountains. Your privacy is further ensured by the fact that there are only three guest rooms here, so the meandering garden paths and the winding trail that leads down to the beach are likely to be yours and yours alone.

Gas fireplaces have been added to the two smaller guest rooms, which also have CD players, antique beds draped with down comforters and cut-lace duvets, private baths, and eclectic country furnishings. The most expensive room (yet still affordable) is the Olympic Suite; it includes similar amenities and is the real reason to come here. Oriental rugs grace sparkling hardwood floors in this airy suite, accented with a hand-thrown pottery sink, a five-headed shower (no kidding), and a cheery sitting area that enjoys views of Hood Canal and the Olympic Mountains.

MANOR FARM INN, Poulsbo
26069 Big Valley Road Northeast
(360) 779-4628
Expensive to Very Expensive
Call for seasonal closures.
Recommended Wedding Site

A country outing can revive city-tired spirits to renewed ardor and ease, and the drive to Manor Farm Inn, through miles of idyllic landscape, is a perfect beginning. Once you arrive, the inn deftly provides the rest of your amorous needs.

Encircled by a white rail fence and friendly farm animals, the French farmhouse blends inconspicuously into the inn's 25 acres of pastoral scenery. Seven cozy rooms and an intimate loft hideaway adorned with simple French country furnishings front a long, open veranda. A fire crackles in the hearth of both the Pig and Sheep rooms, giving them a decisive romantic glow. Although they lack fireplaces, the Carriage and Loft Rooms are our favorites because they survey lovely views of the farm's rolling pastures.

Mornings begin with a friendly knock and a wake-up call of "Scones!"— meaning that hot scones, homemade raspberry jam, and fresh orange juice are waiting just outside your door. Don't forget to save room for a hearty, all-American, three-course breakfast consisting of hot porridge, eggs, bacon, sausage, red potatoes, and sautéed mushrooms. This repast is served in the lovely, countrified **MANOR FARM INN RESTAURANT** (see Restaurant Kissing).

MURPHY HOUSE BED AND BREAKFAST, Poulsbo
425 Northeast Hostmark Street
(360) 779-1600, (800) 779-1606
Moderate

Murphy House is a great getaway for those who don't want to get too far away from it all. Conveniently perched on a residential hillside in the heart of town, this relatively new inn overlooks views of neighboring houses, Liberty Bay, and the Olympic Mountains. The seven guest rooms here are all embellished with a homey mixture of modern and country furnishings. Five have private, albeit standard, bathrooms, and several rooms have small private patios with views. Couples with kissing on their agenda should request either of the two largest rooms in the house; both feature king-size beds, lovely linens, and distant water views. An affectionate bonus: the comfortable common areas offer ample space to snuggle in. In fact, we actually preferred the cozy library, brimming with books and games, to some of the bedrooms. Guests also have access to a handy kitchenette, TV/VCR, and a large selection of movies.

A full breakfast is served in a spacious common area that is warmed by a fireplace and replete with water views.

Restaurant Kissing

JUDITH'S TEA ROOM, Poulsbo
18820 Front Street
(360) 697-3449
Inexpensive to Moderate
Lunch and Afternoon Tea Monday-Sunday

In the mood to share a confection at a cozy table for two? Judith's Tea Room will suit you to a tee. The small country-style dining rooms here provide a charming setting in which to enjoy decadent desserts served daintily on hand-painted china. If you're willing to ignore the adjacent busy street, opt for one of the two-person tables set outdoors on a lovely brick patio enclosed by brass gates.

MANOR FARM INN RESTAURANT, Poulsbo
26069 Big Valley Road Northeast
(360) 779-4628
Very Expensive
Breakfast Daily; Sunday Brunch May-October

Considered by many to be *the* place to eat on the Kitsap Peninsula, the Manor Farm Inn's restaurant is open to the public for breakfast and Sunday brunch only. We recommend arriving early so you can enjoy a cup of hot tea or coffee and take a stroll through the farm pastures to visit the amiable animals. A bell rings when breakfast is ready, and guests are ushered into one of two stark but elegant country-style dining rooms appointed with white linens and fresh flowers. Hot scones, fresh fruit juice, and homemade raspberry jam are followed by fresh seasonal fruit, hot creamy porridge with nuts, baked egg dishes, sautéed vegetables, crêpes with apples, and pancakes, among other wonderful creations.

Quilcene

Outdoor Kissing

OLYMPIC MUSIC FESTIVAL, Quilcene
(206) 527-8839
Ticket prices start at $9
Open weekends from mid-June through early September

From the Hood Canal Bridge, travel west ten miles on the main road (Route 104). Exit at the "OLYMPIC MUSIC FESTIVAL" sign and turn right onto Center Road. The festival entrance is one-half mile ahead. Parking is free.

A rustic turn-of-the-century barn is the setting for the Olympic Music Festival, where members of the highly acclaimed Philadelphia String Quartet perform brilliant chamber music every summer. Hay bales and padded church pews provide seating in the barn, or you may sit outside on the lawn and picnic while classical music fills the air. Come early, before the 2 P.M. performance, and explore the festival grounds. Country paths cover the 40-acre farm, which is home to donkeys, cows, pigs, and goats. Although the rural setting may sound like an unlikely accompaniment for sonatas of

Brahms and Mendelssohn, the experience is thoroughly exquisite. There really is no other festival like this in the Northwest, and it is entirely worth the trip.

Romantic Note: Children under six are not allowed in the barn, but they are admitted on the lawn at no charge. To ensure that you will be able to enjoy the music without the sounds of children scurrying about, the added expenditure for seats in the barn is worth it—and you can still picnic on the lawn before the performance if you'd like.

Port Ludlow

Not yet cultivated by acquisitive developers, Port Ludlow is a sprawling little community that still feels close to nature and is highlighted by awesome views of Puget Sound and the Cascades. Construction of new homes along the water is increasing, but the surrounding area is extremely pleasant, and is a good central location from which to tour the rest of the Olympic Peninsula.

Hotel/Bed and Breakfast Kissing

INN AT LUDLOW BAY, Port Ludlow
1 Heron Road
(360) 437-0411
Very Expensive to Unbelievably Expensive
Dinner Wednesday-Sunday

Perched at the mouth of Port Ludlow Bay, this stately inn resembles a New England estate with clapboard siding, cedar shingles, and a wraparound porch. All of the amenities necessary for a romantic interlude are at your fingertips here: fine dining and creative Northwest cuisine can be found in the relaxed yet sophisticated restaurant on the main floor and there are 37 comfortable, refined guest rooms. Each room has a gas log fireplace, Jacuzzi tub, cozy bathrobes, and a plush down comforter. Mission-style furnishings, wood shutters, minimalist decor, and black and white accents create an elegantly simple ambience. Many rooms also offer vaulted ceilings, king-size beds, and unobstructed water or mountain views. In the morning, an ample continental breakfast is presented in the pleasant, cheerful sunroom.

Romantic Note: The gracious comfort level found here comes as no surprise, considering that the management company that created this relatively new inn specializes in exclusive retreats. One of the inn's sister properties is the highly acclaimed, incredibly romantic **INN AT LANGLEY** on Whidbey Island (see Hotel/Bed and Breakfast Kissing in the Puget Sound chapter).

While the professionalism and decor found at both properties is comparable, we must state that the Port Ludlow setting does not quite compare to the Inn At Langley's. Townhomes closely border one side of the Inn At Ludlow Bay and the grounds have not yet matured to a profuse state. Also, if you are planning to explore the Peninsula, you should know that it is about a 30-minute drive to Port Townsend from here and approximately an hour-long drive to Port Angeles (where the Olympic National Park's boundary begins).

THE NANTUCKET MANOR, Port Ludlow
941 Shine Road
(360) 437-2676
Expensive to Very Expensive
Recommended Wedding Site

The appropriately named Nantucket Manor, with its weathered cedar exterior and stately architecture, looks as if it belongs on a New England seashore. Luckily for Northwesterners, it is located just west of the Hood Canal Bridge. Gorgeous landscaping, a charming gazebo, and abundant gardens grace the yard, and white wicker chairs are set on the front patio, where you can sit and gaze out at the Olympic Mountain range, Mount Rainier, and the waters of Hood Canal.

Upstairs, this same view can be appreciated from three of the five guest rooms. Nantucket is a bright room with dainty rose wallpaper, a king-size four-poster bed, white linens, wicker furnishings, and French doors that open to the expansive front balcony. Pretty antiques and a canopied queen-size bed in the Manor Room are quite inviting, and sage green wallpaper and whitewashed furnishings in the Seaview Room are wonderfully soothing. Both the Manor and Seaview Rooms also have French doors leading to their balconies, and every room has a plush down comforter. To help compensate for the lack of water views, the two remaining rooms, which overlook the gardens, have larger bathrooms with soaking tubs.

A spa tub off to one side of the house is open to all guests, or you may want to warm yourselves in the main-floor parlor, beside a glowing wood-burning fireplace. In the morning, before you set out to explore the area, full breakfasts are served to one large table adjacent to the parlor.

Port Townsend

Port Townsend, a small town at the extreme northeast corner of the Olympic Peninsula, was originally settled in the 1800s. Authentic and lovingly restored period architecture is this town's trademark. Its beautifully cared for, gingerbread-trimmed Victorian homes perch on a bluff overlooking the waterfront, and the nearby parks, boutiques, antique shops, and restaurants project an aura of charm and tranquility. A favorite weekend getaway for Seattleites escaping hectic urban life, Port Townsend is cozy and relatively slow-paced all year long. A walk around the waterfront district and the bluffs above it will give you outstanding views of the Olympic Mountains, Admiralty Inlet, and island-dotted Puget Sound.

Romantic Note: Over the years, Port Townsend has earned a reputation for being the hub of cultural activity on the Olympic Peninsula, with diverse events scheduled from spring through fall. A management company called **CENTRUM**, (360) 385-3102, (800) 733-3608, handles many activities in Port Townsend and the surrounding area, such as the Port Townsend Blues Festival, the Festival of American Fiddle Tunes, Jazz Port Townsend, and the Theater Festival. The Wooden Boat Festival in early September has gained international attention and offers tours and boat races. In nearby Quilcene, the **OLYMPIC MUSIC FESTIVAL**, (360) 527-8839, is another favorite summertime event (see Outdoor Kissing in Quilcene). For general information about local events, you may also contact the **PORT TOWNSEND CHAMBER OF COMMERCE**, 2722 Sims Way, Port Townsend, WA 98368, (360) 385-2722, or drop by on your way into town.

Hotel/Bed and Breakfast Kissing

ANN STARRETT MANSION, Port Townsend
744 Clay Street
(360) 385-3205, (800) 321-0644
Inexpensive to Very Expensive
Minimum stay requirement during festivals

Port Townsend's luxurious past has been beautifully and authentically restored in this ornate 1889 Victorian. Settled on a quiet residential corner, the Ann Starrett Mansion is a sight to behold. A Gothic octagonal tower is the focal point of the mansion, and rich red-and-green-gabled detailing adorns the exterior. The outstanding architectural elements continue inside. Just off the foyer, a free-hung, three-tiered circular staircase spirals up the tower. Be sure to look up at the eight-sided dome ceiling, where beautiful frescoes depict the four seasons and the four cardinal virtues (which are justice, prudence, fortitude, and temperance, if you were wondering).

Classic Victorian elegance throughout the mansion embraces you in stunning splendor. All of the nine mansion guest rooms are plush yet comfortable, with rich color schemes, original period furnishings, antique brass and canopied beds, and lace curtains. Honeymooners have been known to disappear for entire weekends in the Gable Suite, located at the top of the tower. This room is especially grand and private, with a king-size bed, sky-lights, views of the water, and a two-person soaking tub. Downstairs, the carriage house–level rooms are a real romantic bargain if you don't mind a detached bath in some and the lack of a water view. These rooms are still extremely pleasant and cozy, with exposed brick walls, snuggly floral down comforters, and a burbling fountain in the garden just outside. The other rooms also have private baths, some with antique claw-foot tubs.

Right next door is an additional building, the Starrett Cottage, which holds two more rooms. Although they are not quite as grand as the neighboring mansion rooms, both two-room suites offer the ultimate in privacy and spaciousness. The Upper Cottage unit, on the second floor, is boldly decorated in flamboyant, sumptuous Victorian style, with red walls, chandeliers, a gas fireplace, and a Jacuzzi tub for two; the Lower Cottage suite has a more subtle color scheme, a river-rock gas fireplace, and antique oak furnishings. It won't be easy to leave your room, but the award-winning full gourmet breakfast, served in the elegant dining room of the main house, really is worth getting up for.

Romantic Note: One of the main reasons people come to Port Townsend is to appreciate the architecture, and no such tour is complete without a stop at the Ann Starrett Mansion. Be aware that the mansion is open for self-guided tours before guests are able to check in. If you are staying for more than one night, the inn can feel like a museum filled with passing visitors for a few hours during the day. Most likely, though, you will be out touring Port Townsend and the Olympic Peninsula by day, and by the time you return, the tourists will have cleared out and you can delight in the private opulence of this magnificent Victorian as if it were your own.

CHANTICLEER INN
BED AND BREAKFAST, Port Townsend
1208 Franklin Street
(360) 385-6239, (800) 858-9421
http://www.olympus.net/biz/chanticleer/chanticleer.html
Inexpensive to Expensive

Chanticleer Inn is elegant but not imposing. Every detail of this 1876 Victorian cottage radiates luxury and comfort. Pale hardwood floors, cream-colored furnishings, and fine antiques grace the sunny main-floor parlor, and neatly pressed linens, down comforters, feather beds, antique accents, and private baths are found in every room. Three of the main house's four guest rooms lie upstairs; two are quite snug, but one has a Jacuzzi tub and the other has a stunning, intricate antique bed set. Countess is the largest upstairs unit, and it has a king-size bed, pink and mauve accents, lace curtains, and, best of all, a private balcony with a sweeping mountain and water view. Breakfast can be delivered here and enjoyed privately while you savor the landscape of the Olympics, the Cascades, Mount Rainier, Admiralty Inlet, and Puget Sound.

On the main floor, the opulent, creamy white Duchess Room has a crystal chandelier and bed with an antique lace half-canopy. French doors connect this room to the dining room and adjacent parlor so you can enjoy the common areas as if they were your own in the evenings; in the morning, though, if sleeping in past breakfast is your plan, you will be out of luck. However, why would you want to pass up a breakfast like this? A multicourse gourmet extravaganza is served on fine china and sterling silver and accompanied by live harp music every morning.

Romantic Note: An apartment in the adjacent guest house is best suited for families, and the decor is much more casual. If you are spending more than a few nights and want the option of cooking your own meals, though, there is a lot of space for a couple to really move in and be comfortable here. Just don't expect the same level of luxury found in the main house.

HOLLY HILL HOUSE, Port Townsend
611 Polk Street
(360) 385-5619, (800) 435-1454 (outside Washington state)
http://www.acies.com/hollyhill
Inexpensive to Expensive
Minimum stay requirement on weekends

The enthusiastic innkeepers of the Holly Hill House have been wallpapering and painting, scrubbing and polishing, decorating and redecorating, and busily gardening to create a lovely Victorian atmosphere at their bed and breakfast. Their efforts have paid off, and don't worry—they will still have enough energy left to take good care of you.

Elegant antiques fill the main-floor parlor, and a fireplace warms the room. Upstairs, three guest rooms are dressed in handsome Victorian appointments. The spacious Colonel's Room, with its striped navy blue wallpaper, custom-built headboard, and deep soaking tub, overlooks Admiralty Inlet and the Cascades in the distance. Billie's Room also features a water and mountain view and has a pretty blue floral duvet, brass lamps, and a shower in the private bath. Behind the main house, two more guest rooms are located in the Carriage House. Skyview is a favorite because the large skylight above the bed allows stars and moonlight to flow in, but Morning Glory is also a cozy option. Both Carriage House rooms open to the back patio, where flower-pots and wonderful gardens abound, and tea or lemonade and goodies are served each afternoon. Be sure to take a look at the Camperdown elm off to one side of the yard. This unique tree actually grows upside down (you will have to see it for yourselves) and produces enough lush foliage to create a private little alcove perfect for shady summer kissing.

In the morning, a bountiful breakfast is served family-style at two tables in the sun-filled dining room, or out on the back patio on warmer days. Along with your meal of home-baked muffins, fresh fruit, and a hot dish such as egg-and-cheese soufflé with mild chiles and olives, your hostess presents a detailed history of the 1872 home.

JAMES HOUSE BED AND BREAKFAST, Port Townsend
1238 Washington Street
(360) 385-1238, (800) 385-1238
http://www.jameshouse.com
Moderate to Expensive

This striking Queen Anne Victorian—lovingly filled with recovered and refinished period pieces, intricate handcrafted wood moldings, and capacious, unique rooms—is as Victorian as they get in Port Townsend, and that's saying a lot. Of the 12 guest rooms scattered along a labyrinth of hallways, ten have private baths and all are brightened by fresh flower arrangements. The elegant Bridal Suite, with its massive antique furnishings and crisp white linens, is by far the most grand room. It features unsurpassed water and mountain views through bay windows as well as subtle lighting, a wood-burning fireplace, and complimentary champagne delivered at your request. Both the Bay and Chintz Rooms also have fabulous views of Admiralty Inlet and Whidbey Island across the water. Since the James House is set right on the bluff overlooking town, the view really is stunning and totally unobstructed. The Gardener's Cottage, set right behind the main house, is another nice romantic option because of its private entrance and quaint patio that looks out to the verdant lawn, the well-tended gardens, and the water in the distance.

No matter which room you choose, there are plenty of cozy alcoves designed for snuggling. Freshly baked cookies in the afternoon and complimentary sherry are nice extras, but the real treat is the full sit-down breakfast. This morning repast may include fresh scones, a baked pear dressed with a walnut-fruit filling, and a tasty egg-filled croissant dish.

Romantic Option: Right next door, a modest brick house holds another extremely romantic lodging option: **A BUNGALOW ON THE BLUFF** (Very Expensive). This private little unit is managed by the James House, but the style, decor, and setup are dramatically different. It is run more like a self-sufficient vacation rental than a bed and breakfast, and a generous continental breakfast is left for you in the small fridge. Reminiscent of a 1950s bungalow, the room has black and tan furnishings, a wood-burning fireplace, and a picture window overlooking the port and town below. In the spacious slate-tiled bathroom, a corner Jacuzzi tub for two is set beneath a skylight. Kissing here is inevitable.

LIZZIE'S, Port Townsend   💋💋💋
731 Pierce Street
(360) 385-4168, (800) 700-4168
http://www.kolke.com/lizzies
Inexpensive to Expensive
Minimum stay requirement on holidays

With the large number of quality Victorian bed and breakfasts in Port Townsend, it is difficult to specify exactly which ones will suit your romantic taste. Lizzie's is a lovely option and will surely meet all of your needs. Of the seven units, each has a fluffy down comforter and private bath. The bed and breakfast's namesake room is the most regal, with a high ceiling, dark green floral wallpaper, a half-canopied queen-size bed, a claw-foot tub, a wood-burning fireplace, and a cozy sitting area beside a bay window. Sarah's Room has the best view, from a bay-window seat overlooking the water and mountains, and there is a claw-foot tub in the bathroom. Daisy's Room is beautifully opulent, with cream-colored wallpaper, a stylish king-size art nouveau bed, and a view of the sunrise over the bay.

Your friendly hostess serves a generous full breakfast every morning at a huge oak table in the country kitchen, or on the patio when the weather allows.

OLD CONSULATE INN, Port Townsend
313 Walker Street
(360) 385-6753, (800) 300-6753
http://www.oldconsulateinn.com
Inexpensive to Very Expensive
Minimum stay requirement on weekends

If you're smitten with the idea of pampering yourselves in an atmosphere of days gone by, with the modern addition of pleasing creature comforts, then the Old Consulate Inn is exactly right for you. This venerable red Victorian inn has a music room with an antique organ and grand piano, a fireplace-warmed study, a reading nook in the front parlor, and a billiards and game room in the basement. You won't want to miss the handsome wood-framed breakfast area where tea (or lemonade on sunny days) and cookies are served in the afternoon and an assortment of liqueurs and luscious desserts await in the evening. Elegant period antiques abound, and the parlor is filled with collectible dolls and porcelain unicorns.

At the top of the grand oak staircase you'll find eight spacious private rooms, each with its own bath. There are sitting alcoves, turret lookouts, canopied king-size beds, and expansive views of the waterfront. The Master Anniversary Suite, with its antique wood-burning fireplace and four-poster canopied bed, and the lacy Tower Honeymoon Suite, with water views from the pillow and a claw-foot tub in the bedchamber, are especially alluring (and considerably more expensive). Still, each room is such a wonderful retreat that you'll want to leave only for a soak in the outdoor hot tub, which is set in a gazebo overlooking the bay—and for breakfast, of course.

The morning meal, served banquet-style, is a gastronomic fantasy come true. The inn proudly presents its own blend of designer coffee along with seven courses: fresh fruits, liqueur cakes, pastries, gourmet egg dishes, and homemade granolas, to name a few. Savor the relaxed luxury of the Victorian era while you are here—you will return to the real world soon enough.

QUIMPER INN, Port Townsend
1306 Franklin Street
(360) 385-1060, (800) 557-1060
http://www.olympus.net/biz/quimper/quimper.html
Inexpensive to Expensive

The five guest rooms at this grand Georgian-style home are handsomely adorned in unfrilly Victorian style, and three have private baths. Michelle's Room has a brass queen-size bed surrounded by bay windows that face Admiralty Inlet and the Cascades, and a huge bathroom with a six-foot claw-foot tub and pedestal sink. Harry & Gertie's Suite also has attractive antique furnishings and wonderful bay windows facing the water and mountains, but is more spacious, with two rooms separated by pocket doors. The cozy Library Room on the main floor has shelf upon shelf of books lining the walls. If sharing a bath doesn't bother you, Christopher's and John's Rooms have their benefits and are quite a bargain. An outside deck on the second level is lined with colorful flower boxes and provides a common area where everyone can indulge in the view. Breakfast is a bountiful feast, served family-style in the formal dining room.

RAVENSCROFT INN, Port Townsend
533 Quincy Street
(360) 385-2784, (800) 782-2691

Inexpensive to Very Expensive
Minimum stay requirement on weekends and holidays

Sometimes the best way to judge the overall quality of a hotel, inn, or bed and breakfast is to look at the least expensive rooms in the house. If these units are nearly as splendid and comfortable as the more expensive ones, then you are assured of a sensational stay with innkeepers and a staff that really care about their guests. Such is the case at Ravenscroft Inn.

All eight guest rooms in this stately redwood inn are supreme. Many of the lovely suites have French doors that open onto a balcony with views of the bay and mountains; some have spacious sitting areas, canopied beds, and brick fireplaces; and every room has an immaculate, attractive bath, plush down comforters, unlimited privacy, and room to spare. The previously mentioned, least expensive accommodations that instantly won our hearts and kisses of approval are the three secluded garden-level rooms with ex-posed brick walls, floral linens, and smaller windows that view greenery rather than the water. One room also has a fireplace; all of them offer a cozy and affordable option for budgeting lovers.

The top-of-the-line Admiralty Suite is a wonderful romantic splurge. Decorated in whimsical blue and yellow, this exclusive unit has a wood-burning fireplace, a soaking tub, and a fabulous six-foot window seat over-looking the water and distant mountains. The Mt. Rainier Suite shares this incredible view and has a soaking tub for two, while the Fireside Room has a canopied queen-size bed, a wood-burning fireplace, and French doors leading to the expansive second-story veranda.

An imaginatively decorated dining area borders the inn's open kitchen. A brick fireplace warms the cheerful room as your breakfast is served, and a baby grand piano is set off to one side. Your host is a professional pianist, so live music accompanies such creations as a frappé made of frozen berries, bananas, and yogurt; a layered egg dish with tomatoes, onions, and spinach; Cointreau-drenched French toast; and fresh breads. Sheer perfection! The only difficulty you may encounter here is forcing yourselves to leave the splendor when the time comes.

Restaurant Kissing

BELMONT RESTAURANT, Port Townsend
925 Water Street
(360) 385-3007
Inexpensive to Moderate
Lunch and Dinner Daily

The exposed brick-and-wood interior, lofty ceilings, and unhindered water views at the Belmont Restaurant will lure you to stay for lunch or dinner, despite the rather standard menu (burgers and fries, and pasta and seafood dishes that are fine but certainly not the best in the area). The wood booths nestled near the entrance offer the most privacy, but you'll want to request window or outdoor seating to partake in the heavenly waterfront views. If gourmet dining isn't your top priority, the friendly service, reasonable prices, and magnificent view will assure you that you've made the right romantic choice.

BLACKBERRIES, Port Townsend
200 Battery Way, in Fort Worden State Park
(360) 385-9950
Moderate to Expensive
Dinner Wednesday–Saturday; Sunday Brunch

Blackberries isn't like any other state park concession you've ever seen— what a wonderful surprise! Decorated with willow branches arranged halfway up the walls and trimmed with stencils of blackbirds nibbling on the fruits of blackberry vines, this interesting dining room is also adorned with historic local photographs. The attractive decor was inspired by the casual style of the kind of resorts popular a century ago, when Fort Worden was constructed. Innovative Northwest cuisine featuring local ingredients is the focus at Blackberries, and you will not be disappointed. The delicate halibut-and-salmon braid with tangy salal-berry sauce is absolutely grand; and the whiskey-pepper steak, coated with cracked peppercorns and flamed with Jack Daniels, is thoroughly satisfying. Try the blackberry-orange Charlotte for dessert—a rich concoction of ladyfingers and blackberry-orange custard. Yum!

Romantic Suggestion: Before or after dinner, you might want to explore the bunkers and beachfront that are part of historic **FORT WORDEN STATE PARK**. Richard Gere and Debra Winger found plenty of places to kiss while filming *An Officer and a Gentleman* here, and you can too.

Romantic Alternative: Blackberries has opened a second location in the heart of town. **BLACKBERRIES**, 1002 Water Street, (360) 379-1200, in the Palace Hotel, serves breakfast, lunch, and dinner daily. Although the constant flow of traffic (both on foot and in car) outside the windows is somewhat distracting, the Victorian ambience is quite pleasant for a casual lunch.

THE FOUNTAIN CAFE, Port Townsend
920 Washington Street
(360) 385-1364
Inexpensive to Moderate
Lunch and Dinner Wednesday-Monday

If we awarded stars or chef's hats, the Fountain's consistently excellent food and pleasant service would easily earn the highest rating. To earn an equally high lip rating, though, other criteria must be met. Although we'd be the first to admit that we oohed and aahed with pleasure during our meal, when reviewing a restaurant we can't rely on fine food alone—atmosphere counts too.

The super-casual Fountain Cafe's dimly lit, tiny dining room is usually packed with people. Unique green walls, colorful, funky tablecloths, and little bouquets and candles at each of the closely arranged tables impart a familiar Northwest coffeehouse feel. What makes the Fountain so much better than the typical coffeehouse are the creative, delectable dishes cooked up by the talented folks in the kitchen. You can't go wrong when ordering seafood here—it is always fresh. You might want to start with shellfish steamed in wine, garlic, and ginger, and then move on to the locally smoked salmon topped with a cream sauce and a hint of Scotch, garnished with caviar, and served with fettuccine. Dessert choices are just as interesting and delicious (warm homemade gingerbread cake on a bed of custard, in particular), so try to save room!

LONNY'S, Port Townsend
2330 Washington Street
(360) 385-0700
Moderate to Expensive
Dinner Wednesday-Monday

Step into another world at Lonny's—a world of relaxed elegance and old-world Mediterranean ambience. Tawny-colored stucco walls, dimmed track lighting, and cozy booths help set the mood for a memorable evening. This relatively new restaurant is the talk of the town, and for good reason. Not only is the ocher interior warm and welcoming, the food is outstanding. The scent of roasted Italian specialties wafts across the dining room from the copper-accented open kitchen. Fresh organic produce, free-range chicken, and local seafood highlight the menu, and the service matches the flawless meal.

MANRESA CASTLE RESTAURANT
AND LOUNGE, Port Townsend
Seventh and Sheridan Streets
(360) 385-5750, (800) 732-1281 (in Washington state)
http://www.olympus.net/manresa
Moderate to Expensive
Dinner Daily; Breakfast Sunday

Manresa Castle is one of Port Townsend's most recognizable landmarks. Proudly perched on a hill overlooking town, this impressive building was built in 1892 to resemble a Prussian castle. From the 1920s until the 1960s, Jesuit priests used the castle as a training college, but since 1968, it has been operated as a guest inn. Except for a couple of rooms, the castle does not really offer the best romantic accommodations in town, but there is much to be said for the restaurant and lounge.

The stately cocktail lounge is a most irresistible setting for a romantic interlude, and next to it is an unpretentious dining room where tall lace-covered windows, soft lighting, and handsome wood furniture create an intimate, inviting, country-Victorian atmosphere. Dishes from the innovative menu are wonderful. Try the chicken breast Manresa, stuffed with feta cheese, kalamata olives, and artichokes and then dipped in egg batter and baked. Dungeness crab cakes with herbs and spices are another delicious option. Service is attentive and prompt—what more could you ask for (besides dessert)?

Romantic Note: Several years ago, Manresa Castle (Inexpensive to Very Expensive) underwent renovations that were supposed to return this esteemed structure to its former brilliance and glory. Except for some new bedspreads, televisions, and Queen Anne–style dressers, though, most of the 40 Victorian-style rooms still need sprucing up. A little more attention has been paid to the turret suites, which you may want to consider. Self-guided tours of the castle are encouraged. The history is fascinating, the architecture is lovely, and depending on the time of day and occupancy, you can judge the guest rooms for yourselves.

SILVERWATER CAFE, Port Townsend
237 Taylor Street
(360) 385-6448
Inexpensive to Moderate
Lunch and Dinner Daily

Please do not misunderstand the relatively low lip rating: it has nothing to do with the quality of food or service here, which is actually quite good. However, the casual coffee-shop ambience does not exactly tug at the heartstrings. Still, our lunch was so tasty that we must at least mention this little cafe.

Local artwork and brick walls lend character to the room, and a high ceiling, numerous hanging plants, hardwood floors, and unadorned wood tables create a casual ambience. There is a good variety of dishes to choose from—the homemade hummus and tabbouleh plate, served with fresh, soft pita bread, is perfect for a light lunch—and the seafood is consistently fresh and fabulous. An especially inventive and wonderful dish is Oysters Bleu: fresh oysters, bacon, and spinach in a light blue-cheese sauce, presented on fresh black-pepper linguine.

Outdoor Kissing

CHETZEMOKA PARK, Port Townsend

As you head into Port Townsend on Highway 20, turn left at Kearney Street and travel approximately 500 yards to Lawrence Street, then turn right. Lawrence Street goes through Port Townsend's upper business and residential district, then curves to the left (where it becomes Jackson Street); the park is a few blocks farther, on the right.

There are parks and then there are parks, but there is only one Chetzemoka. This ocean-flanked patch of land makes picnicking a treasured outing for two people, particularly a couple looking for surroundings that enhance the aesthetic appeal of bread, cheese, fruit, and wine. Here you can wander through scattered pinery along a cliff with an eagle's-eye view of Admiralty Inlet and Whidbey Island. Thick grass, swings, a footbridge spanning a babbling brook, and a few well-spaced picnic tables make this traditional, picturesque park a standout. Whether your penchant is for a playful or a peaceful diversion, you will be pleased by Chetzemoka Park.

Port Angeles

Port Angeles is more a stopover than a destination. Most of the people who come here aren't looking for a special place to stay, but are only passing through on their way to Victoria or the Olympic National Park. For this reason, budget motels and hotels have sprouted up along the main drag through town like pesky weeds. Thick traffic clogs the roads, and "NO VACANCY" signs continually glow in the summertime air. Only a few inn-keepers have capitalized on the romantic potential Port Angeles has to offer.

Hotel/Bed and Breakfast Kissing

DOMAINE MADELEINE, Port Angeles
146 Wildflower Lane
(360) 457-4174
http://www.northolympic.com/dm
Expensive to Very Expensive
Minimum stay requirement on weekends seasonally
Recommended Wedding Site

Luxurious accommodations are not easy to come by in this neck of the woods, but Domaine Madeleine goes above and beyond the romantic call of duty when it comes to comfort and elegance. Nestled behind tall Douglas firs, this contemporary home perched on a bluff above the Strait of Juan de Fuca offers incredible water and mountain views. The grounds are covered with rhododendrons, flowering perennials, maples, cedars, pines, and an intriguing replica of Monet's garden specially designed by the resident botanist/innkeeper.

Expansive windows throughout the main house allow you to enjoy the captivating view. Hardwood floors, high ceilings, and an impressive basalt fireplace in the living room give the inn a comfortable Northwest feel, while Asian and European antiques add international flair. All four sumptuous guest suites, as well as the newly built private little cottage, come with fresh flowers, a fruit basket, chocolates, and an array of French perfumes. The Ming Suite, which occupies the entire upper floor, includes a free-standing fireplace, a king-size bed, and a 30-foot balcony from which you can watch the sun both rise and set. The Monet Room is decorated in Impressionist style, with pastel tones and windows that face the garden, while the sunny cottage feels entirely private since it is detached from the main house. Remote-controlled gas fireplaces, Jacuzzi tubs or showers for two, scented candles, and magnificent views make each sensuous room an extraordinary lovers' retreat.

If the smell of fresh French bread and remarkable French cuisine weren't so tempting every morning, it would be nearly impossible to get out of bed. But force yourselves and follow your noses! You don't want to miss seafood omelets, crêpes Suzette flamed in cognac and Grand Marnier, or Vesuvial bananas with rum sauce. This four- or five-course extravaganza is served to one large table in the dining room of the main house. The enthusiastic inn-keepers are eager to please and will make you feel right at home—only much more pampered.

TUDOR INN, Port Angeles
1108 South Oak Street
(360) 452-3138
Inexpensive to Moderate
Minimum stay requirement on weekends seasonally

The Tudor Inn provides a good place to rest your weary, travel-tired bodies after a day of hiking in Olympic National Park or touring nearby Victoria. The friendly hosts lived in Europe for ten years and have re-created a bit of European comfort in this historic Tudor home set in a residential neighborhood. Of particular romantic interest is the Country Room with its cathedral ceiling, pastoral mural covering the walls, fireplace, and French doors that open to a private balcony from which you can see the Olympics in the distance. The Tudor Room, appointed with peach walls, dark wood-work, and a four-poster bed with a down comforter and an antique lace bedspread, is another amorous option. The remaining three rooms are on the snug side, but each has a private bath, and the rates are quite affordable.

The lovely main floor, graced by intricate European antiques, provides several comfortable places to relax; we especially liked the living room, with its grand piano, warming fireplace, and plush red velvet couch. A bountiful three-course breakfast is served family-style every morning in the formal dining room.

Restaurant Kissing

BELLA ITALIA, Port Angeles
117-B East First Street
(360) 457-5442
Moderate
Lunch and Dinner Daily

Located on the basement level of a health food store, Bella Italia is a casual retreat. High-backed booths provide a small measure of privacy and wood walls create a warm cozy interior. Service is attentive without being intrusive and the Italian menu has a large variety of pasta, pizza, and seafood dishes to choose from. Unfortunately, the kitchen can be inconsistent. Our linguini with prawns sautéed in garlic, lemon, capers, and white wine was delectable, but the lemon cream sauce that covered the crab ravioli was full of lemon seeds (not exactly tasty to bite into). Thankfully, the classic tiramisu was smooth and creamy as it should be, so our dinner ended on a deliciously sweet note.

C'EST SI BON, Port Angeles
23 Cedar Park Drive
(360) 452-8888
Expensive to Very Expensive
Dinner Tuesday-Sunday

C'est Si Bon, Port Angeles' only fine French restaurant, is at the tip of
every local's tongue when asked about where to have an enamored evening
interlude. The bright turquoise, pink, and purple exterior is slightly garish
but inside the ambience is wonderfully elegant. A massive crystal chandelier
hanging from a vaulted ceiling casts a warm glow upon rich fuschia walls.
Upholstered chairs provide comfortable seating and silk flower arrangements
are placed around the room and on every linen-draped table. The effect is
quite grand, and the room becomes most lovely after the sun sets and the
lights dim. A table by the window is best, where you'll view either abundant
rose gardens, fountains, or the flower-lined brick patio.

Despite the lovely interior, we must warn you that the kitchen can be
inconsistent. Although our Cornish game hen with mushroom stuffing and
rich brown sauce was tender and savory, the daily specials of salmon wrapped
in parchment paper and herb roasted chicken breast were overcooked and
therefore slightly dry. Still, our evening was quite pleasant and service was
swift and friendly—it is just that when an establishment is known as *the*
place to go for a romantic dinner, expectations run high.

CHESTNUT COTTAGE, Port Angeles
929 East Front Street
(360) 452-8344
Inexpensive to Moderate
Breakfast and Lunch Daily

Ask anyone in P.A. (Port Angeles to out-of-towners) where to have a
reliably good, creative, and filling breakfast or lunch, and chances are they'll
answer, "The Chestnut Cottage." For years locals have had a love affair with
the management's tiny downtown establishment, **FIRST STREET HAVEN**
(see Romantic Alternative below), and this little brick cottage has become
just as popular. The casual dining room exudes country charm with its
honey-colored wood interior, well-placed plants, arched windows, and
antique plates and pictures decorating the walls. California-style cuisine
combined with down-home cooking results in flavorful dishes such as
grilled salmon with hollandaise sauce, or California pizza with sun-dried

tomatoes, sautéed mushrooms, artichoke hearts, homemade pesto sauce, and three cheeses. The Caesar salad is another popular item, but we found the dressing a bit heavy. A sweet espresso drink might serve as dessert, but it never hurts to at least look at the dessert tray and be seduced into a chocolate affair.

Romantic Alternative: FIRST STREET HAVEN, 107 East First Street, (360) 457-0352 (Inexpensive) is a tiny cafe that is usually extremely crowded. The hearty breakfasts and flavorful lunches explain why customers keep coming back for more. For breakfast, Haven veggie browns (potatoes sautéed with green peppers, onions, zucchini, and mushrooms and then topped with Swiss and cheddar cheeses) are sure to give you a jump-start for the day ahead. A variety of burgers, sandwiches, and salads are available at lunchtime, and the First Street Haven's baked goods are always great. If you will be trekking around the peninsula all day, you should take an apricot-walnut scone for the road, or make that two—you don't want to fight over who gets the bigger piece.

TOGA'S, Port Angeles
122 West Lauridsen Boulevard
(360) 452-1952
Expensive
Dinner Tuesday–Sunday

With a name like Toga's, you might expect a sheet-clad staff or at least a Greek menu, but you won't find either here—nor will you find a run-of-the-mill small-town restaurant. Toga's (named after the young entrepreneurial chef) is a modestly adorned, family-managed, fine-dining establishment that boasts the most creative menu in town. European sauces and techniques are combined with fresh local ingredients to produce rich, inventive dishes such as baked prawns stuffed with crab and topped by Jarlsberg and Gruyere cheeses, broiled salmon and scallops served with mustard-dill beurre blanc, and classic beef stroganoff served in a crock pot with buttered noodles. A house specialty that you won't find anywhere else on the peninsula is "Jägerstein": the wait staff brings to your table an extremely hot stone, on which you prepare meat or seafood that you have selected. The method is similar to fondue, except that you use the hot stone to cook the food instead of using a pot of hot liquid. Speaking of fondue, that is another favorite here. Desserts are just as decadent as the rest of your meal, so be sure to bring a hearty appetite—you won't want to skip the warm apple strudel with homemade vanilla ice cream.

Outdoor Kissing

DEER PARK
Olympic National Park

Deer Park is southeast of Port Angeles, in Olympic National Park. From Highway 101, turn south at the sign for Deer Park. The park is at the end of a 17-mile drive.

Our recommendation to make the drive to Deer Park comes with a warning. The countless switchbacks and sharp turns you'll encounter on this predominantly unpaved road are hair-raising. With conditions like this, you need to be guaranteed that there's a payoff at the end. Rest assured that there is, and suffer this road's indignities. The reward on a clear day is an enthralling view deep into the heart of the Olympics. And because of the road conditions, you are likely to find yourselves quite alone. Most everyone else will drive the paved road to **HURRICANE RIDGE** (which has an absolutely astounding view of the Olympics), due south of Port Angeles just off Highway 101. The purple mountain majesty of Deer Park will be all yours.

Romantic Note: Ask at the ranger station (open in summer only) about the arduous hike up Blue Mountain. Even your sore legs will thank you for the view at the summit.

OLYMPIC NATIONAL PARK
(360) 452-0330

Trying to describe the wonder and natural beauty of Olympic National Park in one review is an impossible feat. Really, there is so much to experience throughout this nearly 1,500-square-mile park that it is hard to know where to begin. The arresting splendor of every topographical area beguiles the senses. At the top of **HURRICANE RIDGE**, snowcapped peaks extend up to forever; in the forested territory below, old-growth evergreens reach heavenward to mesmerizing heights; deeper into the woods, the **HOH RAIN FOREST** is a mystical Eden draped in moss; and finally, in a stupefying climax, the powerful Pacific Ocean explodes against the western shore of the peninsula. To call this area exalted is nothing less than an understatement. It is a must-see for anyone venturing to the Northwest.

Specific beaches, walks, and sites that are particularly conducive to affectionate moments have been highlighted throughout this chapter under Outdoor Kissing, but it would be hard to find any place in Olympic National Park that does not inspire kissing.

Romantic Suggestion: Take several days to explore this region. Unlike many of our national parks, Olympic stretches so far and wide that most of your day can be spent driving if you have too much area to cover in one day. Call the park or ask your innkeeper for approximate driving times to each of your destinations.

Lake Crescent

Approximately 20 miles west of Port Angeles, Lake Crescent is Olympic National Park's deepest lake. This distinction makes it one of the clearest, most blue, and most beautiful lakes in the entire Northwest. Unfortunately, access to the lake is limited to just a few areas: the small East Beach, which is usually crowded on summer days, a few boat-launch areas, and the shore fronting the Lake Crescent Lodge.

Hotel/Bed and Breakfast Kissing

LAKE CRESCENT LODGE, Lake Crescent
416 Lake Crescent Road
(360) 928-3211
Inexpensive to Expensive
Call for seasonal closures.

A sunny day here may wreak havoc on your senses and emotions. The drive around the perimeter of the lake is a monumental treat (unless you're inclined to car sickness—there are lots of curves). Take the time to see the whole thing, and refresh yourselves with a chilly swim in summer or an energetic hike in the nearby forest at other times of the year.

Lake Crescent Lodge rests on the bank of its enormous namesake, and from your somewhat rustic cabin—heated by a woodstove or a stone fireplace—you can view this glassy stretch of water as it curves around forested mountains that ascend magnificently in the distance. Inhale deeply the fragrant air that permeates this epic landscape. The bond you and your loved one forge amid all this beauty will be strong and everlasting.

The most romantic accommodations at the lodge are the Roosevelt Fireplace Cottages. The furnishings could be called dated, but some might say they give the room character. These cottages do have wood-burning fireplaces and are close to the water's edge, which might make up for the lackluster decor. If one of the Roosevelt Cottages is not available, you may want to consider a Singer Tavern Cottage. Lined up near the main lodge, these units are close to one another and foot traffic passes by between them and the lake, but the peach walls, hardwood floors, and plain interiors make for adequate accommodations. Overall, this property has seen better days, but the rates are not outrageous, and if you want to spend some time thoroughly enjoying the park, this is a good place to call home for a few nights.

Romantic Note: If you're just passing through, stop at the lodge's attractive restaurant (Moderate to Expensive) for a standard, traditional mountain breakfast with robust fresh coffee, a wholesome lunch, or a selection of dinner entrées ranging from king salmon to Hood Canal oysters in a smooth remoulade.

Neah Bay

Outdoor Kissing

CAPE FLATTERY

Highway 101 intersects Highway 112 a few miles west of Port Angeles. Take Highway 112 west along the coast to the town of Sekiu. Twenty miles west of Sekiu is Neah Bay, and Cape Flattery is eight and a half miles northwest of there.

Sekiu is a small, unassuming fishing village with a handful of motels lining the dock. The town is only 28.5 miles from the northwestern tip of the continental United States, which makes it a gateway to some of the most scintillating scenery anywhere. Drive ahead to Neah Bay just so you can gaze along the Strait of Juan de Fuca, flanked on one side by Washington's shoreline and rugged inlets and on the other by Vancouver Island's striking mountainous profile. But don't stop here; the best is yet to come.

Drive farther northwest to Cape Flattery. Here you can camp or just stop long enough to embrace one another and behold nightfall. A 30-minute hike down a wooded trail brings you to an astounding corner of the world. Your urban temperaments will mellow as you watch the cinematic sunset over the rock-strewn beach and the fall of dusk on Tatoosh Island.

Romantic Warning: Be forewarned that the trek to the beach can be treacherous (especially if it has been a wet season), and there is no fence or guardrail along most of the trail. Hiking boots are an absolute must, and you may even want to grab a hiking stick for added support.

HOBUCK BEACH PARK, Neah Bay
(360) 645-2422
$10 per tent per evening
Closed September through mid-June

Call for directions to this private campground.

Outdoor enthusiasts weary of campsites that are merely parking lots with modern amenities for motor homes can find refuge in a tiny piece of paradise stretching along the outer reaches of the Pacific Ocean. Located in the heart of a Native American reservation, this private oceanfront property attracts few tourists. Take your pick of the campsites, which are set back from the ocean (you can't pitch a tent on the beach) and secluded by trees and brush, but have an expansive view of the empty beach. Share a solitary sunset that will surround you in hues of orange and pink. If you keep your eyes open long enough, you might glimpse the village horses running together across the beach or deer wandering near the campsites looking for tidbits.

For those who don't want to rough it, weathered cabins are also available, complete with showers and kitchenettes. The cabins, however, are not next to the water and offer much less privacy.

Romantic Warning: Keep in mind that this area does not cater to tourists. Consequently, the campground office, cabins, and surrounding village are in a state of disrepair. Also, don't leave any of your food unstored or unattended; the crows will carry it away!

SHI SHI BEACH

Drive seven miles southwest of Neah Bay until you come to something that resembles a parking area with signs for the beach. Look over the embankment adjacent to this parking lot and you will see an expansive, empty beach on Makah Bay. Hike from the parking lot through three miles of forest and beach trail to Shi Shi.

In its magnitude and overwhelming presence, this eight-mile stretch of untainted beach rivals any along the entire western coast of the United States. There really are no adjectives equal to the task of describing its hundreds of sea stacks and its cliffs, forest, sand, and waves. And because it takes a bit of stamina to get there, you might find yourselves alone at this edge of the continent.

La Push

Outdoor Kissing

THIRD BEACH

Follow the signs on Highway 101 to La Push, on the northwestern coast of the Olympic Peninsula. There is only one road that goes south of La Push along the coast. Two miles down this road is a small, barely noticeable "THIRD BEACH" sign and an unmarked parking area at the trailhead. A three-quarter-mile walk on a forest path brings you to the beach.

You can run barefoot for two miles along this surf-pounded beach of firm sand, and there are hidden caves and rock formations to explore along the way. At low tide, you can climb onto what at high tide are islands and marvel at tide pools full of trapped sea life. As is true with any vacation outing, day's end will come too soon; be sure to enjoy the fresh air while you can, and take a seashell or some weather-aged pebbles home as a keepsake of your special time together.

Romantic Warning: Beware of the tide, especially on these beaches, where you could easily get trapped by trying to hike around a point or headland during an incoming tide. Know when the tides occur (buy a tide table or copy down the times from the newspaper). Mere guesswork could get you in trouble if you are trying to beat the water.

Kalaloch

Hotel/Bed and Breakfast Kissing

KALALOCH LODGE, Kalaloch
157151 Highway 101
(360) 962-2271
Inexpensive to Very Expensive
Breakfast, Lunch, and Dinner Daily

The Pacific Ocean is Kalaloch's front-yard entertainment and the primary reason to be here. During low tide, take a long, sandy hike along the shore, accompanied by sea gulls drifting overhead. At high tide, the ocean surf resounds in the air. If you would like enough time to enjoy all the tidal phases, stay overnight in the eclectic assortment of accommodations here. The main lodge has nine adequate rooms and a mediocre oceanside restaurant. Farther down, on a bluff overlooking the ocean, are 16 weathered cedar cabins and six older, rustic log cabins. Several of these have wood-burning fireplaces, and most have views of the sovereign sunsets and ethereal seascape. Unfortunately, even in rooms that have been recently renovated, the decor is merely hotel-standard, and the few units that have kitchens are not adequately equipped for much cooking. Still, this is about your only coastal option on Washington's shore, and the setting truly is magical. If you plan to spend most of your time outdoors, maybe you won't mind the less than inspiring interiors. In the evening after dinner, light a fire, turn the lights down low, and launch into a night of ghost stories, giggling, and cuddling.

Outdoor Kissing

HOH RAIN FOREST
(360) 374-6925

On Highway 101 south of Forks, on the northwest side of the Olympic National Park, look for signs directing you to the Hoh Visitor Center, which is 19 miles east of the highway. Inquire there about hikes suitable for your skill level.

The Hoh Rain Forest shows what Mother Nature can do when she has an abundance of moisture to thrive on (150 inches of rain annually). Every inch of ground, including decaying trees, is covered with moss, lichens, mushrooms, ferns, and sorrel. As you pass under this forest canopy, you will also see some of the largest spruce, fir, and cedar trees in the world. Some of the moss-laden evergreens here are 300 feet tall and 23 feet around. On a rare sunny day, streams of light penetrate the thick foliage in a golden, misty haze. Don't even try to restrain the joy and excitement you'll feel with every step. And since you can't restrain the moisture that oozes from the ground, be certain to wear waterproof shoes.

RUBY BEACH

Off Highway 101, approximately nine miles north of Kalaloch.

An easy walk on a well-maintained trail leads down to Ruby Beach. This pebbly stretch of coastline is graced with majestic sea stacks jutting from the ocean. The beach named for the red-colored sand, which contains tiny garnets, and we did find a good number of red speckled rocks along the shore. Although they do not exactly resemble rubies, they could serve as a precious memento of your day at the beach.

Quinault

Hotel/Bed and Breakfast Kissing

LAKE QUINAULT LODGE, Quinault
South Shore Road
(360) 288-2571, (800) 562-6672 (in Washington state)
Moderate to Very Expensive
Breakfast, Lunch, and Dinner Daily

Set in the heart of the Olympic Rain Forest overlooking serene Lake Quinault, Lake Quinault Lodge is a grand cedar-shingled building with hunter green shutters. A massive stone fireplace warms the lobby, and windows face the lake beyond a manicured front lawn that is trimmed by rhododendrons and hydrangeas. Add to this quiet setting a variety of intriguing hikes nearby and the opportunity for a lake cruise just before sunset, and you have an incredible Northwest getaway.

Originally built in the 1890s, then destroyed by fire and rebuilt in the 1920s, Lake Quinault Lodge has seen many visitors come and go. Unfortunately, the lodge has also seen better days. Recent remodeling efforts included new carpeting, bedspreads, and curtains, but the overall effect is a confused combination of rustic wood-paneled walls, wood and wicker furniture, odd lamps, and brass bedframes. The rooms that seem the most pulled-together are the pastel-appointed Lakeside units, but they are located in a separate, more contemporary building, so the lodge feeling is totally lost. Consider a rustic little room in the main lodge so you can at least appreciate the history and authenticity of the place.

If you can focus on the natural wonder of the area, it should be easy to forgive the interior designer here, and you may even forget which way lies civilization. Sometimes you don't need fancy accommodations to find true romance; sometimes all you need is a remote location like this, and your certain someone.

Romantic Suggestion: The Restaurant at Lake Quinault Lodge (Moderate to Expensive) has a captive audience considering the remote location. Thankfully, the kitchen does an impressive job with hearty breakfasts, basic lunches, and traditional Northwest cuisine at dinnertime.

*"A kiss is the anatomical
juxtaposition of two orbicular muscles
in a state of contraction."*

Cary Grant

San Juan Islands

Several of the islands are accessible by ferry from Anacortes, one and a half hours north of Seattle. For information on departure times, call the Washington State Ferries at (206) 464-6400, or toll-free (800) 543-3779 (in Washington).

There are 172 islands in the San Juan archipelago, each one characterized by its own distinctive terrain. As you circumnavigate the most popular island grouping by ferryboat—Orcas Island, San Juan Island, Lopez Island, and Shaw Island—you may be reminded of the island-dotted Caribbean, a notable difference being that the San Juans are much more spectacular in their topography. Of course, you won't see any palm trees here, and because you're about as far north as you can go in the continental United States, the blush on your cheeks will be from the cold and not the equatorial heat. But so much the better: cool cheeks give you a snuggling advantage.

Deciding on the one ideal destination won't be an easy task. You can opt for the convenience of the more populated islands, or, if you have access to a boat, you can homestead on one of the lesser-known islands, setting up camp for a more back-to-basics holiday. Wherever you put down roots, you'll be more than happy with what you discover.

Romantic Note: To save a lot of time and frustration, check with the **VISITOR INFORMATION CENTER**, (360) 468-3663. They can give you good recommendations for outdoor activities and campgrounds. Always check seasonal hours and rates whenever you choose a restaurant or island accommodation.

Romantic Suggestion: Many folks avoid the ferry hassle by leaving their car behind and traveling by bike on the island of their choice. It would be great if the roads were wider to safely and easily accommodate bikes alongside the cars, but this is a great way to enjoy the San Juans if you are up for it. A small but very informative brochure called the *Bicyclists' Touring Companion* is published by **CYCLE SAN JUANS**, Route 1, Box 1744, Lopez Island, WA 98261, (360) 468-3251. The price is $4.95, which may seem steep for a small brochure, but the information included is invaluable and cannot be found anywhere else.

Romantic Alternative: How else can you travel to the San Juan Islands besides on a ferryboat? An exciting (albeit more expensive) alternative is to be flown here in an intimate seaplane. **KENMORE AIR HARBOR**, (206) 486-1257, (800) 543-9595, offers transportation to San Juan Island, Orcas

Island, and Lopez Island, plus a variety of other lip-worthy destinations within the Northwest. Departures are from Lake Union in Seattle, or from Kenmore at the north end of Lake Washington. Call for prices and a detailed schedule.

San Juan Island

San Juan Island is nothing less than a vacation paradise. It is the largest and most developed of the San Juan Islands, and the westernmost destination in the Strait of Juan de Fuca. Replete with restaurants, bed and breakfasts, hotels, and enough shoreline to satisfy any nature lover, it is an island escape par excellence. San Juan Island is also in such close proximity to Vancouver Island that you can often see the mountains from the interior and Victoria's city lights twinkling in the distance.

Hotel/Bed and Breakfast Kissing

ARGYLE HOUSE, Friday Harbor
685 Argyle Street
(360) 378-4084, (800) 624-3459
http://www.pacificws.com/sj/argyle.html
Moderate to Expensive

Located in an appealing residential neighborhood, this early 1900s Craftsman-style home is just steps from the ferry dock and downtown Friday Harbor. Both the main house, with three rather small upstairs guest rooms, and the adjacent private cottage are bordered by shady trees and colorful wildflowers that blanket the rear meadow during spring and summer. Inside the main house, hardwood floors, homey wicker furnishings, and a wood-burning stove fill the common area, while large windows warm the breakfast room with sunlight. Upstairs, all three guest rooms have attractive floral linens, queen-size beds, contemporary furnishings, and private bathrooms (one is inside a room, and the other two are down the hall).

Directly behind the main house is the most private accommodation option: a lovable self-contained cottage fronted by a wooden deck that overlooks the vivid fields of wildflowers. Hanging plants, lace curtains, vaulted ceilings with a skylight above the bed, and floral linens adorn the airy interior, and a small kitchen area is equipped with a refrigerator and microwave for midnight snacks. Bonus: After 10:30 P.M., guests of this cottage have exclusive use of the hot tub, just steps from the door.

Your stay is complete only after you've tasted the full breakfast served in the main house. A hot egg dish such as smoked salmon quiche or French toast, fresh muffins, and fresh fruit are just some of the possible delectables that will help send you on your way.

DUFFY HOUSE, San Juan Island
760 Pear Point Road
(360) 378-5604, (800) 972-2089
http://www.pacificrim.net/~bydesign/duffy.html
Moderate
Minimum stay requirement on weekends seasonally

It is always a treat to find a new romantic bed and breakfast, and we're certainly pleased to have found this stately Tudor-style home flaunting a distant water view and surrounded by grassy fields, colorful flowers, and a fruit orchard. Step inside the ample common area and you'll see that the decor is not like that of your typical bed and breakfast. Native American artwork covers the white stucco walls, and the honey-colored wood floors are tastefully covered with Navaho area rugs. The cream-colored leather couches set in front of a wood-burning stove create a comfortable retreat on a chilly afternoon.

Hidden away on the main and second floors are five traditional guest rooms, all of which have private, standard bathrooms located either in the rooms or down the hall. The Orchard Room is very comfortable, with pink floral linens and a view of the fruit trees below, while Panorama offers a direct water view and an antique bed with a cozy down comforter. Sunset has crisp green and white linens, a partial water view, and the only actual bathtub in the home.

To help get you going in the morning, a three-course breakfast is served at two medium-size tables. The fresh muffins or breads, hot entrée such as sweet French toast, and fresh fruit are all you will need to complete your restful stay.

FRIDAY HARBOR HOUSE, Friday Harbor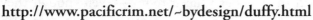
130 West Street
(360) 378-8455
Very Expensive to Unbelievably Expensive
Minimum stay requirement on weekends seasonally

Perched on a unique waterfront bluff overlooking busy Friday Harbor, this massive hotel is a rather imposing figure. With its weathered wood shingles and taupe-and-copper accents, it looks somewhat out of place on laid-back San Juan Island.

Inside, minimalist decor and dark slate floors fill the small lobby; here guests receive their first taste of the ultra-stylish and sleek atmosphere that surrounds all of Friday Harbor House. In most of the 20 rooms, floor-to-ceiling windows showcase unparalleled views of the water and the bustling marina, and on clear days, Orcas Island's Mount Constitution can be seen in the distance. (Try to avoid the Corner Queen rooms—even though they have two walls of windows that overlook the charming marina, they also overlook the adjacent parking lots.) Romantic amenities in all rooms include gas fireplaces, TVs and VCRs, and spacious bathrooms with Jacuzzi tubs (perfect for one, a bit snug for two). In all the Queen rooms, shutters open in the Jacuzzi area so you can view the glowing fireplace while you soak the night away. Unfortunately, the decor feels inert and rigid, with tones of gray, mustard, and black used for the bed linens and carpets; we found them all in dire need of some Northwest charm and warmth. Even so, the setting is beautiful, and the privacy afforded by a large hotel is scarce in the San Juans. A complimentary continental breakfast is served to all guests in the hotel's stunning dining room (see Restaurant Kissing).

FRIDAY'S HISTORICAL INN, Friday Harbor
35 First Street
(360) 378-5848, (800) 352-2632
http://www.fhsji.com/~fridays
Moderate to Expensive

Built in 1891, this gray three-story hotel was a youth hostel before its attractive reincarnation as an island bed and breakfast. Due to it location in the heart of Friday Harbor, noise from the bustling streets can pose a problem for guests seeking quiet refuge; but all will be forgiven once you set foot in the luxurious top-floor Eagle Cove Room. It is hard not to feel pampered here, as you melt in the large two-person Jacuzzi tub set in a beautiful green-and-maroon-tiled bathroom accented with glass bricks and wood. Vaulted ceilings, a king-size bed draped with a sumptuous down comforter, and views of the harbor from a private balcony easily take your mind off the busy town life below.

All of the remaining ten guest rooms at Friday's feature televisions and similar accoutrements. However, most of these rooms share baths, and six of them are on the first floor, adjacent to a large common room, where a continental breakfast is served buffet-style to guests in the morning. Two more guest rooms with king-size beds, jetted tubs, kitchenettes, sofa sleepers, TVs, and computer hookups have been added to the inn's daylight basement, making them highly desirable options if you have to travel unromantically with your whole family. If you have romance at the top of your list, though, you will definitely prefer the Eagle Cove's extravagance and seclusion, and if your budget can handle its slightly steeper tab, you will be elated with what it has to offer.

HARRISON HOUSE SUITES, Friday Harbor
235 C Street
(360) 378-3587, (800) 407-7933
http://www.rockisland.com/~hhsuites
Inexpensive to Very Expensive

Spread out between two adjacent Craftsman-style homes, all five suites at Harrison House have views of the neighborhood surroundings or partial water views, private bathrooms, sitting areas, and either full kitchens or small kitchenettes. In the main house, where four of the units are located, you may want to choose the spacious and attractively decorated two-bedroom suite with hardwood floors, Persian rugs, comfy couches, a wood-burning stove, intricately designed antiques, and a fully stocked kitchen. Although the remaining suites are geared more toward couples (one has a gas fireplace and an outdoor hot tub), they are much smaller and not as nicely decorated as the previously mentioned two-bedroom suite. A garden path leads to the fifth suite and a small cafe that serves inexpensive breakfasts and dinners.

HILLSIDE HOUSE, San Juan Island
365 Carter Avenue
(360) 378-4730, (800) 232-4730
http://www.sanjuaninfo.com/house_1.html
Moderate

Attractive landscaping, a newly built pond, and a trickling fountain greet guests as they wander up the path to this contemporary bed and breakfast, located in a growing residential neighborhood. Six guest rooms are scattered throughout the main floor and basement, and a seventh spectacular suite is perched high up on the third floor. All rooms have distinct themes with plush linens, an eclectic assortment of country collectibles, quaint sitting nooks with comfy pillows, and private bathrooms (either in the room or down the hall). Several offer firsthand views of the 10,000-cubic-foot exotic aviary. Captain's Quarters is decorated in shades of deep blue with abounding nautical paraphernalia, and Primrose has a deep green carpet and pretty floral linens. Nestled in an upstairs loft is the expansive Eagles' Nest Suite, awash in daylight from expansive windows. Cathedral ceilings create a feeling of generous space, and a huge Jacuzzi tub and king-size bed complete this romantic picture. A small private deck overlooks the rapidly developing neighborhood and Friday Harbor in the distance.

Your warm and amiable hosts will encourage you to relax in their comfortable living room and on roomy outside decks with distant water views. In the morning you are guaranteed to enjoy the full buffet breakfast of delicious main dishes, baked pastries, homemade granola, fresh island jams, and plenty of coffee and tea.

LONESOME COVE RESORT, San Juan Island　
5810-A Lonesome Cove Road
(360) 378-4477
Moderate
Minimum stay requirement

Lonesome Cove Resort combines rustic living and secluded island comfort in six delightful log cabins made of weathered cedar wood with cheery red-trimmed windows. All are situated between a sandy beach, perfect for arm-in-arm beach explorations, and a dense forest full of wildlife. You'll often see deer leisurely foraging for fallen apples on the manicured lawns that extend down to the water's edge.

A surprising amount of romance and coziness is found inside the exposed log walls of the cabins. Their prime assets are huge stone fireplaces, full kitchens, and private decks that overlook Speiden Channel and Vancouver Island. Expansive windows allow for wonderful views of the entire cove. The homespun decor is more than a few years old, and the linens are just average, but everything here is immaculate and wonderfully kept up. By the way, the name of this resort is misleading; with the right someone, you won't experience any lonesomeness here.

MARIELLA INN AND COTTAGES, Friday Harbor　
630 Turn Point Road
(360) 378-6868, (800) 700-7668
Expensive to Unbelievably Expensive

Perched at water's edge, this turn-of-the-century seaside inn is a romantic's dream come true. Victorian antiques and crackling fireplaces invite guests to relax in either of the two common areas in the main house. The 11 guest rooms on the main and second floors are on the small side, and because this is an older house, noise can be a problem. But all rooms are extremely cozy, with country Victorian charm, down comforters, antique furnishings, newly renovated white-tiled bathrooms, and views of the nearby water or surrounding flower gardens. Adjacent to the inn is a spa area with a cedar-shake hot tub perfect for a relaxing evening soak.

Seven rustic one- and two-bedroom waterfront cottages are also available. All are charmingly appointed with knotty pine walls, gorgeous refurbished antiques, and wood-burning stoves. If you are staying in the main house, a full breakfast is presented to you in the handsome dining room with views of the water; if you choose one of the cottages, your morning meal will be brought to your door in a basket. Lunch and dinner are also served in the dining room at Mariella Inn (Expensive), where the prix fixe menu offers a four-course taste extravaganza featuring fresh local ingredients. Reservations are a must.

Romantic Note: Mariella Inn and Cottages is currently adding many new facilities and amenities: seven more guest cottages and two condos (all crowded onto the small pristine shoreline), chartered dinner cruises, two tennis courts, and a new 170-foot dock with boat moorage. We hope this new boom in construction does not spoil the intimacy of this sparkling waterside getaway. You'll have to be the final judge.

MOON AND SIXPENCE
VACATION RENTAL, San Juan Island
3021 Beaverton Valley Road
(360) 378-4138
Inexpensive; No Credit Cards
Minimum stay requirement

A sprawling green pasture dotted with colorful gardens encloses this unique island hideaway. Moon and Sixpence is a fully renovated 1902 post-and-beam water tower (one of only three still left standing on the island) with plenty of charm and romance for willing guests. Antique furnishings mixed with homey country appointments fill the three small, cramped levels. The ground level holds a bathroom with a stall shower, while a short staircase takes you to the enchanting bedroom, where a queen-size bed draped in a pretty patchwork quilt awaits your peaceful night's rest. Continue your climb up a wooden ladder to the top of the tower, where a glass-enclosed sitting area offers superlative views of the surrounding meadow and forests. Breakfast is not served at Moon and Sixpence, but the tower is equipped with a small refrigerator and toaster for your convenience.

OLYMPIC LIGHTS
BED AND BREAKFAST, San Juan Island
4531-A Cattle Point Road
(360) 378-3186
Inexpensive to Moderate; No Credit Cards
Minimum stay requirement seasonally and on holiday weekends

Generally, we hesitate to recommend a bed and breakfast where the rooms share baths, for all the obvious unromantic reasons. But Olympic Lights is worth making an exception, and once you experience it you'll know why. Island tranquility is practically guaranteed in this picturesque pale yellow Victorian. It is surrounded by a lush meadow and brilliantly colored wild-flower gardens that overlook the Strait of Juan de Fuca and the Olympic Mountains in the distance.

Inside, the parlor, common area, and five guest rooms are whimsically appointed with soft-sculpted animals and little gold stars, giving this farm-house a carefree ambience. Only one of the five rooms is located on the main floor, and some say it's the most desirable due to its private bathroom and views of the gardens. But don't make your decision until you've seen the four rooms on the snowy white–carpeted second floor. Morning sunlight pours in through the many windows of the room called Ra (named after the Egyptian sun god) which sparkles in cheery colors of cream and white. Olympic affords the best views of the water and Olympic Mountains, and is a picture of beauty with its white linens and floral accents. All four rooms on the second floor share two spacious bathrooms, each with a tub and shower.

Be sure not to oversleep in your comfy bedroom or you'll miss the lavish farm-fresh breakfast awaiting downstairs in the sunny parlor. The scrump-tious hot egg dish, warm scones or muffins, fresh fruit, and coffee will keep you going all morning.

PANACEA, Friday Harbor   😚😚😚
595 Park Street, Reservations through Friday's Historical Inn
(360) 378-5848, (800) 352-2632
http://www.fhsji.com/~fridays
Moderate

To get a clear idea of what to expect from the impressive rooms at Panacea, check out our review of the Eagle Cove Room at **FRIDAY'S HISTORICAL INN** (reviewed above). Both properties are owned and operated by the same people. Although the decor and romantic amenities at Panacea mirror those at Friday's, Panacea offers a more intimate bed-and-breakfast atmosphere. Located in a residential neighborhood, this newly renovated white, Craftsman-style home, complete with wraparound porch and spacious lawn, provides the right setting for a romantic interlude.

Each of the four rooms has enticing floral appointments, classic archi-tectural touches retained from the home's original structure, private entrances, and private baths. A sumptuous king-size bed, a two-person Jacuzzi tub inlaid with hand-painted tiles, and a glass-brick shower are all highlights of the

Sunset Room. The rather dark Mount Baker Room also boasts a large Jacuzzi tub plus a wood-burning stove and a covered porch offering views of the tranquil neighborhood surroundings.

A romantic midnight snack or afternoon picnic can be created in the home's common kitchen, available to guests at any time of day or night. But you won't have to lift a finger for breakfast. A continental buffet including homemade scones, hot and cold cereals, and fresh fruit await guests in the cozy parlor near a mammoth stone fireplace.

SAN JUAN REAL ESTATE COMPANY, Friday Harbor
285 Blair Avenue
(360) 378-5060, (800) 992-1904
Moderate to Very Expensive; Credit Cards For Reservation Only
Minimum stay requirement

There's no place like home—especially when home is on an immaculate stretch of waterfront set amidst pinery on idyllic San Juan Island. These vacation rental homes are not operated as weekend getaways, but if you are fortunate enough to be able to take an eight day-holiday, one of these houses, may be right for you. Dispersed all around the island, the homes vary in style and character and each one has totally different amenities and settings. Fortunately, San Juan Property Company provides a detailed brochure containing all the information you will need to make a decision. Below we list just a few of the homes that struck our fancy as romantic island retreats.

ROCHE HARBOR RABBIT FARM (#5) is perfectly suited for couples. As the name suggests, it is located close to Roche Harbor. Set in the woods with water views through the trees, this fairly new home looks like a weathered old country cottage. The decorating style is not for everyone, but we found it quite charming and unique. A loft bedroom holds a queen-size four-poster bed, and the sunny little bathhouse has a claw-foot tub with shower. The eclectic mix of decor includes hardwood floors, an open-beam ceiling, antiques, a piano, and a bright yellow rabbit-crossing sign. It may sound odd, but if you are interested in something fun and different, this home is a wonderful option, and the easy beach access is an additional bonus.

YACHT HAVEN (#36), another excellent getaway, is also near Roche Harbor. Decorated in a more upscale fashion with cream-colored leather couches and elegant country touches, this two-bedroom waterfront home has fabulous views of Haro Strait, immediate beach access, and a huge front deck with a Jacuzzi tub. Sunsets from this vantage point will leave you speechless, and stargazing is just as wonderful.

Another option is the petite **HONEYMOON COTTAGE** (#14), located just south of Friday Harbor. The frilly pastel touches may be a bit much for some tastes, but this studio-style guest cottage beside a larger home is wonderfully private. A woodstove warms the pale hardwood floors, madrona trees frame the water view from the front deck, and the beach is just down a few stairs.

For the most part, the larger homes that we toured felt like too much house for just one couple, but if you have children in tow or are traveling with another couple, then the extra bedrooms and bathrooms may be essential. In Friday Harbor, **HARBOR VISTA TOWNHOUSE** (#58) is a rather pricey rental, but the in-town location is extremely convenient and views of the marina are excellent. The decor in this contemporary townhouse is somewhat spartan, but there are three bedrooms, two baths, and a powder room. Up-island, perched along the eastern shore, is **EAGLE NEST** (#46), a contemporary three-bedroom home. Awesome water views can be enjoyed from the bright and airy living room or the expansive deck; other amenities include down comforters, a woodstove, and a game room with a pool table.

Staying in a vacation home is an entirely different experience than staying in a hotel or bed and breakfast. At first you may feel like an intruder in someone else's home (you'll find family photos and personal mementos belonging to the owners in most of the houses). By the end of your week here, however, you will feel as if you have become a resident of these precious islands, and you probably won't want to leave.

Romantic Note: Considering that most of these vacation rentals have two or more bedrooms, they do make wonderful getaways for several couples. When split between more people, most of San Juan Property Company's homes fall into the Inexpensive to Moderate range—you need only find other couples who can take a week-long vacation.

TRUMPETER INN, San Juan Island 💋💋
420 Trumpeter Way
(360) 378-3884, (800) 826-7926
http://www.pacificrim.net/~bydesign/trumpet.html
Inexpensive to Moderate

Set in the middle of a grassy meadow dotted with horses and a small pond, the Trumpeter Inn allows for quiet moments in a country-cozy atmosphere.

The cheerful peach and blue exterior is inviting, and inside, the aroma of freshly baked cookies wafts through the five attractive guest rooms and two comfortable common areas. In each guest room you'll find private bathrooms, pretty down comforters, and views of the garden or meadow. Our favorite room is the Bay Laurel, which sports a king-size bed with a burgundy plaid duvet. Large windows spanning three walls offer distant views of Puget Sound and the Olympic Mountains.

Before you begin exploring the island, join other guests at one large table for a delicious morning meal of fresh breads, homemade granola, French toast or smoked salmon quiche, and seasonal fruit.

WESTWINDS BED AND BREAKFAST, San Juan Island
4909-H Hannah Highlands Road
(360) 378-5283
http://www.karuna.com/westwinds
Very Expensive

Where is the ultimate place to kiss in the Northwest, you may ask? Well, even with the stiff competition, Westwinds always comes to our minds. This wood-and-glass home rests high atop a tree-laden hillside on the west side of San Juan Island and has exquisite panoramic views of the Olympic Mountains and the Strait of Juan de Fuca. Luckily, the entire house can be yours, so you don't have to share this magnificent setting with anybody other than your significant other.

An expansive living room with cathedral ceilings, a wood-burning stove, and commanding views of the stunning surroundings welcomes each guest. You know you've arrived at a very special getaway once you discover the adjacent dining room, full kitchen, and two bedrooms with private bathrooms. The most romantic room is the master suite, with its comfy down comforter and large soaking tub. French doors open onto a private deck where you can loll away the morning over the extended continental breakfast. Westwinds is a truly exemplary, one-of-a-kind island getaway.

Romantic Note: Westwinds' steep price can be lessened if you bring along another couple, and there is certainly enough space. To reduce the cost even further, you can bring your own morning goodies instead of having breakfast served.

WHARFSIDE BED AND BREAKFAST, Friday Harbor
Slip K-13: Port of Friday Harbor
(360) 378-5661
http://www.rockisland.com/~pcshop/wharfside.html
Inexpensive
Minimum stay requirement seasonally
Closed November

This is not your run-of-the-mill bed and breakfast in any way, shape, or form. Wharfside Bed and Breakfast is a docked, beautifully restored 60-foot sailboat named the *Jacquelyn*. Anyone familiar with boats might not be surprised by the compact size of the two guest rooms here, but for the less nautically aware, we must explain that these rooms are a lot smaller than any on-land bed-and-breakfast rooms you have ever seen.

Polished hardwood adorns both below-deck rooms, and porthole windows look out to passing boats and ferries. The Forward Stateroom is rather narrow, with an elongated double bed, patchwork quilt, down comforter, and bunk beds. A detached bathroom, located across the main salon, is tiny: there is just enough room for a sink, toilet, and shower. (The shower is shared with the other guest room.) The low-beamed ceiling in the Aft Stateroom is deceiving at first, but this room is actually larger than the other. A velvet settee and a queen-size bed with a burgundy bedspread and down comforter are about all that fits in here. A bathroom with a toilet and sink is tucked into one corner of this room, but shower facilities are next to the salon and shared with the Forward Stateroom.

Homemade (or should we say boat-made?) full breakfasts are served daily, on the deck during sunny weather, or in the snug salon with its skylight, woodstove, and nautical paraphernalia and furnishings. Life aboard the *Jacquelyn* is a cozy and unique adventure. If you can look at the tight quarters as a way to be closer to one another, it is also one of the most affordable options in Friday Harbor.

Romantic Suggestion: Seafood fresh from the local waters is available just down the dock at **FRIDAY HARBOR SEAFOOD**, Main Dock, Port of Friday Harbor, (360) 378-5779. Purchase some precooked crab or shrimp and then enjoy the catch of the day right on the *Jacquelyn's* deck.

Restaurant Kissing

DUCK SOUP INN, San Juan Island
3090 Roche Harbor Road
(360) 378-4878
Moderate
Call for seasonal hours.
Closed December through March

Duck Soup Inn is the restaurant of choice for hungry lovebirds on San Juan Island. Secluded behind a stand of trees, the wood-frame country home overlooks a tranquil duck pond. Country accents and cozy wood booths patterned with colorful cushions create a wonderfully rustic yet elegant setting. If your taste buds and hearts long for savory fresh Northwest cuisine, you've come to the right place. Your evening's menu might include grilled filet mignon with portobello mushrooms and roasted tomatoes, applewood-smoked oysters (the most delicious you'll ever taste), grilled scallops, or prawns sautéed with blackberry vinegar, wild island blackberries, and butter. Be assured that everything on the menu is nothing less than divine.

FRIDAY HARBOR HOUSE RESTAURANT, Friday Harbor 💋💋💋💋
130 West Street
(360) 378-8455
Expensive
Call for seasonal hours.

Located on the main floor of the sleek **FRIDAY HARBOR HOUSE** (see Hotel/Bed and Breakfast Kissing), this polished dining room has an elegant, refined atmosphere. Because the space is small and able to hold only a handful of tables, intimate moments are guaranteed. Floor-to-ceiling windows capture quaint scenes of the picturesque marina, while soothing taupe walls, dark slate floors, fresh flowers at every table, and a glowing fireplace at one end of the room create simple and tasteful surroundings in which to enjoy a superior meal.

Guests will enjoy the decidedly Northwest-flavored menu. We went wild for the Westcott Bay oysters baked with sweet red pepper butter, the breast of chicken baked with chanterelles and tomatoes, and the fillet of wild king salmon flame-broiled with sun-dried tomato butter. A trio of handmade ice creams in a crisp meringue basket put the perfect finishing touch on a wonderfully romantic evening.

ROCHE HARBOR RESORT RESTAURANT, Roche Harbor
4950 Tarte Memorial Drive
(360) 378-5757, (800) 451-8910
Moderate to Expensive
Call for seasonal hours.

Roche Harbor is San Juan Island's second most popular port of call (Friday Harbor sees the most water traffic). This scenic, historic harbor and marina, protected by a tiny barrier island, is a yachting and tourist playground. Every inch of the resort and marina that isn't lined with boats is covered with gazebos, rose gardens, sculpted hedges, and ivy-laden buildings. As you follow the winding brick pathways that weave through the crisp white and dark green New Englandesque buildings, you may feel as if you have stepped back in time.

Bright flower boxes line the waterfront deck of the Roche Harbor Resort Restaurant. Patio furniture is placed around the deck so you can enjoy the sun and the harbor view at the same time. The breakfast and lunch menus offer typical fare, such as pancakes and omelets at breakfast and sandwiches and fries at lunch, but well-prepared seafood is the specialty at dinnertime. Whichever meal you have here, spend some time wandering the grounds—the gardens are truly lovely, and the harbor scene is ever-changing. In addition, guided kayak tours and whale-watching excursions are available. Stop by the information booth at the resort or call the resort's main number (listed above) for information.

Romantic Note: Overnight accommodations are also available at this property. Most of the 20 rooms in the **HOTEL DE HARO**, (360) 378-2155, (800) 451-8910 (Inexpensive to Very Expensive) share baths, but we like the hotel's authenticity and historic charm. Some of the two-bedroom **COMPANY TOWN COTTAGES** have been recently refurbished, and their views of the harbor are fantastic—just be sure to ask for a front-row unit. Waterfront condominiums are also available but are not recommended.

SPRINGTREE, Friday Harbor
311 Spring Street
(360) 378-4848
Inexpensive to Moderate
Call for seasonal hours.

Half the fun of visiting San Juan Island is dining at the Springtree. In fact, on one trip, we actually ate here three times in a row (and that's against travel writers' rules). Located in the heart of Friday Harbor, the Springtree has a white picket-fence entrance covered by an immense Asian elm that helps to shade the red brick courtyard. Guests can dine on this pleasant outdoor patio when weather permits; when it doesn't (which is more often than Northwesterners care to admit), they can dine inside, where floor-to-ceiling windows brighten the restaurant's casual interior. Rust-colored walls adorned with local art, and well-spaced wooden tables lit by single votive candles, set the mood for an enjoyable evening.

Only fresh local ingredients are used in the creative seafood entrées, and the high-quality kitchen consistently prepares one delight after another. We highly recommend the steamed shrimp and mussels in a Thai coconut curry sauce, as well as the baked Westcott Bay oysters with sweet bell pepper butter. Although the menu tends toward vegetarian fare, devout carnivores will be more than appeased.

Outdoor Kissing

AMERICAN CAMP, San Juan Island

From the ferry, exit onto Spring Street and turn left on Argyle Road. Argyle Road jogs around to become Cattle Point Road; at this point, turn left again and proceed directly to American Camp.

The heavily forested terrain in the northern section of San Juan Island gives way to windswept trees carpeted with poppies, wildflowers, wild rabbits, and waving waist-high grass at the island's southern extremity called American Camp. Once you arrive, you can walk down to the enormous sandy beach and investigate the shoreline or meander through spacious meadows composed of sand hills and sea grass. The many opportunities for ducking out of sight make this a perfect site for lovers. You'll be mesmerized by views of the Olympic and Cascade Mountains (both ranges are visible from this spectacular park). From your own personal nook, watch the sun's procession from morning to dusk as it bathes the hills in a rainbow of colors.

Romantic Alternative: If you have the energy and a good pair of shoes, don't miss climbing the beautiful uphill trail from **ENGLISH CAMP** to **YOUNG HILL**. (To reach English Camp from American Camp, take West Valley Road, which turns into Boyce Road, to Bailer Hill Road and turn left. Then turn right on Little Road and right again onto Cattle Point Road. Follow signs to English Camp.) The view will astound you, as will the peace and solitude. You may find yourselves sharing this spectacle with the soaring eagles that make their home in this paradise. You may also come to understand why so many people say that San Juan Island is the Garden of Eden. Leave yourselves at least an hour for this round-trip jaunt.

WHALE WATCH PARK, San Juan Island

On West Side Road near Deadman Bay.

While you're on San Juan Island, be sure to visit Whale Watch Park on the western shore. Two pods of whales make regular trips through this area, and it is from this spot that you're most likely to see these enormous creatures cavorting in play. Even if you don't catch a glimpse of them here, you'll probably witness a sensational sunset with the bay in the foreground and the white-peaked Olympic Mountains in the distance. This is a wondrous, often private section of the island.

Romantic Suggestion: For an even closer look at the island's wildlife, consider a nautical cruise with **SAN JUAN BOAT RENTALS AND TOURS**, (360) 378-3499, (800) 232-6722. This is the chance of a lifetime to come face-to-face with harbor seals, bald eagles, or a pod of orcas, among other magnificent creatures. Join a guided lunch cruise or venture out yourselves on a romantic excursion. There are many other whale-watching tours offered on San Juan Island; look for the flyers posted all over the ferry landing. We suggest calling around to get the exact price and experience you're looking for.

Orcas Island

Horseshoe-shaped Orcas Island is the northernmost of the touristed San Juan Islands, and blends rural landscape and mountain wilderness with several small communities. Eastsound, at the central northern portion of the island, is the largest town. If you need groceries, gas, or a quick lunch, or if you simply want to spend some time wandering through gift shops and little boutiques, this is the place to do it. Beyond Eastsound is Moran State Park, Washington's fourth-largest park, which takes up a good portion of the eastern half of the island and is home to one of the most frequently visited points on all of the islands: **MOUNT CONSTITUTION** (see Outdoor Kissing). There is an abundance of hiking terrain and enough campsites to please any outdoor enthusiast. A good number of esteemed accommodations and restaurants also call Orcas home—maybe you should too (at least for your getaway).

Artists of all types are drawn to these islands because of the natural inspiration found in every direction. Orcas Island has become particularly well known for the wealth of talented potters who reside here. Studios, many of which are extensions of the artists' homes, are scattered around the island, and they are well worth visiting. The wealth and variety of fantastic local artwork and crafts (pottery, paintings, jewelry, and sculpture, to mention just a few) make it fairly easy to find a unique souvenir of your time in this incredible part of the world.

Hotel/Bed and Breakfast Kissing

CABINS-ON-THE-POINT, Orcas Island
Route 1, Box 70
(360) 376-4114
http://www.pacificws.com/orcas/cabinspt.html
Moderate to Expensive; No Credit Cards
Minimum stay requirement

Set sail without ever leaving the shore at Cabins-on-the-Point. Don't worry if you are prone to seasickness—you're not really setting off to sea. The placement of the Heather cabin, perched on a rocky point with water on two sides, just gives you that impression.

It's no surprise that people frequently rent the Heather cabin for weeks at a time; a weekend doesn't feel long enough at this intimate island retreat. The three-room Cape Cod–style cabin is snug but beautifully renovated with hardwood floors, comfortable antiques, a full kitchen, and a wood-burning stove. Best of all, the cozy bedroom has a queen-size bed covered with a down comforter; it has been tucked into a window-trimmed alcove overlooking the water, enhancing the sensation of being on a boat. There are not many places to kiss like this—where you can lounge in bed and watch fiery sunsets linger right above the tips of your toes.

A smaller cabin, Primrose, is nestled among fir trees farther back from the water. Although the setting is not quite as spectacular as the Heather cabin (few settings are), this is still an incredibly cozy little unit. Cedar walls and hardwood floors lend rustic warmth to the bedroom/sitting room, and there is a woodstove in the corner. Down several steps is a petite, fully equipped kitchen with skylights and a separate private bathroom with a shower. A covered porch with patio furniture provides a place to sit and savor the quiet, and a brick pathway leads to a grassy knoll with fantastic views of Westsound.

This same view can also be enjoyed from the outdoor hot tub, framed by madronas and fir trees lit with twinkling white lights. Times can be reserved so you will have the Jacuzzi tub all to yourselves. Last but not least, beach access is another wonderful aspect of staying here. Clam digging is an option when the tide and season allows, or you may want to build a beach fire and toast marshmallows together. Some guests even bring their own kayaks and launch from here. Bon voyage!

Romantic Note: Herb gardens on the property provide the perfect seasonings for a romantic breakfast or dinner, but no meals are included in your stay. Be sure to bring your own groceries.

CHESTNUT HILL INN, Orcas Island

John Jones Road
(360) 376-5157
http://www.pacificws.com/orcas/chestnut.html
Moderate to Expensive
Recommended Wedding Site

What a thrill to find Chestnut Hill Inn, a newly opened bed and breakfast that offers some of the most exquisite accommodations on the island. Perched on a grassy hillside, this pale yellow farmhouse overlooks horse pastures, a red barn, a small pond, and a charming country chapel. Persian rugs on polished hardwood floors, plush couches, French country furnishings, and a marble gas fireplace in the parlor set a casually elegant tone for your stay.

There are just four rooms here, each one a testament to comfort and beauty. Lavish appointments include plush feather beds and down comforters, four-poster or canopied beds, the finest floral linens, and gas-log fireplaces. The Garden Room, decorated in country style with subtle blue tones, has a private entrance and is the only ground-level unit; the other three are upstairs. Deep rose–colored walls, a lace-canopied bed, and dark wood furnishings make the Stable Room a cozy retreat. The Chapel Room features a double-headed glass-brick shower, a massive canopied bed, and, as you may have guessed, a view of the little chapel. And the Pond Room has a claw-foot tub and yellow floral linens on a four-poster canopied bed. It's impossible to single out just one room as the most romantic—despite varying views and color schemes, each one has the same level of opulence as the next.

Tables for two fill the main-floor dining room, where a full country breakfast is served daily. In the summertime, additional tables with comfortable wicker chairs are set on the front veranda overlooking the bucolic landscape.

Romantic Note: Depending on the time of year, different meals and services are available at the inn. In the fall and winter, when many of the local restaurants close, dinner is served here (Expensive). High tea is another event enjoyed in cooler months. In the summer, gourmet picnic baskets can be ordered a day in advance ($29.50 for two people). Ask your gracious hostess for details.

DEEP MEADOW FARM, Deer Harbor   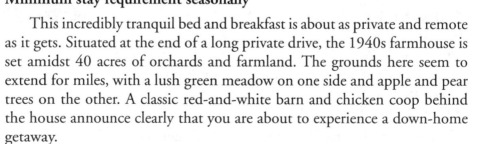
Corner of Cormorant Bay Road and Cedar Valley Road
(360) 376-5866
Inexpensive; No Credit Cards
Minimum stay requirement seasonally

This incredibly tranquil bed and breakfast is about as private and remote as it gets. Situated at the end of a long private drive, the 1940s farmhouse is set amidst 40 acres of orchards and farmland. The grounds here seem to extend for miles, with a lush green meadow on one side and apple and pear trees on the other. A classic red-and-white barn and chicken coop behind the house announce clearly that you are about to experience a down-home getaway.

Inside, American country furnishings and antiques decorate the cozy living room, which extends out to the wraparound deck. Upstairs are two very spacious and comfortable guest rooms with country print wallpapers, antique iron beds with patchwork quilts and down comforters, gabled ceilings, private baths, and plenty of windows for gazing out at the serene landscape. Fluffy robes are provided so you can be sure to enjoy the Jacuzzi spa that is set outside by the barn and fruit orchards. We must also mention another very special aspect of Deep Meadow Farm: the animals. Deer commonly roam the orchards, two cats and two horses reside on the property, and finally there is Dally, one of the most charming and intelligent border collies we have ever met.

In the morning, hearty country breakfasts are served. Morning selections may include delicacies such as Dutch pancakes, eggs Florentine, Southwestern quiche, or blueberry-cornmeal pancakes in addition to the always present fresh fruit juice and hot coffee and tea. A few nights here and you will be thoroughly rejuvenated and relaxed.

DEER HARBOR RESORT, Deer Harbor
200 Deer Harbor Road
(360) 376-4420
http://www.accessone.com/seattle2000/categories/hotels/deerharbor
Expensive to Unbelievably Expensive

A small grouping of A-frames, cottages, and bungalows crowds the shore and hillside next to Deer Harbor Marina—at first glance clearly not the most romantic place to stay on Orcas Island. However, of the 24 units at Deer Harbor Resort, there are several worth recommending. Eight spa cottages are neatly lined up in a row, and each one has an outdoor Jacuzzi tub on the front deck. Inside, pine furnishings and wainscoting, a wood-burning stove or fireplace, a pretty floral bedspread, exposed beams, and dried floral arrangements create a casual country ambience. The simple bathrooms and intrusive televisions are the only hotel-like touches; otherwise you are surrounded by comfort and blessed with a great view of the marina.

As for the other units available, we suggest that you stick with the spa cottages. There are two other weathered white cottages with unobstructed water views that are hard to resist, but they are pretty bare-bones and thus are best suited for families.

Breakfast is not included with your stay, but most of the rooms have coffeemakers and small refrigerators, so you can keep a limited food supply in your room.

Romantic Suggestion: The fairly elegant **HEMINGWAY'S BY THE SEA**, (360) 376-2950 (Moderate) is located just down the hill from the cottages. The restaurant is open only from May through January, but the food is quite good and it couldn't get much more convenient than this.

FOXGLOVE COTTAGE, Deer Harbor
Reservations through the Orcas Hotel
(360) 376-4300
Very Expensive
Minimum stay requirement seasonally

Renting a fully equipped cottage is an ideal way to get a true feeling for the San Juan Islands—you can fully settle in and live by your own vacation schedule (or opt for no schedule at all). Foxglove Cottage, next to Deer Harbor, is an adorable little waterfront cabin. The exterior is painted fresh white with crisp green trim, and the inside is just as immaculate. Although it is petite, once you step inside this taste of contemporary country cuteness you may never want to leave again. The modern white-tiled kitchen is perfect for cooking a lovers' buffet. Share your repast outside on the private deck overlooking the harbor, or inside in the cozy living room warmed by a wood-burning fireplace. Afterward, you may want to take a nice walk—and lucky for you, the beach is just a few steps away.

Deer Harbor Resort is right next door, but most of the cottages' windows face the water or trees, so privacy is still possible. Also, the convenience of having the resort so close means you can spend less time running to the store and more time focusing on each other.

OLD TROUT INN, Eastsound
Horseshoe Highway (Route 1)
(360) 376-8282, (888) 653-8768
Inexpensive to Expensive
Minimum stay requirement seasonally

Richly stained cedar frames this contemporary home set just two and a half miles from the ferry dock on the main road. Designed to resemble a lodge, the atmosphere is warm and inviting. Inside, the entire rear wall of the house consists of one enormous window, so prepare yourselves for the stunning view. The five acres of lavish green meadows, bubbling rock water-fall, wraparound pond, bordering forests, and Turtleback Mountain are all spectacular. Looks like rain? Not to worry. This wondrous view can be enjoyed not only from the five decks but also from the comfortable parlor filled with classic antiques, a brick wood-burning fireplace, and a 1,000-volume library.

There are four guest rooms in the main house and also a detached cottage. The self-sufficient Water's Edge cottage has a kitchenette, fireplace, and, perhaps most enticing, a hot tub overlooking the pond. Two of the rooms in the house share a bath but the two others, the Pond Suite and the Greenhouse Suite, have private baths and queen-size feather beds. The Pond

Suite is larger and has a sauna and an adjoining room with a fireplace and wet bar, but the Greenhouse Suite has the advantage of a private deck and a glassed-in sitting area facing the pond.

Whichever unit you choose, you'll have access to the communal outdoor hot tub. In the morning, a full country breakfast is included. This hearty meal is served just off the parlor at small two-person tables or, weather permitting, outside on one of the decks.

ORCAS HOTEL, Orcas Island
Orcas Ferry Landing
(360) 376-4300, (800) 376-4300
Inexpensive to Very Expensive

The rust-colored roof of the Orcas Hotel is probably the first thing you will see as the ferry pulls into the Orcas Island landing. "Hotel" is really a misnomer here, since that term often conjures up an image of a sterile building with identical rooms and basic detailing, none of which applies to this striking Victorian inn that is trimmed by a white picket fence and a flowering English garden. The view from the wraparound windows in the dining room and lounge—and from many of the rooms upstairs—is striking. From this vantage point you can watch the comings and goings around busy Harney Channel and Shaw Island across the water.

Unfortunately, the majority of rooms in this 1904 landmark hotel are sorely in need of renovation. In terms of kissing-preferred accommodations, we can recommend only two of the 12 rooms here, both of which fall into the Very Expensive category during high season (not exactly a bargain compared with other island accommodations that offer a lot more privacy and designer style). Each of these two units, dubbed the Romantic Rooms, has French doors opening to a sundeck, a private bathroom with a two-person whirlpool tub, a queen-size feather bed, and stained glass windows created by a local artist. The other ten rooms are quite small, with a toilet and sink in the room and a separate shower down the hall.

A full breakfast, served in the hotel's restaurant, is included in the price of your room. Any meal in this window-lined, country-perfect dining room will be a pleasure, and the food, though basic, is quite good.

Romantic Warning: Since this hotel is located at the foot of the ferry dock, there is exceptionally heavy tourist and car traffic during the summer season. The downstairs public rooms can get crowded when there is a delay in boarding the ferry.

ROSARIO RESORT, Orcas Island

One Rosario Way
(360) 376-2222, (800) 562-8820
http://www.rosario-resort.com
Moderate to Very Expensive
Minimum stay requirement on weekends

Rosario has become a community unto itself, and at its heart is the land-mark Rosario Resort. The historic Moran mansion proudly sits at the edge of Cascade Bay in all its glory. Pictures of the sparkling white mansion, its manicured grounds, and its luxurious interior with teak floors and rich mahogany paneling grace Rosario's brochure.

What is not included in the brochure, however, are any pictures of the condo-style buildings that hold the resort's guest rooms. A few pictures of the rooms' interiors are shown, but many visitors come to Rosario expecting to stay in the mansion, or at least in a building with a comparable level of charm and authenticity. Instead, what they get is a hotel-like room that may be located up on the hillside (not right next to the water, as the mansion is) in an apartment-style building. This is not to say that the recently renovated rooms do not have romantic potential: they absolutely do (but *only* the recently renovated ones), and the views of the harbor are indeed stunning. We simply do not want to see our readers disappointed by what they may have been expecting from the brochure.

Now that we have clarified the location of the guest rooms, let us tell you which of the 131 rooms here are best suited for romantic encounters. Rooms in the 1100, 1200, 1300, and 1700 buildings have been redone with cream walls, new linens, comfy furnishings, patios, wet bars, and modern, white-tiled bathrooms. A slight hotel feel is still present, but these rooms are taste-fully appointed and infinitely superior to the rooms that have not been upgraded. If you can ask specifically for a water-view room in one of these buildings, we do not think you will be disappointed with your stay at Rosario.

Romantic Note: Rosario is extremely popular in the summertime, and it can be difficult to get a reservation. Even if you do not stay here, you may want to visit the resort for a meal (see Restaurant Kissing) or tour the Moran Museum, which takes up the second floor of the mansion. You can walk through rooms originally used by the Moran family, who built this mansion as their summer residence. A massive pipe organ fills the music room; during evening historical presentations in the summer this grand instrument is played, followed by a slide show. Call the resort for additional information.

SPRING BAY INN, Orcas Island
Obstruction Pass Trailhead Road
(360) 376-5531
Very Expensive (includes kayak tour)
Minimum stay requirement seasonally

Who else should run this nature lover's paradise, surrounded by wilderness, wildlife, and hiking trails, but two former park rangers? The Spring Bay Inn is approximately two miles south of the tiny town of Olga, completely sheltered from any signs of urban life. On your way, it may seem as if you've taken a wrong turn, but hang tight, watch out for deer, and don't mind the potholed road—the treasure that awaits is worth the bumpy ride.

This mammoth wood house fits in so well with its surroundings that it looks as if it may have grown here along with the adjacent 137 acres of woodland. Inside, the main-floor common area is grand yet cozy, with a 14-foot exposed-beam ceiling, river-rock fireplaces on either side of the room, and comfy couches that just beg to be cuddled upon. Carson and Radcliff, the two extremely friendly resident retrievers, usually curl up on the fluffy white area rugs scattered around the room (after properly greeting you, of course). Expansive windows along one wall look out to a glorious scene of fir trees, the sheltered waters of Spring Bay, and a trail leading to the pebbled beach and the large hot tub there. Private soaking times can be reserved so you can luxuriate while you enjoy each other and the natural beauty around you.

Upstairs, four generous guest rooms share the same forest and water view through six-foot-high windows. Stylish Northwest simplicity is found in every room: nature photography, local artwork, and a mix of antique and contemporary furnishings. A good example of the innkeepers' ingenuity is the driftwood mantel in one room. Patchwork quilts, plush feather beds, wood-burning fireplaces, and a tiled private bath with claw-foot tub and separate shower in every room ensure a comfortable stay. The two larger rooms at either end of the house have private decks, excellent for stargazing or just enjoying the calm bay and tranquil surroundings.

Be sure to see the Ranger Suite which, decorated much like the others, is the largest of the five. This grand main-floor room has the same 14-foot ceiling as the living room, an antiqued brass queen-size bed, a glassed-in reading solarium, a wood-burning fireplace, and its own private entrance. Best of all, this room features a private little courtyard that holds a deep-soaking tub with low-speed jets. Getting comfortable here will not be the least bit challenging. If you think this sounds great, just wait: there's more.

Included in your stay at Spring Bay Inn is a two-hour early-morning kayak tour. Not only is this a great deal, considering that kayak rentals elsewhere on the island start at $35 per person, but it is an incredible way to start your day. Your informative hosts will give you a new appreciation of the serene Orcas Island coastline. They will also have you back at the inn in time for brunch, a hearty and healthy meal that may include a banana-pineapple smoothie, fruit soup, vegetarian sausage, and oat bran waffles topped with fresh strawberries and vanilla yogurt. Breakfast never tasted so good, and kissing in the heart of nature never felt so good.

TURTLEBACK FARM INN, Orcas Island
Crow Valley Road
(360) 376-4914, (800) 376-4914
http://www.specialplaces.com/wa/turtle.sht
Inexpensive to Very Expensive
Minimum stay requirement holidays and seasonally

When the sun begins to warm the air and the colors of the countryside come alive with the glow of daybreak, Turtleback Farm Inn is a delightful place to be. Every corner of this turn-of-the-century farmhouse has been painstakingly renovated by people who clearly were sensitive to the surrounding landscape. The seven rooms with private baths range from charming to more charming (though the less expensive rooms are rather small). Polished hardwood floors, glowing fir wainscoting, and fluffy lamb's-wool comforters endow every room with elegant simplicity, and white curtains and pale-colored linens lend a certain crispness. The welcome omission of televisions and phones in the rooms guarantees a quiet country getaway.

The pastoral setting—80 acres of hills, pastures, ponds, and meadows—will warm your hearts, as will the plentiful breakfast you will enjoy at your own table in the window-enclosed dining room. Served by your gracious hosts, this award-winning meal should keep you going for hours. If peaceful seclusion and a leisurely pace sound appealing, you will be wholeheartedly pleased with your stay here.

WINDSONG, Orcas Island
Deer Harbor Road
(360) 376-2500, (800) 669-3948
http://www.pacificws.com/orcas/windsong.html
Expensive

Built as Westsound's first schoolhouse in 1917, this brick-red home is now a welcoming bed and breakfast. Friendly innkeepers and two friendly dogs will greet you at the door and set the tone for the relaxing time to come. An eclectic mix of furnishings and gold carpet fills the comfortable main-floor living room that is open for guest (and dog) use, and there is a glass-enclosed hot tub area off to one side. This common area is more functional than it is stylish, but the decor in the four upstairs guest rooms is more pleasing.

All of the modest rooms feature antique furnishings, down comforters, robes, and private baths (although the bath for the Concerto Room is detached). Our favorite room is Rhapsody, with its bent willow furnishings, corner gas woodstove, and pretty peach and black linens. Concerto also has a gas woodstove and the skylight above the bed is great for stargazing, but the mismatched gold carpet, green duvet, maroon chairs, and yellowish wallpaper are a little too eclectic for our tastes.

Thankfully, the innkeepers go out of their way to make sure you are comfortable, and the multicourse breakfast served each morning is delightful. While Windsong is by no means fancy, if you can forgive some of the decor's shortcomings, the quiet setting is wonderful.

Restaurant Kissing

BILBO'S FESTIVO, Eastsound
A Street at North Beach Road
(360) 376-4728
Inexpensive to Moderate
Call for seasonal hours.

Generally speaking, Mexican restaurants are rarely romantic—the focus tends to be on good food, generous portions, and a fun atmosphere. Bilbo's Festivo is no exception to this trend, but we must say that Bilbo's does have a unique character. Carved wooden benches surround a blazing fire pit on the outdoor deck, and a lattice covered in foliage conceals the patio from the road. Inside, a stone fireplace and soft lighting embellish the charming interior, which could be romantic if it weren't for the noisy bustle of big groups and families who also frequent Bilbo's. The food is light and mildly spicy, with generous portions and remarkably fresh seafood. This is a local favorite, so reservations are a good idea.

CAFE OLGA, Olga
Horseshoe Highway
(360) 376-4408
Inexpensive to Moderate

Lunch and Dinner Daily
Closed January through February

A few miles south of Mount Constitution is where you will find this charming remodeled 1936 strawberry packing plant turned rustic cafe, art gallery, and gift boutique. As laid-back and casual as the atmosphere is, the food is anything but. Items from the eclectic, health-oriented menu include Sicilian artichoke pie, creamy rich manicotti with walnuts, Moroccan salad brimming with couscous, dates, almonds, and spices, and a Mediterranean plate with hummus, Greek olives, pepperoncinis, and an assortment of fresh vegetables. Breads, soups, and irresistible desserts are always fresh and home-made. As you leisurely dine, you'll have plenty of time to share your thoughts and get to know each other a little better.

CHRISTINA'S, Eastsound
Main Street (Horseshoe Highway)
(360) 376-4904
Moderate to Expensive
Call for seasonal hours.
Closed November until Thanksgiving

Critics from all over the world have been raving about Christina's inventive Northwest specialties for years. The trick is to make sure that Christina herself, the chef and owner, is covering in the kitchen, since she is the one with the magic touch. You can savor fresh local clams, superb salmon, creamy pasta dishes, and vegetarian items that are sheer heaven. Set on the second floor of a gas station and little store, the Craftsman-style dining room with oak tables and chairs, hardwood floors, and wildflower arrangements is island-elegant—not too fancy, but tastefully done. The building is right on the waterfront, and views of the mountains surrounding Eastsound's inlet are fantastic, particularly from the glass-enclosed porch. On sunny summer evenings, the rooftop terrace is an alluring alternative for dinner, and the views up here are even better. For a real taste of the Northwest, Christina's is the place to come.

ROSARIO RESTAURANTS, Orcas Island
One Rosario Way
(360) 376-2222, (800) 562-8820
http://www.rosario-resort.com
Moderate to Expensive

Orcas Dining Room: Breakfast and Lunch Daily; Dinner Seasonally; Sunday Brunch
Compass Room: Dinner Daily

Rosario has two restaurants designed for romantic encounters: the stately **ORCAS DINING ROOM** and the intimate **COMPASS ROOM**. Both dining rooms are on the main floor of the historic waterfront Moran mansion and boast remarkable views. Water traffic passing through Eastsound or docking at the marina includes yachts, sailboats, and floatplanes coming and going—it is a mesmerizing scene.

High ceilings, crisp white table linens, and a peaches-and-cream color scheme lend elegance to the Orcas Dining Room. Window seats are obviously the best, but three walls of windows and the room's terraced layout allow excellent views wherever you are seated. An elaborate seafood buffet is available every Friday, and the Sunday brunch here is wonderfully extravagant. Otherwise, the menu offers typical American fare along with plenty of seafood options. Reports on the cuisine suggest that the kitchen lacks consistency— you be the judge.

Open for dinner only, the Compass Room is a more formal, intimate setting. This area was once the resort's lounge, and all the tables are lined up alongside picture windows, so you really can't go wrong. Fine dining is the focus, so fancier dishes are offered such as checkered salmon and halibut medallions with vegetable julienne and chive sauce, and braised duck breast with poached pear.

Romantic Note: Rosario is probably the most well-known establishment on the island, so reservations are highly recommended. Dress is casual at the resort, but management asks that no tank tops or shorts be worn in the Orcas Dining Room or the Compass Room. A more casual restaurant, the **CASCADE BAY CAFE**, is set aside for the underdressed.

SHIP BAY OYSTER HOUSE, Eastsound
Horseshoe Highway
(360) 376-5886
Expensive
Call for seasonal hours.
Closed December through January

Deer often graze in the orchard leading up to this white Colonial-style house, setting the mood for a splendid evening to remember. Ship Bay Oyster House is nestled on a grassy lawn only yards away from a shimmering bay, so request a window seat and watch the sun set behind the trees. The dining room is simple and understated, done in a tasteful white-and-gray color scheme. We found the tables a bit too close together, but the excess of windows allows ample sunlight (or sunset) to fill the room.

Superior, fresh local seafood is delicious and diligently prepared. Daily specials reflect what came off the boats that morning. Charbroiled Pacific king salmon and Pacific red snapper are excellent. The charbroiled halibut with wild greens and mango dressing is superb. With food like this and a fiery sky in the background, the entire experience is enticingly romantic.

Outdoor Kissing

MOUNT CONSTITUTION, Orcas Island
Moran State Park
(360) 376-2326
Road to mountain closed from late fall to early spring

From the Orcas ferry landing, go north on the Horseshoe Highway and follow signs toward Eastsound. After taking the turnoff into Eastsound, stay on the main road and pass through town. Continue south on this road and you will come to the massive white arch that marks the entrance to Moran State Park. The six-mile road to Mount Constitution is clearly marked, on the left.

From Mount Constitution's vantage point of 2,409 feet, the highest elevation on the San Juan Islands, a breathtaking view stretches to un-believable distances. On a clear day, you can see Mount Baker, Mount Rainier, the Olympics, the Cascades, and the Gulf Islands, not to mention the 171 other islands in the San Juan archipelago and the coastal towns across the water. The easily attained summit boasts a historic stone lookout tower well above the treetops. Even though this site is typically covered with tourists, a visit will be worth your while: the view simply cannot be rivaled. Unquestion-ably, Mount Constitution is a must-see for any island visitor. (Even if you are staying on a different island, it is worth the day-trip to Orcas Island.)

Romantic Option: On the way up the mountain, you will see a turnout on the right for **CASCADE FALLS**. An easy, short hike leads to a fern-lined stream and cascading waterfall. This scene provides a great photo opportunity and could also inspire a kiss or two.

Romantic Suggestion: If you would like to bring along a picnic for a mountaintop meal, make a stop at **ROSES BREAD AND SPECIALTIES**, located at the back of Eastsound Square, just off A Street in Eastsound, (360) 376-5805 (Inexpensive to Moderate). Gourmet meats and cheeses, fresh homemade European-style bread, wine, and a fun variety of locally made items are available for your afternoon feast.

QUARTER MOON CRUISES, Deer Harbor
(360) 376-2878
Very Expensive
Reservations Required
Lunch and Dinner Cruises
Closed November through April

Riding the ferry from Anacortes to the San Juan Islands is a magnificent prelude to a romantic getaway. However, this brief time on the water surrounded by so many other vacationers will probably leave you longing for a private, relaxed cruise around the islands. Quarter Moon Cruises may provide just what you are looking for.

How does an excursion on a deluxe 42-foot motor yacht sound? Gourmet lunch or dinner cruises last approximately three and a half hours, and the menu always includes fresh local seafood, homemade pastas, soup, salad, fresh bread, dessert, and a complimentary Northwest microbrew, Washington wine, or other beverage. On warm summer days, this feast is presented outside on the deck. Even if the weather is not cooperating, the view around you can be enjoyed from the comfortable main salon, where windows line the walls. Up to six people may join you for the ride, but two-person excursions can also be arranged (for an additional fee, of course).

Romantic Option: Quarter Moon Cruises also offers bed-and-breakfast cruises. This type of trip begins with a yacht cruise, during which lunch is served. In the afternoon, the boat sets anchor just offshore and you can paddle in a rowboat to one of the islands. Transportation on-island is provided for whichever activities you like, and you are then transported to a bed and breakfast, where you spend the night. After breakfast, it's back to the yacht for more cruising around the archipelago. Prices vary depending on which bed and breakfast is included, but rates start at $430 per person for a two-night, three-day cruise. This is not exactly inexpensive, but keep in mind that the price includes sailing through the islands for three days, activities such as crabbing or fishing, three lunches, two nights at a bed and breakfast, and any transportation necessary. Bon voyage!

SEA KAYAKING

Osprey Tours, Eastsound, (360) 376-3677, (800) 529-2567
Shearwater Adventures, Inc., Eastsound, (360) 376-4699
Prices start at $35 per person

There is something quite remarkable about propelling yourselves in a two-person kayak through the open waters around the forested islands of the San Juans. It's exciting to be part of nature's aquatic playground, where eagles and gulls swoop down across the water's surface, a variety of seabirds dive underwater, otters and seals dart in and out of the current, and, on rare occasions, a great orca effortlessly glides by. There are no words to describe the sensation of watching the world from this vantage point, and the strength of your arms (or lack of it) has little bearing on the quality of the experience. All kinds of special trips are possible, some of which include time for picnicking, sunbathing, and island exploration. Whichever one you choose, you won't regret the experience.

WHALE WATCHING CRUISES, Orcas Island　　　　
Deer Harbor Charters, Deer Harbor, (360) 376-5989, (800) 544-5758
Orcas Island Eclipse Charters, Orcas Ferry Landing, (360) 376-4663,
(800) 376-6566
Prices start at $35 per person

Orcas Island's name suggests that it is the place to come to view the majestic orca, but it is actually San Juan Island that is best known for whale sightings from the shore. If you are able to get out on the water, however, everything changes and you just may be lucky enough to catch a glimpse of one. What inspires these incredible creatures to put on such a show is not known, but their behavior includes tail-lobbing, in which they wave their sleek black tails above the surface; spy-hopping, in which their heads peek out of the ocean and they seemingly observe the activity around them; and breaching, in which they propel their entire bodies out of the water and then splash with an awesome force. Even when they are just gracefully gliding along with their massive dorsal fins cutting through the water, it is a sight to see. Witnessing such a performance could change your life. Even if you aren't graced by the presence of Orcas, you may well see porpoises, seals, various seabirds, or bald eagles, and just being out on the water is a wondrous experience.

Lopez Island

Although Lopez Island is one of the better-known islands in the San Juan archipelago (it's one of the four on the ferry run), it still seems untouched, with its miles of farmland, rolling tundra, and roaming wild rabbits. Don't be surprised if passersby wave to you from their cars—everybody does, and by the end of your stay, it will have become habit to wave in return.

Hotel/Bed and Breakfast Kissing

BLUE FJORD CABINS, Lopez Island
Elliott Avenue
(360) 468-2749
Moderate; No Credit Cards
Minimum stay requirement on weekends, holidays, and in summers

Romance is Blue Fjord's middle name. It doesn't get much more secluded than these two Nordic cabins nestled in the heart of a 16-acre forest. Both cabins, sequestered beneath groves of cedar and fir trees, are perfect for those seeking to escape everything but each other. Sunlight filters through skylights in both of the simply decorated cabins, which are appointed with open-beam ceilings and wood paneling. Even though the furnishings are plain and the colors a bit out of date, the queen-size beds, full kitchens, large decks with forest views, and privacy on all sides more than compensate.

Just steps from the innkeepers' house is a short nature trail (a five-minute walk) that winds down to Jasper Bay. Savor the stillness as you relax in the gazebo on the beach, with a stunning view of Mount Baker in the distance. You may also catch a glimpse of your only other neighbors (besides the owners): bald eagles, blue herons, and a cluster of sea otters.

Romantic Note: This is not a bed and breakfast, so you'll be expected to supply all of your own food.

EDENWILD INN, Lopez Island
Lopez Village
(360) 468-3238
Moderate to Expensive
Minimum stay requirement on holiday weekends

In some respects Edenwild Inn isn't really a typical Northwest island getaway. Every detail of this sparkling-new, totally elegant, upscale Victorian farmhouse feels somewhat out of place in such rural surroundings. However, the only people who think the Edenwild is a bit too slick for this semi-remote island are the people who haven't stayed here. The Edenwild strikes a perfect balance: you can get away from it all and still enjoy the convenience of uptown amenities. (Now that's romantic.) The eight rooms here are all simply but beautifully appointed with choice furnishings, stunning hardwood floors, and tiled private bathrooms. Some even have fireplaces and views of the water.

Breakfast is a generous display of fresh muffins and breads, blueberry-stuffed breakfast pie with blueberry sauce, orange baked French toast, and a hot baked-egg dish served at two-person tables.

Romantic Note: Something new has popped up at Edenwild Inn recently: a casual restaurant serving a little of everything, from burgers to fajitas to chicken Parmesan. We don't recommend it for romance, but if you're waiting for the ferry and have nothing to do, you may want to give it a try.

INN AT SWIFT'S BAY, Lopez Island
Port Stanley Road
(360) 468-3636
http://www.pgsi.com/swiftsbay
Inexpensive to Expensive
Minimum stay requirement on holiday weekends

Even though the gracious hosts at the Inn at Swift's Bay have become a bit more hands-off than in years past, they still leave no stone unturned in creating an enchanting, luxurious stay for you in their Tudor inn. Tucked behind a stand of cedar trees, just minutes from the beach, the inn fills almost every requirement necessary for a romantic interlude. Lounge in the cozy common rooms adorned with rich colors, floral fabrics, and adorable hand-sewn teddy bears, or stargaze from the private hot tub in the quiet backyard. (You can reserve the hot tub to ensure privacy.)

All five guest rooms continue in the same theme, appointed with soothing colors and a unique elegance. Only three of the five rooms have private baths, but even the two rooms that do share a bath are beautifully endowed with luscious linens and lovely antiques. Both attic suites are particularly alluring, with skylights, queen-size beds, gas fireplaces, generous space, and private entrances.

Make a toast to your love with a bottle of chilled sparkling white wine, delivered to your bedside on request—or, if you're in a literary mood, add an entry to the inn's ongoing write-your-own-mystery. Top off your stay with an exquisite gourmet breakfast served at small two-person tables. The hazelnut waffles and vegetable frittatas are out of this world.

Romantic Alternative: THE HUNTER BAY HOUSE is the other lovable accommodation of the Inn at Swift's Bay. This self-contained, rustically elegant cabin on Hunter Bay is brimming with class and features down-filled sofas and chairs, an impressive sound system with an extensive library of CDs, and lush linens and fabrics. Other amenities include a fireplace, a full kitchen (breakfast is up to you), a private deck, water views, an outdoor hot tub, and access to a private beach. It's a great option if the Inn at Swifts Bay is booked and you would like to stay for at least two nights.

MACKAYE HARBOR INN, Lopez Island
MacKaye Harbor Road
(360) 468-2253
http://www.ohwy.com/wa/m/mackahin.htm
Inexpensive to Moderate
Minimum stay requirement seasonally

Kayakers, beachcombers, and romantics alike can find a haven for their hearts and hobbies in this gracious farmhouse and carriage house overlooking MacKaye Harbor. Each of the five cozy guest rooms in the farmhouse is adorned with a mismatched blend of antiques and country furnishings, plus full or partial water views. Unfortunately, only two of the rooms in the main house have private bathrooms. In the rear of the main farmhouse is the adjacent Carriage House, appointed with a private bathroom, white wicker furnishings, a blue-and-white-tiled floor, and small kitchenette.

MacKaye Harbor House's prime beach setting is what makes it such an ideal getaway, and after the gourmet international breakfast (recipes are available), you can borrow some of the assorted recreational equipment and row off to sea in romantic two-person kayaks.

Restaurant Kissing

BAY CAFE, Lopez Island
Lopez Village
(360) 468-3700
Moderate to Expensive
Call for seasonal hours.

It's a shame the Bay Cafe serves only dinner—we would have gladly come here twice, or even more. The casual, eclectic atmosphere includes colorful artwork and festive dishware displayed on the walls, a wooden kayak hung overhead, and an agreeable mixture of European and American furnishings. The menu is also eclectic. Excellent choices include grilled black tiger prawns with red chili shrimp tamale cakes and mole sauce, as well as the pan-seared, Indian spice–rubbed chicken with dosas, dal, and raita. Both items are sure to tempt you into ordering dessert. (If dinner was this good, how can you go wrong?) Needless to say, the chocolate torte and raspberry cobbler are mouth-wateringly good. Although your meal may take a while to arrive, the staff is remarkably accommodating, and you'll feel comfortable lingering over a glass of wine and pleasant conversation.

GAIL'S, Lopez Island
Lopez Village
(360) 468-2150
Inexpensive
Call for seasonal hours.

Gail's is one of Lopez Island's few lunch spots, but that's not the only reason people flock here. It also features a menu with a wide selection of homemade baked goods and healthy vegetarian options. The carrot ginger soup was delightful the day we were there, and the sesame chicken salad was fresh and tasty. (Lately, we have heard reports of an inconsistent kitchen— and, come to think of it, the garden burger was soggy and unflavorful.) After your meal, be sure to peruse the gourmet desserts that are certain to keep you busy (and satisfied) as you while away the hours until the next ferry. Windows in the airy dining room look out on a patio set beneath a vine-covered trellis, and there are distant water views. Maybe missing a ferry isn't so bad after all.

Shaw Island

Being the smallest of the ferry-traveled San Juan Islands, Shaw Island is also the least populated and developed. The only business establishment here is at the ferry terminal, where a little general store is run completely by nuns (yes, the nuns—in full habit—even rope in the ferryboat). From the moment you step off the ferry, utter tranquility surrounds you and you begin to shed your quick city paces. What is the best way to explore Shaw's natural surroundings, rural country roads, secluded beaches, and nightly sunsets? Pack up a picnic, hop on your bikes, and ride to your own private grassy field. You'll have to share the space only with the occasional deer or blue heron. A day on Shaw Island, with no distractions other than the birds' sweet songs and the pleasant company of each other, will make for a day to remember.

Puget Sound Area

Bellingham

Bellingham's charming historic Fairhaven District, the spectacular beginning of **CHUCKANUT DRIVE** (see Outdoor Kissing), the sparkling waters of Lake Whatcom and Bellingham Bay, and the spellbinding slopes of Mount Baker, only an hour's drive to the east, make Bellingham a transcendent romantic destination. Congenial neighborhoods, Western Washington University, and an overwhelming number of outlet stores are a few of the attractions that have made it one of the fastest-growing towns in the state. Most of Bellingham is lovely, but like any expanding city, several areas are becoming busy and crowded. Luckily, there are still many worthwhile places to seek out together, as well as incredible views of Puget Sound.

Hotel/Bed and Breakfast Kissing

BIG TREES BED AND BREAKFAST, Bellingham
4840 Fremont Street
(360) 647-2850, (800) 647-2850
Inexpensive to Expensive

Old-growth cedars and firs, sprawling green lawns, colorful gardens of wild and domestic flowers, berry bushes, and a flowing creek surround this stately gray Craftsman-style home. Reminiscent of Grandma's house, the eclectically decorated interior retains its handsome original woodwork, including a wood-beamed ceiling and built-in cabinetry around a huge stone fireplace in the common area. Upstairs, the three guest rooms are appointed with fresh flowers, floral comforters or handmade quilts, feather beds, various antique and contemporary pieces, and televisions. Cedar and Rhodie each have their own private bathrooms, and Rhodie's deserves special mention: the floor is an ongoing collage, as guests are encouraged to cut out magazine pictures and shellac them to the painted floral floor. (We know it sounds funky, but it's really quite a work of art.) The third room, Maple, does not have its own bathroom, but it is not rented unless two couples are traveling together, in which case Maple shares Rhodie's bathroom.

Your full country breakfast will most likely include an assortment of freshly baked scones, fresh fruit and juice, and a hot entrée such as fruit cobbler, Dutch babies, waffles, or breakfast frittata. After breakfast, you may want to stroll the grounds with one of the innkeeper's lovable dogs or just sit on the outside porch and take in the tranquil neighborhood setting.

SAIL THE SAN JUANS, Bellingham
3047 West 36th Street, Suite 186
(360) 671-5852, (800) 729-3207
A seven-day chartered tour, with all meals included, costs about $500 per day per couple. Prices vary according to season and number of passengers.

Ahoy, mates! Come sail the San Juans for three days or an entire week aboard *Northwind,* a sparkling, 42-foot Catalina sailboat. This admirable floating getaway is a unique (although expensive) alternative to "stationary" hotels, inns, and bed and breakfasts. Guests have the opportunity to help create the week's flexible itinerary, yet are still pampered by someone else doing the cooking, shopping, and navigating. What could be more relaxing and romantic than sailing with your sweetheart through Bellingham Bay and the magnificent Strait of Georgia? During your tour, you'll stop at both remote and popular destinations in the San Juan archipelago. On occasion, porpoises, seals, and otters play near the boat, and orcas and minke whales are sighted about 50 percent of the time.

Accommodations for one couple traveling alone are located in the bow, where you'll find a snug double bed, blue and white linens, teak accents, and a private head and shower. If you decide to travel with another couple (which is far more economical), you will stay in identical bedrooms in the stern, featuring nautical blue comforters, teak floors and walls, water views through small windows, and a shared head and shower. Although the rooms are snug (just enough space for you and the bed), they are exceedingly cozy and romantic. *Northwind* is also equipped with fishing and crabbing equipment, TV/VCR, a CD player with an extensive library of CDs, a freezer, refrigerator, and foulweather gear.

Gourmet meals, cooked by the crew, are served in the salon. Guests can look forward to a variety of creative dishes, such as eggs, crêpes, blintzes, scones, and fruit for breakfast; sandwiches, salads, and soups for lunch; and fresh halibut, salmon, crab (possibly caught by you that very day), pastas, and chicken dishes for dinner.

With the Olympic Mountains to the south, the Cascades to the east, and nothing but glistening waters and charming harbor towns in between, your sailing adventure will be nothing less than magical.

SCHNAUZER CROSSING
BED AND BREAKFAST INN, Bellingham

4421 Lakeway Drive
(360) 733-0055, (800) 562-2808
http://www.virtualcities.com
Moderate to Very Expensive
Minimum stay requirement on weekends and holidays

For years, Schnauzer Crossing has set the standard for other bed and breakfasts to aspire to, and we are pleased to say that this is still the case. Set on a bluff overlooking Lake Whatcom and surrounded by colorful gardens, perfect lawns, a koi pond, and tall trees, this contemporary home with floor-to-ceiling windows is a dream come true. Every detail necessary for an intimate getaway is here, so you can relax in an atmosphere of comfortable luxury.

Schnauzer Crossing offers two guest rooms, located in the main house, and an elegant guest cottage adjacent to the home. The Master Suite, or King Room, is like a small apartment, with a private entrance from a tree-framed garden, a king-size bed with a floral down comforter, an alcove sitting area, CD player, TV/VCR, wet bar, and wood-burning fireplace. You will never want to leave this suite, especially after you see the huge bathroom with Jacuzzi tub for two, roomy double-headed shower, and sumptuous terry-cloth robes. Not as big or as lavish, but just as lovely, the next-door Queen Room is appointed with a crisp white down comforter on a queen-size bed, colorful views of rhododendrons, a closet library with a wonderful selection of books, and a private bathroom with tub and shower. Two sets of doors shut the Queen Room off completely from the rest of the home, so you will not lack privacy.

The picture-perfect guest cottage, decorated in a subtle Asian motif, is set amidst lofty fir trees. It features a very private wraparound deck, hardwood floors, a king-size bed with a down comforter, a cozy sitting area, TV/VCR with an extensive movie selection, CD player, gas fireplace, and a large Jacuzzi tub in the green-tiled bathroom. A wet bar hidden away in the closet holds the makings for coffee, tea, and hot cocoa, along with an "I-forgot-it basket," filled with everything that you may have forgotten at home, and other fun things you never even knew you needed.

Breakfast is a luscious presentation of gourmet delights that might include sweet rhubarb crisp with hazelnut cream dribbled on top, triple sec French toast with three kinds of syrups, fresh muffins, and a fruit and yogurt parfait. (As good as it sounds, it tastes even better.) If you can pull yourselves away from your room or the breakfast table, take a bike ride on the nearby rural roads or go for a leisurely walk around Lake Padden. Afterwards, you can have a good long steamy soak in the outdoor hot tub, tucked next to the house under the towering trees.

STRATFORD MANOR, Bellingham
1416 Van Wyck Road
(360) 715-8441
Inexpensive to Moderate

Picture a proper English countryside estate—a sprawling Tudor home with a lordly atmosphere, surrounded by rolling emerald hills sprinkled with wildflowers and expansive fields. That's Stratford Manor, which seems curiously out of place in Bellingham. Inside, things are a bit more ordinary, but only a bit. The manor's four large common rooms provide guests with plenty of relaxing space. The four rather spacious, exceedingly comfortable guest rooms, located in one wing of the home, are nicely outfitted with run-of-the-mill traditional furnishings, thick down comforters, small Jacuzzi tubs, gas fireplaces, and Martha Stewart touches. Any of them would be a welcome sight for road- or city-weary eyes.

In the morning, a wake-up tray with fresh muffins and coffee is delivered to your door even before you dress and come down for the generous, delectable four-course breakfast served around the large dining room table. All in all, the gracious hosts and the welcoming atmosphere make a stay here a satisfying and noble experience.

Romantic Note: On the way to breakfast you'll pass through the solarium where the hot tub is located. To say the least, this is a strange configuration, because you literally have to step around the hot tub to proceed down the hallway.

Restaurant Kissing

CAFE TOULOUSE, Bellingham
114 West Magnolia Street
(360) 733-8996
Inexpensive
Breakfast and Lunch Daily

Cafe Toulouse has a consistently stellar reputation as a good lunch spot, and the gourmet delights produced by the serious kitchen are the reason why. The cafe's busy corner location is too distracting to make this place intimate or romantic, but the interior is bright and cheery, and the friendly staff is eager to please. Tantalizing selections from the eclectic menu include chili verde with cilantro pesto, a curried chicken salad with almonds, and cappelini aglio with sun-dried tomatoes, artichoke hearts, capers, kalamata olives, and caramelized onions. We're especially partial to the wood-fired pizzas and calzones, which are always superb.

IL FIASCO, Bellingham
1309 Commercial Street
(360) 676-9136
Moderate to Expensive
Lunch Monday-Friday; Dinner Daily

Il Fiasco ("the flask" in Italian) is still Bellingham's premier dining location, even after a change of ownership. The sophisticated yet intimate interior resembles an Italian country courtyard, with exposed brick, flower boxes, and wood shutters. Soft lighting, tall ceilings with exposed air ducts, and sunny yellow walls with terra-cotta and black accents complete the picture. We suggest beginning your meal with the fresh manila clams steamed with pancetta, fennel, tomato, and garlic, then moving on to the chicken artichoke ravioli or the duck risotto with sautéed shiitake mushrooms, green onions, roasted red pepper, and zucchini. Everything is outstanding.

ORCHARD STREET BREWERY, Bellingham
709 West Orchard Drive
(360) 647-1614
Moderate
Free Tasting and Tour; Lunch and Dinner Tuesday-Saturday

The Northwest has become quite the hot spot for micro-breweries and brew pubs (it's already famous for its coffee companies), so it seemed natural for us to include a select few that meet our strict standards. Don't worry—we haven't changed our format to include any old bar. Traditional "bar food" menus are never worth mentioning, and the rowdiness will certainly trample any feelings of intimacy or romance. No, this new breed is sophisticated and stylish, a place that can be counted on for a very enjoyable evening.

Located at the end of an industrial strip mall, Orchard Street Brewery possesses a simple modern interior with cement floors, bright red accents, exposed air ducts, an attractive open kitchen, and brewery equipment visible behind a solid glass wall. A large oil painting covers one wall, which is much appreciated since the only views are of the parking lot. The food, however, is the real reason to visit Orchard Street Brewery. We thoroughly enjoyed the roasted vegetable turnovers filled with wild mushrooms, artichoke hearts, fennel, pine nuts, and goat cheese, as well as the sesame seared sea scallops served on yakisoba noodles with oyster sauce. The cherry-smoked halibut set on a three-potato ragout surrounded by a tomato–black pepper vinaigrette was outstanding, as was the Thai chicken pizza with marinated carrots, bean sprouts, chicken, and scallions in a zesty peanut sauce. Naturally, you can select a micro-brew to accompany your meal, but even if you are not a beer lover, there is much else to sip.

We would never go so far as to say that this place is particularly intimate or romantic, but the food is exemplary. With such a lack of decent restaurants in Bellingham, we just couldn't pass it up.

PACIFIC CAFE, Bellingham
100 North Commercial Street
(360) 647-0800
Moderate to Expensive
Lunch Monday-Friday; Dinner Monday-Saturday

A soothing combination of blond wooden tables, shoji screens, and Japanese-style overhead lights fills this simply decorated downtown restaurant. Fresh fish and seafood are listed every night, but the curaçao lemon chicken, Penn Cove mussels simmered with garlic, and crab legs and salmon linguine are by far our favorites.

Outdoor Kissing

CHUCKANUT DRIVE 🙂🙂🙂🙂

From Interstate 5, exit to Highway 11 outside of Bellingham or Burlington, following the signs for Chuckanut Drive.

From the moment you embark upon this landmark coastal drive, you'll be dazzled by visual delights. If you're heading south, the exhibition starts with forested cliffs that reach down to the water's edge. On the horizon lies the silhouette of Lummi Island, and in the distance the rugged coastline of Chuckanut Bay. As you continue south, the varying patterns of islands, trees, water, and rocks form a breathtaking panorama. **LARRABEE STATE PARK**, eight miles south of Bellingham, is a perfect place to stop for a walk along the chiseled beach.

Lummi Island

Just north of Bellingham, follow the signs to the Lummi Island ferry landing or the Lummi Casino. The ferry leaves on the hour between 6 A.M. and midnight.

Accessible via a small ferry that docks just west of Bellingham, Lummi Island is just nine miles long and less than two miles wide, with no real town to speak of except for a church, a library, a post office, a fire station, and a general store. It's the perfect place for a quiet bike ride or afternoon picnic.

Hotel/Bed and Breakfast Kissing

THE WILLOWS INN, Lummi Island
2579 West Shore Drive
(360) 758-2620
http://www.pacificrim.net/~willows
Moderate to Very Expensive
Call for seasonal closures.
Recommended Wedding Site

Your senses will be stimulated once you enter this white waterfront home. Embraced by rose arbors, vegetable patches, and herb gardens, this lovely retreat offers scintillating views of the Strait of Georgia and the forested hills of nearby Orcas Island. Four guest rooms are available in the main house, two rooms occupy an adjacent guest house, and a small self-contained cottage sits at the rear of the property. The four rooms in the main house have private bathrooms, heirloom antiques mixed with contemporary touches, plush comforters, and cozy sitting areas. The two upstairs rooms, Sunset and Sunrise, have the best views of either the water or surrounding trees. The Guest House features dark fir paneling and is outfitted in a Scottish Highland theme. Both bedrooms in the Guest House, Heather and Thistle, have comfy linens draped over queen-size beds, antique furnishings, and spacious bathrooms (Thistle has a Jacuzzi tub). The dark wood paneling in Thistle is a bit too dark, but the effect is cozy rather than dreary. A full kitchen and ample living room with a TV/VCR, CD player, and wood-burning fireplace make up the rest of the home, and a door off the living room opens to a private deck with distant water views. The Honeymoon Cottage is adorable and serene; it boasts hardwood floors, a small bathroom with claw-foot tub, floral linens, full kitchen, TV/VCR, and a deck with wonderful views of the water and the colorful gardens.

Elaborate three-course breakfasts are served in the glass-enclosed formal dining room, where fresh breads, creative soufflés, and stuffed French toast with homemade syrups liven up your morning. Later, a delightful afternoon tea (with some of the best shortbreads you'll ever taste) is served in the spacious living room, warmed by a mammoth stone fireplace. Unfortunately, the breakfast and afternoon tea are only available on Saturdays and Sundays, so book your stay accordingly if you would like to partake. If you are staying at The Willows Inn during mid-week, you are on your own for breakfast goodies. But with full kitchens in both the Guest House and Honeymoon Cottage, this shouldn't be a problem.

Bow

Hotel/Bed and Breakfast Kissing

SAMISH POINT BY THE BAY, Bow
447 Samish Point Road
(360) 766-6610, (800) 916-6161
Moderate to Very Expensive

Finding new places is exciting but difficult; finding a bed and breakfast as private and exclusive as this one makes all the effort worthwhile. It doesn't get much more private than Samish Point, which features 43 acres of forested lands, fruit orchards, and sweeping lawns hemmed with colorful flowers. All this surveys panoramic views of Samish Bay and Puget Sound. More than 100 walking trails invite you to set off on your own romantic adventure, and private sandy beaches wait to be discovered.

Of the four guest rooms offered here, one is in the main house, and the other three are in a guest house. If you stay in the main house, you'll want to spend most of your time in the contemporary living room, with its crisp white furnishings and wall-to-wall windows offering impressive views of the water and gardens. The breakfast room is just as elegant, with dark slate floors, tall ceilings with skylights, a wood-burning stove, and more stunning views. Your morning meal may include banana granola, pancakes with home-made berry syrups, omelets, French toast, and fresh fruit. Best of all, you are the only ones who will get to enjoy this wonderful room in the morning, which makes it all the more intimate. Unfortunately, the guest bedroom here lacks much of the splendor and luxury of the common areas, but the contemporary furnishings, queen-size bed, hardwood floors, private bathroom, and private entrance make it a homey and relaxing retreat.

The Cape Cod–style guest house sits across a gravel road in the middle of a grassy lawn bordered by flowers, grazing sheep, and a dense forest. Inside, a cheery living room is adorned with hardwood floors, a river-rock fireplace, gingham couches, and sliding doors that open onto a wooden deck where a hot tub awaits moonstruck lovers. A white-tiled designer kitchen next to the living room is available for use only if you rent the entire house. One guest room is located on the main floor, and it features a king-size bed and pine furnishings. Two more are found upstairs, each with its own private bathroom, patchwork quilts or floral comforters, pine furnishings, and views of the pastoral landscape.

In the morning, a breakfast buffet is set up in the kitchen with cereals, pastries, quiches, and fresh fruit.

Romantic Note: Unless you rent the whole guest cottage (a nice but pricey option), you could be staying here with couples you don't know. Because the cottage is so isolated, this could be a bit awkward. But with so much to explore outside, you will probably never see the other couples.

Restaurant Kissing

OYSTER BAR, Bow
240 Chuckanut Drive
(360) 766-6185
Expensive to Very Expensive
Call for seasonal hours.

This refined and elegant restaurant is a culinary milepost along famous Chuckanut Drive. Only 12 tables fill the pocket-size, knotty-pine dining room, lined with floor-to-ceiling windows that frame breathtaking views of Samish Bay and the San Juan Islands. More tables are available downstairs, but the atmosphere is far less warm and cozy. Unfortunately, service can be slow, but the presentations are always impeccable. The quintessentially Northwest menu features mostly seafood and shellfish. We ordered the grilled salmon with sautéed shiitake mushrooms and radicchio in a balsamic-lemon butter, and it was beyond reproach. The Oysters 222, six Samish Bay oysters with three different toppings, were perfect, and the chocolate indulgence—rich chocolate cake with warm dark and white chocolate sauces drizzled over the top—was an early taste of heaven.

OYSTER CREEK INN, Bow
190 Chuckanut Drive
(360) 766-6179
Moderate
Lunch and Dinner Daily

Only a minute's drive north of the **OYSTER BAR** (reviewed above), but a far greater distance in mood and style, the casual and unassuming Oyster Creek Inn provides a relaxing environment for lunch or dinner. With only a handful of tables in the wood-paneled dining room, everyone has a chance to gaze out the huge windows at towering trees and rugged cliffs. As you would expect, the classic Northwest menu features fresh seafood and shell-fish, and the halibut, prawns, and oysters are flavorful and precisely pre-pared. Entrées are accompanied by your choice of a salad of assorted fresh greens or oyster soup, both of which are exceptional.

Anacortes

Anacortes is well known to ferry-bound travelers headed to and from the San Juan Islands. Even if you've planned on only a brief encounter with this Northwest port of call, unexpected ferry traffic could cause you to miss your boat. Not to worry—there are a few romantic locales where you can while away the hours until the next boat arrives.

Hotel/Bed and Breakfast Kissing

CHANNEL HOUSE, Anacortes
2902 Oakes Avenue
(360) 293-9382, (800) 238-4353
Inexpensive

If you didn't know better, you might bypass this nondescript beige Victorian farmhouse on your way to the ferry dock. Given the chance, how-ever, the Channel House will easily convince you to stay in Anacortes longer than you anticipated. The shiny hardwood floors, Oriental rugs, wood-burning fireplace, and modest furnishings lend a cozy atmosphere to the main floor of the home.

Of the six guest rooms, four are in the main house and two more are in an adjacent cottage. The main-house rooms are all authentically appointed with antique furnishings, lace curtains, down comforters, and spacious private bathrooms. A stately four-poster canopy bed stands in the center of the aptly named Canopy Room, our favorite. Outside, a walkway lined with flowers and plants passes by the not-so-private hot tub on its way to the Rose Cottage. which holds two large suites. Victorian Rose is equipped with a queen-size four-poster bed, whirlpool tub, French doors that open to views of the water, and a warm wood-burning fireplace. Country Rose boasts Laura Ashley linens, sunny yellow walls, a two-person Jacuzzi tub, and another crackling wood-burning fireplace. These two suites are indeed Channel House's finest offerings.

Breakfast can be scheduled for any time, depending on which ferry you may be taking in the morning, and is guaranteed to delight hungry lovebirds. Homemade breads and muffins, a hot egg dish or French toast stuffed with cream cheese and pecans, plus plenty of seasonal fruit, are likely to get your day off to a good start.

MAJESTIC HOTEL, Anacortes
419 Commercial Avenue
(360) 293-3355, (800) 588-4780
Inexpensive to Expensive

It's hard to miss the suitably named Majestic Hotel, a grand four-story building built in 1889, standing tall in the midst of the industrial jostle of Commercial Avenue. French doors open to reveal a pleasant lobby with high ceilings and European decor. The 23 guest rooms have been restored over the years, but we found most of them to be rather spartan and in need of more up-to-date color schemes and romantic amenities. The best options are the fourth-floor Majestic Suites, with skylights, wet bars, refrigerators, marble bathrooms with large soaking tubs, and patios that look out to the courtyard and gardens below.

As you climb the open winding staircase to the mezzanine level for your continental breakfast, look up at the expansive stained glass skylight. For the best views (and the best kissing), be sure to climb to the cupola at the top of the hotel, which is filled with antiques and surrounded by windows.

Romantic Note: THE COURTYARD BISTRO (see Restaurant Kissing), on the main floor of the Majestic Hotel, is an elegant and delightful place for a romantic dinner.

Restaurant Kissing

THE COURTYARD BISTRO, Anacortes
419 Commercial Avenue, at the Majestic Hotel
(360) 293-3355, (800) 588-4780
Inexpensive to Expensive
Call for seasonal hours.

Located on the main floor of the Majestic Hotel, this restaurant is definitely majestic. "Bistro" is a bit of a misnomer, however, because the spacious, airy dining room, with its high ceilings, soft gold walls, and entire wall of windows, is anything but casual. You can't go wrong with the grilled salmon or the savory pasta dishes, and the Northwest seafood chowder is among the best we've had anywhere in the region.

Mount Vernon

Restaurant Kissing

WILDFLOWERS, Mount Vernon
2001 East College Way
(360) 424-9724
Moderate to Expensive
Dinner Tuesday-Saturday

Country charm is the last thing you'd expect to find anywhere near this commercialized strip of neon signs, Food Marts, and gas stations. Fortunately, you can escape the clamor and indulge your fantasies in the seclusion of this creamy white 1930s home. Pretty gardens surround the house, sheltering it from the busy street.

Inside, tables are draped in dark blue linens and tucked intimately in the cozy alcoves of the home's original living and dining rooms. Year-round Christmas lights in the corners add sparkle to the otherwise simple decor. The creative menu lists several innovative seafood and meat entrées. Begin with an appetizer of grilled eggplant with cheese, herbs, tomato, and fennel-infused olive oil, followed by Pacific tiger prawns and linguine with fresh tomato, garlic, basil, and Parmesan in white wine and Pernod. Once you've shared bites of this wonderful cuisine, you're likely to forget about the traffic outside and focus on matters closer to the heart.

La Conner

La Conner is the heart of the Skagit Valley's famous **TULIP FESTIVAL**, which takes place during the last weeks of March and first weeks of April. Its soul is the 1,500 acres of prime farmland that blanket the area with huge swatches of brilliant color. Although this area is assuredly *the* Northwest destination during the festival, every season blesses it with a romantic aura all its own. Hemmed in by mountain ranges and guarded by often-visible Mount Baker, this pastoral valley is also filled with waving cornfields, dairy farms, and acres of lush crops.

La Conner itself is a colorful, picturesque town, and a favorite spring and summer destination. Bordering the Swinomish Channel, it offers a remarkable selection of restaurants, boutiques, antique shops, and bed and breakfasts. The crowds and tour buses calm down in the late fall and winter, after the tulip lovers and vacationers leave, making La Conner a charming corner of Puget Sound for spending time together.

Romantic Note: For more information about the Tulip Festival, call the
LA CONNER CHAMBER OF COMMERCE, (360) 466-4778.

Hotel/Bed and Breakfast Kissing

AN ENGLISH COTTAGE, La Conner
832 South Fourth Street
(360) 466-2067
Inexpensive to Moderate; No Credit Cards
Call for seasonal closures.

Your enchanting English journey begins the moment you open the
wooden green gate and stroll up the brick pathway that leads to the front
door of this weathered wood-shingled home. The two rooms here are both
completely private and steeped in English country charm. The first room,
called the Private Suite, is spacious and handsomely decorated with rug-
covered hardwood floors, antique furnishings, and a wood-burning fireplace.
A white eyelet comforter graces the king-size four-poster bed, which is also
adorned with heavy white drapes that can be drawn closed to ensure a
wonderfully romantic and secluded slumber. A private sitting area with a
hidden TV is next to the bedroom, and beyond that is a large bathroom with
a tiled shower.

At the opposite end of the home is the sparkling Yellow Suite, awash in
sunny yellow and white. The bedroom holds a king-size bed, an antique
armoire, and a pretty painted wash basin. Colorful gardens peek at you
through every window, and a white-tiled bathroom holds a quaint claw-foot
tub. Directly outside the bedroom is a spacious sitting area, with an antique
grandfather clock and a wood-burning stove.

The backyard is filled with magical gardens. In the middle of the
colorful splendor lies a tiny summer house built of recycled weathered wood
panels and mismatched doors and shutters; it looks like something out of an
English storybook.

The final touch is a full gourmet breakfast featuring fresh fruit, warm
scones, and creative egg dishes such as smoked salmon quiche. As you sit at
the round glass table enjoying your meal, you can gaze out huge windows
that overlook an ancient madrona tree and a flowering hillside.

LA CONNER CHANNEL LODGE, La Conner
205 North First Street
(360) 466-1500
Expensive to Very Expensive

The La Conner Channel Lodge boasts a choice location on the bank of the Swinomish Channel. The dark gray shingled exterior is captivating; inside, hardwood floors, a huge stone fireplace, boldly colored area rugs, and beautiful views distinguish the common area. Charm and coziness help to play down the hotel feeling here, but the fire extinguishers and pay phones in the hallways and the metal doors to the guest rooms are hard to ignore. It is clear that at one time, all 40 units were beautifully decorated and tastefully furnished with Northwest flair, but today the worn furnishings and drab linens need more attention and are not reflected in the steep rates. The King Parlor Rooms are still the most desirable, with tall ceilings, Jacuzzi tubs, large tiled showers, fireplaces, and decks that overlook the water below. The Queen Jacuzzi Rooms are also very spacious and nice, with Jacuzzi tubs, tiled showers, wooden shutters, and Northwest prints. To polish off your relaxing stay, enjoy a romantic continental breakfast in the lovely dining alcove.

LA CONNER COUNTRY INN, La Conner
107 South Second Street
(360) 466-3101
Inexpensive to Moderate

This cozy inn is located only a block away from La Conner's busy First Street. The charming wood-shingled exterior is a suitable preview of what's inside. Tired shoppers will appreciate the cozy common area, where comfy couches sit in front of a large stone fireplace. The inn's 28 rooms, spread out between the main inn and an adjacent building, all have spacious private bathrooms and warm gas fireplaces. All of the guest rooms have tall, wood-beamed ceilings, wood paneling on the walls, brass or wooden beds, attractive floral bedspreads, and wood shutters on the windows (which help to muffle the noise from the adjacent street). In the morning, enjoy a continental breakfast served in the common area by the warmth of the roaring fire.

THE HERON, La Conner
117 Maple Avenue
(360) 466-4626
Inexpensive to Very Expensive

Although The Heron is intended to be a Victorian-style inn, the exterior and inside decor are too modern to be completely convincing. Inside, a mixture of antiques and contemporary furnishings fill the common area and the dining room, as well as each of the 12 guest rooms. Private bathrooms, warm comforters and quilts on antique or contemporary beds, TVs, and attractive pine, antique, or wicker furnishings give each guest room a homey country feel. Some rooms have pleasant views of the adjacent meadows, and one special room, called the Honeymoon Suite, has a large Jacuzzi tub set in a sunny corner. Guests in other rooms needn't despair, however; an outdoor hot tub, set against a picturesque backdrop of La Conner farmland, is available to all.

A large continental breakfast buffet served in the inn's downstairs dining room features hot scones, cereals, cinnamon rolls, fresh fruit, and some sort of hot egg dish.

HOTEL PLANTER, La Conner
715 First Street
(360) 466-4710, (800) 488-5409
Inexpensive to Expensive

Even though the rooms in this historic gray stone building are located directly above well-traveled First Street, the hotel's old-world charm makes this a worthwhile destination. Traffic noise is audible here during the day, but the hustle calms down at night, just in time for you to sink into a blissful slumber.

All 12 units boast plenty of country touches and modern amenities, including TVs hidden in custom pine armoires, dried flower arrangements, floral bedspreads atop double or queen-size beds, and wicker furnishings; extra tall windows and ceilings make them feel quite spacious. Small private bathrooms accompany each room, and the old-fashioned tilework and pedestal sinks save them from being too standard. Three rooms look down on a quaint country courtyard where a hot tub awaits in a wooden gazebo. Our favorite room is the Queen Jacuzzi Room, which has a large Jacuzzi tub in the corner near the bed, and a great view of the courtyard through lofty trees.

KATY'S INN, La Conner
503 South Third Street
(360) 466-3366, (800) 914-7767
Inexpensive

Surrounded by a neatly trimmed lawn, colorful perennial gardens, a forested hillside, and a white picket fence, this 1876 country Victorian bed and breakfast is conveniently located just blocks from La Conner's lively heart. Warmth and elegance envelop you in the main parlor, where antique furnishings and family heirlooms mix with tasteful contemporary accents. Upstairs, four small but beautiful guest rooms are chock-full of country-elegant comfort. Ashley's Room, the smallest of the four, features hand-painted

French Provincial furnishings and an antique lace bedcovering. The Garden Room is awash in blue and white, with views of Fidalgo Island and the Swinomish Channel; the Rose Room is done up in pastel pinks and blues; and the Lilac Room, the most spacious, holds a beautiful antique armoire and a cheery white wicker bed. The Lilac Room and the Garden Room have private bathrooms; Ashley's Room and Rose Room share one bathroom (located down the hall) with an antique chain-flush toilet and an elongated claw-foot tub. All four rooms have access to a wraparound deck that offers views of the tranquil neighborhood surroundings and Swinomish Channel. A soak in the enormous hot tub set beneath a white gazebo can be the perfect end to a long day of touring the area.

The friendly innkeepers offer afternoon refreshments in the lovely main parlor. A full gourmet breakfast of baked goods, fresh fruit, and a hot entrée such as French toast or a veggie omelet is served in the formal dining room. If you find it too hard to leave the warmth of your cozy bed, breakfast can be delivered to your door on a silver platter.

Romantic Note: Christian mementos are scattered throughout this bed and breakfast, and your morning meal is accompanied by a Christian prayer led by the innkeepers.

RAINBOW INN, La Conner
1075 Chilberg Road
(360) 466-4578, (888) 266-8879
Inexpensive to Moderate

This impressively renovated turn-of-the-century farmhouse is only a five-minute drive to the busy town center of La Conner, making it a perfect refuge from the mobs of tourists. Although it sits on a heavily trafficked road, a perennial garden and a manicured lawn help shield it from too much noise. You'll also enjoy the sweeping views of the bucolic valley and Mount Baker, a stately old chestnut tree, and the nearby tulip and daffodil fields that blaze with color in the spring. (An outdoor hot tub set beneath a picturesque gazebo offers grand views of the tulips and daffodils when the season is right.) Inside this mammoth home, a snug parlor with a wood-burning fireplace beckons travelers to sit and relax. Three floors of country-rustic rooms, most with lovely pastoral views, are all named after flowers and decorated with floral and calico wallpapers, fluffy comforters, and a combination of antique and contemporary furnishings. All of the rooms have private baths except for the three on the third floor; they share just one bath. The Violet Room and the Heather Room share a large wraparound deck, an ideal spot for reading and sipping iced tea on hot summer days.

A full gourmet breakfast featuring fresh baked goods, fresh fruit, and an ever-changing hot entrée such as brandied French toast or a vegetable frittata is served on an enclosed sundeck. This area is lined with windows and offers intimate tables for two.

WHITE SWAN GUEST HOUSE, La Conner
1388 Moore Road
(360) 445-6805
Inexpensive to Moderate

Just six miles from La Conner's town center, this pleasant bed and breakfast sits on a quiet country road lined with fields and shade trees. A long gravel driveway bordered by commanding poplars takes you to the door of the yellow and white Queen Anne–style farmhouse. A friendly atmosphere is apparent throughout, from the kitchen (always stocked with a plate of freshly baked chocolate chip cookies) to the cozy parlor filled with antique couches and chairs placed near a wood-burning stove. Upstairs, the three guest rooms offer relaxing views of the tranquil surroundings. The rooms are all named for their color schemes: the Yellow Room has sunny yellow walls and a yellow comforter, the Peach Room boasts a pretty patchwork quilt, and the Pink Room features a pale pink comforter and a snug sitting area in a window-lined turret. Unfortunately, all three rooms share just two bathrooms, located down the hall. Luckily, both bathrooms are quite spacious (one holds a large tiled shower, the other an elongated claw-foot tub), and they also afford some of the best views of the brilliantly colored flower gardens.

For more private accommodations, choose the self-contained Garden Cottage, set under huge silver maples on the edge of the property. Amenities include a cedar deck, a comfortable living room, floor-to-ceiling windows showcasing views of the surrounding farmland, a full kitchen, and a capacious loft bedroom. It isn't plush, but it can be your own country home in the middle of this pristine setting.

A continental country breakfast is served in the brightly painted breakfast room to guests staying in the main house. It is delivered to your door if you are staying in the cottage.

THE WILD IRIS, La Conner
121 Maple Avenue
(360) 466-1400, (800) 477-1400
http://www.ncia.com/~wildiris
Inexpensive to Moderate

Every detail at The Wild Iris exudes country refinement and amorous bliss. Although the two-story Victorian-style inn hugs the parking lot, sheer elegance is found inside the parlor and in each of the 20 individually decorated guest rooms. Most desirable of the accommodations are the deluxe Jacuzzi king or queen suites, with elegant contemporary furnishings, plush down comforters, extra-roomy Jacuzzi tubs set near gas fireplaces, and views of the stunning mountains and sprawling valley. Some rooms have romantic white-veiled wrought-iron beds; others feature white wicker or contemporary pine furnishings, and all of the main-floor rooms sport private patios that look out to picturesque farmland. We were most impressed with the fanciful Cloud Room; this room lives up to its name with blue rag-rolled walls, wooden columns, playful white cloud wall murals, and billowy white gauze draped above the king-size bed.

A complimentary gourmet breakfast is served at separate tables in the inn's country-style dining room, where Greek omelets, cheese soufflés, fresh croissants, homemade granola, and fresh fruit are served buffet-style. Guests of the hotel will also want to enjoy the delectable dinners served on Friday and Saturday evenings (available for guests only). We recommend the nova smoked sockeye salmon with French bread and capers, followed by fresh Pacific monkfish broiled and basted with a garlic butter seasoned with lemon, saffron, shallots, and Madeira.

Restaurant Kissing

ANDIAMO, La Conner
505 South First Street
(360) 466-9111
Lunch Saturday-Sunday; Dinner Daily

Because Andiamo is owned by **PALMER'S RESTAURANT AND PUB** (reviewed elsewhere in this section), we had high hopes that the food and service there would match Palmer's. Alas, while the food is equal in quality, the service is inexperienced and inappropriate. We nevertheless enjoyed the superb views of the Swinomish Channel, best seen from the upstairs dining room, where pale green walls are adorned with Italian artwork and the tables are covered with pink linens. The menu is quintessentially Italian, and you can be sure that dishes such as chicken cannelloni with pine nuts and pesto sauce or seafood entrées such as linguine with prawns and bell peppers will be perfectly prepared and presented.

CALICO CUPBOARD, La Conner
720 South First Street
(360) 466-4451

Inexpensive; No Credit Cards
Breakfast and Lunch Daily

We don't need to write much about this darling cafe because the enticing aromas that waft through the open doors and windows will tell you all you need to know. The casual, busy interior is decorated with calico wallpaper, two- and four-person tables, lace curtains, and hardwood floors. The hearty menu features standard and not-so-standard items for varying appetites. We enjoyed the Popeye's Delight omelet of fresh spinach, mushrooms, red onion, tomatoes, and Swiss cheese, as well as the hot tomato-broccoli sandwich with cream cheese, sun-dried tomatoes, broccoli, and red onion topped with melted mozzarella and Parmesan cheese. Still, the fresh baked goods are the real reason to visit this country cafe. Choose from a mouthwatering assortment of warm caramel nut bars, fruit scones, Danish pastries, sour cream coffee cakes, cheesecakes, and Fudgie Wudgie Brownies. The sweet baked items at Calico Cupboard offer just the right amount of gooey goodness for the most delightful sticky sweet kisses.

LA CONNER BREWING COMPANY, La Conner
117 South First Street
(360) 466-1415
Lunch and Dinner Daily

Disregard any image you may have of a loud and smelly brewing company, because this micro-brewery strives to be recognized as a reputable dining spot. Blond wood, bold Southwest colors, copper accents, small tables, and a large wood-burning fireplace fill the warm and inviting interior. Although the menu is rather limited, the selections are surprisingly good. We were quite taken with both the smoked salmon pizza and the pesto pizza.

PALMER'S RESTAURANT AND PUB, La Conner
205 East Washington Street
(360) 466-4261
Moderate to Expensive
Lunch and Dinner Daily

The soft lighting, mauve tablecloths, hunter green carpeting, lace curtains, and wood-beamed ceiling in Palmer's upstairs dining room make it a lovely setting for an intimate evening. Try the fresh halibut rolled in hazelnuts and topped with a sherry beurre blanc; the sautéed sea scallops and prawns with fresh ginger, coconut milk, curry, and toasted cashews; or the herb-roasted chicken with brandied tomatoes and wild mushrooms. Lunch, served in the main-floor pub, is not even half as romantic, but if you order the smoked duck spinach salad or the smoked salmon linguine with capers, red onions, and cream, we know you'll survive.

WHIDBEY ISLAND

By ferryboat: Whidbey Island is accessible from Mukilteo, 20 minutes north of Seattle, and from Port Townsend, on the Olympic Peninsula. By car: Reach Whidbey Island from Anacortes via the Deception Pass Bridge, 90 minutes north of Seattle.

Aside from being one of the most charming, easily accessible islands in the Seattle area, Whidbey Island is also the longest island in the United States. "Longest" is just one more superlative statistic in this realm that irresistibly attracts romantic travelers. If you're looking for a quick escape from city life, Whidbey is an exemplary destination, offering an unusually large selection of engaging restaurants, wonderful bed and breakfasts, spectacular vistas, and idyllic forested parks.

Clinton

The Mukilteo ferry deposits ferry passengers in the small, nondescript town of Clinton, which hosts an odd assortment of small businesses, gas stations, and convenience stores. Clinton itself has nothing to offer for a romantic sojourn, but we discovered some properties in the outlying areas that are undeniably ripe for kissing.

A ROOM WITH A VIEW, Clinton
6369 South Bayview Road
(360) 321-6264
Moderate
Minimum stay requirement on weekends

Converted basement units aren't typically what we look for when it comes to romantic accommodations, but A Room with a View has its share of redeeming features. Nestled on six quiet acres of pastures and trees, the renovated basement of this private contemporary home has a magnificent view of the Puget Sound and the Olympics. Sunsets from this vantage point are exquisite, and the beach is only a short walk away.

In spite of its small size and basement setting, the unit is complete with everything you'd expect in a home away from home: kitchenette, complimentary breakfast fixings, gas fireplace, and TV with VCR. A private entrance ensures your sense of seclusion, and an outdoor deck with a Jacuzzi tub is exclusively reserved for guests' use. Vivid green walls impart elegance to the room, which is furnished with a variety of contemporary furnishings and a king-size wicker bed accented with floral linens and oversized pillows.

Plants brighten up the private bathroom, where a large, handsomely tiled Jacuzzi tub is flanked by two windows that overlook trees in the backyard. We unanimously voted this the best spot to kiss on the premises.

FRENCH ROAD FARM, Clinton 💋💋💋
3841 East French Road
(360) 321-2964
Very Expensive
Minimum stay requirement on weekends

Built in 1918, this quaint little cottage sits deep in the quiet countryside, next to three acres of vineyards. Visited by deer, foxes, and birds, graced with flowers, and surrounded by trees, the charming grounds exude privacy and peacefulness. A vegetable garden provides guests with fresh zucchini and tomatoes to add to dinner (or to take home with you), and a hammock strung between two large trees is the perfect setting for late-afternoon tranquility.

Inside, the cottage is filled with an eclectic mixture of antiques. A sunroom filled with wicker furniture and plants leads to the living room, which has wood walls draped with tapestries, a cozy couch placed in front of a wood-burning stove, and French doors that open to the lawn and a perennial garden. The bedroom is small and bright, with a queen-size bed, lace drapes, and French doors that open to a deck overlooking the vineyard. Perhaps one of the best features here is the large, airy bathroom, which has a stone tile floor and a seven-foot-long Jacuzzi tub next to a window overlooking a flower-covered trellis.

Breakfast is left in a basket in the refrigerator of the cottage's full kitchen. You can eat inside or enjoy an early-morning picnic anywhere you choose on the gorgeous property.

Romantic Note: The owners of French Road Farm have another property that may or may not be of interest, depending on your feelings about truly eclectic decor. This house is located at the end of a long row of nondescript waterfront homes, directly on the sandy beach of Useless Bay next to a 40-acre bird sanctuary. **HOME BY THE SEA**, 2388 East Sunlight Beach Road, Langley, (360) 321-2964 (Very Expensive) offers heavenly quiet and endless views of vast Admiralty Inlet and the jagged Olympic Mountains. Although the property has two accommodations, we recommend only the Sandpiper Suite. Filled with a casual jumble of mismatched furniture and decor, the suite is nonetheless blessed with a fantastic location on the beach. If you are more interested in a gorgeous setting and the many romantic possibilities offered by miles of beach, you may want to give this location a try.

KITTLESON COVE, Clinton
4891 East Bay Ridge Drive
(360) 341-2734
http://www.whidbey.com/kittleson
Expensive to Very Expensive
Recommended Wedding Site

Settled next to the gently lapping waters of Puget Sound, serene, secluded Kittleson Cove is ideal for reconnecting with your loved one. The northeastern exposure affords a spectacular view of the Cascade Mountains and Mount Baker, providing ample proof of the Pacific Northwest's magnetic beauty. Your privacy is assured in the property's two self-sufficient guest suites, both of which feature private entrances, private baths, decks overlooking the rocky beach, stereo systems (bring your favorite CDs!), TV/VCRs, and well-stocked mini-kitchens that include pre-prepared and do-it-yourself breakfast treats. Binoculars are even provided to enhance your enjoyment of the remarkable view. If you are looking forward to keeping civilization as far away as possible, bring dinner fixings and enjoy a waterfront repast.

Decorated with country-style pastel fabrics and floral linens, the homey Beachside Suite is cozy and comfortable. Our favorite aspect of this room is the private hot tub, set on the deck and enclosed by an ivy-covered trellis. In contrast, the three-room Cove Cottage has a beautifully rustic, earthy atmosphere. A stone fireplace warms the deep green and burgundy interior, while a profusion of throw rugs covers the stone floors. (We recommend bringing along slippers in the colder months.) A tall pine four-poster bed with a floral bedspread and matching canopy is lovely, but the bright red Jacuzzi tub in the bathroom is the decisive romantic touch.

Langley

The town of Langley is five miles north of the Clinton ferry dock, on Highway 525.

Balanced on a bluff above the water's edge, the small town of Langley commands mesmerizing views of Mount Baker, the Cascades, and Saratoga Passage. Ice cream parlors, boutiques, and a two-screen movie theater lend old-time charm to the small-town streets. Langley maintains its Northwest look and style without compromising its virtues, which is precisely what makes it such a terrific getaway from life in the fast lane. In the outlying neighborhoods, an abundance of bed and breakfasts appeals to guests with romance and seclusion in mind.

Hotel/Bed and Breakfast Kissing

BOATYARD INN, Langley
200 Wharf Street
(360) 221-5120
Expensive to Very Expensive
Minimum stay requirement on holidays

Nestled in the Langley Marina and Boat Harbor, this aptly named inn resembles an old cannery structure, with corrugated metal roofs and siding. Despite the industrial exterior, the nine guest rooms inside exude straight-forward Northwest style, with platform beds, blond wood furniture, knotty pine detailing, plaid bedspreads and upholstery, and wicker chairs. Each room is also equipped with a galley kitchen, a small balcony from which you can enjoy majestic views of Saratoga Passage and the Cascade Mountains, and a gas fireplace surrounded by black marble. If you're looking for rustic yet elegant simplicity, your hearts will be more than content here.

CHAUNTECLEER HOUSE, Langley
3557 Saratoga Road
(360) 221-5494, (800) 637-4436
Expensive

Ensconced in six acres of lawn and gardens, this picturesque bluff-top cottage overlooks scenic Saratoga Passage. Picture windows frame the gorgeous water views, both upstairs and downstairs. Blond hardwood floors and bright yellow walls give the cottage's interior a crisp, contemporary look. French country antiques are beautifully arranged in the living room, where overstuffed plaid couches flank a brick hearth. You can take turns preparing gourmet meals for each other in the ultra-modern, full kitchen, then enjoy your culinary creations at a two-person table placed next to a bay window with more water views. Revel in the same panorama upstairs in the spacious contemporary bedroom or linger over breathtaking sunsets on your own outdoor deck.

Romantic Suggestion: The property also holds a second beautiful cottage called **DOVE HOUSE** (reviewed elsewhere in this section).

CHRISTY'S COUNTRY INN AND COTTAGE, Langley
2891 East Meinhold Road
(360) 321-1815

Expensive to Very Expensive; No Credit Cards
Recommended Wedding Site
Minimum stay requirement on weekends and holidays

Guests have exclusive use of this picturesque wood-shingled cottage, set beneath a stand of trees on a hillside overlooking a rural valley, the Olympics, and Useless Bay in the distance. Every detail of this hand-worked haven is admirable, from the peaked cathedral ceiling and blond wood accents to the floor-to-ceiling brick hearth and expansive windows. Almost everything you could ever desire is at your fingertips, including a TV with VCR, a CD player, an impressive selection of movies and CDs, and a private deck with an immense hot tub set beneath a canopy of stars at night. The beautifully crafted contemporary kitchen overflows with snacks and breakfast goodies, including fresh fruit, baked goods, and the most decadent homemade truffles you've ever tasted. In the bedroom, a sumptuous four-poster feather bed is covered with a fluffy down comforter and an abundance of oversized pillows. It would be hard *not* to kiss here!

Christy's also offers a second, slightly less private (and less expensive) suite, which takes up the entire upper floor of the owner's private home. Wood paneling and a floor-to-ceiling brick hearth lend rustic appeal to the suite's spacious interior, which surveys the pastoral setting through large bay windows. A fluffy feather bed is the highlight of the master bedroom, but you'll also appreciate the beautiful antiques and views of the distant mountains. Amenities include a TV with VCR and a hot tub set on a private deck (perfect for moonlit soaks). Continental breakfast is served by the gracious hosts at your convenience in the privacy of your own fully equipped kitchen.

COUNTRY COTTAGE OF LANGLEY, Langley
215 Sixth Street
(360) 221-8709, (800) 713-3860
Moderate to Very Expensive
Minimum stay requirement

Conveniently located in a quiet residential neighborhood, just a few blocks from the town of Langley, this lovely country-elegant farmhouse is surrounded by a thick green lawn and colorful gardens. Country Cottage of Langley offers five charming rooms, all with feather beds and down comforters, private entrances, TV/VCRs, stereos, refrigerators, and coffeemakers. Two of the five rooms, found in the main house, have gas fireplaces, small Jacuzzi tubs, and private fenced-in decks. Captain's Cove is decorated from floor to ceiling with nautical knickknacks, deep blue walls, and blue and cream linens. Whidbey Rose is done up in peach and maroon floral linens with lace accents. Two more rooms, Sand N See (yes, it is "see") and Lynn's Sunrise, are located in the gazebo cottage; although they are not as spacious as the first two, they feel more secluded and the decor is relatively subtle. The smallest unit is a renovated creamery that has been transformed into a darling cottage with pine floors, a white eyelet lace comforter, and Dutch doors.

In the morning, you will be handsomely rewarded for getting out of bed: a wonderful gourmet breakfast awaits, including a hot egg entrée, crab quiche, baked goods, and fresh fruit. Breakfast can either be delivered to your room or served in the sunlit breakfast room in the main house, where a magnificent mural decorates the walls.

DOVE HOUSE, Langley
3557 Saratoga Road
(360) 221-5494, (800) 637-4436
Expensive

You'd never guess that this self-sufficient cottage derives its name from its previous incarnation as an actual pigeon coop. Sheltered on six acres of gardens, ponds, and waterfront, the impressively renovated Dove House is magazine material. Red geraniums peek from an antique wheelbarrow in front of this vintage island escape. Cedar walls, bright skylights, and terra-cotta floors give the cottage a rustic disposition. The home is enhanced with Southwestern fabrics and Native American artwork, and colorful hand-painted fish tiles adorn a cozy breakfast nook in the sunny, modern kitchen. (Breakfast provisions are up to you.) In colder months, light a fire in the river-rock hearth in the airy living room, where shelves brimming with arti-facts stretch from floor to ceiling.

A sculpted brass otter clings to the railing in the upstairs loft bedroom, which has been appointed with a handcrafted wooden bed covered with Southwestern linens. Here, large windows offer views of the nearby meadows and a tranquil pond. Pop in your favorite CD and cozy up side by side in the window seat or browse through the interesting collection of artwork and relics that fill every corner of the cottage. We can't think of a better place to seclude yourselves and enjoy the authentic beauty of the Pacific Northwest.

Romantic Suggestion: A second enchanting cottage called **CHAUNTECLEER HOUSE** (reviewed elsewhere in this section) shares the same property.

EAGLES NEST INN, Langley
3236 East Saratoga Road
(360) 221-5331
http://www.pgsi.com/eaglesnest

Moderate
Minimum stay requirement on weekends
Recommended Wedding Site

It's no wonder they call this the Eagles Nest—this large, wood contemporary home is set high on a hill on the outskirts of Langley. Eagles can often be sighted in the surrounding evergreens, and views from the deck and outdoor hot tub are, without exaggeration, spectacular. A floor-to-ceiling stone fireplace and a lovely mural lend Northwest charm to the inn's homey common area. The four spacious, homespun guest rooms are casually and brightly decorated with an eclectic array of modern furnishings. Some have balconies, private entrances, and views; all are great places to call home for a few days of time alone. For the most elegance and seclusion, we recommend the top-floor Eagle's Nest Room, with its many windows.

When you wake in the morning, you'll find a tray of juice and coffee waiting outside your door, followed by a home-cooked breakfast. Be sure to sample a freshly baked chocolate chip cookie and add to the ongoing cookie count. (Last time we were here, guests had consumed more than 40,000 cookies!)

EDGECLIFF, Langley

(360) 221-8857, (800) 243-5536
Very Expensive
Minimum stay requirement

Edgecliff's cottages cater exclusively to romantics. Located in a quiet country neighborhood a mile from Langley, these two cottages are enfolded by lovingly landscaped gardens that overlook distant views of Saratoga Passage and the Cascade Mountains. Paths marked with stepping-stones meander past birdbaths and flowers and trees, inviting you to quietly while away an hour or two.

Set back on the property, the two-story wood-paneled Penthouse is affectionately designed for cuddling and relaxing. An outside stairway takes you up to a snug but handsome apartment that boasts floor-to-ceiling windows, an assortment of interesting knickknacks and quirky heirlooms, and an abundance of country charm. Enjoy the fresh pastoral breezes from the outside deck, where you'll find handcrafted willow chairs. Outfitted with comfy antiques, the living room offers a TV/VCR and a video library, while the impressive kitchenette comes stocked with delectable breakfast treats that might include a hearty mushroom quiche, pastries, breads, and fresh juices. A wood-burning stove provides abundant warmth in the winter.

Upstairs, a loft bedroom holds a grand hand-carved king-size bed draped with luxurious linens. For those who prefer soaking *à deux*, a huge Jacuzzi tub awaits in the black-and-white-tiled bathroom.

Adjacent to the apartment, hugging the bluff, is the unassuming little Cottage, though it's unassuming only from the outside. Inside, antique dolls, country relics, and handmade art pieces clutter the small but charming interior. A cozy living room and full kitchen are enticingly arranged beneath a cathedral ceiling, along with a wood-burning stove and terra-cotta chimney. Filled with more country trinkets and trimmed with romance, the separate bedroom and bath are accessible via a short hallway. In back, under a covered porch, a heart-shaped Jacuzzi tub has scintillating views of the water. White wicker furniture adorns a deck perfect for long conversations.

If you can't decide between the Penthouse or Cottage, don't worry; you will be pleased either way. Besides, it will give you an incentive to return again and try the other one.

GALITTOIRE—A CONTEMPORARY 💋💋💋💋
GUEST HOUSE, Langley
5444 South Coles Road
(360) 221-0548
http://www.whidbey.com/galittoire
Very Expensive
Recommended Wedding Site

Expect the unexpected at this contemporary wood and glass guest house, enveloped by a sloping green lawn and ten tranquil acres of woods. The owner, an architect turned innkeeper, has overlooked nothing in the design of this exquisitely detailed home that caters to the senses. A case in point: a couple concluding their honeymoon at Galittoire decided to take a last morning ramble in the woods. After walking several yards, you can imagine their surprise when they stumbled across a luxurious feather bed nestled in an enchanted forest grove, prepared just for the two of them. Though we can't promise an exact duplicate of this experience, you get the idea.

Only two guest suites are available, located at opposite ends of the innkeeper's house. The smaller (and less expensive) suite has elegant modern appointments, Japanese flower arrangements, and a bed covered with white linens and draped with white fabric. The Master Suite is more of the same, though its sensuality is enhanced by its location at the top of the house, where floor-to-ceiling windows look out to the sky and survey views of the property. Guests in this suite also have the exclusive use of a cozy wood sauna, three-headed tiled shower, two-person Jacuzzi tub, immense hot tub, and an exercise room. On rainy days, guests in either suite can cozy up with a good movie in the sitting room or enjoy the warmth of a fire blazing in a unique pyramid- and heart-shaped fireplace in the living room.

As if this isn't pampering enough, the innkeeper is a master chef and serves a savory two-course gourmet breakfast in the dining room or outside on a large patio. Kiss quietly and stay watchful if you're on the patio: you're likely to see deer.

GARDEN PATH INN, Langley
111 First Street
(360) 221-5121
Inexpensive to Expensive

Is this the path less traveled? Not exactly. But the picturesque brick garden path, cloaked in wisteria and enveloped by nature's scents in spring-time, is a happy contrast to the shop-clad streets of downtown Langley.

You'd never guess this kind of luxury awaits in two suites above a store-front. We prefer the spacious front suite, which offers a view of Saratoga Passage and downtown Langley. Skylights brighten its stately living room, filled with impressive antiques and ultra-modern art. Artistic touches, such as a hand-carved chessboard displayed next to a love seat, give the room a boutique flavor. All the amenities required for a romantic getaway are at your disposal: a fireplace, Jacuzzi tub, VCR, private kitchen, and separate bedroom with a four-poster bed covered with luxurious linens.

On the opposite side of the building, a second smaller suite faces the back parking lot and consequently offers a less interesting view. Still, the suite is lovely, with a gracious daylight-filled sitting room and French country antiques. It, too, has a fully equipped kitchen, a small bedroom, and a pretty private bathroom with a hand-thrown sink and glass-enclosed shower.

Both suites are accompanied by a delicious continental breakfast delivered to your door. You won't regret having chosen this path—this perfect retreat offers the solitude of a garden hideaway and the convenience of an island town.

THE INN AT LANGLEY, Langley
400 First Street
(360) 221-3033
Very Expensive to Unbelievably Expensive
Minimum stay requirement on weekends

For as long as we can remember, the Inn at Langley has been one of Whidbey Island's sleekest, most desirable, and best-known places to kiss. Set high on a bluff, the wood-shingled building overlooks Saratoga Passage, endowing each of the 24 rooms with a glorious view of the mountains and water. Oriental artwork and ultra-modern furnishings lend elegant simplicity to the guest rooms, which also feature private decks, wood-burning fireplaces, and spacious tiled bathrooms. Deep two-person spa tubs are fronted by shower areas the size of small rooms, and both are precisely placed to face the view and the fireplace. Thick comforters and crisp white linens make the comfy beds that much more inviting. Guests who are inspired by the views can access the beach below, via a boardwalk.

The acclaimed "heart of the inn" is a formal country kitchen where guests are treated to a generous complimentary continental breakfast. You can enjoy your breakfast at a large table placed next to a river-rock fireplace or carry a breakfast tray back to the privacy of your room. (We recommend the latter, of course, if you've got kissing in mind.) A Northwest epicurean production is presented on Friday and Saturday nights to guests and visitors alike; reservations are required.

ISLAND TYME, Langley
4940 South Bayview Drive
(360) 221-5078, (800) 898-8963
http://www.traveldata.com/biz/inns/data/isltyme.html
Inexpensive to Expensive

Slow down—you're now operating on island "tyme." Tucked far away from the road and nestled on ten serene acres of woods and pastureland, this recently constructed, multicolored Victorian was built to serve as a country inn, and it shows. Even the entryway deserves mention, with its life-size apple tree stenciled in the corner. The five guest rooms here, located on the main and second floors, feature private baths, queen- or king-size beds draped with beautiful comforters or charming patchwork quilts, and an eclectic assortment of antiques mixed with homey country touches. Though the decor borders on ordinary, the many romantic amenities make up for it. Glowing fireplaces are found in both the Heirloom Suite and Masterpiece; shared or private decks overlooking peaceful views are offered in Turret, Wicker, and Heirloom; and both Heirloom and Turret have large, two-person Jacuzzi tubs set near the bed.

After you've eaten your fill of the full country breakfast, served family-style in a bright, sunlit dining room, you may want to explore the inn's wooded acreage and say hello to the pet pygmy goats.

LOG CASTLE, Langley
3273 East Saratoga Road
(360) 221-5483
http://www.whidbey.com/logcastle
Inexpensive to Moderate
Minimum stay requirement on holidays

Of all the castles you have read about in fairy tales, none is quite like this one. Settled comfortably on an isolated beach with views of Mount Baker, Saratoga Passage, and the Cascade Mountains, this one-of-a-kind home-grown project has taken its owners 18 years to complete.

Each log here—including a wormwood staircase, log breakfast table, and the beams, ceiling, and walls—has an accompanying story of origin, which the owners readily share with all who ask. The rugged, homey ambience extends from the main-floor common area, with its large stone fireplace, to the four cozy guest rooms on the main, second, and third floors. Although the decor is very casual, our favorite is Ann's Room, set in an octagonal turret on the third floor. Here you'll find a double bed, a 1912 wood-burning stove, and surrounding windows that survey panoramic views of Puget Sound and Mount Baker. Guests of this room can take in the evening's sunset on the private deck. Marta's Suite is also engaging, with a king-size bed, a large bathroom with the only tub in the house, an itty-bitty wood-burning stove, and a sundeck with a two-person porch swing. Although the decor in all of the rooms could use some updating, the atmosphere is so warm and inviting, you certainly won't mind.

The three-course gourmet breakfast is preceded by the mouthwatering aroma of freshly baked cinnamon rolls and other baked goods. After you've eaten, you can explore the beach and maybe catch sight of bald eagles, sea lions, or a traveling pod of whales.

Romantic Note: Christian religious items placed along the drive to this property and throughout the inn itself may make some people feel uncomfortable. However, the ultra-accommodating innkeepers are never pushy about their beliefs.

LONE LAKE COTTAGE AND BREAKFAST, Langley
5206 South Bayview Road
(360) 321-5325
http://www.whidbey.com/lonelake
Expensive; No Credit Cards
Minimum stay requirement on weekends

Every time we update this book for a new edition, we run across places that remind us why we re-inspect all previously included destinations, either because they surpass our previous ratings or because they have deteriorated since our last visit. Regrettably, Lone Lake Cottage and Breakfast falls into the latter category, providing one disappointment after another.

The setting of this bed and breakfast is certainly not the problem: all four eclectic (and we mean eclectic) accommodations overlook beautifully serene Lone Lake. But once you step inside your cottage, you'll see that these units fall short of their surroundings. For example, the Terrace Cottage *sounds* nice, with its wood-burning stove, sitting area and breakfast nook, TV/VCR, full kitchen, queen-size bed, and bathroom with Jacuzzi tub; unfortunately the furnishings are extremely tacky and stained, and unwelcoming "warning notes" are posted on the walls. Another example is the *Whidbey Queen*, a houseboat that sits on the edge of the tranquil lake. It certainly *looks* charming and private, but again the decor needs serious updating, and the cramped interior leaves one feeling claustrophobic. The final bothersome feature is the exotic aviary, divided into two huge walk-in cages. The beautiful but exuberant birds get quite excited in the early hours of the morning, and will spoil a good night's rest no matter how soundly you sleep.

To make matters worse, the units' kitchens are stocked with incredibly awful breakfast makings. If you stay any longer than two nights, you'll have to make the two slices of bread, stale muffins, applesauce, cold cereal, and (gasp!) bad coffee last: breakfast is provided for only the first two nights of your stay. Guests deserve more for these prices.

MAXWELTON MANOR, Langley
5278 South Maxwelton Road
(360) 221-5199
Inexpensive

Your first step into this Colonial reproduction home transports you across the country to Virginia, where this 1830s-style farmhouse would fit right in. Tucked in a grove of cedar, fir, and hemlock trees, this modest bed and breakfast has done everything to enhance its 19th-century theme.

A fire pops and crackles in the hearth of the rustic but comfortable downstairs parlor, filled with antiques and knickknacks. The three very austere guest suites are outfitted with more historical antiques and artifacts; although somewhat spartan in decor, they are very authentic. A delicious full breakfast is served in the downstairs fireside kitchen. The best part is the fact that there are only three guest suites here, which means the six acres of forested trails that meander past resident peacocks and friendly llamas are romantically all yours!

NORTHWEST VACATION HOMES, Langley
6497 E Hunziker Street, in the Clinton Landing Professional Building
(360) 341-5005, (800) 544-4304
Moderate
Minimum stay requirement

Romantically inclined couples will appreciate the seclusion of Northwest Vacation Homes' moderately priced rental homes, which range from low-end bungalows to charming waterfront homes. Even though many of them are geared more toward families, you're bound to find something to suit your needs. One of our particular favorites is **HARBOR HOUSE**, a shingled cottage set just above the beach. Though the decor is homey and nondescript, amenities like a TV with VCR, wood-burning fireplace, full kitchen, and expansive deck with an outdoor hot tub and gorgeous water views make it feel extra-special. No matter which home you choose, your romantic interlude is guaranteed to be private and free of distractions.

SARATOGA INN, Langley
201 Cascade Avenue
(360) 221-5801
Inexpensive to Unbelievably Expensive
Minimum stay requirement seasonally
Call for seasonal closures.

Everything about this sprawling country inn would be sheer, immaculate perfection, if only it were on the other side of the street. The inn's spectacular views of Saratoga Passage are disrupted by the main thoroughfare leading into Langley, which can be heavily trafficked in the summer months. Otherwise, the inn is picture perfect, with its classic wood-shingled exterior and wraparound veranda. You'll feel right at home in the inviting and roomy common areas, which are filled with an elegant assortment of comfortable furnishings. Fourteen upscale guest suites are scattered throughout the inn's two stories. The green and taupe color schemes are elegant and enticing, as are the plush floral-patterned linens, down comforters, and decorator pillows. Gorgeous watercolor paintings add even more color and style. Gas fireplaces warm up every room, and beautiful tiles embellish immense walk-in showers in the attractive bathrooms. We are especially partial to the rooms on the top floor, which have cathedral ceilings and the best water views.

If you really want it all (and you're willing to pay significantly more), book the adjacent Carriage House Suite. Designed with couples in mind, this beautifully designed suite embodies romance. Oriental rugs cover gleaming hardwood floors, and a seductive claw-foot tub awaits in the spacious marble bathroom. A fluffy down duvet adorns a gorgeous king-size sleigh bed, and an enormous deck surveys water views across the street. A TV/VCR, CD player, and large open kitchen are additional romantic features.

No matter which room you choose, a generous continental breakfast is included with your stay and can be delivered to your room or enjoyed family-style in the dining room of the main house.

VILLA ISOLA, Langley
5489 South Coles Road
(360) 221-5052
Inexpensive to Moderate
Recommended Wedding Site

More than three and a half acres of towering pines and fastidiously maintained gardens envelop this romantic Italian-inspired escape. Chirruping frogs and a crowing rooster are the only neighbors you'll hear, and if you keep your eyes open you just might glimpse deer or wild rabbits. If one or both of you has a sweet tooth, you've come to the right place: the scent of freshly baked goodies lingers in the air, and guests are invited to raid the fridge for biscotti, tiramisu, and other delectable treats in the evening. Breakfast, served in a dining room that overlooks the flower-laden yard, is equally compelling.

Guests can listen to their favorite CDs and lounge in the elegant, comfortable common areas or retire to the luxury of their own private suite. Named after Italian destinations, all four guest rooms are spacious and exceptionally attractive. The suave and sophisticated Torino Suite is accented with white linens, boutique pillows, and crisp white draperies. (Our only complaint about this room is that the bathroom is detached.) A Jacuzzi tub in a black-and-white-tiled bathroom is the highlight of the Venice Suite. The Florence Room features a wrought-iron canopy bed draped with cascading fabric, and guests in this suite have exclusive access to the adjacent sitting room. (Be warned: the sitting room itself does not have a door and is open to the rest of the house.) Although none of the rooms have much of a view, that doesn't detract from their distinctive sense of style.

Guests who want absolute privacy will appreciate Villa Isola's newest addition: a self-sufficient cottage with a large deck that soaks up the morning sun and overlooks the verdant backyard. Decorated in a contemporary version of 1940s style, the cottage has a fully equipped kitchen (including an espresso machine for caffeine addicts), a wood-burning fireplace, a separate bedroom, and a spacious bathroom with a wonderful Jacuzzi tub.

THE WHIDBEY INN, Langley
106 First Street
(360) 221-7115
Inexpensive to Expensive

Reputedly one of Whidbey Island's finest, The Whidbey Inn looks anything but fine or secluded at first glance. Shops border one side of the inn and a pizza parlor operates above it. However, these drawbacks are all forgiven and forgotten once you step inside your room and survey the serene water views offered by all six accommodations. The three top-floor suites, although a bit spartan in decor, are the most spacious and desirable options. The Saratoga Suite, with bay windows, a marble fireplace, and posh English furnishings, is wonderfully comfortable; the Gazebo Suite has its own private gazebo set outside in the trees, a marble fireplace, and floral linens; and the Wicker Suite is light and airy, with white wicker furnishings and a mint green comforter. The other three rooms are more standard, but still fine options for a peaceful night's rest. A full gourmet breakfast is brought to your room in the morning, complete with a hot egg dish, fresh fruit plate, breads or muffins, and coffee and tea.

Restaurant Kissing

CAFÉ LANGLEY, Langley
113 First Street
(360) 221-3090
Inexpensive to Moderate
Call for seasonal hours.

Greek cuisine, Northwest ingredients, and romance are an unlikely combination, but that's what you'll find at Café Langley. A handful of oak tables and chairs are scattered around the small dining room, which boasts white stucco walls, wood-beamed ceilings, and terra-cotta floors. Though the ambience is more casual than intimate, the tables are spaced far enough apart for semiprivate discussions and a few daring kisses. Daily specials showcase local fish and fresh produce, and every dish is cooked with Greek flair. The service is friendly and attentive; you will be thoroughly satisfied by the time you've finished dessert (the Russian cream is outstanding). Of course, due to the cafe's popularity you might have to wait for a table, but the wait will be well worth your while.

LANGLEY VILLAGE BAKERY, Langley
221 Second Street
(360) 221-3525
Inexpensive; No Credit Cards

Magenta awnings mark the location of this modest bakery tucked into a small array of specialty shops. In any other part of the world it would not be worth pointing out, but in the town of Langley it deserves a mention for its luscious fresh pastries and espressos. If you want a quiet morning repast or have an afternoon sweet craving that needs attending to, this is the best location in town.

THE STAR BISTRO, Langley
201 1/2 First Street
(360) 221-2627
Moderate
Lunch and Dinner Tuesday-Sunday

Too cafe-ish to be really romantic, the Star Bistro is a convenient and colorful place to grab a quick bite to eat on your way through Langley. Situated on the second floor of a downtown storefront, the most striking attribute of this bistro is its bright red walls. Funky contemporary art and a black-and-white-tiled floor add even more pizzazz. Bay windows surround the airy dining room, showcasing views of Saratoga Passage. Service is friendly and efficient, and the moderately priced sandwiches, seafood, and pasta specialties are delicious. We especially recommend the steamed shellfish sampler, which includes Penn Cove mussels and Manila clams served with vegetables and white wine.

TRATTORIA GIUSEPPE ITALIAN RESTAURANT, Langley
4141 Highway 525
(360) 341-3454
Moderate to Expensive
Lunch Monday-Friday; Dinner Daily

Better known for its food than its ambience, Giuseppe's is harbored in a shopping plaza just off Whidbey Island's main highway. Cathedral ceilings with large skylights lend an open, cheerful feeling to the restaurant's three dining rooms. Chandeliers cast soft light on the yellow- and peach-colored stucco walls, and the snugly arranged tables (too snug for kissing comfort) are draped with yellow linens. Dried flowers, candles, pottery, and other knickknacks warm up the otherwise spartan rooms. Noise from the open kitchen is a distraction, but the chef's tasty Italian cuisine doesn't disappoint. Choices are difficult: should you order the superbly fresh antipasto or the homemade minestrone? The wild mushroom ravioli with sun-dried tomatoes or the linguine with mussels, clams, and squid? For dessert, tiramisu is a definite must, but so is the canneloni: pastry shells filled with ricotta, chocolate shavings, and almonds.

Freeland

Hotel/Bed and Breakfast Kissing

CLIFF HOUSE, Freeland

5440 Windmill Road
(360) 331-1566
http://www.virtualcities.com
Unbelievably Expensive; No Credit Cards
Minimum stay requirement seasonally

Situated atop a towering bluff overlooking Admiralty Inlet and surrounded by forest, Cliff House is truly unparalleled in both location and design. It is easy to see why this wood-timbered Northwest contemporary home has won nine architectural awards. Floor-to-ceiling, wall-to-wall windows frame amazing water and forest views, which can also be enjoyed outside from a hot tub or a hammock, depending on your mood. High open ceilings with wooden beams impart a sense of spacious ease, while the natural touch of stone floors, wood-paneled walls, and earth tones throughout is counterpointed by international antiques and modern furnishings. A 30-foot glass-enclosed atrium in the center of the house brings the elements safely inside for your observation. The house holds two upstairs bedrooms, several different sitting areas, a sunken living room with couch and fireplace, and a full gourmet kitchen. Despite the fact that there are no interior doors (except on the bathrooms), every room maintains an abundance of privacy: the house simply flows effortlessly from one level to the next. We prefer the larger bedroom loft, featuring a sumptuous king-size feather bed covered with a down comforter and boutique pillows, and a small Jacuzzi tub in the adjoining bathroom. An extensive video and CD collection is also provided for your enjoyment. Simply put, Cliff House is an island utopia built for two.

SEACLIFF COTTAGE, Freeland

5440 Windmill Road
(360) 331-1566
http://www.virtualcities.com
Moderate; No Credit Cards
Minimum stay requirement seasonally

Located a short distance from **CLIFF HOUSE** (reviewed above), on the same bluff with the same premium view, Seacliff once again proves that the owners of these homes have a rare talent for creating remarkable places where you and your special someone can retreat from the world. Small and rustic, this cozy gingerbread cottage has wood-paneled walls, plush furnishings, a

TV with VCR, and a nice selection of movies. A wood-burning stove keeps the chill away, and the petite kitchen, appointed with weathered wood cabinetry, is stocked with continental breakfast delicacies each day. You won't want to leave the private deck, with its views of boat traffic navigating up and down Puget Sound. Enjoy a quiet meal for two at the picnic table, or pass the afternoon swinging serenely in a hammock. At night, retreat to the bedroom, where a comfy queen-size bed, cushioned window seat overlooking the water, and charming pink-and-yellow-striped wallpaper distinguish this blissful haven for two.

Greenbank

As you head north on Whidbey Island, past the town of Langley, you'll hardly notice when you've come to the town of Greenbank. More a scattering of residential homes than an actual town, Greenbank harbors one of our favorite places to kiss (see Hotel/Bed and Breakfast Kissing). While you're in the vicinity, we also recommend stopping by **MEERKERK RHODODEN-DRON GARDENS**, Meerkerk Lane, (360) 678-1912 (Inexpensive). This 43-acre wooded preserve is a testing site for different varieties of rhododendrons. Gardening buffs can gain valuable knowledge and even buy the rhododendrons in bloom. Those with kissing in mind can simply enjoy the quiet natural scenery while walking hand in hand.

Hotel/Bed and Breakfast Kissing

GUEST HOUSE BED AND BREAKFAST
COTTAGES, Greenbank
3366 South Highway 525
(360) 678-3115
http://www.travelassist.com
Expensive to Unbelievably Expensive
Minimum stay requirement on weekends

Twenty-five acres of gorgeous meadow and forest enfold the six cottages and one suite that comprise this property. Straight out of a fairy tale, these authentic log homes were designed with privacy in mind. Each is surrounded by shady trees and decorated with old-fashioned country touches. Patchwork quilts adorn the feather beds, and the knotty pine walls and oak furniture are endearingly rustic. Petite kitchens, Franklin fireplaces, TV/VCRs, and private spa tubs in some of the cabins supply an abundance of charm and romantic potential. Each cabin is stocked with a generous supply of fresh breakfast items, including eggs from the owners' chicken coops. As if that weren't enough, an outdoor hot tub and heated swimming pool are available for guests to use at their leisure.

For serious romantics with generous budgets, we recommend the spacious, custom-built log mansion, harbored at the edge of a duck pond. It doesn't get more romantic than this, and we should know! Cathedral ceilings soar above the rustic but elegant interior, where a fire crackles in an immense rock fireplace and floor-to-ceiling windows offer views of the pond. Upstairs, an enormous king-size bed covered with luscious white linens takes up most of the loft bedroom, which also has views of the pond. A full kitchen, TV with VCR, stereo, and *two* Jacuzzi tubs will meet your every need. Although we enjoyed examining the cabin's overflowing collection of old-fashioned knickknacks and relics, we were a little put off by the stuffed dead animals (including bears, lynx, deer, and waterfowl), which gave almost too much authenticity to the lodge-like atmosphere. Otherwise, the capacious home provides all the ingredients for ultimate togetherness.

Coupeville

"Why is *this* romantic?" you might ask yourselves, as we did on our way down Coupeville's commercial Main Street. You haven't gone far enough. Sitting directly on the water, the tiny one-street town of Coupeville is as picturesque and old-fashioned as they come. Browse the turn-of-the-century harbor-style storefronts for antiques and trinkets, or stop for homemade ice cream in one of several sweet shops (sure to inspire kisses).

Hotel/Bed and Breakfast Kissing

ANCHORAGE INN, Coupeville
807 North Main Street
(360) 678-5581
http://www.whidbey.net/~anchorag
Inexpensive
Call for seasonal closures.

Built to look like a 100-year-old Victorian home, this newly constructed rambling white inn is located near downtown Coupeville. Sporting a wraparound veranda decorated with white wicker furniture and potted plants, the exterior has a friendly and inviting feel. Inside, the five guest rooms feature quaint pastel floral wallpapers, lace curtains, wicker accents, an awkward mixture of antiques and imitations, and disappointingly standard motel-style bathrooms. Perhaps the best amenity is the water and mountain views from four of the rooms. In the morning a full gourmet breakfast is served downstairs in the handsome dining room.

COLONEL CROCKETT FARM INN, Coupeville
1012 South Fort Casey Road
(360) 678-3711
Inexpensive
Minimum stay requirement

Colonel Crockett Farm's claim to fame is that it was home to Danny DeVito, Michael Douglas, and Kathleen Turner for several weeks during the filming of *War of the Roses*. In spite of its popularity with celebrities, however, this Victorian inn is anything but pretentious. Surrounded by two acres of beautifully tended grounds, the turn-of-the-century farmhouse hugs the edge of Admiralty Bay, overlooking acres of lush meadows that sweep down to the edge of the water. Inside, the inn is reminiscent of Grandma's house, with antiquated colors, old-fashioned decorations, and a variety of family photographs and other personal touches. Though it may be too homey for some tastes, the four guest rooms here offer simple comforts for those seeking refuge from the fast-paced life of the real world.

A series of small two-person tables that overlook the garden fill the small, countrified dining room. A Christian prayer precedes a supreme breakfast of sumptuous egg dishes and heavenly fresh breads and muffins.

Bainbridge Island

Though Bainbridge Island is commonly utilized as a gateway to the Olympic Peninsula, it possesses romantic interest of its own. Peruse the storefronts in tiny **WINSLOW**, and, if you're not in a particular hurry to get to the peninsula, stop in at one of Bainbridge's several lip-worthy locations. For ferry schedules and information, call **WASHINGTON STATE FERRIES**, (206) 464-6400, or toll-free at (800) 843-3779.

Romantic Warning: Because hordes of tourists use the Bainbridge Island ferry in the summertime and on most weekends during the rest of the year, be prepared to contend with horrendous ferry traffic and interminable delays. You can avoid much of the hassle if you leave your car behind; downtown Winslow is within easy walking distance of the ferry.

Hotel/Bed and Breakfast Kissing

BEACH COTTAGE BED AND BREAKFAST, Bainbridge Island
5831 Ward Avenue Northeast
(206) 842-6081, (800) 396-6081
Moderate; No Credit Cards

This enchanting waterfront bed and breakfast is situated next to a marina on Eagle Harbor, just across the water from the Winslow ferry terminal. Large shade trees conceal a handful of staircases that lead to garden-lined footpaths meandering past a greenhouse, patios with water views, and a rushing, rocky waterfall. The four suites have private baths, kitchens, varying water views, private entrances, and a comfortable, unpretentious blend of modern furnishings. Some rooms also have wood-burning fireplaces, and all enjoy the sound of the outdoor waterfall. Your refrigerator comes stocked with provisions for a full hot breakfast.

BOMBAY HOUSE, Bainbridge Island
8490 Beck Road Northeast
(206) 842-3926, (800) 598-3926
Inexpensive to Moderate
Recommended Wedding Site

At first sight Bombay House is simply stunning. Perched on a grassy knoll, the immense gabled Victorian is surrounded by immaculately groomed lawns, trees, and flowering gardens. Continuing in the same gracious theme, the gentrified common area inside features white oak floors, an enormous open brick hearth, gorgeous antiques, and a working loom. The guest rooms are surprisingly (and disappointingly) homey, though still comfortable, decorated with a mixture of modern and Victorian furnishings and knickknacks; only three of the five rooms have private baths.

A filling continental breakfast is served to guests in the large country kitchen overlooking a deck and the water.

Restaurant Kissing

THE FOUR SWALLOWS RESTAURANT, Bainbridge Island
481 Madison Avenue
(206) 842-3397
Inexpensive to Moderate
Lunch Friday-Saturday; Dinner Tuesday-Saturday

This picturesque 1889 yellow farmhouse is wonderfully romantic, which explains the weekend crowds. Elegantly appointed with turn-of-the-century antiques, lace curtains, dried flower arrangements, and leaded glass windows, the house's original living quarters now serve as a semicasual dining room and adjacent antique store. Two-person booths fill the dining room, so you won't have difficulty finding a cozy spot to sample scrumptious Northwest cuisine and savor each other's company. We recommend the lox with capers and onions.

PLEASANT BEACH GRILL, Bainbridge Island
4738 Lynwood Center Road Northeast
(206) 842-4347
Expensive
Dinner Daily

Pleasant Beach Grill is located in a secluded English Tudor-style mansion that has been skillfully renovated, but the atmosphere and food are decidedly Northwest. Beautifully arranged linen-draped tables, accented with china and crystal, are scattered throughout the house's original living areas; window tables survey distant water views. For those who only have eyes for each other, a single table set outside under a white gazebo offers the best seats in the house (weather permitting). As formal as this may sound, the mood and pace are relaxed and comfortable—there is nothing pretentious about this restaurant. Attentive hospitality and imaginative fresh food are the pride of the establishment. The half-dozen or so exotic oyster concoctions will convince you that what they say about these mollusks' aphrodisiac capabilities is true.

After dinner you can step down into the restaurant's petite fireside lounge and sink into one of the overstuffed leather sofas that surround the stone hearth. Sit close together and relax as the crackling fire casts its light on the mahogany-paneled room. For an extra treat, when you're both toasty warm, drive down to the water and watch the twinkling lights of the marine traffic passing through the channel.

Outdoor Kissing

THE BLOEDEL RESERVE, Bainbridge Island
7571 Northeast Dolphin Drive
(206) 842-7631
$6 entrance fee
Reservations Required
Open Wednesday-Sunday

From Seattle, take the Winslow ferry to Bainbridge Island and follow Highway 305 six miles to the north end of the island. Turn right onto Agatewood Road, which becomes Northeast Dolphin Drive. This road leads to the estate. Call for reservations; access is limited to a specific number of people each day.

There are more than 150 acres of meticulously maintained gardens here at Bloedel Reserve, so you're sure to find a peaceful haven for an afternoon interlude. The reserve is a place where the artistic splendor of sculpted plants brings pleasure to the senses. Wander through the bird sanctuary, verdant woods, and Japanese gardens; pause at the reflecting pool; or admire the dense moss garden. All of it is divine. As the brochure for the Bloedel Reserve plainly states: "Man's first recorded home was a garden, no sooner known than lost ... and we've been trying to return ever since." This might not be Eden, but it is the next best thing.

Romantic Note: Picnics are not allowed on Bloedel Reserve's grounds.

Vashon Island

Vashon is accessible via the ferry, either from West Seattle (at the Fauntleroy ferry dock) to the island's north end, or from Tacoma (at Point Defiance) to the island's south end. For information on schedules and directions, call Washington State Ferries at (206) 464-6400 or toll-free at (800) 843-3779. The trip takes less than 30 minutes, so hurry to the bow of the boat and stand watch on the deck to fully enjoy the scenic crossing.

In spite of the fact that Vashon is a quick escape from the city, it remains relatively quiet and undeveloped, with an abundance of rural and residential countryside. Fortunately, it has a wide assortment of favorable places to stay, because you'll want to come back over and over to explore everything this rustic Northwest island has to offer.

Hotel/Bed and Breakfast Kissing

ALL SEASONS WATERFRONT LODGING, Vashon Island
12817 Southwest Bachelor Road
(206) 463-3498
Moderate; No Credit Cards
Minimum stay requirement seasonally

Every season is the right season to enjoy this self-sufficient, very private wood cabin perched directly above Puget Sound. Floor-to-ceiling windows highlight spectacular water views from every corner of the house. For a closer look at the water, you can walk along the beach when the tide is out. The cabin's exceedingly eclectic interior is a blend of modern and dated appointments, including a wood-burning stove (perfect on cold, rainy days), a fully equipped kitchen, a private bath, and a spacious wraparound sundeck. What more could the two of you ask for, besides another weekend away together?

ARTIST'S STUDIO LOFT, Vashon Island
16529 91st Avenue Southwest
(206) 463-2583
Inexpensive
Minimum stay requirement on weekends seasonally

Roosting high above five acres of landscaped gardens and pastures, the second-story Aerial Cottage Loft truly feels like an artist's studio. Stained glass windows (the artist's handiwork), modern art, a wood-burning fireplace, ceiling fans, and brightly colored beams add personality to the uniquely furnished room. Oriental rugs lend color to the parquet floors and lengths of fabric accent a four-poster canopy bed covered with lush linens. A small kitchen, private bath, TV/VCR, and large deck are exclusively yours. Plush robes are provided if you choose to use the sizable outdoor hot tub placed beneath a gazebo (it's also available to other guests). A complimentary breakfast is served directly to your doorstep, and mountain bikes are available for your use. All of this for an exceptionally reasonable price!

Downstairs, the small newly constructed Ivy Room has just as much character, although it's quite different in nature. Mexican saltillo tiles on the floors and peach-colored sponge-painted walls give this room a Southwestern flavor; dried flower wreaths, local artwork, and contemporary linens are additional affectionate touches. Though it is equally private and has a TV/VCR, the Master Suite is our least favorite of the three available rooms here. Brown armchairs, full-length sliding mirrors, and nondescript linens give it a somewhat outdated appearance. A generous continental breakfast is served in the owner's cozy kitchen for guests in the Ivy Room and Master Suite.

BETTY MCDONALD FARM GUEST **COTTAGE, Vashon Island**
12000 99th Avenue Southwest
(206) 567-4227
Moderate; No Credit Cards

Betty McDonald is a well-known children's author (she wrote the *Mrs. Piggle-Wiggle* books), so it's no wonder her enchanting guest cottage is so much like a storybook. Those in the mood for a romantic adventure will best appreciate this property's absolute uniqueness. A creaking staircase climbs past empty rooms with open rafters to the funky but enticing suite, situated on the top floor of an old barn. Oriental rugs and an eclectic array of antiques and modern appointments clutter the spacious suite, which features knotty pine walls; fresh-cut flower arrangements from the surrounding gardens; and a deck that juts out over the hillside to survey magnificent views of the trees and water. Near the back of the suite you'll find a wooden four-poster bed covered with a thick down comforter and a plethora of pillows. Other amenities include a TV with VCR, a CD player, and a rustic but functional private bathroom. A full kitchen is stocked with delicious breakfast items that can be privately enjoyed at your leisure.

Make sure you save time to explore the farm's six wooded acres, complete with flower and herb gardens, a greenhouse, and paths that lead to the beachfront below. Trail bikes are available and can be used to explore Vashon's picturesque countryside and beaches. A stay here is sure to inspire a few stories of your own.

HARBOR INN BED AND
BREAKFAST, Vashon Island
9118 Southwest Harbor Drive
(206) 463-6794
Moderate to Very Expensive; No Credit Cards

Out of place in a quiet neighborhood on Vashon Island, this English Tudor–style bed and breakfast is a refined change of pace. Dark woodwork, towering windows, and fine antiques fill the innkeepers' home with a handsome allure. Admiring the sensational views of Quartermaster Harbor from this vantage point is heart-stirring, to say the least. No matter which of the three guest rooms you choose, it is possible to admire each morning's sunrise right from your pillow. Be sure to nudge your significant other awake to savor the magic together.

The largest guest room here is breathtaking. A king-size four-poster bed sits on a lush deep green carpet, a gas log fireplace provides heartwarming flames, and bay windows front an entire wall. The white bathroom with pink accents continues in the same spirit of seduction: bay windows and mirrors surround a deep two-person Jacuzzi tub where you can scrub each other's backs by candlelight. Though the remaining two guest rooms are somewhat smaller and do not have Jacuzzi tubs, they are equally stylish and comfortable, with the added bonus of being considerably less expensive.

In the morning, allow the skillfully prepared full breakfast to settle, then borrow mountain bikes supplied by the innkeeper to explore miles of enchanting forest trails in nearby **BURTON ACRES PARK**. It is seemingly undiscovered, so you may have the whole area to yourselves.

Romantic Note: The admirable **TRAMP HARBOR INN** (reviewed elsewhere in this section) shares the same owners.

MANZANITA HOUSE, Vashon Island
4616 Midvale North
(206) 633-4230
Inexpensive; No Credit Cards

If privacy is at the top of your priority list, you can't do much better than Manzanita House. Surrounded by tall evergreens, the contemporary wood-shingled and glass rental home can be exclusively yours for a shockingly reasonable price. Though it lacks amenities like a VCR or hot tub, the architecturally impressive house compensates with abundant space and serene quiet. Large picture windows let in ample natural light and showcase glimpses of the nearby water peeking through the trees. Don't expect any frills: the modern appointments are attractive but somewhat sparse and utilitarian. Guests can make use of a fully equipped gourmet kitchen (provisions are your responsibility), a spacious dining room, and three different bedrooms and bathrooms. "Leave it as you found it" is standard operating procedure here, which means guests are expected to make their own beds with the linens provided and clean up after themselves before departure. Not your typical lazy vacation, but with this much space and privacy at these low rates, who minds?

MIMI'S COTTAGE, Vashon Island
7923 Southwest Hawthorne Lane
(206) 567-4383
Inexpensive

Walking into Mimi's small countrified cottage is like walking right into a copy of *Country Living* magazine. Nestled on a residential wooded hillside, the self-contained private bungalow has distant water views and, when the weather is clear, magnificent vistas of Mount Rainier. Knotty pine floors and exquisite woodwork add rustic charm to the cabin's lovely interior. The cottage is accented with antiques, a mismatched assortment of Oriental rugs, a woodstove, and a hand-sewn patchwork quilt draped over the bed. Upon request, the innkeepers (who live right next door) will deliver a full gourmet breakfast to your room. Or, if you'd rather, take advantage of the cabin's kitchen and serve breakfast to your sweetheart in bed.

OLD MILL COTTAGE, Vashon Island
24603 Old Mill Road Southwest
(206) 463-1670
Moderate
Minimum stay requirement seasonally

Slow down your frantic urban pace and revitalize your senses with the sights and sounds of nature at picturesque Old Mill Cottage, where gentle trails wind through ten acres of quiet woods. A hammock sways invitingly between two trees, urging you to stop in your tracks completely. Secluded and self-sufficient, the yellow country cottage faces the owner's home across a vast expanse of lawn. Tranquility and seclusion are the focus here. Colorful rugs are scattered across hardwood floors in the cottage's homey, mismatched interior. Puzzles, a TV with VCR, a CD player, and an eclectic assortment of books provide sufficient entertainment on rainy winter days. Upstairs, a stark sleeping loft with a slanted ceiling holds a four-poster wooden bed covered with blue and white linens and a warm down comforter. The most luxurious spot in the house is the spacious tiled bathroom, where you'll find a large sunken Jacuzzi tub that overlooks a shady grove of trees.

You certainly won't go hungry here. Though a kitchenette is provided for your convenience, an overstuffed basket of baked goodies is delivered to your cottage in the morning. Rain gear and bikes are available for guests' use, and the innkeeper will be happy to guide you to some of the best nature trails on the island.

TRAMP HARBOR INN, Vashon Island
8518 Southwest Ellis Port Road
(206) 463-5794
Expensive; No Credit Cards

The discriminating owners who run the **HARBOR INN BED AND BREAKFAST** (reviewed elsewhere in this section) have restored this early-20th-century home to its former glory. Located across from a quiet harbor, the wood and brick home is surrounded by a sprawling green lawn and sits adjacent to a trout-stocked pond (bring your fishing poles). Not surprisingly, the home itself possesses an elegance akin to the Harbor Inn, though the theme here is historical authenticity. There are even records for the working antique Victrola! A stone fireplace warms the antique-filled parlor, daylight streams through leaded and stained glass windows in the stairwell, and simple country touches make the otherwise stolid upstairs bedrooms inviting. One of the three guest rooms has a private bath and a large two-person Jacuzzi tub; the others share a bathroom down the hall. The good news is that the innkeeper *never* books all three bedrooms at the same time, so the chances are good that the entire house will be yours to enjoy, Jacuzzi tub and all.

Restaurant Kissing

BACK BAY INN, Vashon Island
24007 Vashon Highway Southwest
(206) 463-5355
Moderate to Expensive
Call for seasonal hours.

Locals eagerly recommend Back Bay Inn as a romantic dinner spot, and we can see why. The intimate atmosphere of this Victorian-style inn certainly deserves romantic praise. Subtle lighting, bay windows facing the water, and classical background music create a lovely dining environment. If it weren't for the busy intersection that interrupts the water view, the Back Bay Inn would easily deserve four lips. Although the menu is limited, it does offer delicious and inventive dishes such as polenta served on chanterelle mushrooms or house-smoked salmon fettuccine. We liked our pasta so much we copied down the recipe and attempted our own version at home.

Romantic Note: The Back Bay Inn has four moderately priced and cheery guest rooms, located upstairs above the restaurant. Like the restaurant, they look out onto the busy intersection, and the noise from the dining room is all too audible. Still, we're hard put not to mention them. Charming and attractive, the rooms are decorated with lovingly restored antiques, lace accents, and luscious linens and fabrics. Take a peek and decide for yourselves.

SOUND FOOD RESTAURANT AND BAKERY, Vashon Island
20312 99th Avenue Southwest
(206) 463-3565
Inexpensive to Moderate
Breakfast, Lunch, and Dinner Daily

What a perfect name for this casual gourmet eatery that serves freshly baked pastries and health-conscious cuisine. Large windows with views of trees brighten the rustic but cozy wood-accented dining room, creating a pleasant dining climate. Service is casual and friendly. Take time to savor the subtleties of your meal, indulge in a second helping of fresh bread, and treat yourselves to a delicious homemade dessert. The warm apple pie, dedacent brownies, and lightly glazed blueberry and walnut bear claws are fantastic! After you've eaten your share, we recommend taking a short walk from the restaurant to a guaranteed conversation piece—a child's bike about six feet up in a tree.

TURTLE ISLAND CAFE, Vashon Island
9924 Southwest Bank Road
(206) 463-2125
Moderate
Lunch Monday-Friday; Dinner Monday-Thursday

Located in the heart of Vashon (the biggest and only bona fide town on Vashon Island), the Turtle Island Cafe resides in a storefront on a semiquiet side street. The casual and funky dining room features deep orange sponge-painted walls, hand-painted plates, and pictures of vegetables. Vinyl print tablecloths and a green-and-red-checked tile floor add even more color. The soft harp music playing in the background seems almost out of place here, but provides a soothing accompaniment to your delicious meal. The cafe's eclectic menu offers something for all tastes, ranging from steak and po-tatoes to vegetarian Thai entrées. (We recommend the latter.)

Federal Way

Hotel/Bed and Breakfast Kissing

PALISADES, Federal Way   💋💋💋💋
5162 Southwest 311th Place
(206) 927-1904, (888) 838-4376
http://www.Vacations-ww.com/vacations/palisades.htm
Expensive

We know what you are thinking. Coming to the Seattle area and staying in Federal Way is like visiting Manhattan and staying in Queens. How could we possibly have found a romantic place in less than desirable Federal Way? Well, we have found one, and we think it is definitely worth your while.

Elegance and luxury encompass every room of this dark wood shingled home, located in the attractive Dash Point neighborhood and bordered by myriad trees and views of Puget Sound and the Olympic Mountains. Beautiful contemporary furnishings grace the formal living room, where the honey-colored walls, cathedral ceiling, and tall arched windows create an exquisite spot for lounging in front of the wood-burning fireplace. From the pretty, airy parlor, step through French doors to the veranda, where views of the water through lofty trees are awe-inspiring. Privacy and opulence await guests in the only suite in the house, located on the second floor. Soft cream carpeting blankets the entire space, which includes a study with a small library and writing desk, a large bathroom with an emerald green marble Jacuzzi tub and double-headed shower, and a sumptuous master bedroom with an even better view of the natural surroundings. In here you'll find a gas fireplace warming the queen-size open canopy bed, which is adorned with sumptuous beige and cream linens and a fluffy down comforter. A floral couch rests under a hand-painted dome ceiling, creating a very cozy sitting area, and an antique armoire hides the TV/VCR. Fresh flowers and two fluffy robes await beside the bed.

In the morning, a full breakfast (for just the two of you) is served in the terra-cotta-tiled breakfast room at a lovely wood table set beside a warm stone fireplace. You can look forward to breakfast goodies such as fresh fruit or a fruit smoothie, fresh scones or muffins, and sausage-stuffed French toast or a Southwestern breakfast casserole.

Restaurant Kissing

THE DASHPOINT LOBSTER SHOP, Federal Way
6912 Soundview Drive Northeast
(206) 927-1513
Expensive
Dinner Daily

Located in what used to be a small neighborhood post office, in a charming waterfront area, this small, wood-shingled restaurant is an appetizing spot to enjoy fresh, local seafood. Beige vinyl booths and small tables, each adorned with white linens and a single votive candle, crowd the casual interior. Here, each table affords views of the water and the evening sunset. A skilled kitchen prepares consistently delicious entrées such as the lobster bisque appetizer or the sampler platter, which includes baked Dungeness crab dip, poached prawns, curried calamari, and jalapeño peppers with three different dipping sauces. We highly recommend the pan-fried oysters lightly breaded in panko bread crumbs, the seafood fettuccine with clams, mussels, prawns, and scallops tossed in a garlic-cream sauce, and the Australian rock lobster tails, oven-roasted with butter.

Tacoma

Even though Tacoma is beginning to become a destination spot, it is still not what we would call a mecca of cultural and aesthetic endowments. It does offer a surprising number of attractions, though, including **POINT DEFIANCE PARK** (see Outdoor Kissing), the Tacoma Actors Guild and the Pantages Theater, the Tacoma Art Museum, the Washington State History Museum, and a number of charming waterfront areas and quaint neighborhoods. Once known only for the "Tacoma aroma" (generated by the local pulp mills), the city has blossomed into a desirable place to stop on your way up or down I-5. A surprising number of romantic accommodations and choice restaurants can be found here.

Tacoma is linked to the Kitsap Peninsula by the second Tacoma Narrows Bridge. (The first one, better known as "Galloping Gertie," fell down in 1940.) Bordered by Commencement Bay, Tacoma enjoys awesome ringside views of Mount Rainier.

Romantic Suggestion: Travel west over the aforementioned bridge to the picturesque, quaint town of **GIG HARBOR**, where boutiques, views, and leisurely strolls are the reason to visit.

Hotel/Bed and Breakfast Kissing

CHINABERRY HILL, Tacoma
302 Tacoma Avenue North
(206) 272-1282
http://www.travelassist.com
Inexpensive to Expensive

Once you set foot inside this proud 1889 Victorian, perched on a flowering hillside in a bustling residential area, you'll be surrounded by luxury and elegance, with touches of playful eccentricities. The oak- and fir-lined main foyer and breakfast room are peppered with historical artifacts and original art pieces, and the shiny hardwood floors are blanketed with antique Oriental rugs. Just off the main foyer, through deep red velvet curtains (remnants from the old Pantages Theater), is the comfortable guest parlor, which features a sizable fireplace, stunning antiques, and an expansive literary collection.

Wind your way up the open oak staircase to three of the four guest accommodations, each filled with sumptuous locally crafted linens, rich color schemes, down comforters, fluffy robes, private bathrooms, and wonderfully restored antiques. Our favorite room is the Pantages Suite, where tall ceilings encase a queen-size rope bed draped with beige, cream, and gold linens. This suite also features an attractive tiled bathroom, and a sitting area with an opulent, gold-accented Jacuzzi tub and impressive antique armoire. The Manning Suite, named after the original owner and designer of the home, is also stunning, with a queen-size four-poster rice bed set in the center of the room, and a gas fireplace to warm your toes on cold nights. A large Jacuzzi tub and stall shower are set in a pretty tiled bathroom accessible through sexy purple velvet curtains. The Garden Suite is the smallest of the three but is still lovely, with a cream painted floor, a pretty private bathroom, and tall ceilings. The only disappointment is that traffic noise from the busy street below is audible in all upstairs guest rooms. But when you're surrounded by all this luxury, you won't care.

Affording the most privacy is Catchpenny Cottage, located just behind the main house. The main floor fosters rustic elegance with four walls of exposed dark wood wainscoting that create an exceedingly cozy cabin-type feel. In the center of the room sits a dramatic black wrought-iron queen-size bed, with ribbons and silk flowers entwined in the canopy. A convenient kitchenette is set just off the bedroom, and the warm glow from the gas fireplace puts the finishing touches on this unique room. Upstairs, awash in white and beige, is a quaint sitting area, a bedroom with a queen-size bed, and a bathroom with an antique claw-foot tub and pedestal sink. At this time, this is the only bathroom for these two rooms, but there are plans to install a private bathroom on the main floor that will feature a large Jacuzzi tub. For now, the cottage is rented only to one couple, or to two couples traveling together.

Your stay at Chinaberry Hill is complete only after you've experienced the full country breakfast which can be served in the cheery breakfast room or delivered directly to your room (The latter option is not available for the Garden Suite.) The time you'll spend together at Chinaberry Hill will be time you'll cherish for a long time to come.

COMMENCEMENT BAY BED AND BREAKFAST, Tacoma
3312 North Union Avenue
(206) 752-8175
http://www.bbonline.com/wa/cbay
Inexpensive to Moderate
Minimum stay requirement on weekends seasonally

Set in a quiet residential neighborhood on a slight hilltop that oversees Commencement Bay and stunning evening sunsets, this stately white Colonial home is contemporarily decorated and offers lots of rest and comfort. Three traditional guest rooms are available on the second floor, each with a private bath and comfy floral linens. We suggest you stick with either Myrtle's Room or the smaller Jessie's Room. The former has a private bathroom, TV/VCR, distant view of Commencement Bay, and a wooden four-poster queen-size bed covered in a floral comforter; the latter has a white comforter and view of the water. Laurie's Room is hard for us to recommend because of its overwhelming pink color, which quickly grows tiresome. After you've lounged in front of the fire in the common area or had your daily workout in the small exercise room, you'll want to relax in the outdoor hot tub; it's not too private, but it's certainly pleasant. In the morning, awake to a full breakfast served in the dining room at one long table.

THE GREEN CAPE COD BED AND BREAKFAST, Tacoma
2711 North Warner
(206) 752-1977
http://www.travelassist.com
Inexpensive to Moderate

Aptly named for its Cape Cod–style architecture, this small green-and-white-trimmed home is nestled in a tranquil residential neighborhood just blocks from the quaint boutique-lined Proctor district. The common areas, breakfast room, and three small guest rooms are filled with restored American antiques and attractive contemporary furnishings. As you are guided to your room, make a mental note to return to the living room and stake out one of the comfy bent-willow couches to cuddle up on in front of the warm, crackling fire. Your guest quarters will be located on either the main or the second floor, and appointed with either a king- or queen-size bed. Soothing colors of beige and white envelop the room on the main floor, which features antique photos on the walls, fluffy green robes in the closet, and crisp white linens draped over the king-size bed. A color TV sits out on a stand, and a detached but private white-tiled bathroom lies just outside the door. Upstairs, two more snug but engaging guest rooms await with floral and white linens, sea green or white walls, and more timeless antiques. Unfortunately, both of these upstairs rooms share just one bathroom, which is never romantic, but with prices like these, we don't think you'll mind. A full country breakfast awaits in the morning, or you can opt for an informal light continental breakfast if you're in a hurry.

Romantic Note: Ask the innkeeper about the wedding packages available. They can include special touches such as champagne, fruit, cheese, and chocolates set in your room at turndown time and, in the morning, a full or continental breakfast delivered to your door.

THE VILLA, Tacoma
705 North Fifth Street
(206) 572-1157, (888) 572-1157
http://www.tribnet.com/bb/villa.htp
Inexpensive to Expensive
Call for seasonal closures.

So authentic-looking is this white stucco and red-tile-roofed Italianate mansion that you can imagine it being airlifted here straight from the coast of the Mediterranean. A massive open staircase bordered by tall white pillars makes a dramatic focal point for the main floor. To the right of it, a spacious living room filled with artifacts from exotic lands, as well as cozy couches set in front of a mammoth gas fireplace, creates a comfy retreat. Dried flowers, an antique hutch, and a huge wooden table fill the breakfast room, and an adjacent window-lined solarium is outfitted with cheery white wicker furnishings and myriad thriving plants.

Upstairs, each of the four guest rooms holds a special treat. Set at the top of the house is the Maid's Quarters, the smallest of the four rooms, which is awash in white, with crisp white linens and a white-tiled bathroom. Bright fuchsia walls frame the Garden Suite, with its spacious tiled bathroom and paisley comforter draped atop the queen-size bed. The adjacent sitting area offers cozy couches and a writing desk—the perfect spot for devouring some romantic poetry. In the Rice Bed Room, the beautifully carved four-poster queen-size bed is the main feature. By far the most engaging of the four rooms is the Bay View Suite, which features deep blue walls with white trim, a king-size iron bed draped seductively with a soft white veil, a veranda overlooking the neighborhood, and a gas fireplace set in front of fluffy white couches.

Awake to a full country breakfast of stuffed French toast, fresh fruit, delicious baked goods, and savory sausage or peppered bacon, served in the spacious breakfast room, where colorful gardens peek through tall arched windows.

Restaurant Kissing

LUCIANO'S, Tacoma
3327 Ruston Way
(206) 756-5611
Moderate
Lunch and Dinner Daily

This quaint Italian dinner spot is situated on Tacoma's popular waterfront, between many other unromantic night spots and chain restaurants. Dressed in typical Italian fashion, with colors of deep maroon and black, each table is aglow with soft candlelight. In the background, Italian music lulls diners into a state of *tranquillità*. Guests seeking authentic Italian delights will not be disappointed with Luciano's newly reconstructed menu. Wonderful antipasto choices include the ground polenta topped with Gorgonzola cream sauce and the toasted Tuscany bread topped with fresh Roma tomatoes, garlic, and basil. We also recommend the linguine with mussels, clams, calamari, and prawns sautéed in olive oil, white wine, and garlic, in a plum tomato sauce. The sautéed chicken breast with cracked walnuts, Gorgonzola cheese, white wine, and parsley is satisfying as well. Ask your server about the evening's dessert selections—the perfect end to a very romantic evening.

THE OLD HOUSE CAFE, Tacoma
2717 North Proctor
(206) 759-7336
Expensive
Lunch and Dinner Tuesday-Saturday

Set in Tacoma's charming Proctor district, this old house turned cafe is a delightful setting for an intimate lunch or a romantic dinner. Floral linens drape small tables in the main-floor and upstairs dining rooms, and the crisp white walls in both rooms are accented by pretty floral window treatments. You'll have no chance to forget about dessert here because the host will walk you by the dessert case before showing you to your table; you'll have chocolate decadence imprinted on your brain throughout your meal. We highly recommend the baked Hood Canal oysters layered with dill, garlic, basil, cream, and bread crumbs, as well as the sautéed chicken rotini pasta with fresh mushrooms, sun-dried tomatoes, red onions, and garlic, tossed with a creamy herb sauce.

Outdoor Kissing

LAKEWOLD GARDENS, Tacoma
12317 Gravelly Lake Drive Southwest
(206) 584-3360
$6 general admission
Call for seasonal hours.
Recommended Wedding Site

Once a private estate, Lakewold Gardens is now open to the public, and its ten acres of manicured lawns and gardens are a beautiful setting for a romantic stroll. Exquisitely crafted waterfalls, several shady Japanese maples, and one of the largest collections of rhododendrons in the Northwest combine to create a horticulturist's dream come true. Bring a picnic and sit beneath the mammoth Wolf Tree, or just pick a path that looks empty and steal a kiss among the brilliant color.

POINT DEFIANCE PARK, Tacoma

Follow Interstate 5; take Exit 132 to Highway 16. Exit at 6th Avenue and turn left; then turn right onto Pearl Street, which leads directly into the park.

The enormous display of nature at Point Defiance Park, including the zoo and aquarium, is well worth a special trip to Tacoma. Take your time driving through the park on the serene five-mile drive, dotted with panoramic vistas of Vashon Island, the Narrows Bridge, Gig Harbor, and other beautiful points of interest. Saunter through the prize-winning rose and dahlia gardens or explore any of the numerous hiking and walking trails, so lightly used you can literally kiss for hours and never be seen. Soft grassy banks overlooking a charming pond and fountain are perfect sites for picnic lunches and afternoon naps on lazy days.

Romantic Warning: The gardens and main park areas are popular places, especially on sunny days, but given the park's size and the number of trails, it can be easy to escape the tourists.

Olympia

Unless you've got a penchant for politics or an affinity for beer, Olympia's legislative buildings, courthouses, and prominent brewing company have probably never appealed to your romantic inclinations. But Washington state's capital, harbored on Puget Sound's Budd Inlet, can be a lip-worthy destination as long as you know where to go.

For starters, along the west side of serene **CAPITOL LAKE**, a walking path meanders past **TUMWATER FALLS** and the **OLYMPIA BREWERY**. Farther on, there are viewpoints from which you can appreciate the Legislative Building's landmark marble dome ascending above a wooded hillside. After your walk, you can take refuge from Olympia's busy city center at the **YASHIRO JAPANESE GARDEN**, Plum and Union Streets, (360) 753-8380. Very small but lush and beautifully manicured, the garden is replete with Japanese stone lanterns, an 18-foot pagoda, and footpaths that wander past a bamboo grove, a streambed, a pond, and a miniature waterfall.

Hotel/Bed and Breakfast Kissing

HARBINGER INN BED AND BREAKFAST, Olympia
1136 East Bay Drive
(360) 754-0389
Inexpensive to Expensive

Budd Inlet laps at much of the Olympia shore, and at the Harbinger Inn, guests can admire engaging views of the inlet's east bay and quiet marina. The inn is set atop a steep hillside across the street from the water. Expansive balconies and white columns fortify the majestic turn-of-the-century home, built of gray ashlar blocks trimmed in yellow and gray, and surrounded by manicured gardens. In the backyard, a spring-fed waterfall trickles down the foliage-covered hillside. Visitors are encouraged to kick back and relax here at this comfortable refurbished home, appointed with hardwood floors, antiques, Oriental rugs, and bookshelves brimming with novels. Upon arrival, a complimentary presentation of tea and cookies is offered. Five guest rooms are available here, each with private bathrooms and views of the water or the neighborhood surroundings. Timeless antiques fill our favorite room, the Honeymoon Suite, along with a queen-size bed, private sitting room, and distant views of the Olympic Mountains. Once you've tasted the fresh breads and pastries in the morning, you'll understand why guests rave about the innkeeper's scrumptious and generous continental breakfasts.

Romantic Suggestion: After you've finished breakfast, head several miles north to **PRIEST POINT PARK**, situated on a bank overlooking Budd Inlet. Handfuls of picnic tables are sheltered beneath evergreens, and privacy abounds on the myriad walking paths that traverse the park's wooded acreage.

Restaurant Kissing

SEVEN GABLES RESTAURANT, Olympia
1205 West Bay Drive
(360) 352-2349
Moderate
Reservations Recommended
Dinner Wednesday-Sunday

Enveloped by colorful gardens, this light blue, gabled 1893 Victorian looks more like a private home than a restaurant. Closer inspection reveals that the entire first floor has been converted into a charming eatery where cozy tables draped in mismatched linens are tucked into corners and alcoves of the house's original living and dining rooms. For romantic purposes, the two front dining rooms are preferable, due to the smaller number of tables and the distant views of the water and city. When weather permits, guests can relish the hilltop setting at several tables placed in the shade on the wraparound veranda. Tantalizing menu items include baked Alaskan halibut with a dill cream sauce; avocado seafood crêpes filled with crab, shrimp, asiago and swiss cheese; scallops with ginger and red pepper; and chicken breast sautéed with apples, caramel, lemon juice, and cream. Reservations are hard to come by as a result of the restaurant's popularity, so it's best to call in advance.

Seattle and Environs

Seattle is a big city with a small-town mentality. Its many neighborhoods are fiercely individualistic, almost like separate little villages, with distinct personalities that are reflected in the homes, shops, and people. Despite this diversity, Seattle residents have much in common. This is a town where people don't jaywalk or honk their horns (except the new arrivals, although they are quick to adapt). A true passion for the outdoors is evident in everything the locals do, from bicycling, hiking, and rollerblading to boating, windsurfing, and skiing. Outdoor recreation is a serious year-round pursuit here, although once the sun emerges, so do the locals—en masse.

Seattle's striking setting amid lakes and bays, verdant hillsides, and rugged mountain peaks gives it a serene, beguiling environment with mesmerizing views. Several popular movies, television shows, and national magazine articles have enhanced Seattle's reputation, but the city's growing popularity has taken some of the glitter off this previously untarnishable stone. Traffic can be a living nightmare (it isn't Los Angeles, but some say it's close), housing prices have skyrocketed, and there are days when smog hovers over the horizon. But those drawbacks can't diminish the honeymoon Seattleites have with their city—the ski slopes are only an hour's drive east of downtown; excellent theater, jazz, opera, comedy clubs, and dance thrive here; island getaways are an hour or two away; and the hiking is stupendous. There are enough kissing places here to keep two people preoccupied with romance for a lifetime.

Seattle

Hotel/Bed and Breakfast Kissing

ALEXIS HOTEL, Seattle
1007 First Avenue
(206) 624-4844, (800) 426-7033
Very Expensive to Unbelievably Expensive

Like many of Seattle's downtown hotels, the Alexis is a very exclusive and very expensive place to stay. Where this hotel parts company with the others is that it is also the epitome of luxury, with a quiet and intimate atmosphere and only 109 guest rooms. If you are willing to pay the piper (and a couple of his buddies), you can reserve one of the elegant Fireplace Suites, replete with a wood-burning fireplace, TV/VCR, CD player, tall ceilings, oversized windows, and a formal living room. Spa Suites are equally beautiful and supremely romantic, with a jetted tub for two, opulent linens, richly colored tapestried chairs, and overstuffed sofas. There is no need to go far in the morning, because complimentary continental breakfast is served at **THE PAINTED TABLE**, the hotel's handsome restaurant (see Romantic Suggestion below).

For sumptuous detailing and any service you'd ever want or need, you can't go wrong at the Alexis. So, order room service, light the fire, fill the tub with soft, fragrant bubbles, and get ready for a very special evening.

Romantic Note: Ask about the various packages offered at the Alexis. We love the "Unforgettable Romance" package, which includes two aromatherapy products from the in-hotel Aveda Spa, champagne or sparkling cider, and handmade chocolate truffles waiting for you in your room.

Romantic Suggestion: Whether or not you are staying overnight at the Alexis Hotel, we suggest sharing breakfast, lunch, or dinner at **THE PAINTED TABLE**, (206) 624-3646 (Moderate to Expensive). The peach-colored walls add warmth to the austere, contemporary dining room, which showcases handsome wood paneling, dark wood pillars, a large transom skylight, high ceilings with grand contemporary chandeliers, and a gallery's worth of festive painted plates and modern art by local artists. (Both the plates and the art can be purchased if you fall in love with a piece and want a memento of your visit.) The food here is good, and getting even better, with such entrées as a layered goat cheese and vegetable salad with grilled eggplant and dried tomatoes, pan-seared scallops, herb-crusted salmon, and wild mushroom risotto with root vegetables and roasted tomatoes.

THE BACON MANSION, Seattle
959 Broadway Avenue East
(206) 329-1864, (800) 240-1864
http://useattle.uspan.com
Inexpensive to Expensive
Minimum stay requirement on weekends

Edwardian style abounds in this classic 1909 Capitol Hill mansion. Despite the urban location, the surrounding lawn and flower gardens provide a sense of country relaxation; on nice days, guests can lounge outdoors on the patio to admire the fountain and the adjoining rose garden. The spacious, beautifully renovated interior, comprising over 9,000 square feet of living space, is divided into four levels, all accessed by a winding maroon-carpeted staircase. Downstairs, the fir-paneled library, living room, and dining room are highlighted by leaded glass windows, pastel fabrics, hardwood floors, and Oriental carpets. An extended continental breakfast is served in the dining room at a long, stately table beneath a sparkling chandelier.

The eight guest rooms are not exactly exceptional and they vary in size, but only two lack private baths. Four-poster beds, wicker furnishings, large windows, and tiled bathrooms (one with a claw-foot tub) are offered in most of the rooms. Both antiques and contemporary furnishings are found throughout, creating rather mismatched decor in some of the rooms. The largest unit, the Capitol Suite, offers a fireplace and a view of the city. Behind the mansion, the Carriage House is divided into two units; the downstairs suite is equipped with a kitchenette, wet bar, and a roomy walk-in shower in the tiled bathroom, while the upstairs unit is smaller, but very cozy, with a queen-size bed, sloping ceilings, and a view of the trees and the patio.

CAPITOL HILL INN, Seattle
1713 Belmont Avenue
(206) 323-1955
http://useattle.uspan.com
Inexpensive to Expensive
Minimum stay requirement on weekends seasonally

Dwarfed by the imposing apartment buildings lining this city street, the Capitol Hill Inn is located in a neighborhood that is less than romantic. However, inside this modest teal-colored Queen Anne Victorian, antiques and comfortable furnishings fill the front parlor, which is "guarded" by a friendly miniature poodle named Sarah. Each of the six eclectic guest rooms here are appointed with creative details.

Business travelers will appreciate the convenient access to downtown and the Convention Center, but romantics will be taken with the two ground-floor rooms with double Jacuzzi tubs. The tub in the popular Sherlock Holmes Room is framed by faux marble and sits by a two-sided gas fireplace. On the other side of the fireplace is the bedroom, with rich red walls, an antique carved bed, white shutters, and paraphernalia relating to the famous detective. Just across the hall, the smaller Western Room offers a bright red Jacuzzi tub, handsome navy walls, a brass bed, and Wild West furnishings. The spacious Chutney Room, also on the ground floor, features a gas fireplace in one corner and sunny yellow walls that complement the Ralph Lauren linens on the four-poster pine bed. Like every room, there is a private bath, but the Chutney Room has a shower rather than a tub. Bold color schemes continue in the three upstairs guest rooms; our favorite is the Americana Room, with its rich red walls, and a claw-foot tub and pedestal sink in the ample cedar-paneled bathroom.

In the morning, guests gather around a large table in the dining room to enjoy a filling breakfast of French toast or savory quiche. Afterward, you may want to venture downtown or wander uphill to the Broadway shopping district to get a feel for Seattle life.

THE EDGEWATER, Seattle
2411 Alaskan Way, at Pier 67
(206) 728-7000, (800) 624-0670
Expensive to Very Expensive

Besides the distinction of being Seattle's only waterfront hotel, The Edgewater is best known for two things. First, the Beatles stayed here when the hotel was brand new (it was built in 1962, in time for the World's Fair of that year). Second, hotel guests were once allowed to fish directly from their rooms. You can imagine the messy dilemma that fish flailing across the floor or being stored in the bathtubs presented for the housekeeping staff, and the policy was abolished when the hotel was beautifully renovated to resemble a mountain lodge back in 1988.

While you cannot drop a fishing line from your guest room anymore, the fact that you once could shows just how "waterfront" the Edgewater is—it is built right over the bay. (It should be noted that the hotel's proximity to the water is sometimes accompanied by an unavoidable sea smell.) Half of the 235 guest rooms face majestic sunsets over Elliott Bay with the Olympic Mountains in the distance, and these are the rooms you should request. Prices vary depending on the view, but all of the rooms offer country pine furnishings, sitting areas with comfy armchairs, cheerful plaid comforters on the beds, and picture windows; some also have small balconies. The best rooms in the house (only a handful) face southwest toward the Olympics, while most of the other water-view rooms have partial city and dock views to the north. City-view rooms have the same layout and decor as rooms with a water view, but the parking lot outside the window dominates the scenery and makes these rooms seem small and ordinary.

The bustling waterfront shops, the Pike Place Market, and downtown Seattle are just a short walk from the hotel. Or you can hop on the waterfront trolley that stops right across the street and passes through Pioneer Square before ending its run in the International District.

Romantic Note: Complimentary coffee and hot cider are served in the Edgewater's attractive lobby lounge each morning. Comfortable country-style furnishings and floor-to-ceiling windows overlook the water, and the setting creates the illusion of being on a boat. The hotel's unpretentious restaurant, **ERNIE'S BAR AND GRILL** (Expensive), serves breakfast, lunch, and dinner, and features the same astounding water and mountain views, as well as some impressive entrées. Incredibly fresh halibut is done to perfection and the grilled salmon over a bed of mixed greens with a blackberry vinaigrette is excellent. Sunday brunch here is an event unto itself, an amazing spread of cooked-to-order omelets, hot breakfast specialties, fresh prawns, and delectable desserts.

FOUR SEASONS OLYMPIC HOTEL, Seattle
411 University Street
(206) 621-1700, (800) 223-8772
Unbelievably Expensive

This ultra-posh downtown hotel features more than 450 guest rooms in a centrally located landmark building. The spacious accommodations (some with separate parlors and living rooms) are graciously decorated, but the focus on business travelers is all too apparent. The simple decor and sober beige color schemes certainly won't spark much romance. What will sweep you away, though, are the restaurants, health club, myriad services, gracious concierges, opulent lobby, and boutiques, which are all simply sensational. Once you arrive at the Four Seasons, you'll have no reason to go anywhere else to fulfill your amorous requirements. After your morning workout at the complimentary health club—a lap pool, a 20-person spa tub (which never seems to be in use), and modest workout and weight rooms—you can arrange for fresh coffee, a daily newspaper, and eggs Florentine to be delivered to you pool-side or out on the sunny garden patio.

Located just off the lobby, the **GARDEN COURT LOUNGE** (Moderate to Expensive) is a radiant composite of tea room, lounge, bistro, and ballroom. The immense hall, arrayed with a bevy of trees, marble and carpeted floors, 40-foot-tall windows, and a petite waterfall cascading into a rock pond, offers well-spaced groupings of settees, cushioned chairs, and glass coffee tables. This prodigious dining room changes its agenda as the day progresses: depending on the time and day, you can come here for a Sunday brunch, savory lunch, authentic afternoon tea service, evening cocktails, and late-evening dancing to a small band every Friday and Saturday. The hotel's main restaurant, **THE GEORGIAN ROOM** (see Restaurant Kissing), is one of the most stunning dining spots in all of Seattle. All in all, when you talk about grand accommodations in the heart of downtown Seattle, you're talking about the Four Seasons Olympic.

Romantic Note: Ask about the different packages available, specifically "The Romance" and "The Honeymoon."

THE GASLIGHT INN, Seattle
1727 15th Avenue
(206) 325-3654
Inexpensive to Moderate
Minimum stay requirement on weekends

The Gaslight Inn attracts businesspeople weary of large hotels, as well as traveling romantics in search of rest and relaxation. It is comprised of two turn-of-the-century homes, The Gaslight Inn and Howell Street Suites, located next door to each other on Capitol Hill's busy 15th Avenue.

Guest are sure to find a room that suits their fancy, with 15 striking accommodations to choose from between the two homes. The Gaslight Inn holds eight rooms, each decorated with rich Northwest colors, bent willow and Arts and Crafts–style furnishings, Native American art pieces, museum-quality antiques, and impressive modern glass sculptures. Unfortunately, only six of the rooms have private baths, but to make up for it, two have decks that overlook the backyard pool area and Seattle's skyline, and one room sports a warm gas fireplace.

The home that holds the Howell Street Suites lost most of its old-world charm during the most recent renovation, but the seven attractive suites are still spacious and airy. They feature warm carpeting, richly colored walls, full tiled kitchens, private bathrooms, living areas with comfy couches, and large windows with views of the outdoor courtyard or surrounding neighborhood.

The innkeepers urge guests at both houses to wander about the wood-paneled common rooms in The Gaslight Inn. More antiques and cozy sofas are set in front of a crackling fireplace in one room, and in the other, deep green walls and a deer head mounted over the couch give the look of a Northwest hunter's library. The scent of fresh coffee and local teas awakens guests in the morning, and a continental buffet breakfast is presented on the main floor of The Gaslight Inn.

HAINSWORTH HOUSE BED AND BREAKFAST, Seattle
2657 37th Avenue Southwest
(206) 938-1020
Inexpensive

Built in the early 19th century, this mammoth Tudor-style mansion has an atmosphere of relaxed luxury and comfort. The Victorian decor is impressive, but also homey enough to make one feel compelled to curl up on the soft couch in the TV room and spend a lazy evening watching old Garbo flicks. Only two rooms are set aside as guest chambers; both feature Victorian-style decor, an abundance of English country floral prints, private decks, and private baths. The larger room is by far the nicer, with a fireplace, king-size bed, and an outstanding view of downtown Seattle from the deck and through the large bay windows. The smaller room has a spacious deck overlooking the garden. Regardless of the weather, the ever-changing Puget Sound offers the ultimate in soothing scenery. In the morning you wake to a formal gourmet champagne breakfast.

HILL HOUSE BED AND BREAKFAST, Seattle
1113 East John Street
(206) 720-7161, (800) 720-7161
http://useattle.uspan.com
Inexpensive to Moderate
Minimum stay requirement on weekends and holidays

Renovating a small 1903 Victorian home to this level of immaculate contemporary fashion isn't easy. It is obvious that the owners maintain a consistent level of excellence in every detail, from the lace curtains to the handsome furnishings. Upstairs are three petite but attractive guest rooms, two of which share a small standard bath. Eyelet-covered down comforters are a cozy extra. As well put together and reasonably priced as these rooms are, they are really too small and too close for comfort to recommend wholeheartedly. However, the two garden-level suites have gracious appointments and room to spare. Striking hunter green and burgundy decor, enticing down comforters, separate seating areas with sofas, brightly tiled standard bathrooms, and private entrances guarded by a magnificent willow tree make these a welcome sight for loving eyes.

A full gourmet breakfast is served in the dining room at a somewhat cramped shared table. It would be better if there were more space, but other than that mornings taste great at the Hill House.

HOTEL VINTAGE PARK, Seattle
1100 Fifth Avenue
(206) 624-8000, (800) 624-4433
Very Expensive to Unbelievably Expensive

Romance happens at this conveniently located hotel just blocks away from fine boutiques, department stores, colorful Pike Place Market, and the 5th Avenue Theatre. Elegance and supreme comfort are the hallmark of this intimate, recently renovated downtown hotel. A winery theme plays throughout the hotel's 126 guest rooms, and the suites are named after Washington wineries. Inside the rooms, canopied beds, stately period furnishings, TVs hidden away in wooden armoires, tall ceilings and windows, richly colored tapestried sofas and chairs, sumptuous linens, and small but attractive bathrooms ensure that all your affectionate needs will be met. If your wallet can recover from the blow, you'll find that an especially amorous ambience flourishes in the Chateau Ste. Michelle Suite, with its wood-burning fireplace, four-poster bed, and Jacuzzi tub for two. A competent staff provides attentive service to all guests.

Twenty-four-hour room service is available from the adjacent, lively, and well-regarded **TULIO RISTORANTE**, (206) 624-5500 (Moderate to Expensive). Complimentary evening wine tastings next to a crackling fireplace in the cozy lobby make Hotel Vintage Park a premium addition to the Seattle area, and one not to be overlooked.

INN AT THE MARKET, Seattle
86 Pine Street
(206) 443-3600, (800) 446-4484
Expensive to Unbelievably Expensive

For some, the colorful and intriguing Pike Place Market is one of the most romantic spots in Seattle, and this stylish inn showcases the best this area has to offer. A rooftop patio set with white chairs and tables overlooks one of the best views in the city, with the market, sparkling Puget Sound, and the snowcapped Olympics all laid out before you. Although the decor in each of the 65 guest rooms is fairly simple, all are appointed with French country pine furnishings, cozy down comforters, fluffy robes, TVs hidden in large wooden armoires, and private bathrooms. The guest rooms also feature views of either the Pike Place Market, the water and mountains, or the bustling city streets of downtown Seattle. Breakfast is not served, but with fresh fruit stands and booths of baked goods just steps away at the market, you'll have fun picking out the makings for your morning meal.

LAKE UNION BED AND BREAKFAST, Seattle
2217 North 36th Street
(206) 547-9965
Moderate to Expensive

If ratings were based on decor alone, this bed and breakfast would easily earn four lips; however, we have to consider other factors that can affect romantic potential. Unfortunately the privacy of the smaller of the two bedrooms is limited due to the downstairs location of the bathroom, requiring a trip through the common room. Despite this minor inconvenience, you will be impressed with this contemporary home overlooking the north end of Lake Union.

Guests enter through a landscaped garden enclosed by a six-foot-tall brick wall. Inside, the modest-size interior has plush white carpeting throughout, interesting art pieces, floral arrangements, and overstuffed white chairs flanking a marble fireplace. Sliding glass doors open to a roomy wooden deck featuring a gorgeous view of the lake.

The house can accommodate two couples. The Penthouse is a huge room adorned with willow furniture and a brown marble fireplace. An adjacent solarium, replete with telescope, more willow furniture, and Oriental rugs, connects this room to its separate private marble-tiled bathroom. The bathroom has a shower and a double Jacuzzi tub, with a superb view of the lake and city through sliding glass doors that open to the solarium. The other upstairs bedroom is simple but comfortable (and is the one with the bathroom located down on the main floor). If you can ignore the romantic no-no, console yourselves with the glass-brick-enclosed sauna, piped-in music, and large tiled shower. Both rooms feature down comforters, queen-size beds, and televisions with built-in VCRs. Port and truffles are served in the evening; in the morning, breakfast is served on Lenox china and Baccarat crystal at the hour of your choice.

MAYFLOWER PARK HOTEL, Seattle
405 Olive Way
(206) 623-8700, (800) 426-5100
Expensive

Convenience and charm are tastefully united in this long-standing downtown hotel. Perhaps the word "convenient" is a bit of an understatement when describing the Mayflower: it's located one block from Nordstrom, three blocks from Pike Place Market, around the corner from the Monorail Terminal, and within easy range of more than a dozen espresso stands (a Northwest essential). Built in 1927, the building has been renovated to resemble an intimate European hotel, and for the most part it succeeds. Terra-cotta detailing on the building's facade and the classic elegance of the common areas give the hotel its inviting warmth. In the lobby, huge bouquets of flowers rest upon dark mahogany tables and an enormous crystal chandelier refracts sunlight from large stained glass windows. The adjacent sitting room is perfect for amorous conversation or a quiet evening in front of the fire. Both the lobby and the sitting room are decorated in soothing greens and beiges, with subtle Asian touches that accent the European architecture.

All 173 rooms have mahogany furnishings, plush color schemes, and conservative artwork. The so-called Deluxe Suites are standard rooms connected to a small lounge area with an extra bath. Disappointingly, the bathrooms, which probably haven't seen new fixtures or tiles since 1940, are crying out for renovation. Most of the rooms provide rather unexciting views of the city; however, parts of Puget Sound and Lake Union can be seen from some of the corner rooms.

Downstairs, **ANDALUCA** (see Restaurant Kissing) serves Mediterranean-inspired cuisine in an informal setting. Off the main lobby, **OLIVER'S** (Inexpensive to Moderate) is a stunning spot for refreshments and appetizers. Decorated in deep hunter greens, the lounge boasts magnificent towering windows that filter in sunlight during the day and afford views of Seattle's nightlife after dark. Unlike other restaurants in the Northwest, Oliver's is consistently filled with smoke that spills over from the smoking section. If you can tolerate the smoke, take advantage of the complimentary hors d'oeuvres served weeknights.

SALISBURY HOUSE, Seattle　
750 16th Avenue East
(206) 328-8682
http://www.salisburyhouse.com
Inexpensive to Moderate

Located on a quiet, tree-lined residential street in an old, established Capitol Hill neighborhood, this inviting 1904 Prairie-style house is a peaceful oasis amid the area's colorful but sometimes overwhelmingly busy atmosphere. Downstairs, the handsome common rooms are enhanced with comfortable couches and chairs, polished maple floors, Oriental rugs, fireplaces, and leaded glass windows. On the second floor, a glass-enclosed sunroom filled with wicker furniture and plants overlooks the lush backyard, with views of the manicured lawn, trees, flower gardens, and brick courtyard below. All four guest rooms have queen-size beds with down comforters, attractively renovated baths (one has a six-foot-long claw-foot tub), and a mixture of antiques and contemporary furnishings; two have cozy window seats. The decor is simple and homey, but surprisingly elegant. A full breakfast is served in the morning in the formal dining room.

SORRENTO HOTEL, Seattle　
900 Madison Street
(206) 622-6400, (800) 426-1265
Expensive to Unbelievably Expensive

Very little about the Sorrento bears any resemblance to a typical city hotel. One visit will convince you of that. Built in 1909, the Sorrento Hotel reigned for years as the most romantic spot in the city. Time took its toll, but in 1981 the Sorrento was restored to its previous glory. Today, it continues to be one of the most romantic hotels in the city.

Of the hotel's 76 rooms, the suites are the best, with their exceedingly plush furnishings, large windows, stereos, and formal fabrics. Unfortunately, the bathrooms are dull and the standard rooms are just OK, but everything else is exemplary. Turndown service includes a hot water bottle placed under the sheets for a warm evening snuggle.

Downstairs, the **FIRESIDE ROOM** piano bar holds a stunning, albeit formal, assortment of settees, sofas, and chairs arranged around an imposing hand-painted tile-and-stone fireplace. It is an inviting spot for an early-evening conversation or an after-dinner cognac. And speaking of dinner, the award-winning **HUNT CLUB** restaurant (see Restaurant Kissing) serves consistently fine meals in a radiantly seductive series of mahogany-paneled rooms.

Restaurant Kissing

ADRIATICA, Seattle
1107 Dexter Avenue North
(206) 285-5000
Expensive
Dinner Daily

Perched on a steep hillside overlooking Lake Union, this tall stucco home seems out of place among its industrial neighbors. But when the sun has gone down and the surrounding area is obscured by nightfall, Adriatica looks regal and refined.

Romance and intimacy are the focus here, from the well-spaced tables dressed with classic white linens to the soft lighting shed by antique chandeliers and small table lamps. Unfortunately, recent construction has all but blocked the tranquil view of Lake Union that this restaurant used to showcase with pride. However, the soothing ivory walls, dark wood accents, lovely modern art illuminated by wall sconces, and soft jazz are more than enough to dazzle your senses. A small room at the rear of the restaurant gives patrons an added bonus. Three walls of windows are surrounded by dense trees and shrubbery, creating a stunning greenhouse effect.

In spite of the steep prices, the food here is almost always worth the splurge. If you're having difficulty deciding among the menu's many tasty items, we highly recommend starting with the fresh Penn Cove mussels with red pepper butter, or the grilled portobello mushroom. The evening's risotto rarely disappoints, and the Spanish-style mixed seafood in zesty romesco sauce with peperonata and aioli is a citywide favorite. After you have savored the last bites of your chocolate-espresso soufflé or the phyllo stuffed with dates, walnuts, and brandy, pop up to the second-floor bar—a perfect spot for a quiet drink. Even on Saturday nights, very few people seem to make their way up here, and you are sure to find a secluded table where you can enjoy a long, divine kiss.

AL BOCCALINO, Seattle
1 Yesler Way
(206) 622-7688
Inexpensive to Moderate
Lunch Tuesday-Friday; Dinner Daily

If you're looking for some of the city's finest Italian cuisine in a lively, almost New York–like atmosphere, Al Boccalino should be first on your list. It can get boisterous in here at lunch and occasionally at dinner, but this tiny restaurant is still an extremely charming find. The vintage red brick building is typical of many in the Pioneer Square area. Inside, the floor is covered with institutional green linoleum tiles with multicolored flecks, reminiscent of an old cafeteria. In contrast, wrought-iron-caged windows are framed by floral curtains, white tablecloths are starched to perfection, and service is attentive and professional. Dignified turn-of-the-century lamps hang from the ceiling, spreading soft light throughout the room.

The menu is filled with classic and innovative Italian dishes. The risotto with scallops, prawns, calamari, clams, basil, plum tomatoes, and garlic in a white wine stock is excellent. We also recommend the potato gnocchi tossed in a tomato-basil sauce and baked with provolone, as well as the oven-roasted fillet of salmon stuffed with sun-dried tomatoes and oregano, and wrapped in grape leaves. Stop counting calories after the main course: the tantalizing desserts, featuring homemade ice cream and a sinful chocolate-espresso torte, are bliss-inducing.

ANDALUCA, Seattle
407 Olive Way, at the Mayflower Park Hotel
(206) 382-6999
Expensive to Very Expensive
Breakfast and Dinner Daily; Lunch Monday-Saturday

Everyone is jumping on the Mediterranean bandwagon, but brand-new Andaluca stands out from the crowd. This dark and lively restaurant, housed right downtown in the **MAYFLOWER PARK HOTEL** (see Hotel/Bed and Breakfast Kissing), holds an interesting mixture of old-fashioned wooden booths and groups of tables in assorted sizes, accented by contemporary fixtures, table accessories, and decor. Service is both friendly and helpful, but never intrusive. The creative menu is very small (you may feel annoyed at the lack of choices), but everything is excellent. We remember our meal as a progression of delicious dishes: spicy chicken wings, superb herb bread, and perfectly cooked lamb in a port wine sauce. Our dinner was accompanied by fine wine and capped with truly memorable desserts; the lemon mascarpone custard was elegantly rich, and sharing the warm liquid chocolate cake was a true test of love.

Romantic Warning: The noise level can be overwhelming. This can help fill the conversational spaces if you're here on a first date. (Andaluca is an excellent choice is you want to impress someone with a good meal in an informal atmosphere.) But if you're planning some quiet cooing, go early to beat the crowds or come late, maybe after the theater, for dessert (that warm liquid chocolate cake).

ASSAGGIO RISTORANTE, Seattle
2010 Fourth Avenue, at the Claremont Hotel
(206) 441-1399
Moderate to Expensive
Lunch Monday-Friday; Dinner Monday-Saturday

If it weren't for the crowds (and the accompanying noise), this lovely restaurant on the ground floor of the Claremont Hotel would be perfect for romance. Dimmed overhead lights softly illuminate the beautiful interior, which is separated into two dining rooms by arched doorways. Replicas of Sistine Chapel artwork grace the walls and the cathedral ceiling; a pink-and-green-tiled floor, dried floral arrangements, and miniature stone statues accent the interior. Each table is adorned with peach linens, softly glowing votive candles, and petite clay pots filled with dried flowers. Unfortunately, the restaurant is large and packed with tables placed too closely together for adequate privacy, and the Italian food can be unpredictable. The grilled prawns with goat cheese, lemon, and mint are heavenly; however, the bow-tie pasta served with chicken, zucchini, mushrooms, and onions in a white wine, cream, and tomato sauce is disappointingly bland. To get the most out of Assagio, come early, find a table for two in a corner, and soak up the ambience before the crowds arrive.

CAFE DILETTANTE, Seattle
416 Broadway East
(206) 329-6463
Inexpensive to Moderate
Light Bistro Menu and Dessert Daily

Forrest Gump's mom was right: life *is* like a box of chocolates. Fortunately, at Cafe Dilettante, you know what you're going to get (it's right there on the menu). Cozy, candle-topped tables fill the dimly lit chocolate brown interior, and antique mirrors line one wall. Even if this place weren't so charming, unreformed chocoholics would still be devoted fans. Dilettante chocolates are the stuff dreams are made of—rich, complex, and deeply flavorful. (You may have to try several at the in-house candy counter to decide which is your favorite.) Regrettably, the tables are tightly spaced, and crowds often interrupt the mood. Having said that, sharing a heavenly torte covered in the Dilettante's own fabulously rich Ephemere sauce is still the best way to say good night—except for a kiss, that is.

Romantic Note: Extended hours allow you to drop in for a luscious treat after a movie or late dinner. The cafe stays open until midnight every day except Friday and Saturday, when it is open until 1 A.M. You can also purchase candies or truffles to go if you want to share some later.

CAFÉ SOPHIE, Seattle
1921 First Avenue
(206) 441-6139
Inexpensive to Expensive
Dinner Daily

It is the rare restaurant that improves with age, yet Café Sophie has done just that. Sophisticated elegance coexists here with soothing coziness and casual comfort. The restaurant's high gold-trimmed ceilings and starched white linen tablecloths are softened by the inviting forest green color scheme. Gold-leaf mirrors reflect the soft glow shed by delicate lamps on each table, and one wall is lined with booths framed by rich, gold-tasseled green curtains. The Library, at the back of the restaurant, is worth requesting when making reservations because of its sweeping view of Puget Sound. The fireplace, burgundy velvet seats, tapestry cushions, and book-lined shelves add romantic seasoning to this dining room.

As if this ideal atmosphere weren't enough, the food is truly superior; soups, fresh pastas, and seafood are prepared with the utmost care. Our perfect meal began with herb crêpes with fresh crab, sweet peppers, and citrus-basil crème fraîche, followed by the baked salmon in a ground peanut crust. Café Sophie also serves what could be the best desserts in Seattle.

CAMPAGNE, Seattle
86 Pine Street
(206) 728-2800
Expensive
Dinner Daily

Situated in Seattle's famous Pike Place Market, Campagne serves up superior dinners in an elegant, extremely romantic atmosphere. During summer, outdoor seating is offered in a brick courtyard, where flickering candles give off a dreamy, dim light. Inside, the simple, somewhat sparse dining room has hardwood floors, large fresh flower arrangements, white linens, and expansive windows looking out to Post Alley and the blazing "PUBLIC MARKET" sign. (There is no question as to exactly where you are, no matter where you sit.) The coziest spot here is the lounge, with floral upholstered chairs, muted gold tablecloths, and dark wood accents. The creative French cuisine displays Northwest overtones and will please even the most finnicky palate.

Romantic Note: CAFE CAMPAGNE, 1800 Post Alley, (206) 728-2233 (Inexpensive) is Campagne's more casual but equally attractive little sister. Salad Nicoise (with fresh, deliciously rare grilled tuna), mussels precisely steamed in white wine, and a smooth country pâté are among the memorable, reasonably priced offerings. But be careful when you order: some of the specials are overpriced. Since the cafe is open for breakfast, lunch, and dinner, you can enjoy this quiet, handsome setting any time of day.

CHEZ SHEA, Seattle
94 Pike Street, Suite 34
(206) 467-9990
Moderate to Expensive
Dinner Tueseay-Sunday

At night, after you've quietly watched the Pike Place vendors close up shop, you can climb the wooden stairs that lead to Chez Shea and share an unforgettable gourmet dinner. The restaurant is small, affording all tables a view of Puget Sound and West Seattle. From this vantage point you can watch the sky turn from vivid blue to glowing crimson. Or you can sit right next to the towering windows and gain a clear perspective on the market below.

Dark wood floors, creamy cinnamon-colored walls, arched windows, and high ceilings set the stage for the ultimate romantic evening. The menu at Chez Shea features five different five-course meals, and it changes every six to eight weeks. The French cuisine is consistently and creatively prepared: lamb medallions roasted in a fennel-cumin crust and drizzled with a lemon-olive sauce; chicken laced with sage, prosciutto, and mango cheese; scallops in champagne sauce served in a potato basket; and blackberry mousse are just a few examples. This is the perfect place to take someone special if you both love the market and want ambience oozing with character and charm.

THE CLOUD ROOM, Seattle
1619 Ninth Avenue, at the Camlin Hotel
(206) 682-0100, (800) 4226-0670
Expensive
Breakfast and Lunch Monday-Friday; Dinner Daily

Every cloud has a silver lining, and at The Cloud Room, the silver lining is sparkling city views. Located on the 11th floor of the Camlin Hotel, this petite, sophisticated dining room offers sweeping vistas of the Space Needle, Queen Anne, and downtown Seattle. The gorgeous all-wood interior features marble-topped tables lit by small oil lamps, the perfect setting for a romantic evening interlude.

Service is pleasant but sometimes slow. Thankfully, most of the food is completely worth the wait. The fresh mussels in zesty Thai curry with coconut and cilantro make a succulent starter, and the salmon glazed in brown sugar is excellent. Our filet mignon, however, was overcooked and dry. Despite this inconsistency and several rough touches (the wood needs to be refinished in places), an evening at The Cloud Room can be heaven on earth.

Romantic Note: The piano bar adjacent to the dining room is a popular nightspot. Live music is performed Tuesday through Saturday, and you might want to listen after your meal. On the other hand, if you are just here for a late dinner, lingering smoke may be bothersome.

DAHLIA LOUNGE, Seattle
1904 Fourth Avenue
(206) 682-4142
Expensive
Lunch Monday-Friday; Dinner Daily

Theatrical detailing lightens the formal atmosphere at this popular Seattle restaurant. Outside, the entrance is marked by a humorous neon sign of a chef holding a fish. Inside, a neon "CAFE" sign is at the center of the elegant and sophisticated room, which is distinguished by unique fish lanterns, tall ceilings, vivid red walls, cushy booths, and a mezzanine level. The creative menu changes weekly and lists entrées such as cumin-crusted halibut with autumn squash tamale, sweet peppers, and cilantro crème fraîche; grilled king salmon with baby fennel risotto; and crispy roast duck with a chestnut-honey glaze. The tantalizing meals are wonderfully consistent, and excellent service matches the flawless presentation.

FIGUEROA'S, Seattle
1010 Western Avenue
(206) 682-5799

Moderate to Expensive
Call for seasonal hours.

Like so many other downtown establishments, Figueroa has a split personality. By day, this sophisticated dining room caters mostly to businesspeople who hurry in and out during lunchtime, but at night the scene changes. As the sun sets and the lights begin to dim, the setting softens, the brick walls exude a warm, inviting ambience, and the romantic potential grows.

Professional, attentive service highlights the formal dining experience, and the Euro-Asian menu with a strong Northwest influence is a gourmet revelation. The cuisine is sensational from ginger-braised cod with spicy tamarind sauce, to mushroom risotto with caponata, portobello mushrooms, and goat cheese, to grilled king salmon with black currant–porcini mushroom sauce. And that's just the entrées—dessert items are equally worth raving about, particularly the baked Alaska, a large scoop of homemade chocolate and peanut butter ice cream set on a thin slice of cake that is coated with creamy marshmallow, then toasted and placed beside bananas and a glorious pool of fudge. After a grand finale like that, you are sure to leave here with a smile.

THE GEORGIAN ROOM, Seattle
411 University Street, at the Four Seasons Olympic Hotel
(206) 621-1700
Expensive to Unbelievably Expensive
Breakfast Daily; Dinner Monday–Saturday

If romantic atmosphere is enough to satisfy your appetite, then The Georgian Room deserves a ten-lip rating. Every facet of this distinguished dining room is luxurious and regal. The ornate crystal chandeliers, monumental floral arrangements, two-story Palladian windows, and subdued lighting create a captivating, sensuous atmosphere in which to enjoy very posh dinners that emphasize presentation and flawless kid-glove service. The menu reflects eclectic Pacific Rim and spa cuisine influences; lamentably, the quality of the dishes can range anywhere from very good to disappointing, and at these prices that is almost unforgivable. When we were last here, the grain-stuffed salmon surrounded by morel mushrooms and fennel leaves was good, but the rubbery black morels and pale green fennel looked hideous on the plate and tasted bland. A medley of seasonal vegetables were just steamed, and lacked both seasoning and flair. The split-pea soup poured over a savory clove of elephant garlic was too creamy and had only a vague split-pea flavor. Even the Grand Marnier soufflé seemed short on Grand Marnier. Still, there's that atmosphere, and breakfast is executed with enough style to make The Georgian Room the most luxurious place to spend a morning in the city.

THE HUNT CLUB, Seattle
900 Madison Street, at the Sorrento Hotel
(206) 622-6400
Expensive to Very Expensive
Breakfast, Lunch, and Dinner Daily

A hallowed Seattle dining spot for years, this seductively lit dining room just oozes romance and gentility. Honduran mahogany paneling frames the brick walls throughout the handsome interior. The wait staff performs with panache, and the kitchen lives up to the atmosphere with exceptionally creative and carefully prepared meals. Your every need, including privacy, will be obligingly met. Fresh pheasant, incredibly moist and delicious salmon, and remarkable sauces are highlights of this superlative dining experience. Breakfasts and lunches are more affordable, but still memorable.

IL BISTRO, Seattle
93-A Pike Street
(206) 682-3049
Moderate to Expensive
Dinner Daily

After a day spent listening to guitar-strumming street musicians and bellowing vendors in the Pike Place Market, you can take quiet refuge at this sophisticated hideaway tucked below the market in a quaint, cobblestoned alleyway. Step past the quiet sunken bar to a distinguished dining room where tall antique wrought-iron lamps and candlelight illuminate the interior. Cream-colored walls, hardwood floors, black and white modern artwork, and intimate tables topped with ivory linens create a soothing ambience. In the midst of this tranquility, you'll want to linger over the classic and not-so-classic Italian fare. Even the menu's least intricate items are flawlessly prepared; we were delighted with the gnocci dressed in a sweet tomato sauce and the crostini with fresh goat cheese, roasted garlic, and basil. For a real taste extravaganza, try the grilled and marinated breast of chicken with a delightful wild mushroom sauce; the linguine with fresh fish, shellfish, garlic, basil, and cream; or the pasta with mushrooms, garlic, and hot pepper flakes. Conclude your evening by sharing one of the seductive desserts, and accompany it with an equally seductive kiss.

IL TERRAZZO CARMINE, Seattle
411 First Avenue South
(206) 467-7797
Moderate to Expensive
Lunch Monday-Friday; Dinner Monday-Saturday

This poetic urban nightspot sits right in the middle of what is not the prettiest part of Pioneer Square. Still, you leave the street behind once you enter through a brick archway, past an aqua-tiled fountain cascading into a series of spotlighted ponds. Strategically placed backlighting is reflected by the water, causing the whole courtyard to shimmer and gleam in the night air. This terrace (*terrazzo* in Italian) is the restaurant's "backyard," where tables are set during the summer. Inside, romantic details fill the pretty dining room, which is replete with gleaming crystal, floral-patterned china, and tables adorned with ivory linens and fresh flowers. A high wooden ceiling with exposed beams and pipes, walls decorated with Mediterranean-style plates and paintings, floral fringed Victorian-style lamps, and large plants add eclectic style. Immense floor-to-ceiling, wall-to-wall windows framed by floral drapes view the outside courtyard.

Rest assured that the food lives up to the atmosphere. The kitchen prepares a combination of traditional and daring Italian dishes, with an exceptional antipasto presentation. Your evening can easily be centered around the delicious cuisine and glowing ambience of Il Terrazzo Carmine.

ISABELLA RISTORANTE, Seattle
1909 Third Avenue
(206) 441-8281
Moderate to Expensive
Lunch Monday-Friday; Dinner Daily

Low lighting and rich cranberry walls spark a warm glow throughout Isabella Ristorante's seductive dining room. Crisp white linens and a blue glass vase filled with fresh flowers top every table, and gold brocade curtains block the view of headlights rushing by outside. Once you snuggle into an upholstered booth, you will forget downtown even exists.

Classic Italian cuisine is the specialty here, and portions are more than generous. Hearty pasta dishes include penne pasta with eggplant, smoked mozzarella, ricotta, and tomato sauce, and cheese-filled spinach ravioli sautéed with artichoke hearts, wild mushrooms, and fresh tomatoes. A variety of pizzas and meat dishes are also offered, and the daily seafood specials are reliably fantastic. Service is prompt and attentive.

LA FONTANA SICILIANA, Seattle
120 Blanchard
(206) 441-1045
Moderate
Lunch Tuesday-Friday; Dinner Daily

Nestled at the bottom of a downtown brick apartment building, La Fontana offers precious intimacy. A handful of well-spaced four-person tables accented with single red roses and softly glowing candles or lamps are arranged in each of the two cozy, comfortably elegant dining rooms. In one room, artwork decorates the brick walls; in the other, a wine rack in handsome dark wood cabinetry is tucked to one side, and a painted mural of arches embraced by trailing grapevines covers another wall. Chandeliers hang from the intricately patterned white ceiling, casting a gentle glow on antique clocks and a piano (there is live Italian piano music every Friday evening), and delicate lace window treatments partially shield diners from the street. Classical music accompanies the Italian food, which is spectacular. The fresh black pasta in a smoked salmon cream sauce is rich and delicious, as is the risotto with fresh herbs, olive oil, prawns, garlic, and tomato sauce. On nicer days and evenings, tables are placed in the outside courtyard of the building, where you can enjoy the fountain and flower boxes in addition to each other's company.

LAMPREIA, Seattle
2400 First Avenue
(206) 443-3301
Expensive
Dinner Tuesday-Saturday

Simplicity at its finest describes both the decor and the cuisine at Lampreia. The stylish interior boasts marble floors, mahogany chairs, terracotta-colored walls decorated with modern artwork, and tables topped with white linens and petite candles. Wall sconces and a wrought-iron chandelier provide gentle lighting, and jazz music accompanies your meal. Exposed ventilation ducts hang from the high ceiling, making the room feel a bit industrial, and bad acoustics mean the noise level can be high in proportion to the number of patrons actually present. But once your exquisite meal arrives, you won't notice anything else (except each other, of course). Fresh produce and local fish and meats are the focus of the menu; dishes highlight the individual flavors of each ingredient. Choose from such entrées as breast of pheasant with whipped potatoes, halibut fillet with braised fennel, or lamb loin with roasted pepper. Everything is artfully presented, and the service is exceptional. If appreciating the simpler pleasures of fine dining appeals to you, try Lampreia.

LE GOURMAND, Seattle
425 Northwest Market Street
(206) 784-3463

Moderate to Expensive
Dinner Wednesday-Saturday

Ballard is a neighborhood best known for its Scandinavian heritage, yet Le Gourmand is 100 percent French. This elegant little dining room is tucked away in a modest building that appears to be boarded up at first glance, but take a closer look—the windows are covered only to deflect the sight and sound of traffic outside. Inside, the setting is refined and completely charming. A whimsical pastel mural of a meadow with birch trees covers one wall, and pink crushed silk pillows fill the bench that lines the perimeter of the room.

The appealing ambience is complemented by gracious service and fine French cuisine. Three-course meals are served here, and the daily choices are limited. Delectable starters include the zucchini-mint soup and the blintzes filled with sheep's milk cheese and covered with chive butter sauce. The chicken stuffed with a medley of Northwest mushrooms and served in a savory grape sauce, and the poached king salmon fillet with a creamy sauce of dried salmon and fresh sorrel were unimprovable. The third course, a mixed green salad with edible flowers, is the last one—unless you have spared room for dessert. Be forewarned, the homemade ice creams and sorbets are difficult to resist.

LEO MELINA, Seattle
96 Union Street
(206) 623-3783
Moderate to Expensive
Lunch and Dinner Daily

What a shame you can't eat decor, because this restaurant is nothing less than gorgeous. From the impressive glass-enclosed kitchen to the sultry lighting cast by singularly impressive chandeliers and sconces, Leo Melina sports a dazzling personality. Be that as it may, the kitchen seems dismayed at being upstaged by the inventiveness of the interior designer. Four different entrées seemed to come from four different restaurants. A thick, dry pasta putanesca tasted like someone forgot to add seasoning, the other pasta dish was chewy and completely forgettable, the salmon was nicely done but ordinary, yet the veal was succulent, and covered with a rich, smooth cognac sauce. This establishment needs some polishing if the owners hope to retain their good reputation, which right now appears to be in jeopardy.

MAMMA MELINA, Seattle
4759 Roosevelt Way Northeast
(206) 632-2271

Moderate to Expensive
Dinner Daily

Although we generally hesitate to recommend establishments that get too crowded and noisy, sometimes we just have to make exceptions to the rule. This popular restaurant, located in Seattle's University District, is filled to the brim every Friday and Saturday night, but we still think you should give it a try. Why? Simply because your hearts will soar when you hear the live opera music performed here by the restaurant's proprietor and others, who roam the restaurant's cozy interior while they sing, delivering romance right to your table (they even take requests). Most of the patrons clap for the singers, and cries of "Bravo" often ring out. The result is a lively feeling of community and fun, as well as a fairly high noise level. And although the decor can leave a little to be desired (cream vinyl tablecloths, plastic flowers on each table, worn and slightly stained blue carpeting), the mood is undeniably romantic. In the absence of live singing, Italian music accompanies your meal. Glowing votive candles gently illuminate the restaurant's saffron sponge-painted walls, which are decorated with large, colorful oil paintings depicting Italian scenes, and the tables are arranged well for privacy. Service is friendly and efficient, and the Italian menu delivers highly desirable fare: succulent prawns sautéed in a tangy garlic-lemon-wine sauce and manicotti stuffed with ricotta cheese, spinach, and mushrooms are two especially good choices. And save room for dessert; the sweet tang of the mango sorbet or the divine richness of the almond-raspberry-chocolate cake can be the perfect finale to your meal.

MARCO'S SUPPER CLUB, Seattle
2510 First Avenue
(206) 441-7801
Moderate
Lunch Monday-Friday; Dinner Daily

What is the difference between a supper club and a restaurant? Well, at Marco's there is no difference. This urban eatery features nice low lighting, candles at every table, a bar along one side of the room, and a unique menu featuring world cuisine. Fried sage leaves with a medley of dipping sauces are a must-try appetizer, but deciding on an entrée is more challenging, with choices like the spicy Jamaican jerk chicken, grilled cumin-marinated halibut, and ricotta and pine nut ravioli tossed with arugula pesto.

Tables are situated too close to one another for any intimacy, but service is friendly and prompt, and Marco's is a fun spot. Later in the evening, however, the room turns hectic and noisy, more like a bar, and the smoke can be unpleasant if you are trying to eat dinner.

MAXIMILIEN-IN-THE-MARKET, Seattle
81-A Pike Street
(206) 682-7270
Moderate to Expensive
Breakfast, Lunch, and Dinner Monday-Saturday; Sunday Brunch

Ooh la la—Maximilien-in-the-Market is *très* French and *très* lovely. Antique mirrors line the deep green walls, candlelit tables are spread across the hardwood floors, and large windows take in mesmerizing views of Elliott Bay, West Seattle, and the Olympic Mountains. If your timing is right, your classic French dinner will be accompanied by the Olympics changing color in harmony with the setting sun. The view is absolutely enchanting.

During the week, four-course prix fixe meals are offered, but the menu goes à la carte on Friday and Saturday nights. Fillet of salmon sautéed with butter and wine and garnished with a fine julienne of vegetables, and beef tenderloin in béarnaise sauce are two of the tempting options. Desserts are just as seductive—who can say no to warm profiteroles drizzled with caramel?

Romantic Suggestions: Maximilien-in-the-Market also harbors a petite bar above the restaurant. Polished wood tables and worn upholstery create a more casual atmosphere, and the view is even more astounding than the one from the main-floor dining room. We also recommend Maximilien for an affectionate breakfast. And just think, after a hot latte and fresh pastry, you can spend the rest of your morning exploring the Pike Place Market, right outside the restaurant's doors.

MONA'S, Seattle
6421 Latona Avenue Northeast
(206) 526-1188
Moderate
Dinner Tuesday-Sunday

Tucked between two shops in an unassuming residential area, Mona's is a romantic oasis in an unlikely spot. Tables at this contemporary, fun bistro are topped with white linens and votive candles, and black lacquered chairs with gold cushions rest on the speckled linoleum floor. The sage and saffron sponge-painted walls are decorated with a mix of Renaissance and modern art, collages in funky handpainted frames, and framed mirrors. A high mauve-colored ceiling, ivory window treatments, and wall sconces with softly glowing candles complete the casually elegant decor. The most romantic, private tables flank the entryway; each side has one table, slightly elevated and placed next to floor-to-ceiling windows that overlook the relatively quiet street. And the food is delicious. Try the spicy house paella or the sautéed

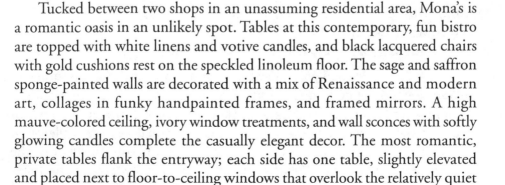

wild mushrooms between potato-parsnip cakes, served with Swiss chard and zucchini in a red pepper vinaigrette.

NIKKO, Seattle
1900 Fifth Avenue, at the Westin Hotel
(206) 322-4641
Expensive
Lunch Monday-Friday; Dinner Monday-Saturday

Japanese dining is not often thought of as particularly romantic. It is usually enjoyed by individuals with a "yen" for uncooked fish and dining ritual, not necessarily for those with snuggling on their minds. Nikko is a rare exception. Every aspect of this restaurant is dictated by the philosophy that beauty enhances taste. From the exquisitely crafted wishing well (sans water) at the entrance to the sponge-painted walls adorned with three-dimensional origami shapes, the interior is filled with elegantly sleek decor. Blond wood accents throughout the dining area are complemented by splashes of deep burgundy, blue, and black. Flower-shaped fans on the ceiling and waitresses in kimonos add the finishing touches. You'll discover that nothing has been left undone, no detail unaccounted for, from the courteous service to the shoes left outside each tatami room. (These private rooms would be perfect for some serious romancing, but unfortunately they are available only for large groups.)

Both eye and palate will find the food pleasing at Nikko. Perfectly fried tempura comes in woven baskets, while sushi is served as elegant swirls of color, adorned with the proper accents. You may order full-course dinners, à la carte, or just fill up at the sushi bar if you like. During lunch on weekdays, all-you-can-eat sushi is offered for $10.50 per person. A *Zen*sational experience!

PERCHE' NO, Seattle
621 1/2 Queen Anne Avenue North
(206) 298-0230
Moderate to Expensive
Lunch Tuesday-Saturday; Dinner Tuesday-Sunday

Perche' No is located only a few blocks from the Seattle Center, home to major theater, symphony, opera, and ballet companies. The restaurant prides itself on being more than willing to work around your curtain call—just tell the wait staff when the performance starts and you'll be out in plenty of time. But you won't want to rush your meal here if you can help it; the ambience and food are well worth admiring. Crisp white table linens, long-stemmed roses, and flickering candles adorn an assortment of well-spaced two- and four-person tables arranged in the two cozy, dimly lit dining rooms.

European artwork, dried flower arrangements, and strands of garlic decorate the walls, while floral drapes shield the restaurant from the busy street outside. Soft Italian music accompanies your meal. Adding a special personal touch, the restaurant's pleasant owner stops by every table over the course of the evening to say hello and make sure you're comfortable.

The homemade pasta selections are outstanding, including the tortellini with Gorgonzola cheese; the fresh fettuccine with scampi, cream, and fresh basil; and the angel-hair pasta with every imaginable "fruit of the sea" (scallops, clams, mussels, shrimp, and more). Dessert is definitely worth the extra time—even if you are in a rush.

Romantic Note: Perche' No offers a dinner/limousine package that includes round-trip limousine service within the Seattle metropolitan area and a four-course dinner ($50 per person, with a two-person minimum).

PIROSMANI, Seattle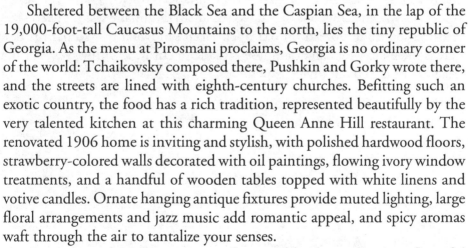
2220 Queen Anne Avenue North
(206) 285-3360
Expensive
Dinner Tuesday-Saturday

Sheltered between the Black Sea and the Caspian Sea, in the lap of the 19,000-foot-tall Caucasus Mountains to the north, lies the tiny republic of Georgia. As the menu at Pirosmani proclaims, Georgia is no ordinary corner of the world: Tchaikovsky composed there, Pushkin and Gorky wrote there, and the streets are lined with eighth-century churches. Befitting such an exotic country, the food has a rich tradition, represented beautifully by the very talented kitchen at this charming Queen Anne Hill restaurant. The renovated 1906 home is inviting and stylish, with polished hardwood floors, strawberry-colored walls decorated with oil paintings, flowing ivory window treatments, and a handful of wooden tables topped with white linens and votive candles. Ornate hanging antique fixtures provide muted lighting, large floral arrangements and jazz music add romantic appeal, and spicy aromas waft through the air to tantalize your senses.

Georgian and Mediterranean influences blend together in a flavorful selection of appetizers and entrées. Tantalizing dishes include spinach pâté; sweet pepper salad; and eggplant folded over a purée of walnuts, coriander, and garlic with fresh ricotta cheese and mint. The breast of duck laced with cinnamon and cardamom and baked with saffron, sumac, onions, and pine nuts, and the fresh salmon marinated in pomegranate juice are both impressive. Authentic ethnic dining of this caliber is not often found in Seattle, which makes a kiss here more inspiring than usual.

PLACE PIGALLE, Seattle
81 Pike Street, at the Pike Place Market
(206) 624-1756
Moderate to Expensive
Lunch and Dinner Monday-Saturday

This highly acclaimed Seattle restaurant features views of the Puget Sound—that is, if you are fortunate enough to reserve one of the few windowside tables. Otherwise, Place Pigalle is small (and usually crowded due to its popularity), with black-and-white-tiled floors that seem to intensify the chatter and wooden tables placed too close to each other for privacy. An open bar is located next to the dining room and fumes from the smoking section invade the whole interior, while the chill from the opening and closing door is irksome to those seated nearby. Perhaps the only opportunity you'll have to be intimate with your loved one here is when you have to get close enough to hear each other over the noise.

If romance is not at the top of your agenda, the best reason to visit Place Pigalle is for the creative menu. Fresh, local ingredients, many from right here in the market, are the focus of the kitchen, but, sad to say, the quality of the food is inconsistent. The charred ahi tuna served with a flavorful wasabi orange oil was amazing, but the sautéed calamari dijonnaise was undercooked, and the sourdough bread on our open-faced sandwich was so hard it flew across the plate when an attempt was made to cut it. Exciting, yes, but not exactly our idea of an idyllic experience.

PONTI SEAFOOD GRILL, Seattle
3014 Third Avenue North
(206) 284-3000
Expensive
Lunch Monday-Friday; Dinner Daily; Sunday Brunch

If you arrive at Ponti expecting savory Italian fare, you may be disappointed. Even though the name means "bridges" in Italian, this is a mecca for fans of Euro-Asian-style meals cooked to utter perfection and beautifully presented. An additional bonus is the view of the ship canal and Fremont bridge. A large floral arrangement is the focal point of the main-floor dining room; deep plum carpeting, dark wood accents, and soft lighting contribute to a very warm atmosphere. White linens and fresh flowers adorn each table, and windows frame views of the bridge beyond the outside patio. Even though the noise level can escalate as the closely placed tables fill up, the room remains surprisingly cozy and intimate. Two small upstairs dining rooms can provide a more secluded evening, but neither of them feels as warm as the main-floor room. In the summer months, outdoor seating is available on two patios that showcase the busy canal.

We suggest beginning your meal with the Dungeness crab spring rolls with a lime-chili dipping sauce. Then move on to the Thai curry penne pasta with scallops, Dungeness crab, and ginger-tomato chutney, or the perfectly seared sashimi tuna with a sake-ginger sauce, cucumber wasabe, and a subtle coconut rice cake. Desserts here are always memorable; sharing one could be a true test of love.

QUEEN MARY, Seattle
2912 Northeast 55th Street
(206) 527-2770
Inexpensive
Breakfast, Lunch, and Afternoon Tea Daily; Dinner Thursday-Saturday

It is easy to drive past this small storefront restaurant and never notice it, although we think it is one of the most romantic restaurants in Seattle. Once inside, you will feel as if you've been transported to the English countryside. This exceedingly charming, polished restaurant has a beautiful interior; we couldn't resist the wood paneling, pleated floral fabric lining the walls and entrance, lace-covered windows, and comfortable wicker chairs placed around a handful of tables set for two.

Fastidious attention to detail and freshness marks every meal. Breakfast is an elaborate display of fresh pastries, granolas, and breads; midday brings light, flaky quiches and generous sandwiches; and dinner is an elegant gourmet event. Beef tenderloin stuffed with Roquefort cheese and mushrooms with a merlot sauce, and pasta with artichokes and smoked salmon in a heavenly cream sauce are both sumptuous. High tea is also a daily offering, and you will be properly impressed with this ritual. But we've left the best for last: dessert. The most outrageous, luscious cakes, tortes, and mousses are made fresh here daily. Chocolate cake with amaretto mousse, marbled cheesecake, and fresh fruit tarts were only a few of the selections available on the night we fell in love with Queen Mary.

REINER'S, Seattle
1106 Eighth Avenue
(206) 624-2222
Moderate to Expensive
Dinner Tuesday-Saturday

It's not the most romantic location, crammed between two city buildings and around the block from a large hospital, but you'll forget that as you're drawn off the street into a colorful garden entryway shaded by trees. As you enter the small dining room, you'll notice that every last corner is filled with polished details. The tables, draped in white linen and set beneath an arched dome ceiling, are surrounded by modern tapestries. Venerable antiques, crystal chandeliers, and lace-curtained windows convey a sense of refined intimacy. Although the tables are arranged somewhat snugly, your privacy is kept intact by the rich ambience of the room. Whether you dine on the extremely fresh grilled king salmon or take advantage of the three-course pre-theater prix fixe meal served nightly (guaranteed to have you in your seats before the curtain goes up), you are sure to satisfy your palate and whet your romantic appetite.

RISTORANTE BUONGUSTO, Seattle
2232 Queen Anne Avenue North
(206) 284-9040
Moderate to Expensive
Dinner Daily

Set above the busy street and defended by gauzy white curtains, Ristorante Buongusto is a deliciously romantic retreat. Inside, the tables are adorned with white tablecloths, spice-colored linen napkins, fresh flowers, and votive candles. A multihued stone floor and soft peach sponge-painted walls distinguish the interior of this quiet, intimate restaurant. A glowing fireplace is built into one wall, which is also softly painted with reproductions of figures drawn by the likes of da Vinci, Michelangelo, and Degas. Low lighting and soft Italian music complete the scene for a perfect meal. And the food is everything you could possibly desire: generous mixed green salads precede flavorful entrées such as chicken tortellini in a light cream and Gorgonzola sauce, and grilled prawns served with garlic, olive oil, parsley, and red pepper. A variety of fresh desserts prepared daily will entice those who love to indulge in the sweeter pleasures in life.

RISTORANTE SALUTE, Seattle
3426 Northeast 55th Street
(206) 527-8600
Moderate
Lunch Monday-Friday; Dinner Daily

If you're in the mood for a taste of Italy's northern and southern countryside, you can't do better than this popular casual Italian eatery. Although it has moved two doors down since we last reviewed it, nothing else has changed. White-and-red-checked linens cover the tables, and fishing nets, buoys, and rowboats hang from the ceiling in two intimate dining rooms adorned with pictures of Italy. While the tables in both dining rooms can feel a little too close for comfort when the restaurant is operating at full capacity (which is often), flickering candlelight and cozy two-person tables help to maintain an amorous mood. Check the chalkboard for daily specials; two favorites are the tortellini with chanterelle mushrooms in a creamy Parmesan sauce, and linguine with clams and mussels in a tangy marinara sauce. Save room for Salute's tiramisu—undoubtedly one of Seattle's best.

ROVER'S, Seattle
2808 East Madison
(206) 325-7442
Expensive to Very Expensive
Dinner Tuesday-Saturday

An unassuming neighborhood setting, a discreet interior, dramatic lighting, white walls covered with pastel artworks, and some of the best continental cuisine you will ever taste are waiting for you at Rover's. Perhaps the decor is a bit too stark to be considered cozy or charming, but flawless, elegant dining can be enticing for those with a discerning palate. In the summer months, you can dine at cozy tables set up in the restaurant's fragrant garden courtyard. The chef here is incredibly skilled, with a world-wide reputation as one of the area's best, and he earns it night after delicious night with dishes such as vegetable flan with a red and black currant sauce; grilled Oregon rabbit with goat cheese, barley ragout, and a heavenly rose-mary sauce; tomato concasse with a goat cheese sauce; steamed lobster with a black truffle sauce; and roasted guinea fowl with celery root purée, cran-berry chutney, and an Armagnac sauce. Unparalleled and outstanding!

SALEH AL LAGO, Seattle,
6804 East Green Lake Way North
(206) 524-4044
Moderate to Expensive
Lunch Monday-Friday; Dinner Monday-Saturday

Serving some of the best Italian food in all of Seattle, this bastion of hearty Tuscany-style cuisine does not disappoint. Enclosed by windows, the small restaurant offers peekaboo glimpses of nearby Green Lake. Candle lanterns and fresh flowers add color to the spartan but elegant two-tiered dining room filled with linen-cloaked tables. Cushioned booths tucked in window alcoves on the lower level offer the most privacy. Service here is extremely gracious, and the food is unforgettable. Windows in the kitchen provide glimpses of the talented chef working diligently on flawless entrées such as wild mushroom and Gorgonzola ravioli with roasted garlic and tomato butter sauce; roasted red pepper pasta and sautéed scallops with cherry tomatoes, scallions and orange zest in an olive butter sauce garnished with crispy fried leeks; and linguine with goat cheese, sun-dried tomatoes, kalamata olives, garlic, and hot pepper flakes. After you've lingered by candle-light over hot coffee and an exquisite dessert, walk hand in hand across the street and enjoy the bustling Green Lake setting.

SALVATORE, Seattle
6100 Roosevelt Way Northeast
(206) 527-9301
Moderate
Dinner Monday-Saturday

Situated in the heart of the Roosevelt District, not far from the University of Washington, Salvatore's is a local romantic favorite. Savory aromas drift from the open kitchen through the small dining room, which is filled with a handful of candlelit two-person tables. If you look closely, you'll notice that people have pasted their pictures onto an Italian townscape painted on the dining room's largest wall. Not your typical mural, but this isn't your typical Italian restaurant. Everything here is wildly delicious, especially the sautéed tiger shrimp with penne pasta, and the "inverted" chicken, stuffed with raisins, garlic, and Parmesan and served in a white wine cream sauce. And the freshly baked desserts—sheer perfection. Our only hesitation about recommending this superior restaurant is the fact that reservations are not accepted, which means you often have to contend with crowds and a long wait for a table.

SERAFINA, Seattle
2043 Eastlake Avenue East
(206) 323-0807
Moderate to Expensive
Reservations Recommended
Lunch Monday-Friday; Dinner Daily

We are told that marriage proposals are a frequent occurrence at Serafina. That may sound romantic, but the reason this is common knowledge is because the proposer practically has to shout across the table just to get the proposee's attention. With many little tables placed very close together, don't count on your evening here being a private affair. Serafina is one of Seattle's most talked about restaurants, so reservations are a must, and it is almost always crowded. The room holds a certain amount of rustic Italian charm, with earth-toned wall murals and low lighting, but ultimately it is the food and not the clamorous atmosphere that makes the whole experience worthwhile.

Cannelloni Serafina with caramelized eggplant and cannelini beans, served on a bed of tomato sauce, is an intriguing—and incredibly flavorful—departure from typical Italian fare. And the spicy gamberi alla puttanesca features the freshest jumbo prawns. Although the menu changes seasonally, you can count on the skilled kitchen for inventive dishes, and desserts are equally pleasing. Service is friendly but, not surprisingly, sometimes rushed.

Romantic Note: Jazz musicians perform nightly, starting at 8 P.M. This would be a romantic plus if it weren't already so noisy, but as it stands now, the music makes whispering sweet nothings nearly impossible.

SOSTANZA, Seattle
1927 43rd Avenue East
(206) 324-9701
Moderate to Expensive
Dinner Monday-Saturday

Madison Park is a charmingly urbane, entirely gentrified Seattle neighborhood, but it isn't so slick that you will feel out of place without your power suit—after all, this is still Seattle, despite the multimillion-dollar homes lining the area. Around the corner from a row of tempting storefronts, you'll find Sostanza, a delightful dining spot with a tender blend of elegance and country-rustic touches. Amber stucco walls, a wood-beamed ceiling, soft lighting, a large gas fireplace (what a shame it isn't wood-burning), and nicely spaced tables fill this Italian trattoria with warmth and comfort. The food is very good, and the wait staff will obligingly (and honestly) lead you in the right direction. For your dining information, the quail is remarkable, and every pasta dish is as fresh and as perfectly cooked as any we've tasted in Italy. After dinner, you can stroll down to Lake Washington, and explore kissing possibilities as you look east to Bellevue and the Cascade Mountains.

SPACE NEEDLE RESTAURANT, Seattle
219 Fourth Avenue North
(206) 443-2150, (800) 937-9582
Expensive to Very Expensive
Breakfast, Lunch, and Dinner Monday-Saturday; Sunday Brunch

Of all the places to dine in Seattle, the Space Needle is without question the most touristy. As Seattle's most indelible trademark, it seems to be on the short list of must-see sites for millions of visitors every year. Why is this flying saucer–shaped tower so popular? Because on a clear day, all of the region's glories are astonishingly visible from up here, from the Olympics to the Cascades to the Puget Sound islands to the green-haloed local neighborhoods. Why are we recommending the Space Needle in a book like this? Because the tables in the two contemporary dining rooms are arranged for surprising privacy, service is excellent, and nothing compares to the ever-changing view as the restaurant makes a full revolution each hour. A summer sunset, candlelight, and fresh king salmon accompanied by this view are worthy of more kisses than we care to count.

Romantic Note: You do not have to pay the usual fee for the elevator ride when you go to the restaurant. This sounds like a great deal because you also have access to the observation deck while waiting for your table or after dinner. However, when you see the prices on the menu (average $25 per entrée), you'll realize it isn't such a bargain after all.

SZMANIA'S, Seattle
3321 West McGraw
(206) 284-7305
Moderate to Expensive
Call for seasonal hours.

Sometimes romantic ambience takes a backseat to incredible cuisine. At Szmania's, a stylish bistro in the upscale Magnolia neighborhood, the atmosphere is lively and not necessarily intimate, but the cuisine is always remarkable. Casual outdoor seating is available in summertime; inside, the sleek interior features dropped lighting over each table and bar seating around the open kitchen. (It's fun to watch the chef and his skilled staff create the masterpieces that will soon grace your table.)

Presentations are lovely, service is impeccable, and every dish is magnificently prepared, with each succulent, mouthwatering nuance intact. Delicious options include white king salmon baked in a crispy potato crust and served with an olive-pesto sauce, and honey and lingcod with sweet balsamic butter accompanied by three different fresh pastas tossed in an ultra-light cream sauce. The Caesar salad here is one of the best and most authentic in the city. For dessert, the perfect crème brulée, strawberry shortcake, or white and dark chocolate mousse can prove almost too wicked. But what's a little decadence between friends?

THAT'S AMORE, Seattle
1425 31st Avenue South
(206) 322-3677
Moderate to Expensive
Lunch and Dinner Daily

When the moon hits your eye and you're in the mood for pizza pie, go to That's Amore. This neighborhood hole-in-the-wall is perfect for those times when you want dynamite Italian cuisine and a nice bottle of wine, but you're too tired to bother with getting all dressed up. Families are welcomed with open arms, so the noise level can be several decibels beyond hushed, but it's far from annoying. The wait staff is both cheerful and professional. The large menu offers a variety of pastas, pizzas, and Italian-accented meat and seafood entrées, and a chalkboard lists nightly specials. Our linguine with wild mushrooms and sun-dried tomatoes in a garlic cream sauce kept a multitude of flavors in perfect balance, and the cheese pizza combined high-quality cheese with a handmade crust. A wall of windows at the back of the long, narrow room frames a territorial view of houses, streets, freeway, the north end of Beacon Hill, and downtown Seattle.

Romantic Note: A lack of air-conditioning here means that the room can get unbearably warm on Seattle's handful of truly hot days.

UNION BAY CAFE, Seattle
3515 Northeast 45th Street
(206) 527-8364
Moderate to Expensive
Dinner Tuesday-Sunday

The Union Bay Cafe offers a touch of casual elegance for dining romantics, although you'd never guess it from the restaurant's location on a heavily trafficked street not far from the University District. This charming cafe has recently moved a few doors down from its previous location, and now finds itself with an updated look and a much cozier ambience. Black-and-white modern art, soothing muted color schemes of mustard and sage, soft music, and tables dressed in white linens and simple votive candles help take your mind off the cars speeding by just outside the window. The experienced kitchen specializes in outstanding seafood prepared with a Northwest flair, and is highly regarded for dishes such as the grilled halibut with watercress pesto, the steamed mussels, and tender salmon fillets. Desserts here are equally tantalizing, and with the cafe's new look, you'll want to linger over them even longer than before.

VIRAZON, Seattle
1329 First Avenue
(206) 233-0123
Moderate to Expensive
Lunch Monday-Saturday; Dinner Tuesday-Saturday

You can experience an authentic taste of Paris without even leaving Seattle at this charming bistro located in the heart of downtown. White linens and fresh flowers adorn each table, and large windows framed by patterned drapes and partially shielded by lace half-curtains look out to the busy street. Yellow sponge-painted walls decorated with colorful artwork brighten the interior, and strings of interesting, funky lights hang from the ceiling. Privacy can be minimal due to the lunchtime crowd of businesspeople and shoppers, but the delicious food more than makes up for it. Each meal is arranged so artfully that you may feel reluctant to eat it, although you'll have no regrets after taking your first bite. The chef takes advantage of fresh local ingredients, so the menu is constantly changing; entrées might include the Brie and coppacola ham sandwich or the grilled Oregon rabbit served with a sweet potato pancake and wild mushroom ragout. A meal at Virazon wouldn't be complete without one of the heavenly desserts—the chocolate-espresso pot de creme, a rich and dense chocolate delight, is perfect for sharing.

Outdoor Kissing

ALKI BEACH, West Seattle

Take Interstate 5 to the West Seattle Freeway exit and the West Seattle Bridge. Cross the bridge, follow Harbor Avenue to the beach, and continue around to Beach Drive.

The waterfront neighborhoods of West Seattle are only a few minutes from downtown Seattle. **LINCOLN PARK**, a large wooded tract just north of the Fauntleroy ferry, faces a spectacular view due west, but Alki Beach, with its northwesterly exposure, has the most expansive, sensational vistas of them all. This long stretch of sandy beach, backdropped by exquisite profiles of the snowcapped Olympics and the silvery waters of Puget Sound, is an incredible place to stroll hand in hand almost any time of year. Unfortunately, a warm summer day can change this flawless stretch of land into a mass of urban congestion. During the spring, fall, or winter, when things are quieter, couples can pass gentle moments here watching the sky and mountains change expressions with the passing hours.

Romantic Alternative: HAMILTON VIEWPOINT in West Seattle, just off California Avenue Southwest, faces the downtown skyline of Seattle. In the evening you can watch as the city's twinkling lights are reflected in the cobalt blue water and the moon's golden glow dances over the surface. This is also a rare vantage point from which to watch the sun rise above Seattle. You won't be the only couple embracing in the moonlight, but you will probably be the only ones snuggling in the early light of dawn.

Romantic Suggestion: PHOENECIA, 2716 Alki Avenue Southwest, (206) 935-6550 (Moderate) has generous windows that look out to expansive views of Puget Sound. Warm yellow and burgundy walls and wooden tables covered in white linen add pizzazz to the handsome setting. Mediterranean cuisine is featured here, and it is handled deftly by the friendly, laid-back chef (who can get overly creative in the kitchen, so ask specifically what's in store or you're liable to be surprised and possibly disappointed). The hummus, roasted eggplant, and couscous salad are all authentic and tasty.

"BHY" KRACKE PARK, Seattle

Located on southeast Queen Anne Hill, north of downtown, at the intersection of Fifth Avenue North and West Highland Drive. It is also known as Comstock Park.

Unless you've read a previous edition of *The Best Places To Kiss* or live nearby, you may not have heard of this park with the funny name. As you drive through the unpretentious neighborhood, you'll probably think nothing of the small, unobtrusive playground on your left. But stop and take another look. "Bhy" Kracke Park starts off as an innocent playground, less than a block long, at the bottom of a hill. On either side of it, landscaped walkways angle upward, meet, then curve around and up, and around and up, to the top of the hill. As you climb, you'll find five tiers of grassy vistas; well-placed park benches, surrounded by dense hedges and vines, face a startling city view. Around each turn is another glimpse of the city, building up to what lies at the top. Unbelievable!

Romantic Note: If you don't want to walk up, drive to the park entrance on Comstock, at the top of the hill, and walk down one tier.

CENTER FOR WOODEN BOATS, Seattle
1010 Valley Street
(206) 382-2628
http://www.eskimo.com/~cwboats
Call for seasonal hours.

Boat enthusiasts of all kinds will feel right at home at this unique wooden boat museum and learning center, which also rents out boats. Wander the docks and inspect turn-of-the-century workboats such as peapods, dories, sharpies, catboats, and skiffs. Then admire leisure boats from a time before the gas engine, including Hampton boats, Poulsbo boats, old canoes and kayaks, Whitebear skiffs, and Stars. If you happen to be an expert sailor, you can rent these boats by the hour and sail around beautiful Lake Union. If not, you'll need to take a series of classes before you can rent one of these beauties. (The classes are interesting, and the atmosphere is exceptionally friendly and inviting.) Whether you spend the day on the water or on the docks, the Center for Wooden Boats is an intriguing spot to spend a quiet afternoon.

DISCOVERY PARK SAND CLIFFS, Seattle

Take the Magnolia Bridge exit off Elliott Avenue and stay to your left. At the first stop sign, turn left onto Magnolia Boulevard and follow it until it dead-ends at the park's southeast entrance.

MAGNOLIA BOULEVARD snakes around the edge of Seattle's exclusive Magnolia neighborhood on the way to Discovery Park. This urban thoroughfare is blessed by a majestic wraparound view of Puget Sound. The cliffs along its southwest border showcase the city and the Olympics. As you follow the drive, you will notice several obvious places to pull off and park. The panoramas from these areas are spectacular, but, unfortunately, they lack privacy. However, if you walk from the grass-lined curb down to the edge of the cliff overlooking the water, the street is no longer visible.

Continue along the road to reach Discovery Park, an unusual area with an amazing variety of trails and terrain. You can hike through dense woods or along sandy cliffs above Puget Sound with unmarred exposure to everything due north, south, and west. Or take the wooden steps leading down through the woods to the shore and ramble along the driftwood-strewn rocky shoreline. While wandering through your new romantic discovery, look for the sand cliffs on the southwest side of the park. During the winter, when sundown occurs in the late afternoon, come stand atop these golden dunes for an intoxicating view of day passing into night.

Romantic Warning: A sewage treatment plant was recently built adjacent to the beach and, unfortunately, there is a strong odor on some days that can repel romantic inclinations. This problem only exists down on the beach (mostly on days when the air is still); a constant breeze helps to keep the air fresh on the cliffs.

HIGHLAND DRIVE, Seattle

From Roy Street on Lower Queen Anne, turn onto the steep part of Queen Anne Avenue North. Two blocks up, turn left onto West Highland Drive and follow it along the southwestern slope of the hill.

This exclusive street, lined with mansions and classic older apartment buildings, offers enviable southwestern views from below the summit of Queen Anne Hill. The intersection of Seventh Avenue West, Eighth Place West, and West Highland faces an especially grand panoramic vista. A grassy knoll nearby offers benches with sweeping, complete views of the city sky-line, Puget Sound, and the Olympic Mountains. With a picnic basket in tow, you can spend an entire summer afternoon up here in each other's arms.

HOT-AIR BALLOONING
Balloon Depot, (206) 881-9699
Over the Rainbow, (206) 364-0995
$99-$145 per person

Call for flight times and meeting locations.

If you're thinking that a hot-air balloon ride sounds like a frivolous, expensive, childish sort of excursion, you're right. It is a Mary Poppins lift-off into fantasy land. After an evening balloon ride, the term "carried away" will suddenly have new meaning.

Departures usually take place just before sunrise or just before sunset, and each ride lasts roughly an hour to an hour and a half. Your first impression will be astonishment at the enormous mass of billowing material over-head and the dragon fire that fills it with air. As you step into the gondola, your heart will begin to flutter with expectation. Once you're aloft, as the wind guides your craft above the countryside, the world will seem more peaceful than you ever thought possible. You will also be startled at the splendor of sunset from way up here as twilight covers the mountains with muted color and warmth. A caress while floating above the world on a cloud-less summer evening can be a thoroughly heavenly experience.

Romantic Note: Some balloon companies serve either a light dinner or a champagne brunch after the flight.

PIKE PLACE MARKET, Seattle

In downtown Seattle, at Pike Street and First Avenue.

Even though it becomes a zoo on summer weekends, there is absolutely no better place than the Pike Place Market for an authentic Seattle experi-ence. Fresh seafood (some of the best crab and mussels you'll ever taste), colorful regional produce, gorgeous flowers, and locally made arts and crafts are just some of the bounty offered at the market. Some of the fish stands feature flying fish (when you select your fish it is tossed raucously from one employee to another), and there are plenty of interesting restaurants (in-cluding Lowell's, where Tom Hanks and Rob Reiner discussed the intrica-cies of dating and tiramisu in the movie *Sleepless in Seattle*). We think visiting the Pike Place Market is one of the most entertaining ways to spend a day in Seattle. Even though it can be crowded, there is still plenty of room for affectionate strolling.

SEATTLE ART MUSEUM, Seattle   💋 💋
100 University Street
(206) 654-3100
$6 per adult; free on the first Thursday of the month
Open Tuesday-Sunday

On University Street, between First and Second Avenues.

Stirring your cultural passions while perusing the museum's permanent collections and special exhibitions can be a stimulating way to spend a leisurely afternoon. You can't miss this sandstone-colored building in downtown Seattle; its entrance is marked by Jonathan Borowsky's immense iron sculpture, *Hammering Man.* Although the transitionally seedy neighborhood around the Seattle Art Museum might bother some tourists, don't let it discourage you—what waits inside is worth checking out. Vast windows line the main floor, allowing light to pour through onto provocative architecture, magnificent statues, and marble floors. Over 20,000 pieces of art are on display for your viewing enjoyment. The museum specializes in Northwest Native and African artifacts, and the atmosphere is intense as well as exotic. Most impressive are the revolving exhibits that visit the museum; the ever-changing environment encourages return visits.

Romantic Note: The museum's grand stairwell, guarded by stone statues and flanked on one side by windows, leads to the small, contemporary cafe, **MUSEUM CAFE**, (206) 654-3245 (Moderate). The variety and quality of the soups and specialty sandwiches served here might surprise you. The vegetarian club sandwich can hardly be eaten without a fork, piled high as it is with grilled eggplant, roasted peppers, cucumbers, sprouts, tomato, and a special onion spread. The warm spinach salad comes lightly steamed in a pancetta-sherry vinaigrette, and would be perfect if it wasn't so heavily oiled. This is a great place to enjoy a latte and each other's company, surrounded by the best in Northwest art. Tables are well spaced, so it is possible to feel intimate in this bright, open cafe.

Romantic Alternative: Sister to the downtown museum, the impressive **SEATTLE ASIAN ART MUSEUM**, 14th Avenue East and East Prospect, in Volunteer Park, (206) 654-3100 (admission $6) is housed in a mammoth art deco building. The superlative collection contains works from Japan, China, Korea, Southeast Asia, India, and the Himalayan countries. Lushly shady **VOLUNTEER PARK** is a wonderful setting for the museum (although a little rough around the edges), and offers some intriguing nooks of its own. Don't miss the conservatory; even in the dead of winter, a loving couple can admire the exotic orchids and fragrant gardenias.

WASHINGTON PARK ARBORETUM, Seattle

From downtown Seattle, drive east on Madison Street to Lake Washington Boulevard East and turn left into the Arboretum.

Many cities in the United States have an area they consider an urban paradise, an essential landmark that transports visitors into a world of greenery that erases the existence of city settings. San Francisco has Golden Gate Park, New York City has Central Park, and Seattle is blessed with the Washington Park Arboretum. This elysian realm is located just south of the University of Washington, near the neighborhoods of Madison Park and Madison Valley, and partly bounded by Lake Washington. Diverse foliage, stunning landscapes, meandering walking trails, and 5,500 different kinds of plants make this an oasis of beauty for city-tired souls. This 200-acre living museum is filled with fascinating arbors and gardens. The fastidiously manicured areas include Rhododendron Glen, with different species and hybrids in a range of sizes; Woodland Garden, with two small ponds and many Japanese maples; Loderi Valley, featuring Loderi hybrids set among magnolias and conifers; and the spectacular Japanese Garden (admission $2.50), filled with tradition and home to formal tea ceremonies in the summer. (Tea is served from April to October, on the third Saturday of each month.) Our favorite times of year for strolling through the Arboretum are spring, when astonishing clouds of white and pink cherry blossoms overwhelm the senses, and autumn, when vibrant fall colors paint the scenery in ardent shades of red, gold, orange, and yellow.

Romantic Note: The Arboretum is open from 7 A.M. till dusk. Whether you venture here on foot or bicycle, please remain on the paved pathways. This ecosystem won't remain long if it is tread upon by humanity.

WASHINGTON STATE FERRIES
(206) 464-6400, (800) 843-3779
http://www.wsdot.wa.gov/ferries
Seasonal fares range from $3.50 (walk-on passenger)
to $7.10 (car and driver)

Utilitarian types may use the Washington State Ferry System only as a means of transportation to and from work, but we romantics take a different approach. What better way is there to get a sweeping view of the majestic mountains surrounding the Seattle area or the many islands scattered throughout the Puget Sound? Granted, it's no *Love Boat*—the decor is tacky and privacy is lacking—but for very little money, you and yours can bundle up for a stroll on the open deck and enjoy a glowing sunset. The crisp sea air is bound to inspire some snuggling. Another option is to make a day of it:

bring a picnic, comfortable walking shoes, and a sense of adventure to explore some of the ports of call, which include Bainbridge Island, Bremerton, Kingston, and Vashon Island.

Romantic Note: The rating of this outing definitely depends on how romantic you want to make it. During rush hour or peak tourist season, lines can be long and crowds can be abundant; at those times you may want to use the ferry only as a means of transportation.

WATERFALL GARDEN, Seattle
Near Pioneer Square
Open Daily

Just north of the Kingdome, at the southwest corner of South Main Street and Second Avenue.

If you weren't looking for it, you could very easily pass by the Waterfall Garden; that would be tragic, for you would miss an opportunity to experience this unique city hideaway. United Parcel Service built this lush urban garden in 1977 as a gift to the citizens of Seattle. (The park rests on the corner originally occupied by the messenger service that eventually became UPS.) Today it remains a cloistered downtown oasis enclosed by stone walls and a wrought-iron gate. Inside, a 22-foot-high waterfall tumbles over granite boulders bordering two sides of the park, its pleasantly noisy rush drowning out any evidence that civilization is right next door. Amazingly enough, 5,000 gallons of water are filtered and recirculated throughout the system every minute. Relax on the stone benches, surrounded by potted plants and rock sculptures, as the light mist revitalizes your spirits. Wrought-iron chairs and tables are scattered about the brick courtyard, making this a convenient place for a refreshing afternoon picnic. Due to its central location, you can rendezvous with someone special here before a football or baseball game at the nearby Kingdome, or before dinner and a night at the theater. You're likely to be quite alone together, except at lunchtime, when businesspeople take advantage of this hidden park.

Mercer Island

This sedate, well-to-do suburb, situated in the middle of Lake Washington, between Seattle and Bellevue, is accessible via the Interstate 90 floating bridge. Most of the island is residential but boutiques and specialty gift shops are thriving.

Restaurant Kissing

SIROCCO, Mercer Island
2448 76th Avenue Southeast
(206) 232-9009
Expensive
Dinner Tuesday-Saturday

Hidden in a row of nondescript offices and businesses, Sirocco is an oasis of Mediterranean warmth and refinement. The handful of linen-cloaked tables are divided between two rooms, both with terra-cotta floors. A mural painted on the wall of the larger room suggests a terrace overlooking the sunny Italian countryside; the smaller room, with its large Oriental rugs and wooden wine racks, resembles a snug study. Unfortunately, the lighting is too bright for a truly romantic mood, and on our visit the background music ranged from soothing classical pieces to somewhat distracting and atonal bebop. An outdoor seating area, screened from the adjacent parking lot by latticework and plenty of plants, is available on fine evenings.

We had no complaints about the food or the friendly, professional service. The menu changes every two weeks in order to take advantage of seasonal and special ingredients, and while the choices are limited, you can count on vegetarian, seafood, poultry, game, and meat dishes. You might start your meal with an appetizer of ricotta cheese and forest mushrooms baked in a tart. Choose a salad (all are made with organic greenery), then feast on roasted lamb served with flageolets and ratatouille, a quail ballontine filled with rich duck mousse and served with red currant sauce, or the perfectly cooked, sweetly tender sea scallops in a saffron cream sauce with baby vegetables. The wine list is exceptional, and after a luscious dessert, you might toast your evening with a mellow glass of Australian port.

Romantic Note: If you find that cigarette smoke inhibits your enjoyment of fine food and affectionate moments, you'll appreciate the fact that Sirocco is 100-percent smoke-free.

Romantic Alternative: While most Asian restaurants cater to casual groups and hungry families, **THAI ON MERCER**, 7691 Southeast 27th Street, (206) 236-9990 (Moderate) offers a distinctly upscale alternative for couples who want to leave the high-chair gang at home for the night. The dim, starkly contemporary room is done up with mint green walls, dark green linen tablecloths, nice crystal, modern vases and artwork, and black laquered chairs. This is a great place to enjoy a wide range of well-prepared, nicely presented Thai dishes.

Bellevue

Over the bridge? No way. Unless it's to head out to the Cascades, most Seattleites refuse to cross Lake Washington to visit the Eastside. They consider everything east of the city limits a desolate wasteland of big malls, little malls, strip malls, and big beige chateaus. But Bellevue, with a primarily affluent population of over 100,000 (it's where Bill Gates lives), and the surrounding towns of Redmond, Kirkland, and Issaquah, are no longer just suburbs of Seattle. Rather, they are seriously yuppified, relatively new, and sprawling communities that feel and look like a patchwork quilt of overdeveloped neighborhoods. In terms of charm and romance, this not a great destination. But for convenience, shopping, and the occasional pleasant surpise, Bellevue and its neighbors should not to be overlooked.

Hotel/Bed and Breakfast Kissing

BELLEVUE CLUB HOTEL, Bellevue
11200 Southeast Sixth Street
(206) 454-4424, (800) 579-1110
Expensive

Mere words cannot adequately portray how stunning a property this is, but we'll attempt the impossible and try to do justice to this 64-room boutique hotel attached to the Eastside's most elite and exclusive health club. Every square foot is a slice of designer heaven. It is hard not to covet one or more of the impressive features, from the pergola-style entry, to the multitextured weaves of the rugs, drapes, and linens, to the radiant wood finishes used throughout the hotel. Intricate, handcrafted furnishings of cherry wood and stone are accented by even more elaborate art and accessories. The handsome patio units on the ground floor are the most inviting, with terracotta tiles and attractive outdoor furniture. The overall impression of spaciousness is understandable given the stately size of the rooms and the extra-high ceilings. Even the bathrooms have an opulent feel, with soaking tubs, separate showers, and marble and granite surfaces. Perhaps best of all is the unlimited use of the health club facilities, which features state-of-the art exercise equipment, tennis and squash courts, an Olympic-size swimming pool, aerobic classes, massage services, saunas, and Jacuzzi tubs.

As sublime as this all sounds, and it is indeed sublime, the potential drawbacks for couples are the more or less corporate ambience mingled with all this finery and, even more distracting, the nearby interstate highway that mars enjoyment of the Northwest landscape.

Romantic Note: The hotel's premier dining room, **THE POLARIS RESTAURANT** (see Restaurant Kissing), is an exceptional place for breakfast, lunch, or dinner.

Restaurant Kissing

AZALEAS FOUNTAIN COURT, Bellevue
22 103rd Avenue Northeast
(206) 451-0426
Expensive to Very Expensive
Lunch Tuesday-Friday; Dinner Monday-Saturday

This quiet Eastside treasure is housed in an unobtrusive brick and clapboard home on a side street in "Old Bellevue" (don't get too excited; this area mostly consists of small, unexciting storefronts that date back to the 1920s).

Inside, you'll find three small, understated dining rooms—two in front, one in back—tastefully decorated with hunter green carpets; tables adorned with white linen tablecloths, candles, and fresh flowers; and a few prints and mirrors on the walls. In season, the most romantic seating is out back in the namesake fountain court, where you can enjoy your meal surrounded by tall ivy-covered walls, iron garden furniture, a delightful mural, and a small fountain and pool with resident goldfish.

You might describe the food here as Northwest continental. The menu changes with the seasons to assure that everything is fresh and flavorful. In the springtime, for instance, you could stimulate your appetites with sautéed Penn Cove mussels with lemongrass and rice wine; linger over mixed baby greens with marinated goat cheese and a port vinaigrette; then savor your entrée—perhaps the peppercorn seared king salmon with citrus and grilled melons or the vegetarian risotto with asparagus, shiitake mushrooms, tomatoes, stewed garlic, and cilantro. And no description can do justice to the desserts; one taste is worth a thousand words.

Romantic Note: On Friday and Saturday evenings, jazz musicians play romantic standards as you eat; share a kiss if you hear "your" song.

Outdoor Kissing

BELLEVUE BOTANICAL GARDEN, Bellevue
12001 Main Street
(206) 462-2749
Free admission

From Seattle, take Interstate 90 or State Route 520 across Lake Washington, then exit onto Interstate 405 and head to Bellevue. In Bellevue, exit onto east-bound Northeast Eighth Street. From Northeast Eighth, turn right onto 120th Avenue Northeast and follow it uphill to Main Street. Turn left onto Main Street; the parking lot for the garden is several blocks up on the right.

Although downtown Bellevue is dominated by cars, this green retreat offers 36 acres of woods, display gardens, and lawns in a quiet neighborhood on Wilburton Hill. Stroll hand in hand as you admire the lush, colorful borders and see if you can find one of the secret paths leading to closer looks (and private kissing places). A half-mile loop winds around, encouraging you to visit the Botanical Reserve, the Rhododendron Garden, and more. Before you leave, share a serene moment in the elegant Yao Garden, a sister-city project with Yao, Japan, and bless the hard work and foresight that make this special place possible.

Romantic Alternative: BELLEVUE DOWNTOWN PARK, located just west of Bellevue Way on Northeast Fourth Street, is a 14-acre oasis of grass and trees across the street from ever-busy Bellevue Square. Futuristic spheres and pylons mark a circular canal, and a cascading waterfall at the south end of the park is a refreshing alternative to the sounds of nearby traffic. A scattering of wooden garden benches and a tiny rose garden are additional amenities. Green and open space is scarce in this part of town, but the park is surprisingly underused, which can be a romantic advantage.

Kirkland

Hotel/Bed and Breakfast Kissing

SHUMWAY MANSION, Kirkland　　　　　　　　　
11410 99th Place Northeast
(206) 823-2303
Inexpensive to Moderate
Recommended Wedding Site

Built in 1909, this four-story, gray-shingled, post-Victorian estate is a curious blend of bed-and-breakfast rooms and banquet facilities. Surrounded by ample parking (enough for 60 cars) and fronted by a busy street, the 10,000-square-foot mansion is surrounded by pretty grounds, with a manicured lawn, flower gardens, and adjacent duck pond. Doors open from the downstairs ballroom to a covered patio area and the backyard, where you'll find an arched trellis draped with climbing roses and a gazebo embraced by wisteria. The mansion is best known as a place to have a wedding: the day we visited, at least five couples were being given tours in anticipation of having their nuptials here. Frequently, wedding parties (over 150 a year) take over the entire property, but when they don't, rooms are also rented out to non-participants (that means the cozy, handsomely decorated common areas may still be inundated with celebrants).

The eight simple guest rooms, appointed with homey Victorian furnishings, patterned wallpapers, lace curtains, dried floral arrangements, and tiled baths, are actually quite nice. Each room has a queen-size bed (some with down comforters) and a private bath (one is detached). Antiques, such as the four-poster cherry-wood bed in one room, add romantic appeal to the otherwise so-so accommodations. In the morning, a full buffet-style breakfast is served downstairs in the handsome dining room.

Restaurant Kissing

BISTRO PROVENÇAL, Kirkland
212 Central Way
(206) 827-3300
Moderate to Expensive
Dinner Daily

One of the prettiest French country-style restaurants to be found anywhere around the Seattle area is situated in the waterfront town of Kirkland. Exposed wood-beamed ceilings, black-and-white-checked tablecloths, and wooden tables and chairs adorn the two small dining rooms. Somewhat stiff although cordial service is typical, but exceptions have been reported. A traditional Provençal menu is straightforward and simply executed, which can be visually disappointing, but the quality is nevertheless very good.

Juanita

Restaurant Kissing

CAFE JUANITA, Juanita
9702 Northeast 120th Place
(206) 823-1505
Moderate to Expensive
Reservations Recommended
Dinner Daily

The white brick home that shelters this welcoming dining spot is draped in lush foliage, hiding an otherwise unattractive location near a shopping

center and main street. The modest interior is simply but beautifully decorated, with a handful of tables, hardwood floors, an open kitchen, and
fragrant flower arrangements. Most appealing are the exceptional views of the
fertile gardens and lush arbors out back, seen through large picture windows.
The menu, written daily on a blackboard, is much admired by eager patrons
who often plan ahead to get a coveted reservation. Fresh, precisely prepared
fish is the restaurant's specialty, but everything, including the homemade
pastas, is excellent. The wait staff is unfailingly polite and efficient, but on
busy nights things can get hurried, and the service may feel more tense then
soothing.

Woodinville

Outdoor Kissing

CHATEAU STE. MICHELLE WINERY, Woodinville
14111 Northeast 145th Street
(206) 488-1133
http://winery.com
Free Tours and Tastings Daily

From northbound Interstate 405, turn east at the Wenatchee/Monroe
exit. Follow Highway 522 east and take the Woodinville exit. Keep right,
and at the second stoplight turn right onto Northeast 175th. At the four-
way stop, turn left onto Highway 202. Go two miles to the winery, which is
on the right side of the road.

Built in the style of a French country chateau, this well-known winery
offers visitors more than superior Northwest wines. The 87 acres of manicured grounds are ideal for lazy strolls after a complimentary wine tasting
and a cellar tour, particularly during the fall harvesting season. The winery's
wine shop offers meats, cheeses, exquisite wines, and truffles—all the essen-
tials for a gourmet picnic you can enjoy in a sunny spot on the soft lawn
or at a picnic table overlooking rows of grapevines and a small pond. A
summer-long series of moderately priced performances, ranging from jazz
to Shakespeare, attracts happy crowds to the outdoor amphitheater.

Romantic Note: Directly across the street is the **COLUMBIA WINERY**,
14030 Northeast 145th Street, (206) 488-2776. The setting isn't nearly as
pretty as its neighbor's, but Columbia's venerable status as the oldest premium winery in the state makes it an interesting stop.

Carnation

Hotel/Bed and Breakfast Kissing

RIVER INN SNOQUALMIE VALLEY, Carnation
4548 Tolt River Road
(206) 333-4262
Moderate to Expensive

While the rural town of Carnation is not the first place you'd think of for a romantic escape, the River Inn provides its guests with a truly serene, tranquil atmosphere. This contemporary home turned bed and breakfast rests on the shores of the Tolt River. The solar-heated indoor pool, saunas, and hot tub add immeasurably to an already ideal setting.

Of the seven rooms here, five are in the main house and two reside in a newly built structure. Two of the five rooms in the main house are fairly small, plainly decorated, and share a bathroom near the pool; they are not recommended. What we do recommend are the two incredibly large, spacious rooms upstairs. Although they are not elegant, they are both exceedingly comfortable. One has a full kitchen, but both have all the amenities you need: a refrigerator filled with fresh juices and mineral water, thick terry-cloth robes, a coffeemaker, a king-size bed, and a shower big enough to be another room. Both rooms offer peaceful views of the Tolt River rushing by.

Outside, the grounds look somewhat unkempt but blend perfectly with the woodland setting. A wonderful riverside gazebo makes a handsome setting for warm-weather dining. Next door is a new building that houses two suites with Jacuzzi tubs. They are rather on the slick side and could use some warming up, but offer more seclusion and style than the other rooms.

Depending on the mood of the innkeeper, breakfast can be a continental array of baked goods or a three-course presentation.

Romantic Warning: One confusing aspect of the River Inn is the number of beds in many of the rooms. The inn seems to be arranged more for groups or families than for solitude-seeking couples, which can detract from the otherwise romantic touches.

Fall City

Restaurant Kissing

THE HERBFARM, Fall City
32804 Southeast Issaquah-Fall City Road
(206) 784-2222, (800) 866-4372

Very Expensive to Unbelievably Expensive
Reservations Recommended
Call for seasonal hours.

In January of 1997, romantics around the region mourned the loss of The Herbfarm's amazing restaurant, which was destroyed by fire. However, the owners hope to rebuild and reopen the restaurant in the very near future. Until then, visitors are still encouraged to come to this remote location 25 minutes west of Seattle to enjoy the abundant, fragrant gardens and the fanciful gift and plant shop.

The Herbfarm has earned national praise for its reverence for the earth's magical bounty and delectable treasures. Before the fire, the dining room was graced with skylights, an open kitchen, bright floral tablecloths, and charming appointments. It was a bit eccentric, but attractive. The menu changed continually but each brilliantly prepared concoction was explained at length by the staff. The parfait mousse of wild mushrooms, zucchini blossoms gently filled with pesto soufflè, rabbit loin steamed in lavender on a bing cherry sauce with sage leaf fritters, herb sorbets, and rosemary shortbread cookies were all paragons of flavor. If all goes as planned, The Herbfarm will continue to be irresistible.

Romantic Suggestion: Once the restaurant reopens, you will have to plan ahead for a meal here. Spur-of-the-moment reservations are almost impossible to obtain, and the dates the dining room is open are even more impossible to predict. So get your calendars out: bookings for the fall/winter season are taken during the last week in August; summer reservations are taken the second week in April, and almost the entire season is full by the end of the first day.

Snoqualmie

Hotel/Bed and Breakfast Kissing

SALISH LODGE, Snoqualmie
6501 Railroad Avenue Southeast (Highway 202)
(206) 888-2556, (800) 826-6124
Very Expensive to Unbelievably Expensive

Salish Lodge has almost everything going for it: a respected name, a celebrated location at the top of Snoqualmie Falls, a brand-new full-service spa facility, and thoroughly romantic guest rooms. All 91 of the plush suites feature ample spa tubs, well-stocked wood-burning fireplaces, and comfortable furnishings that invite tenderness. As you might expect, the outstanding accommodations go hand in hand with outstanding tariffs that increase as the view of the falls improves. A major drawback to this stellar location is the throngs of tourists that invade the place day in and day out, particularly on weekends. (Thankfully, the guest wings are accessible only with guest room keys, so the tourists cannot go everywhere.) Also, only a handful of these exquisite rooms have views of the falls; the rest look out to the road or the power plant upstream.

Romantic Suggestion: If staying here requires an unreasonable investment for your pocketbook, you can still enjoy the extremely intimate, extremely popular **SALISH LODGE DINING ROOM** (Expensive). The restaurant is elegantly appointed with handsome cherry paneling, a wood-burning fireplace, and muted lighting. Almost every seat in the house has a view through floor-to-ceiling windows, but the very best tables are those directly beside the windows that face the falls. Reservations are recommended, so you may as well see if any of those seats are available.

Outdoor Kissing

SNOQUALMIE WINERY, Snoqualmie
37444 Southeast Winery Road
(206) 888-4000
Free Tastings Daily

From eastbound I-90: Take Exit 27 and turn right onto Winery Road; proceed a quarter mile to the winery. From westbound I-90: Take Exit 31 and turn right. After passing factory stores in North Bend, turn left on North Bend Way and proceed about three miles where the road veers left and passes under the freeway; continue a quarter mile to the winery.

If you are heading to the Cascades on Interstate 90 and you want to get a stirring overview of the area you are about to traverse, consider stopping at this hilltop winery. Although there are no vineyards at this location and the actual processing happens elsewhere, the awesome view of Mount Si from the tasting room, gift shop, and picnic area is unbelievable. A bottle of wine is a premium accompaniment to the surroundings.

"*A kiss is something you cannot give
without taking and cannot take
without giving.*"

Anonymous

Washington Cascades

Washington's stretch of the Cascade Range is nothing less than spectacular. To the north, Mount Baker's glacial peak stands guard near the U.S.-Canadian border. South of Mount Baker lies a 300-mile expanse of mesmerizing wilderness that includes national forests, parks, and mountain passes, offering startling views of the range's volcanic giants: Mount Rainier, Mount St. Helens, and Mount Adams. This chain of mountains is liberally supplied with old-growth evergreens, snow-covered cliffs, and countless plummeting waterfalls and spirited rivers. In contrast to the wet, vivid greenery on the west side of the Cascades, the east side of the mountains is authentic Marlboro country—awash in hues of gold, bathed in hot sunshine in summer, and blasted by snowy cold in winter. Almost every square foot of this expanse is magnificent.

The most popular and accessible route through the region is the **CASCADE LOOP**, a series of connecting highways that passes through the northern section of the mountains. (The loop officially begins in Mukilteo, just south of Everett, where you take a ferryboat ride to Whidbey Island and drive to La Conner.) Begin the loop north of Mount Vernon, where State Route 20 heads east. Near the towns of Twisp and Winthrop, continue heading south on Highway 153 toward Pateros. From here, take Alternate Highway 97 south past Chelan towards Wenatchee. Just before Wenatchee, follow Highway 2 heads east across Stevens Pass to Everett. The loop ends just south of Everett.

Driving is the fastest, but not the most intimate, way to experience this area. There are stimulating hikes to consider. To request an informational packet and a catalog from which you can order hiking maps of the area, contact the **NORTH CASCADES NATIONAL PARK**, 2105 State Route 20, Sedro Woolley, Washington 98284, (360) 856-5700. A network of graveled dirt roads branches off the main highways and leads to the paths less taken. These treks of the heart will bring you pleasure and adventure.

Romantic Prelude: If you are heading east to the Cascades from Seattle on Interstate 90 and you want a remarkable look at the scenery you'll be traveling through, stop at **SNOQUALMIE WINERY**, 37444 SE Winery Road, Snoqualmie, (206) 888-4000 (watch for the signs at the Snoqualmie Falls exit); open 10 A.M. to 4:30 P.M. daily. Views of the mountains from the tasting room are unbelievable.

Rockport

Outdoor Kissing

EAGLE WATCHING, Rockport
The Department of Fish and Wildlife
(360) 902-2200

Viewing is possible along State Route 20 between the towns of Concrete and Marblemount during December and January.

Bleak gray skies, negligible daylight, and the mist of Northwest rain can make the heart of the Cascades moderately dreary during the months of winter. Yet despite the inclement weather, December and January are made vibrant when hundreds of bald eagles migrate to the Skagit River during salmon-spawning season. (Salmon die after spawning, which makes the river an eagle's gourmet delight.) All along its banks, eagles soar overhead or perch in clear sight on exposed alpine branches. This profound assemblage is one of the largest in the lower 48 states, and sightings are possible from many points along the road and from eagle-oriented rafting excursions. By mid-March, after all the fish have been eaten and the eagles have dispersed, the Cascades are once again ready for spring renewal.

RIVER RAFTING
River Riders, Inc.
(206) 448-RAFT, (503) 386-RAFT, (800) 448-RAFT
Expensive
Closed October through January

If you are interested in rafting on any of the rivers in the region, call for information and directions on where to rendezvous with your guide.

It doesn't get more visually exciting or relentlessly tumultuous than the Skykomish, Klickitat, Methow, White Salmon, Toutle, and Chiwawa Rivers. If you're in an adventurous mood, several river-rafting companies in the Northwest will provide professional guides to take you down the river of your choice. River Riders is a good, safe company that will give you reliable information as well as an unforgettable adventure.

Once you've decided which river you want to negotiate, the rest is, if you will, all downstream. As you follow the tendril-like course the water has etched through the land, each coiling turn exposes a sudden change in perspective on the landscape. One turn reveals grassy woods adjoining the quiet flow of peaceful water; another magically manifests a rocky tableau penetrated by a bursting mass of energy called white water. The raft's roller-coaster motion accentuates the thrill and glory of the scenery. And the sensation of cold water against your skin as you wildly paddle over and through a whirl-pool can make your heart pound and your senses spin.

Mazama

Hotel/Bed and Breakfast Kissing

MAZAMA COUNTRY INN, Mazama
42 Lost River Road
(509) 996-2681, (800) 843-7951 (in Washington)
http://www.mazama-inn.com
Inexpensive to Moderate
Minimum stay requirement for cabins

Talk about an escape from the real world! The Mazama Country Inn (and the town of Mazama, for that matter) is out in the middle of nowhere, and that is one of its most attractive features. Set among evergreens at the foot of a mountain, the main lodge has 14 exceedingly simple units. The interior austerity would be a romantic drawback if it weren't for the property's sensational location and abundant outdoor amenities and activities. There is something for everyone here: a communal sauna and hot tub, horseback riding, helicopter skiing, cross-country skiing, mountain biking, windsurfing, sleigh riding, and a country-style restaurant where breakfast, lunch, and dinner are served. (During the winter, three full daily meals are included in one reasonably priced package.)

Romantic Alternative: Three is a crowd when it comes to romance, but people traveling in groups will appreciate the inn's five additional rental cabins, located nearby. Amenities vary (and so do the prices) but may include fully stocked kitchens, wood-burning stoves, TV/VCRs, stereos, and even washers and dryers.

Restaurant Kissing

MAZAMA COUNTRY INN DINING ROOM, Mazama
42 Lost River Road
(509) 996-2681, (800) 843-7951 (in Washington)
Inexpensive to Moderate

Even if you're not an overnight guest at the Mazama Country Inn, you'll want to partake of the area's spectacular views and hiking terrain. Dinner here is a perfect way to conclude an exhilarating day in the mountains. A floor-to-ceiling stone fireplace keeps the dining room toasty warm in the colder months, and the soothing interior has a view of gently swaying boughs through tall windows. Although the menu is limited, you won't be disappointed with the Cajun shrimp scampi or daily seafood and pasta specials prepared by an efficient, adept kitchen staff.

Winthrop

Hotel/Bed and Breakfast Kissing

SUN MOUNTAIN LODGE, Winthrop   ♥♥♥♥
1000 Patterson Lake Road
(509) 996-2211, (800) 572-0493
http://www.travel-in-wa.com/ADS/sun_mtn.html
Inexpensive to Unbelievably Expensive
Minimum stay requirement on weekends and holidays
Recommended Wedding Site

Every facet of Sun Mountain Lodge is extraordinary, including the drive there. The road that winds up to this mountaintop resort offers sweeping views of rugged, sculpted peaks and the golden Methow Valley below.

Composed of massive timbers and stone, the original lodge has been beautifully renovated, and the lobby's interior is graced with immense wrought-iron chandeliers, stone flooring, and rock-clad fireplaces. All of the rooms in the main lodge display a Northwest influence, with rugged log walls and ceilings, bent-willow furniture, hand-painted quilts, and local blacksmith furnishings. Twenty-four rooms have luxurious Jacuzzi tubs, and most rooms offer views of the dramatic mountain panorama. (We should mention, however, that some rooms also overlook the roof and consequently retain a hotel-like feeling.)

Fortunately, you won't find fault with the impeccable suites located in the separate, newer wing across from the lodge. Sliding glass doors open to stone patios that survey mesmerizing views of the valley and mountains beyond. Each unit has its own fireplace, elegant willow furnishings, and lush comforters; in winter, you can cross-country-ski out your back door. Couples with privacy in mind will also appreciate the four newly constructed cabin Loft Suites situated at the edge of Patterson Lake. You'll want for nothing in these sizable suites, which include two bedrooms, full kitchens, and private decks with wonderful lake views.

Sun Mountain Lodge also offers every imaginable amenity: two heated pools and an outdoor hot tub, hiking trails, horseback riding, white-water rafting, a golf course, sailboats, sleigh rides, exercise equipment, and mountain bikes. Not to mention the totally outrageous, thoroughly intoxicating heli-skiing packages available for both downhill and cross-country skiers. Fly in to virgin powder runs that will leave you breathless for months to come. At the end of the day, you will need to cuddle very close and review your feats of athletic prowess.

Romantic Note: You don't have to leave the property in search of satisfying cuisine. The **SUN MOUNTAIN LODGE DINING ROOM** (see Restaurant Kissing) is an ideal place to savor spectacular views and Northwest cuisine.

Restaurant Kissing

SUN MOUNTAIN LODGE DINING ROOM, Winthrop
1000 Patterson Lake Road
(509) 996-2211, (800) 572-0493
http://www.travel-in-wa.com/ADS/sun_mtn.html
Inexpensive to Expensive
Breakfast, Lunch, and Dinner Daily
Recommended Wedding Site

Even if you've decided not to take advantage of Sun Mountain Lodge's premium accommodations, at least stop for a while at the restaurant, which is housed in the original section of the lodge. Here the developers wisely left well enough alone: this part of the lodge has always been flawless. A wall of windows allows you to feast your eyes on surroundings that are truly food for the soul. Wrought-iron chandeliers drop from log-ceiling beams and illuminate cozy two-person tables and booths. The menu is equally impressive, and the service is prompt and gracious. Famous for its fresh seafood and hickory- and applewood-smoked duck, not to mention its exquisite desserts, the kitchen lives up to its reputation.

Okanogan

Outdoor Kissing

OKANOGAN NATIONAL FOREST, Okanogan
(509) 826-3275

The Okanogan National Forest is reached from the north and south by Highway 2 and Highway 97. From the east and west, State Route 20 provides access to the forest.

The Okanogan National Forest encompasses an awesome 1,706,000 acres of northern Washington wilderness, bordered by numerous national parks and recreation areas on all sides. Nature lovers will marvel at this region's diverse botany and topography, which ranges from grassland in the lowest elevations to ponderosa pine forests in the mid-elevations to glades of Douglas firs in the higher elevations. Some of the more popular ways to enjoy the enchanting countryside are white-water rafting, hiking, snowmobiling, cross-country skiing, and heli-skiing. For more information about white-water rafting, call **OSPREY RIVER ADVENTURES**, Twisp, (509) 997-4116, (800) 997-4116. Contact **NORTH CASCADE HELI-SKIING**, Mazama, (509) 996-3660, (800) 494-HELI, for information about heli-skiing.

Romantic Must: If your car is more reliable than your legs, embark on a one-hour (each way) adventure up the steep, bumpy gravel road that winds through flower-laden alpine meadows and towering evergreens to **SLATE PEAK**, the highest point accessible by car in Washington state. From west State Route 20, turn left onto Mazama Road and left again onto Lost River Road. Follow this until you see signs for **HART'S PASS**, which will lead you to the top of Slate Peak. From this heavenly 7,500-foot vantage point, snowcapped mountains rise in succession in every direction, and the only audible sounds are bird songs and the gentle murmur of wind sweeping through the trees. A kiss here is likely to take your breath away, if it doesn't change your life altogether.

HART'S PASS serves as a primary trailhead for hikers using the **PACIFIC CREST NATIONAL SCENIC TRAIL**. If you are interested in more information about day or overnight hikes in this area, contact the **OKANOGAN NATIONAL FOREST SUPERVISOR'S OFFICE** at (509) 826-3275.

Chelan

Hotel/Bed and Breakfast Kissing

HIGHLAND GUEST HOUSE, Chelan
121 East Highland Avenue
(509) 682-2892, (800) 681-2892
http://www.lakechelan.com/highland.htm
Inexpensive
Minimum stay requirement on holidays

A quiet hillside above the town of Chelan provides the setting for this pale yellow Victorian home turned bed and breakfast. Manicured lawns and colorful flowers border the charming 1902 residence, and a wraparound porch is filled with white wicker chairs—a perfect place to linger over an iced tea on a hot summer night. Restored antiques mingle with homey touches in the common area, breakfast room, and each of the three guest rooms (located on the second floor). The Rose and Wicker Room is our favorite because it's the only room with a private bathroom; it is decorated in a French Country theme, with white wicker furnishings, green ivy stenciled on the walls, and a private porch that overlooks the sparkling lake. Gramma's Room, with its pretty lace-canopy bed and patchwork quilt, is also lovely but shares a bathroom with the Sewing Room, which is appointed with floral linens and antique sewing machines. Each morning, a full country breakfast is served in the antique-filled breakfast room, where guests can look forward to eggs with Havarti cheese, fresh fruit, country potatoes with rosemary and herbs, and raspberries-and-cream French toast.

Stehekin

Take Highway 20 east toward the towns of Twisp and Winthrop. Continue heading south on Highway 153 toward Pateros. From here, take Alternate Highway 97 to the towns of Manson and Chelan, where you can catch the Lady of the Lake to Stehekin. For information on scheduled departures from either place, call (509) 682-2224 or the Lake Chelan Chamber of Commerce at (800) 4-CHELAN. Flights are also available on Chelan Airways; call (509) 682-5555. For the backpacking route to Stehekin, hikers will want to check with the North Cascades office of the North Cascades National Park, (360) 856-5700.

Otherwise known as "the Enchanted Valley," Stehekin is a geographically unique town, accessible only by ferryboat or plane (no cars) from the towns of Chelan and Manson, or via high-country trails that pass through the Cascade Mountains. (You have to be hardy and well-prepared to take the latter route.) Nestled in the Cascade Mountain Range, the small community with its one-room schoolhouse is situated at the northernmost tip of Lake Chelan and is celebrated for its glorious, dramatic scenery and abundant wildlife. (Watch out for bears!) Many establishments in Stehekin don't even have telephones; locals are often seen pedaling on bicycles to a centrally located pay phone. Jagged mountains line the 55-mile fjordlike lake and are breathtakingly reflected in the cool blue of its glacier-fed waters. The ferry ride takes approximately four hours, and there is only one round-trip crossing per day. Although both the ferry and the town of Stehekin tend to be a bit crowded with tourists on summer afternoons, most people stay only for the day, and even fewer visit in the winter. Once the boat returns to Chelan in the late afternoon, Stehekin's exquisite scenery and hushed seclusion are yours for the taking, and you are sure to find the experience sublime.

Meal options are limited here, to say the least. We recommend **STEHEKIN VALLEY RANCH**, (509) 682-4677, for a buffet-style dinner, and the **NORTH CASCADES STEHEKIN LODGE DINING ROOM**, (509) 682-4494; the latter is located above the ferry dock and is open for breakfast, lunch, and dinner. For a sweeter option, bicycle to the nearby bakery, **STEHEKIN PASTRY COMPANY**, where you can stock up on freshly baked goodies to share later at your leisure. If you really want to feel prepared, we recommend bringing your own foodæthere are no grocery stores out here.

Hotel/Bed and Breakfast Kissing

SILVER BAY INN, Stehekin   😚 😚 😚
10 Silver Bay Road
(509) 682-2212, (800) 555-7781 (in Washington)
Moderate
Minimum stay requirement
Call for seasonal closures.

Silver Bay Inn is a Northwest must for those who want to escape the world at large. Sheltered on the tip of a tiny peninsula dotted with non-descript homes, the inn offers isolation and wondrous mountain and lakeside views that are thoroughly compelling. A hammock overlooking the placid lake sways lazily under a stand of trees, and the manicured grounds and gardens conceal a roomy waterside hot tub, at night lit only by moonlight and shooting stars. Complimentary canoes and bicycles are available, giving guests mobility to explore the surrounding waterways and wilderness.

Part of the inn is a wooden solar home dedicated exclusively to guests (the innkeepers live next door); its privacy is ensured by the fact that it has only three guest rooms. Antiques and country accents convey a feeling of comfort and warmth in the house's cozy private parlor and glass-enclosed breakfast nook, which overlook the water. Patchwork quilts and wood de-tailing add to the charm of each guest room, particularly the upstairs room with its private lake-view deck and large soaking tub.

For the most privacy, we recommend the two neighboring lakeside cabins, comfortably furnished and complete with full kitchens and baths. Breakfast is do-it-yourself in the cabins, but a bountiful continental break-fast is prepared for guests staying in the solar home.

You'll be thankful for the two-night minimum. One evening just isn't long enough at a place like this. Then again, neither are two.

Wenatchee

Outdoor Kissing

OHME GARDENS COUNTY PARK, Wenatchee
3327 Ohme Road
(509) 662-5785
http://www.lakechelan.com/ohme.htm
Closed mid-October through mid-April
Recommended Wedding Site

Just north of Wenatchee, near the junction of Highway 2 and Highway 97A. The gardens are up on the bluff; watch for signs.

It's hard to believe that what is now the lush Ohme Gardens was once desolate desert. Sixty years of painstaking work transformed a dry, rocky wasteland into the fertile mountain splendor visitors enjoy today. Green is the theme here. The gardens are set high on a bluff, and footpaths wander through nine acres of flower beds, splashing waterfalls, and luscious alpine meadows. Natural rock formations emerge from tranquil pools set among evergreens. Views of the Columbia River and Cascade Mountains add to the idyllic setting. A miniature Garden of Eden, this would be paradise on earth if it weren't for the thousands of other tourists who have discovered it. Though the scenery is apt to inspire some passionate kisses, the crowds will certainly inhibit your romantic inclinations.

Cashmere

Aplets and Cotlets are notoriously sweet confections that stick to your teeth and help dentists send their kids to college. They are also Cashmere's claim to fame. Even if you're not partial to Aplets and Cotlets, Cashmere is worth a quick look. This quaint little town is reminiscent of a western frontier town, with old-fashioned balustrades and streets lined with restaurants and antique, sweet, and gift shops.

Hotel/Bed and Breakfast Kissing

CASHMERE COUNTRY INN, Cashmere
5801 Pioneer Drive
(509) 782-4212, (800) 291-9144
Inexpensive
Minimum stay requirement on weekends

If the town of Cashmere is looking for a new trademark (besides Aplets and Cotlets), it could turn to this affable inn as an alternative. Although the tract housing across the street detracts from the romantic mood, this immaculate and affectionately renovated farmhouse is surrounded by meticulously groomed gardens, an acre of apple orchards, and plum trees. Inside, the five guest rooms are on the small side and have been lovingly furnished with eclectic French country decor. Each room has its own private bath. Appropriately decorated in sunflower yellow and white, the Yellow Room has a queen-size bed, a love seat, and French doors that open to a beautifully tiled outdoor swimming pool and hot tub (perfect for moonlit swims). In the lovely Blue Room, views of Mount Cashmere are visible over the top of the surrounding orchards.

The innkeeper is also a gourmet cook (she has actually published her own cookbook!), so it's not surprising that her breakfasts are lavish. Morning brings French toast stuffed with cream cheese, peach schnapps and nectarines, apple-spice muffins, and cantaloupe slices drizzled with homemade mint syrup, among other delicious treats.

Restaurant Kissing

THE PEWTER POT, Cashmere
124 1/2 Cottage Avenue
(509) 782-2036
Moderate to Expensive
Lunch, Dinner, and Afternoon Tea Tuesday-Saturday

Pretty as an English postcard, this small countryside restaurant has an almost exclusively traditional American menu. Lace-covered windows, a handful of tables, and attentive service are the overture, but the talent of the kitchen is the symphony. Hearty, wonderfully prepared down-home cooking is the essence of the menu. Beef pot pie, turkey dinner with all the trimmings (even when it isn't Thanksgiving), and country ham served with rum-raisin sauce are maybe even a little better than Mom made. The deep-dish apple pie is beyond delicious, and large enough for two. Authentic English tea is served every afternoon, and the fresh tarts and pastries are excellent.

Leavenworth

In some ways, the town of Leavenworth is a contradiction. The village's pervasive, tourist-attracting, ersatz Bavarian motif overwhelms most of the storefronts that line Leavenworth's all-too-authentic streets. Even the grocery store, dubbed Safeway Haus, sports a European facade. The alpine influence is almost quaint (and actually lovely in winter, when snow softens the effect)—that is, if you don't mind crowds and if you happen to love wienerschnitzel. Whether or not this environment is conducive to tender snuggling and quiet moments depends entirely on your affinity for things German.

What most people don't realize is that there is more to Leavenworth than meets the eye. Accommodations in Leavenworth are second to none. Concealed in a valley, surrounded by the towering Cascades, Leavenworth has a setting so incredibly gorgeous that even a real Bavarian town would envy it. Just beyond the crest of the bordering foothills lies the astounding **ALPINE LAKES WILDERNESS**, well known for its abundant lakes and vast stretches of stunning mountain terrain. The region is also encircled by thousands of breathtaking acres of evergreen forests in the **WENATCHEE NATIONAL FOREST**. In addition, the **STEVENS PASS, MISSION RIDGE, LAKE WENATCHEE,** and **LAKE CHELAN** recreation areas are close at hand. If your vision of romance includes the great outdoors, you couldn't select a better place to visit: here you can enjoy hiking, cross-country skiing, sleigh rides, white-water rafting, bird-watching, or just simply being together in the masterpiece of nature.

Romantic Note: Long months of exceedingly hot, dry weather in the summer of 1994 led to forest fires that swept through this region's forested mountains. Structural damage was kept to a minimum, thanks to the vigorous efforts of fire fighters from all over (these people deserve medals of honor and plentiful praise). None of the establishments included in this publication were affected in any way. The fires were primarily located in undeveloped forestland; hiking trails suffered the most damage, but because of nature's abundance here, options for wilderness exploring still remain unlimited.

All of this is to say that Leavenworth is alive and well. In fact, it's probably better than ever, due to the community's resilience and renewed efforts to make Leavenworth an enticing, worthwhile destination.

Hotel/Bed and Breakfast Kissing

ABENDBLUME PENSION, Leavenworth
12570 Ranger Road
(509) 548-4059, (800) 669-7634
Inexpensive to Expensive
Minimum stay requirement on weekends

You'll find this newly built inn sheltered at the base of the Cascade Mountains, on a flat residential plain. The white stucco and blond wood exterior, hemmed by a soft green lawn and myriad colorful flowers, is reminiscent of other properties found in Leavenworth, but the resemblance goes only as far as the facade. Hand-carved, arched double doors open to reveal a limestone foyer; a curved wrought-iron staircase winds up, under a stained glass skylight, to seven exquisite guest rooms. Even the least expensive rooms are special, with pencil-post beds, down comforters, TV/VCRs, and private tiled baths. Soft lounging robes are provided for your comfort. For a little extra, you can stay in the lap of luxury in one of the inn's two deluxe suites. Relax in the two-person Jacuzzi tub, or enjoy a water massage in the two-headed shower with four body sprays, found in each of the suites' large Italian marble bathrooms. With the flick of a match, a prearranged bundle of wood ignites in the fireplace, warming your snow-white canopy bed. In each room, flower boxes create splashes of color that peek through every window, and views of the valley and distant mountains can be enjoyed from a cozy window seat or a secluded private deck or patio.

There is no shortage of good places to kiss at Abendblume. We suggest the outdoor Grecian spa inlaid with Italian tiles, or the sumptuous common area where you can snuggle up in front of a crackling fire on one of the overstuffed floral couches. Others may feel that the ultimate place to share a kiss is over dessert, served every evening to guests by candlelight at intimate, two-person tables in the knotty pine dining room. In the morning, a hearty German breakfast featuring sweet breads, a hot entrée, and an assortment of meats and cheeses is served in the same dining room, minus candlelight.

Romantic Note: The hosts at Abendblume are eager to please and are dedicated to romance. Upon request, they will have champagne and chocolates, or wine and cheese, waiting for you in your room. They can even put a red rose on your pillow, dim the lights, and have your favorite soft music playing on the in-room CD player. Ask and you shall receive.

ALL SEASONS RIVER INN, Leavenworth
8751 Icicle Road
(509) 548-1425, (800) 254-0555
Inexpensive to Moderate
Minimum stay requirement seasonally and on weekends

Positioned on a bluff overlooking the Wenatchee River and the tree-covered mountains, this professionally run, country-elegant bed and breakfast caters to those seeking a romantic refuge in the Cascade Mountains. The All Seasons was built to serve as a bed and breakfast, and the spacious common area, filled with country touches and a river-rock fireplace, was designed to showcase views of the surging river and natural surroundings. In the six lovely guest rooms, hand-sewn teddy bears sit atop cozy handmade quilts and floral comforters that drape queen-size beds. Several rooms have private decks or patios, Jacuzzi tubs set near the bed, and sitting areas furnished with restored antique love seats.

Breakfast in the morning is a sumptuous spread of homemade granola, fresh zucchini bread, a kiwi parfait, Mexican tamale pancakes, savory sausage, and German potatoes. Ask for the innkeeper's recipe book if you'd like to try to reenact this unforgettable morning meal back home.

FEATHERWIND'S BED AND BREAKFAST, Leavenworth
17033 River Road
(509) 763-2011
http://www.leavenworth.com/lodging.htm
Moderate
Minimum stay requirement on holiday weekends

This country getaway is a quintessential rural retreat, about 15 miles from the heart of busy Leavenworth. You'll feel as if you've arrived at the middle of the Cascade forest after you finish the winding road that brings you here, but surrounding quietness and natural beauty is what you've come for, right? Tall trees and wildflowers surround the entire property, and a slim rock path winds to the front door of this picturesque, wood-shingled farmhouse. Once you step inside, you'll see that old-fashioned comfort is the focus here. Each of the three guest rooms offers a mixture of country and modern accents, fluffy feather beds draped with pretty floral comforters, cushioned window seats, private baths, and TV/VCRs.

After you've worked up an appetite cross-country skiing around the property's mile-long trail, wandering through the nine wooded acres of Featherwind's, lounging in the large outdoor spa, or swimming under the waterfall that splashes into the outdoor pool (it's small but charming), you'll appreciate the complimentary dessert served every evening to guests. In the early morning, the aroma of piping hot coffee set just outside your door will make it that much easier to get out of your warm bed and enjoy the generous breakfast served in the main-floor dining room.

Romantic Note: Two new guest accommodations have cropped up at Featherwind's: Country Garden Guest Lodge and the Cascade Berry Bunk House. Because the new homes sleep up to 16 people each, they are just too large to recommend for only one couple. However, if you are traveling with another couple or with your entire family, you'll be thrilled with the cathedral ceilings, blond wood accents, propane fireplace, spacious full kitchen, sitting area, and cozy bedrooms in these lodgings.

HAUS LORELEI, Leavenworth
347 Division Street
(509) 548-5726

http://actek.com/HausLorelei.html
Inexpensive to Moderate; No Credit Cards
Minimum stay requirement on weekends

Although Haus Lorelei is conveniently located near Leavenworth's lively town center, you'll find no evidence that the village is only steps away. From the moment you enter this massive riverside beach-stone country mansion, you'll sense that relaxation is at hand, and the stress of the world will magically fade into oblivion.

Homey accoutrements and family pictures adorn the comfortable dining room and common areas, partitioned by a massive beach-stone fireplace. Only eight of the ten guest rooms, each named after a different German fairy tale, can be wholeheartedly recommended. (Of the two less charming rooms, one is furnished with multiple beds and is obviously geared for families, and the other is located in the basement, with the home's recycling and laundry facilities sitting outside its private entrance.) Among the remaining eight pleasant rooms, our favorites are the ones on the main floor that face the Wenatchee River. Featuring magnificent antiques imported from Germany, lace-canopied or four-poster beds covered with down comforters and eyelet spreads, and spacious private bathrooms, these three make wonderfully romantic retreats.

An elegant breakfast is served in the dining room at one long table, or out on the large screened sunporch that overlooks a sweeping lawn and the tumultuous Wenatchee River. After breakfast, you can follow the stone trail to the river's edge or cherish the scenery in the luxurious outdoor hot tub. The attentive hostess and her helpful family are eager to accommodate you and, upon request, will help you plan a rewarding day.

HAUS ROHRBACH PENSION, Leavenworth
12882 Ranger Road
(509) 548-7024, (800) 548-4477
http://www.innbook.com/rohrbach.html
Inexpensive to Very Expensive
Minimum stay requirement on holidays

In many ways, Haus Rohrbach is a quintessential European-style hotel. Ensconced on a forested hillside, with sprawling views of the surrounding landscape, this handsome white stucco and blond wood Bavarian-style lodge holds eight guest rooms, with two other self-contained suites located in an adjacent building. Unfortunately, except for the Wildflower Suite, the rooms in the main lodge feel more like hostel accommodations, with their simple decor and several shared baths. The pleasant Wildflower Suite stands out among the others with a rock fireplace, whirlpool tub, French doors that open to a private deck, and beautiful linens. Just up the hill from the main lodge, in a small white stucco house, are two more luxurious suites called Snowberry and Larkspur. Each suite focuses exclusively on romance and features a floor-to-ceiling rock fireplace that warms the spacious interior, a wall of windows overlooking a private wood deck with views of the peaceful farmland, cathedral ceilings, and a cozy sitting area. You can put on your favorite CD and soak in the oval tiled Jacuzzi tub, snuggle under a cushy floral comforter, or prepare a snack for your sweetheart in the convenient kitchenette. Upon request, the innkeepers will bring a breakfast of Dutch babies, sourdough pancakes, or cinnamon rolls to these suites; otherwise, if you are staying in the main lodge, breakfast is served at long wooden tables. After your morning meal, take a dip in the outdoor pool that affords beautiful views hemmed by colorful flowers.

LEAVENWORTH VILLAGE INN, Leavenworth
1016 Commercial Street
(509) 548-6620, (800) 343-8198
Inexpensive to Very Expensive

At first glance this appears to be just another Swiss-style motel, but upon closer inspection you'll find several deluxe suites here that are anything but motel-like. Hunter green color schemes, lovely fabrics, and plush comforts enhance these surprisingly impressive accommodations. Furnished with lovely four-poster beds, these rooms offer large Jacuzzi tubs, warm gas fireplaces, and comfortable living rooms and dining areas equipped with microwaves and small refrigerators. The views aren't at all interesting, but if you don't open the curtains you can find plenty of romance and solitude inside your suite.

A light continental breakfast of fruit and fresh pastries and breads is served each morning in a small dining room next to the lobby.

MOUNTAIN HOME LODGE, Leavenworth
8201 Mountain Home Road
(509) 548-7077, (800) 414-2378
http://www.mthome.com
Inexpensive to Expensive
Minimum stay requirement seasonally

If seclusion and romance are your hearts' desires, you'll find plenty of both at Mountain Home Lodge. Over the course of the two-mile drive up a steep gravel road that leads to the lodge, Mountain Home's isolation becomes increasingly apparent. In the winter, the lodge's privacy is further enhanced by the fact that the only way to reach it is via a Sno-Cat (a huge snowmobile) driven by one of the innkeepers. The slow, half-hour trip up the mountain is breathtaking, offering views of the snow-blanketed valley. This adventuresome ascent is part of the appeal of this unique bed and breakfast.

Once at the top, you can revel in the wondrous mountain playground and be comforted in the massive wooden lodge, cradled in the center of a sprawling meadow. You'll be graciously welcomed by the friendly innkeepers, who strive to ensure each guest's comfort and privacy. A massive stone fireplace warms the common area, which is furnished with redwood couches and surrounded by wall-to-wall windows that give guests a front-row seat from which to watch the drama of the changing seasons. Each of the ten recently renovated guest rooms are cozy and attractively furnished with Northwest color schemes, cozy log or peeled-pine beds, and restored antiques. All rooms also have private bathrooms and views of the tranquil surroundings. Our favorite is the Cabin Suite, which features a gas fireplace, rustic bent–vine maple furniture, and a lovely Jacuzzi tub.

Just up the hill from the lodge is a sizable log home nicknamed "The Cabin," which is an excellent option if you're seeking lodging for more than two. Although the spacious designer kitchen, expansive living room with stone fireplace, four bedrooms, several bathrooms, spacious basement with computer and fax hookup, and rustic-elegant furnishings create a premium getaway, it is just too large (and too expensive) to wholeheartedly recommend for only one couple.

Evenings back at the main lodge are warm and enjoyable, with hors d'oeuvres and wine served next to the crackling stone fireplace. An adjacent dining area with two-person tables is a cozy spot to enjoy your three gourmet meals, which are included in the price of your stay in the winter. (In the summer, because it's easier to travel to and from the lodge, the meals are extra.)

Whichever season you choose to visit, there is never a shortage of activities. In the winter, cross-country skiing, snowmobile rides, and sledding are all at your doorstep. During the summer, even though Mountain Home Lodge is more easily accessible, it remains just as private and exciting. Without the snow's limitations, horseback riding, hiking, tennis, badminton, swimming, and volleyball are all available for guests.

Romantic Note: In the spring and summer, you don't have to be a guest of the lodge to enjoy the nightly culinary delights. But keep in mind that guests of the inn receive first priority for dinner reservations.

NATAPOC LODGING, Leavenworth
12338 Bretz Road
(509) 763-3313, (800) NAPATOC

http://www.natapoc.com
Expensive
Minimum stay requirement on weekends and holidays

About 15 miles outside the bustling town of Leavenworth, with the surging Wenatchee River literally at your doorstep, seven private log and pine cabins await. Each one is named after a Native American word for a flower or tree. Because the cabins are tucked among 20 acres of tall pines and brilliantly colored wildflowers, privacy here is ensured. Not one cabin is visible from another, and each one has its own private driveway and path down to the river. Unfortunately, most of the accommodations here sleep many more than just two people (the largest cabin sleeps up to 21), so they are just too big to recommend for only one couple.

Don't worry. We wouldn't tell you about this stellar location and then not give you at least one overnight option with which to enjoy it. A wonderfully romantic honeymoon cabin named Stuchin (after the lily flower), offers much comfort and style, and is perfectly sized for just two people. Your spacious front porch has a front-row seat from which to view the rushing river, and is equipped with a bubbling hot tub, barbecue equipment, and deck chairs for long hours of stargazing. Inside, a woodstove warms the living room and full kitchen on the main level. Climb up the open wood staircase to the master bedroom, which holds a queen-size bed draped with a beautiful Native American wedding ring quilt. A pretty stained glass window allows morning sunlight to filter through and wash the room in subtle color, and dried flowers accent the rustic log walls. Because this is not a bed and breakfast, you'll have to bring along your own morning goodies, but coffee and tea are provided.

PENSION ANNA, Leavenworth
926 Commercial Street
(509) 548-6273, (800) 509-ANNA
Inexpensive to Very Expensive

The Bavarian exterior of this bed and breakfast is one more cliche in a town full of cliches, but its immaculate and comfortable interior will be appreciated even by those who think Leavenworth puts out too much of a good thing. Even the lower-end suites have thick down comforters, down pillows, lush carpeting, stately armoires, and dark wood accents. (Plus, these rooms are a steal at $75 a night.) The pricier suites are really not all that pricey, considering that they feature the same European detailing in addition to spa tubs, fireplaces, and sitting areas.

Our favorite suite here is found in an unconventional location. It resides in an old Catholic chapel, adjacent to the property. This sumptuous suite has cathedral ceilings, rich burgundy color schemes, arched leaded windows, a king-size bed, a two-person Jacuzzi tub in the tiled bathroom, and a staircase that leads to what once was a choir loft but is now a second sleeping area. Appropriately, the appointments are baronial and plush; without a doubt, this is a very sexy place to kiss. Unless, of course, you start feeling the need to confess something.

In the morning, all guests are welcome to enjoy an Austrian-style continental breakfast (cheeses, meats, and breads), served in a congenial dining room at tables for two placed around a wood banquette.

PINE RIVER RANCH, Leavenworth
19668 Highway 207
(509) 763-3959, (800) 669-3877
http://www.lakewenatchee.com
Moderate to Expensive

Just off busy Highway 207, only about 14 miles west of the town center of Leavenworth, sits this charming white 1940s farmhouse with an eclectic set of accommodations. There are two upstairs rooms (which need serious updating, and therefore cannot be wholeheartedly recommended); two rooms on the main floor, called Apple Blossom (snug and pretty) and Wildflower (tastefully decorated with a black wrought-iron bed, floral linens, and a gas fireplace); and one outstanding suite, called Ponderosa, set in a small white stucco building adjacent to the ranch house. We highly recommend this very private suite, which features a vaulted ceiling, richly colored linens draped over the huge log bed, windows with distant views of the mountains, a spacious tiled Jacuzzi tub nestled in the corner, and a warm gas fireplace. A small kitchenette, complete with an espresso machine, ensures your sense of self-sufficiency and seclusion. Best of all, you don't have to leave your room until checkout time; a continental breakfast is delivered to your doorstep in the morning, or you can join the other guests over at the main house for Cascade Mountain stuffed French toast or smoked salmon soufflé. In the evening, take time to relax in the hot tub, set on a deck in front of the main house, or explore the property's 32 acres, which include hiking and cross-country-skiing trails with access to a burbling creek.

Soon to have its romantic debut is the Ponderosa Suite's kissing cousin—Lodgepole, named after the lodgepole pine trees in view from this suite's many windows. Guests will love the mammoth pine bed ensconced in deep-colored linens, and the tiled Jacuzzi tub near the gas fireplace. The small kitchenette and cozy sitting area will help carry this suite to ultimate stardom.

RUN OF THE RIVER BED
AND BREAKFAST, Leavenworth
9308 East Leavenworth Road
(509) 548-7171, (800) 288-6491
Moderate to Expensive
Minimum stay requirement on weekends and holidays

This used to be a hidden jewel, but it isn't so hidden anymore. Word has gotten out that Run of the River is one of the finest bed and breakfasts in Leavenworth. Every romantic and practical detail has been attended to with great care and discernment, creating an exceptional place to spend treasured moments together. Surrounded by a picturesque garden bursting with wildflowers and a stone rockery, the expansive contemporary log home achieves a perfect balance between rustic and elegant. Dried flowers accent the warm rooms, and antique quilts cover handcrafted log beds in each of the six distinctive guest rooms. Romantic amenities include soft robes, cozy cuddling nooks, private decks with wood swings, and binoculars for wildlife watching. Three rooms have Jacuzzi tubs, and two have woodstoves. Guests have access to a common deck with spectacular close-up views of the winding Icicle River and Cascade Mountains. Guests also share a large hot tub set in a log pavilion near the river.

Breakfast, served at one large table in the dining room, is a bountiful presentation that may feature fresh fruit or a creative fruit smoothie, a vegetable frittata, organic sausages, and apple cobbler.

Romantic Suggestion: Take advantage of the newly added in-room massage service, sure to put the finishing touches on a wonderfully relaxing time together. Also, don't hesitate to ask the innkeepers more about what this area has to offer. They are very knowledgeable about outdoor activities such as scenic drives, hikes, and mountain-bike trails. Maps and information are available to guests, as is the free use of mountain bikes.

Restaurant Kissing

CAFÉ MOZART, Leavenworth

829 Front Street
(509) 548-0600
Moderate
Lunch and Dinner Daily

Tucked away on the upstairs level of Leavenworth's main shopping street is this elegant retreat where guests can enjoy a romantic and substantial lunch or dinner. Pastel pink linens drape small tables set off in quiet corners, while Mozart's sonatas are heard subtly in the background; white walls with blond wood trim create a perfect backdrop for wall stencils of the restaurant's name-sake. The menu specializes in authentic Bavarian fare with a twist. You'll find such menu items as Schnitzel Wiener Art, which is pork, lightly breaded and pan-fried, served with homemade German potato salad; Konigen Pastete, a puff pastry filled with veal or shrimp in a delicate cream sauce; or Huhnerschnitzel Milano, a chicken breast schnitzel dipped in Parmesan egg batter, sautéed with fresh basil-tomato sauce, and served with pan-fried po-tatoes. The items served here are items that Mozart himself would be proud to sample.

HOME FIRES BAKERY, Leavenworth
13013 Bayne Road
(509) 548-7362
Inexpensive; No Credit Cards
Open Thursday-Monday

Sweet aromas of fresh cinnamon rolls, cookies, coffee cakes, and warm loaves of bread greet you upon entering this tiny country bakery. If you can stop yourself from buying everything in sight (it helps if you don't arrive with an empty stomach), you'll find the perfect assortment of tasty lunch items to pack along and sustain you during a day of exploration in the mountains.

LORRAINE'S EDEL HAUS, Leavenworth
320 Ninth Street
(509) 548-4412, (800) 487-EDEL
http://www.leavenworth.com
Inexpensive to Moderate
Lunch and Dinner Daily

An anomaly in a town of faux Bavarian chalets, this charming country home turned restaurant, located on the edge of town, is a welcome change of pace. Bright red paint trims the white stucco house, which is hemmed by colorful flowers and trees. Inside, the dining room's simple decor is inviting, with hardwood floors, linen-draped tables, antiques, and accents of dried twigs entwined with twinkling white lights. Outside, the patio dining area is embraced by more trees and is softly lit with torches in the evening. Though the ambience is more casual than elegant both inside and out, you can always rely on the skilled kitchen to prepare consistently good entrées. The portobello mushroom and goat cheese appetizer with roasted red bell peppers atop herbed crostinis is a perfect starter; the dill pasta filled with smoked salmon and ricotta in a lobster essence sauce, and the air-dried roast duck in a soy-ginger marinade with a coriander-duck jus, are both delicious and satisfying main courses.

Romantic Note: Lorraine's Edel Haus also has overnight accommodations that we would call "bed and lunch/dinner." Breakfast is not provided, but you get a 50 percent discount off either lunch or dinner at the restaurant. Decorated with lovely country furnishings, the three upstairs rooms have canopy beds and private baths, but noise from the dining room is a definite distraction. What is of interest, and a great kissing bargain to boot, is the self-contained cabin with private Jacuzzi tub, located on the ground floor with its own entrance. This comfortable and cozy spot is yours for $95 a night. (Restaurant noise is still a potential disturbance, but you probably won't mind as much, in light of the amenities you get for the low price.)

Outdoor Kissing
ALPINE LAKES WILDERNESS AND WENATCHEE NATIONAL FOREST

From Highway 2, drive west on Icicle Road, which leads directly into the Alpine Lakes Wilderness and Wenatchee National Forest.

You don't even have to step out of your car to get the full effect of this region's stunning natural beauty. As you follow the Icicle River into the mountain wilderness, you'll feel as if the gates of heaven have swung wide open to receive you. Evergreens flourish on towering mountains that ascend in sheer majesty, their rocky snow-covered peaks cutting into the clear sky above. Those interested in traversing this glorious terrain on foot have unlimited options. Park your car alongside the road and follow one of the many marked trails that wind through the mountain landscape, revealing alpine lakes, meadows, and thriving wildlife.

ICICLE OUTFITTERS AND GUIDES, Leavenworth
2800 Icicle Road
(509) 784-1145, (800) 497-3912
Moderate

Call for a brochure, reservations, and directions to the two available locations; one is in Leavenworth and the other is at 14800 State Park Road on the south shore of Lake Wenatchee.

A great way to explore this area is to take a trek on horseback, and Icicle Outfitters and Guides provides everything from one-hour rides to overnight pack trips. Overnight journeys come complete with meals, pack horses, saddle horses, a well-seasoned wrangler, a cook, tents, and the entire camp setup necessary for a two- to seven-day expedition. This is one unbelievable adventure. You'll cross unspoiled wilderness where pure mountain lakes and streams glisten in the sunshine, the wind rushes through the trees, hawks soar overhead, and snowcapped peaks tower above. As you warmly snuggle by the roaring campfire at night, relaxing after a hearty dinner, you will find yourselves at peace with each other and the world.

Romantic Alternative: EAGLE CREEK RANCH, 7951 Eagle Creek Road, (509) 548-7798, (800) 221-7433, is another full-service horse ranch that offers sleigh, buggy, hay, and trail rides and back-country hiking journeys. The hours of operation can be frustratingly inconsistent, so be sure to confirm your reservation before you make the trip out here.

Mount Rainier

Hotel/Bed and Breakfast Kissing

PARADISE INN, Mount Rainier
Mount Rainier National Park
(360) 569-2275
http://www.mashell.com/mrba.html
Inexpensive to Moderate
Closed October through mid-May

When options are limited, management can get away with murder, or at least, in this case, total neglect. Paradise Inn is one of the only lodges available on Mount Rainier. The views up here truly defy description and are well worth the drive, but the accommodations are awful. Don't be fooled by the lobby, which is an airy, beautiful, open-beamed room built from logs. Large fireplaces and cozy tables and chairs are scattered throughout, providing many tempting places to snuggle up together with a hot drink. When it comes to the rooms, however, it's an entirely different story. Numerous guest rooms are situated along dismal, decaying hallways, and the rooms themselves are at best claustrophobic and sorely in need of renovation, with small windows and dilapidated furniture. It's a shame that the management doesn't do more with this prime property, but the lack of competition for this awesome summer destination has made them lazy. Until things change, we strongly suggest that you spend the night in the valley or bring a tent and save Paradise for daily excursions.

Romantic Note: The other lodge at Mount Rainier is located six miles inside the southwest entrance. **NATIONAL PARK INN AT LONGMIRE**, (360) 569-2411 (Inexpensive) operates as a bed and breakfast during the winter and as a standard hotel during the summer.

Outdoor Kissing

CHINOOK PASS, Mount Rainier
Mount Baker-Snoqualmie National Forest

If you're in the Mount Baker–Snoqualmie National Forest on the east side of Mount Rainier, Highway 410 will take you through the pass.

On a fall afternoon, Chinook Pass is almost too glorious. You'll be so excited by the scenery that you might finish touring and forget to kiss. Take a moment to memorize the image of the golden light bathing hills and lakes. Notice the vivid shades of red and amber that embellish the trees and meadows. Feel the fall air brush your skin while the sun's heat tempers the chill. Sigh. This is a visual gift to share with each other.

Romantic Note: The drive through the pass is loaded with vista turn-outs, hikes with dizzying switchbacks, and meadows that you can explore side by side. Just be sure to travel prepared. Comfortable hiking shoes, munchies (lots of munchies), water bottle, tissues, and a day pack will make Chinook Pass an unsurpassed experience. Also, be considerate of the wilderness. Trails are for people; the rest of the area is for the animals and plants. Responsible behavior on the part of all visitors will keep the beauty intact for many years to come.

MOUNT RAINIER NATIONAL PARK, Mount Rainier
(360) 569-2211
$5 entry fee per vehicle, $3 fee per bicycle

From Enumclaw to the north or Yakima to the east, take Highway 410 into the park. Highway 12 from both the southeast and southwest intersects with Highway 123, which will also take you into the park. On the southwest side of the park, Highway 7 intersects with Highway 706 at the town of Elbe. Highway 706 goes into the park and takes you straight to Paradise, both literally and figuratively.

Using poetic words to describe Mount Rainier is best left to the laureates. For the kissing purposes of this book, suffice it to say that almost every inch of this mountain is romantic and outrageously exquisite. From its dormant volcanic heart to its eternally glacier-covered summit, Mount Rainier is guaranteed to provide superlative panoramic views, memorable hikes, and lasting memories. If it is Northwest drama and passion that you yearn for, this mountain has it.

Several park roads, including some of the main routes onto the mountain, are closed during the winter, so always check for seasonal accessibility. Excellent hiking books are available for this region from *The Mountaineers*

Books. For a catalog, write to 1011 Southwest Klickitat Way, Suite 107, Seattle, Washington 98134, or phone (206) 223-6303.

PARADISE, Mount Rainier
Mount Rainier National Park

Nineteen miles inside the southwest entrance of the park.

A scenic climb by car through lush old-growth evergreens, the spell-binding roar of waterfalls rushing down jagged mountain rocks, nimble deer foraging for greens at the side of the road, brightly hued blue jays, agile mountain goats, regal eagles, lumbering elk, and wildflowers of all kinds make for an unforgettable romantic interlude. Mount Rainier looms before you, draped in majestic snowy white, growing larger and more magnificent the farther you drive up the windy curves toward its peak. Take advantage of the various scenic stops with vantage points of the surrounding park and the mountain beyond. Get out of your car, lean (carefully) over the stone rail-ings, and marvel at the heights to which you've come together. Sunset over the valley of trees below is astonishingly surreal. It's no wonder they call this Paradise.

SUNRISE, Mount Rainier
Mount Rainier National Park

From the north or east, take Highway 410 into Mount Rainier National Park and follow the park map to Sunrise.

If you've always wondered what it must be like at the top of the world, come to Sunrise and fulfill your fantasy, for this is as close to the top of the world as you can drive in the continental United States. When you arrive, there are so many inspiring trails (some relatively easy ones) that choosing one might be harder than you'd like. Your day hike can be a level, leisurely stroll or a strenuous trek up a mountain path, far away from everyone and everything except each other. Nowhere else will you hear such silence.

Ashford

ALEXANDER'S COUNTRY INN, Ashford
37515 State Road 706 East
(360) 569-2323, (800) 654-7615
Moderate

Nestled at the edge of old-growth forest (and, unfortunately, next to the two-lane highway that leads to Mount Rainier), this quaint blue country inn is surrounded by a lush green lawn with winding walkways and wooden benches; the entire property is enclosed in a white picket fence.

Before you settle into a room for the night, you might opt for dinner in the restaurant downstairs. Cozy up in a casual wooden booth with soft cushions, savor the warmth of the wood-burning fireplace, and peek out of the lace-curtained windows that overlook the old wooden waterwheel and surrounding yard (and, in the distance, traffic). Request the fresh trout, typically caught the very same day in the backyard pond, or try the hearty stuffed green peppers. The excellent entrées are accompanied by fresh sourdough bread, and the service is attentive. At the end of your meal, satiate your sweet tooth with a chocolate torte covered in a light raspberry sauce. Now, with a full stomach, you can head upstairs.

The spacious common room has a homey fireplace but is still somewhat disappointing due to sparse furnishings and dim lighting. Some of the 12 guest rooms are much the same, even slightly gloomy, but there are two rooms occupying the tower that you'll be sure to appreciate. First is the Upstairs Tower Suite, a double-decker room with a bright sitting room, furnished with attractive antiques. Carpeted stairs lead you to the loft bedroom, and sunlight filters through the large windows. In the bottom half of the tower is another two-room guest suite; the octagonal bedroom has redwood paneling and wraparound windows. All of the inn's rooms have unique stained glass windows that add a colorful flair to the accommodations.

Complete your evening with a soak in the intimate hot tub, sheltered in a half-enclosed gazebo that overlooks a well-lit pond. (Test the temperature with your toes first—it was too hot to get in the night we were there.) Watch the trout jump across the water's surface, leaving ripples in the silhouetted reflections of the trees, and enjoy the quiet, sweet-smelling breeze emanating from the nearby forest.

Romantic Note: Alexander's has recently added a fully-equipped house and chalet just down the road. Furnished with modern appointments, both houses are family-oriented and can accommodate up to six people. Although these units are designed more for groups, they would be wonderful, ultraprivate places for two.

Stevenson

Hotel/Bed and Breakfast Kissing

SKAMANIA LODGE, Stevenson
1131 Skamania Lodge Way
(509) 427-7700, (800) 221-7117
http://www.skamania.com
Moderate to Very Expensive

Skamania Lodge has been designed to beautifully accommodate conventions and large business groups. As far as romance goes, however, what surrounds the lodge is the real attraction. The lodge overlooks the Columbia River, almost five miles of nature trails cover the 175-acre property, horseback riding is available, the pool and outdoor hot tub are extremely inviting, and the massive main-floor Gorge Room provides a wonderful fireside spot for relaxing and savoring the view. Many of the 195 rooms enjoy this same view and contain Northwest artwork and pine furnishings, but the gray undertones in the bedspreads and carpet create an austere atmosphere. Many rooms have fireplaces to help warm things up a bit, but it would take more than a Presto log to drown out the murmur of voices heard through the thin walls.

Romantic Note: As far as dining options go, you're pretty limited in the town of Stevenson. Thankfully, **THE DINING ROOM** at Skamania Lodge (Moderate to Expensive) offers outstanding Columbia River views and excellent regional cuisine. Tables along the windows are obviously preferred, and the polished oak interior with vaulted ceilings is quite attractive (albeit too large to feel intimate). The coziest area in the whole lodge is the **RIVER ROCK LOUNGE** (Inexpensive to Moderate). Although the menu here is limited, gazing out to the river through floor-to-ceiling windows is heavenly. Or you can gaze at each other (equally heavenly) and bask in the glow of a crackling fire in the huge river-rock fireplace.

Husum

Outdoor Kissing

CHARLES HOOPER FAMILY WINERY, Husum
196 Spring Creek Road
(509) 493-2324
Call for seasonal closures.

Nine miles north of White Salmon, on the way to Trout Lake. Just off Highway 141, near milepost 9, turn west up Spring Creek Road and follow it two miles to the winery.

On your way to or from Mount Adams, be certain to stop at the Charles Hooper Family Winery. A stroll through the vineyards treats you to one of the most exquisite views you will behold anywhere—particularly from June through October, when foliage is most abundant. A large wood-frame building with enormous wooden doors is where the wine is made and can be tasted. Bring a picnic and sit under the lush grape arbor while you nibble on lunch, sip wine, breathe the fresh air, and enjoy each other's company. Take time for this one; your eyes, palates, and hearts will be forever grateful.

Trout Lake

Located about 25 miles north of the Columbia River, Trout Lake is a quiet agricultural community at the base of Mount Adams. For some reason, Mount Adams isn't lauded as much as the other sights in the Cascades, yet this inactive volcano is in a unique position at the south end of Washington state, juxtaposed between the green, lush forests of the western half and the rain shadow of the eastern half. This is a section of Washington's wine country, so the base of the mountain is surrounded with manicured vineyards. Whether you are a snow bunny or you prefer the long, hot days of summer, the endless recreational opportunities in this region will provide all the outdoor entertainment you need for a Northwest escape.

Hotel/Bed and Breakfast Kissing

MIO AMORE PENSIONE, Trout Lake
53 Little Mountain Road
(509) 395-2264
Inexpensive to Expensive

Mio Amore Pensione rests in the small country town of Trout Lake. The snowcapped peaks of Mount Adams and its rolling foothills tower over the little inn's backyard. This early American home has been renovated into a European-feeling bed and breakfast with four lodging options and antique touches all about. Romantic travelers will be interested in the only room with a private bath: the sunny Venus Room, which has violet linens, lavender carpet, a claw-foot tub, and an inviting sitting area overlooking Trout Creek and Mount Adams. As the name suggests, this room is designed for love, and a complimentary bottle of champagne awaits to help set a special tone. Adjacent to the house is the original turn-of-the-century icehouse, which has been turned into a loft cottage. Despite a wood-burning stove, it is still somewhat chilly, with stone walls, sparse furnishings, and no private bath (you walk about 50 feet to the main house to use a bathroom that is shared with the two other guest rooms).

The highlight of your stay will be the gourmet morning meal served by the innkeepers every day. This eye-opening repast consists of luscious homemade tortes, breads, and special Italian baked dishes. Breakfast is complimentary for those staying at the Pensione, and four-course dinners are also available at an additional cost ($50 per couple). The generous dinners feature exotic meats and fresh fish that are selected on a daily basis by the first couple to book their reservation. Mio Amore Pensione is one of the few places where you can combine mountain exploration with European gourmet feasting in proverbial Northwest style and seclusion.

Romantic Note: Reservations for dinner are accepted even if you are not staying overnight. Be aware that because the home is small, even if you are not participating in dinner you will hear the experience from the upstairs rooms between 7 P.M. and 9:30 P.M. Also note that if you do not reserve the only table for two, you will be seated family-style. This may lead to interesting group conversations, but it is not exactly intimate.

SERENITY'S, Trout Lake
Highway 141, Milepost 23
(509) 395-2500, (800) 276-7993
Inexpensive to Expensive

Aren't we all searching for a little serenity? In Trout Lake, Serenity's is not only easy to find and fairly affordable, it is a fine property offering four newly built A-frame chalets. Set amid tall firs and ponderosa pines, these self-sufficient little cabins have everything you need for a mountain getaway. Gas-log fireplaces warm the knotty pine interiors, comfortable contemporary living rooms provide a place to relax, and each unit has a kitchenette where you can prepare your own breakfasts (but no food is included with your stay). Some units have Jacuzzi tubs, while the larger ones have loft bedrooms. Serenity's chalets are not frilly or fancy, but they are an extremely comfortable and private option for couples enamored with the great outdoors.

Romantic Option: Serenity's also operates a relaxed little restaurant (Moderate). A wooden barn adjacent to the cabins offers a pleasant spot from which to enjoy distant views of Mount Adams while sampling continental cuisine. The rustic wood-and-stone interior is cozy and casual, warmed by a woodstove. Share bites of baked Icelandic cod fillet served with drawn butter, or try the breast of chicken Kiev with wild rice dressing. Dally over dessert and savor the serenity while you can.

White Salmon

Unlike the Oregon village of Hood River (see the Oregon Cascades chapter), the towns on the Washington side of the Columbia River Gorge are mostly residential areas where logging and agriculture, not tourist dollars, keep the economy rolling. As in so many small Northwest towns, however, the demand for loggers here is decreasing, so perhaps the focus will shift in the coming years. Until then, White Salmon remains a fairly quiet, nondescript stop along the Columbia River.

Hotel/Bed and Breakfast Kissing

INN OF THE WHITE SALMON, White Salmon
172 West Jewett
(509) 493-2335, (800) 972-5226
http://www.gorge.net/lodging/iws
Inexpensive to Moderate

A testimony to the fruits of a little T.L.C., this remodeled 1937 two-story brick hotel welcomes you with comfortable warmth. The Inn of the White Salmon exudes old-world charm; the lobby and hallways are decorated with refurbished Victorian lamps, framed turn-of-the-century photographs, and old-fashioned patterned wallpaper. The 16 cozy rooms are said to remind guests of Grandma's house, and with good reason. Although many rooms have televisions placed at the foot of the bed and some of the carpeting needs replacing, several rooms have been endowed with affectionate touches that make them conducive to romance. The Honeymoon Suite has plush new carpeting, an enormous king-size bed covered in lush white linens, and a cozy sitting room lit by an intricate metal Victorian lamp. All of the rooms have private baths, and several have attractive wood paneling.

In the backyard, you can follow a wooden walkway past a little hillside bursting with colorful terraced gardens. Dip your toes in the spacious nearby hot tub, well lit at night and enclosed in an attractive latticework fence.

Now for the real highlight of a stay here: an incomparable repast that awaits every morning in the sunny dining room, highlighted with lace table-cloths, lace curtains, and bright floral wallpaper. More than 20 European-style pastries and breads, including baklava and strudel, are set out buffet-style, and you can choose from six savory baked breakfast entrées, including Hungarian flauf (ham baked with Swiss cheese and green onions, seasoned with caraway) and artichoke frittata, with marinated artichoke hearts, Jack cheese, green onions, black olives, and fresh tomato. Even if you aren't guests at the inn, you are invited (and we encourage you) to enjoy this culinary extravaganza ($25.90 for two)—it is a great way to start a day of touring and exploring the Columbia Gorge National Scenic Area.

Goldendale

Hotel/Bed and Breakfast Kissing

HIGHLAND CREEKS RESORT, Goldendale
2120 Scenic Highway 97, Satus Pass
(509) 773-4026, (800) 458-0174

Inexpensive to Very Expensive
Minimum stay requirement on holiday weekends

Part of the romantic appeal of this retreat is the drive that takes you here. The Columbia Gorge is beyond breathtaking, with rugged, parched cliffs and rolling hills ascending on both sides of the surging river. About 20 miles north, you will find Highland Creeks Resort (formerly Three Creeks Lodge): sufficiently isolated, sheltered by woods, and bordering the Little Klickitat River.

Miles from the world at large, nature beckons you to unleash yourselves. Twenty-three units are spread throughout duplex and four-plex cabins here. Every room used to have its own Jacuzzi tub on a private deck, but recent renovations have changed that. Now there are only four rooms with spa tubs (the Highland Suites). This major change may seem like a romantic disadvantage at first, but the results are actually just the opposite. Instead of counting on people coming just for the hot tubs (which needed constant repairs and upkeep), management removed the tubs, refinished the decks, and focused on improving the interiors, which desperately needed the attention. Now the remodeled rooms have Northwest-inspired dark bedspreads and new carpeting to complement the locally made hand-hewn pine furnishings and vaulted ceilings with skylights. Televisions are set out on the dresser in some rooms, which adds a slight hotel-feel, but you might appreciate having the option of renting a movie together (there is no cable). Every room still has a deck facing either the creek or the woods, so you can enjoy nature all around you. The Highland Suites, set in duplexes amidst tall pines, are the most spacious units, with two bedrooms, free-standing fireplaces, and full kitchens. The North Klickitat Rooms are set in four-plexes, which are not quite as private, but some units have awesome creekside settings. Five of the six South Klickitat units have fireplaces, cathedral ceilings, and king-size beds beneath a skylight; all of them face the creek. Renovations were not entirely complete when we visited, but we applaud the efforts so far—all of the changes we saw looked wonderfully promising.

Romantic Suggestion: Exquisite dinners are served in the rustic, exceedingly romantic **RESTAURANT AT HIGHLAND CREEKS RESORT** (Moderate to Expensive). Window seats that face the rushing creek are the best seating option, and you are sure to admire the quality Northwest cuisine served here. Cleanse your palate with the cool sorbet served between entrées, and then settle down to sautéed prawns, flambéed at your table by the competent and gracious staff. Memorable Evening and Romantic Evening packages that include a seven-course meal along with your accommodations are available; call for details and seasonal hours.

Outdoor Kissing

MARYHILL MUSEUM OF ART, Goldendale
35 Maryhill Museum Drive
(509) 773-3733
$5 admission fee
Closed mid-November to mid-March

Who would expect a world-class museum way out here, in the middle of nowhere? Well, right along the majestic Columbia River, you will find just that: the Maryhill Museum of Art, one of Washington state's historic treasures. You will find it hard to believe that this regal mansion, perched upon grassy acres at the river's edge, was originally built in 1914 as railroad magnate Sam Hill's "ranch house." It really is an architectural masterpiece, and now it is home to a surprising number of exhibits, including an extensive Rodin sculpture collection. An ornate group of valuables that once belonged to Queen Marie of Roumania, who was a devoted friend of Sam Hill's, is also displayed.

Romantic Suggestion: About three miles farther east along Highway 14 is another interesting site. Set on a windy bluff above the river is a replica of England's Stonehenge. Sam Hill built this monument as a tribute to the local men who died in World War I.

"*To be thy lips is a sweet thing and small.*"

e. e. cummings

Southern Washington Coast

The southern Washington coast offers many nature-loving possibilities, from forested hillsides to serene stretches of sandy beach to careening whitecapped surf to secluded wildlife refuges. The northern and southern sections of this region have quite distinct personalities. To the north, between Hoquiam and Moclips, the coastline is truly exquisite, but there are few accommodations (romantic or otherwise) to be found. Of course, the area's lack of popularity with tourists and developers can work to your advantage—especially if you have kissing in mind.

To the south, between Leadbetter Point and Chinook on the Long Beach Peninsula, wide expanses of dramatic shoreline are bordered by mile after mile of motel-style properties and condominiums. In general, the area is not only unattractive but also intensely populated. Still, small portions remain pristine, relatively undeveloped, and quite attractive to beachbound couples.

Hoquiam

Admittedly, the small, nondescript town of Hoquiam is the last place you may think of going for romance. However, since there are no hotels or bed and breakfasts worth mentioning in or even near Ocean Shores, you might consider staying at Hoquiam's **LYTLE HOUSE**, just a 20-minute drive from the ocean (see Hotel/Bed and Breakfast Kissing).

Hotel/Bed and Breakfast Kissing

LYTLE HOUSE, Hoquiam
509 Chenault Avenue
(360) 533-2320, (800) 677-2320
Inexpensive to Moderate

Immerse yourselves in the elegance of the Victorian era in a beautifully restored 1900 Queen Anne Victorian, set grandly on a hilltop overlooking Grays Harbor. From your room you can gaze in wonder over a colorful collage of rooftops in the town below.

Much of the house has been kept extraordinarily intact, and its circular second-floor sundeck, majestic front porch, variously shaped windows, and peaked awnings look much as they did in 1900. The house recalls its early years with authentic details: stained glass windows, hardwood floors, kerosene-lamp chandeliers, a coal-burning firebox, and, in the living room, an original mural that was painted for the bride for whom the house was first built.

All but two of the eight guest rooms have private baths, but even those with shared or detached baths are pleasant (robes are provided) and offer something unique: for instance, the third-floor shared bath has a claw-foot European tub filled with live goldfish. (Don't worry, there is a separate shower for the guests' use.) Our favorites are the sunny Rose Room, which embraces you in elegant lace and has a claw-foot tub, and the Windsor Room, which has a detached bath but makes up for this detail with a private balcony overlooking Grays Harbor. The richly appointed Balcony Suite, as the name implies, has a private balcony overlooking the rose garden and a claw-foot tub in the room. The decor is historically tasteful and graced throughout with beautiful antiques.

Your hosts take pride in serving an abundant full breakfast in the plush, deep red dining room, at your own individual table draped in white lace. Choose from a six-item menu that includes specialty omelets, French toast, granola, yogurt, and other standard breakfast items. For a small additional charge, breakfast can also be delivered to your room. Without a doubt, this is the best place to stay in the immediate area.

Moclips

Hotel/Bed and Breakfast Kissing

OCEAN CREST RESORT, Moclips
4651 Highway 109
(360) 276-4465, (800) 684-8439
Inexpensive to Moderate
Minimum stay requirement on weekends and holidays

Shaded by a grove of spruce trees, Ocean Crest Resort is stationed high on a bluff with an unparalleled view of the Pacific Ocean. From the parking lot, the two four-story buildings resemble a standard hotel, with unsightly blue doors marking each of the 45 guest rooms and cars whizzing by on the highway behind you. Don't be deceived; there is much waiting for you inside.

Ranging from comfortable large studios with small refrigerators to spacious two-bedroom apartments with full kitchens, the accommodations all have fireplaces or woodstoves. Most of the rooms have fairly typical hotel decor, except for the studios in Building 5, which have attractive cedar paneling, soft colors, queen-size beds, and newer furnishings. What really makes this place worth your while are the breathtaking views from the large windows and decks found in most of the rooms. (You won't even know you're near a highway—we promise.) And it doesn't stop there. Wind down a beautifully constructed 133-step staircase through a wooded ravine to the beach, which extends for miles in either direction. If you get tired on the way back up, stop and share a kiss in the shade on one of several benches along the way; these perches were seemingly built for just this purpose.

You can luxuriate in the sauna, hot tub, swimming pool, or massage parlor in the recreational facilities, which are located across the street in a contemporary wooden building with vaulted ceilings, skylights, and three tiers of windows. (Remember, these facilities are available to all of the guests, so don't expect much privacy.)

Breakfast is not included in your stay, but we recommend the Ocean Crest's dining room (Moderate) for breakfast, lunch, or dinner. Bay windows reveal spectacular ocean and sunset views, and both the seafood menu and the service are superior.

Copalis Beach

Hotel/Bed and Breakfast Kissing

IRON SPRINGS OCEAN BEACH RESORT, Copalis Beach
3707 Highway 109
(360) 276-4230
Inexpensive to Expensive
Minimum stay requirement on weekends and in summer

Nature enthusiasts are sure to feel at home in one of the 28 cabins tucked amidst 100 acres of spruce trees on a low-lying bluff overlooking the Pacific Ocean. The beige and cedar lined cottages scattered across the property are sheltered by trees and spaced adequately apart, giving each cottage ample privacy and a sense of isolation, perfect for a tranquil weekend getaway. Several of the cabins have direct beach access, and you can wander barefoot from your cabin right into the surf. One-bedroom studios and complete two-bedroom cabins that can accommodate up to four people are available. All are equipped with full kitchens, cooking supplies, wood-burning fireplaces, electric heat for those who prefer it, and fresh linens. Large windows and decks provide wonderful views of the ocean and the surrounding woodland. The unadorned interiors are comfortable, done in pastel colors with throw rugs, brass lamps, and simple artwork. Most of the cabins have been renovated in a more pleasing modern decor, with interesting color schemes and newer decks.

You can get heart-healthy together by hiking along a trail that meanders through the forest. Those not daring enough to brave the ocean's cold can take a dip in the covered heated pool open to guests. Later, treat yourselves to a fresh cinnamon roll or a piping hot bowl of clam chowder, available in the gift shop near the registration office.

Romantic Warning: A possible drawback to this ocean hideaway is its popularity with families in the summertime. Your cabin should provide enough privacy so that the only sound you'll hear is the gentle roar of the ocean. But just in case, you might want to consider coming only in the off-season.

LONG BEACH PENINSULA

The mystery, power, and beauty of the sea have drawn dreamers, poets, and lovers to the shore for centuries, and Long Beach is no exception. Unfortunately, as you pass through the various small towns dotting this peninsula, you cannot help but wonder how the magnificence became entangled with the endless succession of shops, gas stations, restaurants, motels, and urban advertising that line either side of Pacific Highway. Don't let this stop you; the ocean and the sprawling dunes are just moments away.

Chinook

Restaurant Kissing

SANCTUARY RESTAURANT, Chinook
Highway 101 and Hazel Street
(360) 777-8380
Moderate to Expensive
Dinner Wednesday-Sunday

In the sanctuary of a renovated former church, you can sit in actual pews and marvel at your surroundings, including stained glass windows and other structural remnants of the building's past. This distinctive setting might just be the perfect spot for you to pledge your vows all over again. Local seafood is typically a best bet here, but recent reports on service and food quality have been mixed. At least the vast array of homemade desserts hasn't changed, and the unique setting is still noteworthy.

Seaview

Hotel/Bed and Breakfast Kissing

THE SHELBURNE INN, Seaview
4415 Pacific Highway (Highway 103)
(360) 642-2442, (800) INN-1896
Moderate to Very Expensive
Minimum stay requirement on weekends

When you first drive into town and realize that we have recommended an establishment that is right on the main street (and awarded it three lips, no less), you may wonder if we have allowed our requirements to become more lenient. Well, we haven't—establishments are still partially rated on "surrounding splendor"—but The Shelburne Inn has managed to create enough surrounding splendor *inside* the guest rooms that we nearly forgot the road right outside. All of the 15 small rooms and suites in this restored turn-of-the-century inn are furnished with beautiful antiques, comfortably elegant furnishings, down comforters, lace pillows, handmade patchwork quilts, crocheted bedspreads, private bathrooms, and plenty of country-Victorian atmosphere. Many also feature a balcony or deck. Of course, not all rooms are created equal. Some have queen beds, and some have doubles; some face the charming kitchen garden, and some have less inspiring street views (partially screened by frosted windows). A favorite is the pretty corner suite with a sitting area, leaded glass French doors, and an old-fashioned claw-foot tub.

Guests are greeted with a plate of astonishingly rich cookies fresh from a bakery down the street, but the real appetite-pleaser is breakfast. Like works of art, the Shelburne's gourmet breakfasts are designed for eye appeal as well as savory flavor. Feast on treats such as a three-cheese omelet with red salmon caviar or waffles with fresh fruit. Plates are decorated with edible flowers and herbs. After this indulgence, you can hike through a series of dunes to reach the long, smooth beach that this peninsula was named after. Long Beach is vast enough that even when a lot of other people are out enjoying the sand and surf, it doesn't seem nearly as crowded as many other Northwest beaches.

Romantic Note: As much as we adore The Shelburne Inn, we must reiterate that its main-street location is not ideal. In the same breath, we must restate that the rooms here are still worth romantic consideration, and noise is really not a problem unless you open the windows.

Romantic Suggestion: When you book your stay here, we suggest that you also make a reservation for dinner at **THE SHOALWATER RESTAURANT** (see Restaurant Kissing), located on the inn's main floor.

Restaurant Kissing

CHERI WALKER'S 42ND STREET CAFE, Seaview
4201 Pacific Highway (Highway 103)
(360) 642-2323
Moderate
Lunch Wednesday–Sunday; Dinner Daily

It may not look like much from the outside, but this modest, mauve-colored building holds one of the best new restaurants in town. Once the chef at the highly acclaimed **SHOALWATER RESTAURANT** (see Restaurant Kissing), Cheri Walker has moved on to open her own establishment, and her culinary wizardry is as wonderful as ever.

Lace half-curtains shield the view of the busy road outside, while colorful tablecloths and dried floral swags create a casual, country atmosphere. The menu offers a little bit of everything: Northwest-inspired dishes such as pan-fried oysters or grilled salmon with shaved almonds; creative items like homemade sweet-pepper ravioli stuffed with walnuts and feta cheese; and classic, hearty American dishes like country fried steak with mashed potatoes and gravy. Prices are just as friendly as the staff, and meals include homemade bread, salad, and a choice of dessert.

MY MOM'S PIE KITCHEN, Seaview
4316 Pacific Highway (Highway 103)
(360) 642-2342
Inexpensive
Call for seasonal hours.

If you like pie, you have come to the right place. Set in a turn-of-the-century cottage, My Mom's Pie Kitchen is a charming new establishment specializing in (you guessed it) pies. Selection changes daily, but you can usually find apple, rhubarb, pecan, lemon meringue, banana cream, peanut butter, and sour-cream raisin pies on the menu. Three petite dining rooms hold several tables each, and there is also patio seating. Unfortunately, traffic on Pacific Way right out front makes the outdoor option less than refreshing, but cut-lace curtains inside conceal this view. There isn't anything fancy about My Mom's Pie Kitchen, but for a light lunch or an afternoon dessert, this is a worthwhile stop.

THE SHOALWATER RESTAURANT, Seaview
4415 Pacific Highway (Highway 103), at The Shelburne Inn
(360) 642-4142

Moderate to Expensive
Lunch and Dinner Daily

Can food be wildly romantic? At the Shoalwater, the proof is in the pudding, or perhaps we should say it's in the rose-geranium sorbet. No matter what you choose from the imaginative and wide-ranging menu, it will be utterly fresh and delicious, and beautifully presented. Sautéed mushrooms with Dijon mustard, fresh dill, and sour cream; baked halibut with dill pesto, melon relish, and cucumber mayonnaise; roasted pork tenderloin with pecans in a Dijon mustard sauce and an apricot glaze—need we say more? The wine list is extensive, desserts more than live up to the rest of the meal, and service is wonderfully friendly and knowledgeable.

Even if the food at the Shoalwater were merely ordinary, the setting alone would warrant at least a lip or two. The restaurant fills most of the main floor of a turn-of-the-century house that has long been **THE SHELBURNE INN** (see Hotel/Bed and Breakfast Kissing). The dining room features stained- and leaded-glass windows, high ceilings, and well-spaced antique tables and chairs in a warm, country-Victorian atmosphere. Gems like this are rarely found in small towns, which makes the sophisticated atmosphere and worldly gourmet cuisine seem even more special.

Romantic Alternative: The owners of the Shoalwater also operate **THE LIGHTSHIP RESTAURANT**, 409 West Tenth Street, Long Beach, (360) 642-3252 (Inexpensive to Moderate), located in a budget hotel right off the beach. Although the casual interior and standard menu hardly compare with the elegance and gourmet cuisine found at the Shoalwater, the sweeping ocean and coastal views from this vantage point are not to be ignored.

Long Beach

Hotel/Bed and Breakfast Kissing

BOREAS BED AND BREAKFAST, Long Beach
607 North Boulevard
(360) 642-8069, (888) 642-8069
Inexpensive to Expensive

Just one block west of the main highway through Long Beach, you can unpack your bags and take refuge in a quaint beach house ensconced in grass-covered dunes, with a sweeping, undisturbed view of the Pacific Ocean. This bed and breakfast is tightly tucked between other homes, but once inside, you will hardly notice the close neighbors. Unwind in comfortable common areas filled with an eclectic assortment of antique furnishings, a white baby grand piano, and two glowing fireplaces. Listen to a favorite recording from the owners' extensive music collection, or ease into the spacious hot tub in the glass-enclosed sunroom. Done up in attractive black and white tiles, the pleasant kitchen is open to guests, who can help themselves to tea and coffee or fresh muffins at any time.

Choose from four gracious guest rooms, three of which have ocean views; two have private baths. Upstairs, the North Room is the best option, with its own private bath, vaulted ceilings, skylights, whitewashed walls, snuggly comforter, and bountiful sunlight. The second-largest room is the Garden Suite, located on the main floor. Elegant gold and rose appointments dress this room, which looks out to a small, colorful garden. Although the Attic and South Rooms share a bath, they have other romantic assets: the Attic Room features a plush king-size bed with a down comforter and feather bed, while the South Room enjoys incredible sunset views. Plans for a fifth room with a private bath and jetted tub are in the works. The owners are also building a gazebo and spa out in the dunes, so wonderful sunset soaks with the rustle of beach grass all around you will soon be possible here.

In the morning, a delicious full breakfast, complete with hot-out-of-the-oven breads, baked egg dishes, and fresh fruit, is served family-style at the dining room table. Guests in the Garden Suite appreciate the romantic option of having breakfast delivered to their room, but even if you do not get much intimacy during breakfast, you probably won't mind. Your hosts help to make conversation lively, and the food is plentiful. Besides, after your morning meal you can always take a walk, just the two of you, through the dunes to the water's edge or along the nearby boardwalk.

Romantic Note: Next door you'll find a weathered cabin available for rent. It is sparsely furnished and not nearly as well kept as the bed and breakfast, but it does have three bedrooms, a kitchen, one and a half baths, and a working fireplace. It's a perfect getaway for those seeking affordable, roomy, and exclusive privacy with beach access.

SCANDINAVIAN GARDENS INN
BED AND BREAKFAST, Long Beach
1610 California Avenue South
(360) 642-8877, (800) 988-9277
Inexpensive to Expensive
Minimum stay requirement on weekends and holidays

Set in a nondescript residential area, Scandinavian Gardens is a comfortable, affordable bed-and-breakfast option. The spacious Swedish Suite has a two-person soaking tub and a spacious bathroom, but for the most part, the five guest rooms here are austere, with simple Swedish furnishings, Berber rugs, and dated appointments. Added comforts include an indoor spa area with a large Jacuzzi tub and cedar sauna.

Breakfast is served family-style at one large table in the cheerful dining room—not exactly an intimate affair, but you will surely enjoy the abundant array of fresh fruit and homemade Danish pastries. A hot entrée, such as shrimp au gratin or fruit-covered waffles, and savory Copenhagen potatoes are also included.

Ocean Park

Hotel/Bed and Breakfast Kissing

CASWELL'S ON THE BAY
BED AND BREAKFAST INN, Ocean Park
25204 Sandridge Road
(360) 665-6535, (888) 553-2314
http://www.ohwy.com/wa/c/casbaybb.htm
Inexpensive to Expensive
Recommended Wedding Site

Caswell's on the Bay, a newly built Queen Anne Victorian, sits proudly at the edge of Willapa Bay. Tall trees, a manicured lawn, hanging flower baskets, and colorful gardens trim the stately, pastel yellow home, and the view of the tidelands is an ever-changing scene. Unlike a historic Victorian, this house is bright and airy, with high ceilings, plenty of windows, and excellent soundproofing. Five comfortable guest rooms are located on the second floor. Private modern baths, elegant Victorian appointments, and comfortable sitting areas are just some of the amenities you can expect, and two of the rooms have excellent views of the bay. Although the rooms do have a new feeling to them, rich linens and color schemes, ornate antique bedroom sets, and intricate bedside lamps add character.

Of particular romantic interest is the airy Terrace Suite, which has plenty of windows facing the bay and a lovely patio fronting the room. Breakfast can be delivered to this room, so you can enjoy an intimate morning for two. Otherwise, guests enjoy a full gourmet breakfast in the main floor's dining room, at one large table. Even if breakfast becomes more of a social than a romantic event, you can always sneak off to a quiet corner of the veranda afterward and finish your coffee together while surveying the serene landscape.

COAST WATCH BED AND BREAKFAST, Ocean Park
(360) 665-6774
Inexpensive
Minimum stay requirement on weekends

City dwellers often forget how beautiful sunset or a star-filled sky can actually be, but a weekend at the Coast Watch never fails to reacquaint guests with nature's abundant splendor. Escape to one of two spacious, modestly appointed suites in this weathered gray-blue cabin set in the dunes, yards from the ocean. Both suites are full of sunlight; both provide dazzling views of the ocean and dunes, as well as northerly views of the surrounding natural scenery. We preferred the West Suite with its large ocean-view deck, perfect for enjoying sunsets. The North Suite is slightly smaller, and its dark brown carpeting is somewhat dated. Still, both suites are pleasant and unaffected, with simple linens and colors and a mix of contemporary and wicker furnishings.

The conscientious host takes pride in the smallest of details, from the fresh-cut rose on your pillow, to the in-room stereo complete with romantic tapes and CDs, to the delectable fruit-platter breakfast served at your convenience in your private suite. She has even been known to drive for miles, from store to store, to find quality breakfast items to ensure her guests' satisfaction.

This unique bed and breakfast has no common areas for guests outside of their individual suites, which assures unlimited privacy. Additionally, because there are only two suites, you'll feel as if the expanse of beach and grass-covered dunes is yours for the taking. Stroll at dusk and let the waves wash over your feet, or wait until the sun has set and let the stars above enfold you. Is there a drawback to a weekend at the Coast Watch? Only your reluctance to go back to the real world.

Nahcotta

Hotel/Bed and Breakfast Kissing

OUR HOUSE IN NAHCOTTA, Nahcotta
268th and Dell Streets
(360) 665-6667
Inexpensive

Set in a residential area, this three-story cedar-shake house resembles a New England–style home. Abundant foliage and flower gardens trim the building, and an eclectic mix of antiques fills the interior. There are two units here, each one completely private and wonderfully spacious. The First

Floor Suite is handsomely appointed with dark tones and floral accents. A short claw-foot tub is set in the small private bath, and bay windows look out to the gardens. The Second Floor Suite has hardwood floors and is also decorated with a rich color scheme and lovely antiques. This unit is perfect for two couples traveling together because up a flight of stairs adjacent to the living room area, there is another French country-inspired bedroom, a bathroom with a skylight above the tub, and a charming sitting area. Be assured that this third story is rented only if there is a group of people who know each other, so if you are traveling as just one couple, you will not have any shared facilities; you may wish to use the little third-floor sitting area as a nice reading nook.

In the morning, an expanded continental breakfast featuring mammoth cinnamon rolls is delivered to your room. Afterwards you'll be ready for a day of sun and sand on the southern Washington coast.

Restaurant Kissing

THE ARK RESTAURANT, Nahcotta
273rd Street and Sandridge Road
(360) 665-4133
Moderate to Expensive
Call for seasonal hours.

Don't let the nearby oyster farm's industrial equipment, trucks, and buildings distract you from a romantic evening at the Ark. Once inside the small red-painted building that juts out into Willapa Bay, you'll be glad you came. With views of the water on all sides, the restaurant has a wide selection of window tables to choose from. A wood-and-brick interior and large stone fireplace make for a casual but pleasing atmosphere, accented with white tablecloths; colorful flags and knickknacks hang from dark wooden beams overhead.

The Ark is considered one of the finest restaurants on the peninsula, and the real reason to come here is the superb cuisine. Fresh local items are excellent. Try the salmon glazed with Scotch and orange juice, laced with Drambuie, and garnished with crème fraîche; or the lightly breaded, grilled oysters harvested right from Willapa Bay. Save room for espresso or tea and the seductive dessert selections presented on a silver tray. Then sit back and watch as the twinkling stars emerge from the sky beyond your window.

Romantic Note: Before the Ark closes for the winter, be sure to ask about its popular summer Garlic Festival. Reservations for this epicurean festival are accepted only after midnight on Valentine's Day (after all your romantic kissing is done). The menu features every possible (and impossible) appetizer, entrée, and, yes, even dessert, accented with more garlic than you can imagine. Definitely for garlic lovers only.

Outdoor Kissing

LEADBETTER POINT STATE PARK

Take Sandridge Road north past the town of Nahcotta. Turn left onto Oysterville Road and follow the signs to the park.

There are lots of romantic places to walk hand in hand on this peninsula, the most obvious being the beach and dunes. Options include hiking to **NORTH HEAD LIGHTHOUSE** or **CAPE DISAPPOINTMENT LIGHTHOUSE**, both located in Ilwaco, just minutes from Long Beach; the latter is a somewhat steeper proposition. But for assured privacy throughout the year, consider going to Leadbetter Point State Park, at the northern tip of the Long Beach Peninsula. You can wander all day and not run into anybody. But don't wander too far; people have been known to get lost in the wilderness up here. Also, the seasonal appearance of large, aggressive black flies can yield an unforeseen kissing obstacle.

OREGON

Portland

Once you visit Portland, you are likely to become an enthusiast. This growing municipality has two distinct personalities—one urban and the other rural. There is an impressive amount of greenery here, and an amazing variety of terrain for walking, hiking, and exploring. Gardens, parks, forests, and rivers blanket the landscape, and all are meticulously maintained. Then there's the urban side of Portland's character: the upscale charm of Nob Hill, a refurbished neighborhood teeming with restaurants and shops; the growing downtown dotted with art deco buildings and glass skyscrapers; a restored old-town area with all its vintage charm left intact; and the recently developed, affluent riverfront area called RiverPlace. Portland's two personalities are in perfect balance, which is part of what makes the city so remarkable. Whether you are visiting for a day or a week, Portland's earthy appeal is bound to make a lasting impression.

Romantic Suggestion: Portland is home to one of the largest open-air markets in the country. The **PORTLAND SATURDAY MARKET**, (503) 222-6072, is open every Saturday and Sunday, from March through Christmas Eve. More than 200 booths feature a wide variety of handcrafted creations, including just about everything from ceramics to furniture to food. The market extends from the west end of the Burnside Bridge to the Fire Museum, between Front Street and the MAX trolley tracks.

Hotel/Bed and Breakfast Kissing

THE BENSON HOTEL, Portland
309 Southwest Broadway
(503) 228-2000, (800) 426-0670
http://www.holog.com/benson
Very Expensive to Unbelievably Expensive

This grand old hotel has one of the most massive, ornate lobbies in the Northwest. Austrian crystal chandeliers, Italian marble floors, and the building's original Circassian walnut paneling are truly awe-inspiring. The immense, wood-paneled interior is stunning, and the lounge seating is intimate and quiet. Although the entire hotel underwent a $16 million renovation several years ago, the lobby area continues to be the most impressive part of the Benson.

All 280 rooms are comfortable enough, with cherry furnishings, standard baths, and king-size beds strewn with oversized pillows. Compared to the ornate lobby, however, the rooms seem disappointing and drab. The color schemes are fairly conservative (meaning different shades of taupe and gray), and we were hard-pressed to find too many heart-stirring qualities. If you're willing to splurge, consider one of the two Grand Suites. Each has a Jacuzzi tub and a double-headed shower in the bathroom; a four-poster bed; and a sitting area lavishly appointed with chandeliers, a gas fireplace, and your very own baby grand piano. Our only complaint is that the Grand Suites are excessively spacious, almost to the point of being ridiculous. These rooms would be ideal for hosting a party, but they're too large for two people seeking intimate time together.

Romantic Warning: Breakfast is not included with the price of your stay. And for tariffs this steep, that's simply unforgivable. Fortunately, breakfast, lunch, and dinner are available downstairs in the **LONDON GRILL** (see Restaurant Kissing). In addition, the hotel's downtown location allows easy access to a myriad of eating establishments in the area.

THE GOVERNOR HOTEL, Portland
611 Southwest Tenth Avenue
(503) 224-3400, (800) 554-3456
http://www.teleport.com/~peekpa/governor.html
Very Expensive to Unbelievably Expensive

You don't have to be a governor or any other kind of politician to appreciate the stellar accommodations at this refined, historic downtown hotel (although a governor's pocketbook might help). A harmonious mixture of turn-of-the-century decor and modern appointments fills the grand lobby. Fascinating hand-painted murals, found throughout the hotel, pay tribute to Lewis and Clark and the Native Americans they encountered while exploring the Oregon Territory. The subtle, soft hues of the artwork and the original mahogany furnishings make for a warm introduction to your romantic interlude.

Each of the 100 rooms has slightly different decor but all are fairly conservative, with matching upholstered furniture in subtle tones of peach or beige and touches of Northwest art. Standard guest rooms, which are the least costly but still in the Very Expensive price range, lack a view and have a queen-size bed rather than a king. Deluxe guest rooms, which are slightly more expensive, offer considerably more comfort, with separate sitting areas, tall ceilings, and the same dignified decor. The suites are the most luxurious and feature amenities such as gas corner fireplaces, cozy love seats, jetted tubs, abundant space, and skylights that fill the room with sunshine.

Guests at The Governor Hotel can take advantage of the full-service athletic club ($8 daily charge) located on the hotel's lower level. There's just about everything you could ever need to keep in shape, including a lap pool, whirlpool, track, weight room, saunas, and aerobics classes. After a good workout, visit **JAKE'S GRILL**, (503) 220-1850 (Moderate to Expensive) on the ground floor for American grill cuisine breakfast, lunch, or dinner in an informal setting. It's hardly intimate, but the carved wood columns, original tilework, and polished mahogany bar emanate a historic warmth. Try to snag one of the old-fashioned booths where you can pull a curtain to shut out worldly intrusions.

THE HEATHMAN HOTEL, Portland
1001 Southwest Broadway
(503) 241-4100, (800) 551-0011
http://www.holog.com/heathman
Very Expensive to Unbelievably Expensive

When you walk into the dimly lit lobby of the Heathman, your first reaction will be Northwest skepticism. While the geometric art and marble detailing give the interior a distinguished and striking appearance, the modern design and hard finishes make a cold, stark impression. Fortunately, cozy areas are scattered throughout the hotel. Perhaps the coziest is the **TEA COURT**, where tea is served each afternoon and jazz is performed three nights a week. The classic decor, expansive French canvases, rare eucalyptus paneling, large fireplace, and genial quiet make this a suitable place for an afternoon of thoughtful conversation and loving gazes. Upstairs, the Heathman Mezzanine Library, located next to the hotel's bar, has cozy sofas and chairs to snuggle in.

These alluring oases are all the more welcome because the rooms aren't particularly stunning. The 150 rooms are handsome, with all the pertinent amenities, but rather small (unless you spring for a suite). Deep tones of burgundy and gold, marble fixtures in the bathrooms, bamboo chairs and headboards, and original Northwest artwork help enrich the basic hotel style of the understated rooms. If price is no option, why not go all out and stay in the hotel's new Grand Suite? This two-bedroom suite is decorated in shades of yellow and cream, with views of the city from its many windows. Features include mahogany floors, a fireplace, and an inviting king-size four-poster bed in the master bedroom. A two-headed shower and a large soaking tub are luxurious additions to the marble-clad bathroom. This is definitely the most romantic room in the hotel.

For a delicious meal in a sophisticated setting, visit the hotel's restaurant located on the ground floor (see Restaurant Kissing).

Romantic Note: The Heathman Hotel deserves a standing ovation for its commitment to the arts. Not only does the hotel display seasonal exhibits on its mezzanine level, but it also donates a portion of its proceeds to benefit Portland's artistic community.

HERON HAUS, Portland
2545 Northwest Westover Road
(503) 274-1846
Expensive to Very Expensive

Bed and breakfasts are known for being cozy, warm, and congenial. Nothing is quite so affection-producing as a stay in a home where the owners diligently tend to their guests' hearts and senses with such amenities as the aroma of freshly baked morning pastries, a roaring fireplace, cushy furnishings, snuggly quilts covering oversized pillows, and a conspicuous amount of tender loving care. The Heron Haus has all this and more.

This English Tudor home is a huge, attractively furnished mansion in Portland's northwest hills. Features include a solarium and a pool, and the six spacious sun-filled suites—each given a different Hawaiian name—include cozy sitting areas. Many of the rooms have lovely pastel-colored walls, and all have contemporary decor. The bathrooms are so spectacular that you may decide to stay in yours and forget about returning to bed. The Kulia Suite has an ample spa tub that overlooks the city; the Ko Suite has a shower with seven nozzles that will cover every inch of you (or both of you) with pulsating water.

A continental breakfast including croissants, pastries, fresh fruit and juice, and coffee or tea is served in the refined dining room. You probably won't be eager to leave this peaceful setting, but if you have a more hearty breakfast appetite, you're just up the hill from Nob Hill, home to some of Portland's finest eateries.

HOTEL VINTAGE PLAZA, Portland
422 Southwest Broadway
(503) 228-1212, (800) 243-0555
http://www.holog.com/vintage
Very Expensive

If you think the brick exterior and Romanesque architecture of this historic building are impressive, wait until you get inside. The open lobby envelops you in classic, elegant style. More like a living room than a lobby, it has been decorated in rich jewel tones with dark wood paneling, marble pillars, grandiose fresh bouquets, a warming marble fireplace, and sumptuous sofas. As you lift your eyes skyward, take notice of the upstairs hallways and wraparound balconies. A solarium roof draws in sunlight and gives the entire expanse an airy distinction.

In amorous style you can escape the city in any of the 107 rooms, each named after a different Oregon winery. The standard guest rooms are just that—standard—with burgundy and hunter green linens and dark cherry furnishings. The nine Starlight Rooms, however, are a breath of fresh air. Located on the top floor, each of these rooms has an airy conservatory motif, with rattan furniture and pastel color schemes. Their outstanding feature is the view from the 45-degree, solarium-style windows. Here you can gaze at the sky from the comfort of your plush bed, appointed with pastel linens and a fluffy down comforter. If you need more space, the nine two-story townhouse suites are also lovely, with loft bedrooms, winding staircases, full kitchens and living rooms, and private entrances for both floors; some also have jetted Fuji soaking tubs.

Begin your evening with the complimentary sampling of local wines served nightly in the lobby, a decidedly warm overture to a quiet evening in the lap of luxury. In the morning, a complimentary light continental breakfast is served here as well. **PAZZO RISTORANTE**, (503) 228-1515 (Moderate to Expensive) is adjacent to the hotel's ground floor and serves breakfast, lunch, and dinner. The mood here contrasts sharply with the refined elegance of the hotel, embracing you instead with vivid colors and patterns, numerous tables, and steady, lively chatter. Even so, the service is prompt and the northern Italian cuisine is of the finest quality.

Romantic Suggestion: Ask about the hotel's romance packages. Amorous extras may include a chilled bottle of champagne, rose petals scattered over your sheets at turndown time, and continental breakfast delivered to your room in the morning.

JOHN PALMER HOUSE, Portland
4314 North Mississippi Avenue
(503) 284-5893, (800) 518-5893
Inexpensive
Minimum stay requirement on weekends, holidays, and in summers

Registered as a national historic landmark, this bed and breakfast has been well publicized in the Portland area and beyond. The yellow-gold gabled 1890 Victorian house was built as a showcase and it still fulfills that role, displaying a multitude of original antiques. Immaculate grounds and bordering flower gardens nicely outline the house, but the surrounding neighborhood has seen better days and leaves much to be desired.

Inside, the house has been appointed with silk-screened wallpapers, lacy white curtains, and old-fashioned lamps. However, some guests may feel a bit overwhelmed in the common areas, where the abundance of antiques is almost claustrophobic. Those who don't mind the cramped quarters should retire to the parlor each evening for wine and live piano entertainment provided by the on-site innkeepers.

Of the three guest rooms, the Schumann Suite is clearly the most romantic. It's located just off the parlor on the main floor and is the only one with a private bath—and what an unusual bath it is. The stained glass window over the claw-foot tub and the pull-chain toilet are endearing touches, but the dim lighting is a little disenchanting (not to mention inconvenient). The suite itself is decorated in cream and burgundy, and has a lovely Eastlake double bed covered with a hand-crocheted bedspread. Two additional guest rooms occupy the second floor; although nicely decorated, they are a bit on the small side and share a common bath. Four rooms are also available in the adjacent Victorian cottage for guests planning to stay a week or longer.

Romantic Suggestion: Ask the innkeepers about weekend horse-and-carriage rides to and from downtown Portland ($40 round-trip). Also, a formal high tea ($18.50 per person) is served by special arrangement in the ornate dining room from May through October. Once you have indulged in such luxuries, you'll understand why the inn has retained its popularity despite its location and overdone interior.

THE LION AND THE ROSE, Portland
1810 Northeast 15th Street
(503) 287-9245, (800) 955-1647
Moderate
Minimum stay requirement on holidays

Even from a distance it is evident that this grand Queen Anne home holds something special inside. Securely established in a residential neighborhood on Portland's northeast side, it is conveniently, although not romantically, located near a major shopping/business/convention center. But from the lofty cupola and turrets to the grand portico entrance, this is a classic Victorian bed and breakfast through and through with all the commensurate details and affections. Historically accurate furnishings and decor fill every corner. Six distinct rooms, two with shared baths, are found on the second floor. These spacious, richly decorated rooms emanate a sense of comfort and warmth. Standard, snug bathrooms are a drawback but easy to forgive given the other stylish enhancements. Wrought-iron and oak wood beds; cascading draperies in damask, lace, and organza; feathery but firm beds; handsome chandeliers; down comforters; and oversized pillows abound. Guests are presented with a dessert tea upon arrival, and a cordial continental breakfast is served around a large formal table in the stately dining room each morning.

In almost every aspect The Lion and The Rose is impressive, though perhaps a bit overdone if you are not in a turn-of-the-century frame of mind. Given you have a penchant for the past, there are many reasons to choose this side of town for your comings and goings.

MACMASTER HOUSE CIRCA 1895, Portland
1041 Southwest Vista Avenue
(503) 223-7362, (800) 774-9523
http://www.site-works.com/machouse.htm
Inexpensive to Moderate
Minimum stay requirement on weekends seasonally

Inside and out, this turn-of-the-century mansion is reminiscent of grand old-world living. As you walk up to the house, the formal patio, with its Doric columns and Palladian windows of leaded glass, presents a welcoming facade. Once inside, you'll find that everything is elegant, grand, and properly maintained. The antique-filled parlor, however, is so ornately furnished that it borders on being cluttered, a phenomenon that seems to spill over into the dining room and guest rooms as well.

Each of the seven suites is handsome and plush, with down comforters and a variety of antiques; four have fireplaces, and most have separate sitting areas. We recommend the two rooms with private baths. The MacMaster Suite, the largest and most attractive room, is decorated in a safari theme, has a deck with a view, and boasts an unusual bamboo four-poster bed. An attic room, also with its own bath, is nice because it is up and away from the other rooms, although it doesn't feel quite as elegant.

Mornings bring a full breakfast in the dining room featuring innovative vegetarian dishes garnished with fresh herbs from the garden. Awake to a meal of rice couscous, poached egg with zucchini, or lemon and egg-white pancakes. After breakfast, stroll through the recently landscaped garden area next to the house, where potential traffic noise is the only thing to distract you from each other.

PORTLAND'S WHITE HOUSE, Portland
1914 Northeast 22nd Avenue
(503) 287-7131

Moderate
Recommended Wedding Site

Political addresses are usually not romantic, but everything here is totally bipartisan, so there's no need to worry. Greek columns, a fountain, a circular driveway, and an ivory exterior with a west wing and an east wing give this White House an impressive resemblance to its namesake in Washington, D.C. The similarities stop once you're inside, but the bed-and-breakfast refinement continues.

Step into the grand entry hall, complete with oak-inlaid floors and a sweeping banister crowned with gorgeous stained glass windows. Off to the right is an elegant parlor, decorated in cream and pale green, with hardwood floors, chandeliers, and formal settees. To the left you'll find the dining room, where a three-course breakfast is served each morning at one long table.

The six guest rooms on the second floor are quite nice and scrupulously maintained. Five rooms have claw-foot tubs, one has its own veranda, and all have pretty floral wallpapers and antique touches. In addition to being an inviting bed and breakfast, Portland's White House is an ideal place for a wedding: the reception can take place on the lower levels (there's even a dance hall downstairs), and the bridal party can take over the rooms upstairs. The owners of Portland's White House turns their home over for special parties three times a month. If you do want to stay just for the bed and breakfast, the accommodations are gracious and the morning breakfast is wonderful. Weekends can prove a bit hectic when an event is taking place, but during the week everything is peaceful and composed.

RIVERPLACE HOTEL, Portland
1510 Southwest Harbor Way
(503) 228-3233, (800) 227-1333
Very Expensive to Unbelievably Expensive

The RiverPlace Hotel might receive a higher lip rating if it changed its decor and style a little. Its location on the banks of the Willamette River is outstanding, but the prices are ridiculous for the basic hotel-style rooms offered. All 74 rooms have standard baths, mismatched furniture, and unimpressive linens. Some rooms do have separate sitting areas, however, and others have fireplaces. The Grand Suite is the hotel's best attempt at luxury; it is a corner room with water views, a fairly large sitting area with a wood-burning fireplace, and a Jacuzzi tub in the bathroom. (It still isn't worth its steep price tag, though.) The RiverPlace Hotel also owns ten recently redecorated condominiums that overlook the marina. Although these condominiums are nowhere near extravagant, they do have kitchens and decks and the greatest potential for romance. Regardless of which room is yours, you can take advantage of the hotel's on-site athletic club ($8 daily charge), which offers a whirlpool, sauna, indoor pools, racquet courts, and aerobic classes. In the morning, complimentary continental breakfast is either delivered to your room or served at the hotel's handsome restaurant, **THE ESPLANADE** (see Restaurant Kissing).

Restaurant Kissing

ALEXANDER'S, Portland
921 Southwest Sixth Avenue, on the 23rd floor of the Hilton Hotel
(503) 226-1611, Extension 2190
Dinner Monday–Saturday

Although Portland's Hilton Hotel may not be a best place to kiss, its restaurant is worth a visit. High above the city, Alexander's affords incredible views of the Northwest's snowcapped mountains; Hood, St. Helens, Rainier, and Adams are all within sight on clear evenings. The L-shaped dining room is nicely put together, with plush gray carpet, potted plants, and cherry wood accents. Draped in scarlet linens and topped with fresh flowers, the tables are beautifully inviting, although they are arranged a bit more closely than true romantics might prefer. Choose from a variety of seafood dishes, stuffed quail, and filet mignon. Then sit back, enjoy the company, and take in the panoramic view of the city.

ATWATER'S RESTAURANT AND BAR, Portland
111 Southwest Fifth Avenue,
on the 30th floor of the U.S. Bancorp Tower
(503) 275-3600
Expensive to Very Expensive
Dinner Daily
Recommended Wedding Site

Atwater's Restaurant, atop Portland's tallest building, was designed to look like an exclusive uptown residence. From the Oriental accents to the silver service, plush carpeting, and other extravagant touches, it is clear that this is an ultraformal dining establishment. The service is attentive, almost to the point of hovering, but such pampering hardly seems out of place here. In the center of the room stands a glass-enclosed wine display, skillfully etched with wines and grapes, as a tribute to the region's wine-growing achievements. Pale green walls are accentuated by blond wood, and tables are draped with white linens and set aglow by candlelight. The curved, plum-colored booths along the wall are the best spots to snuggle up and enjoy the view. From this vantage point on cloud nine, you can watch the downtown buildings reflect the sun's light until only a silhouette of the mountains is visible through the floor-to-ceiling windows.

Atwater's offers a tempting selection of Pacific Northwest seafood that is artistically presented. Try an innovative appetizer such as the rock shrimp and sugar snap pea risotto, or choose a more traditional starter like the Dungeness crab bisque. It's difficult to decide between the dinner entrées; however, the honey-mustard roasted salmon, served with garlic mashed potatoes and smoked wild mushrooms, is as delicious as it sounds.

Romantic Note: Wednesday through Saturday nights, enjoy live jazz music in the nearby bar area. Although it can get a bit smoky at times, the wood-polished bar offers the same spectacular view as the restaurant and is an attractive spot for a nightcap.

BRASSERIE MONTMARTRE, Portland
626 Southwest Park Avenue
(503) 224-5552
Moderate to Expensive
Lunch and Dinner Daily; Sunday Brunch

Fun-loving and romantic, this delightful restaurant blends relaxed sophistication with casual elegance. The main level features black-and-white-checkered floors, marble columns, old-fashioned hanging lamps, a mammoth wooden bar, and a raised area where live jazz is performed nightly. Overhead, the high ceiling is covered with a splattering of playing cards: the telltale mark of a visiting magician. The interesting, colorful drawings on the walls are worth a closer look—they are the winners of an annual coloring contest the Brasserie holds. (All the tables are covered in butcher paper and customers are offered a handful of crayons, so you can co-create your own masterpiece if the inspiration strikes you.) A lower level, reached via a spiral staircase, features an immense espresso machine and Parisian murals.

Couples of all ages come here to indulge in simple but creative dishes such as French-fried artichoke hearts with sweet dill-mustard sauce; broiled filet mignon with green peppercorn sauce; and saffron angel-hair pasta with olive oil, garlic, tomato, and green onion, topped with sliced broiled chicken breast. You'll be sorry if you don't indulge in at least one of the utterly wicked desserts, so go ahead; and ask for two forks.

CAFÉ DES AMIS, Portland
1987 Northwest Kearney Street
(503) 295-6487

Expensive
Dinner Monday-Saturday

Café des Amis, an effective blend of Northwest atmosphere and gourmet French cuisine, is considered one of the best dinner spots in Portland. Behind the ivy-covered facade are two small, simply appointed dining rooms. Well-spaced tables, sparse white walls, and starched white linen tablecloths offer nothing to distract you from what is truly important: each other. The two dining rooms are separated from each other by a wall of etched glass. Whichever room you sit in, be aware that as the lights soften and dim throughout the evening, the noise level tends to rise. Nevertheless, there's a cordiality about the place that makes for a totally romantic experience.

A sophisticated wait staff delivers intricate entrées to your candlelit table. The pâtés are delicious; the duck, quail, and salmon are perfectly prepared; and the New York steak is the thickest and most tender you may ever experience. And the delectable desserts are sure to make your heart go pitter-patter.

THE ESPLANADE, Portland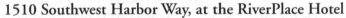
1510 Southwest Harbor Way, at the RiverPlace Hotel
(503) 295-6166, (800) 227-1333
Expensive
Breakfast and Dinner Daily; Lunch Monday–Friday; Sunday Brunch

The Esplanade just may be the most romantic locale along the RiverPlace boardwalk. This elegant restaurant is tucked away in the RiverPlace Hotel to ensure privacy without compromising its excellent view of the marina. Warm shades of sienna, yellow, and brown combine to create an attractive marbled backdrop, seasoned with modern artwork. Cobalt blue linens and maroon cushioned chairs contrast sharply with the warm tones of the walls. Wonderful floor-to-ceiling windows are framed with thick drapery and overlook the Willamette River.

Celebrate the ambience with grilled salmon accompanied by yellow pepper coulis and roasted garlic butter, or try the smoked mushroom ravioli tossed in extra virgin olive oil, feta cheese, garlic, and fresh Roma tomato purée. Across the hotel's lobby is the bar, which offers the same spectacular views as the restaurant and hosts a solo pianist Wednesday through Sunday evenings.

GENOA, Portland
2832 Southeast Belmont Street
(503) 238-1464

Very Expensive
Dinner Monday–Saturday

Genoa has the distinction of being rated one of the best dining experiences in the Northwest. Quite a reputation to live up to, but the skilled kitchen consistently produces culinary feats of excellence. If gourmet dining in a discreet atmosphere is what you're looking for, come to this small storefront location. You can't see inside; cranberry-colored window coverings keep outsiders from peering in and insiders from seeing anything of the outside world. Thick darkness envelops you at the entrance as street noise quickly fades, replaced by the murmur of hushed voices. Dine by candlelight at one of the ten or so tables evenly spaced around the room. With so much intimacy, your attention will be happily concentrated on the food and each other. Once you adapt to the sultry lighting, you'll find a seven-course parade of Italian delicacies that will please your palate throughout the entire evening.

Romantic Note: A no-less-extravagant four-course option is offered Monday through Thursday nights in addition to the traditional seven-course dinner. If you happen to arrive early, enjoy a pre-dinner drink while relaxing in the separate sitting room near the back. It is graciously appointed with comfy upholstered chairs, terra-cotta-colored walls, and plush carpeting.

HEATHMAN HOTEL RESTAURANT, Portland
1001 Southwest Broadway, at the Heathman Hotel
(503) 241-4100
Moderate to Expensive
Breakfast, Lunch, and Dinner Daily

Attentive service and skillfully prepared French dishes make for a memorable evening of fine dining at the Heathman Hotel Restaurant. Just about anything off the menu will be worth your while. Tempting entrées include halibut confit, served with olive oil–whipped potatoes, tomato compote, and julienne of snow peas; and the angel-hair pasta with Manila clams, forest mushrooms, and Asiago cheese. Breakfasts are as elegant and carefully created as the dinners.

A contemporary interior of teak and marble sets the stage at this lively, downtown restaurant. Black leather booths and white linen–covered tables fill the dining room, while an open kitchen at the back displays the chef's culinary feats. Glass sectional dividers and large windows have been etched with stylish art deco designs. One of the restaurant's most notable features (besides the food) is the artwork decorating the walls; Andy Warhol's

Endangered Species series brings color to the otherwise understated decor, and continues into the lobby of the adjacent hotel (see Hotel/Bed and Breakfast Kissing). A small bar area next to the restaurant is a cozy spot for an after-dinner drink. The only drawback here is the business conversations taking place around you.

HIGGINS RESTAURANT AND BAR, Portland
1239 Southwest Broadway
(503) 222-9070
Expensive
Lunch Monday–Friday; Dinner Daily

Looking for a special dinner spot after a busy day in the city? Look no further than Higgins. Unwind in the simple elegance of this modestly appointed downtown restaurant. The main dining area is tastefully adorned with purple and green swaths of fabric, decorative vases, and potted plants. Polished wood accents throughout lend the interior a glowing warmth. Two floors of dining rooms are filled with white linen–covered tables and booths, set beneath tiny triangular lamps. A lower, separate room is more intimate, with dark wood paneling and candlelight.

Seafood at Higgins is always fresh and skillfully prepared. We recommend the pan-fried Alaskan razor clams or the broiled pavé of Alaskan halibut served with olive and garlic mashed potatoes, basil vinaigrette, and vegetables. A honey-glazed loin of pork with grilled Walla Walla onions, ginger-plum chutney, and almond couscous is a wonderful alternative to fish, and desserts are superb.

IL FORNAIO, Portland
115 Northwest 22nd Avenue
(503) 248-9500
Moderate
Lunch and Dinner Daily

Although *Il Fornaio* means "the baker" in Italian, this upscale eatery is not your average bakery. Sure, it has a deli area, the *panetteria*, which offers a wide selection of fresh breads and pastries, sandwiches, salads, Italian coffees, and beverages; but it's better known for its dining accommodations. Il Fornaio is a fast-paced dining spot perfect for some romantic fun.

The pale yellow exterior matches the sunny disposition of the interior. Skylights and abundant windows allow sunlight to stream in unhindered, while clusters of dried flowers, garlic cloves, hanging baskets, and copper pots adorn the walls. To the right is a casual area peppered with little wooden tables for two. Maroon booths line a curved wall of windows, and next to the bustling kitchen area is an open bar hosting twin television sets. For more intimate interludes, you may wish to sit in the formal dining area to the left of the entrance. Here, black-and-white photographs have been enlarged to fill the red terra-cotta-tiled walls. White linens, elegant sconces, and views of lush greenery create a more refined setting in which to enjoy the zesty Italian cuisine.

Both lunch and dinner feature superb entrées ranging from pizza to pasta to poultry. Try the ravioli filled with lobster, ricotta cheese, and leeks, served with a savory lemon-cream sauce. For a creative change of taste and some lively style, celebrate at least one special occasion at Il Fornaio.

LONDON GRILL, Portland
309 Southwest Broadway, at The Benson Hotel
(503) 295-4110
http://www.holog.com/benson
Expensive
Breakfast, Lunch, and Dinner Monday-Saturday; Sunday Brunch

An elegant refuge from the city streets, the London Grill's plush dining room is a den of refinement. Crystal chandeliers, large floral arrangements, ornate wall sconces, and finely upholstered armchairs help set a formal, sophisticated mood. Visitors dine by candlelight beneath an arched ceiling, surrounded by lovely wood paneling. Although extremely tasteful and polished, this dining room is almost too formal to be considered cozy or intimate.

Interesting menu choices range from fresh ahi tuna, sautéed with garlic and ginger and served with a lemon Szechuan sauce, to London Grill steak Diane, prepared tableside with mushrooms, garlic, shallots, and a hint of brandy. We've heard it said that ostrich will soon be added to the menu, though we have to admit that we're somewhat hesitant to try it. At one time, *Glamour* magazine listed the London Grill as one of the six most romantic restaurants in the United States. We're not nearly that enthusiastic, as our lip rating implies, but you certainly should give it a try and compare notes.

MARRAKESH MOROCCAN RESTAURANT, Portland
1201 Northwest 21st Avenue
(503) 248-9442
Moderate
Dinner Tuesday–Sunday

Enter the hidden world of Marrakesh, where all outside distractions are quickly swallowed up in thick darkness, dissonant musical rhythms, and tantalizing aromas of Moroccan spices. Sexy and plush, every inch of the restaurant is draped with intricate fabrics of red and gold. Cushy couches line the perimeter of the two interconnecting dining rooms. Small, beanbag-like cushions are strewn around knee-high tables to provide low seating beneath lamps of colored glass. Overhead, large pieces of fabric have been swept up and gathered at the ceiling to form an intimate, tentlike ambience. You can order à la carte, but most prefer the five-course dinner that includes salad or lentil soup, an appetizer, your choice of entrée, plus mint tea and dessert. From the moment you step inside until your last bite of couscous, your senses will be stimulated and your passions aroused.

Romantic Note: Be sure to bring your sense of adventure when dining at Marrakesh, for Moroccan food is typically eaten with the fingers. (Don't worry; utensils are provided for less daring types.) Also, exotic belly dancers entertain visitors most Friday evenings.

PALEY'S PLACE, Portland
1204 Northwest 21st Avenue
(503) 243-2403
http://www.teleport.com/~paleys
Expensive
Dinner Tuesday–Saturday

Portland's Nob Hill is blessed with many lovingly renovated neighborhood shops and restaurants; each is more interesting than the last, and several are among the best Portland has to offer. Paley's Place lives up to this area's reputation with its dedication to fine cooking in a relaxed setting. The attention given to maintaining an attractive, unpretentious place is reflected in the modest interior filled with white linen–covered tables, hardwood floors, eclectic knickknacks, and pastel green walls.

The menu offers well-prepared and graciously served seasonal American cuisine. Begin your meal with a goat-cheese salad or the soup of the day. Dinner entrées range from pasta to duckling confit to braised halibut. Save room for the desserts here, for the soufflés will sweep you off your feet.

TABLE FOR TWO, Portland
Briggs and Crampton Caterers
1902 Northwest 24th Avenue
(503) 223-8690
Expensive

Reservations Required
Lunch Tuesday–Friday
Closed December

If it weren't nearly impossible to get a reservation, this would be a premier, four-lip lunch destination. Why are reservations so unattainable, you ask. The answer is simple: this restaurant, located in a Victorian home, has only one table, and it serves only one meal a day. That's right, lunch for just two people is served once a day, four days a week. (Reservations are available on a quarterly basis.) Don't think that the managers are slacking, though; they keep quite busy with the real specialty of the house: catering, which they do beautifully. The menu is always a surprise, but it is sure to include six savory Northwest-inspired courses made from the freshest local ingredients.

Butter-colored walls, low lighting, high ceilings, floral linens, and mismatched china create a cozy feeling in the dining room. The single table is adorned with a vase of fresh flowers and is set by a window looking out on a plant-filled sunporch. The whole experience feels more like dining in the intimacy of a friend's home.

WATERZOIES NORTHWEST, Portland
2574 Northwest Thurman Street
(503) 225-0641
Moderate to Expensive
Lunch Tuesday–Friday; Dinner Tuesday–Saturday; Sunday Brunch

This restaurant with the funny name is situated in a gray Victorian home at the edge of Portland's Nob Hill district. You can't miss it: it's the only house on the block with a bright purple door. Inside, three informal dining rooms provide a bright and airy atmosphere in which to enjoy a hardy entrée like bouillabaisse, snapper, porterhouse steak, or hunter's stew. Or simply make a meal out of fresh grilled portobello mushrooms topped with a demi-glace sauce. The restaurant is sparsely decorated, but colorful napkins and candle holders provide welcome splashes of color against the glare of super-white tablecloths and walls. In back of the restaurant is a small patio area framed by hedges. Weather permitting, more casual dining takes place outside beneath colorful sun umbrellas.

Oh, and about the funny name … *Waterzoies* refers to a Belgian fish stew. If your curiosity is piqued, you'll just have to order a bowl and try it for yourself.

ZEFIRO, Portland
500 Northwest 21st Avenue
(503) 226-3394

Expensive
Lunch Monday–Friday; Dinner Monday–Saturday

Several upscale eateries have recently emerged in Portland's Nob Hill neighborhood, but Zefiro is definitely the one everyone is talking about. Everything about this crowded and lively place is dramatic, from the bright saffron-colored walls to the innovative food. Slick black chairs encircle tables covered in starched white linens, while track lighting crisscrosses overhead like artificial tree branches. The bar area is more informal but no less sophisticated, with round copper tabletops and geometric wall designs. Throughout the restaurant, the striking color scheme is further enhanced by black and gold contemporary artwork on the walls. A mustard-colored velvet curtain provides the backdrop for a row of black leather booths where friends and lovers convene to laugh the night away.

Intriguing appetizers include seafood tapas and Asian ravioli. For dinner, don't miss the grilled Alaskan coho salmon, wrapped in grape leaves and served with grilled Japanese eggplant. And the saffron risotto with rock shrimp, tomatoes, and *gremolata* is as rich and delicious as it sounds. Finish off your meal with either the gelato *affogato*, milk chocolate ice cream drowned in espresso, or the nectarine tarte Tatin, served warm with a side of vanilla ice cream.

Outdoor Kissing

JAPANESE GARDENS, Portland
611 Southwest Kingston Avenue, in Washington Park
(503) 223-1321
$5 entrance fee
Open Daily

From downtown Portland, drive west on Burnside Street. Turn left onto Tichner Drive and then right onto Kingston. The gardens will be to your right in Washington Park.

Here is a prime spot for rest and reflection: five and a half acres of gardens, pagodas, statues, and carefully sculpted shrubs. Considered one of the most authentic Japanese gardens outside of Japan, these gardens remain relatively secluded from the rest of Washington Park because they are enclosed by a wall and located high on a hilltop, at a place where heaven and earth seem to meet. Enjoy the stark simplicity of the Sand and Stone Garden, or take in spectacular views of Mount Hood and downtown Portland from the deck of the Pavilion. Gravel pathways lead you to a koi-filled pond, where a weeping willow gracefully drapes her long arms into the tranquil water. This is nature's simplicity at its best.

MACLEAY PARK, Portland

Macleay Park is one of many entrances to Portland's Forest Park. You can enter Macleay off the Thurman Bridge near Franklin and 32nd Street Northwest, or at the end of Forest Park in northwest Portland off Cornell Road.

Macleay Park is really a park within a park, as well as a gorgeous example of nature's ability to thrive in the midst of a city. This lush green wilderness is strewn with 152 acres of surging creeks and hiking trails. Visit some of the wildlife viewing areas, or if you're really ambitious, follow the Wildwood Trail approximately 13 miles to **PITTOCK MANSION** (reviewed below). Macleay Park is just one of the almost limitless doorways into Forest Park. This immense park rests on the northeast face of the Tualatin Mountains and is the largest city wilderness in the United States. It affords so many kissing places that if you're not careful, you'll risk a lip or two.

Romantic Note: Another doorway into Forest Park is **COLLINS' SANCTUARY**, run by the Portland Audubon Society, 5151 Northwest Cornell Road, (503) 292-6855. This area of untamed landscape is not very well known even though its secluded beauty is near the heart of the city. Intriguing trails and paths lead you to private corners of this 67-acre wildlife area.

PITTOCK MANSION, Portland
3229 Northwest Pittock Drive
(503) 823-3623
$4.25 entrance fee
Open Daily

From downtown Portland, drive approximately two miles west on Burnside Street, following the signs to the mansion.

This stately home, replete with beveled glass windows and a red-tiled roof, is essentially a museum. A walking tour through the mansion reveals its regal interior, ornately appointed with embossed wallpapers, hardwood floors, velvet furniture, and Oriental rugs. There's a wood-paneled library, a grand old parlor, and an elegant dining room eternally set for formal occasions. Rising upward near the center of the house is a marble staircase with an intricately carved banister. The exterior of the mansion is just as lovely as the interior. Well-kept grounds beautifully frame a view of Portland, seemingly nestled in an abundance of distant trees. Stroll the grand walkways behind the mansion, and cherish the sunset in the shadows of fine architecture.

Romantic Note: Almost hidden from sight among the foliage surrounding Pittock Mansion, the **GATE LODGE RESTAURANT**, (503) 823-3627, is a delightful place for lunch or afternoon tea. The interior is nothing special, but this is a pleasant enough location to enjoy quiche or a hot crab sandwich after touring the mansion. Call for reservations.

RIVERPLACE, Portland

From downtown Portland, take Southwest Market Street east to the river, where it dead-ends at RiverPlace.

RiverPlace doesn't seem the least bit romantic to us. How can a half-mile-long arcade of condominiums, stores, and restaurants be intimate and endearing? But so many couples can be seen strolling hand in hand along this Willamette River development that we can't ignore its apparent romantic appeal. There are enough options here to offer something for everyone regardless of taste or budget.

RiverPlace begins with the **RIVERPLACE HOTEL** (see Hotel/Bed and Breakfast Kissing) at the northern tip of the walk. This is an exquisite European-style building with overpriced, hotel-like accommodations. We would, however, encourage you to try the distinctive, much-admired restaurant adjacent to the lobby, called **THE ESPLANADE** (see Restaurant Kissing). The lobby bar here is one of the most romantic in town.

As you continue walking, you'll have a view of the water on one side and a series of handsome condominiums on the other, along with a dozen or so boutiques and eateries. Farther down, you'll pass more restaurants with water views. The constant hum of traffic is not exactly tranquil but, romantic or not, RiverPlace is worth a stroll—and perhaps a stop somewhere along the way for a glass of wine, a cappuccino, or whatever else may catch your fancy.

SAUVIE ISLAND, Portland

Take Highway 30 north to the Sauvie Island Bridge, about 11 miles from downtown Portland.

When you feel the need for wide-open empty space, take a drive to this vast pastoral oasis. Sauvie Island is a popular Portland getaway, but its size ensures that you'll never feel crowded. You can enjoy relatively isolated beaches and numerous hiking trails through wetlands, pastures, oak woodlands, and spotty sections of coniferous forest. More stretches of sandy beach can be found on Oak Island, a much smaller land mass connected to the northeast end of Sauvie Island by a natural bridge.

Romantic Warning: Sauvie Island can be covered in smog when other parts of the area are clear. Check the horizon before setting out. Also, you should be aware that gasoline and drinking water are not available on the island.

TRYON CREEK STATE PARK, Portland

Head south from Portland on Interstate 5 to the Terwilliger exit. Travel two and a half miles due south on Southwest Terwilliger Boulevard to get to the park.

This park offers easy walks along gently rolling red-bark paths that cut through thick forestland. Don't expect wide vistas or places to sit in the sun; it is usually shady and moist here, not to mention a little muddy in the winter. Whether you walk for miles or just a few hundred feet, the two of you will feel safe, unhurried, and alone here.

WASHINGTON PARK ROSE
TEST GARDENS, Portland

From downtown Portland, drive west on Burnside Street. Turn left onto Tichner Drive and then right onto Kingston. The gardens will be to your left in Washington Park.

William Shakespeare once wrote, "Of all flowers methinks a rose is best." If you agree, then you'll surely be in heaven at the Washington Park Rose Test Gardens, where just about every shade of rose is on display. Breathe in the deliciously sweet fragrance as you stroll hand in hand along the brick pathways or pass beneath rose-covered arbors spanning stone stairways. The park itself has a supreme location, overlooking the city and the Willamette Valley. From the fragrant, endless rows of rosebushes to the unhindered view of Portland and the mountains beyond, this is pure embracing territory, acre after magnificent acre. It's a perfect place to come to enjoy quiet afternoons, brilliant sunsets, or twinkling evening lights.

Willamette Valley

A 30-minute drive southwest from Portland brings you into the Willamette Valley, home of the famous Oregon wineries. Embraced on the west by the gentle countenance of the Coastal Range and on the east by the glacial peaks of the Cascades, this area has much to treasure. You could call this region the Sonoma Valley of the Northwest, but that wouldn't do it justice. The Willamette Valley is far more stunning than Sonoma, and the wineries, although young, offer an acclaimed selection of wines any enophile would appreciate.

Numerous wineries are scattered throughout this picturesque area, each with its own attitude regarding the art of winemaking. Many of them feature vineyard-draped hillsides, a rathskeller-style tasting room, or a restful country setting. Still others are plain roadside buildings that make up for their lack of atmosphere with the excellence of their wines. Whether you choose to visit one or all, whether you choose to consume or not, your entire winery-hopping tour will be an intoxicating joy. And if you're pleased by what you taste, purchase a bottle or two for a toast to happy memories of a vintage visit.

To better acquaint yourselves with the myriad wineries in the region, contact the **OREGON WINEGROWERS' ASSOCIATION**, 1200 Northwest Front Avenue, Suite 400, Portland, OR 97209, (503) 228-8403, (800) 242-2363. Its yearly publication, *Discover Oregon Wineries*, is an excellent brochure that will help you with your tour. **GRAPE ESCAPE WINERY TOURS**, (503) 282-4262, provides transportation from Portland and tours of several wineries in the Willamette Valley. Appetizers, a gourmet sit-down lunch, and dessert are included in the tour price ($60 per person). Call for more details. If you'd like to explore the area by less conventional means, book a hot-air balloon flight with **VISTA BALLOON ADVENTURES, INC.**, (503) 625-7385, (800) 622-2309.

Outdoor Kissing

WINE TASTING, Willamette Valley

Pinot noir is the crowning glory of the Willamette Valley. Grapes mature as late as October in this region of mild winters and warm, dry summers. The following vineyards, listed alphabetically rather than by preference, are only a sampling of the more than 50 wineries in the area. Come find a favorite for yourselves.

ELK COVE VINEYARDS, 27751 Northwest Olson Road, Gaston, (503) 985-7760; open 11 A.M. to 5 P.M. daily. The octagon-shaped building offers breathtaking views from its attractive tasting room and banquet hall. Outside, picnic tables are set on a grassy knoll overlooking 60 acres of vineyards.

ERATH VINEYARDS, 9009 Northeast Worden Hill Road, Dundee, (503) 538-3318, (800) 539-9463; open 10:30 A.M. to 5:30 P.M. daily. Join other wine connoisseurs in this cedar-enhanced tasting room/gift store. A covered picnic area overlooks the vineyards and provides shelter in the sweltering heat of summer.

REX HILL VINEYARDS, 30835 North Highway 99W, Newberg, (503) 538-0666; open 11 A.M. to 5 P.M. daily. This vineyard has one of the most elegant tasting rooms around. The interior has been tastefully put together with peach and brick walls, dark wood antiques, Oriental rugs, and a massive stone fireplace. Follow a barrel-filled tunnel to a viewing area overlooking large vats of fermenting wine. Outside, its terraced picnic area is just as lovely, with colorful flowers, vine-draped arbors, and plenty of lawn space.

TUALATIN VINEYARDS, 10850 Northwest Seavey Road, Forest Grove, (503) 357-5005; open 10 A.M. to 4 P.M. on weekdays and noon to 5 P.M. on weekends. Sip to your hearts' content in the pine-interior tasting room, or sit outside in a picnic area shaded by cherry trees that overlooks the valley and vineyards.

Newberg

Hotel/Bed and Breakfast Kissing

SPRINGBROOK HAZELNUT FARM, Newberg
30295 North Highway 99W
(503) 538-4606, (800) 793-8528
Moderate to Expensive

For all its sophisticated comfort and gracious amenities, Springbrook Hazelnut Farm has retained a certain amount of country charm. The 8,000-square-foot, Craftsman-style farmhouse sits on 60 acres of prolific hazelnut trees, with expansive flower gardens, a large vegetable and herb garden, a swimming pool, and a tennis court out back. Next to the farmhouse is a peaceful pond often visited by local blue herons.

Inside, bright yellow walls and polished hardwood floors adorn the elaborate entry hall, and a glass-enclosed sunporch is filled with wicker furniture and hanging plants. Wide hallways lead guests to their antique-filled rooms. Although artistically adorned, all four rooms in the main house share bathrooms, and traffic noise from the nearby highway can be distracting. A full country breakfast is served on antique china in the fruitwood-paneled dining room. Awake to the aroma of rhubarb muffins, crêpes with asparagus, or chicken and apple sausage. As you might have guessed, creative hazelnut dishes are the house specialty.

The completely private Carriage House sits out back behind the main house. You'll want to move into this fully functional, apartment-like hideaway. Its interior is bright but soothing, with hardwood and painted-wood floors and an abundance of windows. There's even a claw-foot tub in the bathroom. The lovely open kitchen is equipped with modern appliances, pretty bone china, and a full breakfast stocked in the refrigerator, including homemade jams, muffins, eggs, pancake batter, and sausages for you to whip up at your own convenience. If you are touring the wine country, the delightfully independent Carriage House is a promising place to set up temporary housekeeping.

Restaurant Kissing

THE COFFEE COTTAGE, Newberg
808 East Hancock Street
(503) 538-5126
Inexpensive
Lunch, Dessert, and Coffee Daily

Romance might not be the primary reason to stop here, but not many self-respecting Northwesterners can go very long without a cup of coffee, preferably served up as a latte, cappuccino, or mocha. This region has literally hundreds of places to imbibe this dark, aromatic liquid, in some of the most out-of-the-way locations you can imagine. The Coffee Cottage is a very affectionate spot to take an unhurried coffee break and look for a good read in the bookshop. Order a cup of freshly roasted coffee at the espresso bar, and then visit the in-house bakery for a muffin or two. Wood tables are arranged on hardwood floors around the shop's perimeter, but you might opt to sit on the outdoor garden patio. You're right next to the highway, so it can be noisy at times, but you can still enjoy a warm day, iced lattes, and a light lunch.

Romantic Note: The Coffee Cottage opens as early as 6:30 A.M. most days for those who need to jump-start their mornings with a cup of joe.

Dundee

Restaurant Kissing

RED HILLS PROVINCIAL DINING, Dundee
276 Highway 99W
(503) 538-8224
Moderate
Lunch Tuesday–Friday; Dinner Tuesday–Sunday

We had no idea that fine dining even existed in the small town of Dundee—that is, until we found the Red Hills. An appetizer of Montrachet (a mild cheese with a texture resembling feta) wrapped in a grape leaf and served with roasted garlic is heavenly. The grilled salmon with mango salsa enhanced by cilantro, mint, and sweet onion is perfectly prepared, and the chicken quarter braised in pinot noir, onion, mushrooms, and grapes is a dish we'll be trying to re-create for a long time. If you happen by at lunchtime, sink your teeth into a focaccia sandwich piled high with mozzarella, cucumber, lettuce, tomato, onions, and a healthy dose of pesto. An extensive wine list provides the finishing touch to any meal.

The two provincial dining rooms are set on the main floor of this renovated Craftsman-style home. Each one holds a mere ten tables and is simply adorned with a mismatched assortment of china plates. The worn hardwood floors and dark woodworking are rather ordinary, and the partially lace-curtained windows don't conceal the busy highway right outside. Still, the service is efficient and friendly, and the food is a connoisseur's delight.

TINA'S, Dundee
760 Highway 99W
(503) 538-8880
Expensive
Lunch Tuesday–Friday; Dinner Daily

This small, homegrown restaurant is gaining a considerable reputation in the Newberg/Dundee area. Everyone is talking about the food, and it *is* pretty incredible. We recommend the appetizer of warm chevre with hazelnuts and roasted garlic. An ever-changing menu sports mouthwatering entrées like grilled rabbit with honey mustard and garlic or grilled leg of lamb with pinot noir sauce. You're sure to fall in love with the peach and brown-butter torte for dessert, and who can possibly resist homemade ice cream? You certainly won't walk away hungry from this place.

Why the low lip rating, you ask? Well, let's just say that the ambience leaves a lot to the imagination, even for us romantics. First, the location isn't the best; the entrance is merely steps away from noisy Highway 99, although the dining room is relatively quiet once you get inside. Second, worn carpeting, conspicuous baseboard heaters, and distractingly eclectic artwork are not exactly mood-inspiring. Fortunately, the ten or so tables are nicely adorned with white tablecloths, flowers, and glowing candles. Finally, there's the service: it's slow. It's so slow that you might have to peek your head into the kitchen to announce your arrival. Once seated, you'll find that a single blackboard with the menu listed on it is passed from table to table. While this is a charming idea, it means you must wait to see the menu until others around you have made up their minds. Overall, Tina's would be a real find if only the ambience were as impressive as the food.

Dayton

Hotel/Bed and Breakfast Kissing

**WINE COUNTRY FARM BED AND
BREAKFAST AND CELLARS, Dayton**
6855 Breyman Orchards Road
(503) 864-3446, (800) 261-3446
Inexpensive
Minimum stay requirement on holiday weekends

Spend some time walking around the 13-acre property, or stroll through the stables where the Arabian horses are kept. Relax on the porch of this renovated 1910 stucco farmhouse and take in the all-encompassing view of the valley, mountains, and vineyards. With such magnificent scenery all around, it's understandable that the inside of this bed and breakfast pales in comparison to the outside. Outdated furnishings and abundant knickknacks are a constant theme throughout; fortunately, each of the common rooms is equipped with large windows, perfect for viewing the spectacular scenery from just about every part of the house. Mornings bring a generous breakfast served in the dining room on the main floor. From this vantage point, you can savor the view along with the food.

All six rooms in the main house are small but cozy, with antique furnishings and private baths. Some share the wondrous view, one has a wood-burning fireplace, and all are comfortable, with quilts or country floral bedspreads. A recently built tasting room on the premises is a lovely addition. Located next door to the farmhouse, it is available for private parties or drop-in guests. Inside, wrought-iron chairs are clustered around tables draped with burgundy and ivory linens, and an entire wall of unfinished wood is a charming touch. And the views are just as incredible from here as from the rest of the property. On the second floor of the wine-tasting building is a two-room Honeymoon Suite (Expensive). It is modestly furnished and decorated in shades of scarlet and white. A four-poster canopy bed entwined with wispy fabric is complemented by leafy green vines painted along the ceiling. This lodging isn't fancy or refined, but it is a secluded spot where civilization seems a million miles away.

Romantic Option: The Arabian horses aren't just for show. Buggy rides and country picnics can be arranged; just ask the innkeeper for details.

McMinnville

McMinnville is the largest city in Yamhill County, but it's hardly a sprawling metropolis. Its quaint downtown area has a definite hometown feel to it that's rather charming. With Highway 99W as its backbone, the town spreads outward into residential areas until it eventually fades into lonely farmland.

Hotel/Bed and Breakfast Kissing

STEIGER HAUS, McMinnville
360 Wilson Street
(503) 472-0821, (503) 472-0238
Inexpensive to Moderate

Steiger Haus looks as if it belongs in the Swiss Alps instead of in the residential neighborhood where it is located. Nonetheless, we are glad this chalet-style bed and breakfast is here in McMinnville—it's a much more easily accessible location than Switzerland, and you won't need a translator.

Rich colors, plants, and natural wood throughout the house create a warm atmosphere, while bay windows and skylights allow sunlight to flood in. Colorful couches and chairs are situated around a brick fireplace in the contemporary living room; a second, more modest sitting area is shared by guests staying in the upper-level rooms. All five guest rooms have private baths, but our favorites are the Fireside and Treetop Suites. The Fireside Suite feels somewhat tucked away from the other rooms and has a private deck and a wood-burning fireplace. The Treetop Suite, as its name suggests, is on the top floor. It is appointed with a Quaker-style pine bed, bay windows overlooking the grassy yard and healthy gardens below, and a large soaking tub set beneath a skylight in the bathroom. In the morning, make your way to the wood-accented kitchen area. Friendly conversation is sure to accompany a delicious breakfast of raisin-bran muffins, fresh fruit, and a hot entrée such as quiche or crêpes. The Alps were never this homey!

YOUNGBERG HILL VINEYARD
BED AND BREAKFAST, McMinnville
10660 Youngberg Hill Road
(503) 472-2727
http://www.youngberghill.com
Expensive
Recommended Wedding Site

We can't think of a better base for touring Oregon's wine country than this grand farmhouse set on a hilltop surrounded by vineyards and pristine farmland. A winding gravel road brings you up to an illustrious view of the valley, mountains, and rolling hills. And just so you can soak up as much view as possible, the entire house is surrounded by wide decks.

The determined innkeepers have managed to blend the charm of a country bed and breakfast with the modern comforts of an inn. Each of the five comfortable rooms is pleasantly private, and the 50-acre property is large enough to keep you from feeling that you're constantly bumping into other guests. Two of the rooms have brick fireplaces, one has a cathedral ceiling, and all have down comforters and antique-style oak furnishings. What is outstanding is their commanding view of the area.

A full breakfast here might include eggs Benedict with fresh fruit and homemade muffins, served at one large table in the breakfast room. Watching the sun rise behind Mount Hood and Mount Jefferson while enjoying this hearty morning meal should give your day a beautiful start.

Restaurant Kissing

CAFÉ AZUL, McMinnville
313 Third Street
(503) 435-1234
Inexpensive
Dinner Tuesday–Saturday

OK, so it's not the most romantic place we've ever dined, but this colorful restaurant in downtown McMinnville is a good place for a casual date on those jeans-and-T-shirt sort of days. Café Azul (the Blue Cafe) isn't blue at all; in fact, it's a very cheery shade of yellow. Decorating the walls is an odd splattering of Mexican artwork, including dishes, rugs, woven baskets, and statues. Tiny lights and a haphazard array of colorful animal figurines adorn the front windows. Booths coupled with wood tables fill the restaurant, but the best spots are the two curved booths at the front. Toward the back you can hear a woman patting tortillas into shape. If the decor doesn't lift your spirits, the food certainly will.

Café Azul serves up generous portions of authentic dishes from southern Mexico. The menu includes everything from tacos to tostadas to huevos rancheros. If you can figure out how to pronounce it, we recommend ordering the *tlacoyos*: masa rounds filled with pork and topped with cheese and salsa. And you can't leave without sampling the traditional Mexican dessert called *pavé*, a flourless, bittersweet chocolate cake covered with raspberry sauce. After your meal, venture to the small deli/espresso area in back, where you can pick up a latte to go.

NICK'S ITALIAN CAFE, McMinnville
521 East Third Street
(503) 434-4471
Moderate
Dinner Tuesday–Sunday

As the name suggests, Nick's Italian Cafe is a casual place, but a meal here (typically lasting two and a half hours) is a serious dining experience. There is a different fixed menu every night, but dinner is always a five-course Italian extravaganza that features creatively prepared homemade pastas, soup, fresh-from-the-oven bread, salad, and a garlic-laced entrée. Although it is not included in the fixed menu, dessert is definitely worth saving room for.

Nick's has two dining rooms; the one in back has exposed brick walls, but the most romantic tables are the private little wood booths in the front dining room. A single candle tops every table, and low lighting makes the wood interior glow.

THIRD STREET GRILL, McMinnville
729 East Third Street
(503) 435-1745
Expensive
Dinner Monday–Saturday

Do you believe in love at first bite? We do, now that we've experienced a meal at the Third Street Grill. Begin your evening with an appetizer of wild mushrooms and Brie baked in a puff pastry on roasted garlic cream. Entrées are prepared with the freshest seasonal ingredients and explode with intricate flavors. We recommend the hazelnut-crusted halibut with citrus butter and wild rice pilaf, and the seared Yamhill pork tenderloin stuffed with sun-dried cherries and a sweet bourbon sauce. Top it all off with profiteroles for dessert. A meal this good will make a believer out of you.

Located next to the old train station, this 100-year-old house is neatly trimmed with flower boxes and a white picket fence. Its gray exterior only hints at the subtle refinement inside. Taupe walls, cherry-wood accents, and thick gray carpet conspire to set the mood in the three dining rooms on the main floor. Linen-draped tables are topped with fresh flowers and candles, and encircled by cushioned chairs. Burgundy and floral curtains frame the windows. A similar dining room upstairs, fronted by a lovely sitting room, is reserved for private parties and overflow. In good weather, more informal dining is available outside on the patio, though the view isn't much to rave about.

"*You are always new. The last
of your kisses was ever the sweetest…*"

John Keats

Oregon Coast

It is probably safe to say that no other state has a span of highway quite like Highway 101 in the state of Oregon. This winding coastal highway runs the length of the state, and almost every mile is filled with awe-inspiring scenery that will literally take your breath away. Thank goodness there are many turnoffs, parks, trails, coves, inlets, and ravines where you can stop and drink in the view at your own leisurely pace.

Constant, temperamental mood swings in the weather enhance the boundless drama of this area. At times the mixture of fog and sea mist creates a diffuse screen through which the world appears like an apparition. Other moments bring a haunting quiet as a tempest brews on the horizon, where ocean and sky converge. Yet even on the calmest summer days, the unbridled energy and the siren song of the waves unleashing their power against beaches, headlands, and haystack rocks have a spellbinding impact. Time shared on the Oregon coast can rekindle your relationship with the world—and with each other.

Not only is the scenery stupendous, but the two of you can also indulge in a multitude of activities here, such as hiking through coastal rain forest, beachcombing, hunting for agates, clamming, exploring tide pools, kite flying, and whale watching. Until you've attempted each of these, you haven't truly experienced the Oregon coast.

After whetting your appetite with all these heartfelt images, we must warn you about one major drawback: summers and most weekends can be maddeningly crowded, with traffic jams reminiscent of a big city and beaches overflowing with people instead of sea gulls and crustaceans. All of the places we recommend take the concept of solitude and seclusion quite seriously, but there is only so much they can do. It is essential that you keep the popularity of the area in mind when planning your getaway. This way you have a better chance of getting away from it all instead of finding it all there when you arrive.

For information on **OREGON COAST PARKS AND RECREATION AREAS,** call (503) 378-6305. For up-to-the-minute camping information from March through Labor Day, call (800) 452-5687 or (503) 731-3411. Be sure to bring along proper beach attire and gear: bathing suits in the summer, jeans and warm sweaters all year long (just in case—after all, this is the Northwest), as well as plenty of towels, a blanket or two, and a bucket with shovel for clamming or agate hunting. Hundreds of secluded, totally accessible beaches line the road; be prepared so that when the mood strikes to splash in the surf or walk hand in hand through the sand, there won't be anything stopping you.

Romantic Warning: Although this might sound like an exaggeration, it isn't: there is an almost interminable procession of motels bordering the coast and abutting Highway 101. Most of these are appropriately labeled "motel," but some refer to their facilities as "inns," "cottages," or "resorts." Several of them do have alluring views, real fireplaces, and efficient kitchens, but they are still motels—assuredly OK places to stay, but by the standards of this book not the least bit romantic. If you would like a list of these places for the entire state (and you might if you will be traveling with children and/or pets), contact the **OREGON LODGING ASSOCIATION**, 12724 Southeast Stark Street, Portland, OR 97233, (503) 255-5135, and ask for their concise guide, *Where To Stay In Oregon.*

Astoria

Occupying a peninsula near the mouth of the swelling Columbia River, Astoria became well known when John Jacob Astor's fur traders established a trading post here in 1811. During the early 1800s, Astoria operated as a port for the North West Company and the Hudson's Bay Company, and eventually grew into the bustling commercial port it remains today. Unfortunately for romantics, an industrial atmosphere permeates most of the town, overshadowing even the lovely Victorian buildings clustered on its hillsides.

Romantic Note: We were hard-pressed to find a restaurant in Astoria that would please both the palate and the heart. You may want to fill up on breakfast and then head south down the coast for more amorous dining options.

Hotel/Bed and Breakfast Kissing

FRANKLIN STREET STATION
BED AND BREAKFAST INN, Astoria
1140 Franklin Street
(503) 325-4314, (800) 448-1098
Inexpensive to Moderate

Although the Franklin Street Station isn't situated in the most attractive of neighborhoods (mortuaries and tired apartment buildings are hardly conducive to romance), the interior of this 1900 Victorian home will surely set the mood for encounters of the heart. A stately grandfather clock and an old-fashioned settee, among other lovely antiques, fill the dining room, and the adjacent breakfast room is a sunny place to begin your day over Belgium waffles or spinach quiche.

All five guest rooms are cheerfully decorated in pastel colors with pretty floral wallpapers. Each room has a different combination of amenities, including partial river views, private mini-decks, wet bars, claw-foot tubs, and charming headboards. A queen-size bed with a beautiful woven canopy is the centerpiece of the Lewis and Clark Room on the main floor, while the Astor Suite upstairs has a trundle bed (geared more for children) and frilly white drapes. The best room in the house is in the attic, accessible via a private staircase. Named the Captain's Quarters, this room has its own fireplace, TV/VCR, wet bar, tiny sitting area, and partial glimpses of the Columbia River. Amorous extras like satin sheets and breakfast in bed are available for all guests at an additional charge.

ROSEBRIAR HOTEL, Astoria
636 14th Street
(503) 325-7427, (800) 487-0224
Inexpensive to Moderate

Astoria's oldest established bed and breakfast sits on a hillside overlooking the town center. Recognized as a historic landmark, this magnificent 1902 neoclassical home has been beautifully restored to retain much of its charm while offering modern-day comfort. The stately white building rises above a landscaped garden, and a small veranda fronts the columned entrance. Inside you'll find an old-fashioned front desk and a cozy parlor with red fir paneling, overstuffed floral couches, and a fireplace with a handsome wooden mantel.

A room in the 1885 carriage house offers the most privacy, as well as a kitchenette, fireplace, soaking tub, and several stained glass windows. Upstairs in the main building, ten more guest rooms are handsomely decorated with sage walls, mahogany furnishings, and elegant moldings. Generous windows grant sunlit views of the Columbia River that are only slightly obstructed by the town below. Several of the larger rooms have fireplaces and soaking tubs, as well as couches and chairs covered in plush burgundy and refined beige. However, after serving as a convent for 20 years, the Rosebriar could use some warming up; the rooms are a bit too spartan and sterile. In the morning, seductive aromas will lure you to the dining area, where you can feast upon such goodies as Finnish pancakes, baked pears, or salmon frittata.

Gearhart

What distinguishes the exclusive seaside town of Gearhart from all the other communities hugging this end of the Oregon coast? We think it's the picture-perfect Northwest-style homes lining the quiet residential streets and the expansive beaches that go on for miles, where you can literally drive onto the sand and find your own secluded stretch of heaven. (And it is heaven.) Northwesterners want to keep this area a secret. Well, it still is, because we won't tell anybody, right?

Romantic Note: Romantic accommodations are scarce in the town of Gearhart, so look for lodgings in nearby Seaside instead. Gearhart is really more for day trips to the beach than for overnight getaways.

Restaurant Kissing

OCEANSIDE RESTAURANT, Gearhart
1200 North Marion Drive
(503) 738-7789
Moderate
Call for seasonal hours.

In this town of breathtaking beaches and fabulous seaside homes, the only place that even vaguely resembles a tourist attraction is the sprawling condominium vacation complex directly behind the weather-worn Oceanside Restaurant. Fortunately, once you enter the restaurant you won't be aware of anything except the exhilarating beach panorama. The window-enclosed dining room—complete with brick-faced walls, oversized chandeliers, and a vaulted cedar-beamed ceiling—faces windswept sand dunes and the sparkling Pacific Ocean in the distance. What a view! And our dinners, fresh salmon and the angel hair pasta with fresh crab and shrimp in a rich pesto sauce, were served with a wonderful sunset on the side.

PACIFIC WAY BAKERY AND CAFE, Gearhart
601 Pacific Way
(503) 738-0245
Inexpensive to Moderate
Call for seasonal hours.

If you want to taste absolutely sensational baked goods, this unassuming, rustic cafe is the place to order hot espresso and fresh cinnamon rolls for two. The cheerful yellow and gray exterior is set off by a green-striped awning. Inside cranberry-colored tables with hunter green chairs surround a wood-burning fireplace. An eclectic array of old-fashioned knickknacks and photographs decorates the walls, and a small brick courtyard offers outdoor seating overlooking quiet Cottage Street. In spite of the laid-back nature of the staff, everything is immaculate and nicely presented. Lunch is superior, with generous sandwiches, delicious soups, fresh breads, and exact seasonings. All this, and the expansive empty beaches of Gearhart only a stone's throw away.

Seaside

At first glance there is almost nothing romantic about Seaside, a town where much of the ocean has been obscured by hyperactive motel developers with no sensitivity to the landscape. In the summer, families flock here by the thousands to frequent the arcades, mini-malls, and popular beachfront. Fortunately, you can still find plenty of space to breathe and kiss on the vast beaches at the north and south ends of town. In the off-season you might even find yourself alone on Seaside's famous Prom, a mile-and-a-half long cement trail that meanders along the beachfront, near the thundering surf. You'll also find plenty of romantic inspiration at many of the newer properties that have sprouted up over the past few years. Stay away from the video arcades and the kid-lined streets of the town center and you may actually find Seaside an enchanting locale, especially when school is in session and there is nary a child in sight.

Romantic Warning: Seaside's restaurants leave much to be desired, and we strongly recommend that you head just a little farther south to Cannon Beach for a truly romantic repast. Nevertheless, if you just don't feel like getting in your car, we can recommend one affectionate spot in the heart of town (see Restaurant Kissing).

Hotel/Bed and Breakfast Kissing

BEACHWOOD BED AND BREAKFAST, Seaside
671 Beach Drive
(503) 738-9585
Inexpensive
Minimum stay requirement on weekends
Call for seasonal closures.

Enveloped by whispering pines and well-kept gardens, Beachwood feels surprisingly remote and quiet despite its proximity to the center of town. The only sound you'll hear is the rumbling ocean, one block away. When the innkeepers renovated this gabled Craftsman-style home, they paid attention to all the right details. Hunter green carpeting throughout the rambling home contrasts with crisp, whitewashed walls. A fire warms the stately living room, which is filled with comfortable antiques and intriguing memorabilia. (Ask the friendly innkeepers to fill you in on the home's romantic history; they'll be more than happy to oblige.)

Romantic possibilities abound in the four guest rooms, appointed with attractive antiques, leaded glass windows, lace curtains, and country-style fabrics. Sunshine streams through two walls of windows in the Astor Room, where you can enjoy the sights and sounds of the nearby ocean from a cozy, cushioned window seat big enough for two. Windows surround three sides of the newly added Veness Suite, which has a TV and VCR, cheerful decor, and a private bath. The smaller Lewis and Clark Room has a private detached bath, a comfy queen-size bed covered with a beautiful handcrafted patchwork quilt, and interesting wood detailing. The premier Holladay Suite features a bounty of pillows piled on a four-poster canopy bed, a gas-burning brick fireplace, a TV and VCR, a private sitting room, and (best of all) a gorgeous black-and-white-tiled two-person spa tub.

You certainly won't go hungry here. Bowls of chocolate and other candies are scattered throughout the inn and much too tempting to resist (especially around the holidays). Breakfast is served in the formal dining room, and the menu is outstanding. Pumpkin pancakes, Spanish-style eggs served with fresh salsa, and French toast stuffed with cream cheese are a few of the entrées you may find upon awakening.

FOUR WINDS MOTEL, Seaside
820 North Promenade
(503) 738-9524, (800) 818-9524
http://www.ohwy.com/or/f/fourwind.htm
Inexpensive to Moderate
Minimum stay requirement on weekends

Calling the Four Winds a motel doesn't do this Victorian-style building justice. In reality, there is very little here that is reminiscent of a motel. Compared to the economical and somewhat rundown properties in the surrounding neighborhood at the north end of Seaside (far from the crowds), this property gleams like a diamond in the rough. Many of the rooms here have ringside views of the expansive grassy sand dunes that stretch to the water's edge. Here, sea gulls' cries rise above the roar of the surf and the nearby promenade invites you to take a sunset stroll or early-morning bike ride.

In addition to stellar views in 12 of the units, each of the 18 rooms features a fireplace, wet bar, and private deck or porch. Whitewashed wood furnishings and fresh flowers give the otherwise standard interiors an upscale feel.

GILBERT INN, Seaside
341 Beach Drive
(503) 738-9770, (800) 410-9770
http://www.abba.com
Inexpensive
Minimum stay requirement on weekends and holidays
Call for seasonal closures.

A white picket fence surrounds this picturesque yellow Victorian, one block from Seaside's popular beachfront. In the height of summer, when throngs of tourists are a force to be reckoned with, the inn's location on a corner intersection in the heart of town can feel like a disadvantage—until you step inside, that is. Once you've checked in, you'll find that Seaside's crowds simply fade into oblivion. Tongue-and-groove fir paneling lends rustic elegance to the spacious common areas, where comfy, overstuffed sofas hug a brick hearth.

Recent renovations have ensured that even the smallest of the inn's ten guest rooms have plenty of comfort and charm. Fluffy down comforters and handfuls of pillows embellish antique beds in every room. Fir paneling gives homespun appeal to rooms in the older wing, where we discovered our favorite room of all: the Turret Room. A circular wall of windows allows ample sunlight in this cozy room, which is furnished with an inviting four-poster cherry-wood bed. The newer wing contains a series of brightly done suites with wicker furniture, handsome wood armoires, antique trunks, country fabrics, and private bathrooms. If seclusion is a priority, ask about the inn's four next-door units, hidden behind a lattice fence. Full kitchens, hand-hewn fir beds, antiques, and affectionate details distinguish these private hideaways.

Cinnamon-raspberry French toast or blueberry pancakes might be featured in the generous morning meal, which is served at individual white wrought-iron tables tucked in a lovely pink breakfast nook that you enter through French doors.

RIVERSIDE INN, Seaside

430 South Holladay
(503) 738-8254, (800) 826-6151
Inexpensive
Minimum stay requirement on holidays

Before we tell you why this is one of our favorite kissing bargains on the coast, several romantic warnings are in order. First, this historic 1907 inn is harbored on one of Seaside's busiest thoroughfares. Second, the stores and rundown houses in the surrounding neighborhood leave much to be desired.

Third, most of the rooms here are much too small and homey for kissing comfort. That's the bad news. Here's the good news: the Riverview Annex. Set behind the main building, the Annex overlooks the peaceful Necanicum River. The four suites in this building have deliciously thick down duvets and sliding glass doors that open onto semiprivate decks with beautiful, and surprisingly quiet, river views (just past the parking lot). Vaulted ceilings in the two upstairs suites are especially enticing, although impressive wood detailing and brightly tiled kitchens give every unit stylish charm. For close-up views of the river, seek out the nearby communal deck perched at the edge of the river—it's a great place to catch up on those long discussions you've been too busy to make time for.

You don't have to worry about any interruptions in the morning. A hearty complimentary breakfast that changes daily is included with your stay and can be delivered directly to the privacy of your room.

SEA SIDE INN, Seaside
581 South Promenade
(503) 738-6403, (800) 772-7766
Inexpensive to Moderate

One of Seaside's celebrated landmarks is the paved promenade that borders the enormous sandy beach that stretches alongside the ever-changing Pacific Ocean. As exceptional as this sounds, the beachfront is marred by a series of rather bland, timeworn motels near the town's center. Nevertheless, in the midst of this aesthetic lapse, we found a splendid, recently constructed country inn that pampers guests who have a flair for the unusual. Bird's-eye views of the sprawling dunes and crashing surf appear to be within arm's reach of the inn's eclectic lobby, engagingly appointed with vividly colored modern art and a hodgepodge of trinkets, including a basket of wind-up water toys. Guests can relax with a glass of wine or a micro-brew in this comfortable ocean-view setting, which also doubles as a sometimes noisy local bar.

Eccentricities continue throughout the inn; a golf ball collection and tacky stuffed animals are showcased in the hallways, and there's much, much more. The Logo Golf Ball Room features a miniature putting green; in the Rock 'n' Roll Room you can sleep in a bed made from a '59 Oldsmobile. Our three favorite suites are less peculiar and more romantic. In the Northwest Timber Room, cathedral ceilings soar above an immense four-poster king-size log bed accented with swags of twisted green fabric. An open staircase climbs to a loft bathroom, where you'll find the best surprise of all: a green-tiled soaking tub and a sexy glass-enclosed shower. A gas fireplace and full-on ocean views complete this picture-perfect setting. Next door, the Clocktower Room features similar luxuries: a cathedral ceiling, fantastic ocean view, spa tub, and gas fireplace. A large round bed distinguishes this room from its neighbor. Last but not least is the Bubble Room—the brightest room in the house and probably our favorite. Here, colorful fish accent a blue-tiled spa tub and glass-enclosed shower cozied in the corner; this mini-suite also has spectacular ocean views.

A full, bountiful breakfast is served in the large common room, made remarkably inviting by floor-to-ceiling windows and a beachstone fireplace.

Romantic Option: Depending on reservations and the season, you can enjoy a four-course prix fixe dinner at the Sea Side Inn. If you're lucky enough to find the chef in, you will be treated to a country-fresh meal that is flavorful and rich (maybe even a little too rich). The fresh salmon, stuffed trout, and the fresh shrimp are all delicious.

Restaurant Kissing

VISTA SEA CAFE, Seaside
150 Broadway
(503) 738-8108
Inexpensive
Call for seasonal hours.

Renowned for its gourmet pizza, the Vista Sea Cafe inhabits a bright yellow turn-of-the-century storefront several blocks from the beach. Hungry diners congregate in cushioned booths in the airy dining room, which features yellow walls, hardwood floors, potted ferns, and lacy white curtains that shield patrons from the crowds passing by outside. Design the pizza of your dreams with a vast selection of gourmet toppings and after one bite you'll understand why this charming cafe has become so famous.

Cannon Beach

As you approach Cannon Beach, you may not believe your eyes. The cliffs and ocean here seem to stretch out to infinity, and massive rock outcroppings dot the shoreline. More than seven miles of firm sand and rolling waves beckon dreamers and lovers to roll up their jeans, hold hands, and stroll at the edge of the churning surf. At low tide you can stand at the base of a free-standing monolith called Haystack Rock, the third-largest of its kind in the world and a true natural wonder, and feel humbled by its towering dimensions.

Evenings here provide another chance to appreciate the glory of the sea and the sky. The Oregon coast has been nicknamed the "Sunset Empire" for good reason. As the sun begins to settle into the ocean, brilliant colors radiate from the horizon, filling the sky like a golden aurora borealis. At first the light penetrates the clouds as a pale lavender-blue haze, transforming suddenly into an intense yellow-amber, and culminating in a blazing red that seems to set the sky on fire. Then, as dusk finalizes its entrance, the clouds fade to steely blue-gray and the sky changes its countenance to cobalt blue and then to indigo. Slowly the moon takes a central place in the evening heavens, and its platinum rays seem to dance on the surface of the water. When the weather cooperates, this performance occurs nightly at Cannon Beach and along the entire Oregon coastline.

Of course, there is more to Cannon Beach than gorgeous beachfront. Boutiques, gift shops, and restaurants entice tourists into the charming weathered storefronts than run the length of the town, and local artists display their handiwork in working studios and impressive galleries. We recommend stopping at **ICEFIRE GLASSWORKS**, 116 East Gower Street, (503) 436-2359, to watch the talented glassblowers perform artistic miracles.

Romantic Warning: On warm summer days, Cannon Beach can be overwhelmed by tourists, traffic, and congestion that seem out of place in such a serene, tranquil setting. Farther south along the coast, the quiet towns of Manzanita and Oceanside (both reviewed elsewhere in this chapter) are excellent alternatives to Cannon Beach on crowded summer weekends.

Hotel/Bed and Breakfast Kissing

ARGONAUTA INN, Cannon Beach
188 West Second Street
(503) 436-2601, (800) 822-2468
Moderate to Unbelievably Expensive
Minimum stay requirement seasonally

While some of the appointments at the Argonauta are more second-hand than homey, its beachfront location makes it well worth a stopover. Poised at the ocean's edge, this weathered gray seaside complex comprises three small apartments and two homes. Though the smaller units lack ocean views, they are imaginatively decorated and cozy, boasting plush linens and wood-burning fireplaces. Two even have fully equipped kitchenettes. Similar amenities are featured in the spacious three-bedroom Beach House, which can actually accomodate up to ten people and is geared more toward families. Whether you bring along the kids, another romantically inclined couple, or keep the space all to yourselves, you'll be mesmerized by the panoramic ocean views showcased on the glass-enclosed sundeck. You can also appreciate the convenience of a full kitchen, the romance of a stone fireplace, and the seclusion of a private deck and lawn. In the neighboring two-story Town House with two bedrooms, glass doors slide open to an ocean-view deck. Other comforts include fluffy down comforters, a stone fireplace, a full kitchen, and an eclectic assortment of antiques.

CANNON BEACH HOTEL
AND RESTAURANT, Cannon Beach
1116 South Hemlock
(503) 436-1392
Inexpensive to Moderate
Minimum stay requirement seasonally

If only the Cannon Beach Hotel were situated directly on the beach, it would be a rare find; instead it is located on busy Hemlock Street, and as a result can get quite noisy. This turn-of-the-century building was once a boardinghouse for loggers, but it has been renovated, at least on the inside, to resemble a European-style hotel. Outside, the exterior retains a Northwest feel with weathered shingles, green awnings and shutters, and striking white trim. Inside, the formal yet inviting lobby is done up with taupe walls, pine accents, and sage chairs that face a marble fireplace.

All nine rooms are quite handsome, with polished wood furnishings, Italian duvets, hunter green and burgundy color schemes, and original local artwork. Some of the more expensive rooms have couches, small dining tables, gas fireplaces, king-size beds, and single-person spa tubs. (Despite all this classic elegance, the European formality and somewhat sparse decor may seem a bit too sterile for a true Northwestern experience.) Each morning, freshly baked scones and seasonal fruit are delivered to your room in a basket and left for you to savor in privacy.

Romantic Suggestion: Adjacent to the Cannon Beach Hotel is a European-style cafe called **JP'S AT CANNON BEACH**, (503) 436-0908 (Moderate). Sit outside or at one of the mahogany tables in the sunny bistro area, or snag a couple of bar stools near the counter. Wherever you end up sitting, this is a wonderful spot for a casual lunch or dinner.

CANNON BEACH VACATION
RENTAL HOMES, Cannon Beach
(503) 436-2021
Very Inexpensive to Unbelievably Expensive; No Credit Cards
Minimum stay requirement

If privacy is as important to you as being near the ocean, these are the people to talk to. Seclusion is the specialty of this property management company, and they will be more than happy to set you up with the private home of your dreams—at least for a while. The 16 homes in their rental pool range from modest to spectacular; their price tags do too. Some are so close to the ocean, the surf practically rolls through your front door. Those without ocean views are within walking distance of the beach and offer tranquil seclusion in peaceful forested settings. Even the smallest rental homes are impressive and beautifully maintained, appointed with modern furnishings and all the amenities you could ever want (and often many more): TV/VCRs, stereos, CD players, washers and dryers, full kitchens with dishwashers, wet bars, whirlpool or Jacuzzi tubs, queen-size beds, ocean views, and the list goes on and on. Each property is unique, so be sure to get a good desciption when you call to book a reservation and specify exactly what it is you are looking for. Fortunately, no matter what home you select, you're in good hands here.

THE COURTYARD, Cannon Beach
964 South Hemlock
(503) 436-1392
Moderate to Very Expensive
Call for seasonal closures.

More like a group of attractive apartments than a hotel, The Courtyard offers a world of privacy and contemporary elegance. This two-story, wood-shingled building surrounds a lovely brick courtyard, where neat rows of flowers and a burbling fountain reside. Seekers of solitude will be delighted to find that the front desk, located a block away at the Cannon Beach Hotel, is conveniently out of sight and out of mind. With all this privacy, you'll have no choice but to cuddle up and enjoy your time together.

Each unit has a private entrance via the central courtyard, and all 13 are tastefully appointed with cherry-wood furnishings, modern kitchenettes, gas fireplaces, Jacuzzi tubs, and tiny patios. Thick Italian down duvets, dust ruffles, and large fluffy pillows grace the beds, while brilliant oil paintings add a finishing touch to the taupe walls and subdued color schemes. When you've had your fill of peace and quiet, venture a short block to the beach or relax in the common area on the first floor. No matter how you decide to spend your time, The Courtyard offers a secluded haven in which to explore the desires of your heart.

HALLMARK RESORT, Cannon Beach
1400 South Hemlock
(503) 436-1566, (800) 345-5676
Inexpensive to Very Expensive
Minimum stay requirement seasonally

Set high on a hill above the crashing surf in the heart of Cannon Beach, this sprawling clapboard complex surveys a residential hillside and the majestic ocean beyond. Spectacular water views of this caliber rarely (if ever) come at such affordable rates, making this otherwise very standard hotel worth checking into—literally. Dated fabrics, linens, and furnishings lend a motel flavor to most of the property, but fireplaces, fully equipped kitchens, and beautifully tiled Jacuzzi tubs are decidedly romantic touches in many of the suites. Private decks with ocean views outside nearly every room provide further kissing incentive. As its name implies, the Hallmark Resort offers everything you would expect from a full-scale resort, including an indoor recreation center with a heated pool, whirlpool spas, dry sauna, exercise room, wading pool, and even guest laundry facilities.

HEARTHSTONE INN, Cannon Beach
107 East Jackson Street
(503) 436-1392
Inexpensive to Moderate
Minimum stay requirement seasonally

This unobtrusive contemporary building, hidden by gently swaying willow trees, looks more like a residence than an inn. Inside are three studios and one suite, all with vaulted cedar ceilings, beach-rock fireplaces, skylights, stained glass windows, and fully equipped kitchenettes. Unfortunately the decor is somewhat dated and the furnishings are modest at best. Nevertheless, due to its location in an out-of-the-way corner of Cannon Beach, this rustic cottage is a refreshingly private and welcome place to stay.

STEPHANIE INN, Cannon Beach
2740 South Pacific
(503) 436-2221, (800) 633-3466
http://seasurf.com/~smmc
Expensive to Unbelievably Expensive
Minimum stay requirement on weekends seasonally

When it comes to indulgent beachfront accomodations, the Stephanie Inn stands alone. After an evening here, you'll understand why this relatively new property set at the ocean's edge has become so popular. The surf practically laps at the foundation of the sprawling, contemporary inn. A fire is always aglow in the river-rock hearth in the front parlor, which is furnished with comfortable overstuffed sofas; impressive wood detailing and hardwood floors scattered with Oriental rugs create an inviting but elegant ambience. Help yourselves to a handful of locally made saltwater taffy or fresh cookies (available at all hours) on your way to the elegant fireside library, which overlooks spectacular ocean views through a wall of bay windows. Aperitifs, wine, and hors d'oeuvres are served here in the early evening, accompanied by delicious sunsets. A complimentary breakfast buffet is served in the inn's mountain-view dining room every morning (dinner is also available; see the Romantic Suggestion below).

The inn's 46 sophisticated rooms are all equipped with plush terry-cloth robes and four-poster beds draped with beautiful floral linens, and nearly every room has a corner Jacuzzi or whirlpool tub, private deck, and gas fireplace. Chocolates left on your pillows with the evening turndown service make you feel extra pampered. The Mountain View rooms are the least expensive units in the inn, but also the least romantic—they face the parking lot. If you can, splurge for an ocean view; the views of the vast sandy beach, crashing surf, and jagged sea stacks are indescribably beautiful.

Romantic Note: The Stephanie Inn will do almost anything to make your stay special. Ask about their "special occasion" packages, which can include everything from surprising your beloved with a birthday cake upon check-in to sprinkling flower petals on the bed at turndown. (Do keep in mind that there is an additional fee for these extras.)

Romantic Suggestion: Dinner at the Stephanie Inn is a lingering four-course, prix fixe affair that can take several hours. The chef will sometimes greet you personally at your table and describe in advance the culinary wonders you are about to encounter. Though the dining room itself does not face the ocean, ample windows showcase mountain views (across the parking lot), and crisp linens and candlelight create an opulent dining atmsophere.

SURFSAND RESORT, Cannon Beach
Ocean Front and Gower
(503) 436-2274, (800) 547-6100
Moderate to Expensive
Minimum stay requirement on weekends and holidays seasonally

You'd never guess the Surfsand was once a Best Western motel, at least not if you have the good fortune of staying in one of the property's newly constructed luxury suites harbored right on the beach. Every one of these rooms is appointed with maple wood accents, impressive linens, and elegant contemporary furnishings. Private decks or patios showcase panoramic views of the ocean and Haystack Rock, gas fires blaze in every hearth, and the pounding surf resounds throughout the building. We are especially partial to the rooms on the fourth floor, which offer peaked ceilings, gorgeous corner Jacuzzi tubs, and seductive glass-enclosed showers. (Guests are also encouraged to make use of the property's indoor pool and Jacuzzi tub.) Though breakfast is not included in your stay, a kitchenette in nearly every room is a convenient alternative for those who are willing to plan ahead and bring their own provisions.

Unfortunately, the remaining rooms in the older building still show signs of the property's past. Dated color schemes, linens, and furnishings are functional but not impressive, and views of the ocean are obscured by neighboring buildings and a very large parking lot. The rooms with fireplaces and Jacuzzi tubs offer some romantic potential, but pale in comparison to the property's newer units.

Romantic Note: Surfsand Resort also manages several oceanside rental properties in the area, ranging from Moderate to Expensive. Some of these homes are the most enviable places to stay on the coast. Imagine a handsome, traditional Oregon coast home that fronts the crashing surf, with scintillating views of the awesome scenery (awesome is an understatement). Now imagine yourselves sharing blissful solitude. Anything else you imagine is between the two of you.

TURK'S HOUSE IN THE TREES, Cannon Beach
50 Highway 101
(503) 436-1809, (503) 436-2274, (800) 547-6100
Unbelievably Expensive
Minimum stay requirement on weekends and holidays seasonally

A recent $30,000 renovation has restored Turk's reputation as one of the Oregon coast's most extraordinary places to kiss. Supported by stilts on one side, this unusual home was crafted from rough-cut spruce and fir and juts out over the western slope of a steep, forested hillside. A wraparound deck surveys compelling views of the Oregon coastline; salty breezes rustle the branches of the towering evergreens and gently caress the untamed ferns and foliage that enfold the property. The interior is equally stunning, with cathedral-style pine ceilings and an abundance of floor-to-ceiling windows. Bright blue tiles accent the spacious sunken kitchen, where a basket of breakfast goodies (cider, hot chocolate, baked goods, and fresh fruit) awaits guests upon arrival. A wood-burning stove sheds more than enough warmth to heat the entire home, and interesting knickknacks add charm. You won't want for space in the spacious two-level master bedroom, which has an open rock-lined shower and an oversized spa tub set overlooking the trees. You can also cozy up under a patchwork quilt on the king-size bed and watch a fire crackling in the bedside hearth. An open loft bedroom with several additional beds is designed more for kids, but can also accomodate another romance-minded couple if they don't mind the limited privacy.

If you are looking for something inexpensive (especially in the summer), ask about the modest cottage or studio next door, both of which enjoy quiet views of the trees and distant ocean. Mismatched furnishings and dated linens make these choices homey rather than romantic (worthy of only one lip), but skylights, TV/VCRs, a whirlpool bathtub or a steambath shower, and the convenience of kitchenettes help to compensate.

THE WAVES OCEANFRONT MOTEL, Cannon Beach
188 West Second Street
(503) 436-2205, (800) 822-2468
Inexpensive to Unbelievably Expensive
Minimum stay requirement on weekends seasonally

It doesn't get more eclectic than the sprawling Waves Motel. The enormous property meanders for several blocks along the water's edge, offering a hodge-podge of accommodations. Some units have scintillating views of the ocean and are perfectly designed for cozy twosomes; others overlook the cement parking lot and are geared more for a family of five. For guaranteed inspiration, we recommend choosing a unit in La Colina or the Flagship Building; rooms in both have unobstructed ocean views, and the resonant sound of the surf striking the steadfast shore is a welcome reminder of just how far behind you've left city life. La Colina is cozy and somewhat rustic; rooms in this building feature open beams, river-rock fireplaces, and nondescript furnishings. Rooms in the Flagship Building are slightly more spartan but still enticing, with pine furnishings, fireplaces, and tiny decks (which could use fresh paint). Ocean views, down comforters, and slate fireplaces in the Southwind units also ensure romantic possibilities; modern amenities such as Jacuzzi tubs and upscale kitchens are alluring as well. Steer clear of the rooms in the Garden Court, which lack ocean views and suggest a typical economy motel.

Romantic Alternative: If space is a priority and price is not an issue, consider renting the Waves' ultra-private **OCEAN HOUSE** (Expensive to Very Expensive), located one block from the beach in nearby Tolovana Park. Due to its size, this large contemporary split-level home draws more families than couples, but it has everything you could ever want in a romantic get-away. Pop your favorite movie into the VCR or cook up a memorable feast for your partner in the fully stocked kitchen. Later, start a fire in the hearth of the upstairs master suite, where you'll also find a king-size bed, wet bar, and jetted tub. A washer and dryer and a double garage offer all the conveniences of home. Best of all, the beach is just down the street.

WHITE HERON LODGE, Cannon Beach
356 North Spruce
(503) 436-2601, (800) 822-2468
Expensive
Minimum stay requirement on weekends seasonally

Sea gulls soar above the foamy waves that roll onto the beach in front of this Victorian-style complex, located just north of Cannon Beach. Sea grass sways at the edge of the front lawn, eventually giving way to a vast expanse of sand. In spite of its proximity to Cannon Beach's town center, the quiet residential area around the lodge remains peaceful and enticing. The six relatively new units here are comfortably appointed and fully equipped. Private decks look out to the shore and fireplaces glow with inviting warmth. Lace curtains lend privacy to the cozy bedrooms, and the beds are adorned with thick floral comforters. Spa tubs, private baths, and full kitchens are additional luxuries. Whether you opt for the duplex, which can accommodate up to five people, or settle on one of the studios, with just enough room for two, you'll have all the space you need to spoil yourselves with utter relaxation and quiet.

Restaurant Kissing

BISTRO, Cannon Beach
263 North Hemlock Street
(503) 436-2661
Moderate
Call for seasonal hours.

Nestled within a cluster of small shops, this Tudor-style cottage fronts a charming little outdoor patio a comfortable distance away from the main thoroughfare. Past the bustling bar area, you'll find a snug dining room handsomely appointed with peaked ceilings, dark wood trim, green table-cloths, and glowing candles. A plethora of rural knickknacks, everything from dried flowers to plates, baskets, plants, and birdcages, covers the white stucco walls, and soft track lighting creates a cozy atmosphere in which to enjoy some of the best food in town.

You might begin your feast with the mouthwatering Manilla clams dipped in herbed broth and drawn butter, then move on to the spicy spaghetti marinara with fresh vegetables or the baked salmon served with leeks, asparagus, and an intriguing black bean sauce. All entrées may be ordered à la carte or as part of a full dinner that includes antipasto, soup, salad, and fresh bread.

Although Bistro is slightly noisier than most places we recommend for amorous encounters, the constant hum can work to your advantage by drowning out neighboring conversations and possible kitchen clamor. The tables are far enough apart to ensure all the privacy you need for a kiss or two.

CAFE DE LA MER, Cannon Beach
1287 South Hemlock Street
(503) 436-1179
Expensive
Call for seasonal hours.

After a late-afternoon or early-evening stroll along the beach, head inland to quaint little Cafe de la Mer. The outside of this tiny blue house is fronted by planters overflowing with tulips and greenery, and the rustic interior has been simply but pleasantly decorated. Wall sconces shed soft light on a handful of tightly packed tables adorned with colorful flowers, pink linens, and candles in one room; a second dining room, although less intimate than the first, is more spacious, with a row of windows lining an entire wall. The attentive staff consistently delivers enticing dinners and superior service. Fresh seafood entrées include a savory bouillabaisse and delicate petrale sole, to name only a few. Save room for dessert, because the white satin tart with marionberries is as smooth and luscious as it sounds.

LOCAL SCOOP, Cannon Beach
156 North Hemlock Street
(503) 436-9551
Inexpensive
Call for seasonal hours.

There was a time when a boy would take a girl to the local ice cream shoppe and they would share whatever gooey offering they could handle with two spoons or two straws. Well, times have changed, and Local Scoop has updated that innocent setting with striking Northwest flair. Towering pine ceilings, floor-to-ceiling windows, wrought-iron tables with cushioned chairs, and an authentic soda fountain counter set an appropriately sweet mood. Yes, during the summer and on weekends parents may be treating their children to a sugar rush. But during off-hours, after a long stroll along the beach on a sunny afternoon, order a soda with two straws and stare into each other's eyes until the last slurp is gone. Enjoy your refreshments outside on the brick wraparound patio if the day is sunny and warm, or huddle inside near the antique wood-burning stove if the weather is less cooperative.

Outdoor Kissing

ECOLA STATE PARK, Cannon Beach
(503) 436-2844, (800) 452-5687 (for reservations only)
$3 entrance fee per vehicle
Recommended Wedding Site

Two miles north of Cannon Beach, off Highway 101.

State parks are not usually considered good places for conducting affectionate business. They may be well kept, they may offer supreme scenery, but they also tend to be crowded and inundated with RVs and kids. Ecola State Park is an exception. The character of this area is so exceptional, the potency of the sights so remarkable, you won't notice anyone but yourselves and the splendor of nature.

Ecola State Park begins just outside Cannon Beach and extends nine miles north toward Seaside. From the park's entrance, a narrow road winds seaward through a dense forest, where emerald green moss clings to tree branches above a fern-laden carpet of undergrowth. Even on the foggiest days, Ecola Point is a good place to catch a sunset; fog simply means fewer crowds and more mystical scenery. The point offers expansive views of Haystack Rock, and you can also watch the tumultuous surf crashing against the basalt headlands; past erosion and landslides have sculpted these headlands into the rugged panorama we enjoy today.

From Ecola Point, continue northward either by foot, following a two-mile trail with views of the coastline, or by car, winding farther into the forest until you reach the wind-sculpted trees of **INDIAN BEACH**. Hold hands as you take in views of Tillamook Rock, a 100-foot-high sea stack of basalt that broke away from the mainland years ago and now stands roughly a mile offshore. Tillamook Head, the cape separating Seaside from Cannon Beach, was traversed by the Lewis and Clark expedition in 1806; nowadays it is explored by scenery-seeking hikers. (Watch for the sign at Indian Beach marking the six-mile Tillamook Head National Recreation Trail.) Both Ecola Point and Indian Beach offer grassy picnic areas overlooking sandy beaches. What better place to inspire romance than in the heart of nature?

Tolovana Park

Outdoor Kissing

HUG POINT, Tolovana Park

Four miles south of Cannon Beach, off Highway 101.

Even when the parking lot is full, there is still plenty of room at this windswept beach to feel like you're all by yourselves. If you find yourselves at Hug Point during low tide, give in to your curiosity and permit those kids inside you to play for the duration of your stay. The soaring cliffs along the beach are gouged with caves and crevasses of varying shapes and proportions. For the timid there are gentle tide pools and rocky fissures where you can easily observe marine life. For the more daring there are dark, ominous sea caves in which to hide. When your exploring is done and the tide reclaims your playground, the grown-ups in you can end the day by watching the dazzling sunset over the Pacific while you hug.

Arch Cape

ST. BERNARDS—A BED AND BREAKFAST, Arch Cape
3 East Ocean Road
(503) 436-2800, (800) 436-2848
Expensive to Very Expensive
Minimum stay requirement on weekends

Without a doubt, St. Bernards is one of the most exclusive places to stay on the coast. So why didn't we award it the four lips it deserves? Unfortunately, one of the innkeepers has a tendency to be inappropriate to the point of being offensive or rude. If you're good about boundaries, this shouldn't pose a problem. If not, you may want to reconsider, despite the splendor of this impressive property.

Ensconced on one and a half acres of lovingly landscaped grounds, St. Bernards surveys views of the ocean across the street. Reminiscent of an old-world castle, the expansive wood-shingled chateau is like a treasure box waiting to be explored, with its collection of unusual European antiques, unexpected staircases, and dramatic guest rooms. The foyer holds a picturesque table topped with melted candles and handwoven baskets; an extensive wine cellar brims with vintages from all over the world. Plush white carpets extend throughout the home, which is accented with French doors, beautiful tilework, and pieces from the owners' private art collection. A carousel horse is the highlight of the spacious living room, where an afternoon social hour is celebrated next to the warmth of a blazing fire.

The inn's seven guest rooms are bona fide masterpieces, and all of them enjoy distant ocean views. White lace and pale peach walls decorate the Tower Room, which hosts a Louis XIV carved bed and a raised sitting area with a handsome settee situated beneath a pointed turret. Commanding center stage in the blue and white Ginger Room are a pair of magnificent 200-year-old twin Austrian beds that stand over seven feet tall! For a taste of the French countryside, request the Provence Room, with its cathedral ceilings, authentic French linens, terra-cotta floors, and French doors that lead to a private terrace. A wood-accented tiled Jacuzzi is an added luxury here. The appropriately named Gauguin Room, decorated in muted shades of purples, pinks, and peaches characteristic of Gauguin's artwork, showcases a unique headboard made from an antique Polynesian porch railing.

Breakfast at St. Bernards is an all-out affair. French country pine tables clustered beneath a peaked turret in the conservatory allow lovely views of the patio garden area. One of the innkeepers is a former chef, and she spoils her guests with gourmet goodies like broiled grapefruit, cranberry upside-down coffee cake, and a corn bread and Dungeness crab quiche, all presented on fine china and crystal.

Manzanita

The town of Manzanita is nestled between the endless Pacific Ocean and the base of the Neahkahnie Mountains. Although this small, nondescript village has grown a bit over the past few years, it remains relatively undiscovered by tourists, particularly in comparison with Cannon Beach and Seaside. For beach roaming, kite flying, or an exhilarating day by the sea, this area is sheer perfection. Manzanita is close enough to Cannon Beach for you to take advantage of the nightlife and many dining spots, yet far enough from the crowds to give you a comforting sense of calm.

Hotel/Bed and Breakfast Kissing

THE ARBORS BED AND BREAKFAST, Manzanita
78 Idaho Avenue
(503) 368-7566
Inexpensive
Minimum stay requirement on weekends and holidays
Call for seasonal closures.

Cozy up in the country after a windblown day spent exploring Manzanita's vast sandy beaches and flourishing tide pools. Set just a block from the beach in a quiet residential community, this freshly painted English-style cottage is embraced by gardens and a white picket fence. Choose between two small but comfortable guest rooms with hardwood floors, well-maintained private baths, and glimpses of the ocean. Thick down comforters and patchwork quilts drape inviting antique brass beds in both of the modestly decorated rooms. Breakfast is a generous assortment of muffins, scones, a baked entrée, and fruit, served family-style in the homey downstairs dining room. At these reasonable rates, you couldn't ask for more—you'll feel rejuvenated and ready for another day at the beach.

THE INN AT MANZANITA, Manzanita
67 Laneda Avenue
(503) 368-6754
Moderate to Expensive
Minimum stay requirement on weekends seasonally

Set amid coastal pines and spruce trees, this contemporary Northwest inn sits a mere 200 feet from Manzanita's seven-mile stretch of beach. Guest rooms in the main building are a hybrid of sunny log cabin and comfortable hotel room, with pine and cedar walls that rise dramatically to form vaulted ceilings, and private decks that allow partial views of the ocean through the treetops. The rooms are further enhanced by all the amenities a couple could ever need to ensure romance: two-person Jacuzzi tubs, old-fashioned gas fireplaces, stocked wet bars, and firm, cozy beds with down comforters. All that's missing are a few personal touches to warm up the somewhat barren interiors.

Adjacent to the main building is a stunning two-level cottage. The two units in this cottage are both decorated in subtle shades of nautical blue with wood paneling, Jacuzzi tubs, and small decks. Captain's beds with down comforters are tucked into cozy sunlit nooks separated from the living area by curtains. The downstairs unit has a full kitchen; however, advantages in the upstairs unit include a vaulted ceiling, a superior view, and a skylight over the bed for stargazing.

Three new units have recently been added in a second cottage, giving guests a total of 13 rooms from which to choose. The downstairs unit in this cottage has a full kitchen, but the two units on the second floor offer better views of the nearby ocean. Other amenities include Jacuzzi tubs, fireplaces, and interiors of dark green and washed wood. Considering the prices and the luxurious Northwest-style comfort, the Inn at Manzanita could easily become one of your favorite getaways along the coast.

MANZANITA RENTAL COMPANY, Manzanita
32 Laneda Avenue
(503) 368-6797, (800) 579-9801
Inexpensive to Expensive
Minimum stay requirement

If you've ever fantasized about living on the rugged Oregon coast with the pounding surf as the backdrop to your comings and goings, you're in luck. Manzanita Rental Company has a remarkable assortment of homes that you can call your own (for a little while anyway). The 60 or so rental properties range from loft studios to spacious five-bedroom homes. Some have breathtaking ocean views; others are set back in wooded glens secluded from the rest of the world by old-growth trees. Interiors range from beach-frolic residences best for families to unique designer abodes that will delight the most finicky of travelers. Kick off your shoes, cuddle on the deck as you drink in the view, and revel in your home away from home on the Oregon Coast.

OCEAN INN, Manzanita
20 Laneda Avenue
(503) 368-6797, (800) 579-9801
Inexpensive to Moderate
Minimum stay requirement

Situated at the very end of Manzanita's main thoroughfare, the Ocean Inn is literally perched on a white sand beach that reaches down to the ocean's edge. As advantageous as this sounds, the timeworn motel across the street detracts from the otherwise ideal location. Still, the four mini-apartments in this recently remodeled clapboard building are all endearing places to stay. Wood-burning stoves in three units warm the knotty pine interiors, which are accented with floral wallpapers and country antiques. Contemporary full kitchens (breakfast provisions are your responsibility), TV/VCRs, full bathrooms, and even private garages ensure that you will have all the comforts and conveniences of home. Two of the suites are equipped with French doors that slide open to private outdoor decks where you can sit and watch the waves roll onto the shore for hours on end. Who could ever tire of these views?

Restaurant Kissing

BLUE SKY CAFE, Manzanita
154 Laneda Avenue
(503) 368-5712

Moderate to Expensive; No Credit Cards
Dinner Wednesday-Saturday

Casual is the word for the Blue Sky Cafe (the waiters and waitresses seem quite comfortable in their jeans and T-shirts), yet the food is anything but ordinary. Organic ingredients are used in such remarkable entrées as the fresh ahi tuna served with coconut curry rice and the goat cheese layered with fresh herbs, sun-dried tomatoes, artichoke hearts, garlic, and olives. We fell in love with the red snapper baked in parchment with feta, Nicoise olives, and Sambuca liqueur. And the lobster salad with papaya, blood oranges, and mango dressing is impeccable. As you can see, the menu is more than tantalizing—it is downright seductive. Leave room for dessert, because anything prepared here is worth the effort.

JARBOE'S IN MANZANITA, Manzanita
137 Laneda Avenue
(503) 368-5113
Moderate to Expensive
Call for seasonal hours.

Jarboe's is a must for an intimate, truly gourmet dinner. This charming, exceedingly small restaurant is situated in a wood-shingled cottage not far from Manzanita's beach. The cozy dining room is decorated with crisp white walls, simple artwork, and innovative flower-pot lamps that hang from the vaulted ceiling. The crayfish bisque is perfect, and the mesquite-grilled pizzetta with garlic and Asiago cheese is superb. For your main course, try the duck with lamb sausage or the ahi tuna prepared with roasted peppers and grapefruit. If you have difficulty deciding between the many enticing entrées, why not simplify the matter by choosing the three-course prix fixe dinner? Garden-fresh garnishings are sure to accompany whatever you choose. With all this romantic potential, we regret to add that the service can be inconsistent, especially as the evening draws to a close.

QUEEN BESS, Manzantita
411 Laneda Avenue
(503) 368-4255
Moderate to Expensive
Call for seasonal hours.

It doesn't seem possible that a town this small could be home to two outstanding restaurants—the **BLUE SKY CAFE** and **JARBOE'S IN MANZANITA** (see previous reviews). When it comes to the Queen Bess Tea Room, however, outstanding is a bit of an understatement. This is a culinary experience *par excellence*.

Don't be disappointed by the plain exterior; for once you step inside the dining room, you'll know you have passed from the ordinary to the sublime. Exquisite statues and vases, beautiful Oriental rugs, and elegant floral arrangements that seem to overflow with fruit are set off by the regal maroon walls. Twelve tables are evenly spaced around the room, draped with white and maroon tablecloths, and crowned with slender candlesticks. In the back stands a beautiful pulpit from an English cathedral; a shoji screen shields the entryway from the rest of the dining room. From the polished wood parquet floors to the immaculate tea sets displayed overhead, everything seems to shine with refined elegance.

Each course in the prix fixe dinner is made from the freshest and finest ingredients, and artistically presented. Begin with the ahi tuna prepared carpaccio-style and served with an Asian vinaigrette over fresh vegetables. Outstanding main courses include the filet mignon with wild mushroom sauce and the chinook salmon cooked in champagne and dressed with a Vietnamese- and French-inspired sauce. Even the house salad is impressive, with 15 different types of organic lettuce! And desserts are simply heavenly. You'll agree that each course is nothing short of a gastronomical masterpiece.

At Queen Bess, visitors are treated like honored guests and welcomed as family. World-renowned chef Mity Harding emerges from the kitchen at the end of the evening to personally greet her guests, and thinks nothing of spontaneously sharing her good fortune with others. She may, for example, decide to open one of her expensive French vintage wines and sell it by the glass so that her guests can say they have, at the very least, had a taste of the good life. This is hospitality at its finest. Queen Bess successfully combines extraordinary cuisine with wonderful service in an idyllic atmosphere. Does it get any better than this?

Romantic Suggestion: Queen Bess prepares picnic baskets for starry-eyed lovers who wish to dine at the beach. Baskets are available for a refundable $10 deposit, and you can specify which type of meal you would like: meat, fish, or vegetarian. Each basket comes with a bottle of champagne, silver place settings, and enough food to satiate the most passionate palates.

Outdoor Kissing

OSWALD WEST STATE PARK

Ten miles south of Cannon Beach, on the west side of Highway 101. Look for signs pointing the way.

Oswald West State Park is one of the most inspiring campgrounds in these parts—just ask any Northwest camping enthusiast. Its superior desirability has to do with its mode of access. In order to set up camp, you must walk a quarter of a mile down a rain-forest path, wheeling a cart (provided) with your things piled on top. This short jaunt tends to eliminate feather-weights and RVs, giving you and your loved one much-needed privacy. The forested setting is within arm's reach of the water, with footpaths that take you briskly down to a 13-mile stretch of surging surf. The scenery to the south is a succession of overlapping mountains jutting into the ocean; their dark jagged profiles are silhouetted against the distant horizon. White sand, effervescent surf, and a rock-clad shore make exploring here a treasure hunt.

Oceanside

Located about eight miles west of the main road on the small peninsula that forms Tillamook Bay, Oceanside offers sweet reprieve from the crowds that haunt the coast in the summertime. Harbored right on the coast, Oceanside is small and unassuming, which is part of its charm. There are only a few dining and lodging establishments worth recommending here, but the magnificent Oregon coastline is invitation enough. As the mist mingles with the cries of seabirds along this stretch of inviting rugged beachfront, you'll find the stresses and cares of your busy life simply fading away.

Romantic Suggestion: For magnificent views of the surrounding area, head east to nearby Tillamook and hop on a "gull-wing" aircraft at **TILLAMOOK AIR TOURS**, (503) 842-1942. Private charters, scenic tours, and whale-watching expeditions are available daily. Twenty-minute tours are $30 per person; 30-minute tours are $40.

Hotel/Bed and Breakfast Kissing

HOUSE ON THE HILL MOTEL, Oceanside
1816 Maxwell Mountain Road
(503) 842-6030
Inexpensive to Moderate
Minimum stay requirement on holidays

Balanced atop one of the highest points along the entire Oregon coast, these pale blue, contemporary buildings boast absolutely spectacular ocean views. A telescope in the motel's lobby area allows you to witness the migrating whales that occasionally breach on the horizon or the hundreds of resident sea lions basking in the sun on rocky outcroppings. It's a shame the owners haven't done more with the rooms here, which don't begin to live up to the property's views. The accommodations are clean and well maintained, but the cheap linens, artwork, and furnishings are more functional than attractive. Floral linens and a private deck in the Honeymoon Suite make it feel relatively upscale, but it's still disappointing. Nevertheless, with views of this caliber at your fingertips, a stay here can make you feel a little closer to heaven, and a lot closer to the mesmerizing sea.

Restaurant Kissing

ROSEANNA'S RESTAURANT, Oceanside
1490 Pacific Northwest
(503) 842-7351
Inexpensive to Moderate
Breakfast, Lunch, and Dinner Daily

Roseanna's is Oceanside's only oceanfront restaurant. In fact, except for the little coffee shop down the road, it's literally the *only* restaurant in town. But even if there were a number of dining establishments to choose from, we would still highly recommend eating here. Views of the ever-changing ocean surround this vintage Northwest dining establishment. An assortment of shells and other eccentric seaside trinkets ornament the dining room's pink walls; pink floral tablecloths and green plastic chairs create a casual mood, augmented by swivel stools that flank a counter in the front of the restaurant. While Roseanna's atmosphere is easygoing, the kitchen takes its job seriously, producing healthy breakfasts, lunches, and dinners. The menu highlights regional cuisine and fresh seafood; expect salads chock-full of crisp, fresh vegetables, and seafood done to perfection. In the evening, nature prepares another treat to enhance your meal: an ambrosial sunset for two.

Romantic Warning: Roseanna's doesn't accept reservations, and due to Oceanside's limited dining options, the wait for a table here can be *ridiculously* long. But look on the bright side. You'll have time for a stroll on the beach, and the longer you wait, the more likely you are to enjoy a late summer sunset while you dine.

Outdoor Kissing

THREE CAPES SCENIC LOOP

North of Tillamook you will see signs for the Three Capes Scenic Loop. Turn west off Highway 101 and follow the signs along this loop to Cape Meares, around and south to Oceanside, and down to Pacific City, where the loop rejoins Highway 101.

Near Tillamook, Highway 101 abandons the seashore and veers through a long stretch of overdeveloped and unsightly shopping areas. To avoid these distractions, we recommend taking a scenic detour along the Three Capes Scenic Loop. Even at the height of summer the tourists seem to be elsewhere, and you can explore this exquisite passage at a slow, cruising pace. You'll begin near Tillamook Bay, where wispy trees outline marshy mudflats and fishing boats dot the horizon. Follow the winding road toward **CAPE MEARES STATE PARK**, where you can survey the ocean from forested hilltops. Migrating seabirds and resident orcas, sea lions, and porpoises are easily seen from this exquisite vantage point, and waterfalls trickle down jagged rocky cliffs into the crashing waves below. Though Cape Meares does draw crowds on hot summer days, if you follow signs to the park's wind-sculpted Sitka spruce (better known as the Octopus Tree) and the private lookout beyond, you'll find a bit more privacy and breathtaking views of the coastline.

Continue inland (by car) toward Oceanside and Netarts, where the road drops back to sea level. Both hikers and romantics will appreciate **CAPE LOOKOUT STATE PARK**, which has gorgeous walking paths that lead down to the beach and nature trails that climb to the tip of rocky lookout points. Unfortunately, easy-access camping facilities here also mean more crowds.

Near the end of the loop, stop at **ANDERSON VIEWPOINT**, a precipitous mountain bluff just south of Oceanside that overlooks everything north, south, and west—it's a supreme location for a picnic. Just a little farther south you'll find vast expanses of sand dunes along the placid shores of Sand Lake.

Netarts

Restaurant Kissing

MARINA'S RESTAURANT, Netarts
4785 Netarts Highway West
(503) 842-8525
Moderate
Call for seasonal hours.

You could easily miss this enticing Italian restaurant, tucked away in a renovated roadside convenience store, but that would be a shame. The adept kitchen staff more than makes up for what the restaurant lacks in exterior charm. Knotty pine walls lend a rustic flavor to the restaurant's two dining rooms, which are dressed up with eclectic local artwork, floral window treatments, and hunter green tables. Though at first glance the menu seems to offer little more than steak and seafood, this restaurant has won local acclaim for its delicious Italian fare. The sautéed scallops, manicotti, and antipasto are all sheer perfection. After one bite, Marina's will have your vote of approval too.

Sandlake

Hotel/Bed and Breakfast Kissing

SANDLAKE COUNTRY INN, Sandlake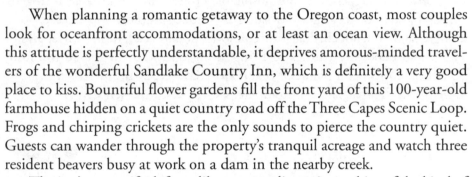
8505 Galloway Road
(503) 965-6745
Inexpensive to Expensive
Minimum stay requirement on weekends seasonally

When planning a romantic getaway to the Oregon coast, most couples look for oceanfront accommodations, or at least an ocean view. Although this attitude is perfectly understandable, it deprives amorous-minded travelers of the wonderful Sandlake Country Inn, which is definitely a very good place to kiss. Bountiful flower gardens fill the front yard of this 100-year-old farmhouse hidden on a quiet country road off the Three Capes Scenic Loop. Frogs and chirping crickets are the only sounds to pierce the country quiet. Guests can wander through the property's tranquil acreage and watch three resident beavers busy at work on a dam in the nearby creek.

The inn's countrified, farm-like surroundings give no hint of the kind of elegance and luxury that await you in the four very private suites. New innkeepers tend to all the affectionate details to ensure that your stay is comfortable. The smell of freshly baked cookies and sweet apple cider permeates the house, enticing guests to stop for refreshments in the homey downstairs parlor before checking into their rooms. Creaking hardwood floors give historic flavor to the unusually elegant rooms, while dramatic floral fabrics and wallpapers add personality. The spacious Honeymoon Suite is situated behind a curtain at the top of the stairs in the original farmhouse. (The connecting rooms in this spacious suite have doors that can be closed for privacy.) A double-sided fireplace warms the suite's master bedroom and extra sitting room, where you'll find a TV/VCR, French doors that open onto a private outdoor deck, and a wood-paneled bathroom with a Jacuzzi tub for two.

Downstairs in the Timber Room, sumptuous linens drape a four-poster king-size bed, French doors open onto a private deck and gardens, Oriental rugs cover hardwood floors, and a large bathroom boasts a sunken Jacuzzi tub set behind lace draperies. The Rose Garden Room is smaller but equally charming, with a netted canopied bed and a sitting area that faces an abundant flower garden. For total privacy we recommend the neighboring self-contained Cottage, with its atrium doors that open onto a deck beside a burbling creek. In the inviting bedroom, a gleaming black Jacuzzi tub offers views of the garden. A full kitchen, cozy breakfast nook, and TV/VCR are additional luxuries.

Because the owners value your privacy almost as much as you do, an overwhelmingly generous three-course breakfast is delivered for you to enjoy undisturbed in your room. Imagine waking to fresh-squeezed orange juice, grapefruit with raspberry sauce, lemon bread, and green chile soufflé with fresh salsa. The menu changes daily, making every morning a special event.

Romantic Suggestion: Your hospitable hostess can also provide a "Togetherness Basket" of local goodies such as smoked salmon and cheese, sourdough baguettes, hot cheddar-broccoli soup, potato salad, fresh fruit, sparkling cider, and chocolate truffles to bring along on a tour of the surrounding splendor. Consider a picnic at **SAND LAKE** (see Outdoor Kissing), just a mile down the road, for an exemplary Northwest experience.

Outdoor Kissing

SAND LAKE, Sandlake

From southbound Highway 101, take the Sandlake turnoff, go 5.5 miles to Sandlake Grocery, and turn right onto Galloway Road. Follow Galloway Road until it dead-ends at a campground. Turn left just before the campground entrance at a sign that reads "FISHERMAN'S DAY CAMP," and follow this road into the parking lot. The lake and estuary are on the other side of the sand dunes.

Seabirds seek refuge at this quiet lake and estuary surrounded by sandflats and grass-covered dunes. When the tide is out, you can walk around the perimeter of the lake and explore the tide pools that eventually merge with the raging Pacific. Astonishingly, this exquisite beach area is not popular with locals or tourists (we don't know why), and the odds of having the beach to yourselves are in your favor. We can't think of a better place for an inspirational romantic interlude.

Pacific City

Restaurant Kissing

FISHES, Pacific City
33200 Cape Kiwanda Drive
(503) 965-6789
Moderate
Call for seasonal hours.

Everybody's talking about this new restaurant set a short distance from Cape Kiwanda's shoreline. Candles and bottles of virgin olive oil dress up tables draped with burgundy and white tablecloths. Pastel fish murals surround the colorful dining room, and an individual fish has been hand-painted on every chair. If you sit at a window table, you'll be able to glimpse the ocean past neighboring residences and a newly constructed micro-brewery.

Though the tables are a little too close together and the pop rock music in the background is far from romantic, the chef here never disappoints. The meal begins with delicious fresh rolls accented with herbs. Next, savor the seared jumbo scallops with whole roasted mushrooms and glazed parsnips, or the vegetarian pasta served with a light pesto sauce and freshly grated Parmesan cheese; both are superlative. Try to restrain yourselves from eating too many rolls so you can save room for a delectable homemade dessert. After dinner, take a moonlit stroll along Cape Kiwanda's nearby beachfront, where rocky cliffs ascend above the foam-capped surf.

Cloverdale

Hotel/Bed and Breakfast Kissing

HUDSON HOUSE BED AND BREAKFAST, Cloverdale
37700 Highway 101 South
(503) 392-3533
Inexpensive

A white picket fence surrounds this pale gray and blue Victorian, found just off the busy highway. If not for the sight and sound of speeding traffic, the home's pastoral views of surrounding green pastures would be picture perfect. Fortunately, traffic slows down as evening falls, and when it does you'll appreciate the Hudson House's old-fashioned setting. Faded Oriental rugs cover hardwood floors in the inn's timeworn interior, appointed with homey antique furnishings. Family heirlooms and photographs make three of the four guest rooms a little too homespun for our romantic tastes, but the Laura Room is worth mentioning. Located on the second floor, this cozy two-room suite has beautiful wood detailing and an interesting sloped ceiling. Pretty old-fashioned wallpapers enhance the hand-sewn patchwork quilt that covers the antique brass bed, creating comfortable country ambience. Best of all, you can enjoy views of the rural landscape through a wall of bay windows in the bedroom. In the morning, after you've eaten more than your share of a bountiful breakfast served family-style in the small dining room, you can work off the extra calories by exploring the surrounding area on bicycles provided by the innkeepers.

Lincoln City

Lincoln City isn't a destination around which to plan a romantic itinerary. Use it instead to fill a shopping list or take advantage of Oregon's tax-free outlet stores. To its credit, Lincoln City does offer two kiss-worthy spots for dining after a long day of shopping; however, you would do better looking elsewhere for romantic accommodations. This section of the Oregon coast is too commercialized to feel like the Northwest getaway most of us are expecting.

Restaurant Kissing

BAY HOUSE, Lincoln City
5911 Southwest Highway 101
(541) 996-3222
Expensive
Call for seasonal hours.

This weathered building, all by itself on a steep bank off the main highway, is hardly what you'd call a showcase. But pull over! Bay House enjoys a flawless view of tidal Siletz Bay, the driftwood-strewn shoreline, and the flow of the calm clear blue water. Just about every table is blessed with its share of the lovely scenery. The newly renovated interior is elegant and modern, with large bay windows, deep colors, abstract paintings, and cozy private booths. On the menu you'll find an enterprising assortment of Northwest creations made from local fish and meats. Meals here are consistently outstanding. The shellfish pan roast with pasta cakes is remarkable, and the herb-crusted rack of lamb with port demi-glace is unbelievable. Equally wonderful are the desserts; if you forget to save room, at least order one and sample it together.

KERNVILLE STEAK AND SEAFOOD HOUSE, Lincoln City
186 Siletz Highway
(541) 994-6200
Moderate to Expensive
Dinner Daily

From its weathered wood exterior to its knotty pine interior, this is a casual, down-home eatery where portions are more than generous. The emphasis is strictly on meat and seafood dishes; although appetizers often include deep-fried Kernville potatoes or mushrooms sautéed in a garlic-wine sauce, that's where the vegetables start and stop. We loved the fresh halibut encrusted in Parmesan, but the teriyaki steak was drenched in an overly sweet sauce. Those with large appetites can tackle a king cut of prime rib, the steak and prawns dinner, or a bucket full of sweet butter clams. You might not experience elegant intimacy here, but you are right on the Siletz River where great blue herons often feed at the water's edge. So sit back, admire the view, and enjoy the hearty fixings.

Gleneden Beach

Restaurant Kissing

CHEZ JEANNETTE, Gleneden Beach
7150 Old Highway 101
(541) 764-3434
Expensive
Lunch Monday-Friday; Dinner Daily

Thick branches curl around the roof and walls of this stone-fronted home resting snugly upon a vine-covered hill. The interior is divinely elegant, yet remarkably cozy and welcoming, with two blazing fireplaces warming the softly lit dining rooms. Soothing piano music envelops you as you gaze out the windows at the lush foliage and flowering trees. Velvety green drapery, lush carpet, regal high-backed chairs, and tables set with bone china and crystal create a thoroughly intimate and romantic atmosphere in which to enjoy delectable French dishes.

Just about everything is made from scratch at Chez Jeannette, from the oven-fresh herb baguettes to the enticing homemade desserts. We suggest you begin your meal with the escargots à la bourguignonne or the ragout of wild and button mushrooms served on toasted bread. As for the main course, you certainly can't go wrong with any of the chef's nightly seafood, game, or pasta selections. (Our spinach pasta with scallops was superb!) One look at the dessert tray and we guarantee you won't escape without a little taste of heaven.

Depoe Bay

Depoe Bay is the Oregon coast's prime spot for whale watching, especially from December through April, when cetacean migration is in full swing. Regardless of whether you come here to whale watch or not, this small strip of a town is an entertaining place to spend a day. Massive waves crash endlessly against its rocky shores. There is no beach separating the town from the sea, just formidable black rocks rising up out of the water. Sun-starved Northwesterners usually hope for clear days, but witnessing a turbulent storm here is a moving experience, not soon forgotten.

Hotel/Bed and Breakfast Kissing

CHANNEL HOUSE INN, Depoe Bay
35 Ellingson Street
(541) 763-2140, (800) 447-2140
http://www.newportnet.com/channel
Inexpensive to Very Expensive

If you're looking for a cozy getaway spot with fantastic ocean views, Channel House Inn is definitely worth a visit. Don't let its rather ordinary appearance disappoint you: a world of closeness with each other and the sea awaits inside. Appropriately named, this towering blue building sits high upon the rocky cliffs of Depoe Bay and overlooks one of the world's smallest channels (only 50 feet wide). The interior displays a nautical theme, from the whales etched into the glass doors at the entrance to guest rooms with names like Channel Watch, The Bridge, and Crow's Nest. Scattered throughout the hallways are maritime antiques such as brass ship fittings, a polished captain's wheel, and part of an archaic diving suit.

Almost all of the 12 contemporary units feature views of the waves crashing against the venerable coastline. The larger, more desirable oceanfront rooms and suites have their own private decks, where you can lie back in a steaming hot tub for two and watch the evening sun disappear beneath the sea. After a relaxing soak, let the gas fireplace warm and dry you while the stresses of life seem to ebb away. In rooms like Whale Watcher, the bedroom seems to jut out over the water like the cliffs themselves; here you can lie in bed, surrounded by two walls of windows, and bask in the sights, sounds, and smells of the ocean in total privacy. (Boat traffic during the day may be your only company.) Each room is decorated in subtle shades of blue, with pine furnishings and a pair of binoculars for whale watching. In the morning, head downstairs to the cheery breakfast nook for a buffet of fresh fruit and pastries.

Outdoor Kissing

FOGARTY CREEK STATE PARK, Depoe Bay
$6 day-use fee for parking

One mile north of Depoe Bay, on Highway 101.

Fogarty Creek State Park may not look like much at first; the signs from the highway lead you east to a rather unattractive parking area with a few picnic tables scattered about. But once you leave your car behind and take the pedestrian underpass to the other side of the highway, you're in for a treat. This small, intimate stretch of sandy beach is an ideal setting for picnics and whale watching. Take in the dramatic display of waves and mist as the turbulent surf breaks against the rugged rock formations or, if the sea is in a more tranquil mood, explore sea life in the peaceful tide pools. Such a striking seascape is bound to inspire a kiss or two.

Otter Rock

Hotel/Bed and Breakfast Kissing

INN AT OTTER CREST, Otter Rock
301 Otter Crest Loop
(541) 765-2111, (800) 452-2101
Moderate to Very Expensive
Minimum stay requirement on holidays.

If it's natural splendor you're seeking, the Inn at Otter Crest offers more than its share. From the moment you turn off the highway and embark upon the curvy descent to the inn, the magic of the area is clearly evident. One moment the road hugs a perilous cliff; the next it disappears beneath dense canopies of foliage. Disappointingly, once you reach the inn's entrance, it is also clearly evident that the accommodations do not come close to matching the quality of the surroundings.

The half-dozen or so gray wooden buildings scattered over the property's 35 acres are overdue for refurbishing. All 150 units are individually owned and decorated by private owners; the inn simply rents out vacant rooms to guests when the owners have not reserved them. Rates vary, depending on the decor and amenities of each room. Most are modestly appointed with outdated furnishings, full kitchens, standard baths, and private entrances. Some come equipped with TVs and VCRs as well, and all suites and studios have fireplaces. On the positive side, each room has a private deck that allows incredible views of the craggy coastline and the churning ocean beyond. (This is the perfect place to catch glimpses of the gray whales and seals that occasionally visit the coves.) It's doubtful that these extremely average rooms will spark romance, but the quiet tranquility of the property is bound to turn your thoughts inward toward matters of the heart.

At the foot of the hillside, **THE FLYING DUTCHMAN RESTAURANT** (Moderate to Expensive) features wonderful views of the ocean, although the food will leave your palate wanting. Nearby you'll also find the community saunas, heated outdoor pool, hot tubs, and outdoor sports area.

Newport

Don't be dismayed by your first impression of this small, nondescript seaside town. Once you step beyond the commercialized strip of Highway 101, the dramatic ocean surf and wide stretches of sandy beach are a lover's paradise.

Hotel/Bed and Breakfast Kissing

NYE BEACH HOTEL, Newport
219 Northwest Cliff Street
(541) 265-3334
Inexpensive to Moderate

Gleaming brightly amidst its rundown neighbors, this relatively new cosmopolitan hotel is a diamond in the rough, so to speak. The hotel's striking shingle-sheathed facade has been painted a shade of chile-pepper red. Inside, the color scheme is equally eye-catching, with a hunter green lobby and banisters accented with splashes of taupe and cranberry. The lobby is also home to several lovebirds and canaries that twitter at guests from the safety of their cages.

Overall, this hotel is more eclectic than romantic. All 18 guest rooms are identical, with fireplaces, bent-willow love seats, small private baths, thick down comforters, and black-lacquered bed frames imported from Holland. For the purposes of our book, we recommend the six rooms with Jacuzzi soaking tubs and unobstructed ocean views. In a half-hearted attempt to decorate the maize-colored walls, a few theater posters have been tacked haphazardly around the rooms; unfortunately, they do little to liven up the unusually spartan, hostel-like atmosphere. Still, if you slightly open the sliding glass door to your tiny balcony, you can doze off together to the continuous melody of the nearby ocean surf.

Romantic Note: For a casual lunch or dinner, simply head downstairs to the brightly decorated oceanfront **NYE BEACH CAFE** (Inexpensive). Your senses will be overstimulated by the red-and-yellow-tiled floor, the colorful posters peppering the walls, and the eclectic mix of Mediterranean, Caribbean, and Mexican food on the menu. Hanging from the ceiling are pots of plants and cacti, with their branches reaching downward like long tresses of hair. To top it all off, a small bird aviary is located outside on the main deck. This place is anything but boring!

OCEAN HOUSE BED AND BREAKFAST, Newport
4920 Northwest Woody Way
(541) 265-6158, (800) 562-2632
Inexpensive to Moderate

For more than ten years Ocean House has maintained its reputation as a treasured place to stay. Rain or shine, you will find many reasons to prolong your visit. A sweeping lawn and meticulously maintained gardens envelop this blue-painted wooden home. A private staircase winds down to Agate Beach, where five miles of firm sand summon those who want to shed their shoes and comb the beach for seashells and agates. A series of cedar decks strategically placed along the bluff take full advantage of sunset's magic, and the homey common rooms, including a glass-enclosed sitting room, share this same enchanting perspective.

Recent renovations have turned the Ocean House's five guest rooms into luxurious, ultra-romantic retreats. Even the smallest room, Melody's Room, has been beautifully redecorated with light blue walls, a white eyelet coverlet and pillows, and a bathroom that boasts a spacious black and white Jacuzzi tub. Michelle's Room has an adjacent glass-enclosed sunroom with magnificent ocean views. Don't let the name of our favorite room deceive you—Mom's Room is not your typical extra bedroom. Cathedral ceilings soar above a king-size bed covered with lush linens and colorful pillows. French doors open onto a private porch where you can sit and listen to the sound of the surf. Guests can also luxuriate in a corner Jacuzzi tub situated in the wonderfully spacious white-tiled bathroom. The Overlook Room has its own fireplace and a wraparound porch that surveys the gardens and the ocean. An inviting bed covered with white embroidered linens is framed by picturesque bookcases artistically adorned with baskets, books, and seashells. Unusual wallpapers accent the bathroom, which also boasts a corner Jacuzzi tub. The remaining two rooms offer more of the same, with the bonus of beautiful ocean views.

A satisfying breakfast is served family-style in the unpretentious kitchen; it's not the best arrangement for romantic considerations, but with all these other distractions for the heart, this is easily overlooked.

STARFISH POINT, Newport
140 Northwest 48th Street
(541) 265-3751
Expensive

Set atop an oceanfront bluff, the six condominium-style units at Starfish Point have bay windows that emphasize stunning views of the ocean. (For an even closer look at the water, guests can follow the well-groomed but steep trail leading down to the outstretched shore below.) Each two-bedroom, two-story modern unit is a spacious townhouse that provides everything you could possibly think of (and more) to ensure a totally luxurious getaway: a full kitchen, sunken dining and living room, stereo, TV/VCR, fireplace, private decks, and two bathrooms. A spacious tiled Jacuzzi soaking tub set under skylights and overlooking the ocean is the romantic highlight of every unit. In contrast with the luxurious amenities and architecture, we must warn you that the decor could use some sprucing up—particularly the dated green carpeting, drab linens, and unattractive artwork.

TYEE LODGE OCEANFRONT
BED AND BREAKFAST, Newport
4925 Northwest Woody Way
(541) 265-8953, (888) 553-TYEE
http://www.newportnet.com/tyee/home.htm
Moderate

Named for the Chinook word for salmon, this newly renovated contemporary home embraces the Native American heritage of the Pacific Northwest. Sited on a cliff overlooking the ocean, Tyee Lodge offers breathtaking views of Agate Beach and Yaquina Head from almost every part of the house. Each guest room honors a different local tribe, with names like Tillamook, Siletz, and Alsea. All five are sparsely appointed, with green and burgundy color schemes, down comforters, queen-size beds, private baths, pine furnishings, wrought-iron mirrors, and somewhat barren cream walls. The Yaquina Room has an inviting bay window for watching the waves roll in on the beach below. The Chinook Room outshines the others, with its gas fireplace, bathroom skylight, and extraordinary view to the southwest.

If you're adventurous types, follow the switchback trail down to the sandy beach, where you can explore tide pools to your hearts' content. Or catch a brilliant sunset from the outdoor firepit. More serene souls will find contentment in the sunlit grand room, which has been tastefully decorated in subtle greens and beiges, with large windows facing the sparkling ocean. Snuggle up in the plaid overstuffed chairs near the slate fireplace as you sip complimentary coffee or tea. In the adjacent dining room, there is a glass etching of the lodge's trademark: a salmon done in traditional totemic style. Mornings here begin with a full breakfast of fresh cinnamon rolls and smoked salmon quiche. Honeymoons, anniversaries, and other special occasions often merit breakfast in bed, so be sure to make arrangements with the innkeepers beforehand.

Waldport

Hotel/Bed and Breakfast Kissing

CLIFF HOUSE, Waldport
1450 Southwest Adahi Street
(541) 563-2506
http://www.virtualcities.com
Expensive to Very Expensive
Minimum stay requirement on weekends and holidays

Everything about the Cliff House is deliciously romantic. A superlative renovation has turned this small seaside home, perched on a cliff overlooking the clamorous surf, into a beguiling retreat from the world at large. The tasteful interior is filled (and we mean *filled*) with intriguing antiques, heirlooms, and several pairs of chirping birds in cages. The cozy downstairs common area, which boasts a vaulted ceiling, knotty pine walls, impressive hanging ferns, and a beach-stone fireplace, is the perfect place for snuggling together on a velvet couch and admiring the ocean view.

All four guest rooms are plushly decorated and adorned with chandeliers and exquisite European antiques. The Library offers full frontal views of the glorious sea from the pillow of your queen-size rice canopy bed; in the Morning Star Room, you can enjoy the fresh ocean air on your own balcony. The Bridal Suite features supreme privacy, in addition to its ocean views, queen-size sleigh bed, wood-burning stove, and a large Jacuzzi tub in the fully mirrored (including the ceiling) bathroom. Breakfast is served to this room each morning at a small table, overlooking the thunderous waves.

For everyone else, breakfast is served on pretty blue glass dishes at one large table in the oceanfront breakfast area. After your morning meal, be sure to take advantage of the large, adjacent common deck, which has a panoramic view of the ocean to the north, west, and east. In the center of the deck you'll also find a massive hot tub with massaging jets that move up and down your spine. As we said before—deliciously romantic.

Restaurant Kissing

YUZEN, Waldport
10111 Northwest Pacific Coast Highway
(541) 563-4766
Inexpensive
Lunch and Dinner Tuesday-Sunday

Wooden booths tucked next to tall windows and vaulted ceilings with twinkling white lights intertwined in hanging green plants create an attractive atmosphere in this otherwise casual Japanese restaurant. The friendly staff brings one delight after another: flavorful teriyaki, fresh sushi, and scrumptious tempura. With literally no other romantic restaurant choices in Waldport, you'll be as pleased as we were with this tasty find.

Yachats

In spite of its popularity as a tourist destination, the tiny oceanfront town of Yachats retains a spirit and appearance of obscurity, lacking the urban sprawl that proliferates in many of the other coastal towns along Highway 101. Luckily, Yachats is unlikely to change, as it is protected from developers by several surrounding state and federal parks. Harbored in the Siuslaw National Forest, Yachats is one of the few places where the coastal mountain range actually merges with the shoreline. The hiking terrain ranks with the best on the coast, and the beaches are relatively remote and empty. Better yet, Yachats has some of the most impressive and romantic bed and breakfasts in the area.

Hotel/Bed and Breakfast Kissing

ADOBE RESORT MOTEL, Yachats
1555 Highway 101
(541) 547-3141, (800) 522-3623
Expensive to Very Expensive

If it weren't for the Adobe Resort's spectacular oceanfront location and handful of romantic suites (six out of 95, to be exact), we wouldn't have dared to recommend this otherwise drab property. The prevailing atmosphere is reminiscent of an economy roadside motel, but this annoyance fades into oblivion once you set foot in one of the Adobe's spacious ocean-view rooms. You can hear the waves crash against the rocky shore only feet away, and watch the sunset cast wondrous colors on the sky and sea. Cedar paneling and wood beams add texture to the standard and rather outdated decor, but it's the spa tubs, fireplaces, and proximity to the ocean that really set the amorous mood.

Plan ahead. Do not make your reservations here on the spur of the moment, because the Adobe's six best (and only recommendable) suites are in high demand.

KITTIWAKE, Yachats
95368 Highway 101 South
(541) 547-4470
Expensive
Minimum stay on weekends and holidays
Call for seasonal closures.

The ocean views seen from this massive white contemporary home are so sensational, you'll wonder if the innkeepers ever experience high tide in their living room—the careening ocean surf seems *that* close. Each of the three light and airy oceanfront rooms is superbly appointed with brightly colored coordinating linens (handmade by the innkeeper herself), lovely wood furnishings, and French doors that open out to the crashing surf. In two of the rooms, guests can appreciate the inn's gorgeous location from the vantage point of a large private Jacuzzi tub.

You can walk along the beach at any time of day or night in any season, thanks to the innkeepers' thoughtful supply of beach amenities, which includes boots, hats, scarves, rain ponchos, warm jackets, and flashlights. You might want to take an extended walk before breakfast to whet your appetites for the extravaganza to come: fresh nectar and juices, home-baked coffee cake, and lox and bagels (and that's just for starters). The main dish might be a hearty farmer's breakfast, stuffed crêpes, or a breakfast strudel made with phyllo and Brie. This feast is served to guests at one shared table, which isn't great for kissing, but with this array of goodies your appetites will keep you too busy to remember your lips anyway.

Romantic Note: A continental breakfast is also available for light eaters on the go.

MORNING STAR, Yachats
95668 Highway 101
(541) 547-4412
Inexpensive to Expensive
Minimum stay requirement on holidays

At first glance, you might not expect too much from this small store-front bed and breakfast set directly next to busy Highway 101. But we strongly urge you to take a second look, as we did: Morning Star is full of small surprises. Although the common area and breakfast nook are somewhat cluttered with the innkeepers' personal belongings, ignore them and head to the back of the house, where French doors open up to an outdoor hot tub sporting some of the best views around. All three guest rooms are located on the upstairs level and are named after famous artists. Each one is appointed with plush linens, private bathrooms, and art that corresponds with the room's name. The most impressive room, named Icart, has an intricate queen-size steel canopy bed with Oriental fabrics, a gas fireplace, rich window treat-ments, and a brightly tiled private bathroom that doesn't quite go with the room's decor, but is still spacious and pretty. O'Keeffe has great ocean views, a black Jacuzzi tub in the bathroom, and pastel linens; and Matisse, along with unfortunately audible traffic noise, has a king-size bed and a peekaboo view of the water. After you have enjoyed your full country breakfast, wan-der over to the adjacent Morning Star Gallery, which is run by the innkeeper and filled with wonderful local art and crafts.

THE OREGON HOUSE, Yachats
94288 Highway 101
(541) 547-3329
http://www.virtualcities.com
Inexpensive to Moderate
Minimum stay requirement on weekends and holidays seasonally

The owners of Oregon House have made this one of the most difficult bed and breakfasts to describe, because the ten units are so dramatically different from one another. Fortunately, this oceanfron getaway is as capti-vating as it is nonconformist. Perched on a cliff and embraced by a well-trimmed lawn and tall evergreens, the handful of accommodations overlook the blue Pacific from a quiet, peaceful setting. Three units have rambling, family-oriented floor plans; two others are charming self-contained cottages; two more share a spacious townhouse arrangement; one is a cozy loft studio; another is a very tiny (and very inexpensive) creekside room; and a room in the main house operates like a bed and breakfast (it's the only unit that gets a full-service breakfast in the morning). What these units have in common are floral fabrics and wallpapers, country accents, and a variety of amenities: Jacuzzi tubs, fireplaces, skylights, dining nooks, decks, patios, and full kitchens. They also offer everything from a glimpse to a full view of the ocean.

Due to the vast spectrum of accommodations, be very specific about what amenities you desire and exactly what you will be getting when making your reservation; some of the rooms are much nicer than others, depending on your romantic needs.

SEAQUEST BED AND BREAKFAST, Yachats
95354 Highway 101
(541) 547-3782, (800) 341-4878
http://www.seaq.com
Moderate to Very Expensive
Minimum stay requirement on weekends seasonally

If we could award a five-kiss rating to this bed and breakfast we would. Everything you could possibly want in a romantic getaway is here (and much, much more). Residing a mere 50 feet from the ocean's edge, this contemporary 7,000-square-foot wood home exemplifies Oregon coast architecture at its best. The five beautifully designed guest rooms feature bright pastel linens and wallpapers, down comforters, beds piled high with comfortable pillows, private entrances, and tantalizing views. Shutters open from the bedrooms onto spacious Jacuzzi soaking tubs in the tiled bathrooms.

A crackling fire warms the glass-enclosed dining and living room—a perfect spot to enjoy the full buffet-style breakfast. Morning repasts may include homemade granola and jams, fresh cakes, pastries, and a delicious croissant stuffed with eggs, cheese, and mushrooms. The enthusiastic innkeepers are a delight, but clearly specify if you want privacy—during breakfast you may encounter unwanted social introductions.

SERENITY BED AND BREAKFAST, Yachats
5985 Yachats River Road
(541) 547-3813
Inexpensive to Expensive

Don't make the mistake of bypassing this outstanding romantic destination simply because it is not on the ocean. It is a haven filled with unexpected luxury and opulence, located on a 13-acre sweep of lawn lined with red alders and kissed by distant ocean breezes.

We had difficulty choosing between the four ornate guest suites because each one has been lavished with sensuous details and appointed according to its unique theme. Alt Heidelberg, the smallest suite, features a double bed and antiques from Heidelberg, Germany; Bavaria, brimming with Bavarian knick-knacks and accented with beautiful blond wood, holds a Jacuzzi tub. Europa has an enticing assortment of fine European antiques, including an iron bed draped in blue and white linens. The most opulent room is Italia, also called the Honeymoon Suite, with its white-veiled wrought-iron canopy bed, tall ceilings, and large Jacuzzi tub. French doors in each room open to private decks or patios overlooking the nearby gardens and distant mountains.

If you can tear yourselves away from your romantic oasis for breakfast, you certainly won't be disappointed. The innkeeper is known for her authentic German-style breakfasts, served at one shared table in the main house, amid European antiques and lace curtains.

ZIGGURAT, Yachats
95330 Highway 101
(541) 547-3925
Moderate to Expensive
Minimum stay requirement on holidays
Call for seasonal closures.

Believe us when we tell you that Ziggurat is truly unique, an architecturally striking specimen of coastal escapism. True to its name, the building is a towering four-story shingled pyramid that sits on a grassy bluff overlooking the untamed ocean. The inn's interior, equally unusual, is somewhat schizophrenically appointed with a strange combination of slick gray tile and laminate, black carpeting, homey accents, and handsome locally crafted furniture.

The two spacious guest rooms, One East and One West, take up the lower level of the home. Both sport wraparound windows, scintillating views, comfy linens, and a slick ambience. One West is the most alluring by far, with its immense round glass-brick shower, mirrored ceiling, and private deck accessible via French doors. One East has a canopy bed, rather spartan decor, and a private sauna.

A full, carefully prepared breakfast is served in the ultra-modern (almost space-age) dining room, accompanied by extraordinary views of the ocean. Although there are only two guest rooms, until you get used to the multi-level, maze-like floor plan, you can actually get lost.

Restaurant Kissing

LA SERRE RESTAURANT, Yachats
160 West Second Street
(541) 547-3420
Moderate
Breakfast Sunday; Dinner Wednesday-Monday

La Serre remains one of our favorite dining spots along the Oregon coast. Unlike most other restaurants in this neck of the woods, it is neither too formal nor too casual; the interior is decorated with thriving greenery, oak tables, and hardwood floors. Fresh, local seafood is the busy kitchen's specialty. We recommend starting your meal with the steamed mussels and clams with drawn butter and lemon, before moving on to, say, the honey-curried scallops with a light curry glaze, or the filet mignon wrapped with bacon and topped with sautéed mushrooms in a light cream sauce. Service can be a bit slow due to the restaurant's popularity, but the wait is well worth it. A meal at La Serre will satisfy both your palate and your need to be close to your special someone.

Outdoor Kissing

DEVIL'S CHURN AND CAPE PERPETUA, Yachats

Two miles south of Yachats, just off Highway 101, on the west side of the road. Look for the signs to the turnoff.

If you thought the drive from Cannon Beach to Yachats was awesome, you ain't seen nothing yet. Every mile between Yachats and Gold Beach is stupendous. The coast is even more rugged and mountainous, and bordered on the east by the Siuslaw National Forest. The vista turnoffs along this stretch of highway are all located on soaring cliffs that offer arresting panoramas of the coastline due south and north. Take your time during this drive and take advantage of every wayside opportunity for kissing and viewing.

Two of the best places to observe the astounding mixture of rock, sand, and surf are the **DEVIL'S CHURN** and the 2,700-acre **CAPE PERPETUA SCENIC AREA**. The Devil's Churn is accessible via an exciting descent down a steep flight of wooden stairs that leads to a rocky, narrow channel. At the exchange of tides, the movement of water through this natural cut into the land is electrifying. If you feel like stretching your legs, stop at the Cape Perpetua visitor center, which offers hiking maps for a diverse range of easy to difficult trails. An auto tour map is also available for those who want to see the area by car; the drive is fantastic.

Romantic Suggestion: TILLICUM BEACH STATE PARK and BEACHSIDE STATE PARK, (541) 563-3220, both offer campsites (without RV hookups) located a stone's throw from the beach. There are plenty of trees to protect your tent from the wind, so the nearby ocean is a sterling bonus, not a shortcoming.

Florence

There is nothing remotely romantic about *new* Florence, which straddles Highway 101 and is noted for its overabundance of gas stations and mini-marts. For romantic moments, we endorse the nearby seaside and sand dunes, and historic **OLD TOWN FLORENCE**, harbored on the Siuslaw River. In the relatively quaint surroundings of Old Town Florence you can park your car and browse through the gift, coffee, and sweet shops ensconced along the placid riverfront.

Hotel/Bed and Breakfast Kissing

BLUE HERON INN, Florence
6563 Highway 126
(541) 997-4091, (800) 997-7780
Inexpensive to Moderate
Call for seasonal closures.

Located next to the highway and across from the Suislaw River, the Blue Heron Inn was undergoing renovation at the time we updated this book. Landscaping of the yard was still in progress and the Bridal Suite was under construction. From the looks of things, however, the Bridal Suite will turn out to be the most desirable room of all with its high ceilings, open double shower and Jacuzzi tub, and views of the yard and river. The other four rooms are charmingly decorated with floral wallpaper, lace curtains, patch-work quilts and floral bedspreads, dried floral arrangements, and antiques; some offer river views, while others overlook the serene backyard. Most of the bathrooms are standard, but one does have a sunken tub—a notable romantic plus.

A full breakfast is served downstairs in the dining room. The adjoining living room is very casual, with a fireplace, television, books, and binoculars for bird-watching. Using the common areas of this inn can seem too much like you're visiting a friend or relative instead of sharing a cozy getaway, but the overall feel is still quite comfortable, and the area offers plenty of opportunities to watch birds and wildlife.

COAST HOUSE CABIN, Florence
(541) 997-7888
Very Expensive; No Credit Cards
Minimum stay requirement

A short lantern-lit trail meanders through a grove of evergreens to this round, cedar-shake rental home set high on a towering cliff overlooking the blue waters of the Pacific. An expansive deck complete with outdoor shower offers a stunning view of the mesmerizing terrain. (Please note that the deck is somewhat perilous due to its height and lack of fencing.) Inside, throw rugs cover hardwood floors and a woodstove provides heat. Floor-to-ceiling windows in the comfortable living room allow a poignant view of the ocean through lofty pines. Ladders lead to two sleeping lofts, where you can stargaze through windows and skylights. In the bathroom, a claw-foot bathtub sits next to windows with more views of the ocean. While the house does provide a full kitchen, a microwave oven, and a stereo along with a collection of tapes and CDs, there is no television or telephone to distract you from each other.

THE EDWIN K BED AND BREAKFAST, Florence
1155 Bay Street
(541) 997-8360, (800) 833-9465
http://www.moriah.com/inns/or/ccoast.html
Inexpensive to Expensive

Beautifully tended flower gardens trim this lovingly refurbished turn-of-the-century white home, located on the edge of Old Town Florence and across the street from the river. (Unfortunately, the inn's river views are obstructed by a building and a large parking lot.) The innkeepers have a talent for historic renovations, and they are equally adept at creating thoroughly comfortable guest accommodations.

In the main house are six guest rooms, all named after seasons and times of the year. We prefer the four very spacious upstairs guest rooms, appointed with stained and leaded glass windows, period antiques, contemporary pastel fabrics and linens, and private patios that look down on a rock waterfall. Unfortunately, the cream carpeting is stained in places, and the decor is somewhat outdated. Each room has a designer bathroom, containing a large tiled shower or Jacuzzi tub, that opens to the bedroom. (The toilet is just as visible, which might make you as uncomfortable as it made us.)

Two additional countrified guest rooms are located on the main floor, just off the antique-filled common area, but they are not as lavish as the upstairs rooms. A relatively new addition is a rental apartment located in a recent add-on to the home. Unfortunately, this unit is even less enticing than the two main-floor rooms, with drab, motel-like furnishings, a visually intrusive television, and thin linens. It does have a full kitchen, however, as well as a washer and dryer.

If you are staying in the main house (breakfast is not served to the rental apartment), your morning will conclude with a generous full breakfast served at one large table in the formal Victorian dining room.

THE JOHNSON HOUSE, Florence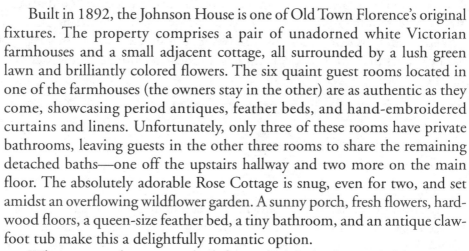
216 Maple Street
(541) 997-8000, (800) 768-9488
Moderate
Call for seasonal closures.

Built in 1892, the Johnson House is one of Old Town Florence's original fixtures. The property comprises a pair of unadorned white Victorian farmhouses and a small adjacent cottage, all surrounded by a lush green lawn and brilliantly colored flowers. The six quaint guest rooms located in one of the farmhouses (the owners stay in the other) are as authentic as they come, showcasing period antiques, feather beds, and hand-embroidered curtains and linens. Unfortunately, only three of these rooms have private bathrooms, leaving guests in the other three rooms to share the remaining detached baths—one off the upstairs hallway and two more on the main floor. The absolutely adorable Rose Cottage is snug, even for two, and set amidst an overflowing wildflower garden. A sunny porch, fresh flowers, hardwood floors, a queen-size feather bed, a tiny bathroom, and an antique clawfoot tub make this a delightfully romantic option.

When you awake, you can look forward to the innkeepers' pleasant conversation as you enjoy sweet French toast, fresh fruit, homemade muffins and breads, and a hot egg dish, all served at one large table in the main house.

MOONSET, Florence
(541) 997-8000, (800) 768-9488
Very Expensive
Call for seasonal closures.

For reservations and directions, call the phone numbers listed above or write to: Jayne Fraese, Box 1892, Florence, OR 97439.

Specifically designed as an intimate romantic oceanfront getaway, this phenomenal property is owned and operated by the people who own **JOHNSON HOUSE** (reviewed above). Octagonal in shape, Moonset is a one-of-a-kind contemporary home set on an acre of meadow and trees. The interior of this architectural masterpiece sports wood-paneled walls; a loft bedroom with a king-size bed adorned with colorful goosedown pillows and comforter; and wraparound floor-to-ceiling windows that showcase views of the nearby woods, the sprawling ocean dunes, and the blue waters of the Pacific Ocean in the distance. The full sunken kitchen (breakfast is up to you) and tiled bath are modern and luxurious, and romantic amenities include a sauna, outdoor Jacuzzi tub and shower, and a wood-stocked fireplace. When you tire of being indoors, retreat to the circular decks outside and get closer to nature and each other.

Outdoor Kissing

SANDLAND ADVENTURE DUNE BUGGY RIDES, Florence
85366 Highway 101
(541) 997-8087
$30 per hour; $50 deposit

The Oregon Dunes National Recreation Area is one of the most beautiful sections of this coast, and much of it is accessible only by dune buggy. Renting one of these nifty, though potentially dangerous, little vehicles opens up the phenomenal ecosystem of the dunes to your personal perusal. Imagine 600-foot sand dunes dotted with wisps of sea grass, secret lakes, and unusual islands of trees. The area is immense. During the summer you are likely to run into reckless kids (hopefully not literally), but depending on how you navigate your excursion, you can cleverly avoid them.

Charleston

Outdoor Kissing

CHARLESTON STATE PARKS, Charleston

The town of Charleston is south of Coos Bay, on a small peninsula 30 miles due west of Highway 101.

This trio of state parks south of town are well marked and well worth the detour from the main road. Despite the fact that they are separated from one another by only a few miles, each one has its own distinctive personality and mood. The northernmost park is **SUNSET BAY**, where majestic forest and cool sandy earth flank a small, calm ocean inlet. **SHORE ACRES**, a bit farther south, is where the remains of an estate sprawl on a cliff soaring high above the coast. Intriguing paths ramble over rock-strewn beaches gouged with caves and granite fissures where the water releases its energy in spraying foam and crashing waves. This park is renowned for its extensive formal gardens, which are maintained to resemble their former glory. Don't miss the numerous lookouts. The most informal park is **CAPE ARAGO**, an outstanding picnic spot high above the shoreline with a northern view of the coast. It is best known for the sea lions and harbor seals that can be seen romping in the surf or sleeping languidly on the rocks below.

Bandon

Bandon is one of the few relatively undiscovered seaside towns along the Oregon coast, although that won't last much longer. Real estate signs abound, which isn't surprising. The beach here is more spectacular and interesting than any of the more popular sites farther north, with a multitude of haystack rocks that rise in tiers from the ocean. There are only a few noteworthy restaurants in this small community, and an even smaller number of bed and breakfasts. If you yearn to retreat from the busy coastal towns, this small beachside community is definitely your answer.

Hotel/Bed and Breakfast Kissing

LIGHTHOUSE BED AND BREAKFAST, Bandon
650 Jetty Road
(541) 347-9316
Inexpensive to Moderate

Comfort should be this bed and breakfast's middle name. The sunken common room, furnished with a mismatched combination of cozy beige couches and eclectic antiques, is a good example of what we mean. A telescope propped in the corner allows closer views of Bandon's historic lighthouse (the inn's namesake) and nearby Coquille River.

All five guest rooms have side glimpses (some better than others) of the water, plus private bathrooms, and a varied assortment of romantic assets: one new suite has a fireplace and a whirlpool tub set in a glass-enclosed bathroom, one has a bedside view of the river, and another has its own private deck overlooking the water. The inn's decor is definitely outdated, but the gourmet breakfast helps compensate.

Restaurant Kissing

HARP'S, Bandon
130 Chicago Street
(541) 347-9057

Expensive
Dinner Daily

Harp's is acclaimed up and down the coast for its superlative cuisine and gracious service. Situated in a small, unassuming weathered building in Old Town Bandon, the restaurant has an equally casual interior, with dark wood tables, wood paneling, and soft lighting. Walls cluttered with prints of the sea, an abundance of green accents (including the blinds, carpet, tablecloths, and walls), and a smattering of plants add to the charm. While the decor could use some updating, the food is nothing short of superb: the salmon with capers marinated in vermouth is impeccable, and the halibut in a hot pistachio sauce is even better. Save room for a freshly baked dessert, or top off your meal with a glass of port served with walnuts and cheese.

LORD BENNETT'S, Bandon
1695 Beach Loop Road
(541) 347-3663
Moderate
Lunch and Dinner Daily; Sunday Brunch

Named after Bandon's founder, this contemporary wood restaurant sits across the street from the beach and serves traditional fare, with an emphasis on seafood. Floral paintings and silk flowers enliven the modern dining room's temperate mood, and long, narrow windows showcase views of the surf. We've heard locals rave about Lord Bennett's, but after we ate there, we couldn't figure out why. The food was only mediocre, and the service at times was slow. The real attraction is the stellar location. The panorama of jagged coastline, sparkling water, and haystack rocks is spellbinding.

Outdoor Kissing

FACE ROCK WAYSIDE, Bandon

Turn off Highway 101 at the signs indicating Beach Loop Drive.

Many sections of beach and shoreline along the Oregon coast claim to possess unparalleled views and the most stupendous scenery. Though the competition is tough, there are no real winners due to the multitude of spectacular locations in this area. Yet, if we had to cast a vote, we would choose the beachfront at the Face Rock wayside. The rock-studded water and damp, firm expanse of sandy beach are truly without equal. Memories of your time here will linger long after you've gone.

Langlois

Hotel/Bed and Breakfast Kissing

FLORAS LAKE HOUSE BED AND BREAKFAST, Langlois
92870 Boice Cope Road
(541) 348-2573
Inexpensive to Expensive
Call for seasonal closures.

If you windsurf (or want to learn how), this place has a definite kissing bonus. Floras Lake is one of the few lakes located directly next to the ocean where you can actually windsurf. (It's the proximity to the ocean that makes the windsurfing so ideal.) The owners rent sailboards and wet suits, and even give lessons. But you don't have to windsurf in order to appreciate this lovely wood and brick contemporary home. The four attractive guest rooms are very spacious, designed with cathedral ceilings and abundant windows, and decorated with antique beds, patchwork quilts, wicker furnishings, and pastel accents. Two rooms have fireplaces, and all have private entrances that open onto a wraparound deck facing the beautiful gardens, Floras Lake, and the ocean in the distance. Before or after the continental breakfast buffet, take a long walk on the beach. It remains empty most of the year, so you can privately kiss to your hearts' content.

Romantic Alternative: A small campground called **BOICE COPE CAMPGROUND** sits directly on the shore of Floras Lake, hidden by trees from the bed and breakfast. If camping is more your style, try this wonderfully secluded spot, which is protected from the ocean. You can still rent sailboards and wet suits from Floras Lake House.

Gold Beach

Hotel/Bed and Breakfast Kissing

INN AT NESIKA BEACH, Gold Beach
33026 Nesika Road
(541) 247-6434
Inexpensive to Moderate; No Credit Cards

One of the last stops for romance before the California border is this recently built Victorian-style home. It is located in a residential neighborhood, on a steep bank overlooking the dramatic Pacific Ocean. Each of the four spacious and tastefully decorated guest rooms has a ringside view of the crashing surf and brilliant sunsets. Three of the rooms have black marble fireplaces, and all have whirlpool tubs in private bathrooms, mismatched homey touches, thick down comforters, feather beds, lace curtains that billow in the breeze, and cozy sitting areas.

Breakfast is served at a common table in the formal dining room, along with more ocean views. You can take your coffee out on the enclosed sundeck after you feast on warm scones, pecan French toast, and pancakes stuffed with peaches. Morning delights like these will keep you going all day long.

TU TU' TUN LODGE, Gold Beach
96550 North Bank Rogue
(541) 247-6664
http://www.el.com/to/tututunlodge
Expensive to Very Expensive
Minimum stay requirement seasonally
Call for seasonal closures.

Prepare to be enchanted. Located seven miles from Gold Beach, Tu Tu' Tun ("People by the River") is nestled in the heart of a quiet forested valley, next to the winding Rogue River. Ivy cloaks the wood pillars that flank the cedar lodge, colorful flower boxes line the stairs, and the manicured grounds envelop a heated outdoor lap pool and terraced gardens.

The lodge's 16 comfortable and attractive rooms, two suites, and two private homes have a distinctive Northwest flavor; all are decorated with unique art pieces, sumptuous linens and fabrics, and open-beamed ceilings. A tile entryway, wool carpeting, and a small refrigerator are additional features. Some units offer slate fireplaces; others are blessed with sliding doors that open onto private balconies or patios where guests can relish river views from a "moon soaker" tub. (Be sure to specify the amenities you desire; only five rooms have hot tubs, and only six have fireplaces.) Fresh flowers enliven each room, and turndown service and fresh cookies are provided nightly. The only accommodation here that does not have a river view is a private three-bedroom home sheltered in an apple orchard that is frequently visited by tame deer.

For an extra charge, breakfast, hors d'oeuvres, and dinner are served in a comfortable common lodge, warmed in winter by a crackling fire in an immense river-rock fireplace. Unfortunately, all of the meals are served family-style at several round eight-person tables, which precludes the possibility of a romantic encounter. However, at the time this book went to press, plans were being made to accommodate guests who desire more privacy by offering candlelit dinners for two in the comfort of your own room.

" *There are swords about me to keep me safe: They are the kisses of your lips.*"

Mary Carolyn Davies

Oregon Cascades

Columbia River Gorge

In Oregon, Interstate 84 borders the south side of the Columbia River and Highway 14 runs parallel to it on the north side of the river in Washington state. Several bridges span the river between Oregon and Washington. Reviews of kissworthy places on the Washington side of the Columbia River Gorge are included in the Washington Cascades chapter of this book.

The Columbia River Gorge is a most fitting region to include in this kissing travelogue. The 60 miles or so of scenery formed by the river carving its way through the Cascade Mountains create a kaleidoscope of heart-stirring images. To travel this passage is to sense the magic afoot in the emerald mountains to the west and blazoned across the sunburnt mountains and grasslands to the east.

The Gorge is a vast collage of all the intensely beautiful things the Northwest has to offer. There are scores of ponds, mountain lakes, and trails, but the waterfalls are undoubtedly the most remarkable natural feature. Depending on the season, they rush to earth in a variety of contours and intensities. **ONEONTA FALLS** drops abruptly off a sheer ledge for several hundred feet. **ELOWAH FALLS** sprays a fine, showery mist over deciduous forest, while **PUNCH BOWL FALLS** pours into crystal-clear Eagle Creek. **UPPER HORSETAIL FALLS** is forced out in a jet stream through a portal centered in a wall of rock, and **WAHKEENAH FALLS** rushes over rocky steps and beds of stone. Wherever you happen to be in the Columbia River Gorge, its stunning natural pageantry will make you feel that you've found paradise.

Outdoor Kissing

COLUMBIA RIVER GORGE NATIONAL SCENIC AREA 💋💋💋
U.S. Forest Service
(541) 386-2333

The Columbia River Historic Highway begins at the Ainsworth Park exit or the Troutdale exit on Interstate 84 (east of Portland) and extends east roughly 30 miles.

This highway, the first paved road to cross the Cascades, was constructed in 1915 and is reported to be an engineering marvel. Once you drive this sinuous, moss-covered work of art, you will swear it was really built by wizards. There is none of the commercialism you associate with road travel; you won't be bothered by neon, billboards, superhighways, traffic signs, or speeding cars. This is one scenic route that really accentuates the scenery. In the days when it was built, driving was called touring, and cars moseyed along at 30 miles an hour. You can go a tad faster through here now, but not much, and why bother? You won't want to miss the falls, hikes, and roadside vistas that show up suddenly along the way.

Romantic Warning: In summertime, when family vacations are under way, this can be a very crowded strip of road. The best time for romance here is when school is in session.

Romantic Option: We don't generally recommend tourist attractions; the crowds associated with them usually prevent intimate moments and privacy. The restaurant in **MULTNOMAH FALLS LODGE**, Highway 30 East, Troutdale, (503) 695-2376 (Moderate) is indeed a tourist attraction, and were it not for one unbelievable feature this would be just another Northwest wood-and-stone dining room serving three decent meals a day. That attraction, of course, is the lodge's namesake, a plummeting waterfall that spills a dramatic 620 feet, almost in the lodge's backyard. This spectacle makes any snack or meal here a momentous occasion.

Troutdale

Set at the west entrance of the Columbia River Gorge, Troutdale is located 25 miles west of Hood River and 20 miles east of Portland. New development and residential areas cover most of the town, but there is one noteworthy stop on your way into or out of the Gorge.

Restaurant Kissing

BLACK RABBIT RESTAURANT, Troutdale
2126 Southwest Halsey, at McMenamins Edgefield
(503) 669-8610, (800) 669-8610
Moderate to Expensive
Breakfast, Lunch, and Dinner Daily

As most Portlanders know, the McMenamins have a corner on the Northwest microbrew market. With more than 32 pubs and brewpubs in Oregon and Washington, their popularity is continually growing. With this site, however, they have crossed over into another industry: fine dining and accommodations. The modestly elegant Black Rabbit Restaurant is a fabulous place for a generous meal of Northwest specialties and gourmet delights. Wall sconces cast subdued light upon the dining room and its hardwood floors, Persian rugs, and high-backed wood booths. The dining room was understaffed the night we visited, but the wait staff remained friendly and the food was excellent.

Romantic Warning: Overnight lodging at **MCMENAMINS EDGEFIELD** (Inexpensive to Moderate) is not for everyone. Built in the early 1900s as the county's poor farm, this complex of buildings eventually became a nursing home. It was nearly demolished in the late 1980s, but the McMenamins stepped in with big plans. We applaud the rescue and restoration of this historic property; unfortunately, however, the guest rooms have retained the sterile feeling of an institution. Thin bedspreads, shabby rugs, and detached baths down each hall add to this cold ambience. The extravagant murals along the walls and doors are interesting, but the surreal theme throughout the work is somewhat eerie. If you are a big fan of the McMenamins brewpubs, you might be able to appreciate the charms of this property and enjoy the several on-site pubs and movie theater. Otherwise, the drafty halls and funky artwork will probably not tug at your heartstrings.

Hood River

Though the Columbia River Gorge is visually stunning, and the trails, natural wonders, and fruit-laden countryside are totally splendid, it has yet another attraction: windsurfing. Hood River is at the heart of this activity, and here is where to find the reliably exciting air currents that windsurfers relish. Sit and watch these enthusiasts and their multicolored sails whip across the Gorge, or get out there and try it for yourselves—several places in town offer classes.

Hotel/Bed and Breakfast Kissing

COLUMBIA GORGE HOTEL, Hood River
4000 West Cliff Drive
(541) 386-5566, (800) 345-1921
http://www.gorge.net/lodging/cghotel
Very Expensive to Unbelievably Expensive

Vast, meticulously maintained grounds surround the Columbia Gorge Hotel, a prestigious Spanish-style villa set on a high, forested bank above the Columbia River. Wah Gwin Gwin Falls tumbles down the bluff in front of the hotel, and guests can watch windsurfers test their skill across the river's waves. This landmark hotel was built in the 1920s by a Portland lumber baron. The grandeur of the hotel is immediately apparent in the lobby, and the elegance continues in the hotel's restaurant, **COLUMBIA RIVER COURT** (see Restaurant Kissing).

Upstairs, the 42 guest rooms may be a letdown after you see the main floor. Each suite is attractive enough, with Queen Anne–style furniture and floral accents, but the thin bedspreads and televisions placed in plain sight are less than amorous. Rooms in the Unbelievably Expensive range have a view of the river, which is great, but everything else is still ordinary. More than anything, it is the price tag on these accommodations (for rooms with or without a view) that makes you expect more than what you get. One saving grace is that a phenomenal six-course breakfast is included with your stay (nonguests pay $45.90 for two). This meal takes approximately 90 minutes, and the delicious courses of fresh fruit, hot apple fritters, oatmeal, three eggs, breakfast meat or grilled Idaho trout, golden hash browns, biscuits, and buttermilk pancakes seem never-ending. Even if you were not completely thrilled with your room, you will surely leave the hotel smiling after this morning feast.

HOOD RIVER HOTEL, Hood River
102 Oak Avenue
(541) 386-1900, (800) 386-1859
Inexpensive to Expensive

Visit yesteryear and spend an evening in Hood River's oldest hotel. This venerable 1913 red brick building is located in the core of downtown Hood River. The lobby summons you through stylish French doors into the handsome embrace of posh sofas, large potted plants, and high ceilings that allow the room to fill with profuse sunlight in the morning. You'll know this is a vintage hotel when you take your first ride in the antique elevator with a brass door that you pull shut yourself, a time machine–like experience.

Upstairs, hallways with high ceilings and Oriental carpets lead to your room. None of the 41 guest rooms escape the perpetual hum of traffic beyond, but if you can get used to this (after all, you are downtown), you're likely to appreciate these accommodations. The two-bedroom suites with full kitchens, hardwood floors, Oriental carpets, antique mirrors, and plenty of windows feel more like apartments than hotel rooms. The less expensive rooms are smaller but also cozier, with personal touches like dried floral wreaths and canopied beds. From some, you can even catch a glimpse of the Columbia Gorge beyond the nearby buildings, roads, and railroad tracks. This is a nice option for those who want the romance of staying in a historic building and the convenience of being downtown, but don't want to pay exorbitant prices.

Romantic Note: A restaurant called **PASQUALE'S** (Inexpensive) is adjacent to the downstairs lobby, and you might consider having breakfast or lunch here (neither is included with your stay). The atmosphere is casual, and the fare ranges from creamy pasta dishes to homemade minestrone soup served with a baguette.

Romantic Suggestion: If a day trip to Mount Hood or a breezy picnic by the river sounds intriguing, pick up provisions at **THE WINE SELLERS**, 514 State Street, (541) 386-4647 (Inexpensive). In the back of this charming gift and flower boutique is a little coffee shop that also sells gourmet foods and a large selection of local wines.

LAKECLIFF ESTATE BED AND BREAKFAST, Hood River
3820 West Cliff Drive
(541) 386-7000
Inexpensive to Moderate; No Credit Cards
Call for seasonal closures.

Rather than staying in the costly accommodations at the Columbia Gorge Hotel, consider a sojourn at Lakecliff Estate Bed and Breakfast, only a half mile down the road from the hotel. This large, beautiful, historic summer home is tucked away on three magnificent acres of prime Columbia River property. Almost every room in the house has a commanding view of the river. An outside deck at the back of the house is perfect for lounging and gazing, as is the pleasant sunroom with wicker furniture and floral cushions. All four rooms are spacious and totally appealing. The Garden Room is an especially cozy hideaway, with dark green linens, views of the surrounding garden and woods, thick quilts, a native stone fireplace, and a private bath. Emily's Room, decorated with light florals, has a river view and is the only other room with a private bath. The two rooms that share a separate shower and bathroom each have a stone fireplace, a washbasin in the room, plush carpets, and attractive decor.

A hearty breakfast awaits you in the morning, making this bed and breakfast an easy place to call home. Breakfast is served family-style to one large table, which might be a minor romantic inconvenience but usually becomes a fun, sociable time for all.

STATE STREET INN, Hood River
1005 State Street
(541) 386-1899
Inexpensive
Closed September through April

Centrally located on a residential street, this handsomely renovated Craftsman-style home with oak floors and leaded glass windows is a bright and airy place. The four guest rooms are all named after states the owners have lived in, and each is decorated appropriately. The California and Maryland Rooms are the most spacious and have views of the Columbia River and Mount Adams through leaded glass windows. The potential drawback is that two bathrooms are shared between the four rooms, but for the price, the quality, and the delicious breakfast, State Street Inn is a great option. If simple comfort is high on your list of priorities, you'll be thrilled to stay here.

Restaurant Kissing

COLUMBIA RIVER COURT DINING ROOM, Hood River
4000 West Cliff Drive, at the Columbia Gorge Hotel
(541) 386-5566, (800) 345-1921
Expensive to Very Expensive
Breakfast and Dinner Daily; Lunch Monday-Saturday

As befits an elegant 1920s country estate, the dining room at the Columbia Gorge Hotel is adorned with fine crystal, silver, and pastel tablecloths. Still, the main attractions are the arched bay windows which overlook the river through tall trees. If you plan on being in the neighborhood, you may want to consider a morning stop here. The "world-famous farm breakfast" is pricey if you aren't a guest, but you may end up saving money because you surely won't need lunch after this six-course extravaganza. Dinner is an equally elegant affair, and the menu offers gourmet Northwest fare such as fresh halibut baked with morel mushrooms, and poached salmon with roasted red peppers and dill pesto. Try the chef's signature wilted spinach, smoked duck, and bacon salad, prepared and flambéed tableside. Service is professional but not always swift (probably because the restaurant is always full).

STONEHEDGE INN, Hood River   💋💋💋
3405 Cascade Drive
(541) 386-3940
Moderate to Expensive
Call for seasonal hours.

Considered one of the state's best-kept romantic secrets (according to an Oregon newspaper poll), Stonehedge consistently lives up to its well-deserved reputation. It is set away from the town up a pothole-filled gravel road, concealed by dense shrubbery, and identified only by a beat-up sign that gives no clue as to what lies beyond. This century-old, stone-clad home is an intriguing find. The former dining and living rooms have been beautifully transformed to accommodate intimate seating in a homey setting, the windows face the woods and gardens outside, and the food is classic continental with a Northwest accent. Entrées are incredibly fresh and generously accompanied by soup, salad, and fresh warm bread.

Mount Hood

At 11,235 feet, Mount Hood is Oregon's highest mountain. It is also one of the most popular winter destinations in the state. The skiing is outstanding, and there are many trails where you can hike in the summer. For the most part, accommodations in this region (including the towns of Government Camp and Welches) cater to outdoor enthusiasts; guest rooms tend to be plain, because most of the people who come here spend the majority of their time outside, not in their rooms. The rugged beauty of the area is likely to make up for any shortcomings in romantic accommodations, though, and your time here is sure to be relaxed and casual—something all Northwesterners can appreciate.

Hotel/Bed and Breakfast Kissing

INN AT COOPER SPUR, Mount Hood
10755 Cooper Spur Road
(541) 352-6692, (888) 541-6894
Inexpensive to Expensive
Minimum stay requirement on holidays

Best described as a romantic anomaly, this lodge definitely has all the outward signs of a provincial mountain snuggery. At the foot of a gentle, less-traveled slope, definitely off the beaten path (about a half hour from the Timberline ski area), a log gateway guards a stone path leading to a charming wood cottage that houses the lodge's restaurant. Inside, you will be greeted by more distinctive woodwork and the aroma of either just-baked pies or freshly grilled thick steaks. The 14 rooms and cabins have the same type of exterior, and the interiors are all wood, with stone fireplaces. Almost a dozen hot tubs wait outdoors to assuage tired, over-skied muscles. (They all occupy the same cement slab, so there is no privacy, but they are soothing for skiers just the same.)

Who could deny how quaint and cozy all that sounds? And it is, but only up to a point. What you'll discover is that the homey, ultrabasic decor and furnishings and laid-back atmosphere make this more a place for hiking or skiing chums than a haven for starry-eyed lovers. Though this may not be exactly the intimate destination you were looking for, if it is ski season, the Inn at Cooper Spur has mountain hospitality aplenty and all the warmth and social activity you could want.

TIMBERLINE LODGE, Mount Hood
South Side of Mount Hood
Reservations: (503) 231-5400, (800) 547-1406
General Information: (503) 272-3311
http://www.teleport.com/~timlodge
Inexpensive to Very Expensive
Minimum stay requirement on holidays

Mount Hood stands as an overwhelming example of nature's potency and formidable genius. Near the summit, there rests an example of human tenacity and creativity: Timberline Lodge. This grand structure was built in 1937, during the Depression, as part of President Roosevelt's WPA (Works Progress Administration) program to create jobs. Every aspect of the building is endowed with character and masterful craftsmanship, evidenced in metal filigree, stone chimneys, archways, and massive hand-hewn beams. The handcrafted metal-strapped furniture, wall murals, patchwork bedspreads, and intricately arranged wood rafters are further testimony to this hard work and artistry.

There are 60 guest rooms in the lodge, but the ten Chalet units are beyond rustic, with bunk beds and a shared bath. Fireplace Rooms have the most romantic potential, with all-wood interiors, but we must warn that the authenticity of the units makes for less than plush surroundings. The rust-colored bedspreads are endowed with the original appliqués, and some of the furniture and curtains are stained or water-damaged. Still, if you are here primarily to enjoy the great outdoors, this handsome, historic lodge and the riveting countenance of Mount Hood together will create a scene of rugged romance perfect for two.

Romantic Note: As you may expect, the peak season here is winter, when skiing is in full force. This popular mountaintop destination isn't a secret and can be booked year-round, so be sure to plan ahead.

Government Camp

FALCON'S CREST INN, Government Camp
87287 Government Camp Loop Highway
(503) 272-3403, (800) 624-7384
Moderate to Very Expensive
Minimum stay requirement on holidays and in the Mexicalli Suite

The gracious hosts here are eager to make you feel right at home in their cozy bed and breakfast. Five rooms are available in the contemporary chalet-style mountain house, and each has a private bath, in-room telephone, and a forest or mountain view. The Mexicalli Suite is the only ground-level unit, making it a particularly private option. Bright colors, a wrought-iron-and-pine bedframe on the queen-size bed, and a two-person Jacuzzi tub make it even more sumptuous. Up a flight of stairs, the Master Suite, adjacent to the dining room, has a four-poster queen-size bed, knotty pine walls, and a luxurious hot tub on the back deck—this is a favorite room for romantics. The Safari and Cat Ballou Rooms may be a bit overdone for some tastes, with stuffed animals and wild prints in one and rich red velvet, satin, and lace accents in the other, but the Cat Ballou Room is the only room with a king-size bed. There is a comfortable sitting area on the third floor with a television, a VCR, and a stereo for guests' use. Common areas throughout the house are homey and furnished with various collections from the innkeepers' family and travels.

In the morning, fresh muffins are delivered to your room with a hot beverage. The full gourmet breakfast in the dining room, which follows this "appetizer," should keep you satisfied until well into the afternoon.

Romantic Note: If you visit Falcon's Crest in the winter, you should know that from the day after Thanksgiving through the month of March, the inn celebrates an extended Christmas. Each room has its own custom-designed tree and is dressed with garlands and lights.

Romantic Suggestion: Elegant dinners are served in the inn's dining room, and we highly recommend an evening here. Six-course Euro-American extravaganzas are the specialty, and you will surely be satisfied by a main course such as Cornish game hens stuffed with apricot stuffing or prime rib with horseradish sauce. Reservations for dinner are required at least 24 hours in advance, and the price starts at $65.90 per couple.

MOUNT HOOD INN, Government Camp
87450 East Government Camp Loop
(503) 272-3205, (800) 443-7777
Moderate to Expensive
Minimum stay requirement on holidays

Although the Mount Hood Inn is obviously a chain hotel that borders the highway, the accommodations here are more pleasant than those at the better-known **RESORT AT THE MOUNTAIN** and the **INN AT COOPER SPUR** (both reviewed in this chapter). All of the 56 rooms are tastefully decorated with matching linens, comforters, and curtains; plush new carpeting; and contemporary natural-wood furniture. The pastel decor and nondescript hotel interiors may not be incredibly stylish or impressive, but many rooms also offer private, beautifully tiled, two-person Jacuzzi tubs—perfect for ski-weary bodies. Given the fact that the mountain setting is just moments away, this might be a better option.

Welches

THE RESORT AT THE MOUNTAIN, Welches
68010 East Fairway Avenue
(503) 622-3101, (800) 669-7666
http://www.theresort.com
Inexpensive to Very Expensive

Rushing waterfalls, dense forest, and diverse wildlife fill this area with raw natural beauty. Finding a place to stay amid all the gorgeous scenery is not always easy, though. You should call far in advance to make a reservation, especially during the height of ski season—and even then, you might be out in the cold. However, your chances are better at this resort, which offers 160 guest rooms.

We would not usually recommend a resort of this magnitude, not only because its size reduces your sense of privacy, but also because the grounds resemble an apartment complex and the rooms are reminiscent of a standard hotel. Nevertheless, the setting is sublime; the resort is nestled in 300 acres of evergreen woodland in the foothills of the Huckleberry Wilderness Area of the Mount Hood National Forest. It's truly a special place to be in any season, but it's particularly spectacular when the grounds are covered in snow.

Catering to sports enthusiasts, the resort has golf courses, tennis courts, an outdoor heated pool, a Jacuzzi tub, a fitness center, hiking trails, volleyball, and more. It is a perfect place for athletes, but for those of you who have come looking for some peace and quiet, we suggest walking in the stillness of the woods and drinking in the enthralling mountain views. As you fill your lungs with the sweet, fresh air, you will be thankful for this mountain vacation spot, even if it was your only option.

Romantic Note: Dinner at **THE HIGHLANDS**, (503) 622-2214 (Moderate to Expensive) is a must. Not only is it conveniently located in the resort's complex, but it offers serene intimacy in an elegant green-and-peach room with a view of the evergreens and grounds beyond. Lobster bisque, salmon piccata, and hazelnut-chicken linguine are just a few of the dishes you can relish by candlelight.

Sisters

Hotel/Bed and Breakfast Kissing

BLACK BUTTE RANCH, Sisters
13243 Hawksbard Road (Highway 20)
(541) 595-6211, (800) 452-7455
Inexpensive to Very Expensive
Minimum stay requirement

For some, a romantic retreat consists of shutting out the world for hours or even days and focusing solely on each other. Others interpret romance to mean exploring the world actively together, side by side or hand in hand. You can have the best of both at Black Butte Ranch, although it caters more to those who want to see and do it all.

Encircled by seven impressive mountains, the ranch is set on a flat, grassy plain sparsely covered with ponderosa pines, meandering streams, and fertile meadows. Your interlude begins in the registration lodge, an unusual three-story building with open wood beams, high ceilings, terraced landings and stairways, cozy nooks and crannies, and a live tree growing through its center. Encircling glass windows give you calming views of the distant plains, the glorious mountains, and the nearby lake which is dotted with geese in the summer. The ranch-style interior makes you feel as if you've really gone out West.

You can rent one-, two-, or three-bedroom condominiums, all set in contemporary gray wood complexes with wood walkways and views of the grounds. Inside, the suites feature high ceilings, fireplaces, full kitchens, and ranch-style decor that can look somewhat dull and outdated, depending on the condo. One- and four-bedroom homes scattered around the ranch are also available for rent. Because each home is privately owned, furniture, amenities, and decor vary significantly from one to another. Neither luxurious nor elegant, Black Butte is nevertheless a pleasant place to enjoy some country privacy together.

For a real taste of ranch life, the stables are moments away. Befriend a horse, and take a guided tour on horseback in the silent, lush backwoods. Choose from various trail rides (some include a barbecue dinner in the barn afterward), design your own ride, or get lessons if you're a tenderfoot. As if this were not enough, Black Butte Ranch offers the standard resort amenities: tennis courts, four outdoor swimming pools, bike rentals, jogging trails, golf courses, and sufficient restaurants. Needless to say, these activities are not geared toward intimacy, but you never know. Life is full of surprises.

CASCADE COUNTRY INN, Sisters
15870 Barclay Drive
(541) 549-INNN, (800) 316-0089
Moderate

Set among sprawling farm fields on the outskirts of Sisters, this contemporary gabled country inn is an unexpected surprise. Even more surprising is the fact that the inn is adjacent to a small community airport (it's so small it's hardly noticeable). Guests with access to small private planes can almost literally fly through the front door.

The abundance of windows in this newly built country home creates a sunny ambience, amplified by cheery touches. Daylight pours into the comfortable common living room furnished with floral-patterned couches. Stained glass transom windows in each of the six guest rooms look out to views of the Cascade Mountains. Dried flowers, patchwork quilts, and Christian quotes and Bibles (the latter of which may be too prolific for some tastes) fill every room, sometimes to the point of overflowing. Hand-painted murals and stenciling give each room its own unique, and sometimes too-busy, country flair.

We definitely have our favorites. The Angels Room has a beautiful wrought-iron canopy feather bed draped with white lace fabric, as well as a beautiful stained glass window that diffuses light above the fireplace. In the Bridal Suite (appropriately called Mi Amor), honeymooners are greeted with champagne and decadent locally made fudge. A fireplace, a Jacuzzi tub, and beautiful views of the Cascades ensure romantic possibilities here. Although Victoria's Secret is one of the smallest rooms, we found it unusually charming, with its blond hardwood floors and its headboard painted to resemble a fence post. Those with a penchant for flying are the only ones who will really appreciate Wild Blue Yonder, located in an actual hangar, a short walk from the inn. This lodging is filled with flying memorabilia, including an aircraft radial engine, which provides the base for a glass-topped table in the room's center.

Evening refreshments and a complete gourmet breakfast are included with your stay, as is the use of the inn's mountain bikes, which can help you explore Sisters' rugged, rural terrain.

Bend

Parched in the summer and frozen in the winter, Bend is a lively resort community set in the heart of the Oregon Cascades. Summertime brings white-water rafters, hikers, bikers, rock climbers, and families; in the winter, skiers hit the slopes. More akin to Marlboro Country than a captivating Northwest enclave, Bend's primary romantic draw is the great outdoors. In the summer, musicians with the Cascade Festival of Music perform jazz, pop, blues, and classical music along the river at Drake Park. Mount Bachelor and the Deschutes River are a short drive away, and more than a dozen parks and national forests offer unlimited adventure. Whatever the season, activities abound, and lovers of the outdoors love Bend.

Hotel/Bed and Breakfast Kissing

INN OF THE SEVENTH MOUNTAIN, Bend
18575 Southwest Century Drive
(541) 382-8711, (800) 452-6810 (in the U.S.)
Inexpensive to Unbelievably Expensive

For those dynamic couples who just can't sit still, the Inn of the Seventh Mountain is ideal. Trips down a coursing white-water river, challenging mountain trails, sturdy mountain bikes, a large pool where roughhousing is considered acceptable, lots of hot tubs, roller skating, horseback riding, and a world-class golf course are right outside your door, and that's just in the summer! Winter brings a whole new set of activities such as ice skating, snowmobile touring, sleigh rides, and, of course, skiing at nearby Mount Bachelor. Outdoor activities are the specialty here, and the inn's knowledgeable staff will be happy to set you up with the activities that interest you most.

We recommend this inn for active, outdoor-oriented people only, because you won't want to spend too much time in your room. The 400 condo-like accommodations are privately owned and reflect each proprietor's individual tastes, ranging from tacky '70s decor and "resort simplicity" to contemporary accoutrements. Although most rooms have views of the forest and snowcapped Mount Bachelor, the furnishings tend to be dismal, outdated, and plain. A fireside studio or loft room is your best bet, because the layout of these rooms offers ample space.

Romantic Note: The pace here is almost always vigorous and busy. In summer the inn becomes the setting for family vacations, and the winter months bring the ski crowd. Off-season, when kids are in school and the first snows are still a few weeks away, is the best time to enjoy each other while participating in as many activities as you desire.

LARA HOUSE BED AND BREAKFAST, Bend
640 Northwest Congress
(541) 388-4064, (800) 766-4064
Inexpensive

One of the oldest homes in Bend, Lara House was built in 1910 and sprawls graciously on a residential corner, offering views of tranquil Drake Park and Mirror Pond from a large front porch and bay windows. Your hostess will welcome you with a genuine smile and offer a cup of her steaming, delicious spiced cider. The common rooms are dignified, with well-polished hardwood floors, a brick fireplace with close-by comfy armchairs, and antique sofas. A cheery, glass-enclosed sunroom serves as a breakfast room. Guests also have access to an outdoor hot tub, perfect for soaking weary skiing, biking, or hiking muscles at the end of a busy day spent outdoors.

Though all of the five guest rooms upstairs are comfortable and have private baths, they are also exceedingly homey and mismatched. The hand-sewn quilts give queen-size beds an antiquated appearance, and the dated antiques, fabrics, and color schemes could use some updating. However, the prices here are extremely reasonable, and the innkeeper goes out of her way to ensure that your stay is enjoyable. Enjoy an ample full breakfast of stuffed French toast, fresh fruit, and almond-flavored coffee served at your private table in the solarium. You'll probably agree that although Lara House is not exceedingly elegant, it's still a wonderful place to let your hair down, loosen your tie, and liberate your hearts.

PINE RIDGE INN, Bend   🙶🙶🙶
1200 Southwest Century Drive
(541) 389-6137, (800) 600-4095
http://www.empnet.com/bchamber/bmotel.htm
Moderate to Very Expensive
Minimum stay requirement on holidays
Recommended Wedding Site

Popular with outdoor enthusiasts, this newly built inn is perched on a several-acre bluff above the raging Deschutes River. Considerably smaller than the area's other sprawling resorts, Pine Ridge caters to the romantically inclined, offering the ultimate in personal attention and seclusion. Amenities in most of the inn's 20 guest rooms include private baths, gas fireplaces, TV/VCRs, kitchenettes, Jacuzzi tubs, and evening turndown service. Despite a distinctive hotel-feel, even the least expensive rooms are wonderful. Rich green linens cover four-poster beds, and a gas fireplace warms a cozy sunken living room. Nine guest rooms have lovely views of the river and surrounding trees. Our only complaint is that the remaining 11 rooms face less than desirable views of the parking lot.

For a relatively reasonable price (considering the going rates in Bend), you can enjoy Pine Ridge's designer Honeymoon Suite: 900 square feet of sheer Northwest luxury. Ralph Lauren linens cover an enticing king-size bed, and a fire blazes in the stone fireplace in the winter. Intriguing nature artwork accents striking mauve-colored walls. A two-person Jacuzzi tub is the centerpiece of the large airy bathroom, which also has a glass-enclosed shower. Best of all, two private decks and expansive windows offer glorious views of the river below.

Wine and cheese are served in the early evening in a communal fireside parlor, and a delicious complimentary full breakfast can be served in the privacy of your own room.

RIVER RIDGE AT MOUNT BACHELOR
VILLAGE, Bend
19717 Mount Bachelor Drive
(541) 389-5900, (800) 452-9846 (in the U.S.)
Inexpensive to Unbelievably Expensive
Minimum stay requirement

Now this is romantic! Balanced high atop a steep ridge above the ever-changing Deschutes River, the River Ridge condominium units are a luxurious dream come true. Each exquisitely detailed unit has surrounding windows, a private deck with an outdoor hot tub, and upscale, stylish furnishings. A plethora of pillows makes the expansive couch a perfect spot to cuddle together by the gas fireplace and relish the views. Blond wood and plentiful sunlight highlight the modern, fully stocked kitchen; in the spacious bedroom, sumptuous linens adorn a comfy king-size bed. A second, indoor spa is featured in the contemporary white-tiled bathroom.

Nestled in the heart of Mount Bachelor Village, this series of sprawling, two-story contemporary buildings is privately owned, but available for rent through the Village's registration office. You can choose to rent executive, one-, two-, or three-bedroom suites, all of which are seductively sensuous. The executive rooms are the smallest but least expensive—a real bargain. All of the rooms have the same sumptuous decor, but the executive rooms have less square footage and lack forest or river views. Although the one-bedroom suites don't have a spa or kitchen, they do have plentiful space for two, and enough opulence and natural beauty to last a lifetime. The two- and three-bedroom suites are the *crème de la crème*, each sporting a complete kitchen, a hot tub on the deck, a Jacuzzi tub in the master suite, a gas fireplace, and an Unbelievably Expensive price tag.

Fortunately or unfortunately, depending on how you look at it, the River Ridge is part of a bigger resort. This means that there will be more people in the surrounding area, but it also means that as guests you will have access to all of the Village's amenities. You can bring your fishing pole and fish the Deschutes River, take a romantic walk on the nature trail that runs through the Village and next to the Deschutes, and tone your muscles at the athletic club. In the warmer months you can splash in the outdoor pool; in snowy seasons, you can ski Mount Bachelor, just 20 minutes away.

One- and two-bedroom suites in various other buildings at the Village are also available. Decorated individually by their private owners, many of these rooms are adequate and comfortable. There's a wide variety to choose from, so you're sure to find one that's right for the two of you. Just keep in mind that they don't come remotely close to the River Ridge, in either price or decor.

ROCK SPRINGS GUEST RANCH, Bend　　　　　　　　💋💋
64201 Tyler Road
(541) 382-1957, (800) 225-DUDE (in the U.S.)
http://www.empnet.com/bchamber/bmotel.htm
Moderate to Expensive
Minimum stay requirement on holidays and in summer

Step off the dusty trail and unpack your saddlebags, pardners; you've reached the Ponderosa. To adequately portray this diamond-in-the-rough location, we should probably rhapsodize about the 12,000 arresting acres of mountain scenery and rambling streams, or elaborately describe the rustic cabins and the large outdoor hot tub and swimming pool. But the essence of Rock Springs Guest Ranch is not revealed by such particulars; rather, it is displayed when you traverse this land on horseback with the one you love, the breeze cooling your brow and the balmy summer sun tanning your face.

Vacations at the ranch are a family affair and a social affair as well; some groups return year after year to see old friends and have fun with their whole family. Your stay lasts one week, and lodging, three hearty meals a day, horseback riding, and all activities are included in one fee. All of the 26 dated but cozy cabins have knotty pine walls, many have wood-burning fireplaces, and some have loft bedrooms. The hospitable, qualified staff plans separate daily activities for the youngsters and grown-ups, something both parents and kids appreciate. Meals are served family-style at large wooden tables in the casual main lodge, and horseback rides are taken in groups every morning.

If you are looking for total privacy and luxurious seclusion, try somewhere else. But if a playful and casual escape is more your style (and you want to bring the kids along), we suggest giving Rock Springs Guest Ranch a call.

Romantic Note: Rock Springs operates as a guest ranch for ten weeks each summer and is also open briefly around Thanksgiving and Christmas. The winter stays are shorter and are more geared toward skiers, but horseback riding is still available for those who bring warm clothes and a sense of adventure.

Restaurant Kissing

BROKEN TOP CLUB RESTAURANT, Bend
61999 Mount Washington Drive
(541) 383-7600, (800) 382-7690
Moderate to Expensive
Lunch and Dinner Tuesday–Sunday; Sunday Brunch
Recommended Wedding Site

We usually recommend steering clear of exclusive country clubs for romantic encounters, but Broken Top Club is an extraordinary exception to our rule. Set at the edge of a sloping, emerald green golf course, Broken Top's dining room overlooks tall stands of evergreens, a shimmering pond, and views of Broken Top Mountain in the distance. Floor-to-ceiling windows wrap around the expansive series of dining rooms, which are accented with natural wood, crisp white linens, and candlelight. For the most intimacy and comfort, request that your meal be served in the front lounge. Here, immense windows showcase the spectacular setting, and a fire roars in a floor-to-ceiling hearth. Cathedral ceilings and Northwest artwork create a stylish atmosphere. You can cozy up together on a plush, oversized couch and enjoy savory crab cakes served with mascarpone cheese and caviar, grilled salmon with papaya-mango confetti, or sea scallops and mussels in saffron. Desserts are little slices of heaven. Best of all, you'll have all the privacy to really enjoy each other's company, up close and personal.

TOOMIE'S THAI CUISINE, Bend
119 Northwest Minnesota
(541) 388-5590
Moderate
Lunch and Dinner Daily

Set in the heart of downtown Bend, this expansive dining room has oversized windows with views of the storefronts across the street. Curtains blocking this less than inspiring view would be a welcome addition. This space once housed a popular Italian eatery, but the only remnants of this European past are the columns and archways commonly found in Italian restaurants. Bright and airy by day and dimly lit at night, Toomie's dining room is appointed with Eastern artifacts, sculptures, and wall murals. Red tablecloths with Thai prints drape snugly arranged tables illuminated with candle lanterns. A gracious wait staff serves up tantalizing Thai food. You can't go wrong with anything on the menu, but we were particularly impressed with the sweet-and-sour lemongrass-and-coconut soup and the just-right spicy vegetarian Phad Thai.

WESTSIDE BAKERY AND CAFE, Bend
1005 1/2 Galveston Street
(541) 382-3426
Inexpensive
Breakfast and Lunch Daily

Be prepared to wait in line, because this is arguably one of Bend's most popular breakfast spots—especially on the weekends. In this casual and funky space, Walt Disney posters and goofy stuffed animals decorate knotty pine walls in a rambling series of dining rooms. While there's certainly nothing romantic about the ambience, the adept kitchen staff has a special knack with pancakes, waffles, omelets, and decadent pastries. The Westside is a perfect place to fill up before an adventure-filled day outdoors.

Outdoor Kissing

CASCADE LAKES HIGHWAY

From Highway 97 just south of Bend, turn west onto Cascade Lakes Highway and follow the signs.

Depending on the season, adventurous souls (with good snow tires) can journey together on this 89-mile paved loop with stirring views. Mount Bachelor, the Three Sisters, and Broken Top tower overhead in astonishing panoramas. Celebrate the area's beauty, stopping frequently for closer looks at the numerous lakes, streams, and unique environments, all teeming with wildlife. Take a moment to bird-watch at the osprey observation area, or investigate lava caves with the aid of the provided flashlights and hard hats. Keep your eyes open for deer, rabbits, hawks, and other wild creatures that inhabit this heavenly domain. We can't think of a more opportune spot for kissing, as long as you don't cause traffic to back up (maybe you should pull over).

Sunriver

Hotel/Bed and Breakfast Kissing

SUNRIVER RESORT, Sunriver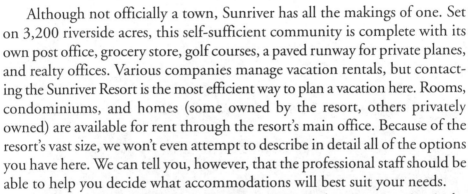
1 Center Drive
(541) 593-1000, (800) 547-3922
http://www.sunriver-resort.com
Moderate to Unbelievably Expensive
Minimum stay requirement on holidays and in summer

Although not officially a town, Sunriver has all the makings of one. Set on 3,200 riverside acres, this self-sufficient community is complete with its own post office, grocery store, golf courses, a paved runway for private planes, and realty offices. Various companies manage vacation rentals, but contacting the Sunriver Resort is the most efficient way to plan a vacation here. Rooms, condominiums, and homes (some owned by the resort, others privately owned) are available for rent through the resort's main office. Because of the resort's vast size, we won't even attempt to describe in detail all of the options you have here. We can tell you, however, that the professional staff should be able to help you decide what accommodations will best suit your needs.

Like most resorts in the area, the Sunriver Resort's main attraction is the surrounding mountains, rivers, scenic beauty, and all of the available outdoor activities. Unlike many resorts, Sunriver is sufficiently spread out, so you aren't forced to have a family experience even if you are traveling without children. Most of the guest rooms are decorated in typical hotel style, but if you ask for a room numbered in the low 100s or 200s, you have a good chance of getting a partial-mountain-view room that doesn't necessarily cost more. Sunriver's homes and condominiums are more spacious and come complete with full kitchens, two bathrooms, wood-burning fireplaces, private decks, and varying decor. For the most upscale (and the most expensive) accommodations, you can rent one of the executive homes, most of which have three or more bedrooms, a hot tub, a stereo, and an attractive interior, in addition to daily maid service, a fruit basket, coffee, and souvenir mugs. If you're able and willing to pay the considerable price, these homes are a choice option for special occasions.

*"No-one could tell what lay beyond
the closed chapter of every kiss."*

Lawrence Durrell

Southern Oregon

From magnificent national parks and forests to a world-renowned Shakespeare festival, Southern Oregon offers something for everyone. Outdoor enthusiasts will appreciate river rafting on the Rogue or touring Crater Lake, while even the most discriminating traveler will enjoy Ashland's highly acclaimed theater and gourmet restaurants. Whichever your preference, or if you care to combine outdoor and cultural activities as many Northwesterners do, Southern Oregon is a unique, worthwhile destination unto itself.

Steamboat

The riverside community of Steamboat is located on Highway 138, approximately 38 miles east of Interstate 5 and the town of Roseburg. Besides the wonderful forested hillsides of the Umpqua National Forest and the rushing waters of the Umpqua River, Steamboat is also home to one of the most popular fishing resorts in the state.

Hotel/Bed and Breakfast Kissing

STEAMBOAT INN, Steamboat
42705 North Umpqua Highway (Highway 138)
(541) 498-2411, (800) 840-8825
Inexpensive to Very Expensive
Call for seasonal closures.

It may feel like the middle of nowhere, but the Steamboat Inn is approximately halfway between Interstate 5 and Crater Lake, in the heart of the Umpqua National Forest. The remote location along the rushing North Umpqua River is the primary allure of this rustic lodge. Hiking to a dozen different waterfalls, wading in the river, and fly-fishing are on the lineup of possible activities. If the great outdoors is not calling you, other options include perusing the inn's library beside a gas fireplace, or relaxing in your own deep soaking tub (almost half of the rooms offer this amenity).

Fifteen different units in a variety of shapes and sizes are available. The five Hideaway Cottages set in forested surroundings are spacious and particularly private. Each one features comfortable furnishings, knotty pine walls, a white-tiled soaking tub, a wood-burning fireplace, a small kitchenette, and a spacious bedroom and living room area. The only thing lacking is a river view. If a view of the rushing North Umpqua appeals to you, opt for one of the two higher-priced River Suites, which feature king-size beds, soaking tubs, fireplaces, and private decks that overlook the river. Finally, at the inexpensive end of the price spectrum, there are eight very small wood-paneled Streamside Cabins without any extras except a pleasant common veranda that overlooks the river. Some rough edges, such as dated artwork and worn furnishings, serve as a reminder that many guests come here to fish, not to kiss, but the rusticity is part of the fun of this lodging, and the secluded setting really does allow you to get away from it all.

Romantic Note: The inn is known for its Fisherman's Dinner (Expensive), served in the dining room around a long wood-slab table. Meals include aperitifs, hors d'oeuvres, a hearty main course and savory side dish, Oregon wines, and a grand dessert. The set menu changes nightly and isn't always fish (despite the name), but the food is always plentiful and good. Family-style seating encourages a warm, conversational atmosphere around the table. Although it may not be a romantic encounter, the Fisherman's Dinner is a great value, considering all of the food and beverages included, and you should give it a try at least one night during your stay. Reservations are required; try to reserve at least two days in advance if you have any special requests or dietary restrictions.

Crater Lake

Hotel/Bed and Breakfast Kissing

CRATER LAKE LODGE, Crater Lake
Rim Village
(541) 830-8700
Inexpensive to Moderate
Call for seasonal closures.

1995 marked the grand reopening of Crater Lake Lodge. During its six-year restoration, most of the original 1915 building was torn down and rebuilt, and modern amenities were added. The renovated lodge sits on the southern rim of the Crater Lake caldera near Rim Village, where it proudly displays its stone-and-wood exterior accentuated with chalet-style shutters. Inside, an extensive collection of black-and-white photographs and a detailed display area recount the history of the original building and its recent transformation.

You won't find any phones or TVs in the lodge's 71 guest rooms. But don't worry: there's plenty of entertainment right outside your window. Half the rooms offer incredible views of Crater Lake, and the other half face the Klamath Lake basin. Sparsely decorated, the rooms could use some warming up; however, they do have contemporary oak furnishings and cushioned window seats. All are decorated in maroon and hunter green, with rather ordinary linens and small private bathrooms. Rooms on the third and fourth floors have intriguing sloped ceilings. Four spacious loft rooms are also available, but unfortunately these rooms are better suited for families than for couples looking for a romantic getaway.

After a day of outdoor adventures, take in the breathtaking views of Crater Lake from the lodge's large patio area or enjoy Northwest cuisine served fireside in the dining room. One of the original stone fireplaces still stands in the main lobby, where Douglas fir floors, columns made from tree trunks, and walls of stone and wood create a rustic Northwest ambience not soon forgotten. Next to the lobby is the Great Hall, which was part of the original 1915 lodge. Here you'll find hardwood floors adorned with throw rugs, a second stone fireplace, and an assortment of Adirondack-style furniture. In such a setting, you can almost imagine the lodge's earliest visitors gathered around the tables playing cards, the smoke from the men's cigars slowly floating upward. With so much history and surrounding splendor at your fingertips, you're sure to experience serene togetherness at this Northwestern retreat.

Romantic Suggestion: June through August is the busiest time at Crater Lake Lodge. Consider making reservations as early as January if you plan to visit during the summer months.

Outdoor Kissing

CRATER LAKE NATIONAL PARK, Crater Lake
(541) 594-2211, (541) 830-8700
$5 per car

Crater Lake is off Highway 62, 80 miles northeast of Medford, and 60 miles northwest of Klamath Falls.

It's hard to fathom the dimensions of this volcanic formation, cut into the earth thousands of years ago by forces that make the Mount St. Helens eruption look like a firecracker on the Fourth of July. At 1,932 feet deep, Crater Lake is the deepest lake in the United States, and the seventh deepest in the world. A towering border of golden, rocky earth encompasses this inconceivably blue body of water. It is an astounding spectacle to behold. You can drive around the entire perimeter (except in the winter) with fascinating vistas all around, take a two-hour boat ride from Cleetwood Cove to Wizard Island, or hike the trails down to the lake and embrace amidst scenery that will take your breath away. Alas, the caravans of tourists during the summer can also take your breath away, and mar what is otherwise some pretty good kissing ambience. Snow lasts nine months of the year here, which is good news for cross-country skiers; trails ranging in length from one to ten miles are available for skiers of all levels. Springtime is the best season for fine weather and privacy. Remember, Crater Lake is on the east side of the mountains, so rainfall and cloudy days occur infrequently.

Romantic Note: For overnight accommodations, we recommend the recently renovated **CRATER LAKE LODGE** at Rim Village (see Hotel/Bed and Breakfast Kissing). Camping at the **MAZAMA CAMPGROUND**, (541) 830-8700, is also an option for those who can't get enough of the crisp mountain air.

Merlin

Near Grants Pass, Merlin is a small, mostly residential community approximately one hour north of Ashland.

PINE MEADOW INN, Merlin
1000 Crow Road
(541) 471-6277, (800) 554-0806
Inexpensive to Moderate; No Credit Cards

Hospitality counts for a lot, and the welcoming innkeepers at the Pine Meadow Inn go out of their way to make you feel right at home. Set in a quiet rural area, upon a grassy, wooded knoll, this large country home was styled after a Midwestern farmhouse. The owners were diligently involved in designing and building the house and cultivating its gardens. From the abundant vegetable garden, fruit trees, and pretty flowers around the house, to the serene koi pond and the house itself, the tender loving care they have invested is evident.

The comfortable, homey furnishings in the main-floor living room are indicative of the comforts that await in the four upstairs guest rooms. Each room has its own private bath, but the Willow Room is the largest, with English antiques, a sitting area, and a window seat that views Mount Walker in the distance. Both the Heather and Garden Rooms look out to the gardens and woods, but the Garden Room also has a bay window overlooking the koi pond. Finally, the Laurel Room is furnished with oak antiques, a handmade quilt, and lace curtains. A long window seat is perfect for stargazing or watching the sun rise.

As much as possible, produce from the gardens is used to create healthy gourmet breakfasts and vegetarian specialties each morning. The country calm, country cooking, and country cordiality found at the Pine Meadow Inn makes for a very special retreat.

Grants Pass

Restaurant Kissing

THE COUNTRY COTTAGE CAFE 💋💋
AND TEA ROOM, Grants Pass
2315 Upper River Road Loop, at Meadow View Country Gardens
(541) 476-6882
Inexpensive
Lunch and Afternoon Tea Monday–Saturday

Ah, high tea is such a cultivated afternoon activity, and in such a charming setting, you really can't go wrong. Since this casual tearoom is located at Meadow View Country Gardens, there is a lot more to do here than just sip tea. Three different gardens—one for organic vegetables, one for herbs, and a classic English flower garden—can be toured before or after your meal, and the Harvest Room, which sells just-picked produce, allows you to take fresh vegetables and herbs home with you.

Everything in the restaurant is homemade, using Oregon-made products, organic produce, and herbs from the gardens whenever possible. Lunch options include a variety of sandwiches and fresh soups. High tea includes the traditional scones with hand-whipped cream and jam, lemon tarts, dainty finger sandwiches, home-baked shortbread, and, of course, a pot of tea. The open-air covered patio with skylights is a quiet, lovely setting where romance is free to bloom along with all of the flowers around you.

Jacksonville

If you haven't visited Jacksonville before, there are several excellent reasons why you should make this town a stop on your romantic itinerary. Four distinct seasons sweep across the area's rolling hills, distant mountains, and pristine farm country, filling them in turn with sultry warmth, stunning colors, and mild frosts. During the summer, don't miss the exhilarating **BRITT FESTIVALS** (see Miscellaneous Kissing), the town's outdoor music and performing arts series. In addition, Jacksonville is conveniently located for **RIVER RAFTING ON THE ROGUE** (see Outdoor Kissing), and only 15 miles from Ashland and the **OREGON SHAKESPEARE FESTIVAL** (reviewed elsewhere in this chapter). Trolleys and horse-drawn carriages tour downtown on most summer days, and quaint shops and historic museums are abundant. First-class bed and breakfasts and restaurants are found here, some of which are thoroughly romantic.

Jacksonville is remembered as the first place gold was discovered in Oregon during the 1850s gold rush. Today it remains a truly charming, revitalized Old West town that gives only the subtlest hint that it is a tourist attraction. You will be pleased to discover this lovely escape.

Hotel/Bed and Breakfast Kissing

JACKSONVILLE INN, Jacksonville
175 East California Street
(541) 899-1900, (800) 321-9344
http://www.mind.net/jvinn
Inexpensive to Very Expensive

This landmark brick hotel is set in the heart of Jacksonville. Built in 1861 and lovingly restored over the years, the Jacksonville Inn blends old and new to create comfortably elegant lodgings. All of the eight second-floor rooms have exposed brick walls, private baths, handsome antique armoires, oak furnishings, comfortable beds, and a great deal of polish. The blue-toned Peter Britt room even has a wonderful whirlpool tub—not exactly authentic, but very luxurious. A full breakfast of your choice is served in the inn's famous Victorian dining room (see Restaurant Kissing), which is a romantic must even if you aren't staying here.

In addition to the inn's rooms, there are three charming, private guest cottages, approximately a block away. A white picket fence trims these side-by-side cottages, and gardens line the walkways. Two are newly built, with vaulted ceilings, large Jacuzzi tubs with steam showers, and double-sided gas-log fireplaces. The older cottage is also a wonderful little hideaway, with country Victorian furnishings, a lace-canopied bed, a gas fireplace, a kitchenette area, and a steam shower with Jacuzzi tub. A fruit-and-champagne breakfast can be delivered to these cottages, but you may want to walk over to the inn for a fine breakfast that will tide you over until dinnertime.

TOUVELLE HOUSE, Jacksonville
455 North Oregon Street
(541) 899-8938, (800) 846-8422
http://www.wave.net/upg/touvelle
Inexpensive to Moderate

Don't make a wrong turn as you pull into Touvelle House; the driveway adjacent to that of the bed and breakfast leads to the Jacksonville Cemetery. Although a night here might be an interesting diversion, you'll have a much better time at this congenial bed and breakfast housed in a massive Crafts-man-style home and framed by shady black oak trees.

After you've been greeted by the personable innkeepers, saunter through the inn and soak in the grandeur of the common areas: the great room, where plush couches and chairs sit beside a grand stone fireplace; the bright sunroom, with its floor-to-ceiling windows; and the stately dining room, dignified by an antique built-in buffet. The loving work that went into this place is unmistakable; extraordinary attention to detail is apparent throughout. Each of the six rooms has an individual style, but most have queen-size beds and all have private baths. The Garden Suite is dressed in pastel floral prints; Prairie West features early Jacksonville charm with bent willow furnishings and a handmade quilt; and the Americana, patriotically furnished in burgundy, white, and navy blue, has a lovely outdoor patio. All are impeccable places to temporarily call home.

A dip in the outdoor pool and spa provides welcome refreshment at the end of a hot summer day. (Summer days here can be unbearably hot, so the pool really is a treat.) Generous three-course breakfasts are served on fine china with antique crystal each morning, and the cooking is just as wonderful as you would expect from everything else here.

Restaurant Kissing

BRIT-ISH FARE TEAHOUSE, Jacksonville
235 California Street
(541) 899-7777
Inexpensive
Lunch and Afternoon Tea Daily
Call for seasonal closures.

Fronting this historic home is a small gift shop selling a rather odd assortment of English treats and boutique dresses, but just down the hall is where the kissing begins. Three charming tearooms, each with only four tables, has been decorated to honor a different British Isle. The pretty English tearoom has a crystal chandelier, an old-fashioned woodstove, and pink-and-white floral wallpaper. The Welsh room features dark wood detailing and cream walls adorned with wreaths of dried flowers. And the Scottish room, situated near the kitchen, is accented with tartan wallpaper. No matter where you sit, you can partake in this little taste of Britain.

In terms of style and decor, this small restaurant wholeheartedly resembles a British teahouse; unfortunately, the food is rather disappointing. We found the finger sandwiches to be light on creativity but heavy on butter, the scones disappointingly stale, and the choice of teas virtually nonexistent (the house tea is the only flavor available). Ordering a bowl of soup seems to be your best bet.

JACKSONVILLE INN RESTAURANT, Jacksonville
175 East California Street
(541) 899-1900, (800) 321-9344
Moderate to Expensive
Breakfast Daily; Lunch Tuesday-Saturday; Dinner Daily;
Sunday Brunch

One of the better-known restaurants in the area, this plush, demurely lit dining room is constantly busy. We are not sure what all the commotion is about; the service is not worth raving about, and parts of the extensive menu leave much to be desired. The salmon crêpes with cream sauce were mushy and the sauce too thick, and the spanakopita was greasy and tough. You are better off ordering the simpler entrées, because they can be delicious. Meat dishes, particularly the filet mignon and the fresh fish, are just fine and quite tender.

The dining rooms themselves are definitely romantic settings for any meal. Burgundy linens, exposed brick, and old-fashioned lamps create a quaint atmosphere in the main-floor dining room. The lower-level dining room is more intimate-feeling, but the stone walls can make for poor acoustics. Consider coming to the Jacksonville Inn for Sunday brunch—champagne from local wineries is served with the meal. If you choose carefully, this can be a four-lip dining rhapsody. If not, well, you can still kiss.

Romantic Note: Lovely accommodations await upstairs (see Hotel/Bed and Breakfast Kissing).

MCCULLY HOUSE INN, Jacksonville
240 East California Street
(541) 899-1942, (800) 367-1942
http://www.wave.net/upg/mccully
Moderate to Expensive
Dinner Daily; Sunday Brunch Seasonally

World-class cuisine is not necessarily what you expect in a small town like Jacksonville, but it is exactly what you will encounter at the McCully House Inn. This historic federal-style mansion sits proudly at the edge of Jacksonville's downtown area. Remarkable gourmet cuisine is served in three separate dining rooms, each with its own distinct character. The first dining room, where you enter, feels much like having dinner in someone's elegant home, with its glowing fireplace and warm peach-toned walls. The next room, done in a dusty blue color scheme, is equally elegant, but the lights are kept low to create an intimate mood. A sunny indoor garden patio with floor-to-ceiling windows looking out to flower gardens is the final option; it's also the most casual, but patio chairs with green-and-white-striped cushions and striking local artwork make it quite inviting as well. On warm days or for special events, outdoor seating at umbrella-shaded tables may be arranged.

Not only are the dining rooms lovely, but the dinner itself is a culinary treat. You can order something fairly simple from a bistro menu (prices are less than $10 per entrée for slightly smaller dishes), but it is worth the extra few dollars to try something more complicated from the internationally inspired main dinner menu. The sautéed prawns in peanut sauce served with Chinese vegetables and black bean butter sauce are absolutely succulent, and so is the wild mushroom–stuffed pork loin with port-Dijon sauce. Be sure to give the dessert menu a once-over. Your willpower is stronger than ours if you can resist the chocolate afterlife *pave*, a concoction of two thin slices of Belgian bittersweet-fudge brownies layered with dense chocolate-espresso ganache, topped with a dollop of whipped cream, and served on a bed of strawberry sauce. Don't miss the chance to eat here; it will leave you with a satisfied glow.

Romantic Note: Although the three second-story guest rooms at the **MCCULLY HOUSE INN** (Inexpensive) have been nicely renovated and decorated with antiques, it is nearly impossible to escape the noise from the kitchen and dining rooms. If accessibility to the fabulous first-floor restaurant is important, this is the place to be; but be forewarned that noise is a potential problem as late as 10 P.M.

Outdoor Kissing

RIVER RAFTING ON THE ROGUE ❧❧❧
Adventure Center, (541) 776-4932, (800) 444-2819
Noah's World Of Water, (541) 488-2811, (800) 858-2811
Orange Torpedo Trips, (541) 479-5061, (800) 635-2925
Rogue/Klamath River Adventures, (541) 779-3708, (800) 231-0769
Prices start at $50 per person

Many of the rafting companies offer pickups in Jacksonville and Ashland.

The area between Grants Pass and the coast (where the Rogue River empties into the Pacific) has attracted more than 45 different rafting and boat companies that offer all kinds of excursions down the Rogue River or the Upper Klamath River. Some of these jaunts are totally tame, letting you float freely in the midst of towering pines and mountains, while others are radically exhilarating, making you shoot rapids and navigate rocky channels. Boats built for one, two, eight, or even larger groups are all part of the Rogue adventure; what you choose depends on skill and your level of confidence in yourself and each other. A trip down the Rogue might seem touristy, but once you challenge the rapids and feel the thrill of riding a waterborne roller coaster, everyone else disappears and it is only the two of you and the river.

Miscellaneous Kissing

BRITT FESTIVALS, Jacksonville
(541) 773-6077, (800) 882-7488
http://www.mind.net/britt
Ticket prices range from $16 to $35

Two blocks from downtown Jacksonville.

From June through early September, Jacksonville is filled with crowds attending the annual Britt Festivals. This summer-long series hosts internationally recognized musicians, bands, and dance ensembles, as well as a handful of comedians and musical-theater troupes. All perform under the stars in an outdoor amphitheater, surrounded by ponderosa pines and madrona trees, on land that was once the estate of pioneer photographer Peter Britt. Bring a blanket and find your own stretch of musical heaven on the hillside facing the stage. Just about every type of music is represented: classical, jazz, rhythm and blues, folk, country, and rock. The lineup changes seasonally, so call ahead for details and tickets.

Talent

Just north of Ashland is Talent, a small village that is little more than a stretch of two-lane highway dotted with businesses. Chances are that you will pass through Talent on your way to or from Ashland without even noticing the intriguing little restaurant that is a desirable kissable destination.

Restaurant Kissing

NEW SAMMY'S COWBOY BISTRO, Talent
2210 South Pacific Highway
(541) 535-2779
Expensive; No Credit Cards
Reservations Required
Call for seasonal hours.

All right, all right, we know what you are thinking: how can romance and Sammy the Cowboy go together? Well, we weren't so sure at first either. From the outside, this bistro looks like a downright funky roadside shack: several shades of bright, vivid colors adorn the exterior walls, and a flashing arrow (with lots of bulbs missing) is the only sign indicating the restaurant. As you enter the first set of doors, you may wonder if you are in the right place. Venture on: half of the romantic fun is what awaits inside.

Attractive country wallpaper, pastel accents, Fiestaware, and candles on the tables allow you to forgive the outside and appreciate what you've found—a dining room reminiscent of a quaint little dollhouse. The kitchen's emphasis is on fresh, regional ingredients, and the food here is some of the best in the Northwest. The teensy dining room holds only six tables, so you'll have to make reservations up to three months in advance to taste for yourselves. We recommend the baby vegetable stew with new potatoes, snow peas, asparagus, onions, and carrots combined with cheese, pesto ravioli, and morel mushrooms. Try the grilled quail Provençal with rice pilaf? If you are looking for a unique experience and you are able to plan far in advance, New Sammy's Cowboy Bistro will not let you down.

Ashland

Ashland marks the southernmost point covered in this book. Tranquil neighborhoods, a dynamic downtown area teeming with shops and restaurants, a world-class cultural center, pristine countryside, and mountainous terrain bordering fertile river valleys make up the utopian world of Ashland. Not only is the town attractive and its numerous accommodations among the best in the Northwest, the Ashland theater season, beginning in February and running through October, makes Broadway pale by comparison (this is not an overstatement). It will take only one visit to make both of you sustaining members of Ashland's annual **OREGON SHAKESPEARE FESTIVAL** (see Miscellaneous Kissing).

There is more to do in this small, quaint area than in almost any other town in the Northwest. Besides the in-town activities, you can try whitewater rafting down the nearby Rogue or Klamath Rivers (see Outdoor Kissing in Jacksonville), horseback riding, hiking with llamas, mountain climbing, and, during the winter, downhill and cross-country skiing, available minutes away on Mount Ashland. The town is chock-full of wonderful bed and breakfasts, and many offer very enticing winter rates. In summer, lodging reservations should be made months in advance because rooms book quickly when the weather is hot and the theater is in full swing. If you are having a hard time finding a place to stay, **ASHLAND'S B&B RESERVATION NETWORK**, (541) 482-BEDS, (800) 944-0329, is a very helpful service.

Hotel/Bed and Breakfast Kissing

ANTIQUE ROSE INN, Ashland
91 Gresham Street
(541) 482-6285
Moderate to Expensive
Main house closed November through January

As you begin your ascent up the steep stairs leading to this beautifully renovated Queen Anne–style home, you'll know right away that something special is in store. Romance inhabits every corner of the house, which is decorated with authentic Victorian furnishings, cream-and-white lace curtains and table coverings, Oriental rugs, and enough antiques to make you think you've traveled back in time.

An abundance of love and attention has gone into all three guest rooms. The Rose Room is nicely tucked away upstairs and features a king-size four-poster bed with down comforter, a uniquely carved wood fireplace, a private balcony, and a separate sitting area with an antique fainting couch. The Lace Room is also located upstairs and has a canopied oak Victorian bed and a delightful private bath with a claw-foot tub. The smaller Mahogany Room is set directly off the downstairs entry hall, which means that other guests can be heard coming and going. Still, this room is just as lovely as the others, with rich mahogany walls, antique wedding photos, a queen-size four-poster bed, lace curtains, and a private bathroom with an antique claw-foot tub. For the ultimate in privacy, the newly opened Rose Cottage, right next door to the inn, is a two-bedroom retreat with a fireplace, Jacuzzi tub, skylights, lace-canopied four-poster beds, and, as you would expect from the looks of the main house, many elegant antiques. Gourmet breakfasts are delivered to this unit to allow for a thoroughly private encounter.

Full gourmet breakfasts are served downstairs in the formal dining room for guests staying in the main house. The long table is topped with lace and crystal, and the satisfying meal features fresh fruit, homemade breads and pastries, a variety of egg dishes, and plenty of hot coffee and tea.

COOLIDGE HOUSE, Ashland
137 North Main Street
(541) 482-4721, (800) 655-5522
Inexpensive to Expensive
Minimum stay requirement

We have said it before and we will say it again: Ashland's Main Street is not the most tranquil location for a bed and breakfast. On the other hand, it *is* one of the most convenient places to stay if you do not want to bother with hopping in and out of your car and finding a parking spot whenever you go to town. Coolidge House is a finely restored Victorian just two blocks from downtown. Manicured shrubs and gardens adorn the front yard, and flower baskets line the porch. There are six rooms here, four in the main house and two in the Carriage House behind it. Rooms in the main house vary in size, but all have a private bath and are furnished with gorgeous antiques. The Baker Suite, dressed all in blue, features a lovely 1880s hand-painted French bed set, and the bathroom features a claw-foot tub and a pedestal sink. Romantics will especially love the regal Parlor Room, with its hardwood floors, fabulous window seat, luxurious furnishings, and spacious bathroom with Jacuzzi tub for two. The Rose and Garden Rooms are smaller, but an antique iron bed and claw-foot tub make the Rose Room a cozy choice. The Garden Room is a sunny place with white wicker furniture, a handmade quilt, and views of the garden.

Out back, the Carriage House rooms have the advantage of being larger, but the lovely antique collection remains, for the most part, in the main house. The contemporary style of these rooms is a bit of a letdown if you've had the opportunity to admire the furnishings throughout the main house. However, these two units should be considered both for the extra space they offer and for the fact that they are tucked behind the main house, which means noise from Main Street is hardly evident. The Cottage is a two-room suite with a gas fireplace, television, and huge round Jacuzzi tub. The Sun Suite (available in summer only) is appropriately named given the bright and airy feel of the room. Vaulted ceilings and white wicker furniture contribute to this effect, and there is also a gas fireplace and a whirlpool tub for guests to enjoy.

Full gourmet breakfasts are presented each morning. Depending on the season, you may enjoy your morning meal in the dining room, on the flower-trimmed brick patio behind the house, or on the second-story balcony at charming white iron tables for two.

COUNTRY WILLOWS BED AND BREAKFAST, Ashland

1313 Clay Street
488-1590, (800) WILLOWS
http://www.willowsinn.com
Moderate to Expensive

Things just keep getting better at Country Willows. This agrarian ranch estate two and a half miles from downtown Ashland has been a wonderfully kissable destination for years, but the enthusiastic innkeepers keep improving things. Who knows—if they keep up the good work, we may have to create a 5-lip category!

A river flows by the property, so rushing water fills the air with gentle sounds. Willow trees and horse pastures border the farmhouse and renovated barn, and a duck pond sits at one edge of the property. This bucolic scene can be enjoyed from almost every part of the house. Four rooms are located on the second floor of the farmhouse, where an expansive deck with willow furniture provides a place to sit and appreciate the country landscape. Across the yard and right beside the pond is an individual unit called The Cottage, which has a pot-bellied woodstove, a kitchenette, and a little patio. Our only hesitation in recommending this particular room is that you may wake to quacking and honking from the resident ducks and geese outside your door. Still, this is a nice private option.

For the ultimate in privacy and comfort, the remaining Barn Suites have to be the absolute best places to kiss on the property. The most recent addition is the luxurious Pine Ridge Suite, a stunning, spacious room with a fireplace, high open-beam ceilings, skylights, and a dazzling slate bathroom with a two-person open shower and a Jacuzzi tub for two. The fresh Northwest-style decor—a peeled-log bedframe on the king-size bed, pine furnishings, and coordinating pine-tree wallpaper and linens—creates an overall effect that is simply glorious, yet entirely tasteful. Our other favorite is the Sunrise Suite, a masterpiece of white-stained pine furnishings. A secluded deck overlooks the river, there is a gas-log fireplace, and a wonderfully enormous bathtub is nestled in an alcove and surrounded by bay windows that overlook the trees. A smaller, less fancy version of this suite is the adjacent Bunk Room, with similar stylish furnishings, skylights, and a private deck. The Hayloft Suite, with a kitchenette and sitting area on the entry floor and a bedroom with skylight on the upper level, is handsomely appointed in hunter green and rich burgundy.

Sunrise is accompanied by fresh coffee, homemade breads, and whatever gourmet creation the inspired innkeepers can think of. The pleasant sunroom, with several tables for two, is a lovely breakfast area. Last but certainly not least, we must also mention the huge heated pool out back and the hot tub where you can steam away every care from your city-tired bodies. Impressed yet? Obviously, we were. It is places like Country Willows that inspire us to keep kissing and telling.

COWSLIP'S BELLE, Ashland
159 North Main Street
(541) 488-2901, (800) 888-6819

http://www.cowslip.com/cowslip
Moderate; No Credit Cards

Once upon a time people sought out bed and breakfasts just for a clean and simple place to stay overnight. Today, ask anyone who frequents bed and breakfasts why they choose to stay at an intimate inn rather than a hotel, and the answer is often "For the breakfast, of course." In honor of this tradition, breakfast at Cowslip's Belle is an event in itself. Served on the main floor of this 1913 Craftsman bungalow, breakfast is an extravagant affair that may include fresh fruit, homemade coffee cake, and brandied peach Dutch babies or cornmeal crêpes with shrimp-vegetable stuffing. Needless to say, you will not be left hungry.

Roses and honeysuckle cover the arbor leading to the front door. Inside, the four guest rooms are renovated on a revolving basis, so they are all beautifully kept up. Every room is named for a flower cited in a Shakespearean play. Our favorite rooms are the two in the adjacent carriage house and the Rosebud Suite in the main house; each has a private entrance, a down comforter, and the softest linens you've ever snuggled in. A ringing telephone in the main house may be the only thing to distract you in the sunny Rosebud Suite, but the two rooms in the carriage house feel especially private. They are tucked away by a teeming flower garden in the backyard. Cuckoo-Bud has a daybed and a magnificent four-poster bent-willow canopied bed entwined with roses. It also features an antique stained-glass window, a beamed ceiling, and a star-quilt wall hanging. Love-in-Idleness has a beautiful antique brass bed and a damask love seat. The furnishings throughout are wonderful, and some of the bathrooms are adorned with brass fittings and shiny Italian floor tiles. Air-conditioning in all four rooms provides comfort during the sweltering heat of summer.

At night, when you return from the theater, you will find a tucked-in teddy bear and homemade, hand-dipped chocolate truffles placed lovingly on your pillows. Now this is the kind of pampering you could get accustomed to.

GRAPEVINE INN, Ashland
486 Siskiyou Boulevard
(541) 482-7944, (800) 500-VINE
Moderate
Minimum stay requirement on weekends
Call for seasonal closures.

Given the abundance of high-quality establishments in Ashland, innkeepers face some stiff competition. Fortunately, the GrapeVine Inn has just the right blend of style, elegance, and comfort to distinguish it from the rest.

This Dutch Colonial home has a lovely wraparound porch and a colorful garden with a trellised patio and charming gazebo. A contemporary common area on the main floor features bent-willow furnishings, hardwood floors, and a Southwestern motif, giving the space a unique and comfortable look.

Upstairs are two of the guest rooms, both named after wines. Chardonnay, decorated in golden tones, has a sitting area with a fireplace, along with a stunning queen-size French iron bed wrapped with iron vines and draped with muslin. Cabernet features a deep burgundy comforter on a queen-size iron bed. Both rooms are elegant and cozy, and each has a spacious tiled bathroom. Guests enter the third room, the Grape Ivy Suite, through its trellised garden entrance near the back of the house. Its bright and airy atmosphere is created by soft green carpet, white-and-green ivy-patterned linens, a sitting area with fireplace, a private bath, and a full kitchen. All three rooms are graced with down comforters.

A full breakfast, served at the antique pine table in the dining room, features fresh fruit, creative egg dishes, blintzes, freshly baked breads and sticky buns, and fresh coffee and tea. In hot weather, guests can choose to eat outdoors in the garden gazebo. During their stay at the GrapeVine Inn, guests are presented with a complimentary bottle of wine from a local Oregon winery. Enophiles and even casual wine appreciators will find it extremely romantic to be surrounded by grapes and the precious elixir they yield.

MORICAL HOUSE GARDEN INN, Ashland
668 North Main Street
(541) 482-2254, (800) 208-0960
http://www.abba.com
Moderate to Very Expensive
Minimum stay requirement seasonally

Although Main Street may not be the very best location for a bed and breakfast, the thoughtful innkeepers at Morical House have done everything possible to downplay this point and welcome you in casual elegance. This flawlessly renovated Eastlake-style Victorian farmhouse is somewhat concealed from the road by shrubbery. Five guest rooms are located on the upper floors of the main house, and two newly constructed garden units sit in the backyard. Color schemes and styles vary in each guest room, but the ones in the main house are embellished with antiques and have private baths. Foxglove, an elegant top-floor unit with all-cream interior, lace curtains, and a claw-foot tub, has views of the neighboring valley that stretch for miles. Garden Party is tastefully done in pastels, and The Berries, with a portion of exposed brick from the old chimney, is handsomely appointed with dark burgundy wallpaper. The remaining two main-house rooms are just as attractive as the others but they face Main Street, so road noise is noticeable.

Behind the house, a beautifully maintained lawn and garden stretches back to a pond, and a sundeck surveys the surrounding farmland with the Cascades as a backdrop. A veritable arboretum of trees frames the yard, and pleasant sitting areas all over the property allow you to relax and enjoy the lovely surroundings.

The best rooms are those you'll come to last; these magnificent rooms are worth waiting for—and worth planning your vacation around. Set off to one side of the gardens is a modest new building that resembles a carriage house. The two lovingly crafted units inside epitomize a romantic traveler's dream come true. Though the styles are different, both have exquisite furnishings, corner gas-log fireplaces, two-person Jacuzzi tubs, and king-size beds with piles of pillows and top-quality linens. Personal touches in each of the garden rooms include locally crafted stained glass and etched windows, hand-carved mantels, and stunning watercolors. As for added conveniences, both garden rooms have their own temperature controls, air-conditioning, wet bar with fridge, and coffeemaker.

An integral part of your stay at Morical House is the hearty country breakfast, beautifully presented on fine china or colorful glass dishes. In the afternoon, enjoy wine and hors d' oeuvres while discussing the plays of the season with your friendly hosts and other theater-going guests.

MT. ASHLAND INN, Ashland
550 Mt. Ashland Road
(541) 482-8707, (800) 830-8707
Inexpensive to Expensive
Minimum stay requirement seasonally

Enjoy breathtaking views as a winding road leads you high into the Siskiyou Mountains. Sheltered by pine trees near the summit of Mount Ashland, this handcrafted cedar cabin will make you feel like lacing up your hiking boots and shrugging on your Northwest flannel. Every effort has been made to make the Mt. Ashland Inn a nature lover's retreat. In wintertime, the inn provides lightweight high-tech snowshoes for adventurous, snow-clomping types. Downhill and cross-country skiers will find ecstasy only three miles away at the **MOUNT ASHLAND SKI AREA** (see Outdoor Kissing). Spring and summer bring beautiful weather, budding wildflowers, and the opportunity to explore the Pacific Crest Trail, which cuts through the inn's 40 acres. (The owners' two energetic golden retrievers will gladly accompany you on hikes.)

A cedar-log interior adds charm to the Mt. Ashland Inn. The main living room resembles a cozy mountain lodge, with peeled log columns and a 17th-century fireplace carved out of a massive stone wall. Some of the guest rooms are on the snug side, but all five are appointed with handmade quilts, Early American furnishings, and private bathrooms (although one is a detached bath across the hall). Especially romantic are the McLoughlin and the Sky Lakes Suites. The second-story McLoughlin Suite is decorated in deep blue and maroon, with a rose-marble gas fireplace at the foot of the bed. A lovely rectangular window above the king-size bed perfectly frames Mount McLoughlin, while Mount Shasta stands off to the south. Situated on the ground floor, the Sky Lakes Suite has a delicate waterfall cascading over a rock wall beside a two-person Jacuzzi tub. Although this suite does not have a cedar-log interior like the other rooms, it offers plenty of extras, including a wet bar with microwave and refrigerator, a log-arch doorway to the bathroom, and a private entrance.

Days at the Mt. Ashland Inn start in the main-floor dining room with a full breakfast of baked apples with walnuts or warm spiced grapefruit, followed by an entrée like the mushroom egg puff with homemade turkey sausage. Afterward, venture outside to the inviting wraparound deck, where you'll find clear, crisp views of Mount McLoughlin and Mount Shasta. Air as fresh as this is good for the heart.

A long day of hiking or skiing can tire even the most energetic outdoor enthusiasts. Instead of driving into town, why not let your dinner come to you? Plan ahead and ask the innkeepers about gourmet dinner baskets that can be delivered to the inn from local restaurants.

Romantic Note: Due to the sometimes snowcapped location, traction tires and/or chains may be required during the winter.

NIGHTINGAIL'S INN, Ashland
117 North Main Street
(541) 482-7373
Moderate; No Credit Cards
Minimum stay requirement seasonally
Closed November

Set on busy Main Street, this pale yellow home is conveniently located a block and a half from downtown Ashland. When we visited, the house's decor was described to us as "vernacular with Queen Anne accents." Translation: NightinGale's Inn is a rather odd mix of Victorian touches and standard, rather ordinary decor. The contemporary red and green plaid chairs seem out of place in the old-fashioned sitting room, and the TV room is, well, just your average TV room. Perhaps the only endearing (and historical) features are the stained glass windows and vintage photographs throughout the house.

Upstairs, all three guest rooms are named after flowers and have private bathrooms, down comforters, and pretty homemade quilts. Unfortunately, only the Lily and Camas Rooms have some amount of romantic potential. The Lily Room, although sparsely decorated, offers views of Grizzly Peak and has a two-headed shower in the bathroom. The Camas Room has lavender walls, a pedestal sink, and a four-poster bed covered with a purple and green quilt. In the mornings, a family-style breakfast is served downstairs in the handsome dining room. Weather permitting, we recommend eating outside on the patio in the backyard, where you can enjoy your German pancakes or waffles among the fruit trees and roses.

THE PEDIGRIFT HOUSE, Ashland
407 Scenic Drive
(541) 482-1888, (800) 262-4073
http://www.opendoor.com/pedigrift
Expensive
Call for seasonal closures.

A white picket fence frames this cheerful blue and white 1888 Queen Anne Victorian set in a quiet Ashland neighborhood. Judging from the historic exterior, one would expect to find a clutter of antiques and an elegant array of furnishings inside the home, but instead it is freshly appointed in a combination of contemporary and classic styles. The original maple hardwood floors are polished to a high sheen in the parlor, where green leather couches sit beside an Italian granite gas fireplace. Adjacent to the parlor is the open, airy breakfast room, where full breakfasts are presented in the morning and beverages, cheese, and crackers are offered each afternoon. Later on, after the evening performances are concluded, a warm dessert à la mode is set out here for all guests to enjoy.

There is only one guest room on the main floor, the East Room. High ceilings, pale hardwood floors, antique furnishings, and a window seat make this our favorite room. The remaining three guest rooms are upstairs. Two are best suited for groups of three, since they are furnished with both a queen-size and a twin bed, but the last room, Cypress, is a pretty cozy choice. It is considerably darker than the rest of the rooms, but antiques and a claw-foot tub lend authentic charm.

PEERLESS HOTEL, Ashland
243 Fourth Street
(541) 488-1082, (800) 460-8758

http://www.mind.net/peerless
Moderate to Very Expensive

A bold name like "The Peerless" sets up lofty expectations in a traveler's mind. Luckily, this relatively new inn lives up to its name by offering a memorable and unique-to-Ashland experience. With colorful flower boxes adorning the windows and an old Coca-Cola sign painted on one outer wall, the exterior of this turn-of-the-century brick building gives no indication of the magnificent polish found inside. Upon entering the elegant lobby, however, you'll begin to see the romantic potential. Finally, your room will take your breath away.

All six of the grand rooms have massive wall murals or intricate stencilwork, towering 12-foot ceilings, original woodwork, rich colors and fabrics, and glistening hardwood floors with Oriental rugs. Although each room is different, a flamboyant and stylish Victorian theme is prevalent throughout, with antiques, queen-size beds, and sumptuous furnishings and linens. Suite Three has side-by-side claw-foot tubs and a spacious sitting area adjacent to the bedroom; the French-influenced Room Five has a two-person Jacuzzi tub set beneath a skylight; and Suite Seven has a four-poster mahogany bed, jetted tub for two, and two-person shower. The sitting room for Suite Seven is done in a wild safari theme that is almost too much, but the rest of the suite is painted a calming green tone and the windows are draped with sheer white material to create an overall soothing feeling. Turndown service is provided in the evening, but you are otherwise left alone once you check in.

After an early morning bicycle tour around town (bikes are supplied by the inn), return for an expanded continental breakfast. It is served buffet-style in the plant-filled sunroom, filled with wicker furniture and tables for two. The traditional array of fresh fruit and dry cereal is fine, but the additional dish (an apple custard the day we stayed) can be disappointing. On the other hand, if you prefer a lighter breakfast, you should be satisfied.

PINEHURST INN AT JENNY CREEK, Ashland
17250 Highway 66
(541) 488-1002
Inexpensive to Moderate
Breakfast, Lunch, and Dinner Wednesday–Sunday; Sunday Brunch
Call for seasonal closures.

Nestled in the Cascade Mountains a good distance from the nearest city or village, this unassuming country inn is just about the most enchanting place for miles around. Once a stage stop along the Applegate Wagon Trail, the original inn was restored as a roadhouse in the 1920s. Today, as in days gone by, the Pinehurst Inn offers travelers a secluded spot to rest after a long day on the road.

The inn's entry room is all cedar and pine, with a huge stone fireplace for luxuriant heat. Just beyond the parlor is the restaurant, with its rich scarlet wool carpet, cream walls, and lace curtains. At the back of the restaurant stands an antique wood-burning stove that warms the dining room in winter-time. These touches, along with the antique chairs, wood tables, and peeled-log columns, create a rustic setting in which to enjoy innovative Northwest cuisine. You certainly won't want to miss the delicious English muffins or the homemade desserts.

Upstairs the simple guest rooms offer views of the surrounding woods and Jenny Creek. One of the suites has burgundy walls and an old-fashioned stained glass window above the entryway. Room Five has a wedding-ring quilt, a bent-willow headboard, and an extra-long tub. All six rooms feature down comforters, antique furnishings, and private baths with claw-foot tubs and showers. These rooms aren't exactly suitable for high romance, but the entire experience is unique and serene.

Enjoy views of the property's 23 acres from the inn's wraparound porch. Or relax in the screened patio overlooking ponderosa pines and a terraced garden. An upstairs sunroom, filled with wicker furniture and hanging plants, provides an amazing panorama of the forested mountainside. Over-all, the breakfast is superb, and the hospitality is unparalleled. If getting away from civilization is what you want, you'll be happy at this out-of-the-way location.

When making reservations, ask about the Pinehurst Inn's year-round package that includes both breakfast and dinner with your lodging. This package is quite economical when you consider the restaurant's convenient location and the quantity of food you receive (you can order whatever you'd like, and you can eat as much as you want). Dinner usually begins as early as 4:00 P.M. to accommodate theater-goers.

Romantic Warning: For those wishing to attend Ashland's Shakespeare Festival, the Pinehurst Inn's distance from the town center may be a serious disadvantage. Evening theater performances in Ashland can get out as late as midnight, and the slow, uphill, winding drive to the inn isn't enjoyable when you're tired or when it's dark outside.

THE QUEEN ANNE, Ashland
125 North Main Street
(541) 482-0220, (800) 460-6818
Moderate to Expensive; No Credit Cards

The Queen Anne is one of the more appealing Victorian bed and break-fasts in Ashland. Lovingly renovated, the bright, stately exterior features well-tended English gardens, abundant rose bushes, a handcrafted stone waterfall, a white gazebo, and an outdoor deck with views of the Cascades. Unfortunately, this 1880 home also overlooks busy Main Street, and traffic noise can be a problem.

Inside, the four ample guest rooms have lace curtains, cozy sitting areas, and private baths with antique claw-foot tubs. All are extremely sunny and comfortable, with queen-size beds and old-fashioned patchwork quilts. Lady Lora is appointed with pine furnishings and decorated in pretty blue pastels. It is the only room located on the main floor and has a detached private bath across the hall. In the evening, its French doors open onto the parlor, providing exclusive use of the sitting area (the parlor is closed to other guests during this time). Upstairs, the Queen Victoria Room features a lovely antique vanity and an old-fashioned pedestal sink, as well as a cozy bed tucked away in a small bay window. Distant views of the garden and the Siskiyou Mountains can be seen through the chintz flowered curtains in the Prince Hal Room. The most spacious room in the house is the King George, in which the bedroom is connected to a sitting area by an arched doorway. A six-foot-long claw-foot tub and double vanity adorn its bathroom.

Fresh breads and hot coffee and tea accompany a full breakfast in the morning. Nectarine smoothies, French toast, chicken crêpes with asparagus, and strawberry and blackberry compote are just a few of the savory dishes prepared by the innkeepers.

ROMEO INN, Ashland
295 Idaho Street
(541) 488-0884, (800) 915-8899
Expensive to Very Expensive
Minimum stay requirement seasonally

Although the Romeo Inn is desperately in need of tender loving care, we decided to again include it in this book, with hopes that the motivated new owners will breathe fresh life into this grand old dame. Perched on a grassy knoll, the Cape Cod–style Romeo Inn was one of the first professionally run bed and breakfasts to open in Ashland. The exterior has been beautifully maintained, and gorgeous terraced gardens surround a backyard hot tub, pool, and patio. It is the six country-style guest rooms, however, that need serious attention. Each room has a private bath, but the calico prints are worn, many furnishings are out of date, and the carpet in many rooms needs to be replaced. For now, the spacious Stratford Suite is your best bet. It is detached from the main house, and has a two-person whirlpool tub under a skylight, vaulted ceiling, and complete kitchen. Overall, the prices are too high for such uninspiring interiors, but if you spend your days enjoying the pool and garden area, then it may be worth it for you and your Romeo (or Juliet). Outstanding full breakfasts are another noteworthy event; you can dine on the patio in summertime or inside on cooler morns.

Romantic Note: Keep in mind that redecorating efforts had just begun when we toured the property. Our lip rating reflects what we saw at press time, but the plans for improvement sounded promising. Like you, we will have to wait and see.

SHREW'S HOUSE BED AND BREAKFAST, Ashland
570 Siskiyou Boulevard
(541) 482-9214, (800) 482-9214
Inexpensive to Moderate
Minimum stay requirement on weekends

Shrew's House is closer to Ashland's main street than we'd like it to be, but other details make this a great (and affordable) bed and breakfast. The main house is a 1920s Craftsman, with a cluttered, antique-filled sitting room. Two units in back of the main house contain the inn's four guest rooms. Each room has a private bath, a kitchenette, and its own private entrance (some with shared porches). One room is decorated with pretty blue and pink florals, and has a king-size bed with a half-canopy. Theater memorabilia and a river-rock fireplace adorn another. The gold and cream Baroque Room has a king-size bed, Jacuzzi tub, fireplace, Empire sofa, and wood-burning stove. Small but airy, the Princess Room is a steal with its half-canopy and sit-down steam shower. All rooms have wet bars, color TVs, and private phones (a plus for any bed-and-breakfast traveler). Unfortunately, the rooms at Shrew's House have a slight motel-like feel, and the small swimming pool next to the cottages does nothing to convince us otherwise.

In the morning, enjoy a breakfast of freshly ground coffee, homemade whole-grain breads, and lavish fruit presentations, delivered to your room upon request or served outside beneath a canopy.

WATERSIDE INN, Ashland
70 Water Street
(541) 482-3315
Very Expensive to Unbelievably Expensive; No Credit Cards
Call for seasonal closures.

You could call these gracious apartment-style suites a home away from home, but only if you live in a super-stylish, antique-filled designer home. Even if you do happen to be so blessed, you will still envy the style with which each room here has been outfitted. The intense innkeeper was once a cinematic set designer, and she has used her appreciation of sumptuous, intriguing (and sometimes flamboyant) details to distinguish each suite. The Normandy, Kafuzo, and Taos Suites are the loveliest options; the other two could use some refreshing touches. The suites we recommend offer a dining and living room with plush furnishings and 20-foot ceilings, a TV/VCR and stereo, an incredible full kitchen, a sensuous bedroom with down comforters, overstuffed pillows, and floral fabrics, a full loft, and wraparound windows facing a babbling stone-scattered creek. A full hot breakfast is served on the lower creekside patio every morning. Long hours can be spent at the Waterside Inn, listening to the flow of rushing water and enjoying each other's company.

WEISINGER'S VINEYARD COTTAGE, Ashland
3150 Siskiyou Boulevard
(541) 488-5989, (541) 482-5481, (800) 551-9463
http://www.weisingers.com
Expensive
Minimum stay requirement seasonally
Call for seasonal closures.

Ultimate privacy and a feeling of total seclusion are the draws here. Or could it be the pretty contemporary country furnishings? Or maybe it's the wooden deck with a large outdoor hot tub, just three steps from your front door? You'll have to be the judge. We think it's all this and more.

In your own private cottage set on ten acres of luscious vineyards and quaint farmland, you and your love will have a time to remember. The petite modern home has everything you could want for an affectionate interlude: a comfy floral love seat positioned directly across from a gas fireplace, a private hot tub on the outside deck, a TV/VCR and stereo hidden away in an attractive armoire, air-conditioning, and a basket of wine, cheese, crackers, and light breakfast items awaiting your arrival. The full kitchen is stocked with utensils, a toaster oven, and a microwave, but you're on your own if you would like a breakfast of more than just pastries and coffee.

In the spacious bedroom, where green-and-white decor sets the mood for rest and relaxation, you'll find a queen-size bed, ivy-patterned linens and wallpaper, and a skylight perfect for midnight stargazing. The only drawback to this place, and we mean the *only* drawback, is that you can hear the road from the outdoor deck. But with the bubbling Jacuzzi tub and the undeniably serene surroundings, we guarantee you won't be too bothered.

Romantic Suggestion: Check out Weisinger's tasting room and gift shop, just across the driveway and parking lot. If you discover some vintages that you are especially fond of, or if you need wine for a picnic or other outing, take advantage of the wine discounts offered to overnight guests.

WINCHESTER COUNTRY INN, Ashland
35 South Second Street
(541) 488-1113, (800) 972-4991
Moderate to Very Expensive
Call for seasonal closures.

Located on a side street in downtown Ashland, the Winchester Country Inn is a lovely Queen Anne Victorian with a neighboring carriage house. Bountiful flowering gardens line the walkway, and a charming gazebo sits in the front lawn. Here is a place where the elegance of the Victorian era radiates in grand style, but the comforts and conveniences of the twentieth century abound.

Eighteen guest rooms are available, all quite lovely. At the lowest end of the price range are the 12 Victorian Rooms, some of which have claw-foot tubs and antique furnishings. The helpful, professional staff will gladly assist you in choosing a room, but we found the slightly more contemporary suites and carriage house units to be especially endearing, with two-person Jacuzzi tubs, gas fireplaces, and space to spare. Both the Belvedere and Barbara Howard Suites also have bay windows overlooking the tiered gardens and lovely grounds.

A full gourmet breakfast with a choice of three different entrées is served in the main-floor restaurant, which we highly recommend as a dinner destination (see Restaurant Kissing). You should also inquire about the Winchester Country Inn's off-season getaway packages, which include overnight lodging and breakfast along with a four-course dinner for two. Prices for the packages do not exceed the Very Expensive range, which is a great deal in this part of the world.

Romantic Warning: With the popular restaurant downstairs, there is a potential for noise disturbance in the second-story rooms of the main house.

WOLFE MANOR INN, Ashland
586 B Street
(541) 488-3676, (800) 801-3676
Moderate
Minimum stay requirement seasonally

The very pink Wolfe Manor Inn, a large two-story Craftsman bungalow, is poised on a corner in a residential area. Victorian-era antiques and lace curtains beautify the main-floor parlor and formal dining room of this relatively new bed and breakfast. Upstairs, five modest guest rooms await, each with a down comforter and private bath, and all but one with air conditioning. Mementos of the innkeepers' family and travels adorn each of the rooms. Madeleine's Memories, done in a turn-of-the-century theme with an antique iron bed, is dedicated to the owner's mother and filled with family keepsakes. Norman's Nook is furnished with Norman Rockwell memorabilia and has a large bathroom, while Alyce's Alcove is a small room with a cut-lace duvet, lace curtains, and a window seat. The last room has two full-size beds, so it is not geared toward couples, but it is interestingly decorated in an African safari theme. The style may seem out of place in this old home, but the carvings and masks that line the walls are from the innkeepers' exotic journeys abroad.

Breakfasts such as broiled grapefruit, vegetarian quiche and fried potatoes, or poached eggs and turkey ham on English muffins are served here, at two long tables in the dining room. After you have enjoyed your morning meal, walking to Ashland's shops or to a matinee is quite convenient from here.

Restaurant Kissing

CHATEAULIN RESTAURANT, Ashland
50 East Main Street
(541) 482-2264
Expensive
Dinner Daily

Conveniently located in the heart of Ashland's theater district, this ivy-covered French country restaurant will win a place in your hearts. Inside, the subtle lighting is augmented by flickering candlelight. Exposed brick walls are decorated with champagne bottles and copper kettles, and rosy stained glass windows frame the restaurant's bar area. Lace window treatments, scarlet carpeting, and dark woodwork create a romantic milieu. The seating is intimate—perhaps too intimate (meaning too close to other diners), particularly just before showtime. Still, the food produced by the serious kitchen is excellent, and the menu changes seasonally. Creatively prepared pâtés and veal dishes with subtle sauces are the specialties here, and the seafood is always fresh and delicious. Desserts at Chateaulin border on euphoric, so save room for one of our favorites: the Chambord pot de creme with raspberry coulis. This is one of the most romantic restaurants we've encountered in Ashland.

Romantic Suggestion: If dinner at Chateaulin isn't feasible, the next best thing is a visit after the final curtain call for drinks and dessert. The bar is open until midnight.

DRAGONFLY BISTRO, Ashland
70 Water Street
(541) 488-4262
Moderate to Expensive
Call for seasonal closures.

Since this restaurant is open in the summer months only, your window of opportunity to dine here is rather small. Visit the Dragonfly on a hot summer afternoon for a chance to treasure the creekside setting at its best. An expansive brick patio stretches alongside Lithia Creek, and tables with umbrellas are placed around the deck for casual dining. At times, the rushing stream is so loud that it is hard to hear each other, but the sound of flowing water is absolutely mesmerizing.

Unfortunately, the food (tropical French when we visited) does not always live up to the fantastic setting. Given the restaurant's short season, it seems that the kitchen is having a hard time finding its stride and a good resident chef. One way to enjoy the lovely surroundings with a minimal chance of disappointment is to come here before a show just for wine and appetizers. Dining al fresco and then walking to the theater, only about a block away, makes for an enchanting, European-style evening.

THE FIREFLY, Ashland
15 North First Street
(541) 488-3212
Moderate to Expensive
Call for seasonal hours.

Pardon the pun, but the whole town is abuzz about The Firefly, the latest addition to Ashland's illustrious dining scene. Fresh flowers, brass sconces, and blue-glass accents help warm the modest dining room, but the real draw here is the inventive world cuisine. Does giant sweet potato and sage ravioli with hazelnut brown butter pique your curiosity? How about smoked quail with wild rice and lingon-marionberry sauce, or salmon wrapped in rice paper with prawn fried rice and spicy red bean sauce? Save room for dessert—doesn't lemon meringue tartlet with strawberry coulis sound delectable? Not only will a meal here satisfy your curiosity about trying new and interesting foods, but it will also more than satisfy your appetite.

IL GIARDINO CUCINA ITALIANA, Ashland
5 Granite Street
(541) 488-0816
Moderate
Lunch Thursday–Friday; Dinner Daily

You'll surely succeed in wooing your beloved at Il Giardino. This family-run restaurant is both casual and personal, with family photographs and colorful art deco advertisements covering the bright blue walls. Italian-speaking waiters deliver steaming hot pasta dishes to linen-draped tables while opera music plays in the background. Just off the dining room, a garden patio allows for al fresco dining beneath wisteria vines and hanging baskets of flowers. No matter where you sit, be aware that the restaurant is usually too noisy and bustling for intimate conversation; you may just want to gaze into each other's eyes and let the food speak for itself.

Authentic Italian cuisine is prepared with the utmost care and expertise here. We highly recommend the linguine with clams in a light tomato sauce, or the capellini with tomato and basil. You'll want to linger over the black ravioli stuffed with shrimp-and-salmon mousse and topped with a light cream sauce. Even the classic spaghetti Bolognese is a masterpiece. *Bravo!*

MONET RESTAURANT, Ashland
36 South Second Street
(541) 482-1339
Moderate to Expensive
Call for seasonal closures.

Contemplate an exquisite French meal, with every dish more delectable than the last, and you'll have only a hint of what awaits you at Monet. Culinary masterpieces include smoked salmon wrapped around a heavenly avocado mousse, creamy broccoli soup drizzled with sour cream, and Mediterranean linguine with sautéed artichoke hearts, sun-dried tomatoes, olives, and mushrooms. Most meals come with fresh whole-grain French bread. From appetizers to entrées, all portions are unexpectedly generous, so be sure to save room for dessert.

Named after the famous French Impressionist, this restaurant is as pretty as a picture. A delightful garden area outside, filled with plants similar to those in Monet's garden, is a perfect spot for dining in the summer. Emulating the colors of the artist's palette, the interior has been decorated in pale pinks and greens, with peach curtains framing the front windows. The walls are covered with French batting and adorned with replicas of Monet's oil paintings. Fresh flowers, floral tablecloths, and elegantly comfortable chairs complement each table. Our only complaint is that the tables are a little too close together, but all is forgiven once the formal procession of delicacies begins.

PLAZA CAFE, Ashland
47 North Main Street
(541) 488-2233
Inexpensive
Call for seasonal closures.

Local art and pottery displayed on brick walls, a high ceiling with track lighting, and mismatched wood tables contribute to the personality of this casual dining room. The Plaza Cafe's style may not be particularly extraordinary or intimate, but the atmosphere is mellow enough for quiet conversation over a flavorful lunch, and the food is excellent. A creative, California-inspired menu offers healthy soups, salads, and sandwiches, and is enhanced by daily specials. The blackened snapper tacos with a side of mango salsa are spicy, sweet, and savory, and the chicken and mushroom linguine in pesto sauce is excellent. Like most Ashland restaurants, the Plaza Cafe can be very busy in the summer, but service here still tends to be swift and friendly.

PRIMAVERA RESTAURANT AND GARDENS, Ashland
241 Hargadine
(541) 488-1994
Expensive
Call for seasonal hours.

Located on the lower level of the **OREGON CABARET THEATRE** (see Miscellaneous Kissing), Primavera earns a full four lips for romantic ambience, but only one lip for food quality. This averages out to a two-and-a-half-lip rating on our kissometer. It's too bad, really; such an elegant restaurant ought to serve equally wonderful cuisine. The dinner menu is full of creative-sounding dishes such as mustard-fennel halibut with tomato-mint compote and saffron couscous, and eggplant-and-rice-stuffed roasted pepper with crisp polenta and green sauce. Such creativity, however, is best left to those who have mastered basic culinary skills.

To add to our disappointment, we found the menu setup rather odd. Like many restaurants, Primavera offers its guests a choice between full dinner entrées or lighter bistro fare. However, Primavera's wait staff asks for your preference as soon as you arrive (before you've seen either menu), so they can seat you in the appropriate part of the restaurant. And once you've made your decision, you can't order items off the other menu. That's a lot to decide before you even sit down.

Food and service aside, though, this restaurant is truly striking. The dining room has all the makings of a 1920s style speakeasy, with its etched bronze-and-black pillars, subdued lighting, handsome floor-length curtains, and baby grand piano at center stage. Walls of dark blue and fiery orange are adorned with colorful exotic canvases of dancing gypsies. Crystal sparkles on the white-linened tables, small lamps at each table give the room a subtle glow, and black-lacquered chairs add to the overall drama. Weather permitting, the lush terraced garden patio at the rear of the restaurant is laced with tables for dining beneath the stars.

THAI PEPPER, Ashland
84 North Main Street
(541) 482-8058
Moderate
Lunch Friday; Dinner Daily

Authentic Thai cuisine—heavy on the curry and impeccably fresh—is a spicy change of pace from the European-oriented cuisine offered by most of the restaurants here. It's such a welcome change of pace, in fact, that this became our favorite lunch spot in Ashland. In the summer, sip Thai iced tea and dine outside on the patio, where birch trees border flowing Ashland Creek. You'll have to speak loudly over the sound of rushing water, but the stream's sounds are soothing and help to muffle the noise from Main Street, which is right above the restaurant. Inside, the setting is contemporary, with glass-brick walls that allow light to reflect throughout the all-white interior. The single inside dining room has a casual and airy atmosphere, but it doesn't really compare with the charm of the patio.

Spend a midsummer night's eve here eating tiger rolls with cream cheese, crab, and shrimp, dipped in sweet hot-and-sour sauce; green coconut chicken curry with lemongrass and fresh spearmint; and juicy shrimp with coconut peanut sauce and fresh spinach. Thai food is always great for sharing, and this is some of the best we have ever had.

Romantic Warning: Despite our rave review, we have to report that Thai Pepper cannot be counted on for swift service. In fact, service can be terribly slow, and in a town where visitors are often in a hurry to make a show, this is a huge problem.

WINCHESTER COUNTRY INN, Ashland
35 South Second Street
(541) 488-1115, (800) 972-4991
Moderate to Expensive
Call for seasonal hours.

Competition is stiff in Ashland, but ask anyone where to get a fine meal and great service, and they are likely to mention the Winchester Country Inn. The restaurant is on the main floor of a renovated Queen Anne Victorian; tables are placed casually throughout the library, living room, and dining alcove, with plenty of privacy and space in between. Windows look out onto tiered gardens where you can also dine, and the mood is always cordial and relaxed. The kitchen specializes in international cuisine, and prepares it with finesse and skill. The Teng Dah beef, a filet mignon marinated in soy, garlic, nutmeg, anise seed, and lemon zest, is incredible; and the boneless chicken breast stuffed with pears, currants, and ricotta and served with brandy cream sauce is rich yet subtle. Warm bread and soup or salad come with your meal, and there is a different prix fixe meal each night—an affordable option to consider if you have a large appetite. Service is prompt and eager to ensure that you will make it to your performance.

Romantic Note: The Winchester Country Inn is also a lovely place to spend the night (see Hotel/Bed and Breakfast Kissing).

Outdoor Kissing

LITHIA PARK, Ashland

Located in Ashland's theater district.

Lithia Park is a national historic landmark that begins in the heart of Ashland's theater district and extends southward for roughly a mile. With more than 100 acres of forest, lawns, ponds, and flower gardens, there's plenty of space for intimate moments in this lovely playground. Stroll arm in arm beneath the ponderosa pines, or share a kiss on one of the small bridges spanning a burbling creek. Rhododendrons, dogwood trees, azaleas, and forget-me-nots grace the park with their brilliant displays of color each spring. Abundant picnic benches throughout the park create the perfect dining spot among 100 different kinds of trees and shrubs. Immaculate trails eventually become unpaved as you wind your way upward to a panoramic view of Ashland and the valley beyond. Lithia Park also features tennis courts, a volleyball court, a children's playground, and a small open-air amphitheater used for performances by local entertainers.

MOUNT ASHLAND, Ashland

At the heart of the Siskiyou mountain range, 18 miles southwest of downtown Ashland.

The town of Ashland is crowned by the 7,500-foot summit of Mount Ashland. In winter, outdoor buffs hit the more than 100 miles of cross-country ski trails that snake their way through forests, across open fields, past crystal-clear mountain lakes and flowing rivers, and over rolling hill-sides. The views are spectacular. As you glide over endless stretches of white powder, you can see the peaks of the Cascade Range to the north and Mount Shasta to the south. Mount Ashland is considered one of the most challenging downhill ski areas around, with more than 23 runs catering to intermediate and advanced skiers. For information on skiing, call the **MOUNT ASHLAND SKI AREA**, (541) 482-2897. In spring and summer the steep trails are equally challenging and beautiful, and perfect for hiking.

Miscellaneous Kissing

OREGON CABARET THEATRE, Ashland
First and Hargadine
(541) 488-2902
Ticket prices range from $11 to $18
Call for seasonal closures.

After several nights of Shakespeare and contemporary drama at the Festival, try a taste of musical comedy at the Oregon Cabaret Theatre. Don't let the name deter you; this is not a small, crowded, noise-filled room, but a handsomely decorated theater that has transformed the interior of Ashland's historic First Baptist Church. Stained glass windows throw muted light onto the dark green walls. Suspended overhead is an enormous crystal chandelier that has been transplanted from a vintage movie palace. Tables draped in burgundy linens and adorned with glowing candles line the tiered first floor and the second-floor balcony area. Just about every seat in the house has an excellent view of the stage.

The Oregon Cabaret Theatre is a professional (non-Equity) company that performs some of the most innovative musical theater around. Many of the productions are original and some are well-known off-Broadway hits, but all are delightfully entertaining. Shows change every two to three months, so call ahead to find out which show is currently playing.

Romantic Warning: Dinner at the Cabaret Theatre is prepared by **PRIMAVERA RESTAURANT AND GARDENS** (see Restaurant Kissing) and is completely unappetizing. Somehow the food gets worse on its way from the restaurant to the theater. Our pasta shells with three-cheese filling could best be described as a soupy mess, and our salmon dish came drowned in a pathetic marinara sauce. Most of the desserts were disappointing as well. (How can you mess up chocolate?) We recommend making your own dining arrangements beforehand and then arriving at the theater in time for the show. If you do decide to split a dessert during intermission, the vanilla-and-peanut-butter ice cream pie, better known as "Dick Hay Pie," is your best option.

OREGON SHAKESPEARE FESTIVAL, Ashland
(541) 482-4331
Tickets start at $20 in summer; prices are slightly lower in spring and fall

Centrally located in downtown Ashland.

For those who have a passion for Shakespeare, what could be more romantic than snuggling close together at dusk in an outdoor Elizabethan theater, listening to romantic love poetry from England's leading authority on the subject? At the Oregon Shakespeare Festival, you can see a variety of the master's works in several different theaters (both indoor and out) in downtown Ashland. Who would have imagined that such a small town would be home to the oldest existing full-scale Elizabethan stage in the Western Hemisphere? Season after season, the costumes are spectacular, the sets are imaginative, and the acting is superb.

If you are not a Shakespeare fan, don't let that stop you from attending; Shakespearean drama is only one component of each season's theatrical offerings. Established in 1935, the Festival boasts one of the largest regional theater companies in the United States, and it performs plenty of contemporary plays that will surely spark your interest. You can call the Festival directly for tickets, or phone the **SOUTHERN OREGON RESERVATION CENTER**, (541) 488-1011, (800) 547-8052, a professionally run ticket agency that can help you with both tickets and lodging.

"*A kiss is a lovely trick designed by nature to stop speech when words become superfluous.*"

Ingrid Bergman

Index